THE
FINAL SOLUTION

**The Attempt to
Exterminate the Jews of Europe 1939-1945**

GERALD REITLINGER

Jason Aronson Inc. • *Northvale, New Jersey* • *London*

Library of Congress Cataloging-in-Publication Data

Reitlinger, Gerald, 1900-1978
  The final solution

  Originally published: London: Vallentine, Mitchell, 1968.
  Bibliography: p. 531
  Includes index.
  1. Holocaust, Jewish (1939–1945)   I. Title.
DS135.E83R4   1987   940.53 15 03924   87-17130
ISBN 0-87668-951-9

For Venetia

Contents

PART I

THE SEARCH FOR THE FINAL SOLUTION

v

CONTENTS

PART II

THE FINAL SOLUTION IN PRACTICE

CONTENTS

CONTENTS

MAPS

Foreword

Gerald Reitlinger's *The Final Solution* was the first significant historical work to tell the story of what was then nameless—and is now known as the Holocaust. Reitlinger's book began the process of understanding what happened and why. Yet after more than a third of a century and after two editions, the work is neither a relic of early scholarship nor an antiquarian collectors' item. Written only seven years after the end of the war, this book still has the power of its initial freshness and the excitement of its then new discoveries. Although *The Final Solution* is an objective piece of history, written by a distinguished English historian who is master of understatement and irony, the pain of immediate loss and outrage at the perpetrators screams forth from each page.

In the thirty-four years since its initial publication, Reitlinger's pioneering effort has been joined by others. Raul Hilberg's *The Destruction of the European Jews* examines the *Endlosung* from the perspective of the perpetrators. That is its strength, also its limitation. In *The War Against the Jews,* Lucy Dawidowicz writes of the experience of the victims and of the ideology of the perpetrators. She presumes that one will also learn elsewhere how the Holocaust unfolded and the inner world of the *universe concentrationaire.* Nora Levin has also written a large text detailing the unfolding of events from 1933 to 1945, which engulfed the Jewish people in a catastrophe without precedent and brought to an end a millennium of Jewish culture and civilization. And there have been textbooks by fine scholars such as Yehudah Bauer and John Roth and Richard Rubenstein, books that condense the story for students. These scholars had the benefit of Reitlinger's work. They also had access to additional material. Over the decades new sources had been opened from then secret archives. Thousands of books and tens of thousands of new documents informed their scholarship. And they had time for research and the requisite distance.

Privileged is the man who was present at the beginning, who shaped the questions to be posed, and whose work endures after other masters have tried their hand.

There are now more specialized works dealing with one aspect or another of the issues first raised by Reitlinger. Isaiah Trunk's *Judenrat* examines the Jewish councils appointed by the Nazis and charged with limited responsibility for the ghettoes. Neither Trunk's questions nor his answers differ significantly from the measured assessment of the Jewish councils offered by Reitlinger, who early on understood the differences between Lodz, Vilna, and Warsaw, and who grasped the interplay between the personalities of ghetto leaders Chaim Rumkowski, Jacob Gens, and Adam Czerniakow and the objective conditions of their ghettoized communities. Because of Trunk's work, critics no longer need be as disturbed if Reitlinger's portrait of the *Judenrat* is a bit too condemnatory at one point or too laudatory at another.

There are now specialized works that deal with each of the countries described by Reitlinger—France and Italy, Hungary and Poland, Denmark and the U.S.S.R. There are also fine biographies that deal with major and minor figures of the era—perpetrators, bystanders; heroes, survivors, and victims. The role of the Allies has been examined in detail in large works and specialized monographs. Even the role of the press, the shifts in U.S. State Department policy, and Jewish communal responses have been subjects of extensive research.

Nevertheless, Reitlinger's historical insights have stood the test of time. At points, they are modified by later research, and changes of tone and nuance are suggested by new works, yet the overriding impression is that much of the new research has further documented Reitlinger's initial conclusions.

The historian is now blessed with thousands of memoirs to read. Survivors have told their stories again and again. There are works that deal with individual camps—or even with subdivisions of slave labor camps—and works that grapple with German business and with the structure of the German military, but when Reitlinger wrote his work, almost none of this material was known. Major documentation has emerged from the Nuremberg trials, and Reitlinger read this voluminous material with a seriousness of purpose and a healthy skepticism. As a scholar who has read in this field for almost two decades, I found my respect for Reitlinger growing with every passing page. He had learned so much, so soon.

Examples abound. Like Hilberg, Reitlinger follows the bureaucratic struggles in the aftermath of *Kristallnacht* to solve the problems of the insurance companies. If Jews had to be compensated for damaged property, the insurance industry would have sustained a difficult loss. The solution: the Jewish community was immediately fined a thousand million marks, a new drive for Jewish emigration was begun, and the damage done would have to be repaired by the Jews themselves without benefit of insurance.

So, too, Reitlinger carefully traces the collapse of the policy of emigration and the three stages of annihilation: starvation in the ghettoes, a policy that might have taken some five years, but the Nazis were not willing to wait for nature to run its course; the *Einsatzgruppen*; and finally the extermination camps. He stresses the background of the mobile killing group leaders such as Otto Ohlendorf, a Ph.D.; Ernst Bieberstein, an ordained minister; and Erwin Schulz, an attorney. Similarly, he portrays the dependency of the S.S. on collaboration by the indigenous occupied populace, yet local militia were ineffective and could only make a limited contribution to the murder of Jews. "Without discipline or ideological urge, the mere expectation of plunder could not make men kill enough," Reitlinger writes.

Each step of the way, Reitlinger assesses the role of the bureaucracy and the leaders of the Reich. He rejects a passive role for the German bureaucracy. The broad guidelines of policy were set elsewhere, but the implementation of the policy required extraordinary initiative and diligence. The destruction proceeded under its own momentum. Hitler, Reitlinger writes, did not have to intervene except to suggest a change of policy and a new direction.

The Final Solution is not without its critics. In an early review of the first edition, Philip Friedman took the author to task for some hasty generalizations and interpretations as well as minor inaccuracies. Some of these were corrected in the second edition, others were not. And with the proliferation of scholarship on the Holocaust, the contemporary scholar may have a more subtle understanding of what happened. None of this should detract from our administration of Reitlinger's accomplishment.

The Final Solution is also not without controversy, yet it does not invite controversy. Reitlinger's estimate (guesstimate) of Jewish dead is low. He offers a figure of approximately 4.5 million, more than half a million less than Hilberg and 1.5 million less than the traditional number of six million. Yet, serious historian that he is, he details the assumption of his guesstimate in a carefully crafted appendix that is serious in purpose and in tone. Taken together with Hilberg's essay on the numbers question at the end of his revised and definitive edition of *The Destruction of the European Jews*, the reader is given ample ammunition to silence the revisionists if truth alone were at issue.

Reitlinger's understanding of Adolph Eichmann concurs with Hannah Arendt's much criticized treatment of the banality of evil. Reitlinger's 1952 edition was revised after the Eichmann trial. He carefully studied the documents of the trial and measured his original insights against the new information that surfaced a quarter of a century ago. He too is critical of the trial, dispassionate yet respectful. Yet, unlike Arendt, even when he is critical, his tone is measured, and he is never judgmental or aloof. Never rebellious or angry at the victims and the survivors, he describes the events as he sees them. The purposes of the trial, he writes, were "to show that Israel had secured the greatest persecutor of the Jewish race in all history and brought him to justice; secondly, by means of a cloud of witnesses, to exhibit the fortitude of a generation of survivors." Parenthetically, he adds, "Only the second end was achieved successfully." Yet now, a generation later, we know that the Eichmann trial was a turning point in Israeli, Jewish, and world awareness of the Holocaust. The painful questions raised by the trial and the interest generated in the Holocaust have led to an abundance of research and artistic interest in the event.

Reitlinger is also measured in his assessment of what Hitler achieved. The war had not meant the end of the Jewish people. Even the deaths of millions of Jews "had not hidden the reality of his failure from Hitler himself."

Reitlinger wonders about what lessons can be learned from the Holocaust. "The future could no longer be awaited with the ancient resignation of the East. Only through a new use of privation and a new use of loyalty could existence be endured at all." Only four years after Israel's birth, Reitlinger understood that the destiny of the Jewish people was linked with the State of Israel. He concluded that "in the trials of a newly created nation and not in the up-to-date installation at Birkenau lay the Final Solution of the Jewish Problem."

Perhaps, perhaps!

Of course, for the believing Jew there is no finality to history save the Messianic end. But for the foreseeable future the Jewish people have chosen to stake their future on their reentry into history as a sovereign state in the land of Israel.

Michael Berenbaum

Acknowledgments

In my search for documents and for links in the chain of evidence I have received precious help from a number of persons to whom I must acknowledge my indebtedness and gratitude.

First and foremost, I must thank Dr. Alfred Wiener, founder and director of the Wiener Library in Manchester Square, London. This unique centre for the study of contemporary Central European history has seldom, if indeed ever, failed to provide me with the appropriate printed sources, in addition to which I would have been very hard put to it without Dr. Wiener's personal experience and advice. Among the very patient ladies of the library staff I must particularly thank Dr. Eva G. Reichmann, who has kept a close scrutiny on the German press on my behalf, filing numerous items relating to post-war trials and juridical proceedings that are essential to my story.

I must thank Mr. E. J. Passant, librarian of the Foreign Office, for permission to study in 1949–50 the documents and transcripts from the Nuremberg trials, which were then deposited in the archives section of the library in Princes Street, Westminster. It was the only classified collection from these immensely bulky materials which was available in England, and I could not have gone far without it. In the same connection, I must thank Major F. Elwyn-Jones, M.P., a member of the British prosecution team both at Nuremberg and at the trial of Field-Marshal von Manstein. To Major Elwyn-Jones I owe the loan of an almost complete collection of documents, relating to the persecution of Jewry and extracted from the enormous files of the Wilhelmstrasse case, none of which had then been printed.

I am much indebted to the staff of the *Centre de Documentation Juive Contemporaine* for their assistance during my stay in Paris, when I was able to fill several gaps in the story, thanks to the stencilled, photographed, and original documents in their possession. To M. Leon Poliakov, archivist at the *Centre*, my debt is twofold, first, for his personal advice and second, for the heavy use that I have made of the several admirable sequences of documents that he has edited for the *Centre*'s publications, *L'Etoile Jaune, La condition des Juifs en France sous l'occupation Italienne*, and for the monthly review, *Le Monde Juif*. M. Poliakov's book, *Breviaire de la haine*, came out

xiii

ACKNOWLEDGMENTS

when about three-quarters of the present book had been written. In a sense we are rival chroniclers, but it is not, I think, a head-on collision. M. Poliakov is content to let the documents speak—and in a very dramatic fashion—whereas I have had to let the documents, even when exceptionally vivid, take second place to the reconstruction of the sequence of events.

I must thank the staff of the Rijksinstituut voor Oorlogsdocumentatie and particularly Dr. Louis de Jong for assistance during my Amsterdam visit and for enabling me to study original German documents, while to the Danish Embassy in London I am indebted for permission to study documents from the Werner Best trial, copies of which were kindly sent to London on my behalf. I am, moreover, indebted to several persons for unique material in their possession. Dr. Norbert Masur, of Runebergsgatan, Stockholm, most generously presented me with a typed German transcript of his pamphlet in Swedish, *En Jude talar med Himmler*. Miss Helga Melchior sent me an English precis from Stockholm of the strange narrative of Mejer Neuman of Volove in Ruthenia. Mr. Joseph Zigman, of the Motion Picture Branch of the Information Services Division in the Office of the US High Commissioner in Germany, sent me stills from what is probably the only cinematographic record of a gas-chamber. Dr. Gaddo Glass, of the Comitato della Communita in Trieste, gave me valuable information on the fate of Trieste Jewry.

Finally, I must thank Mr. Barry Sullivan, who has passed a fine-tooth comb through the thicket that grew from my researches and who has extracted not a few thistles; and Mr. Kenneth Duke, sub-editor of the German Foreign Office Documents, now emerging in many volumes from Whaddon Hall, Buckinghamshire, who kindly read most of my typescript and arrested the public career of several howlers. Mr. H. C. Stevens, who translated and summarised some of the Polish printed sources, also earned my gratitude.

GERALD REITLINGER

Beckley, Sussex, November 1952

xiv

THE FINAL SOLUTION

Part I

The Search for the Final Solution

CHAPTER 1

Forced Emigration and Pogroms before September, 1939

1. The Nuremberg Laws and the consequences of Munich

'THE Final Solution of the Jewish Problem' was a code-name for Hitler's plans to exterminate the Jews of Europe. It was used by German officials after the summer of 1941 in order to avoid the necessity of admitting to each other that such plans existed, but previously the expression had been used quite loosely in varying contexts, the underlying suggestion always being emigration. It is probable but by no means certain that the choice of terms had been in the first place Adolf Hitler's.

What did Hitler mean by 'the Jewish problem'? A glance at Hitler's writings and speeches shows that there were *two* Jewish problems, and that though Hitler entangled them together, they demanded quite separate treatment. Firstly there was 'the conspiracy of World Jewry,' by which Hitler meant the power of Jewish-led international finance to do Germany harm. It had lined up the forces of the world against the Kaiser,* it had created the *Diktat* of Versailles, it had excluded Germany between the wars from her natural markets, and by an unholy alliance with Bolshevism it had cheated her of her lawful territorial claims. Secondly there was 'sub-human Jewry,' the proletarian Jewish masses, spreading westwards from the reservoirs of Eastern Europe, which had contaminated German blood and would still do so, unless checked.

*It may be noticed that William II, who was not generally considered an anti-semite, made this discovery about the same time as Adolf Hitler. Dr. Friedrich Schmidt-Ott, a former Prussian Minister of Education, who interviewed the ex-Kaiser at Doorn in 1921, writes: 'He was persuaded that the First World War had been instigated by the Jewish Masonic Lodges in France, Britain, and Italy, and he provided me with highly questionable literature on the subject.' (*Erlebtes und Erstrebtes*, 1860-1950 [Wiesbaden, 1952].)

3

Hitler, as we shall see, believed (*page 22*) that the victory of Germany in a second world war would mean the extinction of World Jewry as a political power. He also believed that it would mean the physical extinction of the Jewish masses, wherever he might find them, but while the former required total victory over a second continent, since the roots of 'World Jewry' were in the Western hemisphere, the latter could be achieved even through partial or temporary victory, since the biological centre of European Jewry lay close at hand. Thus at a quite early stage in his conquests Hitler abandoned all his plans to undermine the capitalistic power of World Jewry in favour of the progressive massacre of European Jews, as they fell into his net. Hitler was led by his *Gefuehl* or intuition to pursue the easier prey, the proletarian Jew, largely to the exclusion of the very sort of Jew whom he most attacked. For at every stage of the programme of deportation and massacre it was possible for Jews with hidden capital to buy their lives. It was under Hitler's very nose that the exemption traffic flourished most. The more impoverished a community of Eastern Jews, the more savage and complete its destruction, but in Germany social position and education could be a title to a Jew's survival even in a concentration camp. Although throughout the war Hitler continued his diatribes against Jewish finance, at no moment did he seriously attempt to stop the Gestapo trafficking in the lives of Jewish property-owners.

It was not only that Hitler chose the easiest course but that, as he became immersed in the conduct of total war, he lost interest in the devilish thing that he had started. Whether there were areas in South-East Europe, where the extinction of the Jewish masses was incomplete, or whether there were pure Jews still living at liberty in his own Reich capital ceased greatly to concern him any longer. Only towards the end of the war he appears to have become aware of the extent to which his orders had been disregarded and of the scale on which European Jewry had survived, a fact which he acknowledged in the political testament which he dictated in the Reich Chancellory bunker on April 30th, 1945 (*page 477*). But having started the machine working, Hitler was generally content to assume that it continued to do so and by all the rules the machine under these conditions

4

should have run down altogether. A brief excursion into the past is, however, necessary to explain why this did not happen.

By the middle of 1934 the two million brown-shirted members of the SA or Storm Detachments, the party militia, had fallen into the hands of a clique of radicals, led by a certain Captain Roehm, who had been a sort of filibuster-adventurer in Latin America. Frightened of a real revolution within a revolution, Hitler was pursuaded by Goering to allow a massacre of Roehm and his followers and the disarming of the SA. The control of the police forces of the Reich now devolved by natural process to Hitler's own bodyguard, the *Schutzstaffeln* or 'Protection Formations,' known more generally as the SS. The head of this party-elite guard had been since 1929 Heinrich Himmler. Thus, as *Reichsfuehrer* SS, Himmler acquired in 1934 the control of an organisation which can only be described as a 'State within the State.' Not only did it include Heydrich's secret political police or Gestapo and under it all the complicated ramifications of the German police system, but in the next five years Himmler built up a series of departments of the SS, which duplicated practically every department of the Government so that there was no sphere of life, not even the armed forces, which was not immune from police interference. This 'State within a State' was something that Hitler had never envisaged in his own writings. The only thing with which it could be compared was the Russian NKVD, for which Hitler professed no admiration ; but he knew its dangers and therefore kept at the head of it a man who was not a member of his own intimate court and whose actions would always be jealously reported to him.

In 1929, when the SS was still subordinate to the SA, the post of the *Reichsfuehrer* had not been important and it had fallen to Himmler, the least colourful of the party 'Bonzes.' A member of the Gestapo's Foreign Intelligence Service, Willi Hoettl, has produced the attractive theory that the immense power, which later accrued to Himmler, was created for him by his subordinate Heydrich—and created as a camouflage screen for his own activities—and that after Heydrich's death it suited Hitler to keep Himmler on because he was a mere stooge and easy to manage.[*1] This is probably a half truth. Although less forceful and unscrupulous, Himmler was probably a better intriguer and

*Source references will be found, chapter by chapter, on *pages 542-590.*

5

place-hunter than Heydrich, who was capable of revealing himself for the ill-tempered ungovernable brute that he was, and who probably would not have realised his ambition of supplanting Himmler had he lived.

The key to the enigmatic rôle of Heinrich Himmler lies in his physical appearance. Whereas Heydrich looked like a night club king, Himmler looked like a myopic bank clerk. And Himmler, in spite of his undoubted personal popularity and his capacity for organisation, was timid. He was never at ease among the splendid Nordic specimens whom he chose instinctively to be his police satraps.* With Hitler Himmler's fear was pathological and this alone made him the perfect instrument to carry out Hitler's plans for the Jews, for if he hesitated—and he did so more than once—then Hitler's court, Goebbels, the Minister for Propaganda, and Bormann, the chief of the Party Chancellory, both of them fanatical anti-semites, had only to jog Hitler's elbow.[2]

Apart from its significance in the creation of Himmler and his organisation, the massacre of Roehm's followers on June 30th, 1934, had a second and equally important bearing on the future destruction of European Jewry. The advent of National Socialism was a political revolution without any dispossessed class and the Jews alone presented a target at which the rabble leaders, the 'old party-fighters' of the Brown Shirts or SA, could direct their animal spirits after the disappearance of the Communists. In this situation there was as yet no implication of the racial extinction

---

*The official short life of Himmler in 'Der Grossdeutsche Reichstag,' 1943, shows that he had been a sergeant-major in the 11th Bavarian Infantry Regiment in the First World War, when he was only seventeen. Himmler himself reminded Count Bernadotte and Dr. Felix Kersten of this rather extraordinary circumstance, but Carl Gebhardt, head of the Hohenlychen hospital, who had known Himmler intimately since the age of twelve, when he went to the school run by Himmler's father, told a different story. He declared at 'The Doctors trial' that Himmler's father, who had been a tutor to the Royal Family of Bavaria, arranged to keep young Heinrich on a farm. I think this is extremely typical of Himmler. The 'Jenghhiz-Kahn' day-dreams recorded by Dr. Kersten, and which can be studied in the original in the transcript of Himmler's Metz and Posen speeches (see page 297), came from the habit of living up to the company he was keeping, particularly the police major-generals. Those who knew Himmler best found him as Dr. Gebhardt found him, 'not original, not a split personality, but very industrious.' (Francois Beyle, 'Croix Gammé ou Caducé,' Neustadt, 1950, pages 219-220.)

of the Jews. But in the second phase of a revolution, the secret-political-police phase, revolutionary passions are no longer a free market. They are, as it were, rationed. There is no more beer-house brawling and indiscriminate parading of uniforms and banners. The State Enemy must now be defined by police regulations and every man of the true breed and the right thinking must be allotted his inferiors.

That was the implication of the victory of Himmler and Heydrich in June, 1934, when they were called in by Hermann Goering, the Prime Minister of Prussia, to make an end of the pretensions of the 'old party-fighters.' For the Jews the meaning of this victory was not revealed till more than a year later in the publication on September 15th, 1935, of the most murderous legislative instrument known to European history, the Nuremberg Laws. Even then, though for the first time since feudalism the law recognised two degrees of humanity, it was probably not at all evident to the Jews of Germany that police-made pogroms on Russian Tsarist lines were implicit in the new decrees.

The character of these Nuremberg Laws was twofold. There was first the Reich Law of Citizenship which established two degrees, the *Reichsbuerger* who must be of pure German blood, and the *Staatsangehoeriger* who was a subject but not a citizen. The 'law for the protection of German blood and honour' was complementary, for it added the principle that the two should not cohabit together in wedlock or out of it.[3] Thus the Reich Law of Citizenship was a basic law. Its thirteen supplementary decrees trace the whole course of Hitler's anti-Jewish action down to the last supplementary decree, which was not published till July 1st, 1943, when the Reich was theoretically 'Jew-free' and which made the Jew an outlaw, wholly at the mercy of the police and without access to the courts.[4]

In 1938, shortly before the Munich agreement, when the Fifth Supplementary Decree had just expelled the Jews from the last of the liberal professions, Franz Stuckart, the man who had not only drafted the Nuremberg Laws but largely promoted them, wrote that the aim of racial legislation had now been achieved. Many of the decisions reached through the Nuremberg Laws would 'lose their importance as the Final Solution of the Jewish Problem is approached.'[5] This phrase, of course, was not yet a camouflage-term to conceal race-murder,* but the meaning of the sentence is clearly that the laws were intended not to make the situation of the Jews permanent but to remove all reason for such a situation. The Jews were meant to leave the Reich for good. Yet at this precise moment there loomed another alternative. War might break out before the last Jew had left the Reich and what would be the fate of the Helots in a nation harnessed to total war ? The correct answer was provided on November 24th, 1938, in an article in the SS newspaper *Das Schwarze Korps*, which declared that 'the fate of such Jews as the outbreak of war should still find in Germany would be their final end, their annihilation (*Vernichtung*).'[6]

Thus the surrender of Chamberlain and Daladier at Munich on September 29th had a special significance for Jewry in the Greater Reich. They were henceforward not merely prisoners of the Nuremberg Laws, waiting to be ransomed, but future hostages for any political demands that Hitler might make on other countries. Hitler's unexpected success must have made him revise his views on Jewish emigration. He must have reflected that what he called International Jewry would be less inclined to pull the strings of interventionist war if he kept some hundreds of thousands of Jews in pawn and showed what he might be prepared to do with them. As if to give expression to this thought, a decree was published on October 5th, only a week after Munich, annulling all Jewish passports and imposing a special emigration permit on all Jews leaving the Reich.[7]

It was perhaps reluctance to part with hostages that induced Hitler to countenance the Schacht emigration plan in the following December, but in reality it is seldom possible to discern the drift of Hitler's private policy behind the conflicting actions of his ministers. This decree of the Ministry for Interior was made in the interest of an 'orderly' emigration policy. It represented the wishes of the economic agencies of the Government to get the most out of Jewish assets, while easing the drain of foreign exchange and the stampede of Jewish mental capital for which

---

*I have purposely avoided the word 'Genocide,' which was coined at the International Nuremberg Trial of 1945-6 and used by the prosecution throughout the subsequent Nuremberg trials. I consider that this hybrid combination of a Greek and a Latin word is no asset to the English language as it says nothing which cannot be conveyed in plain speech.

they still had some use. The decree was in sharp conflict with the policy of the Gestapo and its formidable chief, Reinhardt Heydrich. The irony of this situation was that the men who inspired the articles in *Das Schwarze Korps,* the future exterminators, saved thousands of Jewish lives by forcing total emigration, while the moderates, like Hjalmar Schacht, with their long-term schemes and procrastinating tactics assured the future supply for the gas chambers.

The failure of the Western Powers to support a small nation suggested to Heydrich and the advocates of total Jewish emigration that small nations might be used as compulsory dumping-grounds for Jews in Germany. Already before Munich the Polish Government perceived that they might be faced with the dumping of the 60,000 Jews of professed Polish nationality who resided in Germany. They therefore passed a decree invalidating the passports of those who lived outside Poland, unless these passports received a special stamp which could only be procured in Poland itself after submitting proof of authenticity. Those who failed to do this by October 29th became stateless.

In Warsaw the German Ambassador von Moltke asked for an extension of the time limit,[8] but in Germany Heydrich watched the clock. On the 28th some 15,000 Jews with Polish passports, who were due to become stateless at midnight, were served by the police with deportation notices. Some of them were taken in passenger trains to the Polish border, but, since this was found to be closed, they turned back and the passengers were released to their homes.[9]

Heydrich resumed the attempt a few days later. This time 10,000 Jews were bundled into goods trucks, taking only what they could carry, and put out in the fields near the frontier-station, Sbonszyn.[10] Many of the old and infirm died in the days that followed from exposure and only the efforts of the American Joint Distribution Committee in getting the Jews quartered in a number of Polish towns averted real disaster.[11] The organisation of Heydrich's first mass deportation differed little from that of the deportations to Auschwitz in 1942-44.

In spite of the protests of the Polish Government, there were more deportations over the East Prussian and Silesian borders in

May and June, 1939.[12] There is in existence a circular signed by Schumberg, an official of the Foreign Office department 'Deutschland,' which handled Jewish questions. It was sent on January 25th, 1939, to every German legation and consulate.[13] The writer admits with no bashfulness that the Jews were deported to Poland *after* the publication of the Polish decree. Poland had been singled out for this treatment because of her huge Jewish population and her proneness to anti-semitism. Then he writes this sentence:

> 'The poorer and therefore the more burdensome the immigrant Jews to the country absorbing them, the stronger that country will react and the more favourable will the effect be in the interest of German propaganda.'

This sentence perfectly defines the new German policy towards Jewish emigration which was brought about by the Munich Agreement.

2. The Week of Broken Glass

The deportations of November, 1938, have a double significance. They showed the Jews what to expect, should Hitler occupy territories in the East, and they may have been the immediate cause of the murder of Ernst vom Rath. For Herschel Grynszpan, the murderer, was the son of one ot the Jews who had been put across the Silesian border at Sbonszyn.

On November 7th, this boy of seventeen, who had been visiting an uncle in Paris, waited on the steps of the German embassy in order to kill the ambassador, Count Johannes von Welczek. Did Herschel Grynszpan hope personally to end the era of appeasement by embroiling the French Government with Hitler or was he a mere catspaw of higher agencies—as German propaganda maintained? If the latter, he must have been singularly badly briefed, for only a simpleton or a victim of delusions could have believed that ambassadors habitually came out in the passage to interview strangers or that they were as young as the unfortunate third secretary who was sent to take a look at Grynszpan. And the murder was doubly pointless, for the man destined to be the successor to Wilhelm Gastloff, the second German martyr to the Jews, was being watched by the Gestapo on account of his railings against the National Socialist régime. Nor was Ernst vom Rath in the least degree an anti-semite. We shall never know the real motives of Herschel Grynszpan, for, certain that the French Government would not be in a hurry for a public trial, Goebbels on November 7th, 1938, was able to put any interpretation he liked on the vom Rath murder without fear of controversion

On November 9th Hitler, according to his habit, celebrated the anniversary of his idiotic *Bierhalle* plot of 1923 by marching with the party leaders to the Feldherrnhalle in Munich. Before the subsequent dinner at the city hall Hitler was informed that vom Rath had died of his wounds. Goering, who was not at the dinner, declared at his trial that Hitler left the table early without making an announcement. It was Goebbels who imparted the news to the diners. According to the President of the Party Court, Major Walter Buch, Goebbels revealed that 'spontaneous' reprisals against the Jews had already begun.[14] Goering was by this time in his sleeping-car on the way to Berlin. He learnt of the night's pogrom at the Anhalter Station, where the train arrived in the morning, and where he seems to have assumed at once that Goebbels was responsible. The same impression was received by Walter Funk, the Minister for Economics, who telephoned Goebbels that morning, getting back the retort that the pogroms were his own fault for having failed to eliminate the Jews from economic life, when told to do so earlier in the year. Hitler, according to Goebbels, had now issued new decrees to that end.[15]

Goering saw Hitler that afternoon and complained to him that the pogroms would make a bad impression abroad, coming so soon after the Munich agreement, and that, if they continued, the Four-year Economic Recovery Plan would be jeopardised—with all of which Hitler seemed to agree. It was only in the evening, after he had seen Goebbels, that Hitler insisted on going on with his plans for a collective punishment of the Jews.[16] This story, however, does not account for the immense gusto with which Goering announced Hitler's measures on November 12th. That both Funk and Goering, on trial for their lives at Nuremberg eight years later, accused the dead Goebbels, cannot mean very much.

Clearly the plans for the simultaneous pogroms throughout Germany had been laid at the first news of the shooting of vom Rath. The incidents of the night of the 9th could not have been staged at a few hours notice. Hitler, moreover, exploited the success of the night's work to invoke the wrath of the German people as an excuse for putting into operation the measures for the complete economic spoliation of the Jews, which he had planned in the previous April. Thus he may have ordered the pogroms himself. On the other hand, the party radicals had a motive for forcing his hand. The butchery of Roehm's followers on June 30th, 1934, had established the SS as the unique armed police force of the party. In the next four years the SS had encroached into every sphere of government and this had only been tolerated on account of recurrent states of emergency, due to Hitler's challenges to the foreign powers. Then on September 29th, 1938, Mr. Neville Chamberlain had spoken of ' Peace in our time.' If this meant German disarmament, what would become of the SS ?* If, as Hans Gisevius suggests, Hitler planned the pogroms ' to keep revolutionary passions from cooling,'[17] the SS had everything to gain from them and in particular the *Reichsfuehrer* SS, Heinrich Himmler; but Ulrich von Hassell, who had the best private intelligence service in Germany, was told by Guenther Schmidt, commander of Himmler's bodyguard, that Himmler was not informed till the night of the 8th that he disapproved of the action and that for the next two days he kept his bodyguard confined to barracks.[18] This is rather typical of Himmler, who did not like conspiracy and who had kept well in the background during the suppression of the alleged ' Roehm Putsch ' on June 30th, 1934—the event that had brought him to power. Such orders as have survived implicate only Heydrich, who was well capable of acting over his chief's head.

*If the pogroms were staged in order to challenge Western opinion and to stop Hitler coming into line with the Munich spirit of appeasement, the results could not have been better. Dirksen, the German Ambassador in London, reported on November 17th that there was no longer any chance of Mr. Chamberlain opening discussions, based on the Munich protocol, that Mr. Chamberlain had suffered a loss of prestige, and that even the British supporters of friendship with Germany had become pessimistic. It is needless to insist how extremely truthful was this report, sent to Ribbentrop, a man who disliked the truth above everything. (*Documents on German Foreign Policy. 1918-1945.* Series D., Vol. IV, No. 268.)

Although Reinhardt Heydrich was the real engineer of the Final Solution, which bore the marks of his genius long after his death, his name was little known on November 9th, 1938, except in inner party circles. Thirty-four years of age, tall, willowy, and with a long razor-edged but strangely girlish face, this most fanatical of racialists had few of the physical attributes of a Nordic hero—and the matter was not unnoticed. In 1934 a baker in his home town, Halle, had asserted that Heydrich's father, the Dresden music-tutor Bruno Heydrich, was born of a Jewess. Thereafter it was said that the head of the Security Service went to the length of carving his grandmother a new tombstone with the name Sarah omitted.[19]

Heydrich began his strange under-cover career in 1931 when he suddenly left the navy and the post of chief intelligence officer to the Baltic Command, having, it was said, been forced to resign by Admiral Raeder for compromising the virtue of a shipyard director's daughter. A few months later he won the favour of Erich Koch, the party Gauleiter for East Prussia, and was recommended by him to Himmler—the result, according to Willi Hoettl, of Heydrich's attentions to Frau Koch. At first a mere political officer in Munich, Heydrich soon became head of the Berlin Gestapo, where, by whetting his unique appetite for blood in the executions of the alleged leaders of the June, 1934 *Putsch,* he made certain of his destiny.

With the SS in unchallenged ascendancy over the 'Old Party Fighters' of the SA, Heydrich now ran the Security Service (SD), the Gestapo and the Criminal Police. At the head of the German police system was Himmler, and Himmler was nominally under the orders of Frick, the Minister for Interior, but, in so far as Heydrich was concerned, both these authorities were a legal fiction at any rate until September, 1939, when the SD and Security Police were merged as the Main Security Office (RSHA). Moreover, on the night of November 9th, 1938, Hitler or Goebbels could have done nothing without Heydrich, whose SD officials alone were in a position to contact the riot-raisers and stop the local police intervening. In fact there has survived a copy of Heydrich's teletype, which was circulated to the State Police:

'Because of the attempt on the life of the Legation

13

Secretary vom Rath in Paris, demonstrations against the Jews are to be expected to-night, November 9th-10th, throughout the Reich. The Police Presidents are to get in touch with the Gauleiters in order that they may adjust their measures to the following conditions.'[20]

Heydrich goes on to explain how damage to German property is to be avoided. Shops and flats may be destroyed but they must not be looted. Synagogues may not be fired when they endanger adjacent houses. A further circular, signed by Heinrich Mueller, Heydrich's chief of the Gestapo, orders the State Police officials to arrest 20,000 to 30,000 Jews, above all, persons of wealth. The ' sharpest measures' are to be taken against those who resist with arms, synagogue archives must be secured and those of Cologne are to be sent to the SD.[21]

Heydrich took great care to provide himself with an alibi and this suggests that he was more than a mere executive for Hitler or Goebbels. On the night of November 9th he was not in Munich with Hitler and the party leaders but in an hotel in Nuremberg with Werner Best, one of his Gestapo chiefs, according to whom Heydrich feigned complete ignorance when a neighbouring synagogue went up in flames and only issued orders to the State Police after he had been able to contact Himmler in Berlin over the telephone.[22]

On November 11th Heydrich sent a report to Goering, according to which 191 synagogues and 171 apartment-houses had been set on fire and 815 shops looted.[23] Only 117 participants in the riots had been arrested but 20,000 Jews had been taken into ' protective custody,' half of them being sent to Buchenwald camp.[24]* There had been 36 Jews killed and 36 badly wounded. Next day, however, Heydrich admitted an under-estimate. The

---

*According to Eugen Kogon, the exact number of Jews sent to Buchenwald after the ' night of broken glass' was 9,815. Buchenwald was at this time barely a year old but it already contained some 2,700 Jews who had been brought there in June and August. The new arrivals were not admitted to the still reasonably equipped main camp, but left with the barest comforts of existence in the ' Little camp.' This camp was dissolved on February 13th, 1939, when most of the ' November Jews' had been ransomed, but quite a considerable number had died. Later in the war the ' Little camp' was revived as an overflow camp, whenever large transports arrived, and it was destined to fulfil an even worse rôle in the destruction of Jewry in January-April, 1945 (*see pages 458-459*).

real number of looted shops was 7,500. Three months later even a party court admitted that the riots had been organised at a considerably higher level than the members whose conduct was under examination; after which pronouncement the court expelled five members from the party for the crimes of rape, theft, and murder, and suspended a few others, but begged the Fuehrer to quash the sentences that had been passed in the State Criminal Courts.[25]

The pogroms were only the unofficial penalty for the murder of vom Rath. The official penalty was not announced till the 12th, when Goering held his inter-ministerial conference in the Air Ministry building. Although three out of the seven numbered parts are missing, the minutes of this meeting, which lasted from 11 a.m. to 2.40 p.m., occupy 10,000 words. Nevertheless, the illustrious company had no primary decisions to take. They had only to comment and to listen to the rich voice of the *Reichsmarschall*, who seems to have been in his best form, having just had instructions from the Fuehrer that the Jewish question was to be 'co-ordinated and solved, now, once, and for all, in one way or another.'[26]

With the comforting sense that they lived in a totalitarian State, where everything was ordered over their heads, the members of the conference were not unduly serious. The tone was set by the interchanges between Goebbels and Goering. Goebbels wanted special railway coaches for Jews. Goering suggested that this might mean providing Jews with seats when Germans were crowded out. Such Germans should 'need no regulation to kick a Jew out of his seat and make him sit alone all the way in the lavatory.'

The professional bureaucrats Stuckart, Funck, Woermann, von Krosigk, and Fischboeck were not quite so light-hearted but the standard excuse that they struggled against the storm does not stand up very well. If Funk proposed that the Jews should retain the shares in their own firms, it was, as he explained, because he feared that their sale would depress the stock market. When Heydrich opposed the creation of ghettoes—for precisely the reasons that he later advanced for liquidating their inhabitants —Funk was all for the ghettoes. But Schwerin von Krosigk, Minister of Finance, who had been an Oxford Rhodes Scholar,

15

thought the ghettoes 'not very nice.' For the Foreign Office, Woermann wanted to protect *foreign* Jews. He feared that the U.S.A. might retaliate against German assets.

The most difficult problem, set them by the Fuehrer's decrees, was insurance. Goering supposed that they need not pay up, but a certain *Reichsgruppenleiter* Hilgard, who had been invited to speak for the insurance companies, warned them that most of the freeholds concerned were Aryan-owned, in particular the looted Markgraf establishment on Unter den Linden, that Aryan owners had suffered a loss in plate-glass alone of six million marks and that this glass could only be replaced against foreign currency. Moreover, Herr Hilgard continued, failure to pay up would ruin the confidence of foreigners in German insurance.

For this Heydrich offered a simple solution. Herr Hilgard should pay up, but the money should go to the Finance Minister and the victims should be compensated by their Jewish tenants. No, said Hilgard, the claims were likely to exceed double the year's insurance revenue. In great exasperation Goering turned on Heydrich, ' I wish you had killed two hundred Jews instead of destroying so many valuables.' 'There were thirty-five killed,' Heydrich replied. But, when on trial at Nuremberg, Goering declared that he had been so rattled by Goebbels's idiocies that he had said this ' in a moment of bad temper and excitement.'[27] A compromise-suggestion of Schwerin von Krosigk's was adopted, by which some of the thousand million mark fine was to relieve the burden of the insurance companies. ' Hilgard, you can consider yourself damned lucky,' Goering boomed. Hilgard, who probably thought he had got into Bedlam, protested. ' The fact that we will not have to pay all the damage you call a profit.' Thereupon the great bulk of the *Reichsmarschall* towered before the insurance broker. ' Just a moment. If you are legally bound to pay five millions and all of a sudden an angel in my somewhat corpulent shape appears before you and tells you that you may keep one million, hang it, isn't this a profit ? I should like to go fifty-fifty with you or whatever you call it. I have only to look at you. Your whole body expresses satisfaction. You are getting a big rake-off.'

Herr Hilgard made one more expostulation and was told to see to it himself that less windows were smashed—for the pogroms were still proceeding. Then he withdrew from the meeting and the curtain of history was drawn over him. A memorandum of the conference, made by Woermann of the Foreign Office, shows what Hitler's brief to Goering meant by 'co-ordinated and solved.'[28] All Jewish enterprises were to be taken over by State-trustees and sold to Aryans, the owners receiving merely book-entry securities, bearing fixed interest. A few exceptions might be made in favour of the promotion of export, but works of art, real estate, securities, and jewellery would be taken over on similar terms. The questions of extending the forced labour decree to the Jews, of confining them to ghettoes, of banishing them from all places of recreation, of banning their children from German schools, were to be examined by select committees. There was to be an immediate community fine of a thousand million marks. There was to be a new drive for Jewish emigration, and the damage done in the pogroms was to be paid for by the Jews themselves without benefit of insurance.

Three of these orders had been published that very morning as decrees in the *Reichsgesetzblatt,* the order eliminating the Jews from economic life, the order to pay the thousand million mark fine, and the order to defray the riot damage. The ban on German schools followed three days later and on November 28th the ban on places of recreation. Not till many months afterwards, on March 4th and April 30th, were the Jewish labour-conscription decress published and the law which limited Jewish tenancies to transactions between Jews—the first step towards the ghetto.[29] In announcing the thousand million mark fine Goering remarked:

> 'That will work. The pigs will not commit another murder. Incidentally, I would like to say that I would not like to be a Jew in Germany now. The second point is this. If in the near future the German Reich should come into conflict with foreign Powers, it goes without saying that we in Germany would first of all let it come to a reckoning with the Jews.'

In later years Goering was responsible for a certain amount of intervention on behalf of Jews. In April, 1940, he suspended the expulsions from the incorporated Polish territories and in the

17

Autumn of 1941 he obtained a respite of rather more than a year for the families of Jewish armament workers in the Reich. Goering was also responsible, according to his friend Karl von Bodenschatz, General of the Air Force, for a number of interventions on behalf of individual Jews whose cases had been reported to him.[30] Of these three sorts of intervention, the first was due to Goering's fear of foreign repercussions, the second to his anxiety for the arms production programme, and the third to his personal vanity. Goering's real feelings regarding the Jews will be found in his singularly unbridled utterances of November 12th, 1938. On two subsequent occasions, in January, 1939, and July, 1941, Goering was to confer a general brief on Heydrich to 'solve the Jewish question.' Not only was Goering perfectly aware of the methods by which Heydrich carried out this brief, but he retained, as *Reichsmarschall*, personal authority over Heydrich and on occasions was able to exercise it (*see pages 44-5 and 83*). Goering must therefore be considered just as responsible for the exterminations of 1942 as he was for the forced emigrations of 1938. Nor should it be forgotten that Heydrich, to whom Goering showed such obvious hostility in the minutes of November 12th, 1938, was his own creation. For it was Goering's dread lest Roehm's plans for a revolutionary Wehrmacht should achieve a Bolshevik system in 1934, that had brought about the SS State.

3. The Schacht Plan and Its Failure

The clash between Heydrich and Goering, which enlivens the minutes of November 12th, 1938, concerned Jewish emigration. Heydrich was content to push Jews over the 'Green Frontier' after the Gestapo had extracted such ransom as it could. Goering, no less than Heydrich and *Das Schwarze Korps*, expected to settle finally with the Jews if war should break out, but in the meantime he preferred to sell them more methodically and at a higher price, payable in foreign exchange. This difference emerged clearly when Heydrich boasted how in the eight months since the *Anschluss* he had forced 45,000 Jews to leave Austria, whereas from the 'old Reich' only 19,000 had been permitted to leave, the success being due to his own strategy of forcing the Jewish *Kultusgemeinde* to collect foreign exchange holdings from rich Jews in order to finance the emigration of the poor. Here Goering expostulated: 'But, children, did you ever think this out? It doesn't help to extract hundreds of thousands from the Jewish rabble this way. Have you ever reflected that this procedure may lose us so much foreign exchange that we may not be able to hold out?'

With affected meekness Heydrich agreed that the best annual figure might be 8,000-10,000 Jewish emigrants, but he meant nothing of the kind. He had just rounded up 20,000 Jews whom his agents had selected for the concentration camps on account of their wealth or social standing. By putting the screws on these 'November Jews' he could find the passage money for several times their number—that is if Heydrich was not interfered with. But at this particular moment, November 12th, 1938, there were signs that Heydrich and the Gestapo might lose their undisputed empire over the bodies of German Jewry.

The efforts to make German Jewry an international responsibility had culminated in July, 1938, in the Evian Conference, out of which had emerged an Intergovernmental Refugee Committee under the direction of Mr. Rublee of New York. On October 18th, after a request from the British and U.S. ambassadors that Mr. Rublee should be heard in Berlin, Ribbentrop received the following report from his permanent State Secretary, the Baron Ernst von Weizsaecker:

> 'The committee had intended, in order to prove its worth, to enter into discussions with the German Government. It would then be established in Germany that we— for obvious reasons—were not willing to provide the Jews with foreign currency and thus the committee would reach its ultimate object, namely, to prove that it was again German obstinacy which was responsible for the misery of the Jews. I was not able to recommend Mr. Rublee's journey simply for the sake of making Germany the scapegoat.'[31]

After this report from the alleged philo-semite von Weizsaecker it is perhaps not surprising that Mr. Rublee had received no invitation to Berlin by November 10th, when the U.S. Ambassador left Berlin as a protest at the pogrom. But Goering, seriously concerned two days later at the economic consequences of another drain of foreign exchange holdings through Heydrich's 20,000 new hostages, put up a plan of his own, which was to send Fischboeck, the Minister for Economics in Austria, to submit emigration proposals in London.[32] The final outcome of Goering's plan was that Hitler approved the dispatch of Schacht, the President of the Reichsbank.

The proposal which Schacht discussed in London during December with Lord Bearsted, Lord Winterton, and Mr. Rublee was roughly as follows: The German Government were to freeze the assets of the Jewish community which were to become the security for an international loan, repayable in twenty to twenty-five years. On the assumption that the Jewish assets were worth 1,500 million marks, there would be enough foreign currency to finance an orderly emigration of the Jews of the Greater Reich in three to five years.[33] Schacht then returned to Germany and at Berchtesgaden on January 2nd, 1939, he had a long personal discussion with Hitler concerning the reception of his proposals in London. Hitler was apparently impressed, for three days later he appointed Schacht Special Delegate for the promotion of Jewish emigration.

Hitler now for the first time openly opposed the rough-and-ready methods of Heydrich and the Gestapo. The Foreign Office were instructed to withdraw their opposition to Mr. Rublee's visit[34] and the negotiations with the Intergovernmental Refugee Committee were transferred to Berlin. Then on January 20th came Hitler's famous quarrel with Schacht, who was dismissed from his presidency of Reichsbank after refusing to agree to increase the note circulation. For a time the negotiations of Helmuth Wohltat, head of the Foreign Credits Control Office, with Messrs. Pell and Rublee were broken off. Although they were resumed at the request of the U.S. Consul-General and the Italian Ambassador,[35] they proved quite fruitless, since Hitler, in violent reaction against Schacht, now refused to give up the Jewish community's assets.

There was the same stumbling-block in April, when Wohltat was allowed to go to London to discuss a limited Jewish emigration to Rhodesia and British Guiana. Schacht actually maintained in his final speech at Nuremberg that the Western Powers had lost an opportunity in December, 1939, when his plan still had

Hitler's backing. 'Had the plan been carried through, not a single German Jew would have lost his life.'[36]

Is one really to believe that Hitler would have financed Jewish emigration during the war merely to honour the Schacht loan or that the Allies would have accepted Jews from the Reich throughout the wartime blockade? And even if the Allies accepted some 300,000 Jews, who were under Hitler's rule in January, 1939, what of the subsequently occupied territories where over four millions perished?

Hitler had toyed with Schacht's project for barely six weeks. On January 24th, four days after Schacht's dismissal, the omnipotence of the Gestapo in Jewish emigration affairs received the standing of a decree. Goering had to write to Frick that a Central Emigration Office for Jews would be established within his ministry with Heydrich at the head. Two of Frick's officials would serve in this office, but this was merely the old fiction that the SS were part of the Ministry of the Interior. Goering's mandate to Frick—which must have been most uncongenial to him—empowered Heydrich to ' solve the Jewish question by emigration and evacuation in the way that is most favourable under the conditions prevailing at present.'[37]*

At the conference of November 12th Goering had mentioned casually that Hitler was considering a Jewish settlement in Madagascar and now significantly the word ' evacuation ' was coupled with ' emigration.' On February 7th the Foreign Press in Berlin was invited to an important Press conference, addressed by Alfred Rosenberg, who at this time directed a somewhat nebulous ' Foreign Political Office.' The *Voelkischer Beobachter* reported his words as follows[38]:

> ' What territories are the democracies willing to provide for the purpose of settling some fifteen million Jews ? The Jewish millionaires and multi-millionaires will have to place their means at the disposal of, let us say, the office of

---

*It must be noticed that the word *Endloesung*, which plays such a part in Heydrich's renewed brief from Goering on July 31st, 1941, does not occur in this first brief. Nevertheless, on November 6th, 1941, Heydrich wrote to Quartermaster-General Wagner (*see page 308*) 'I have been entrusted for years with the task of preparing the final solution of the Jewish problem.' Presumably Heydrich dated his trust from January 24th, 1939, but he had not always been engaged on the same solution.

the Evian Conference. If millions of Jews are to be settled, elementary humanity towards the Jews demands that they shall not be left to themselves, but that the colony be placed under administrators trained in police work. There is no question of establishing a Jewish State, but only of a Jewish reserve.'

Where precisely did Rosenberg intend this penal colony under alien police administrators to be ? In Madagascar, on which Hitler had no territorial designs, or in that Russian *lebensraum* of which Rosenberg was the persistent advocate ? The whole concept implied war and the annexation of territory, but of that contingency Hitler had spoken in the least equivocal terms and as recently as January 30th in a speech to the Reichstag which lasted two hours and twenty-two minutes : [39]

'To-day I will once more be a prophet. If the international Jewish financiers inside and outside Europe should again succeed in plunging the nations into a world war, the result will be not the bolshevisation of the earth and thus the victory of Jewry, but the annihilation of the Jewish race throughout Europe.'

The words were inserted in an immense and rambling speech, but they were not spoken at random. In years to come Hitler was often to remind listeners of his prophecy and on at least five occasions he repeated the words verbatim in public.[40]

4. Heydrich and Eichmann

The next act in the drama of the Final Solution began five weeks later on March 15th, 1939, when Hitler marched into Prague and proclaimed the German Protectorate of Bohemia and Moravia. For the first time Hitler governed a region predominantly hostile in feeling and foreign in speech. Though Czechoslovakia had capitulated without firing a shot, virtually there was martial law for the next six years. The Germans gave their orders, the puppet Government of Dr. Hacha merely ratified them. Thus an immense mass of Jews were delivered to the Gestapo without even that minimum of protection which the law still accorded the Jews of Germany. There resulted a forced emigration on a scale that had not been reached even in Austria, some 35,000 Jews leaving the protectorate in the next six months.*

Heydrich was assisted by the historic status of the Czech Jews in achieving this clearance. For generations the Council, elected by the Prague community, had administered relief to the Jews of the whole country. The Germans therefore made the Prague Jewish Council the unique medium through which a Jew could approach them, a complete bureaucracy of thirty-two departments. It had taken far longer to achieve such results in the Old Reich, where the creation of the *Reichsvereinigung* of German Jews was preceded by years of forcible amalgamation of the existing Jewish charitable organisations.

On July 26th, 1939, a branch of the six-months old ' Central Office for Jewish Emigration' was set up in Prague by a certain Captain Eichmann. In spite of Goering's mandate of January 24th, Eichmann belonged to Heydrich's Security Service. Thus in Prague, as in Vienna, the Gestapo worked in the actual building of the Jewish Community Council[42] and it was the task of the Council to provide a daily quota of Jewish emigrants. If the emigrants were not produced and their capitation fees were not paid, it might be a concentration-camp matter. Thus the poorest members of the community tended to be the first to go, because those who were known to have property had to negotiate with the Gestapo on their own. The 'quota Jews' demanded by Eichmann were dumped with their exit permits at ports and frontiers. Thousands were put aboard German ships with bogus Latin-American visas or with British permits for Palestine. Some were left to roam the high seas for weeks on end, as in the case of the passengers of the Hamburg Amerika liner *Saint Louis,* which sailed for Cuba in May, 1939.

In the beginning Eichmann demanded the emigration of 70,000 Jews within a year. Dr. Kafka, the President of the Prague Community Council, protested that the funds of the Council had been blocked. Eichmann then threatened to take 300 Jews a day,

---

*In March, 1939, the Jewish population of Bohemia-Moravia was swollen by refugees from Austria and Sudetenland and may have numbered 122,000, or even 129,000. By October, 1939, on the eve of the first mass deportation to Poland, the number had fallen to 90,147.[41]

street by street, and send them to Dachau and Merkerlgruen, 'where they will become very keen on emigration.'[43] Somehow the money was forthcoming. Had the war not broken out five weeks later, Eichmann's demands might have been satisfied in full. In the meantime the freezing of Jewish funds, the seizure of Jewish business, and the dismissal of Jewish employees had caused a rush to the capital. In October, 1939, though 35,000 Jews may have left the country, the Prague community had grown from 35,425 to 46,170 Jews.[44] Some 8,000 had been forcibly brought in from the smaller towns through a police decree of August 11th.[45]

Thus the state of mass destitution, foreseen by the writer in *Das Schwarze Korps,* was brought within sight and Prague seemed about to recover its historic closed ghetto. But Heydrich, as we have already noticed, was not partial to ghettoes. He had obtained the necessary excuses of overcrowding and epidemics. The next move was massed deportation, as soon as spare territory became available, first in Poland and later in Soviet Russia. But wherever they were to go, the Jews were made the instrument of their own expulsion. The Prague Community Council was to provide the model for the Jewish Councils (*Judenraete*) which in the towns of Poland and Russia in 1941-43 registered the names of their flock, brought them to the assembly place, and eventually followed them to the execution pits and death camps.

This system was the undoubted invention of Heydrich, who had applied something like it to the Vienna Jews, immediately after the Anschluss of March, 1938, and had boasted of the results at Goering's conference of November 12th. As to Eichmann, although he was to brag seven years later to the Nuremberg witnesses, Willi Hoettl and Dieter Wisliceny, that he had contrived the death of five million Jews, he was no more than Heydrich's executant and it was in the Central Emigration Office that he served his apprenticeship.

Since Eichmann may be alive to-day, more may come to light concerning the position he finally acquired in the SS hierarchy, but the files of the Foreign Office department 'Deutschland III' have already shown that the functions of the Jew-inquisitor were neither autocratic nor secret. (*See pages 72, 74, and 96.*) Other Eichmann legends have been shattered by the discovery of his personal service record, as kept by the SS staff office. Such, for instance, the legend that he was born in Palestine, in the German Templar colony of Sarona.[46] The prosaic truth has not, however, stopped the creation of new legends, that Eichmann was in Egypt in 1948, recruiting escaped German prisoners to fight the Jews,[47] or that he had returned to Palestine after the war *as a Jew*.[48]

In fact Eichmann was born in March, 1906, at Solingen of a family who were formerly domiciled in Elberfeld, but who moved to Linz in Austria during Eichmann's infancy. His father was head of an electrical construction company.[49] Thus he grew up in a purely Austrian atmosphere, acquiring an Austrian turn of speech and a passion for riding, which was noticed in his Budapest heyday of 1944, when Dr. Kastner perceived Eichmann's bandy-legged walk.[50] Eichmann was originally trained to follow his father's calling and in all his documents he describes his civil occupation as 'mechanical engineer,' but he had to abandon his technical studies in 1925 when his father was ruined by the inflation.

In 1927 Eichmann had to become a salesman for the firm Vacuum Oil A.G. and in 1931 his disappointment found an outlet in joining the Austrian National Socialist Party. In July, 1933, he crossed the German border and for the next fourteen months trained with the 'Austrian Legion' at Lechfeld near Passau. In September, 1934, Sergeant Eichmann was transferred to the more congenial surroundings of the Berlin head office of the SD or Security Service, where at first he was employed compiling a card-index on Freemasonry. Subsequently he had charge of the office museum, where he got interested in Zionist documents and acquired a smattering of Yiddish and Hebrew, M. Poliakov believes that Eichmann was sent to Palestine in 1937 to make contact with the Arab rebels, but that he was expelled[51] by the British authorities after 48 hours ; that Eichmann then went to Cairo, where he made friends with Haji Amin Husseini, the ex-Mufti of Jerusalem. But at the time of this alleged Palestine visit, Eichmann was only a sergeant-major in the SS, serving in unannexed Vienna as a Gestapo spy. Eichmann's friendship with the Mufti probably dates from 1942-44 when the latter was an accredited Arab plenipotentiary, living in Berlin and maintaining contact with Eichmann's office.

Eichmann's real career began on August 1st, 1938, a few months after the *Anschluss*, when he was put in charge of the Vienna Jewish emigration office. His recommendation for promotion to the rank of captain, dated January 30th, 1939, reads: 'Eichmann directs the entire Jewish emigration.'[52] From Vienna Eichmann was moved to Prague and from Prague to Berlin, where on January 30th, 1940, he attended Heydrich's great conference on the resettlement of Jews and Poles (*see pages 44 and 45*). A few months later Eichmann was in charge both of the Central Emigration Office and the Jewish investigation department of the Gestapo, the two offices having been amalgamated as Bureau IVA, 4b, of the *Reichssicherheitshauptamt* or RSHA, the Reich Main Security Office.

'IVA, 4b,' with its own four-storey building at 116, Kurfurstenstrasse, became in the years 1941-44 the headquarters of the Final Solution, the hub of the entire spider's web of deportation and massacre. Yet in theory it was a very humble institution. Amt IV meant the Gestapo, Section A was its internal activities department, of which No. 4 was a subdivision investigating religious cults, and IVA, 4b a further subdivision concerned with Jews. Thus it ranked with more than a hundred obscure offices of the RSHA* and, in keeping with this camouflage, Eichmann was destined never to rise beyond the SS rank of an *Obersturmbannfuehrer* or Lieutenant-colonel. This, Eichmann's last promotion, was achieved on October 29th, 1941, shortly after the revival of deportations from the Reich. During the subsequent blood-bath it was Eichmann's rôle not to look too important. Only in Budapest after March, 1944, did he permit himself to become a public personality, possibly because he had the support of Kaltenbrunner against Himmler.

Dr. Kastner's portrait of the Eichmann of this period is that of an SS satrap, cynical, boastful, hard-drinking, and maintaining a smart mistress, but the photograph published by M. Poliakov, taken probably ten years earlier when Eichmann had just joined the SD, is of a less worldly character.[53] Of this earnest student face, only the queer glittering eyes remain unchanged in the

---

*For instance, the office 'VIF, 4a' of Major Krueger which manufactured forged foreign banknotes in Sachsenhausen camp for the use of the counter-intelligence service, Ausland-Abwehr. (Case XI NG 5508, and *see page 454*.)

photographs attached to Eichmann's personal service file in 1944. One wonders whether Eichmann did not choose his assignment because his colleagues teased him on a Jewish appearance. Psychologists at least should be interested in Eichmann's explanation of his lack of party 'sports insignia'—a gratuitous explanation in any case—'on account of an injury to my hand.'[54]

Eichmann's career was that of a German civil servant, absorbed in his work and getting no glory from it. He married a commonplace little woman who bore him three daughters—the family who, he intended, should die with him when he committed suicide, as he informed his friend Wisliceny in February, 1945. But Wisliceny was to see Eichmann again a day or two before the capitulation of Germany. It was at Alt-Aussee in Salzkammergut, the last headquarters of Kaltenbrunner and the Reich Main Security Office. Eichmann then told Wisliceny that he had procured his family false papers and that personally he was going to hide in the mountains 'till the forthcoming conflict between East and West' (see pages 480-1).

More than seven years have passed and Eichmann's body has not been found. We do not know whether he fulfilled his boast that 'he would leap into his grave laughing because the feeling that he had five million people on his conscience would be for him a source of extraordinary satisfaction.[55] In any case the murders in which Eichmann had a direct hand numbered less than a million, for his connection with the massacres in Poland and Russia seems rather remote. He was a Grand Inquisitor without a vestige of glamour or romantic mystery and he may be summed up in the words of his friend Dieter Wisliceny, the man who recommended him for his first commission[56]:

> 'Eichmann was in every respect a painstaking bureaucrat. He at once recorded in the files every discussion he ever had with any of his superiors. He always told me that the most important thing was to be covered at all times by one's superiors. He shunned all personal responsibility and took care to shelter behind his superiors—in this case Mueller and Kaltenbrunner—and to inveigle them into accepting liability for all his actions.'

5. Emigration After the Outbreak of War

On July 6th, 1939, Heydrich's empire of death was complete. The latest annexe to the Nuremberg Laws, 'the Tenth Decree, Supplementing the Reich Law of Citizenship,' had transformed the *Reichsvereinigung*, the amalgamated Jewish relief organisations of the Old Reich, into an official Jewish bureaucracy, controlled by the Chief of the Security Police and SD.[57] The Jews were close prisoners of the SS State. They had charge of their own taxation and social services, it is true, but they had lost most of the limited rights of appeal to the common law of the country which the original Nuremberg Laws had left them. They lived in a ghetto without walls.

Under cover of the 'Tenth Decree' the expropriation of Jewish firms was carried out without even the compensation in nominal Government stock, stipulated in the decree of November, 1938, but the process was slow and at the beginning of the war there were still a few Jewish private banks and some firms which exported furs and textiles. There was no vocation for the majority of the 375,000 Jews of the Greater Reich, including Austria and the Protectorate, from whom complete destitution was only averted through the labour conscription decree of March 4th, 1939. Even so, the number who had work was insufficient. For instance, there were only 20,000 Jews who were employed, in the Berlin community, which numbered 95,000 at the outbreak of war.[58] The conscription decree required the Jews to be employed in building and landwork, but in practice the armaments-industry was allowed to take on skilled Jews who were thereby protected from deportation till as late as February, 1943, particularly in Berlin and Breslau (*see page 161*).

The outbreak of war on September 1st, 1939, brought no change in the legal status of German Jewry. Emigration was permitted up till October 1st, 1941, when extermination in the Eastern ghettoes had been going on for months. Several neutral countries remained open to the golden key, the Atlantic could be crossed, even Palestine could be reached. Till June 20th, 1940, refugees with the necessary means could sail from Italian ports and from June 20th, 1940, to November 11th, 1942, they could make their way, though with increasing difficulty, through unoccupied France to Lisbon or Casablanca. In May, 1941, the Gestapo complained that French Jews used these limited facilities to the prejudice of permitted Jewish emigrants from the Reich.[59] Even Jews in Poland could at first escape the German terror. Italy could be reached through Slovakia and Hungary, and the Black Sea ports through Rumania. There was an extensively used route to China and Japan through Lithuania and the USSR.

It is extremely difficult to assess the number of Jews who escaped after the outbreak of war, but it is known that, during the two and a half years' existence of the unoccupied zone in France, the organisations HICEM and Joint Distribution Committee cleared 10,000 Jews through Lisbon and 1,200 through Casablanca.[60] The outbreak of war with Japan found some 20,000 European Jewish refugees living in Shanghai and 4,000 in Kobe, the majority of whom had arrived since September, 1939. The heyday of this emigration was between the fall of France and a month or two before the invasion of the Soviet Union, when the Russians stopped the transit traffic.

Possibly as many as 13,000 Jews from the Old Reich alone left voluntarily in the first two years of the war (*see pages 491-2*), a figure that need not surprise in the light of the exodus across Europe to Palestine in 1947. In other words, one in sixteen could afford to buy their ransom from the Gestapo.* Hitler may have been kept ignorant of this practice or he may have condoned it, but no such doubt surrounds Himmler and Heydrich. The former, having regarded Jewish emigration as a source of revenue for the SS during the first two years of the war, made several attempts at collective bargaining years after Hitler had ordered the Final Solution. The attitude of Heydrich is harder to understand. When entrusted with the programme of murderous deportations in the summer of 1941, he carried out his task without the least pity or

---

*The official *Reichsvereinigung* statistics for the Old Reich show 215,000 Jews living there in September, 1939, and 163,696 on October 1st, 1941, when the emigration ban was published.[61] Of the loss of 51,000 Jews, 6,500 were accountable to the deportation to the South of France in October, 1940, and 1,400 to the deportation from Stettin to Poland in February, 1940. A much greater loss was entailed in these two years by the growing excess of deaths over births, which Himmler's statistician, Dr. Korherr, put as high as 85 per thousand[62] a year (*see Appendix 1*).

deviation, but he seems at no time to have hindered the departure of the Jews in order to retain them for future extermination.

The crime of Herschel Grynszpan, which had served its purpose as the excuse for the penal decrees of November, 1938, achieved a fresh significance at the outbreak of war. Grynszpan was now not merely the Jewish conspirator who had sought to embroil Hitler with France, he was the living symbol of the International Jew who had brought about the war. On September 20th, 1939, Goebbels published a 'yellow book,' called 'Grynsz-pan and his accomplices,' which was written by Wolfgang Dierwege, a councillor in his ministry.[63] But from this point on the Germans seem oddly to have neglected the possibilities of the Grynszpan legend, even after the collapse of France in June, 1940, when Grynszpan fell into their hands. It was significantly in December, 1941, when mass murder was extended to the Jews of the Reich, that it was first thought expedient to stage a State trial. Dierwege, who was sent by Goebbels to Paris to collect witnesses, succeeded in interviewing M. Georges Bonnet, the Foreign Secretary of Munich days. According to Dierwege, M. Bonnet was ready to testify that he had been compelled to declare war on Germany by the same Jewish influences that had delayed bringing Grynszpan to justice.[64]

At this moment the whole fabric of the plan for a great State trial before the eyes of the world began to totter. Goebbels did not like the rôle of M. Bonnet, and all the party leaders disliked the revival that the trial would create for the hero-worship of vom Rath, who typified the Junker opposition. Early in April Thierack, the future Minister of Justice, was substituted for Roland Freisler, who was to judge Grynszpan in the Berlin People's Court. Thierack ordered a certain Weimann to act as Grynszpan's counsel[65] and to Weimann he sent, printed in the prosecution brief, a weapon to wreck the vom Rath legend. It was an anonymous letter, written by a Jewish refugee in France, accusing vom Rath of protracted homosexual relations with Grynszpan. Double-crossed and furious, Goebbels had to persuade Ribbentrop and Abetz to drop their plans for the trial. On May 11th, 1942, it was postponed sine die.

Here the mysterious figure of Herschel Grynszpan disappears from history. No trial was needed if it was merely a question of getting rid of a Jew. The Germans had only to put Grynszpan on one of the Auschwitz trains, which were soon running according to time-table. Strange to say, in May, 1940, Grynszpan had been at liberty. The train which was to take him with other prison-inmates from Paris to Toulouse was bombed near Limoges. Grynszpan demanded to be taken to prison, even when the *Procureur* of the Republic wanted to put him in an hotel.[66] Somehow this gesture of fatalism by the young man, who had brought such misfortune on his race, seems to symbolise the attitude of the Eastern Jews in the ordeal that lay before them, an attitude that still defeats speculation.

CHAPTER 2

Deportation, 1939—1941

1. The Strengthening of German Folkdom

On September 1st, 1939, when the first German troops crossed the Polish frontier, ill-founded optimism was rife. The Poles were expected to last out long enough to benefit from the slow mobilisation of the West. Few realised that the eighteen days of Polish resistance were a remarkable achievement for a nation which was not equipped for armoured warfare. In the speculation of the day there was little curiosity concerning the fate of the largest national group of Jews in Europe—2,732,600 in September, 1931, perhaps 3,250,000 in September, 1939. Under the secret terms of the Ribbentrop-Molotov pact of August 23rd about 1,170,000 of these Jews passed under Russian rule. Making a liberal deduction for fugitives, nearly two million Jews must have fallen into German hands by September 18th.

In the wake of the German armoured columns moved the lorries and motor cycles of the *Einsatzgruppen,* the 'action groups' of the Security Police and SD, Heydrich's men who had organised the pogroms of November 9th, 1938. Pogroms indeed broke out in almost every town with Jewish inhabitants and they began on the first day of the campaign. It was not hard for these experienced *agents provocateurs* to pursuade the Polish population to console themselves for the miseries of defeat. But the 'little terror' of September-November, 1939, was not comparable with the methodical massacres undertaken in 1941 during the invasion of Russia. The outrages of 1939 lacked the signs of a co-ordinating touch ; nor were they confined to the SS and police troops, for Wehrmacht units of every description indulged in them.[*1] They seem to have become worse after the fighting ended

*It is impossible not to agree with Mr. R. T. Paget, K.C., M.P., that the evidence, taken by the Polish Commissions after the war, has very little probative value. It consists mostly of isolated narratives that are hardly ever confirmed from other sources. But because of this absence of legal proof there can surely be no grounds for advancing a counter-hypothesis. Mr. Paget writes that 'The German Army behaved well,' 'atrocities were few and far between,' 'The conduct of the German Army had been correct.' Educated survivors who lived through this period in Poland do not confirm this view, nor does the correspondence of liberal circles in Germany.[2]

and it was not till the establishment of civil government in the middle of November that they were suppressed.

Whereas in June, 1941, the independence of the police units in the rear areas of the army was defined with meticulous care after long conferences, in September, 1939, there seems to have been only a hint from the Fuehrer that the SS were privileged and that the animal spirits of the men were not to be discouraged in Jewish relations. On September 14th, for instance, two SS men, a sergeant and a gunner, were court-martialled for the murder of fifty Jews. Having worked them all day at bridge-building these two men drove the Jews towards evening into a synagogue and shot them. The court reduced the murder charges to manslaughter and pronounced sentences of nine years' and three years' imprisonment. After some correspondence, the Commander-in-Chief, Von Brauchitsch, failed to confirm even a mitigation of these sentences, which he declared had been quashed under the terms of a general amnesty. For the gunner Ernst the Judge-Advocate had pleaded that ' as an SS man he was particularly sensitive to the sight of Jews. He had therefore acted quite thoughtlessly in a spirit of adventure. An excellent soldier, not punished before.'[3]

The case was public enough to attract comment in Germany. On October 19th the former Ambassador, Ulrich von Hassell, entered an accurate description of this very affair in his diary, accusing the part played by Brauchitsch,[4] though he asserts that the Fields-Marshals Reichenau* and Blaskowitz protested at other ' SS bestialities.' If it was indeed the case that every atrocity practised on the Jews in Poland was due to the SS, then the SS man must have had an unusual talent for ubiquity ; for at this moment the rank and file of the SS, both the reserve troops and the Death's Head *verbaende* (most of whom were guarding concentration camps in Germany) numbered no more

---

*That Reichenau, who wrote the notorious order of the day of October 10th, 1941, on ' sub-human Jewry,' should have been associated with such a protest is remarkable, but von Hassell perceived the explanation. Reichenau, who had been chief of the Wehrmacht Chancellory under the Weimar Republic, did not share the confidence of the Nazi leaders in a victory over the Western Powers, with whom he desired peace. As a man ' who heard the grass grow,' Reichenau perceived a danger to conciliation in the atrocity stories (*see page 231*).

than 26,000 and were insufficient to produce an infantry division.[5] These figures make the impotence of the Wehrmacht generals all the more incomprehensible. In the later stages of the war, when the Waffen SS numbered 500,000 men and produced thirty field divisions, there was some reason for their respect of Himmler.

When complaints reached them, the High Command took little more than routine action. Thus on the night of September 10th, 1939, when Hitler was at Southern Army Headquarters in an old castle at Konskie, between Lodz and Kielce, his favourite actress and film producer, Leni Riefenstahl, rushed into the office of Major-General Langhauser, the chief intelligence officer. She had seen twenty-two Jews shot and could not continue work with her film unit. Langhauser made a report to the commander of the Southern Army, von Manstein, who ordered ' investigation and immediate action in all cases,'[6] but the incidents continued to take place in the Southern Army area for another two months.

The tame acquiescent attitude of Brauchitsch, the impotence of the generals, all derive from the policy pursued by Field-Marshal Keitel, chief of OKW, the Higher Command of the Armed Forces. On September 12th, shortly before the fall of Warsaw, Admiral Canaris, Chief of Counter-Intelligence, protested during a conference in the Fuehrer's railway train at the proposed repressive measures against the Polish intelligentsia, nobility and clergy. Keitel's excuse was that Hitler meant to use the Security Police if the Army failed to execute his orders. A civilian would then sit at the elbow of each military commander. This apparently was the terrible vision which drove a German Field-Marshal to condone mass murder.[7] Von Bock told Fabian von Schlabrendorf that Hitler had made this threat before the war,[8] presumably at the Obersalzburg Conference of August 22nd, of which Manstein, Rundstedt, and even Franz Halder, who kept the minutes, preserved only the haziest recollection.[9] It would seem that Hitler did not mention the Jews at Obersalzburg, but there was a further conference on Hitler's train in Poland on September 18th where, according to Brigadier-General Erwin Lahousen, Ribbentrop produced a crack-brain scheme for inciting the Ukrainians against ' Polish farmers and Jews.'[10]

It does not seem that at this period systematic extermination of the Jews was considered. In all probability Hitler had made his plans before the war for the annexation of a large part of Poland to the Reich, for the expulsion of all Jews from this territory, and for the application of the 'November Laws' to the Jews wherever he might find them or put them. In this connection the report of a secret conference, addressed by Heydrich on September 21st, is of great significance since Heydrich carefully circulated it among the higher military administration in Poland. As a first step to the *Final Solution of the Jewish Problem*, Heydrich declares, all country-dwelling Jews must be moved into the towns. In the territories, due for incorporation, the Jews must be grouped handily in a few urban communities. Except in the densely populated Jewish area east of Cracow there must be no Jewish communities of less than 500 souls and these only where the railway passes. Each is to elect a Jewish Council of not less than 24 members and the chief responsibility of the Jewish Council is to be the transportation or reception of the Jews who are to be moved. The classification and registration of the Jews is to be carried out by the Action Groups of the Security Police and SD.[11]

This is an exceedingly prophetic document but, as was often the case with Heydrich, his plans looked too far ahead. Even when the death camps began to function, more than two years later, only half the Jews of the incorporated territory had been expelled and it had not been possible to move all the Jews to towns situated on the railways. Furthermore, Jewish affairs were not destined to remain the private preserve of the Security Police, for the establishment on October 12th of a civilian administration in the unincorporated part of Poland created for Heydrich an unamenable partner in the person of Governor Hans Frank. Nevertheless, a huge shuffling of the Jewish population did in fact take place. It was, Hitler told the Reichstag in his 'peace plan' speech of October 6th,[12] one of the six German cardinal aims in the Eastern area that all minority problems should be solved and the living space organised according to nationalities. An experiment would therefore be made in regulating and organising the Jewish problem in Poland.

For the moment Hitler's purpose was not so much that Jews should live among Jews and Poles among Poles as that Germans should live among Germans. On the day of the 'peace plan' speech Himmler acquired a new post, that of 'Reich Commissioner for the Strengthening of German Folkdom,' *Reichskommisar fuer die Festigung Deutsches Volktum* or RKFDV.[13] He was called upon to bring back to the Reich all racial Germans living under foreign Governments, to eliminate all alien influence in Reich territory, and to create new German colonies in occupied territory by the resettlement of racial Germans, or *Volksdeutsche*, returning from abroad.

The terms of the October 6th decree, vague, unrealistic, almost self-contradictory, seem designed for the character of Himmler himself. They are the clue to all his wilder acts and utterances and they absorbed a large part of his energies during the three years of German victory. They engendered the day-dreams recorded by Himmler's masseur and confidant, the Baltic German Felix Kersten ; dreams of the revival of the Carolingian kingdom of Burgundy, of the transplantation of the Dutch to Russia, and of the English to the Baltic States, of the elimination of dark-haired Germans, the abolition of German cities and the legalisation of bigamy among a blonde warrior caste, living in feudal castles in the Urals, drinking the milk of the wild mare of the steppes and breakfasting on mineral water.[14]

Hardly less fabulous were the memoranda, drafted at various times in the RKFDV office by pupil-thinkers. Thus Dr. Wetzel advocated that the Poles should be compelled to practise birth control. They should be taught that it was a divine law to be industrious and obey the Germans. Reading would not be required nor counting beyond 500.[15] In March, 1940, Himmler presented the report to Hitler, who found it 'very good and correct,' but only suitable for a limited edition. In May, 1942, another reporter of RKFDV, one Dr. Abel, had a plan for the 'progressive elimination' of the Russian race. Abel, an anthropologist attached to the Higher Command, wanted to Germanise all Nordic Russian types and send the rest to Siberia.[16] Wetzel differed slightly from Abel. His 'General Plan—East of the Reichsfuehrer SS' of April 27th, 1942, favoured selective birth control.

Nevertheless, in spite of the obtrusion of this favourite form of German professorial speculation, the purpose of the RKFDV office was severely practical. Two secret protocols to the famous

Moscow pact had been signed by Ribbentrop on September 27th, 1939. These permitted the Russian sphere of influence to include Lithuania. For their part the Russians promised to facilitate the transfer to the Reich of racial Germans dwelling in their occupied territories. German officials were even to be allowed into these territories to direct the emigration.[17] It was expected that 40,000 of the 110,000 Baltic Germans and most of the 134,267 Germans living in the Russian share of Poland would leave for the Reich immediately. One day they would be followed by 135,000 racial Germans dwelling in Bessarabia, which was still in Rumanian hands. These people were to be accommodated in the incorporated Polish territory and in Austria and the Bohemian Protectorate,[18] from which the Jews would be removed in order to create living-space.

By a decree of October 8th, 1939,[19] the provinces that had been lost to Poland in 1918, together with the province of Lodz, were reincorporated into the Reich, which thus became the possessor of approximately 650,000 more Jews.[20] Two days later Himmler announced that 550,000 of these Jews were to be deported at once to 'unincorporated Poland,' together with all Polish intellectuals and Poles suspected of being anti-German. A start would be made with Danzig and Posen. These Jews would be sent to the region between the rivers Vistula and Bug, and eventually they would increase the Jewish population of the 'General Government,' the name given to the unincorporated territory, to about two millions.[21] A speech made by Governor Frank in January, 1940, in his capacity as President of the Academy of German Law, shows that he feared still more extreme measures from Himmler. A million and a half Polish peasants were to be brought into the General Government from the incorporated territory and *all* the Jews of the Greater Reich and Bohemia-Moravia.[22] To this Frank protested that space could only be created in the General Government, which had a normal population of twelve millions, by the removal of Polish labourers to Germany and by the hindrance of 'Polish biological reproduction.' Both the protest and the remedy were typical of Frank in that there was nothing humanitarian about them. As to the importation of Jews, about which Frank constantly grumbled, the murderous solution was completely congenial to him.

At Nuremberg Frank was different. In the months of captivity preceding his trial he had become reconciled to the Roman Church and his contrition before the judges seemed genuine. Virtually he pleaded guilty to the extermination of the Polish Jews by admitting a share in the ' collective responsibility' for the gas chambers, of which, however, he claimed ignorance. ' My conscience will not allow me to throw the responsibility on these small people . . . a thousand years will pass and the guilt of Germany will not be erased.'[23]

The effect of these courageous words was spoilt by the pleas, subsequently put up by Frank and his witness Josef Buehler, that the massacre of the Jews in Poland was wholly due to the police chiefs, Krueger and Globocnik, whom Heydrich had forced on Frank, a man devoted by his very profession to the rule of law. But then Frank enjoyed the split mind that was so common in Hitler's entourage. In May, 1945, he refused in a moment of exaltation to destroy the 42-volume journal of his acts and speeches, which reposed in his bedroom in the Berghof Hotel at Neuhaus in Bavaria. Later the knowledge that the Americans had his journal caused him to slit his wrists and throat in a determined suicide attempt.[24]

This journal is indeed a frightening document, scarcely credible in its cold inhumanity, but it certainly shows that Frank was at loggerheads with the SS and police. His first threat to resign was made on November 19th, 1939,[25] when Himmler appointed Friedrich Krueger, a former Strasbourg book-seller, to be police chief in the General Government. Krueger had to carry out Himmler's resettlement plans, which meant economic chaos to Frank as a responsible Governor. Only in the plan to liquidate the Jews did Frank find himself in agreement with Krueger and his police chiefs. Six weeks before Heydrich had disclosed the meaning of the 'Final Solution' at the Gross-Wannsee conference, Frank was openly discussing it with his Cabinet. 'Do you think they will be settled in villages in the Ostland ? . . . Liquidate them yourselves! ' (see pages 51, 99, and 247).

The breach between Frank and the SS was most complete in the summer of 1942, when Himmler proposed to expel Poles from the purely Polish Zamosc area in the course of an arbitrary and experimental settlement of racial Germans from various countries—and this at a time when Frank actually expected an agricultural surplus from his territory in addition to supplying manpower for Germany and services for the Eastern Front. In that month of July Frank stormed through the German universities, advocating before the law students a return to constitutional rule (see pages 157-8).[26] As a consequence of this Frank was all but arrested. He was stripped of his party honours, he ceased to be Reichskommissar for Justice, and Goebbels urged Hitler to dismiss him from his governorship. 'Hitler no longer has any respect for Frank,' he wrote.[27] But there Goebbels was wrong. Hitler had an uncanny respect for a man who could four years later retain his thrusting jaw and Nazi strut in the shadow of the gallows. Frank remained Governor-General long enough to see his enemies, Krueger and Globocnik, removed; long enough too to see the Russians in the outskirts of Cracow, his capital which he had planned to make a German city. Frank had won his war with the SS, but the Russians had won the war with Germany.

For the extraordinary Government, set up in what Hitler intended to be the Polish State of the future, the legalistic and unplastic mind of Hans Frank was mainly responsible. There were no Quisling Polish Ministers. Most of the elaborate Polish system of local government was set aside. The country—a third of pre-war Poland—was divided into four laende and 40 kreise. Only the bezirk, the smallest unit, could be governed by Polish subjects and even these were for the most part members of the racial German minority. Forty thousand German-born civil servants battened on a country 'half the size of Italy' and Frank at his trial thought this number insufficient.[28] No Pole could be happy under such a régime, but Frank thought he had a remedy for that. He made the lot of the Jews still less happy.

2. The First Deportations into Poland

The first period of Jewish deportations lasted from October, 1939, to March, 1940. Unlike the second period, which began in October, 1941, the Jews were deported neither to closed ghettoes, concentration camps nor gas chambers. They were merely assigned a residence in existing Jewish communities in the region between the Rivers Vistula and Bug, where many towns were practically ghettoes already. The immediate plan was to turn out enough Jews, Poles, and Czechs from the enlarged Reich to create a living for the incoming racial Germans. That this plan was never fully carried out was due to a number of causes, among them a typhus epidemic, an unwelcome leakage of information to the foreign press, and finally the fact that the racial Germans, even when screened and vetted by the agencies, RUSHA and VOMI, failed to settle down and get rich on what the Jews had been forced to leave.

What had happened can be studied in a German official report, made at the end of 1941 when the return of Germans from the remaining Baltic States and from Greater Rumania had brought the number of immigrants to 497,000.[29] These people lived in reception areas, from which 1,200,000 Poles and 300,000 Jews had been expelled into the General Government. In theory, therefore, each German occupied the space of three Poles and Jews. Yet, in July, 1942, 120,000 of them were still housed in camps. A year later, in August, 1943, when the returned *Volksdeutsche* numbered 546,000, there were 99,500 in camps or temporarily employed[30] and 22,000 of them were encamped near Lodz in complete idleness and destitution. It may be said that Jews were being killed to maintain them, for it was on behalf of this Lodz camp that the party Winter Relief Fund had requested the bloodstained clothing of the victims of the neighbouring Chelmno death institute[31] (*see pages 137-8 and 250*). The Race and Settlement Office in Lodz were also promised by Oswald Pohl in February, 1943, a share of the mountain of Jewish clothing collected in Auschwitz camp and in the Lublin depots of 'Einsatz Reinhard.'[32]

It should be stressed that this was the month of Stalingrad when even more *Volksdeutsche* were streaming West. For instance, 2,000 Germans from the Caucasus had just reached the Black Sea evacuation port of Yaisk.[33] Yet the German economy had not absorbed the first migration from Volhynia which had crossed the Rivers San and Bug with such a fanfare of trumpets in December, 1939.

Thus was formed the nucleus of the German *displaced*

Pre-War Poland as partitioned between 1941 and 1944.

41

persons. Himmler, the son of a history tutor to a Bavarian prince, had planned a new *Voelkerwanderung* in accordance with the cast-iron racial theories on which he had been nurtured and in violation of historical biology. Himmler's victims, the Slav nations, continued after the war the work Himmler had began and to-day nine million displaced Germans live in the Federal West German Republic, unwanted, under-privileged, and almost foreigners, the germ-bearers of the vindictive German militarism of the future.

It was easier to move Jews than to move racial Germans, because the Jews were not allowed to take much property. Moreover, deportation to other Polish towns was regarded by Jews as a less evil fate than incorporation in the Reich. Already during the 'eighteen days' war' some 60,000 Jews had moved East. On February 12th, 1940, Artur Greiser, Governor of the Warthegau, that is the former Polish provinces incorporated in Germany, reported that 87,000 Jews had been removed from Danzig-West Prussia[34] and only 1,800 remained. Bromberg had been declared free of Jews on November 14th, 1939,[35] Thorn, Graudenz, Kalisz, and Posen were cleared by February, but much greater masses remained in the Lodz region, 180,000 of them in Lodz city. Of these, some 20,000 were sent to Warsaw, Cracow, and Lublin in December and January, including a large proportion of intelligentsia, but this movement was not resumed.[36] In March, 1940, when the deportations into the General Government were suspended, Lodz retained 80 per cent of its pre-war Jewish population.

The future ghettoes of the General Government reflected this movement. Losses, due to flight during the 'eighteen days' war,' were more than made up. Warsaw recovered its 360,000 Jewish inhabitants, the Cracow community grew from 58,000 to 68,000, Czestochowa from 28,000 to 33,000, Kielce from 19,000 to 25,400, and Lublin from 37,000 to 42,000.[37] A mass of Jews—estimates vary between 25,000 and 60,000—were pushed into the small Jewish towns of the Lublin province from which there was a constant drift, unhindered by the Germans, into Lublin itself.

Lublin province also received the Jews from Bohemia, Vienna, and Stettin. There seems to have been a scatter-brained scheme by which 40,000 of the Baltic Germans were to go to Bohemia,[38] in order to create a German belt between the Czechs and the Slovaks. No less than 70,000 Czech peasants were uprooted, besides 12,000 to 20,000 Jews dwelling in the towns of Tetschen, Maerisch-Ostrau, Bogumin, and Bruenn. The number of Germans who took their place was small and out of all proportion. They were mostly Reich Germans of the industrial and clerical ranks.[39]

The original exchange scheme provided that the displaced Czech and Viennese Jews should be moved to an agricultural reserve in Eastern Poland. Their centre was to be near the small town of Nisko, west of the River San and south of Lublin. The first transport left Maerisch-Ostrau (Ostrava Moravska) on October 12th, 1939. It carried building materials for Nisko and German constructional engineers as well as settlers. At first the scheme received publicity in the German press but this was soon dropped.[40] Survivor reports are even scarcer. A Jew who was deported from Vienna on October 20th, 1939, travelled by passenger train, taking two-and-a-half days. He recorded that the passengers were relieved of nearly everything they possessed on the twelve-mile march from Nisko station by guards from the SS Death's Head *Verbaende*.* Only a few skilled workers were chosen for the so-called settlement which possessed not so much

*At this period the rank and file of the SS belonged either to the reserve troops or to the Death's Head *Verbaende*, the latter becoming the nucleus of the numerous SS field divisions (all of which had names) which were recruited during the war. To be a member of the *Totenkopfverbaende* at this period was to be a member of the party bodyguard, and, in fact, most of the *Verbaende* were still employed guarding concentration camps. Later there developed a strong distinction between the *Totenkopfverbaende* and the SS *Totenkopf* Division, which, originally recuited from party stalwarts, became a field division like any other, made up with conscript drafts. The presence of *Totenkopfverbaende* troops at Nisko in October, 1939, seems to find an explanation in the Nuremberg evidence of Seyss-Inquardt, who had been at this time Civil Commisar with the High Command in Poland. He had learnt that the Jews who were deported from Vienna had arrived without preparation and were in ' serious difficulties.' He had complained to Buerckel, the Gauleiter of Vienna, and on November 9th he wrote to Himmler asking that the SD should take control of the deportees. He believed that these were ' wild deportations,' carried out in Vienna by party members and assisted by Globocnik, who had not yet been made Higher SS and Police Leader in Lublin. This introduction of the name of Globocnik, who was still in disgrace (*see pages 245-46*) is a little uncertain, since the purpose seems to have been to shield Seyss-Inquardt's co-defendant Kaltenbrunner, who was then Security Police Commander in Vienna. (PS 3398 and IMT XVI 168.)

as a roofed hut. The remainder were left at a bridge over the San and told to ' join their friends, the Russians,' who incidentally were only fifty miles away.[41]

The author of this report managed to find shelter with a Jewish family, but most of the Jews, who were destined for Nisko and who survived the marches and exposure, made their way to the still unenclosed Lublin ghetto, where, as Max Freiherr Duprel wrote in March, 1942, ' in filthy dens, dugouts, and catacombs the Jew feels at home '[42]—and where they were considered picturesque, for in November, 1939, Herr Veit Harlan paid a visit in order to photograph ghetto scenes for the Nazi version of the film *Jew Suess*.[43]

These deportations from Vienna to Lublin affected about a sixth of the community and were a wartime continuation of the forcible evacuation of the poorer Jews at the expense of the *Kultusgemeinde*. The two movements in October, 1939, and February, 1940, involved 11,200 people[44] who were eventually distributed either in Lublin town or in the small almost entirely Jewish towns along the then Soviet border, the towns which in March, 1942, were to become transfer stations for the extermination camp at Belsec.

The Reich Jews were not easily assimilated to the conditions of the impoverished Jewish communities of Eastern Poland, nor did the local Jews welcome them. The lack of proper food, clothing, shelter, or sanitation produced a typhus epidemic. In December, 1939, the Commander-in-Chief, East, Field-Marshal Blaskowitz, reported that children arrived in the deportation trains from the incorporated territory frozen to death, and that people were dying of hunger in the reception villages.[45] The Swiss Press got hold of the report sent to Himmler by a high SS officer,[46] according to which the death-rate among the Jewish deportees to the Lublin province was thirty per cent. Nevertheless, after an extremely cold spell of weather, orders were given for the resumption of the deportations at a full-dress conference of the Reich Main Security Office, summoned by Heydrich on January 30th and attended by Eichmann. At this conference the Race and Settlement Office asked Himmler's authorisation to deport 30,000 gipsies from the Greater Reich.[47] It was followed on February 12th by a meeting between Himmler and Goering at his country house at Karinhall near Berlin to arrange for the removal of a further 30,000 racial Germans from the Lublin province in order to make room for the Jews. But Himmler was persuaded by Goering to wait till the migration of racial Germans from across the Russian border was complete.[48]

The unfulfilled threat to expel Germans in order to bring in Jews was the last of the 'Jewish State' of Nisko. The region was part of the patrimony of the Counts of Zamosc, about whom Himmler, with the aid of his friend Globocnik (see pages 159 and 245), was shortly to discover a Teutonic mythus. Zamosc, the centre of the 30,000 threatened racial Germans, was visited by Himmler himself on July 21st, 1941. A Fuehrerhof was founded and the town was renamed Himmlerstadt. The region was now intended to become the nucleus of a German corridor extending from the Baltic to the Carpathians.[49]

With the revival of the Jewish deportations in midwinter the German Foreign Office became alarmed at the reactions of the foreign press. On February 15th von Weizsaecker submitted to Heydrich's office a report in the Neue Zuercher Zeitung that the expulsion of the Jews of Stettin had been ordered—it had in fact been decided at Heydrich's conference on January 30th.[50] Heydrich paid no attention and at the end of February the Governor of Stettin received orders from the Ministry for Interior to proceed. Having discovered that Heydrich had sent the orders under the Ministry letter-heading, the Governor cancelled them, but too late to stop Heydrich,[51] and in the first week in March about 1,200 Jews began leaving Stettin for Lublin. From Lublin station they had to walk fourteen hours in a snow blizzard to Piaski and on the march seventy-two persons were frozen to death. A child of five, who survived, had to have both hands and feet amputated. By March 12th the dead numbered 230. The rest lived in sheds and barns without luggage, money, or overcoats. Moreover, on that day another 160 Jews from the Pomeranian town of Schneidemuhl arrived in the neighbourhood. The local Jewish communities would do nothing to feed these Jews from the Reich and the Governor of Lublin province, Zoerner, tried to shift the responsibility on to the Security Police, who had begun the action.

The report on the march to Piaski, which was sent from

Frank's office to Lammers of the Reichschancellory and thence to Himmler, claimed that on the 14th the deportations were still continuing,[52] but on March 23rd Goering ruled that all deportations into the General Government must cease.[53] Even so, on the 29th Helmuth Wohltat, Goering's man in Heydrich's Jewish emigration office, had to ask the Foreign Office to deny a rumour, which had started in the U.S. Embassy, that Berlin would be included in the deportation measures.[54] On the other hand, Artur Greiser protested that Goering's order applied only to Stettin and that Goering had promised Himmler at Karinhall that the deportations from Lodz into the General Government would be resumed; even Frank had agreed to receive them.[55] But Greiser, having sought a new ruling from Goering in vain, had to report on May 8th that the action would be suspended until the last of the racial Germans had arrived from Volhynia. By now half the Jews and ten per cent of the Poles had been expelled from the incorporated territory.[56]

Two days later the great offensive began in the West and the entire situation changed. For the next sixteen months the deportations to the General Government were influenced by the official pretence that there was to be a reserve for European Jewry in Madagascar (*see pages 76-79*). Thus on July 12th Frank told his Cabinet chiefs that he had persuaded Hitler to include the Jews of the General Government in the Madagascar scheme and that in any case no more Jews would be coming from the Reich.[57] Yet Hitler had just told Baldur Von Schirach the exact contrary, namely, that the 50,000 Jews surviving in Vienna must go to a 'closed settlement' in the General Government.[58]

On October 2nd, 1940, Schirach reminded Frank of this, while sitting next to him at dinner at the Fuehrer's headquarters. Gauleiter Erich Koch of East Prussia also reminded Frank that he would have to take the Jews of the incorporated district, Cieczanow or Zichenau.* As Frank bridled with anger, Hitler stopped the argument with a long speech.[59] Two months later Frank was warned by Reich Chancellor Lammers that the Viennese Jews would have to be resettled before the end of the

*In fact, the Jews of Cieczanow were not finally evacuated till December, 1942, when they were sent to Auschwitz.

war[60] —but somehow Frank contrived in October, 1941, that they got no further than Lodz in the incorporated territory.

On deportations from the incorporated territory as opposed to deportations from the Old Reich, Frank was less successful. As originally planned by Himmler for January, 1941, there was to be a deportation of a further 831,000 Poles and Jews into the General Government,[61] reduced subsequently to 200,000 Jews. The actual number, moved between February and May, seems to have been 72,000. They were taken from towns west of the Vistula into the Warsaw Ghetto, raising its population to 430,000 or more and giving it the largest death rate of any urban area in the world (*see page 59, footnote*).

3. Deportations Inside the General Government

Heydrich's plans of September 21st, 1939, show that he regarded the native Jewish population of Poland as something to be moved about from day to day, and in fact resettlement actions were continuous right up to the time of the first exterminations in March, 1942. The policy was to get as many Jews as possible into the bigger ghettoes. Those who had to be left behind in the smaller communities were moved from one place to another to prevent their taking root. There were, however, many changes of mind on this subject. On April 14th, 1940, Frank announced that he would make Cracow, his capital, a Jewless city and a year later some 35,000 Jews were ordered to leave. And yet in September, 1941, some 7,000 country-dwelling Jews were brought into the Cracow Ghetto.[62] At Lublin, where throughout 1940 some 40,000 to 50,000 Jews were packed into a ghetto which normally contained only a portion of the pre-war population of 37,000 Jews, another 12,000 were suddenly added between March 10th and 13th, 1941, most of them from Cracow. At the same time 14,000 Lublin Jews, including a large illegal community, were expelled to the 'Jewish reserve' towns, Chodel, Lubartow, and Belzyce.[63] Yet on October 17th, 1941, Frank was worried because there were again more than 40,000 Jews in the Lublin Ghetto. He proposed the immediate deportation of 1,100 of them beyond the Bug river.[64] Thereafter, and until the opening of the Belsec extermination camp in March, 1942, the shuttling of Jewish communities to and fro in 'Lublinland' became completely chaotic and purposeless (*see pages 251 and 255, footnote*).

The official excuses for the resettlements were varied and ingenious. On January 28th, 1942, the Jewish Council of the small town of Wisznice in Lublin province complained that 150 Jews had been dumped on them 'barefooted or naked.' The German *Landkommissar* explained simply that he had thrown four Jewish communities into one in order to keep a better eye on black-market activities. 'No deaths have occurred on account of the resettlement.'[65] At Kazimierz on the Vistula, east of Warsaw, the excuse was quite original. The place was 'a romantic painter's nook' and the Jews were turned out in the course of a 'beautification action.'[66]

The futile fussiness of most of the resettlements, ordered by Heydrich or Krueger, was equalled by Frank's own experiments of this order, but sometimes Frank would register practical objections because he feared that the overpacked ghettoes, even when walled and guarded, meant a danger of epidemics to their Aryan neighbours. Hence the occasional release of more food and medical supplies and the occasional reduction of ghettoes that had reached saturation. Hence, too, the remarkable survival in the ghettoes of a society which was expected to die out, but which after two years' blockade had not lost all the graces of life.

❊   ❊   ❊   ❊

One further form of deportation, practised by the Germans in Poland, remains to be studied, the deportation or encouraged migration of Jews across the newly established Russian border. It is an obscure subject inasmuch as the precise number of Jews, both of those who lived in pre-war Poland and of those who fell into German hands after the invasions of September 1st, 1939, and June 22nd, 1941, is not known. The decision to make the General Government a dumping ground for Jews from further West probably allowed for a compensatory eastward movement. It certainly accounts for the reluctance of the German authorities to readmit Jews who had fled in their first panic through the Russian lines.

Thus an order from the Supreme Command of the Army, dated September 20th, 1939, enjoins unit commanders to prevent the recrossing of the Rivers San and Bug by fugitive Jews.[67] On the 25th, hundreds of Jews, who were trying to return home, were turned out of the town of Jaroslaw at half an hour's notice and pushed across the San river on rafts, where they were fired on by German Security Police or left to drown. From Southern Army headquarters Von Manstein proclaimed that the Jews 'were drifting back into Upper Silesia,' but the Russians had not yet begun to ship the Jews back to the Germans by force. On October 14th, when some Jews were deliberately dumped on the Russians at Sokal, there was no counter-action. But when a Jewish doctor crossed the River Bug at this point on November 5th, he was imprisoned and put back across the frontier with a group of Jews and the whole party barely escaped shooting by the German guards.[68]

A formal protest by the Russians on November 15th obliged the Germans to open the frontier at several points for the return of Jews, but the dumping still continued. On December 5th Field-Marshal Keitel appealed to Weizsaecker to bring Foreign Office pressure to bear on those responsible for the deportations.[69] On December 8th, Governor Frank noted in his diary a considerable movement of Jews to the Eastern frontier.[70] Seven hundred Jews from Hrubieczow and 1,200 from Chelm were put across the River Bug that day. The Russians sent them back and during the march a number of stragglers were shot by the German guards.[71] Apparently shootings of returned Jews by the SS became a regular occurence and on January 11th, 1940, Ulrich Von Hassell notes that M. Potemkin had brought them to the attention of the German Ambassador in Moscow, Count Von Schulenburg.[72] About this time, however, the Foreign Office intervened and the dumping at the border ceased.

The Jews who were deported to Russia came mainly from towns near the newly created border, Chelm, Hrubieczow, Jaroslaw, Lankut, and the German part of Przemysl. The voluntary emigrants, who came from all parts of Poland, must have been many times more numerous. According to the post-war Polish Commission of investigation they numbered 300,000.[73]*

A part of these may have been swept up after June 22nd, 1941, in the German invasion of Russia and eventually killed. But the Russians only accorded the right to remain on the spot to such Jewish refugees as they considered eligible for immediate Soviet citizenship and most of them were deported to the Urals and South Siberia. In January, 1943, these deportees were allowed to choose between Soviet citizenship and Polish citizenship, the latter entailing repatriation after the war. By June, 1946, when the offer expired, 157,400 Jewish exiles had returned from Russia to Poland[75] but clearly this was only a small proportion of the whole, which included not only the 300,000 Jews who fled from German-occupied Poland, but those Jews whom the Russians had deported from the Soviet-occupied part of Poland or who fled from there eastwards after June 22nd, 1941. When it is considered that at least 1,170,000 Jews lived in this territory in September, 1939, and that, quite apart from the deportations, the escape of a third of them may well have been practicable, then the number of Jewish refugees, received into Russia from pre-war Poland becomes not 300,000 but at the least 700,000 (*see Appendix 1*).

Apart from the 157,400 who returned to Poland, the fate of these refugees is absolutely unknown. The populations of the annexed regions, whom it was considered necessary to move into the interior, were not treated with any special tenderness. The best that can be said is that the Jews were not the subject of racial discrimination, but that, together with Poles, Lithuanians, Rumanians, and others, they took their chances against a hard climate, primitive camps, and chaotic organisation. Unless the Soviet authorities choose to establish a new Jewish census, this very large question of survivors from former Poland must remain unanswered.

The history of the first stage in the deportation of Jewry, the

---

*At the end of 1942 Dr. Korherr reported to Himmler that quite apart from Jews 'evacuated to the East' the General Government had lost 427,920 Jews since September, 1939, by excess death-rate and voluntary emigration.[74] If we allow a quarter of a million for the former (*see page 244, footnote*) we get a figure which, when a proportion is added for the incorporated territory, may well reach 300,000 (*see Appendix 1*).

stage that ended in October, 1941, shows that the Germans were sensitive to American opinion and until June 22nd to Russian opinion. Thus, while the conditions were invariably murderous, deliberate mass murder was not practised. It is significant that Frank used the words: 'Liquidate them yourselves' nine days after Pearl Harbour and that the first gassings in Poland took place at the end of that year. It may even be doubted whether the 'Fuehrer Order' to exterminate Russian Jewry would have spread west of the former Russian demarcation line, if the United States had not entered the war on December 7th, 1941.

CHAPTER 3

The Ghettoes, 1940-1942

1. Economic Elimination

IN 1939 the Germans entered Eastern Europe, bringing with them the cast-iron theory that no country could be harmed by the loss of its Jews. The Jews either did no work or their work was unnecessary or pernicious, and besides they were not numerous enough to matter, for even in 1933 the Jews had furnished less than one per cent of the population of Germany and two per cent of Austria and Czechoslovakia. But the conclusions, which could be drawn from such figures, could not be applied in 1939 to Poland, where the Jews made up ten per cent of the population, while in every large town they were at least 25 per cent and in some small towns 100 per cent. The Jew in the view of National Socialist economists was always a trader and a middleman and generally a parasite, feeding on the productive system. In reality barely half the trading population of Poland was Jewish, while Jews accounted for 20 per cent of the artisans and factory workers, 12½ per cent of the professional men, and 11½ per cent of the transport operators.[1] In the textile towns, Bialystok and Lodz, the Jews managed most of the factories.

In Poland the party-economists were deceived by appearances. Though there seemed to be no Jewish working-class, a depressed Jewish middle class had become a proletariat. In Eastern Galicia an industrial enterprise might consist of a single family or even a single worker, propped up against his machine at the window of some lime-washed one-storey house. Often these workers had to compete with large organised concerns that did not employ Jews. Moreover, the very large numbers of people, dependent on a single worker, frequently represented a concealed form of unemployment. The unemployed, classed by the Germans as 'work-shy' and 'asocials,' occupied themselves in a variety of ways typical of the structure of an Eastern country, in mendicancy, study, and prayer, in black-market activities, in hope. Even in the Soviet Union ancient tribal habit had barely changed after a quarter of a century of revolution. The competition of collectivism had merely increased the pressure on the medieval Jewish economic system.

The German programme was simple. The Jews must be expelled from private trade and industry and put to manual labour. Those who could not be employed need not be kept alive. On this point, as we have seen, Governor Frank was in agreement with the police bosses of the SS, but other German agencies, more directly concerned in war-time production, objected that you could not get the best even out of an unskilled worker if you killed off all his family—or if you deprived him of the incentives offered to others. These objections never got very far. From Himmler downwards every German, concerned with the government of Poland, busied himself killing the goose that laid the golden egg. Thus on December 21st, 1940, Max Frauendorfer, head of the Labour Office in Frank's bureaucracy at Cracow, published a decree forbidding the payment to Jews of sickness, holiday, overtime, and bonus payments, and abolishing all regulations on their hours of work.[2] Yet Frauendorfer kept Ulrich Von Hassell posted on SS atrocities and finally resigned his post in Poland in disgust and went to the front as a soldier.[3]

A systematic treatment of the Jewish question after the invasion, as opposed to mere looting and pogroms, dates only from the establishment of the *Judenstern* or distinctive Jewish badge. It was tried out at Wloclawek in the incorporated territory on October 24th, 1939, at the inspiration of a German town commissioner. A badge was also decreed by Governor Waechter at Cracow on November 18th, but the general decree for the whole General Government was not issued by Frank till November 23rd. The six-pointed star had to be worn on a white brassard ten centimetres wide. A similar mark had to be placed on all Jewish shops, offices, and apartments.[4] It was the first decree to depart from the practice of the German Reich, for nearly two years were to pass before the Gestapo ventured to subject the Jews, who were to be seen on the streets of Germany and Western Europe, to this medieval indignity.

Like its medieval prototype which had made the Jews the

property of the king, the Jewish badge guaranteed the bearer his life and no more. He could not travel on trains or public vehicles without a permit or leave the place of his registration or visit certain streets or parks. He could still be arrested without warrant and carried off for any sort of work. In November, 1939, many wearers of the badge already longed for the things that were meant to go with it, the walled and sequestered ghetto and the autonomous rule of the Jewish elders.

Closed and guarded ghettoes were clearly intended at the time of Heydrich's secret recommendations of September 21st, 1939 (see page 35). In practice they had to wait till the Aryanisation of Jewish shops and works was almost complete. Even so, at Lodz, the Jewish pawnbrokers were permitted to carry on in the town after the closing of the ghetto.[5] At Vilna, at a time when the Jewish population had already been much reduced by massacres, the Jewish chimney sweeps had to be allowed out to pursue their vocation.[6] A host of unexpected problems such as these caused the deferment of the creation of the Lodz and Warsaw Ghettoes to April and November, 1940, respectively. At Lublin, Radom, Cracow, Tarnow, and Kielce, where there were Jewish communities of 25,000 and more, the ghettoes were not enclosed till March or April, 1941.[7] In the half-Jewish towns of Eastern Galicia, which the Germans did not occupy till June, 1941, the ghettoes were never enclosed at all. There was consequently the possibility of flight from the prison ghettoes to the theoretically free Jewish communities. For instance, when the Lodz Ghetto was formed, the richer families fled to Warsaw.[8]

The Germans had little cause for concern. Already the Warsaw Jews were forming a voluntary ghetto for their own protection. The Germans could rely on this instinct to huddle together even when the death camps had functioned for two years. A town would be emptied of Jews by massacre, declared Jew-free and then declared open to Jews again—and still fugitive Jews would return (see pages 270-271).

The history of the ghettoes falls into four phases. In the first they were only intended to stop the Jews trading, since dispossession was not enough and a Jew, who was allowed to move freely, might open shop again. In the second phase the

Jews were to die of hunger. In the highest circles it was openly admitted. Thus, in October, 1941, Governor Frank announced a reduction of the Jewish rations in Warsaw in the following words: 'During the winter the death-rate will doubtless go up, but this war involves the total annihilation of Jewry.'[9] The third phase began in March, 1942. The Jews, who were not directly employed in essential industries, went to the execution pit and gas-chamber. The last phase began with the Warsaw rebellion of April, 1943. With the exception of Lodz, where the solution was deferred another sixteen months, the ghettoes were emptied and even razed to the ground. In 1944 the labour camps were the only places, apart from the Lodz Ghetto, where the Jews of Poland had a right to survive.

The plan of the second phase, namely, to exterminate the Polish Jews by hunger, should have been realised in a matter of months, but for human fallibility. A Jewish medical commission, which examined the subject during the deportations to Warsaw, came to the conclusion that extinction of the ghetto by famine alone might take five years,[10] but this took into consideration certain realities due partly to the Germans' fear of epidemics and partly to their corruption. For the ghettoes never entirely lost the power to bribe and the business of guarding the ghettoes was delegated not only to Germans but to Poles and police from neighbouring countries. Even the so-called fanaticism of the SS was not bribe-proof.

In theory the ghetto could have no intercourse with the outside world, except through German agencies such as the *Transferstelle*, in the case of Warsaw[11] and the *Ernaehrungs- und Wirtschaftsstelle* (Victualling and Supply Office), in the case of Lodz.[12] Through these agencies the products of the factories and co-operative workshops in the ghettoes as well as the estimated output of the labour commandos, which were sent to work outside, were exchanged for just such rations as the police chose to distribute. Inside the ghetto the rations were distributed again through the *Judenrat* or Jewish Council, a bureaucracy which might, as in the case of Warsaw, employ as many as 5,000 people.

Under famine conditions the *Judenrat* had to decide who should live and who should die, but in practice the decision was partly taken out of their hands, since a great deal of production in the ghetto and commerce with the outer world went on unofficially. It proved impossible on either side of the ghetto wall to prevent smuggling. Sometimes it was done through sewers and holes in the wall by small boys, but often it was done quite openly in lorries and carts—even when mass exterminations were in progress.

Practical-minded Germans foresaw this situation from the beginning. Thus the ghetto system was roundly attacked at Rosenberg's conference on the Jewish problem, held at Frankfurt in April, 1941. The speaker was Professor Peter Heinz Seraphim, of Goettingen University, author in 1938 of a sort of anti-semitic encyclopedia of Eastern Europe, attached in 1943 to the Armaments Ministry in the Ukraine and in 1949 an advocate for the return of lost German territory.[13] Seraphim declared at Frankfurt that forced labour was economically unsatisfactory, that an encircling wall did not create a closed economy, particularly where government offices were situated in the ghetto and a main thoroughfare traversed it—all of which was confirmed by Governor Frank six months later, when he admitted that the Warsaw Ghetto had been supplied since the beginning with illegal rations.[14]

At Lodz, exit without a pass was forbidden as early as April 30th, 1940. On May 10th passes were required for Poles and Germans visiting the ghetto. The inefficiency of the control is shown in a complaint of August 24th that a Pole had been arrested, while selling passes inside the ghetto. He claimed that the German Criminal Police employed him to extract valuables from the Jews this way.[15] Nearly a year after the establishment of the Lodz Ghetto, the German civil administrator, Hans Biebow, considered the passage of Jews in and out of the ghetto considerable enough to cause epidemics in Germany.[16]

No penalties were considered too severe for breaking out of the ghetto. An order of the Lodz *Schutzpolizei*, dated April 14th, 1941, required not only Jews going in and out of the ghetto without a pass to be shot at sight, but also Jews inside the ghetto who ventured near the barbed wire. A sentry of the *Kriminalpolizei* reported on December 1st, 1941, that he had shot an old woman for putting her hand through the wire to steal a turnip off a cart.[17] Inasmuch as strict obedience meant a lingering death from hunger, the death penalty could not be effective. At one time 170,000 people in the Lodz ghetto were guarded by a police force numbering only 600. The barbed wire was not complete along the ten-mile perimeter. As late as February 3rd, 1942, the Police President complained that the ghetto fence in the south-east consisted of boards and plain wire.[18]

In Warsaw the problem was even worse. In Lodz 40,000 out of the 160,000 Jews were employed in July, 1941, making textiles and equipment for the Germans.[19] In Warsaw, where there may have been at this time more than 430,000 Jews, there was much less employment available. The black market with the Aryan section was correspondingly vaster. Nor was the police so effective as in Lodz, which in November, 1939, had been made a Reich city under the name of Litzmannstadt, its *Buergermeister* and thirty-six city councillors being drawn exclusively from the 90,000 racial German inhabitants. The 370,000 Aryan Poles were even forbidden schools and newspapers in their own language.[20] Warsaw, with its 1,200,000 inhabitants, could not be handled this way. It had not capitulated without a fight and the Germans were never really comfortable there. Moreover the 360,000 Warsaw Jews of 1939 had spread beyond the old ghetto district. They were the least sequestered of the Polish Jewish communities and as a result the creation of a ghetto caused great hardships for the Aryan population. The Germans could thus no longer rely completely on Polish anti-semitism.

2. 'The Jewish State'

The walling-in of part of Warsaw began in the late summer of 1940. It was an oblong measuring about a mile by two and a half and it included, besides the medieval ghetto, the long straight streets of the industrial quarter, running north of the railway station. At its north-east corner the ghetto nearly touched the Vistula and it was bisected by the main artery to Posen and Berlin.

The cutting out of this lump from the heart of Warsaw was at first disguised as a quarantine measure. All persons, Aryans as well as Jews, who took up residence in Warsaw were compelled to live in the enclosed section.[21] In September, 1940, it contained, besides 240,000 Jews, some 80,000 Aryan Poles. Much of the enclosure, then completed, consisted of barbed wire or fencing, for the continuous brick wall was not finished till the summer of 1941. No one however doubted that the enclosed region would be turned into a ghetto.

On October 16th, 1940, a decree was published, allowing a fortnight for the 80,000 Poles to move out of the 'infected section and for 120,000 still dispersed Jews to move in. The effect of this decree was to concentrate 360,000 Jews in an area which normally housed 160,000 people.

Most of the surviving Jewish business concerns outside the ghetto wall were now Aryanised, but certain workshops were permitted to move in. The exchange of apartments between Poles and Jews was a matter of individual bargaining, but the density of the population inside the walls rose to 5.5 per room. As one would expect, even in what was to become their prison those with negotiable assets could still buy superior accommodation.

On November 15th, without warning and overnight, guarded barriers were erected across the fourteen open entry points. The terror and chaos were unimaginable, for more than 100,000 normally employed persons had now to find work within the restricted space. To belong to the conscript labour commandos, even to the commandos which were sent to prison camps along the Russian border, became in some quarters a dearly sought privilege.[22] The overlarge population of black-coated workers, swollen by deportees from Lodz and Cracow, had to jostle each other for posts in the bureaucracy of the *Judenrat*, in the police force or *Ordnungsdienst*, or in the coveted service of *Hausmeister* to the apartment houses.[23] The factories, licensed by the Germans, the tolerated co-operative workshops, and the few permitted retail stores, were quite insufficient to employ the remainder.

Nevertheless, in the first few months of the ghetto the Germans were ready to make a few concessions. On February 18th, 1941, the Jewish Council was allowed to raise a loan from German banks on the security of the blocked Jewish deposits.[24] Three synagogues, including the main synagogue in Tlomaczek Street, were reopened, and in April schools were licensed for 5,000 of the 50,000 ghetto children. Several international relief societies, including the American Jewish Joint Distribution Committee, were allowed offices in the ghetto. Gifts from abroad were permitted through the post and Swiss medical equipment made up in part for the loss of the Czyste hospital.[25]

With the deportations into the Warsaw ghetto from the towns West of the Vistula, there began in February-May, 1941, a marked deterioration.* The refugees, dumped in bombed buildings and cellars by the Jewish Council, became a source of epidemics. In July, 1941, no less than 17,800 of them, including 3,300 children, were classed as destitute.[28] Of the whole group only six or seven thousand were alive a year later, when, since they possessed no *Ausweise* or labour cards, they were the first to go to the Treblinka gas chambers. Dr. Michal Mazor, a former welfare officer in the Warsaw Ghetto, mentions cases that he saw of shelter dwellers who joined the Treblinka column voluntarily, rather than endure life as they knew it.[29]

The attitude of the Jewish Council towards the problem of destitution seems to have been defeatist. It was left to the amalgamated welfare societies, known as KOM and by the Germans as JSS (*Juedische Soziale Selbsthilfe*), to provide a daily meal of soup. By the end of 1941 there were 100,000 people living on this soup[30] which had sometimes to be made of hay.

Even at this time luxury was achievable in the ghetto. The *sobre* factual narrative of Dr. Michal Mazor acknowledges this as much as the juvenile and artless gossip of Mary Berg. There were black-market restaurants on Lesno, Sienna, and Galianza Streets, besides cafés, night clubs, and brothels. Right up till the time of the 'resettlement action' most things could be got at a price. In Lesno Street a cabaret was able to buy its way out of a German demolition order, after Auersbach, the ghetto commissioner, had heard a song sung in English.[31] Yet all this time

*The Jewish Council carried out a census of the ghetto on January 1st, 1941, showing 378,979 persons. According to Du Prel 72,000 Jews were moved in, so that, allowing for the fantastic death-rate, there must have been at least 430,000 ghetto inhabitants in May.[26] Nevertheless, on July 22nd, 1942, when the resettlement action began, the population was again 380,000.[27] So there was an excess death-rate of 50,000 in fourteen months.

corpses were thrown out into the streets naked, so that their room-mates could keep their rags.

Governor Frank told Curzio Malaparte that the Jews were dirty, diseased, and dying, because they preferred it that way.[32] Others have suggested that the Jewish Council could have pieced out what there was on Socialist principles. But the corruption was above the Council's heads in the German administration office and the German police. Without smuggling and illicit profits the ghetto could not have lived at all. Furthermore, the ghetto had to borrow from the Germans the principle that only the exceptionally useful were worth preserving. The choice was expressed by Emanuel Ringelblum, Director of the Inter-Aid Committee, ZTOS, in a diary that he buried in the ghetto[33]:

' Communal kitchens do not solve the question. They prolong existence but the end is inevitable. . . . Reduced to soup and dry bread, those who eat from the public kitchens are slowly dying. . . . The tragic question remains to be answered. Must that which is insufficient for life be dispensed with a drop-counter or should a small group of the elect be helped to the utmost ? '[*]

As we have already seen (*page 47*) it had been intended in January, 1941, to bring even greater numbers of Jews to Warsaw. One may wonder whether Hitler, who had already laid his plans for the invasion of Russia, was not preparing the final annihilation of Polish Jewry a year before it actually began. It may be noticed that as early as July 4th, 1941, Dr. Marder, the *Regierungspraesident* of the Lodz region knew that the *Aufloesung* of the Lodz Ghetto was under discussion and this word, *dissolution,* had often a personal and physical sense in the Nazi vocabulary. Yet only as recently as June 3rd, the ghetto commissioner, Hans Biebow, had protested at a plan to ship the remaining 100,000 Jews of the Warthegau *into* Lodz ' where the famine at present raging would be increased sevenfold.' By September, however, both plans were dead (*see page 85*).[35a]

---

[*]The official figures supplied to the Germans by the Warsaw Jewish Council show 44,630 deaths in 1941, over 10 per cent of the population. Not more than 15,780 were deaths attributable to the typhus epidemic.[34] *Gazeta Zydowska,* the Cracow Jewish newspaper, licensed by the Germans, shows the increase in the death-rate after the arrival of the refugees, 2,041 deaths in April, 1941, 3,881 in May, 4,280 in June, 5,700 in September.[35]

Not much can be made of these orders and counter-orders except that in the early summer of 1941 the highest authorities already regarded the ghettoes as collecting places for further massed deportations, though the reduction of the Lodz Ghetto did not begin till the following January and that of the Warsaw Ghetto not till July 22nd, 1942. Thus, some 400,000 Warsaw Jews were permitted to survive an entire year in the shadow of the massacres of Russian Jewry. Even as late as May, 1942, the Warsaw Ghetto was considered a paradise, compared with Lodz, and sums of 20,000 zlotys were paid for the privilege of being smuggled into the Warsaw Ghetto by the Kohn-Heller transport service.[36]

Nevertheless, the decline in the standards of life was again accelerated in the Warsaw Ghetto in the autumn of 1941, when a more severe blockade was timed to coincide with the first big massacres in the Russian ghettoes. The usual excuse of 'epidemics' was invoked. On September 9th, 1941, Frank told his Cabinet[37] that there were 2,405 cases of typhus. The death penalty for leaving the Warsaw Ghetto must therefore be enforced. Recently only eight persons out of 45 who were charged, had been convicted and there were 600 cases pending. He had therefore received 'with gratitude' the police decree which permitted the shooting of Jews on the roads.

A few weeks later Frank announced from the Palais Bruhl a reduction of ghetto rations.[38] Whereas the Polish population received the very low ration of 45 ounces of bread a week, the Jews would get 33 ounces. Sugar was to be ten ounces a month, marmalade three and a half ounces a month, and fats less than two ounces. Special distributions would be necessary whenever it was possible to make them, but the ration itself could not be increased. Mary Berg has described in her diary what was perhaps the first of Governor Frank's 'special distributions.' On December 1st, a load of condemned frozen potatoes intended originally for the Russian front, reached the ghetto.[39]

In September the ghetto Post Office had been forbidden to handle foreign mail. It was the end of parcels from neutral countries.[40] Finally, on December 17th, the German Post Office refused to accept mail out of the ghetto, citing as usual, the excuse of epidemics. Thus, for the next seven months the Warsaw ghetto was virtually blacked out from observation, though in July, 1942, 'resettlement' actions stirred the exiled Polish Government in London and their excellent courier service again put the Warsaw Ghetto before the eyes of an indifferent world. Since 'Pearl Harbour' the American welfare organisations had been withdrawn.

Living space was reduced as well as food. On October 23rd, 1941, the Warsaw Ghetto lost its north-eastern sector, including the Tlomaczek Synagogue. In December the Jewish cemetery at the north-west angle was walled off on the grounds that coffins were used for smuggling. The practice continued, nevertheless, under the eyes of the German guards posted in the cemetery and in the narrative of a Jewish doctor, who escaped to Switzerland in 1943, it is stated that many of the arms used in the ghetto rebellion were brought back in the empty coffins.[41] Franz Blaettler, the Swiss Red Cross driver who visited the cemetery on January 30th, 1942, accompanied by a Jewish policeman, saw the immense mass-burial pit and recorded that 90 per cent of the corpses were dead from hunger, but this narrative could not be published till 1945 on account of the Swiss neutrality censorship.[42]

Blaettler also saw a smuggler caught, while entering through a hole in the wall. Although there were executions in the ghetto every day, it appears that this smuggler got no more than a beating. The truth was that the Gestapo were themselves interested in the smuggling. Since the Jewish Council were deemed incompetent to prevent it, the Gestapo appointed a special commission, independent of the Council, to combat the black market. The commission, known from its address in Lesno Street as the *Trzynastika* or thirteen, had its own 'green armlet' police. Some ghetto survivors have denounced it as an organised gang of racketeers, enjoying through its leader, Chaim Ganzewich and his associates, the protection of the Germans. These witnesses, however, differ as to whether the Germans removed the 'Thirteen' as early as May, 1942, or whether the 'Thirteen' were liquidated by the forces of the ghetto rebellion.[43]

Accusations of corruption such as this, though in a lesser degree, have been made against the Jewish Councils of all the Polish ghettoes, but the subject is beset with many difficulties.

The theory that the Germans picked the Jewish Councils at random or that they deliberately appointed scoundrels may be dismissed altogether. As in the West, Heydrich's agents enlisted the help of the relief organisations. These had great power in communities where there was always a big element of destitution. Conscripted under pain of death to act for the Germans, the relief organisations became at once soup-ladlers and policemen and symbolically the Warsaw Jewish Council used the premises of the former *Kehillah* or community relief centre. To reduce the population to the soup kitchen level, to amalgamate the soup kitchens into one Gestapo-controlled bureaucracy was generally an easy matter, given the isolation of the Jews in Poland, except in such enormously complicated communities as Warsaw. Here the situation somewhat resembled France where the Jewish organisations avoided being swept up altogether in a *Reichsvereinigung* on the German model (*see page 306*).

Thus, in Warsaw, the President of the Jewish Council, the *Obmann* or *Judenaelteste,* never came anywhere near being a ghetto dictator though such dictators were common, for the National Socialist system reposed on dictatorship at every grade. The Germans found it easier to get their quota of work or lives, if a single man was made responsible for them. These presidents did not have long to exercise their ambitions. The record of their fate is one of suicides and executions. Dr. Adam Czerniakow of the Warsaw *Judenrat* was allowed to own a motor-car. His almost regal state became the butt of the ghetto cabaret artists. Yet he committed suicide in July, 1942, sooner than be associated with the German 'resettlement.' Czerniakow's successor, Dr. Lichtenbaum, was removed by the Germans, on the eve of the ghetto rebellion having never been more than a cypher.[44] Dr. Bieberstein of Cracow was sent to Auschwitz as early as the summer of 1940.[45] Dr. Rotfeld, of Lwow, committed suicide during the October 1942 action. His successor, Dr. Landsberger, was hanged from a balcony with ten colleagues.[46] At Kolomia the *Judenaelteste* or Jewish President, Dr. Horowitz, committed suicide during the final action in the presence of the German police.[47] Other instances can be quoted by the dozen.

At Lodz, however, the Germans chose a president in October, 1939, who suited their purposes for nearly five years. Mordechai

Chaim Rumkowski, the manager of a Jewish orphanage, was known for his skill in raising subscriptions.[48] Besides this gift, which had such obvious appeal for the Germans, Rumkowski possessed resiliency. He was ordered to appoint a Jewish Council, who were then imprisoned as hostages. Badly beaten up while trying to obtain their release, Rumkowski was forced to appoint another council[49] but thereafter was not physically molested. He was treated like a dog outside the ghetto but allowed to be a king within the barbed wire. He issued currency notes bearing his signature, and postage stamps, engraved with his portrait, a genial elderly philanthropist with a cloak and a flowing mane of white hair, who moved about the ghetto in a respectable broken-down carriage. Rumkowski believed that the position the Germans had accorded him could be used to save Jewish lives during the resettlements. Thus in September, 1942, he marched to the station with the children whom the Germans had demanded—for had not the Germans spared his own orphanage?[50] Even in August, 1944, when close on 100,000 Lodz Jews had been 'resettled,' he sponsored the treacherous 'appeal' of the ghetto administrator, Hans Biebow.[51] Then, perceiving the trap he had baited, he voluntarily boarded the train for Auschwitz, where he was seen going into the gas chamber (*see page 303*).

The distribution of food and the allocation of labour in the Lodz Ghetto was Rumkowski's personal monopoly. There can be no question that he was efficient. He made the ghetto so essential to the German economic ministries that it outlasted Warsaw and Bialystok by a year and more. But this form of ghetto dictatorship was something unusual. The normal ghetto government was a police state reposing on the Jewish *Ordnungsdienst* or police force, who were in some cases quite independent of the Jewish Councils and took their orders straight from the Gestapo, to whom they were responsible for delivering their quota of live bodies; in the early days for labour assignment or genuine resettlement, but later for the execution places. Yet, long after they had discovered the truth, the men of the *Ordnungsdienst* earned their exempted status and wore their German-pattern blue uniforms. Dr. Michal Mazor, the most impartial of witnesses, declares that during the great Warsaw 'resettlement action,' a Jewish police officer inspired as much fear as a German and that the

Ordnungsdienst even revealed the hiding places of children.⁵² Sometimes they trafficked in Jewish lives. At Vilna they grew rich on the sale of employment certificates.⁵³ At Kovno, however, Dr. Gringauz absolves all but a few of the *Ordnungsdienst* of collusion with the Gestapo. Whatever their rôle, the end of the *Ordnungsdienst* was always the same. As soon as they had outlived their usefulness to the Germans, they were collectively shot —usually by a trick as at Minsk, where they were decoyed away to fight a fire (*see page 288*).⁵⁴

The commander of the *Ordnungsdienst* was frequently a baptised Jew who had held a commission in the Polish Army, such as Colonel Szerynski, who commanded a force in the Warsaw Ghetto, which numbered at one time 1,650 men. His deputy, Lejkin, who commanded early in 1942 while Szerynski was in prison, was photographed in *Voelkischer Beobachter* over the caption, 'The Jewish Napoleon.' Nevertheless, the power of these men could be real.⁵⁵ Thus, another Jewish professional soldier, Jakob Genns, the commander of the *Ordnungsdienst* in Vilna, made himself independent of the Jewish Council. In the autumn of 1942 the Germans recognised him as overseer of all the ghettoes surviving in Lithuania and White Russia, and he was saluted by the Lithuanian militia.⁵⁶ Like Rumkowski, Genns deceived himself that his personal usefulness to the Germans could be the means of saving Jewish lives—a genuine self-deception since in the end he chose to surrender himself for execution sooner than escape and so cause mass reprisals.

During the 'resettlement actions' the power of the *Ordnungsdienst* became intolerable, for frequently they alone decided how the numbers to be delivered to the Germans should be made up. In Lodz, Lieutenant Rosenblatt told Dr. Friedrich Hielscher, a member of the German resistance circle, that he contrived to select those who were past enduring the life of the ghetto and he arranged to keep aged couples together on the road to the gas chamber, but he was sorely troubled with his conscience.⁵⁷ Jakob Genns on the other hand preferred to brazen his activity. In October, 1941, he declared that by delivering a few Vilna Jews he had saved thousands from the Ponary death pits. Genns was then confronted by the Vilna rabbis with this sentence of Maimonides:

' When the idolater shall say unto you " Deliver to us one of your people that we may slay him, but if you refuse we shall slay you," then let all consent to perish and let no single Jewish soul be delivered freely to the idolater.'[58]

Perhaps the best answer to the rabbis would have been that there were no machine guns in the twelfth century. The Jewish policeman, who bought himself a reprieve of weeks or days by delivering his countrymen at the collecting station or *Umschlagsplatz*, was no more to be blamed than the Jews in the death camps, who were made to search the secret places of the gassed corpses for valuables and whose own reprieve might be reckoned only in hours. To-day, however, a burning hatred pursues the Jewish Councils and the *Ordnungsdienst* beyond their nameless graves. In November, 1949, the Bulletin of the Jewish Historical Institute of Poland announced that henceforward it would continue its studies on strict Marxist lines. In particular it would investigate the members of the Jewish Councils, their political affiliations, personal fortunes, and relations with the Germans.[59] It is rather sad to recall how little of this spirit there was in the first post-war researches of the Central Jewish Historical Commission of Poland.

The record of the amalgamated relief associations, the *Juedische Soziale Selbsthilfe,* seems to have been better than that of the Jewish Councils, particularly in the case of the bigger ghettoes where they were almost independent. Membership was voluntary and since there was practically no Gestapo control, the committees were not banned as collaborationists by the Jewish political parties. In Vilna, the committee was a symbol of independence, known affectionately as the National Assembly.[60] Even so the Germans had to recognise the committees. On February 10th, 1942, for instance, a complaint from the welfare committee in the small community of Wisznice had to be dealt with on an official plane by the Ministry of the Interior in Cracow.[61] In the course of time the Jewish Councils became absorbed in the task of placating the Germans, while internal government fell more and more on the shoulders of JSS, in particular the foremost duty of financing the soup kitchens. In Vilna, for instance, the workers in the labour commandos gave up two days' wages a month, two marks, and on this it was contrived that no one died of hunger[62] but there were seldom more than 20,000 Jews in the Vilna Ghetto and the problem was not comparable with that of Warsaw with its 100,000 daily soup kitchen meals.

3. Jewish Labour and Labour Camps in the General Government

Finance is the most mysterious part of the ghetto mechanism, for the civil administration of the Polish towns could not rate or tax the ghettoes, because in theory they had no income. The legitimate output of the Warsaw Ghetto could only be handled by the Transfer Office which was in the control of the SS. In return for these goods the Transfer Office issued rations and materials to the ghetto, but only after its agents had taken an enormous profit—a profit which was shared with certain Jewish entrepreneurs such as the trolley-bus proprietors, Kohn and Heller. As a result of such profiteering it generally happened that the ghettoes remained a liability on the civil administration. Thus, in July, 1941, the *Regierungspraesident*, Dr. Marder, complained that the town of Lodz bore the cost of the special police control and traffic arrangements in the ghetto. In September, Dr. Marder's successor, a colourless little member of the Reichstag called Dr. Uebelhoer, declared that these charges would be increased by the proposed immigration of Jews from Wloclawek. It was a situation unique in the history of local government that a third part of a city, the size of Birmingham, had been made destitute by the action of the police.[63]

It might be expected that with wages fixed at two marks a day, the ghetto could at least pay its way, but it seems that in Lodz this was not the case. In this same month *Oberbuergermeister* Ventski complained that only 80 per cent of the cost of the ghetto, then containing 140,000 people, was defrayed by work.[64] It was, nevertheless, the boast of the SS chiefs that they had harnessed Polish Jewry to productive tasks. Thus, in May, 1940, Major-General Friedrich Krueger, Frank's Higher SS and Police Leader, a former Strassbourg bookseller who looked like a fat village policeman, contributed this paragraph to Du Prel's guide to the General Government: [65]

> 'A no less extensive even if less thankful task of social responsibility had and has still to be performed by the men of the SS and police. The work-shy Jewish rabble had to be brought to their appointed work-places. If, thereby, many a Jew was able for the first time in his life to perform a productive and generally useful task under the compulsion of the police, it must above all be remembered that the commitment of all Jews to labour was indirectly brought about by a substantial police contribution in a field of important problems.'

What was this commitment to labour? In Lodz eight per cent of the Jews died of hunger in a year and yet their work paid for only 80 per cent of the cost of the ghetto. Such was the 'substantial police contribution.' The police were controlled by Heydrich, to whom ghettoes were no permanent solution of the Jewish problem and with whom Jewish labour, which meant Jewish survival, was not popular.

Only a small part of the Jewish population was given an opportunity to work. The German administration recognised two sorts of Jewish labour, work in the clothing and equipment factories in the ghettoes and work in the navvying camps and commandos outside. The decree of October 26th, 1939, made all male Jews liable to serve on public works for as much as two years. The conscription age was later extended between the limits of 14 and 60 years and the *Judenraete* were made responsible for furnishing the contingents.[66] In this way close on 500,000 Jews became liable for the heaviest labour, yet only 80,000 were employed in the summer of 1941 and probably never more than 100,000.[67] There was no difficulty in finding volunteers. More than half were employed in the daily commandos or in camps near Warsaw and Lublin. In addition there were till October 1940 some 30,000 Jews in construction camps along the Bug and San rivers, where the so-called Otto line was being built as a defence against Russia. This was considered the worst assignment with a very high death rate. Very different was the position of the 8,000 Jews in the Warsaw labour commandos, working for private German contractors, receiving four zlotys or two marks a day and living at home. In July, 1941, however, some 1,580 men from these commandos were returned to the ghetto, because the contractors refused to feed them.[68]

The Jews in the labour camps were hired out to civilian contractors by the Security Police, the civil government, or the municipal authorities. Everywhere there was gross embezzlement. The Higher SS and Police Leaders were not at first subordinated to an economic office of the SS. In the Lublin province, Odilo Globocnik—later the chief of the extermination programme—founded Jewish co-operative workshops and then turned them into labour camps for his own benefit. In July, 1941, Himmler visited Globocnik and became so perturbed at his friend's profits that he drafted the first plan for a centrally-administered concentration camp at Lublin, which was to take over all these workshops.[69] But Lublin or *Majdanek* concentration camp was not ready till 1942, and even then the SS Economic Office did not effectively get control of Jewish labour in Poland till Globocnik had gone and a million and a half Jews of the General Government had been murdered.

In fact the Germans, with their competing systems of control, were unable to use the entire Jewish population of the General Government as labour conscripts till the autumn of 1943, when they had killed off nine-tenths and in particular had eliminated all the ghettoes ; for as long as there were ghettoes there was to some extent free and competitive Jewish production. For instance, in August, 1941, there were 3,000 Jews employed in the Warsaw co-operative workshops. They made as much as 100 zlotys or 50 marks a week and received a daily free meal.[70] In the Cracow co-operatives the master-tailors could make 180 zlotys, nominally £4 10s., a week. In Warsaw the ghetto administrator, Auersbach, encouraged the growth of technical schools and courses. The motive for these deviations from the strict German code concerning the Jews was corrupt. An unlicensed workshop could always be suppressed by the police or the economic administration. The workers could then be forced to bring their labour and machines to German entrepreneurs, who enjoyed the protection of those authorities.

The Warsaw Ghetto rebellion has made the name of one of

these German entrepreneurs notorious. The career of Walter Toebbens was indeed sensational. In 1934, at the age of twenty-five, he had quitted the Bremen firm of Leffers Brothers, where he was employed as a coffee-roaster. Within the next four years Toebbens acquired, on the cheap, seven shops belonging to expatriated Bremen Jews. In October, 1939, he was recommended by the Bremen Chamber of Commerce to Lautz, the newly appointed *Geschaftsfuehrer* for the General Government, who was in charge of forty officially recognised district-wholesalers. Lautz and Toebbens went into partnership. Early in 1941 they moved into the Warsaw Ghetto and with next to no capital soon acquired 12,000 to 15,000 Jewish workers. After July 22nd, the beginning of the great 'resettlement' action, Toebbens was able to sell his protection certificate for fantastic sums and to obtain his labour force virtually for nothing—until the day when he had to hire it from the SS, and even then he was able to share his profits with Globocnik (*see page 294*).

Toebbens, whom Himmler once accused of 'making himself a millionaire on Jewish labour,' was not deserted by his luck even after the war.[71] An agile man of thirty-seven, he jumped the extradition train to Poland on November 22nd, 1946. Somewhere he must live, certainly in freedom, possibly in wealth, in spite of the sentence of the Bremen *Spruchkammer*, or Denazification Tribunal, passed in his absence in May, 1949, of ten years' labour camp.[72]

CHAPTER 4

The Madagascar Project:
The Deportations to Lodz and Russia
June, 1940—January, 1942

1. The Effects of the Conquest of the West

In the six weeks between May 10th and June 25th, 1940, not less than 350,000 Jews of Western Europe passed under German rule, a third of them being refugees from the Greater Reich, while a further 130,000 Jews came indirectly under German orders in Vichy territory. These half-million Jews of the West presented Hitler's policy with a harder problem than the two million Jews of German-occupied Poland. The sword had dangled over the heads of Eastern Jewry since the Russian pogroms of the early eighties. Compact ghettoes, a separate civil register for Jews, and an organisation of the anti-semitic forces were all at the disposal of the invader. But in the West Jews, who did not speak the tongue of their neighbours and who huddled in communities which could be conveniently encircled, were a minority—even when the less assimilable portion of the Reich refugees was added to their number. As to the native-born Jewish communities, the absence of a special registration made even physical identification difficult for the Germans, while the small ratio of the Jewish to the Gentile population facilitated dispersal. Whereas towns like Warsaw, Lodz, Odessa, Minsk, and Kiev were a third or more Jewish, Amsterdam was the only city West of Budapest with even a ten per cent Jewish population.

Before the problem of registering Western European Jewry Heydrich hesitated. Although a 'statut des Juifs' was exacted from the Vichy Government on October 3rd, 1940, it was not till March, 1941, that a special French Commissariat for Jewish Questions was established and that Jewish stamps were put on

71

identity cards. A Jewish Council, controlled by the Gestapo on the German and Polish model, was not set up till the summer— with what inadequate results will be seen in Chapter 12.

The Germans could not achieve a reliable Jewish census in the West. Even in Holland, where the occupation of the main cities within four days of a surprise invasion precluded flight, the Germans could not tell how far the normal Jewish population had been increased by their own refugees. In Belgium the Germans believed that 30,000 Jews had escaped to France, and in France they believed that huge numbers had reached the Free Zone. Thus on January 20th, 1942, Heydrich quoted a Gestapo figure of 700,000, whereas the real number in the Free Zone was certainly less than 130,000.[1] Even after November 11th, 1942, when the Free Zone was occupied, the German experts at 72, Avenue Foch, could not get at the true figures. During the first few months after the capitulation the Germans did not care how many Jews lived in the Free Zone, since it was considered a Jewish dumping-ground and not part of the privileged Europe which was to be made ' Jew-free.' The Foreign Office shared the views of the Security Police, in particular Ribbentrop's pleni-potentiary in France, the former Karlsruhe drawing-master Otto Abetz. Examined in 1948-49 in the Wilhelmstrasse case and again at his own trial in Paris, Abetz explained that he had supported the expropriation of the stateless Jews and their expulsion to the Free Zone, but that he had done so as a blind, knowing it would not succeed.[2] The truth, however, seems to be that this action against the stateless Jews would have succeeded only too well if Heydrich had not overplayed his hand.

Abetz did in fact submit his proposition regarding the state-less Jews to Heydrich on September 10th[3] and the mechanism through which this was done deserves study, since this was the beginning of a new and very close liaison between the Foreign Office and the Security Office of the SS State. Abetz's proposal passed through the hands of one Dr. Martin Luther, the head of the Foreign Office department ' Deutschland,' which had normally been the liaison office with the Ministry for Interior. This unpleasant person was a creature of Ribbentrop's and at the same time a powerful agent of Heydrich and the Gestapo, a dual rôle which eventually led Luther to conspire against

Ribbentrop's person and so land himself in Sachsenhausen Concentration Camp, from which he never came out alive.*

Luther, a companion of Ribbentrop in his champagne-selling days, had entered the ' Bureau Ribbentrop ' in 1936 in the modest capacity of a forwarding agent in charge of office equipment and was so enabled to make himself very useful when Ribbentrop was redecorating the London Embassy in Carlton House Terrace.[4] Promotion to department 'Deutschland' in the Foreign Office proper followed in May, 1940, as his reward. Ribbentrop's chief motive seems to have been to annoy the old-guard diplomatists like Ernst von Weizsaecker, whom Luther called 'old women and Father Christmasses,' and whom he used to address in official correspondence as ' Dear party-member.' For their part, the scandalised diplomats had to console themselves with the thought that Luther's ruffians (they numbered over 200) lived in scattered office buildings, not even in the Wilhelmstrasse, but somewhere near the Zoo, into which hostile territory they could send an occasional spy such as Hans Haeften, the nephew of Frau Brauchitsch.[5]

For three years Luther had Ribbentrop's unqualified support. In April, 1941, this Dahlem furniture remover was able to help his old political friends by persuading Ribbentrop to appoint five new Ministers to the Governments of South-East Europe from among the discredited group leaders of Roehm's Storm Detachments of 1934, men who had nothing to recommend them but their capacity to shout and intimidate. This was because in Luther's company Ribbentrop fancied himself a revolutionary and was able to vent the essentially snobbish spite which he felt

---

*The circumstances of Luther's fall in April, 1943, are still rather mysterious. The best account was given by Weizsaecker's successor, Steengracht von Moyland, during the 'Wilhelmstrasse case.' Luther's plot against Ribbentrop was revealed by two private individuals whom he had threatened with the Gestapo, so Luther was forced to denounce Ribbentrop openly when the latter ordered an inquiry. The SS were, however, disloyal to the man who had served the late Heydrich so well. Himmler's adjutant, Karl Wolff, sent Ribbentrop a copy of Luther's charges. Hitler thereupon wanted to hang Luther but Ribbentrop persuaded him to send him to Sachsenhausen. The nature of the charges have not been disclosed, but Ulrich von Hassell believed that Luther was plotting to replace Ribbentrop with the SS man, Werner Best. (Case XI, transcript 9760-9768, examination of Steengracht. Defence document books, IIb, 75-6, and I, 5-6.)

towards the professional diplomats, as a man with a spurious *von* to his name. Yet at the Nuremberg trial Ribbentrop was not averse to boasting of the small diplomatic post he had occupied in Constantinople in the First World War and of his alleged family connection with Ambassador Dieckhoff (IMT X, 154).

Between Ribbentrop's thwarted snobbery and his anti-semitism there was a recognisable link and there lay the appeal of Martin Luther, who had made anti-semitism his life's work. Through his control of the department ' Deutschland III ' Luther now acquired sole competence in Foreign Office dealings in the Jewish question. ' Deutschland III,' moreover, was in daily, almost hourly, contact with Eichmann's office in the Kurfuersten-strasse. During the whole of its existence from June, 1940, to April, 1943, the department was directed by Franz Rademacher. As a consequence we shall hear as much of Rademacher as of Luther. His career therefore merits some description.

Before entering the diplomatic service Rademacher had been in practice as a barrister, but in 1940, when he was thirty-four years old, he patriotically abandoned his post of legation secretary in Montevideo in order to enlist in the navy. This, according to Rademacher's own story,[6] angered Ribbentrop so much that he was sent to Department ' Deutschland ' as a punishment. He was not able to leave it and follow his original inclination till the fall of his chief, Martin Luther.

For the next three years Rademacher's name was to appear on every sort of incriminating document relating to Jewish deportations and, on one occasion at least, relating to massacres of Jews (*see pages 360 and 364*), yet somehow after the war Rademacher had a charmed life. He avoided trial because he was needed as a witness and he avoided giving evidence because he was awaiting trial. At the beginning of 1950 it was discovered that Rademacher was at liberty, the private secretary of the Hamburg cigarette-manufacturer, Philip Reemstsma.[7] Rade-macher was not finally brought before the Nuremberg *Schwurgericht* till 1952, when—on March 17th—he received a sentence of three years and five months' imprisonment.

Whether signed by Luther or Rademacher, the directions of Department Deutschland to the diplomatic representatives in occupied or satellite countries betray a consistent skill in shifting the responsibility on to the Governments in question. This skill was certainly not Luther's, whose direct diplomatic contacts were of the most bludgeoning kind (*see page 416*). It is in fact Heydrich's skill of which we get the first glimpse on September 20th, when Abetz received his consent through Luther to the proposals for the stateless Jews in France. Heydrich insisted that the arrests—it was believed that there would be 40,000 in Paris alone—should be made by the German Security Police and not by the French. Nevertheless, Abetz was instructed to persuade the Vichy Government to 'take the first initiative so that it may sign for it and bear the responsibility in the event of failure.' It was, therefore, Abetz's task to provide the Vichy Government with a legal pretext. He proposed that the emigré Jews in France should be declared collectively to have forfeited their nationality. And so, on October 4th, 1940, the Vichy Government responded with a 'Statut des Juifs' which anticipated by a full year the notorious '11th Decree Supplementing the Reich Law of Citizenship' (*page 87*).[8]

By the end of 1940 this statute had effectively deprived 30,000 Jews in the Occupied Zone and 20,000 Jews in the Free Zone of their liberty. Yet in a Nuremberg affidavit Abetz declared[9] that he had recommended the deportations into the Free Zone because in this way the emigré Jews could acquire the 'support of French Law.' In fact the Jews lost their freedom, whichever zone they stayed in. For in the Occupied Zone the Germans interned them at Drancy, Pithiviers, or Beaune la Rolande, while in the Free Zone the Vichy authorities interned them—and under far worse conditions—at Gurs, Les Milles, or Rivesaltes.

The Abetz plan was short-lived. Heydrich killed it by including Jews living in the German Reich in the deportations to the French Free Zone. This was the affair known as 'Action Buerckel' which took place on the night of October 22nd, 1940, when 7,450 Baden and Saarland Jews were removed, some of them at twenty minutes' notice. They were collected by the local police under the orders of the Gestapo. The greater part—the official figure was 6,504 Jews—were bundled into nine goods trains and dragged across France to the camp of Les Milles near Aix en Provence and to Gurs and Rivesaltes in the Pyrenees.[10] 'The operation,' Eichmann proudly declared to Luther, 'was scarcely noticed by the public.' The Jews, who were involved in 'Action Buerckel,' consisted of elderly people and children who were not needed for the German war potential. Many were ill or bedridden and there were numerous deaths on the journey. The French camps could at first provide neither food nor accommodation and on October 29th General Stuelpnagel, the Military Governor in France, transmitted to the Foreign Office a protest from General Doyen of the French armistice commission.[11] This was followed up on November 19th with a request from Marshal Pétain that the Saar-Baden Jews be returned to Germany, which Ribbentrop told Weizsaecker to 'treat in a dilatory manner.' Six days later Stuelpnagel was informed that the Foreign Office would take no action. The Saar-Baden Jews were not set at liberty. After November, 1942, when the Vichy camps fell into German hands, those who were still alive were sent to Auschwitz.*

Pétain's protest was ignored and yet the deportations were not repeated. There was henceforward strict injunction against using the Free Zone as a dumping ground, even for Jews resident in France. Higher authority, from whom Heydrich concealed his plans, had intervened. As a rule Hitler did not like to give up potential hostages and this may explain why he interfered with Heydrich's plan. The explanation may also be that Heydrich's action conflicted with the Madagascar project, Hitler's interest in which had been announced by Goering as far back as November, 1938 (see page 21).

Jewish colonisation in Madagascar was an old proposal. It had at one time commended itself to the Polish Government, which finally, in 1937, sent a commission to report. Of this

---

*A month after the action Luther was asked to provide a copy of the Vichy Government's protest for Wilhelm Frick, the Minister for Interior, with a view to disciplining the two Gauleiters, Josef Buerckel of Lorraine-Saarland and Robert Wagner of Baden-Alsace. It would, therefore, appear that the Gauleiters had taken secret instructions from Heydrich without informing Frick, who was nominally Heydrich's superior. The minutes of Wagner's trial—he was shot by the French at Strassbourg in October, 1946 —should elucidate some of this mystery. As to Buerckel, who nearly became Heydrich's successor in place of his companion of *Anschluss* days, Ernst Kaltenbrunner, he committed suicide at the end of the war. Gauleiter Robert Wagner should not be confused with Gauleiter Julius Wagner of Silesia, who was dismissed in 1940, or Gauleiter Adolf Wagner of Bavaria, who died in 1943.

commission, one member, Major Lepecki, considered that 15,000 Jewish families could be settled on the Ankaisina plateau, while two other members, both Jews, declared that only small groups could be settled and that they would be exposed to tropical epidemics.[12] The suggestion that Madagascar could take millions of people never arose. We must now therefore seriously consider the evidence, whether Hitler at any time believed in the Madagascar project or whether it was used as a cloak to hide the real plans for the Final Solution which were maturing in his mind. The report of the Polish Government in 1937 had several repercussions, for not only did Goering speak of the Madagascar plan on November 12th, 1938, but on December 7th M. Georges Bonnet, the French Foreign Secretary, told Ribbentrop in Paris that the French Government was thinking of shipping 10,000 Jewish refugees there.[13] But the Wilhelmstrasse only learnt of a general Madagascar plan at the time of the fall of France. The two circulars, sent out from Luther's department, were dated July 2nd and August 15th, and signed[14] by Rademacher, but the second circular shows that the details had been worked out by Eichmann, since the enclosures are signed by his assistant Dannecker and bear the letterhead of Kurfürstenstrasse 116.[15] This fits in with the assertion made by Dieter Wisliceny, a close friend and associate, that Eichmann was commissioned to draw up a Madagascar plan in August and that Dannecker, the future organiser of the Jewish deportation trains to Auschwitz, was employed in research on Madagascar at the French Ministry for Colonies,[16] and that the matter occupied Eichmann for the next year.

We need not linger too long over the inconceivably unrealistic proposals of August 15th. The colony was to be an autonomous Jewish reserve under a German police-governor. An inter-European bank was to finance the emigration of *four million* Jews and there was to be a shipping pool big enough to take them all within a few years to Madagascar. All this was taken seriously for, according to a later memorandum from Luther,[17] Heydrich obtained Himmler's approval of the plan before the end of the month and also submitted it to Goering as *Reichsmarschall*. We are led to suppose that these authorities gave the go-ahead signal to Eichmann and that during the next year, when scarcely a ship left Europe except by tolerance of the British Navy, he was making all the necessary preparations. Clearly it was the most harmless year in Eichmann's life.

We are also led to suppose that all this was changed by the invasion of Russia. Yet the curious thing is that not once in that eventful year did either Hitler, Goering, or Himmler mention Madagascar in their speeches and that, even on March 28th, 1941, when Rosenberg spoke of a 'distant reservation for the deportation of European Jewry,' the name Madagascar was omitted.[18] What then is the evidence that Hitler ever discussed Madagascar at all?

Paul Otto Schmidt, the Foreign Office interpreter, recollected that on June 17th Hitler observed to Mussolini 'One could found a State of Israel in Madagascar.'[19] Luther, writing to Ribbentrop a year after the event, recalled how in August, 1940, Hitler had informed him through Abetz of his intention to evacuate all the Jews of Europe.[20] Abetz for his part remembered this interview, which he placed at August 3rd, 1940, but declared that Hitler meant evacuation *to the U.S.A.*, which he thought capable of absorbing several million Jews.[21] Against this there is good evidence that by evacuation Hitler still meant evacuation to Poland and that the fall of France had not changed his plans in the very least. Thus Baldur von Schirach declared that he was summoned by Hitler to his field headquarters at the end of June, 1940, and told that he intended to settle the Jews of Vienna in 'the General Government'—in other words, that he would resume the deportations which had been suspended only a few months previously.[22]*

Felix Kersten claims that he was told by Himmler that he had been summoned to Hitler's field headquarters after the

---

*Hitler, according to Dr. Picker, made a remark when dining at his headquarters that if the Jews did not emigrate after the war to Madagascar or some other Jewish national State he would round them up, town by town. The fact that this threat was made on July 24th, 1942—the third day of the great Warsaw 'resettlement'—seems to confirm the camouflage nature of Hitler's allusions to Madagascar. On May 29th, according to Dr. Picker—and also an unpublished fragment of the Goebbels diary—Hitler had said that it was better to send the Jews to Africa than to Siberia, 'a climate which would certainly not make them vigorous and full of resistance.' (Henry Picker. *Hitler's Tischgespraeche*, Bonn, 1951, pp. 118, 311.)

capitulation of France and informed that he would have to undertake the progressive extermination of European Jewry. Himmler told Kersten that he had personally urged the Madagascar project and that he protested to Hitler, but in vain.[23]

This admittedly third-hand picture of Hitler, already intent on the Final Solution, being offered the Madagascar plan to keep him quiet is repeated in a second testimony that is unfortunately open to the same objections. At his trial in 1947 Viktor Brack of the Fuehrer's Chancellory (see pages 79, 82, and 176) stated that at the end of March, 1941, 'when it was no secret in higher party circles that the Jews were to be exterminated,' he. and his colleagues of the Fuehrer's Chancellory had suggested to Hitler a Jewish settlement in Madagascar, of which their chief Philip Bouhler should be the governor.[24]

One would surely expect that, if Hitler had been actually entertaining such a proposal for the past nine months, the members of his secret chancellory would know something about it. One is forced to conclude that the Madagascar project was intended mainly to ease the burdens of the Foreign Office in preventing the free emigration of Jews from Axis territories. As such the fiction died hard. It was not till February 10th, 1942, that Rademacher sent the Foreign Office departments a new ruling:[25]

'The war with the Soviet Union has in the meantime created the possibility of disposing of other territories for the Final Solution. In consequence the Fuehrer has decided that the Jews should be evacuated not to Madagascar but to the East. Madagascar need no longer therefore be considered in connection with the Final Solution.'

On receiving this circular, Weizsaecker's Under-Secretary, Woermann, asked Rademacher where, in view of the importance of this decision, he had got his information and was told by Luther a fortnight later that 'personal talks with Heydrich had made the Madagascar plans of his office obsolete.' But Woermann's question and Luther's reply were nothing but a façade, intended for the record, for on January 20th, Luther had attended Heydrich's conference at Gross-Wannsee and sent Woermann a copy of the murderous proposals contained in the minutes (see page 99).

2. The Fuehrer Order

According to Field-Marshal Keitel, it was at the beginning of December, 1940, that Hitler first ordered plans for an invasion of Russia, but the General Staff were not assured of its imminence till March, 1941.[26] At this period Jewry experienced a noticeably different climate in every part of German-occupied territory. Thus, in February-May there was a revival of deportations into the General Government and in March the remainder of the large Polish ghettoes were enclosed. In France and the Low Countries the much postponed registration took place, while in February there was a mass deportation of Dutch Jewish hostages to the German concentration camps and in May the first round-up of foreign Jews who had received French naturalisation.[27] That these steps, which were taken on the orders of Himmler, were linked with the development of Hitler's first extermination order there can be little doubt. It should be noted, too, that Rosenberg's allusion to a ' distant reservation ' was made on March 28th, five days before he was made Hitler's adviser on Russia as a prelude to becoming *Reichsminister* for the occupied Eastern territories, and that the occasion was a momentous one, the opening of a conference on the Jewish Question at which the vassal-States were represented by five Minister-presidents or State-secretaries.[28]

The actual Fuehrer Order for the execution of Jews, gipsies, racial inferiors, ' asocials,' and finally Soviet political commissars, was communicated to those responsible for its execution in stages. Field-Marshal Keitel recollected a conference at Hitler's headquarters in the first half of March, where Himmler was given extensive plenipotentiary powers, covering all police actions which would become necessary in the occupied territory.[29] A broad hint of these ' police actions ' was conveyed by Keitel himself in a High Command instruction, dated March 13th, 1941.[30]

' By order of the Fuehrer, the Reichsfuehrer SS has been given special tasks, arising from the conclusive and decisive struggle between the two opposing political systems. Within the limits of the set tasks the Reichsfuehrer SS acts independently upon his own responsibility.'

At a conference on March 30th Keitel revealed to the army commanders that they would have to execute political commissars who fell into their hands, or else hand them over to the Gestapo.[31]* Thereupon, Generals Leeb, Bock, and Rundstedt urged Walter Brauchitsch, their Commander-in-Chief, to protest. Brauchitsch admitted at Nuremberg that he had not done this because he had believed in his own capacity to kill the Fuehrer Order by strict injunctions to his troops against excesses.

Did the army commanders also learn of the order to exterminate Jews? Ohlendorf, an accused police general with a spite against the High Command, said they did,[32] but General Halder, who, as Chief of Staff, kept the most careful minutes of Keitel's conference, made no such entry.[33] Moreover, Ohlendorf himself, who was present in the latter part of May at the discussions between Wagner, the Quartermaster-General, and Heydrich, denied that the execution of Jews was then discussed.[34] All this is inconclusive and still more so the argument of von Brauchitsch that Wagner could not have been a party to Heydrich's true plans because his convictions led him to take part in the July 1944 plot and subsequently to commit suicide.[35] As we shall see, Wagner was more than once a party to Heydrich's plans and, as to the July, 1944 plot, even an extermination group commander like Nebe could take part in it. Moreover, Schellenberg and Ohlendorf—and perhaps even Himmler himself—gave the plot a friendly wink while it had a chance of success.

The part of the Fuehrer Order concerning the execution of Jews was at any rate never put on paper and even those to whom it was passed were not all informed at the same time. Ohlendorf got his orders in June from Streckenbach, of Heydrich's Personnel Office,[36] while two other extermination group commanders, Erwin Schulz and Walter Blome,[37] were briefed in the same month in the course of a lecture, given by Heydrich to a select

*Helmuth Greiner, who kept the war diary of the Wehrmacht, records a much earlier conference, at which Hitler mentioned the order to kill political commissars—on March 3rd. Hitler then adopted a rather peculiar reasoning. It would be impossible for the Germans to restore capitalism in Russia, especially as this would encourage Russian national feeling. Instead they must set up 'dependent Socialist States with a minimum of military strength.' Therefore the Communist organisers and political commissars must be shot. (Helmuth Greiner. *Die Oberste Wehrmachtfuehrung, 1939-1943. Wiesbaden, 1952.*)

audience in his office in the Prinz Albrecht Strasse But another of these commanders, Otto Rasch, deposed that he only learnt of this part of the Fuehrer Order when serving in Russia at the end of August,[38] at which time massacres of Jews had already begun on all sectors of the front.

Viktor Brack's statement that these matters were 'no secret in higher party circles' in March, 1941, is mitigated in force by the fact that this was his defence for having written Himmler a letter on the 28th advocating mass sterilisation; but there is a strong suspicion that soon after the first conferences on the Fuehrer Order, its full nature and implications were known to Goering. On May 20th a circular was dispatched by Eichmann's office, the Jewish section of the Gestapo, warning all German consulates that Goering had banned voluntary emigration by Jews from France and Belgium, firstly because it hampered similar emigration from the Reich and secondly because 'The Final Solution of the Jewish Problem' is undoubtedly close at hand.[39] The circular, moreover, was signed by Himmler's intelligence chief, Brigadier Walter Schellenberg, who on this precise date represented Heydrich in his negotiations on the Fuehrer Order with Wagner—a significant circumstance.

Goering, as we have already seen, had been responsible since January, 1939, for Heydrich's brief to evacuate Jews from the Reich, a brief which he was on occasion able to withdraw (see particularly page 21, footnote). Any extension of Heydrich's powers demanded a fresh brief from Goering as Reichsmarschall and in this case, the intended mass-deportation to Russia of all Jews in German hands, we possess a copy. It is described as a supplement to Heydrich's instructions of January 24th, 1939, and it is dated surprisingly late, July 31st, 1941, when the extermination groups had been nearly six weeks in Russia.[40]

> 'I herewith commission you to carry out all preparations with regard to the organisation, the material side and financial viewpoints for a total solution of the Jewish question in those territories of Europe which are under German influence. If the competency of other central organisations is touched in this connection, these organisations are to participate.

' I furthermore commission you to submit to me as soon as possible a draft showing the administrative, material, and financial measures already taken for the execution of the intended final solution of the Jewish question.'*

At Nuremberg Goering was singularly little pressed by Mr. Justice Jackson as to what was meant by the word *endloesung* in this document. Goering said it meant not *final* solution but *total* solution and he was allowed to get away with that.[41] Jackson apparently failed to perceive that both the words *Gesamtloesung* and *Endloesung* were used in this document and that Goering has made him accept the same translation for each. Goering's plea was that he had merely asked Heydrich, the appropriate authority for Jewish emigration, for information on the progress achieved—a ridiculous plea, for how could Goering help knowing that Heydrich was in charge of the massacres in Russia and that he would do the same to any Jews that were deported there ? It is difficult to imagine that Goering, who was then at the height of his power, holding the offices of *Reichsmarschall*, Prime Minister of Prussia, Plenipotentiary for the Four-Year Plan, and Commander-in-Chief of the Air Force, did not realise what Hitler was demanding from Himmler and Heydrich. We know at least that, very much later, on January 20th, 1942, when Heydrich openly admitted that the intention was murder, Goering's State Secretary, Neumann, did not object, except to ask for the exemption of certain Jews in the armament industry.

We have noticed (*see pages 44-5*) that in March-May, 1940, Goering stopped the deportations into Poland for fear of diplomatic repercussions. We shall also see that in October, 1941, he was able to mitigate the deportations from Berlin in the interests of the armaments industry. Thereafter, his interventions for Jews were limited to private favours. Thus Goering, as Prime Minister of Prussia, did nothing to prevent the mass-deportations from

*' . . . beauftrage ich Sie hiermit, alle erforderlichen Vorbereitungen in organisatorischer, sachlicher und materieller Hinsicht zu treffen fuer eine Gesamtloesung der Judenfrage im deutschen Einflussgebiet in Europa.
  Sofern hierbei die Zustaendigkeiten anderer Zentralinstanzen beruehrt werden, sind diese zu beteiligen.
  Ich beauftrage Sie weiter, mir in Baelde einen Gesamtentwurf ueber die organisatorischen, sachlichen und materiellen Vorausmassnahmen zur Durchfuehrung der angestrebten Endloesung der Judenfrage vorzulegen.'

Berlin at the beginning of 1943. In fact, by this time, he was sunk in sloth and debauch and he scarcely intervened in anything, but there is no evidence that Goering at any moment made a stand on principle against the Final Solution and his only Nuremberg defence was the fatuous one that he knew nothing about it.

3. The Reich Jews Deported to Lodz

Among the fragments of Goebbels's diary, which have been recovered since part of it was first published, are his accounts of two conversations with Hitler in August, 1941.[42] In the first, Hitler speaks of the coming deportations. The Berlin Jews, he says, will have to go to the East as soon as possible, as soon as transportation means are at hand. 'Then they will have to make their living in a much harder climate.' In the second fragment Hitler alludes to his prophecy of January 30th, 1939, that another world war would mean the annihilation of the Jews and he notes that in the past few weeks it has been fulfilled 'with almost unnatural precision.' Hitler concludes by saying:

> 'And as regards the Jewish question one can verify to-day that a man for example, like Antonescu, proceeds in these matters in a far more radical fashion than we have done up to the present, but I will not rest or slacken until Jewry has incurred the last consequences.'

There is a certain slyness in this remark, in which Hitler suggests that the massacres and deportations by the Rumanians had been ahead of his own programme. We shall see, when dealing with the persecutions in Rumania (*pages 201 and 398*), that the German Security Police commanders were in the smug position at this time of restraining the Rumanians from 'uncontrolled' executions and deportations. Yet the Rumanians were not leading the Germans but following them. Antonescu knew that in the wake of the Wehrmacht in Russia the Security Police murdered the Jews wherever they found them, and that by pushing his Bessarabia and Bukovina Jews into German rear areas, he would make them an embarrassment to the field commanders and an easy prey for the Security Police under the terms of the Fuehrer Order. Similarly in Hungary in this same month of August the

Government of Laszlo Bardossy drove part of its recently acquired Jewish population of Carpathian Ruthenia into Russian Podolia, where, after a conference between Quartermaster-General Wagner and the Police-General, Franz Jaeckeln, about 11,000 of them were massacred near Kamenetz-Podolsk (*see page 413*). At the same time the Hungarians expelled some 16,000 Jews of the recently occupied Yugoslav Bachka province into the ghetto created by the Germans in Belgrade (*see page 359*). Now at Belgrade there was a puppet Serb Government and a Reich plenipotentiary and the problem of disposing of this overcrowded ghetto became a Foreign Office matter. Among the suggestions that entered Ribbentrop's mind was shipping the Jews down the Danube to be dealt with by the Rumanians. There followed the inconceivably callous correspondence described in Chapter 14, in which Ribbentrop learnt from Heydrich through Rademacher that the Hungarians and Rumanians had jumped the gun and that 'not even German Jews could be sent at present to the General Government or to Russia.' Eichmann could, therefore, only suggest that the Jews in Belgrade be shot on the spot.

This, be it noted, was on September 12th, a full six weeks after Heydrich had received his brief from Goering, and in fact no deportations left the Reich till the middle of October and even then the first trains got no further than Lodz, which was neither in Russia nor in the General Government. But the decision to use Lodz was certainly made as early as September, for on the 24th the German *Buergermeister* knew quite accurately the number of Jews he was to expect.[43] There were several reasons for the substitution of Lodz. The clearing of the Russian ghettoes for the reception of the Reich Jews had been delayed. The Transport Command of the Wehrmacht maintained a ban on the use of the Russian railway system. Finally, Heydrich was obliged by the terms of his brief to consult other ministries, 'where their competency was involved.' In fact on October 4th he had been forced to hold an inter-ministerial conference, where he complained of the demands made in every quarter for exemption and the fact that no one would exert himself to replace Jews with other workers. Heydrich then attacked Georg Leibbrandt, Rosenberg's representative, because the Ministry for the

Eastern Territories had shown so little inclination to go into the question of the Jewish settlement, and he spoke threateningly of another conference where the whole undertaking would be put in the hands of the Security Police 'in all its ramifications.'[44] Altogether, Heydrich was in an extremely thwarted and ugly mood.

Heydrich's chief obstacles were in Berlin. Goebbels noted in his diary in August that, though there remained 77,000 Jews in Berlin, only 26,000 were at work,[45] but in reality this was an enormous proportion, since Goebbels only recognised conscript-labour. Not all Jewish labour-conscripts were roadmakers and field labourers at 75 Pfennige an hour according to the decree of March 4th, 1939 (see pages 17 and 28). Many were skilled men and key-workers in the armament industry. It was therefore Heydrich's endeavour to deport the victims first and hear the complaints later. In this way, thousands of Jews were got out of the Reich before their exemptions had been confirmed by ministerial decree. Thus, the memorandum of the Ministry of Justice, which exempted both Jews in essential work and the partners of mixed marriages, did not circulate till November 21st[46]; that of the Labour Office, exempting the families of labour-conscripts, not till a month later.[47] It was only at the Gross-Wannsee conference of January 20th that the various degrees of privilege among German Jews were fully acknowledged by Heydrich and this accounts for the chaotic and indiscriminate character of the Lodz and Russian deportations, as compared with the very cautious deportations from the Reich in 1942.

Another difficulty was the legal status of the deportees. Although Jews from the Greater Reich had been sent to the General Government in large numbers in October, 1939-April, 1940, it was not certain whether they still retained their position under the Nuremberg Laws as *Staatsangehoerige* or second-degree citizens. Under the 'Reich Law of Citizenship' a Jew, who emigrated, forfeited both property and citizenship, but how could this concern a Jew deported against his will? On July 7th, 1941, Franz Stuckart, State Secretary in the Ministry for Interior, proposed that the 'freewill of the Jews concerned' be declared immaterial.[48] This proposal was not actually made law in the form of 'the Eleventh Decree supplementing the Reich Law of Citizenship' till November 25th, when tens of thousands of Jews had already left for Lodz and Russia.[49] It was then pointed out that the 20,000 Jews, who had been deported to Lodz, were still in Reich territory and therefore entitled, even in the ghetto, to any pensions or annuity payments that became due to them. Stuckart got round this by invoking a decree of the Ministry of Finance, dated July 14th, 1933, which confiscated the property of anyone deemed 'hostile to the people and State.'[50] It was under the terms of this decree—which had to be invoked each time—that the flats of the deportees were sealed by the Gestapo and their contents collected by the Finance Ministry in warehouses or in the commandeered lounges of hotels to be sold at auction or distributed to camps and hospitals.[51]

The deportation decree of October 14th is signed not by Heydrich but by Lieut.-General Kurt Daluege, chief of the regular German police[52] or *Ordnungspolizei*. This is not really surprising. Although in theory the regular police was independent of Heydrich's Security Office, Daluege only stayed in office through serving Heydrich, as a consequence of which numerous companies of regular police were drafted to Poland and Russia in 1941-42 to take orders from the Higher SS and Police Leaders and to play their part in the massacre of Jewry. Nevertheless, among the Nuremberg documents it is only the two deportation orders of October, 1941, and the report (*page 323*) of a journey to Marseilles in 1942 that incriminate this rather colourless policeman in the Final Solution. Daluege, who succeeded Heydrich for a time as Protector of Bohemia, was hanged in Prague in October, 1946, having been tried on a totally different indictment. It is a loss to history that Daluege was not arraigned at Nuremberg.

The 19,287 Jews who were sent to Lodz between October 16th and November 13th, came not only from Berlin but from Vienna, Prague, Cologne, and other cities of the Greater Reich.* Even

---

*According to a *Schutzpolizei* report from Lodz dated November 13th, 1941, the total was made up as follows: 4,187 Jews from Berlin in four trains commencing October 19th, 5,486 Jews from Vienna in five trains, 5,000 from Prague, 2,007 from Cologne, 1,034 from Hamburg, 1,134 from Frankfurt, 984 from Dusseldorf, and 512 from Luxembourg, which was then included in the Reich.[53]

when spread out over four weeks the movement disorganised railway traffic. The trains were delayed, the sidings were blocked, the detrainment of thousands of helpless people with their bundles was hampered by the construction of the corridor coaches ; later the Gestapo learnt their lesson and ordered cattle-trucks. For three weeks additional guards had to patrol the Lodz Ghetto by night, while the dazed multitudes were herded to and fro in search of billets.[54]

In Poland the *Herrenvolk* rarely put on their best perform-ance. At the other end the operation was by contrast almost perfect, free from the mass-pillage attending such operations in the Balkans, free from the individual pillage that went on in occupied territory. The victims were allowed to take 50 kilograms of luggage, 100 marks in currency, and three days' provisions, if they could find them. They received a final notice of two hours from their own *Reichsvereinigung* and they had to extinguish the fires and electricity in their flats and hand over the keys. Then they boarded the lorry, which was accompanied by a single policeman. In the smaller places, such as Wuerzburg, they joined a pathetic overloaded column which marched to the station, scarcely noticed by the crowds on the streets.[55]

Eichmann did not as yet risk trusting the whole operation to the Jewish *Ordnungsdienst* as he did in the light of experience in Poland during the deportations from Berlin at the beginning of 1943. At this time the number of Jews was thought too large for such a risk and in Berlin there was a particularly high proportion of young and able-bodied people.* But Eichmann underestimated the despair and resignation of the last remnant of German Jewry. A remarkable feature of the Gestapo deportation lists is the high proportion who could not be collected for 'resettlement' because they were found to have committed suicide. Among a transport of 523 Berlin Jews which was to have left for Poland on April 3rd,

---

*In Vienna it was just the reverse. Of the 43,700 Jews who survived in the summer of 1941 only 7,000 were between the ages of 18 and 45, and of these only 1,953 were males. As compared with 2,412 children and adolescents there were 20,000 people over 60 years of age and two-thirds of the entire Jewish population were females.[56] Not less than 19,000 of these poor people were packed in unheated trains for a week on end or more and left to face the Russian winter of 1941-42 in the utter destitution of the ghettoes—that is if they were not sent straight to the execution pits.

1942, there were 57 suicides.* Out of 717 who were destined for
the Esthonian transport on October 3rd no less than 208 were
entered as having killed themselves.[56a]

Dr. Ella Lingens-Reiner, a woman who did not lose her sense
of human values in the Hell of the Birkenau *Frauenlager,* noticed
this peculiar weariness of life among the German Jewish internees
and her explanation is so admirable that I must quote part
of it[56b]:

> ' Here it must be remembered that the strongest and most
> active of the German Jews had emigrated in the years
> between 1933 and 1939. Those who stayed on were
> practically without contact with the anti-Fascist movements
> of their country. They had been enslaved and kicked,
> humiliated and half-starved longer than the others. They
> were without energy, they were weary to death. And
> in their stubbornness, their fanatical love of work and
> their shattering respect for uniforms, they were very
> " German." '

In 1941 a neutral press that still included the U.S.A. was
allowed to observe the start of the Berlin deportations. The
New York Times heard of the deportation notices on October 6th.
Ten days later this newspaper discovered that the Levetzow and
Muenchener Strasse Synagogues had been closed and filled with
straw mattresses in preparation for the round-up. On the 28th,
when three trains had left Berlin in ten days, the *New York Times*
reporter wrote with some exaggeration that the deportations were
' almost daily.' He had been able to get within 200 yards of one
of the trains in a suburban goods yard, where he had seen the

---

*At one time these suicides had caused grief to the Ministry of Finance.
When the 11th decree supplementing the Reich Law of Citizenship was
published on November 25th, 1941, the *Oberfinanzpraesident* of Baden
complained that some Jews who had been marked for deportation on
October 22nd, 1940 (*see page 76*), had committed suicide too soon for
their property to be confiscated under this decree. After the publication of
the decree the question of the suicides presented no difficulty. They were
counted as having already been deported. The Gestapo confiscated their
property as belonging to ' persons hostile to the People and State ' and the
Act was formally published in the Reich and Prussian Gazettes. (Copy of
original Berlin Gestapo file by courtesy of H. Tuch, Jewish Restitution
Organisation, Berlin-Dahlem. *See also infra, page 100, footnote.*)

Jews unloaded from canvas-topped lorries and the members of the Jewish *Reichsvereinigung* attending the departure. Surprisingly the censors allowed him to mention the intervention of the Wehrmacht to save its armament-workers and the sympathy felt by the masses for the Jews.[57]

This sympathy was largely of the passive kind in which Germans excel, though on November 1st Ulrich von Hassell recorded that the population was so disgusted that the party leaders were inspired to distribute leaflets, saying that the Jews were to blame for everything and that all who sympathised with them were traitors.[58] It was only a month before the deportations that the Berlin Jews had been forced to wear the Jewish badge for the first time. A few sympathisers wore the badge too, but the police soon took care of that. Of a much more memorable kind was the gesture of a 65-year-old Catholic priest, Provost Lichtenberg, who paid for it with a slow death in a concentration camp. On November 11th the Provost declared in the course of a sermon, preached in St. Hedwig's Cathedral, that he wished to share the fate of the Jews, deported to the East, in order to pray for them there.[59]

We have already seen the conditions that awaited the deportees in Lodz (*see ˌpages 60 to 61*) where 14,000 Jews had died in eighteen months and where the density of population was expected to rise to seven to a room, where the old wooden tenements were too infected to be used and where people had to sleep in factory hangars.[60] Lodz was probably only meant to be a half-way house for Russia till the railways became available again, but why this choice? The explanation seems to be that among Heydrich's tribulations there had been a protest from Governor Frank, to whom he had to give an assurance—falsely—that there would be no more ˌdeportations to the General Government[61] (*see pages 99 and 247*).

Some of the deportees were redeported, after their arrival in Lodz, to an unknown destination, taking a minimum of luggage.[62] A letter from Rosenberg's office, dated October 25th, shows that it was intended to select the able-bodied to work behind the Eastern front. Later, there were some rumours that Jews had been sent from Lodz to the land reclamation scheme in the Pripet Marshes and to the Jewish agricultural colonies near

Krivoi Rog in the Ukraine,[63] but it is certain that by far the greater part of the 19,000 Reich deportees, together with a small number deported later from Antwerp (*see page 343*), died in 1942 during the systematic reduction of the Lodz Ghetto.*

Letters to these people were merely returned to Germany with the inscription 'Gone away, address unknown.' However, before the end of 1942 a Gentile woman returned to Berlin from the Lodz Ghetto, having been illegally deported by Heydrich, along with her Jewish husband. She told Rabbi Leo Baeck, the President of the *Reichsvereinigung*, the true story of the Chelmno gassing vans and the part they played in the resettlement.[65]

4. The Deportations to Russia

Daluege's second order, dated October 24th,[66] records that 50,000 Jews from the Greater Reich and Protectorate were to leave for Minsk and Riga, the movement to be completed by the end of November, 1941. In fact it did not begin till November 14th and the numbers that were sent hardly exceeded 30,000. Moreover, an essential part of the plan was cancelled, namely Eichmann's proposal to set up the first gas-extermination centres near these two towns.[67] Some light is thrown on both matters by the telegram, sent by Brigadier-General Braemer, the military administrator at Riga, on November 20th and addressed to Hinrich Lohse, the Reich Commissar for the Eastern territories. It says that orders had come from Army Group Centre to stop all Jewish deportation trains, because the railways had got to be cleared for supplies for the front. 'The bringing in of Jews from the Reich is in my opinion quite impossible.'[68]

It is evident that Field Marshal von Bock, commanding Army Group Centre, was not able to stop the deportation trains since a train reached Riga from Berlin only nine days later. Subsequently the protests of the Wehrmacht were successful and after

*The figures of the former Lodz Jewish Council show that 10,527 foreign Jews were 'resettled' from Lodz while 6,247 died in the ghetto. Dr. Korherr's report to Himmler, dated March 23rd, 1943, indicates that there were then only 4,049 Jews left in the Lodz Ghetto who were not Polish.[64]

the end of January no more Jewish deportation trains entered occupied Russian territory, though only two-thirds of Daluege's programme had been fulfilled.

This is a mystery which cannot as yet be elucidated but a still more mysterious circumstance accompanied it. The plan to fill the emptied Russian ghettoes with Reich Jews, which was only known to a most restricted circle in Germany and only referred to in carefully camouflaged language, was common knowledge among the inhabitants of the occupied territory even before Daluege had issued the deportation order. For on October 20th Brigadier-General Erwin Lahousen of Canaris's *Ausland-Abwehr* had learnt from one of his intelligence sergeants apropos the massacre in Borissov, that 'the people were saying that the houses of the dead Jews would soon be occupied by Jews from the Reich.'[69]

As we shall see in Chapter 10 the newly created ghettoes in Riga, Kovno, and Minsk were systematically emptied in order to provide room for Reich Jews in precisely the way anticipated by the inhabitants of this remote White Russian town. Heydrich's extermination experts must have been garrulous.

The largest number of deportees went to Riga, 20,000 according to one of the *Einsatzgruppen* reports, 15,000-18,000 according to a ghetto survivor, Dr. Max Kaufmann.[70] Jeannette Wolff, who was to become Deputy-Mayor of Western Berlin, counted eleven transports including her own, an exceptionally large one, which left Dortmund for Riga on January 25th, 1942, with 1,350 people.[71] But at least three additional trainloads went straight to the death-pits in the Riga Forest, for instance, a train which left Berlin on November 27th and arrived in time for the 'Bloody Sunday' massacre (*see pages 218-219*). A second death train arrived from Prague on January 13th and a third from Vienna on the 19th.[72] At the Shirotava railway station in Riga a small selection was made for the labour camps, but apparently not more than seventy to eighty young men were found in each death train. The statement in the long report, sent to Heydrich by Major-General Franz Stahlecker, that half the Jews were admitted to the Riga Ghetto and half to the two labour camps, seems to be quite misleading. In the case of train-loads which were not exterminated outright, the majority of the people were taken to the ghetto.*

The Kovno transports are more difficult to trace and they were even more murderous. Only a small portion of the Jews from the Greater Reich were admitted to the ghetto. Most of them went direct to 'Fort No. 9,' where they were kept some days prior to being shot in the neighbouring execution pits. A Lithuanian guard testified before the Russian State Commission of 1945 that there were two executions of 3,000-4,000 Reich Jews on December 10th and 14th, 1941.[74] A ghetto survivor testified that in January or February, 1942, the Prague and Vienna Jews rebelled in Fort No. 9 before being shot. The Reich Jews, who began arriving in Kovno from Berlin, Hamburg, Duesseldorf, and Prague at the end of November, numbered 15,000 according to this witness, but the real figure was probably determined by the number of Kovno Jews who had been shot—apparently 10,000 (see page 217).[75]†

The deportations to Minsk seem to have been timed to coincide with two huge 'actions' in the White Russian Ghetto on November 6th and 20th. One transport can be identified with certainty as leaving Berlin on November 14th. Others came from Hamburg, Bremen, Vienna, Prague, and Brunn in Bohemia, but on December 16th the Commissar-General, Wilhelm Kube, wrote that only six to seven thousand Jews had appeared in place of the expected 25,000. Apparently this was the final figure. Kube complained that they included numerous ex-Servicemen and other Jews who should have been exempted, but he got no satisfaction from Heydrich.[76] As we shall see in Chapter 11 the fate of the Jews sent to Minsk was particularly drastic. Only 2,600 survived

---

*From surviving Gestapo files and other sources the following transports can be traced which were admitted to the Riga Ghetto: from Nuremberg leaving on November 29th, from Stuttgart on December 4th, from Hamburg on December 12th, from Cologne on the 13th, and Duesseldorf on the 14th. In January the following can be traced: from Vienna on the 2nd, from Berlin on the 13th, 19th, and 25th, and from Dortmund on the 28th. The Berlin transports in January totalled only 2,392 people between them. It would appear from these indications that a figure of 15,000 for all the Riga transports, including the 'death transports,' might be rather high.[73]

†According to Gestapo reports to the Higher Finance President, Berlin-Brandenburg, a transport left Berlin for Kovno on November 17th.

the 'resettlement' of June 28th-30th, 1942, and not one survived the final resettlement of September, 1943.

It is nevertheless an astonishing fact that the German ghettoes in Russia continued to exist for two years. It was due to the constant intervention of the Wehrmacht, who appreciated the qualities of the Reich Jews as workmen and clerks, and to the reprieve, caused by the death of Heydrich in June, 1942. This was followed in August-October by a short revival of the Russian plan, in which a few thousand Reich Jews were deported to Riga and Esthonia.[77] But the appointment of Kaltenbrunner to fill Heydrich's long vacant post in January, 1943, brought the end of the ghettoes in sight. It was Kaltenbrunner who made up Himmler's mind for him (*see page 281*).

CHAPTER 5

The Gross-Wannsee Conference and the Auschwitz Plan

1. The Gross-Wannsee Conference

We come now to a most remarkable conference to which the events described in the last chapter irresistibly led. Deportations to Russia from Hungary and Rumania had begun 'spontaneously,' systematic deportations from the Reich had followed later. It now remained to co-ordinate the two movements, to devise a grandiose deportation plan for the Jewry of all Axis-Europe and to obtain the necessary collaboration of the ministries of the Reich. Still acting under the brief conveyed to him by Goering on July 31st, 1941, a copy of which was attached to each invitation, Heydrich wrote to the Ministries on November 29th. The conference was convened for December 8th.

It appears that this invitation reached the Foreign Office two days after a reception, at which the Bulgarian Minister, Popoff, had asked Ribbentrop whether 'like treatment could not be accorded to Jews of all nationalities,' and Ribbentrop, having found the suggestion 'not uninteresting,' had asked Luther to prepare a report.[1] Luther did so and sent the report to Weizsaecker with the reminder that only Spain, Italy, and Hungary had objected to the suggestion raised by Popoff. Weizsaecker then sent Luther's report to Emil Albrecht of the legal department of the Foreign Office in the hope that it might be buried there for some time[2]—a favourite device when dealing with 'Department Deutschland.'

Popoff was certainly not speaking for his own Government, which proved most reluctant to carry out anti-Jewish measures. In fact one wonders whether Luther did not insert this incident, which really had very little significance, in his memorandum of

August, 1942, in order to persuade Ribbentrop that he had not been taking orders from Heydrich. It is true that Heydrich issued the invitations to his conference two days *after* Ribbentrop's reception, but according to Josef Buehler, this was not the first invitation he had received (*page 247*). Since August, Ribbentrop had been trying on his own to get Jews deported East from Serbia and had come up against Heydrich's veto and on December 6th he briefed Luther to bring up this matter at Heydrich's conference.[3]

The conference, which Heydrich again postponed from December 8th to January 20th, took place finally in the office of the International Criminal Police Commission 'Am Grossen Wannsee No. 56/8.'[4] It was in the Western sense a secret conference, but in Germany, where the ministry chiefs could meet and make decisions without having to answer questions in Parliament, it was no different from any other ministerial conference. Thirty copies of the minutes were circulated. The incomplete copy, used by the Prosecution in the Wilhelmstrasse case, bears the number 16 and the initials of Von Weizsaecker.[5*] It mentions fourteen members of the conference in addition to Heydrich. Five of them represented the SS and police, the remainder represented the interested ministries, including the office of Governor Frank. The SS and police were represented by Heinrich Mueller and Adolf Eichmann, of the Gestapo head office, by Schoengarth and Lange, of the Gestapo in Poland and Latvia, and by Otto Hoffmann, of the Race and Settlement office. Of the SS men, Major Lange was a particularly relevant figure, for it was he who had been in charge on November 29th of an execu-

---

*In the 'little Wilhelmstrasse' case, the trial of Franz Rademacher, in February-March, 1952, the plea was made that Rademacher and the late Weizsaecker had merely put their signatures to a 'protocol,' of which they took no cognisance. This now rather moss-grown excuse was effectively countered by the evidence of the former head of the press and news department of the Foreign Office, 'Minister' Dr. Paul Otto Schmidt, who explained the mystic sentence, scribbled in the margin with Weizsaecker's brown pencil, 'Aber nicht fuer Presseschmidt.' Schmidt claimed that he was the only department chief from whom the circulation of the protocol had been withheld and that this was because Goebbels had complained to Ribbentrop of Schmidt's indiscretion. (*Frankfurter Allgemeine Zeitung*, 26.2.52. *Das Freie Wort*, Baden, 6.3.52.) [This was not the Paul Otto Schmidt who was Hitler's interpreter.]

tion near Riga, where for the first time German Jews coming straight from the Reich—in fact from Berlin—had been slaughtered *en masse*. It was no doubt Lange to whom Heydrich particularly alluded on January 8th, when he wrote to Hoffmann that it had been necessary to postpone the conference 'on account of events in which some of the invited gentlemen were concerned,' though in the general planning of the massacre it is probable that all five SS men were involved. Incidentally only one of them, Brigadier-General Schoengarth, who had the misfortune to fall into British hands, was hanged after the war.

But if the five SS members of the conference were up to their necks in blood, there is no reason to suppose that the nine civilians, all of whom have explained the innocence of the rôle they played at Gross-Wannsee, could have been shocked by anything that Heydrich said. Franz Stuckart for instance, who represented the Ministry for Interior, had heard a month earlier about this particular Riga massacre from his expert on Jewish matters, Bernhard Loesener, and, if the letter from Riga was news to Loesener, it certainly was not news to Stuckart. When Loesener had begged to be allowed to resign his duties (in which he eventually succeeded) Stuckart told him sternly: 'Herr Loesener, do you not know that all this takes place by order of the highest authority?'[6] This no doubt explains the warmth with which Stuckart supported Heydrich's proposal that half-Jews should be allowed the alternative of sterilisation.

Heydrich opened the conference on January 20th with a long review of Jewish emigration since 1933 and of the present state of Jewry in Axis countries. He described how the war with Russia had made the Madagascar project out of date and then he came to the gist of the matter.

'In big labour gangs with separation of sexes the Jews who are capable of work are brought to these areas (in the Eastern occupied territories) and employed in road building, in which task undoubtedly a large part will fall out through natural diminution. The remnant that is able finally to survive all this, since this is unquestionably the part with the strongest resistance, must be given treatment accordingly, because these people, representing a natural selection, are to be regarded as the germ-cell of a new Jewish development, should they be allowed to go free.'

It may be said of these sentences that, though they were circumlocutionary, the words of the German language must have lost their meaning altogether if they failed to convey to the members of the conference and those who subsequently read the minutes, that the slow murder of an entire race was intended. It may also be said—but this the conference could not know—that these sentences depicted accurately what actually happened to ' the Jews who are capable of work,' for Heydrich was discreet enough not to mention the rest. If the labour camps of Poland and Auschwitz are substituted for the roads of Russia (whether or not this was a deliberate camouflage will be discussed later) it makes Heydrich's prediction accurate up to a time far beyond his own death.

It was a strange anti-climax that Heydrich should have to follow up this pronouncement with a long catalogue of all the types of exemption which he had tried to prevent. The Jews who were exempted from deportation, including those over 65 years old as well as Jews with serious disablements or decorations from the First World War, would go to a special ghetto, possibly the town of Theresienstadt in Bohemia which Heydrich, as *Reichsprotektor*, had just requisitioned. The half-Jews would be sterilised but not deported. Those with only one Jewish grandparent would not be molested unless they could be considered as Jews on account of an ' exceptionally unfavourable appearance ' or unless a ' bad political or police appraisal had shown them to conduct themselves like Jews.'

If there was any protest at this monstrous weapon which was levelled against countless Germans, should anyone choose to mention them to the Gestapo, that protest is not recorded in the minutes. On the other hand the minutes show Heydrich acquiescing very meekly in the exemption of Jewish war workers, which was demanded by Goering's State Secretary, Neumann. Heydrich, however, had realised that he might have to surrender over this as early as October 4th (*see pages 18 and 86*). The exemption, of course, did not extend to Jews of the General Government who were the subject of a special address to the conference by Josef Buehler, representing Governor Frank. They were denounced as carriers of disease, unfit for work, and black-marketeers. Neither the demands of labour nor the dearth of transport stood in the way of *their* resettlement.

Buehler had clearly been instructed not to insist on protocol. Frank had told his Cabinet that Buehler was to attend a conference on resettlement and he had used these words: [7]

> 'Do you think that they will be settled in villages in the Ostland? That is what we are told in Berlin, but why all this ceremony? We can do nothing with them either in the Ostland or in the Reichskommisariat Ukraine, so liquidate them yourselves!'

In the face of Frank's words, Buehler's plea, made at Nuremberg in 1946, that Heydrich had convinced him before the conference that an orderly settlement was intended, seemed astonishing rubbish, even though at that time Buehler's own contribution to the discussion at Gross-Wannsee was not known. No one at Gross-Wansee could have supposed that if two million Jews were disease bearers and unfit to work, they would become any less so if they were moved from Poland into Russia. Hence, the coyness of the conference minutes, which record no resolution concerning the General Government. Rademacher in forwarding Luther's report on the conference to Weizsaecker described the ninth item on the agenda extremely cryptically as 'a matter for the Governor-General, to be started in the General Government (disease carriers, illegal traders, majority unable to work).'[8]

The annexe to the original minutes mentions five resolutions. Their significance is as follows. Throughout German-occupied territory Jews of German, Croat, Slovak, and Rumanian nationality, as well as all Jews by definition stateless, were to be deported to 'the East.' Among these were included the Jews, expelled by the Hungarians to Belgrade. As yet, there was no mention of the Jews of French, Dutch, or Belgian nationality, but the Slovak, Croat, Bulgarian, and Hungarian Governments were to be informed that the Germans were ready to evacuate their Jews for them to 'the East.' It was not, however, recommended that these Governments should be hurried. Although the Reich was now at war with the U.S.A. and the Wehrmacht was wintering quite a bit short of Moscow, the new Europe was nevertheless expected to be permanent.[9]

2. The Russian Plan Superseded

The Gross-Wannsee conference was no more than a luncheon party, convened for twelve o'clock and finished the same afternoon. Yet to the Foreign Office and the decree-drafting agencies, which had been represented there, the conference offered work for two years and the prospect of a whole series of further conferences with Heydrich's Reich Main Security Office (*see pages 173-175*). In fact, the problems of foreign Jews, of Jews in mixed marriages, and of half-Jews were never solved at all. The arguments with the Security Office went on, while the latter carried on the work of murder with little hindrance from German bureaucracy—the death of Heydrich actually increased the pace.

Since the end of September, 1941, Reinhardt Heydrich had added to his post of head of the Security Police and SD—and incidentally head of the entire German police system—the protectorship of Bohemia and Moravia. According to Willi Hoettl, Heydrich hoped, by demonstrating his ability to be an administrator as well as a policeman, to attain the position of Minister for Interior and so give orders to Himmler and the entire SS.[10] But Heydrich with his ugly and easily excitable temper lacked the true skill of an intriguer and it is doubtful whether he would ever have fulfilled this ambition, even if the first step had not killed him. On May 29th, 1942, as he drove from Prague to his new country residence at Panenske Brezany, a hand bomb of British origin was thrown at his car near the village of Lidice by one of a group of Czech partisans. For six days Heydrich endured the agony of a severed spine, expressing, it is said, deep contrition for his actions. This did not interfere with the celebration of the old Teutonic rites of human sacrifice at the hero's grave. Some 1,339 persons were executed in Prague and Bruenn and 199 in the village of Lidice, which was razed to the ground.[11] In Berlin 152 Jewish hostages, who were arrested at Goebbels's request on

May 29th, were executed,* while in Poland the 'Resettlement Staff' of Brigadier-General Globocnik dedicated themselves henceforward to Heydrich's *manes* under the name of 'Einsatz Reinhardt.'

For more than six months Heydrich's post remained vacant, since Himmler apparently did not trust anyone sufficiently to fill it. During these six months the great mass deportation of Jews from the Western countries was started and reached its greatest height. Those who were not killed outright on arrival 'fell out' at their work from 'natural diminution' as predicted by Heydrich within a few months, but this happened not in Russia but in the Reich itself—at Auschwitz.

Now the last deportation trains had left for Russia within a few days of the Gross-Wannsee conference and in March, when deportations of Jews from the Reich were resumed, the victims were sent no further than the Russian-Polish demarcation line to be dealt with in Poland inside the framework of the 'Einsatz Reinhardt' massacre programme. A few of these transports, particularly those from France and Slovakia, which started running

*An undated fragment of Goebbels's diary, which includes a remark of Hitler's, recorded by Dr. Henry Picker on May 29th, contains also this passage: 'I shall go on with the arrest, which I have planned, of 500 Berlin Jews and I will warn the leaders of the Jewish community that for every Jewish plot and every Jewish attempt at rebellion 100 to 150 Jews who are in our hands will be shot.' (Copy Rijksinstituut fur Oorlogsdocumentatie, Amsterdam.) The threat was carried out more than literally. The following communication was sent on June 5th, the day Heydrich finally died, by the *Staatspolizeistelle* of the Gestapo, Grunerstrasse 12, to the *Oberfinanzpraesident* of Berlin-Brandenburg. (Courtesy H. Tuch. Jewish Restitution Centre, Berlin-Dahlem.)

Subject : requisition of assets of Jews.

'Herewith I send you a list of Jews who were arrested in a special action on May 29th, 1942, and have in the meantime died. At the same time I enclose statements of the property belonging to them. This cannot be negotiated, unless declarations of value are provided. I have requested the Reich Minister for Interior to establish the "hostility to people and State" of the Jews in question and to facilitate the requisition of their property.'

I do not know a better illustration than these two documents—one of them an accidental find among the rubble—of the Police State in action. Apart from these two laconic references no record survives of this great massacre, which was conducted in the secrecy of a prison and from which there are no survivors.

at the end of March, were, however, directed to Auschwitz. The question therefore arises whether the stupendous plan for making Auschwitz the extermination centre for all European Jewry had not been decided *before* the Gross Wannsee conference and whether Heydrich's allusions to 'the occupied Eastern territories' were not a camouflage for the benefit of the civilian representatives who might have some qualms concerning 'falling out through natural diminution' in the Reich itself.

There exists a document which suggests that at the time of the Gross-Wannsee conference Himmler was trying to carry out a policy totally different from Heydrich's, for on January 26th he telegraphed as follows to Major-General Gluecks, his inspector of concentration camps[12]:

'During the next few weeks 100,000 Jews and 50,000 Jewesses will be sent to concentration camps, which will have to deal with major economic problems and tasks. Major-General Pohl will inform you of particulars.'

Oswald Pohl, on trial for his life in the summer of 1947, denied that anything more than a fraction of the number of Jews, mentioned by Himmler, was sent to German concentration camps in the few weeks in question[13] and this was indeed the truth. Himmler's plan may have been frustrated by Heydrich, for he seems to have sent this dispatch as the first move in a bid to remove Heydrich, now well preoccupied in Prague, from his control of the concentration camp system. Under an arrangement, dating from December, 1939, the economic administration of the camps through Oswald Pohl depended on Himmler, while discipline was maintained through Gluecks, the inspector, who came under Heydrich; but on February 1st, 1942, Himmler followed up his dispatch to Gluecks by a decree creating a new department of the SS known as *Wirtschafts- und Verwaltungshauptamt*, the Economic and Administrative Head Office or WVHA.[14] Oswald Pohl was thereby put in charge of all the works departments of the SS. Furthermore Gluecks's Inspectorate of the Concentration Camps was now no more than 'Amt D,' a subdivision of Pohl's empire, which was ruled from his great mushroom wartime-establishment in Unter den Eichen at Berlin-Lichtenfelde.*

Pohl was promoted as part of a long-cherished plan of Himmler's to get the utmost use out of the concentration camps, which he regarded less as a contribution to war production than as means for financing the SS, should it ever lose the support of the head of the State. Thus the creation of WVHA produced one of Himmler's recurrent drives for efficiency in the camp labour system. The nature of the system itself invariably doomed these drives to failure, but of this fact Himmler seems never to have been truly aware. It was in this state of unreal thinking that he wrote to Heydrich from the Fuehrer's headquarters on December 5th, 1941, that Hitler had commissioned 100,000 cubic feet of granite from the quarrying camps for his great plan to rebuild Berlin after the war. Five thousand masons and 10,000 bricklayers would have to be trained in readiness. The concentration camp inmates' lot must therefore be alleviated, their rations and clothing increased, the discipline relaxed, and the incentives improved.[17] If Himmler's dispatches of December 5th and January 26th are considered together, it can be inferred that Himmler wanted not only to stop the wastage of concentration camp inmates in the interest of the finances of the SS, but also to make similar use of the doomed Jews in occupied territory—this being the origin of the plan for a huge Jewish camp at Auschwitz.

Here, however, we come up against the testimony of a much-implicated person, Lt.-Colonel Rudolf Hoess, who was for three and a half years the commandant at Auschwitz and

*It may have amused Himmler in February, 1942, to hand some of Heydrich's power to a fellow naval officer, but, in fact, Himmler had perceived the merits of Oswald Pohl, then a paymaster-captain, as early as 1933, when he met him at a banquet in Kiel.[15] In Pohl, who even at his trial in 1947 looked astonishingly like a ship's purser, Himmler must have recognised a nature as parsimonious as his own. Pohl maintained at Nuremberg that, though Himmler attacked Gluecks's softness, Gluecks succeeded in maintaining the independence of his own office—which remained at Oranienburg—in everything except labour allocation and that he continued to take orders from Heydrich till Heydrich's death.[16] The court, nevertheless, held Pohl fully responsible for the conditions in the concentration camps. As one of the seven 'Red-jacket men' he spent three and a half years in the Landsberg death-cells and was not hanged till June 8th, 1951.

who took Gluecks's place as acting inspector of concentration camps towards the end of the war. Hoess stated that he was summoned to Himmler's presence as early as June, 1941, when Auschwitz was still a very small camp, and told that the extermination of the Jews of Europe would take place in Auschwitz because of its suitability as a railway junction. In July Hoess received further details from Eichmann, who visited him in the camp, but in the meantime Hoess had already been to Treblinka death camp in Poland to study gassing methods. Hoess came back with a poor opinion of Treblinka and decided to experiment on his own with 'Zyklon B' crystals, which he used effectively soon after Eichmann's visit[18] (*see pages 144-5*).

Here then we have Himmler deciding on Auschwitz more than six months before the Gross-Wannsee conference and at a time when Heydrich had not received his brief for the 'Final Solution' from Goering. Hoess, however, though a very frank witness, had a habit of confusing several incidents together in his memory, for in another affidavit[19] he declared that he went to Treblinka at a time when 80,000 Jews from the Warsaw Ghetto had been exterminated, that is to say in August, 1942, nearly a year after his own first experimental use of 'Zyklon B.' This would confirm—as appears clear enough from other evidence—that it was in the summer of 1942 and not in the summer of 1941 that Himmler decided on Auschwitz as the extermination centre for the Jews of Western Europe, having in fact waited till Heydrich was dead.

The curious inverted megalomania which caused Hoess to write a statement, admitting the murder of two and a half million persons, also caused him to boast of a secret trust, imposed on him by Hitler in the summer of 1941. Yet the first of the two converted barns in the Birkenwald could only accommodate 250 victims for gassing. When it was ready for use, either in March, 1942, or a little earlier, it was not even intended specifically for Jews but for getting rid of the sick in the camp, and it was not till many months later that an order arrived restricting its use to Jews and Gipsies.

In reality Himmler preferred Auschwitz to the other Polish death camps, not because of its railway junction, which was nothing exceptional, but because of the camouflage status it had acquired through the plans to make it the centre of a huge synthetic oil and rubber industry. These plans were well advanced in the summer of 1941, and it may well be that at this time Himmler already had his eye on Auschwitz as an alternative to Jewish camps in Russia. It is also possible that at the time of the Gross-Wannsee conference Himmler added his objections to those of the Transport Command of the Wehrmacht against continuing the deportations to Russia. Nevertheless, he was not able to brief Mueller, Eichmann, and Hoess with the Auschwitz plan till after Heydrich's death on June 4th, 1942.

3. The Auschwitz Plan

Auschwitz camp or Oswiecim had quite a long history behind it. The nucleus of the camp, including the notorious punishment block, No. 11, was an Austrian cavalry barracks, for till 1918 the frontier between the Hohenzollern and Hapsburg monarchies had passed within a few yards of it. It was built on poor marshy ground inside the junction of the Vistula and Sola rivers, a forlorn place, from which, nevertheless, the winter fogs would sometimes clear sufficiently to enable a forest of factory chimneys to be seen to the west and the snowy peaks of the Tatra sixty miles to the south. It was not a beauty spot and Baedeker's description is unpoetic:

> 'The railway to Cracow continues north-east past Auschwitz (348 kilometres from Vienna), an industrial town of 12,000 inhabitants, the former capital of the Piast Duchies of Auschwitz and Zator (Hotel Zator 20 bedrooms), whence a secondary railway runs *via* Skawina to Cracow (69 kilometres in three hours).'

Perhaps for a guide, published in September, 1943, Baedeker's 'Generalgouvernement' was too terse. According to Perry Broad, a member of the Auschwitz political department (of American origin), passengers used to crowd to the train windows to get a glimpse of the crematorium chimneys.[20]

In February, 1940, the former Austrian barracks were occupied by a constructional company of the Wehrmacht, but Gluecks wrote to Himmler that they might be made suitable for a quarantine camp.[21] Instead the site was chosen as a concentration camp for Poles in 'political detention,' a camp on the German model but intended for exceptionally dangerous people, fugitive Polish officers and members of resistance movements. Before the official opening on June 14th some of the historic figures of the Auschwitz scene had already arrived, Hoess, who was then only a lieutenant, was accompanied by Kramer, his adjutant, who became known to the British press in 1945 as 'the Beast of Belsen.' With them were two of the most accomplished mass-killers whom even the Death's Head *Verbaende* of the SS could produce, Lieutenant Graebner, head of the 'political department,' and the *Rapportfuehrer* or camp marshal, Sergeant Palitsch ('Wilhelm Tell'). In addition there arrived thirty *Prominenten*—German convicts carefully picked for their strength and brutality, who acted as labour overseers during the life of the camp.[22]

At Nuremberg Hoess was to testify that the cruelties of Auschwitz were the result of permanent overcrowding and the impossibility of maintaining any real supervision, but, in fact, Hoess, the ex-convict, was not chosen for nothing. During the period before the construction of Birkenau and the continuous arrival of Jewish transports, that is before March, 1942, Auschwitz had already the worst possible reputation. Individual acts of sadism flourished. The German guards and *kapos* feared the Polish internees more than victims of their own race, and believed that they could only protect themselves by absolute terrorism. There are very few Auschwitz survivors whose term of residence goes back so far, but one of them, the Polish officer Zenon Rozanski, was admitted to the camp early in 1941 with a registration number as low as 8214. He has described what life was like when there was only one Auschwitz camp, no gas chambers, and still very few Jewish inmates, and, in particular, the 'penal company' who were permitted neither bedding nor extra clothing in winter, who were forbidden to go sick, and among whom a Jew could not live more than ten days.[23] He has also described the 'cork wall,' adjoining Block 11, the domain of Graebner and Palitsch, where unwanted Gestapo prisoners, Polish partisans, or Russian political commissars were daily disposed of.

Zenon Rozanski's narrative ends in July, 1942, when

the Jewish transports were beginning to reach Auschwitz from the Western countries. Paradoxically, the advent of the racial murder programme brought an alleviation of the lot of the Aryan internees. The régime, under which scores of men were executed at a time at the whim of a mere *kapo* or an NCO of the SS, came to an end. The gas chamber was restricted to the Jews. When the Warsaw intellectuals arrived in the Birkenau *Frauenlager* in August, 1944, Kristina Zywulska could tell them with assurance: 'What an idea, they only burn Jews! Don't worry.' But the Gipsies in Auschwitz who cherished the same belief were deceived (*see pages 448-9*).[23a]

In most narratives of Auschwitz survivors there is one personage lacking—Rudolf Franz Hoess. It seems that Hoess took no pleasure in attending the mass-executions and the selections of the sick for the lethal syringe, which were already a weekly if not a daily feature of Auschwitz life in the autumn of 1941. Hoess remained the quiet bureaucrat in the background, leaving such spectacles to the then *Lagerfuehrer*, Captain Fritsch. For Hoess was an exceptional person. The common law criminals or 'Green triangles' were the aristocracy of the German concentration camps. As *Kapos* and *Vorarbeiter* they could terrorise the work gangs, as *Blockaelteste* and *Blockschreiber* they could make Hell of the sleeping huts, as *Lageraelteste* they became at night monarchs of their own kingdom, when the SS had withdrawn. Yet they could be eliminated at a stroke of the pencil as easily as any other internee. Hoess was unique in leaping the barrier into the ranks of the SS. Not only did he rise to command a camp group of 60,000 inmates, but at the end of the war this man, who—as convict or gaoler—had spent the whole of his professional life in prisons, negotiated with representatives of neutral countries as a high official of the SS administration. Finally, Hoess went underground to emerge in Schleswig in March, 1946, as a day-labourer who admitted blandly to the murder of two and a half million people.

Hoess was born in 1900, the son of a small shopkeeper in Baden-Baden, a pious Catholic, who destined him for the priesthood and who used to 'punish him with prayer,' with the result that at the age of twenty-two he broke with the church and joined the infant National Socialist party.[24] At the end of 1923 young

Hoess, now a bookkeeper, was implicated in the 'vengeance-killing' of the schoolmaster Walter Kalow, who had denounced Leo Schlageter, the Nazi proto-martyr, to the French. He received a life sentence.

For ten years Hoess was a common convict. According to Konrad Morgen, he made the acquaintance in prison of the future Head of the Party Chancellory, Hitler's private secretary, Martin Bormann, whose protection was to prove so valuable that the SS 'always treated Hoess like a raw egg.'[25] In spite of this testimony the victorious party was slow in recognising Hoess's services. It was not till the end of 1934 that he was taken from one prison to another and made a 'blockleader' in Dachau camp. His commission as 2nd lieutenant in the Death's Head *Verbaende* dated only from 1936.

In 1944 Hoess's SS service file recorded that he had been not only a good camp commander but 'a true pioneer in this field, thanks to new ideas and new methods of education.'[26] It was a belated recognition of his merits. The new camp at the ends of the earth to which Hoess had been assigned in May, 1940, was no sugar plum after six years on the staff of the biggest camps in Germany, and it never became one. For instance, in May, 1944, when the 'Beast of Belsen' was posted back to Auschwitz from Natzweiler, Frau Kramer learnt to her mortification that it was because her husband had failed to rise beyond the rank of captain.[27]

After reading Hoess's muddled and verbose affidavits and Dr. Gilbert's record of his conversational powers, one is forced to conclude that the authorities must have found Hoess useful but dull-witted. In the photographs, taken in his prime, the political enthusiast, who had found his way to murder even in 1923, looks like an adequate lance-corporal but with the pale, rather dilated eyes of those who find life hard to understand.

The facts of Hoess's career make it seem extremely improbable that Himmler really entrusted him with the secrets of the Final Solution at a very early stage. On the contrary, there is evidence that Hoess was slowly dragged into a plot which he could not have understood and which was perhaps only decipherable in 1948 when evidence was assembled for the trial of the I.G. Farben directors.

It started early in 1941 when there was a scheme to evacuate 7,000 Poles and 4,000 Jews from Auschwitz town in order to add more buildings to the camp, which then housed only 7,000 people. After a ruling from Goering it was decided only to move the Jews, and these left in April for the neighbouring industrial town of Sosnowiece.[28] The significance of this was that the great chemical combine, I. G. Farben of Frankfurt, had just obtained permission to build a synthetic fuel-oil and rubber factory in Upper Silesia in a neighbourhood where concentration camp labour could be obtained. At the end of April Hoess learnt from Himmler himself that he was to supply the labour for the heavy work of construction—a project which Hoess did not at all like. Consequently the I. G. Farben directors complained at a building conference in the following October that Hoess had provided only 1,300 of the 2,700 labourers, and that he objected to Polish and German political prisoners being employed at the building site, which was at Neudachs, several miles from the camp.[29]

At the next building conference between the I. G. Farben directors and the SS constructional department, which took place on November 16th, it was decided to build a new detainees' camp at Monowitz, close to the factory, and to employ for this purpose 12,000 Russian prisoners of war. But Himmler had already authorised Hoess to construct what was allegedly a prisoner-of-war camp at Birkenau, three miles south of Auschwitz town and nowhere near the *Bunawerk* factory, and it was on this project that the Russians were employed.[30] By the middle of April, 1942, two of the first stone buildings at Birkenau were complete, and the camp contained 1,350 Jews from Slovakia and France, but most of the Russian construction team had died already from sheer neglect.[31] Only 450 remained alive.

In this way the *Bunawerk* project, with its ministerial sanctions and building conferences, served as a cover for the creation of the future 'selection' camp at Birkenau. Work also began at two adjacent farm buildings, which became the gas chambers, but it was not till January, 1943, that the first *Bunawerk* factory was completed, having absorbed conscript labour of all nations, including British prisoners of war.[32] With the opening of the factory Himmler revived its use as a cover for the Final

Solution, and in March recruitment for *Bunawerk* was made the pretext for the final comb-out of the Berlin Jews from the armament industry and the extermination of three-quarters of them, while in May *Bunawerk* became the pretext for a revival of Jewish deportations from Holland (*see pages 162 and 336*).

Although begun in November, 1941, Birkenau did not become an international extermination centre till the daily transports from France, Belgium, and Holland started running in the second half of July, 1942. Previously small groups of Jews had been sent to the gas chamber by lorry during the first resettlement actions in Cracow, Sosnowiece, Dabrowa-Gornicza, and Bielitz. The period of these actions was from April to June.

The very reliable report of the Birkenau infirmary registrar or *Blockschreiber*, who escaped to Hungary in April, 1944,[33] declares that there was a selection for the gas chamber from the train which arrived from Paris (Drancy) on June 22nd, 1942 (*see page 312*), but the little evidence that is available suggests that this did not become a general practice for some weeks. Even in August selections which sent more than thirty per cent to the gas chambers were exceptional.

It took some time for the inmates of the camps to realise the full significance of the smoke from the Birkenwald. The place was outside the camp area and its growth had been quite independent. It was only in April, 1944, that the trains brought the victims to a place within sight of the *Frauenlager*. Previously they were picked out at Auschwitz station, or at Cosel, fifty miles up the line. Hence the extraordinary ignorance, shown in the narratives of quite well-informed survivors, concerning the size, date, and origin of the death transports. The new arrivals, who had been through the selection, were too dazed and exhausted to remember many details. Dr. Lingens-Reiner, who was in a position to observe that selections from the *Frauenlager* ceased temporarily after her own arrival in February, 1943, was apparently quite unaware of the gassing of German Jewish transports in the following month. It was only in August that she saw the flaming chimney and the endless procession of lorries passing the wire-zone on the way to the new gas chamber and heard the cry of the internees, 'It's started again.'[33a] And even then she could not trace the origin of this transport.

The flotsam of war has disclosed a little—a very little—of the 'Office end' of the business, but it is likely that the true delegation of authority will never be discovered, by which it was possible to take hundreds of men, women, and children at a time—later on thousands—and consign them to one anonymous death without so much as entering a name or stamping an identity card and this too in the German Reich, the most paper-bound bureaucracy in the world. Hoess, who was always excessively vague, said that he received orders for mass gassings directly from the Main Security Office. After some pressing he admitted that they were signed by Eichmann, of the Jewish section of the Gestapo, rather than by Mueller or Kaltenbrunner, who signed the Auschwitz execution warrants.[34] But Lt.-Colonel Rudolf Mildner (see pages 170 and 347) believed that written or oral orders for the extermination of Jewish transports went through Pohl and Gluecks—and Mildner, who was head of the Gestapo for all Upper Silesia and had witnessed the gas chamber at work, was in a position to know something.[35]

Certain teletype messages, which give detailed figures of the selection for the gas chambers, confirm Mildner's view. These were sent by Captain Albert Schwarz, the labour-commitment officer at Auschwitz, to Colonel Gerhardt Maurer in Gluecks's 'Amt D' at Oranienburg (pages 162-3 and 168-9). Schwarz, moreover, signed a Nuremberg affidavit before his extradition to Poland in 1947[36] in which he put all the blame for the selections on Gluecks and Maurer. Furthermore, he declared that Gluecks had always exercised full control over the medical services at Auschwitz through his office 'D II,' and was therefore responsible for the SS doctors who conducted the selections.*

Pohl, while not rebutting this evidence, denied that he had any authority over Gluecks—a shadowy man who went underground before the end of the war—because even after Heydrich's

---

*The evidence of Major Karl Sommer, who was Maurer's deputy, contradicts Schwarz's affidavit, but neither of these witnesses was aware at the time of the Concentration Camp Case at Nuremberg that the teletype messages had survived—and both were clearly lying. Unfortunately Maurer was not captured till February, 1947, after the indictment had been filed. Since it was decided that he should be extradited to Poland, he was not subpœnaed as a witness. Maurer was condemned to death at Cracow in the Auschwitz case on December 22nd, 1947. (Trials of War Criminals, 1951. V.676ff.)

death Himmler continued, in secret, to give Gluecks the orders that Heydrich would have given him. It was Himmler's policy, Pohl declared, never to consult two of the chiefs of his administrative offices at once, nor would he have a representative of each office on his personal staff. Himmler believed that in this way he could stop them forming cliques.[37] The Nuremberg tribunal seems to have been rather impressed with this explanation, for—though in view of the other charges the matter was academic—they acquitted Pohl of direct participation in the gas-chamber exterminations, leaving the guilt to the vanished men, Gluecks, Mueller, and Eichmann.

To my mind there is another explanation of Schwarz's teletypes to Maurer. The Office DII sent instructions to Auschwitz explaining how the Jews from certain transports were to be employed, but Schwarz seems completely to have ignored such instructions. The decision in fact rested with neither of these men but with the two SS doctors who separated the groups by merely pointing with their walking-sticks on the Auschwitz siding. And again these doctors were guided solely by the percentage of able-bodied people in the transport and the vacancies reported by the camp leaders. Throughout the twenty-eight months of selections at Auschwitz the procedure was by rule of thumb. Children under fifteen, men over fifty, and women over forty-five went to the gas chambers. To save the SS difficulties all mothers who accompanied young children went to the gas chambers, irrespective of their age.

At first this rule was interpreted liberally. A comparison between the detailed registration lists of the trains which left Holland for Auschwitz before August 8th, 1942,[37a] and the Birkenau camp *Appell* roster shows that at this time over-aged men and boys must have been entered on the camp strength and given registration numbers. After August 8th the discrepancy was the other way. The figures for the arrivals from the French camps suggest that already 70 per cent were being sent to the gas chamber.

Thenceforward it seems to have become an assumption in German bureaucratic circles that one-third of the Jewish deportees were fit for labour, but in fact the selections were governed persistently by the age-and-sex rule of thumb and by the sick-list, so that the variations were enormous. Moreover, under the principle of 'the survival of the fittest' the later transports to Auschwitz brought better human material. Precise figures for registered entries in the Birkenau male camp appear again between October 21st, 1943, and October 30th, 1944, when Dr. Otto Wolken, the *Lagerschreiber*, was able to record twenty-six transports which were admitted to the quarantine section 'B IIa.' These figures, preserved in secret, can be presumed accurate, but Dr. Wolken could not obtain the figures for the women's quarantine and he only knew the rough guesses of survivors—in some cases confirmed from other sources as surprisingly accurate—for the *complete* strength of the transports. His figures suggest that, when allowance is made for the women, the survival rate in the last year of the gas chamber may have exceeded 40 per cent, though this was not applicable to the Hungarian transports which do not figure on the quarantine list.[37b]

In all probability there was not, so long as the rule of thumb was observed, any necessity for special instructions *via* Eichmann and the Auschwitz political department or *via* Gluecks, Maurer, and Schwarz. Hoess himself, in a written statement to Dr. Gilbert,[38] the Nuremberg Court psychiatrist, wrote that each transport was preceded by a teletype from Eichmann which contained the unvarying formula ' to be treated according to the directives for *special treatment (Sonderbehandlung*—the code name for gassing). But no lists of names accompanied the trains and only Eichmann was permitted by Himmler to keep any record of the extermination actions. Hoess, who was obliged to destroy such records of these transports as he possessed, could only guess at the numbers gassed. His own estimate, given to Dr. Gilbert and later to the Warsaw court—and incidentally a complete denial of his first voluble confessions—was 1,135,000,[39] but Eichmann had told him in April, 1945, that, according to his own report to Himmler, the number was two millions and a half. In reality it is very unlikely that the true aggregate figures for the Auschwitz gas chambers, as distinct from the death-budget in the camp, are even as high as three-quarters of a million (*see page 461*). For Eichmann merely lied, as was his habit, to impress Himmler and quite possibly never received the figures at all, which were all the time piling up in Maurer's office at Oranienburg, where most of them were destroyed.*

The procedure, adopted for the Auschwitz transports, was in fact typical of the Final Solution as a whole. It proceeded by its own momentum. No day-to-day authority was needed for the work to go on ; on the other hand, nothing short of an order from Hitler could stop it. The statement of Himmler's field adjutant, Lieut.-General Karl Wolff, that 'Hitler did not know that the extermination of the Jews was going on' is an over-simplification,[40] but it is probable that, unless he was considering major policy changes, Hitler did not bother to receive reports about it.

The automatic nature of murder by standing-orders produced results that were totally illogical. In July, 1944, when the Jews from the Lodz and Kovno Ghettoes, the Polish and Baltic labour camps, were evacuated to Germany, it depended purely on the route the train took whether they had to run the gauntlet of a gas-chamber selection in Birkenau. Dr. Lingens-Reiner was admitted to Birkenau in February, 1943, an Aryan political prisoner, along with eleven Jewesses, who underwent no selection because they were civil delinquents from prison who were entitled to a legal existence so long as they had a criminal dossier. And this led Dr. Lingens-Reiner to draw the only permissible conclusion.[41a]

> 'For a Jew there were only two possibilities of certain escape from the gas chamber. He had either to have stolen silver spoons or to have worked in an underground movement.'

4. The Auschwitz Plan in Action

A greater mystery than the administrative procedure, by which the arrivals in Auschwitz were exterminated, is the motive which caused at first the overwhelmingly greater part, but later a proportion, varying between a fifth and a third, to be admitted to the strength of the camp. At certain periods

*When Himmler wanted a balance-sheet of the deportations and resettlements early in 1943 he did not employ Eichmann but Dr. Korherr, his own statistician.

entire transports were admitted and the total number, who were registered in the camp books between 1940 and 1945, Aryans as well as Jews, is said to be 363,000.[41] Yet these people were spared only to die a more miserable death, generally within a few weeks or months. Apparently able-bodied young men and women were spared the gas chamber merely to demonstrate that Auschwitz was a working camp. At Nuremberg the witness, Mme Vaillant-Couturier, put it this way[42]:

> 'Nobody was interested in the output. We were beaten for no reason whatsoever. It was sufficient to stand from morning to evening, but whether we carried one brick or ten was of no importance at all.'

It was the opinion of this witness that the Jews who were selected for the camp were not intended to remain on the ration strength during the largely unproductive winter months and that for this reason the transports were mostly timed to arrive during the spring and summer. Those who remained alive by the autumn were picked out in the arbitrary selections from the infirmary to go to the gas chamber.

In the main this view is justified. The arrival of massed transports invariably overfilled the Birkenau camp and its subsidiaries, even though the greater part were gassed. The number of men and women in Birkenau camp was seldom less than 30,000 and, during the Hungarian deportations in May-June, 1944, it may have exceeded 70,000. As we have seen, Birkenau had been intended for Russian prisoners of war, whom the Germans scarcely regarded as human beings, and camps of this kind without drainage or foundations were not suited for long occupation. The huts were of a kind formerly used by the Wehrmacht for stables. They possessed no glazed windows and were ventilated by clerestories. Not unsuited for a Russian winter, the design had every demerit during the rest of the year. Normally this type of hut housed 52 horses or, alternately, 300 men in three-tiered bunks, but in the transport season the number of inhabitants would be doubled or trebled. The water supply and latrine pits were then hopelessly inadequate and inside the huts the clay floors became disease-traps.[43]

In March, 1942, when this camp was first used, a transfer

115

from Auschwitz main camp was regarded as an almost certain death sentence, and yet overcrowding in Auschwitz had already made it the worst camp in Germany and the first to resort to the extermination of the sick. Hoess's gassing experiment of September, 1941, was carried out on invalids, and the weekly selections began during the following winter. Henceforward, every season of Jewish transports was to bring its train of epidemics, foremost among them spotted typhus. The first season of all set the standard pattern. The strength of the Birkenau male camp rose from 16,274 on July 15th, 1942, when the daily transports from the West were instituted, to 23,010 on August 8th. At that moment it had already become necessary to stop work at the Bunawerk factory and the entire Auschwitz area had to be cordoned off for two months.[44] There then began what was called a 'delousing action,' a systematic clearing of the infirmaries into the gas chamber. It was an innovation in the interest of decency, for hitherto the two Polish *Volksdeutsche* doctors Entress and Zinkteller had made selections of a different kind. The naked invalids were given phenol injections through the heart in the open corridor of the infirmary. 'The professor,' the sanitary orderly Clair, could do many such operations in an hour, and in March, 1942, the typhus season was closed with a mass clearance of this kind.[45]

In the Institute for War Documentation in Amsterdam may be seen a solitary volume of the Death Book, which was smuggled out of the Auschwitz Staff Office during the evacuation. This huge volume contains the death certificates for only five days— September 28th to October 2nd, 1942—yet there are 1,500 of them.[46]* Here one may see how Dr. Kremer became bored with the normally recognised causes of death and invented new ones

*The previous twenty volumes of the Death Book must have covered longer periods than five days each, if the 33,000 registered deaths had accumulated since the opening of the camp in March, 1942. On this assumption the deaths during the first six months of Birkenau had averaged 160 a day. Between July 16th and August 19th they can be deduced from a fragment of the daily roll-call roster. The registration numbers of the new arrivals rose from 47,087 to 60,043, but the roll-call figures went up only from 16,246 to 22,925. There was therefore a deficiency of 6,276 heads or 179 a day. The roll call shows that the daily deficit varied from as little as 16 to as much as 391. (Netherlands Red Cross, *Auschwitz Deel I and II*.)

such as 'weakness of the heart muscles.' But there was a reason for these absurdities. With a death rate running almost as high as at Belsen in February-April, 1945, there was officially no typhus in Auschwitz. Kremer and his like, terrified of being hauled over the coals, copied into the death certificates the fanciful diagnoses of internee doctors, who were trying to save their patients from the 'transport list' or the phenol syringe. Under Kremer's predecessor, Ferdinand Entress, the certificates had been made out in advance,[46a] but their immense number had caused an inquiry to be made from Oranienburg. The phenol injections were stopped and Entress was transferred to Monowitz. Bogus death certificates continued, nevertheless, and it was not till July, 1943, that discharge certificates or *Entlassungen* were made out for the condemned.[46b]

During a 'delousing action' such as that of September-October, 1942, the camp doctors attended almost daily gassings, and of these Dr. Kremer—a professor of Muenster University who was hanged at Cracow in December, 1947—kept an astonishing diary[47]:

September 2nd—Present for the first time at a special action at 3 a.m. Compared to this, the inferno of Dante seems a comedy.

September 5th—Present this afternoon at a special action from the women's camp (Mussulmen) (*see pages 458-9*), the worst I have ever seen. Thilo, the medical officer for the troops, was right when he told me this morning we are at *anus mundi*. In the evening at approximately eight o'clock present at a special action of Dutchmen.

A much simpler calculation was made for the *Frauenlager* by Dr. Ella Lingens-Reiner. On the day of her arrival, February 20th, 1943, the strength of the camp was about 13,000, and it had been in existence since the end of March, 1942. Since her own registration number was 36,088, there must have been 23,000 deaths in eleven months, or rather less than 69 a day. (*Prisoners of Fear*, London, 1948, page 52.)

In March, 1944, when registrations in the Birkenau male camp passed the 180th thousand, a new series was started to prevent internees making such disturbing calculations. The only result was to spread the belief that millions had died in the camp. It was only after the war that it was possible to check the number of camp registrations: 253,000 men and 110,000 women. (Friedman, *This was Oswiecim*, page 14.)

Men want to take part in these actions because of the special rations they get, consisting of a fifth of a litre of schnappes, five cigarettes, 100 grammes of sausage and bread.

September 6th-7th—To-day, Tuesday, excellent lunch, tomato soup, half a hen with potatoes and red cabbage, a marvellous vanilla ice. . . . In the evening at eight o'clock outside for a special action.

September 9th—Present in the evening at my fourth special action. How many doubles have I got in this world ?

Kremer managed to get himself transferred elsewhere on November 18th, after he had taken part in eighteen selections, but the pattern was maintained for two more years. After the deportations from Greece in the spring of 1943 came the typhus epidemic in the autumn and the two huge selections on September 3rd and October 22nd.[48] In December the women's infirmary was cleared completely after the 'third typhus epidemic,'[49] and again at the end of July, 1944, there was a scarlet-fever selection in the women's camp following the Hungarian deportations. Typhoid followed immediately afterwards with the Lodz deportations,[50] so that the routine of epidemics and selections went on till the end of the gas chambers.

Only Mme. Vaillant-Couturier's theory accounts for the failure to prevent the epidemics, which could have been done by dispersing the new arrivals among other camps. At the very moment when the Birkenau camp was having its first 'delousing action,' there was a man-power panic in Germany, following the realisation that there would be a second winter campaign in Russia. Thierack, the Minister for Justice, was prepared to knock the fabric of German law to pieces in order to pressgang 35,000 Eastern workers into the concentration camps without so much as a police charge (*see pages 158-159*). Yet this moment, the beginning of October, 1942, was chosen to transfer all the surviving Jews in the German concentration camps to Auschwitz and Lublin—and Hoess welcomed it. He wrote to Maurer that, though the proposed transfer of the Polish detainees from Auschwitz would disrupt the whole organisation, there was no objection to bringing more Jews to the camp. 'On the contrary, they are urgently needed here.'[51]

Urgently needed for what? It was not till the summer of 1944, long after the rule of Rudolf Hoess, that Birkenau became a labour depôt for the Silesian factories and for various other German concentration camps, to which Jews were once more admitted. For two years only a fraction of the starved and ailing Birkenau population had been employed at all. An employment roster for May 11th, 1944, when the Birkenau male camp contained the not abnormal figure of 17,589 detainees,[52] shows that only 6,269 were at work, mostly employed in camp fatigues. There were 11,311 who did no work at all, being classed as 'immobile,' 'unemployable' and 'unassigned.' They were distributed in a variety of sick blocks and quarantine blocks and they included the 3,027 Jews of the Theresienstadt family camp, who were destined to be gassed on June 20th (*see page 170*) and 4,500 in the gipsy family camp, half of whom were gassed on August 2nd (*see page 188*).

Quarantine at Auschwitz was a sinister word. New arrivals who had escaped the gas chamber went into quarantine and also internees who were about to be moved to other camps. Hoessler, the commandant of the Birkenau *Frauenlager*, declared at the Lueneburg trial that he also sent internees to the isolation block when it was proposed to change their work, but there is abundant evidence that the *Revier* was for these people only an ante-room for the crematoria.

The enormous literature concerning Auschwitz covers mainly the last eighteen months of its existence when chances of survival improved. That people of intelligence and education are still living to write of such experiences is due to the categories of sheltered employment in the infirmaries, the Staff Office, the camp orchestra, and the 'Canada' sorting-commando. The first category was the largest. In order to delay the death of the deportees by a few weeks the camp medical service developed an inexhaustible appetite for prisoner-doctors and nurses. Even the gas chambers had their autopsists to enable Dr. Mengele to record the inherited characteristics of the *sub-human* for the Berlin Institute of Racial Biology.[53] These protected workers stood their chance of typhus in the pestilent sleeping-huts, but at least they were not liable to be wheeled back to camp after their day's work on a hand-cart and propped up dead at evening roll-call.

Some truly fantastic survivals of the German-Jewish intelligentsia may be singled out. Jeannette Wolff, a former City Councillor of Bocholt, was sent to the Riga Ghetto in January, 1942, as the mother of a large family and already past the age at which women deportees were selected for death. She survived nearly two years of the ghetto and another eighteen months, spent in the terrible camps of Kaiserswald and Stutthof and among the Hungarian Jewesses of the Todt organisation's trench-digging commandos. Now, after the extinction of almost all her relations, she fills the honoured post of Deputy Mayor of Western Berlin.[53a]

Philip Auerbach, a pharmacist, survived not only two years of Auschwitz and the Buchenwald 'Little Camp,' but more than four years during which he was under sentence of death for high treason. Nearly half of this he spent in the Gestapo cellars of the Prinz Albrechtstrasse. Unfortunately, the arts of surviving in a condemned cell and a concentration camp served him too well after the war as chief of the Jewish restitution office in Bavaria, and his trial and suicide in August, 1952, were infinitely more tragic than the fate he had escaped.

These are cases of people who in astonishingly different ways were exceptionally gifted with the instinct of self-preservation. At the opposite end of the scale we have the Talmudic students of Eastern Europe, penniless, unworldly, proverbially helpless and utterly unassimilated to the German way of life, and yet the caprice of the SS guards would sometimes spare a *Melammad*. Both Yankiel Wiernik at the death camp Treblinka in 1942-3 and Primo Levi in Auschwitz in 1944 met such oddities, performing the function of *Scheissmeister* or timekeeper at the latrines in all the trappings of Galician Orthodoxy that National Socialist youth found so excruciatingly funny.[53b]

The outstanding features in all Auschwitz narratives are the lack of food, the dirt and promiscuity, the ill-treatment by German internee *kapos* and by NCOs of the SS, the idiotic and homicidal roll-calls, and the human experiments conducted by the German medical profession. It should, however, be pointed out that, while overcrowding created a much greater death-roll, in none of these respects was Auschwitz different from other German concentration camps, once the selections had replaced indiscriminate murder in the camp. That prisoners should be cheated of their food and forced to ' organise' in order to live, that they should be beaten to death at their work in order to give their guards exercise, that they should drop from exhaustion at evening *Appell* because of the inability of these guards to count, were inevitable things, given the nature of their masters.

In the early days the concentration camp had been a place where 'State enemies' received either a swift and lasting discipline or death. To deal with the 'scum of mankind' only the scum of mankind was competent, therefore habitual criminals were selected for the work from the German gaols. At that time they were no doubt adequate for their purpose, but it seems almost inconceivable that Himmler believed that he could obtain real discipline and real effort for the war machine under the rule of these same *Prominenten* and their friends, the old hands of the SS Death's Head *Verbaende*.

Generally speaking, Himmler knew what went on but without understanding the causes, as, for instance, on December 28th, 1942, when he ordered the concentration camp death rate to be reduced at all costs, and in July, 1943, when he ordered Konrad Morgen to investigate embezzlement among the camp commanders.[54] But on the whole Himmler was too busy at his field headquarters to trouble over concentration camps until the moment came when he had to think of working his passage with the Allies.

From this lack of any responsible supervision the internees could sometimes benefit. The older German concentration camps, which dated from 1933, gradually developed among their inmates an antidote to the Heydrich system. The camp commanders were forced to rely to some extent on trusted political detainees of long standing and, through these men, there grew up secret committees, dominated by the Communists, which could protect a favoured detainee and even arrange the death or transfer of a particularly murderous German convict. In the main camp at Auschwitz, which remained to the last a camp for Polish and German Aryan political offenders with the Jews in a minority, the secret committee grew, as it did at Buchenwald, to great power and contrived to secure for its protégés a life that was almost human.[55] But Birkenau never had such a committee, because the population was always changing. Even the prevalent language of the camp might vary between Slovak, Dutch, Greek, and Hungarian. The Jewish *kapos* could not be organised to neutralise the power of the German convicts, for the administration picked them from the German Jews who lacked sympathy for Jews from the East. Jews, moreover, were not allowed to reach the higher grades of the prison hierarchy and, after February, 1944, even the posts of the Jewish hut commanders and their adjuncts were abolished.[56]

As a result, there was an utter lack of resistance. Only in' the infirmaries could a Jew survive and at the same time do some good for his fellow-men. Organisation was out of the question. The very word meant in the prison vocabulary to fend for oneself by cheating others. Dr. Marc Dvorjetski describes a trainload of Jews who are being taken from the Vilna ghetto to a concentration camp. They rejoice that they have not been liquidated, and then a man who has been in such a camp turns to them and says: 'You will take the food from each others' mouths.'[57]

Thus the great mass of men and women, who worked outside the privileged commandos in 1942-43, could only hope to last a matter of weeks. The 257 names in the 'death-book' which could be traced by the Dutch Red Cross were of people who had been in the camp from four to seventy-two days.[58] They stayed on their feet at work or *Appell* from twelve to fifteen hours a day on a diet of watery turnip soup till they became *Mussulmen*, wrapped in a scrap of blanket and waiting their turn for the syringe or the gas-chamber lorry.

CHAPTER 6

The Gas Chambers

1. "The Charitable Foundation"

THE lethal chamber as a means of killing criminals or unwanted pets is an old conception. Adapted to the almost daily destruction of thousands of people, it represents a considerable technical advance—perhaps its sponsors would have preferred the word 'progress.' For this advance no single man can claim the credit, though one Nuremberg witness seemed to want to do so. The development of the gas chambers at Birkenau, which during June, 1944, may have disposed of 6,000 lives a day and on one occasion 10,000, sprang from two separate chains of experiment. There was, on the one hand, the decontamination of large camps by hydrogen-cyanide gas or 'Zyklon B' and, on the other, the administering of 'euthanasia' to the insane by carbon-monoxide poisoning.

The latter came first, for it was practised as early as the end of 1939 at Hitler's orders, but Hitler's interest in gassing went back even further. In 1924 he had declared in 'Mein Kampf' that 12,000 to 15,000 Jews should have been killed by poison gas at the beginning of World War One.[1] It seems that Hitler had already an obsession for gas and the reason is not far to seek. He had himself been gassed in 1917.

The first clue to the origin of the gas chambers came very late in the Nuremberg trial. On August 7th-8th, 1946, Major Georg Konrad Morgen gave evidence on behalf of the SS as an indicted organisation.[2] A former judge of the Stettin *Landgericht*, Morgen had been transferred at Himmler's request in July, 1943, from the SS military courts to the Criminal Police in order to investigate embezzlement in the concentration camps. He was given full powers of arrest, which he used on Koch and Hoven of Buchenwald, Goeth of Plaszow, and Graebner of Auschwitz.[3] He seems to have been a boastful man of some

123

integrity, though not enough.* Although he knew how to keep his mouth shut when the clues became dangerous, he got the reputation of a Nosey Parker in SS circles, who made his life irksome when the Americans confined him in Dachau.[4] In the end Morgen's fellow-captives overcame their repugnance, recognising in him a man whom the Allies might consider respectable. He was therefore put up as a defence witness on the extermination camps of Auschwitz and Poland.

Morgen's case was that the extermination camps were not run by the SS at all and to prove it he told an astonishing story. In the late Summer of 1943 he learnt from the commander of the Security Police and SD in the Lublin region of Poland that there had been a wedding in a Jewish labour camp which had been attended by 1,100 guests, including many German SS men. The investigation of this fantastic charge led Morgen to another camp, 'rather peculiar and impenetrable,' which was run by a certain *Kriminalkommissar* Wirth. From this man Morgen learnt that the Arabian Nights' story was absolutely true. The Jewish wedding banquet was part of a plan by which Wirth induced Jews to serve in four secret camps, where they had to exterminate their own brethren.

Under the names of Treblinka, Belsec, Sobibor, and Chelmno the Nuremberg Tribunal had heard of these camps long before August, 1946, but Morgen gave them a new interpretation. In particular he insisted that the administration was not in SS hands. Wirth's daily orders, which Morgen had seen, came, not from the Reich Security Office, but from the Fuehrer's Chancellory at

*Attempts by German witnesses for the prosecution to discredit Morgen's integrity were, in the absence of documentary proof, less damaging to him than his own special pleading. There is, for instance, no means of checking the statement of his colleague, the SS judge, Lieut.-Colonel Kurt Mittelstedt, that in the summer of 1944 Morgen drafted a leaflet to be distributed by the SS among the deportation trains. This leaflet was alleged to have incited the Jews not to throw away their valuables or surrender them to the Hungarian gendarmerie, but to conceal them, because they would need them in Germany, where genuine employment awaited them (Case IV, No. 1875, printed in *Le Monde Juif*, April, 1952) (*see also page 424, footnote*). A further charge against Morgen needs to be answered. Hoven, the Buchenwald doctor, was accused of poisoning a colleague. Eugen Kogon declares that, in order to elucidate this mystery, Morgen callously tested the effects of alkaloid poisons on Russian prisoners of war. (*Theory and Practice of Hell. London*, 1950, *page 265.*)

No. 4, Tiergartenstrasse, and they were signed 'Blankenberg. But by this time, when the Nuremberg trial had lasted ten months, the court had had their fill of concentration camps and gas chambers. A man who talked of the wonderful view, the grass, and the flowers at Buchenwald and who had noticed no SS men at Auschwitz, could not be taken seriously.[5] And so Counsel for the Defence was told not to waste time and Sir David Maxwell-Fyffe omitted to cross-examine Morgen.

Nevertheless, a few months later, the 'Doctors' Trial' demonstrated the importance of Morgen's clues. There was no doubt of the historicity of Blankenberg and Wirth, 'the Savage Christian' to his unlucky subordinates,[6] and there was no doubt of the existence of the 'old empty institute' at Brandenburg an der Havel, where Wirth had first practised extermination on the insane. But in his rather far-fetched attempt to exculpate the SS, Morgen made a serious mistake. He mentioned that Wirth's commando worked under the code-name 'Einsatz Reinhardt'[7] and it was of course already abundantly established that the director of 'Einsatz Reinhardt' had been the normal Higher SS and Police Leader for Lublin province, Major-General Odilo Globocnik*

Thus it was brought to light that the 'Mercy Killers' had served under the mass-murderer Globocnik. The same men, doctors as well as police officers, who had allegedly worked for human welfare, had built up an organisation that tortured and killed millions of normal beings. Why this proved so easy is partly explained in the testimony of Dr. Karl Brandt, the *Reichskommissar* for Health, who was condemned to death on August 28th, 1947[8]:

> 'In 1935 Hitler told the Reich Medical Leader, Wagner, that, if war came, he would take up and carry out this

---

*In fact the link between Wirth and Globocnik was made still more obvious. Morgen mentioned a second visit to Lublin early in 1944 when he discovered that Wirth and his camp-guards had gone to Istria. Later he learnt that in the month of May Wirth had been killed in a street fight with Tito's partisans. The same story of a street fight in Istria was told by Kaltenbrunner's counsel to account for the death of Globocnik, whom Himmler had made Higher SS and Police Leader for Trieste and the Adriatic coast in September, 1943. Globocnik is also said to have committed suicide in Carinthia in June, 1945 (*see page 357*), to avoid capture by a British patrol. Wirth's death has not been established.

question of euthanasia because it was easier to do so in wartime when the church would not be able to put up the expected resistance.'

The defendants at the 'Doctors' Trial' were not backward in citing pleas for euthanasia from the most liberal sources, as well as precedents for the gas chamber from democratic countries. Mercy killing is undoubtedly one of the problems that modern Western society has created for itself by becoming increasingly institutional—and one of the most glaring faults of Germans living in the National Socialist State was their implicit confidence in institutions. It was left to institutions to decide that a person was a mental defective, an incurable bearer of disease, or simply an *asocial* type, definitions that the least wave of popular or engineered panic could expand. Even in peace time National Socialism, with its morbid insistence on youth and health, had almost made illness a crime. The plea of *bouches inutiles* which justified every massacre of Jews had its roots in notions of national economy and even of social welfare. Thus the language of welfare workers found its way into the reports of the Security Police, who combed out the Jewish settlements in Russia in the autumn of 1941[9]:

> 'In the town of Janovici contagious diseases, accompanied by fever, broke out. It was to be feared the disease might spread to the city (Minsk) and the rural population. To prevent this happening 1,025 Jews were shot. This operation was carried out solely by a commander and twelve men.' (Daily situation report No. 92, September 23rd, 1941.)
> 'A second action consisted in applying special treatment to 812 men and women, all persons without interest from the racial and intellectual point of view.' (Daily situation report No. 124, October 25th, 1941.)

In Germany the calculated slaughter of lunatics and incurables had just ceased at the time of these extremely typical reports from the Russian Front. Public opinion had taught Hitler that an *asocial* person, although a nuisance, might still be a German. If, however, the *asocial* belonged to a subject race, public opinion was dumb. Hitler's greatest asset was his inferiority complex. He knew well that Germans would put up with anything, provided that something worse was reserved for 'lesser breeds.'

Hitler's dangerous gamble with German sentiment had taken place at exactly the moment he had predicted to Wagner. His handwritten note to Philip Bouhler bears no date, but according to Karl Brandt it was made a secret decree at the end of October, 1939, and backdated to September 1st[10]:

> 'Reichsleiter Bouhler and Dr. Brandt are charged with the responsibility for expanding the authority of physicians who are to be designated by name to the end that patients, who are considered incurable in the best available human judgment after critical evaluation of their condition, can be granted mercy killing (*der Gnadentod gewehrt werden kann*).'

The National Socialist hierarchy produced no figure more shadowy than this Philip Bouhler, who was said to have committed suicide in Goering's country house at Karinhall during the last battle in Berlin. Since 1934 he had conducted the Fuehrer's Chancellory, which, distinct from the Reich and Party Chancellories, existed for no other purpose than this, the preparation of decrees that were never published and could not be seen. For so sinister an office Bouhler's personal appearance was not intriguing. In 1939 he was forty years old, curiously soft-faced and juvenile. Peering through thick-rimmed spectacles, he looked more like an American college-boy than a lieutenant-general of the SS. In 1922 he had abandoned the Munich philosophy school to help float the National Socialist newspaper *Voelkischer Beobachter*. He had sat on numerous committees concerned in party education and he was now engaged in purging the German school book. Later, in March, 1942, when other fruits of his pedantic wisdom were blooming in Poland, Bouhler was to publish 'Napoleon, the Comet-Path of a Genius,[11]' which Hitler read in bed, fascinated by the description of a European Plan, almost as good as his own, which had been wrecked by the machinations of the English.[12]

According to Viktor Brack, who served under him, it was the mild reputation of Philip Bouhler which caused Goering, Himmler, and Frick to recommend him for the euthanasia organisation, the natural choice being Dr. Leonardo Conti, head of the Health Department in the Ministry for Interior. But Conti, a blue-eyed Swiss from Lugano, was also under the authority of Martin Bormann, who combined the office of chief of the Party Chancellory with being Hitler's confidential secretary. Bormann was the *pur des purs* of the National Socialist race fanatics and he was already reported to have said that the euthanasia programme would in no respect be limited to incurable lunatics—in which he was probably predicting its ultimate use. In this conflict with the big men of the Cabinet, Hitler's brown shadow did not altogether lose, for the outcome was that Bouhler and Conti exercised a dual authority.*[13]

It is hardly possible to thread the maze, formed by the relationship of the three chancellories with the Health Department, since Philip Bouhler, Herbert Linden, and Leonardo Conti all appear to have taken their lives after the war. The maze baffled the inquisitive as successfully in 1947 as in 1939, though Viktor Brack had survived to face the judges. This man of modest intellectual attainments was no physician but a student of economics. Brack's father had attended Frau Himmler in 1929 during her *accouchement*,† and Viktor Brack, aged twenty-four, had then become the chauffeur and intimate of the future

---

*An entirely different version was given before the Nuremberg International Tribunal by Hans Lammers of the Reich Chancellory, who declared that Hitler in fact chose Conti to direct the programme. Thereupon Conti had gone to Lammers, the only genuine legal expert in all three Chancellories, to get his position legitimised, an action which reduced Hitler to such fury that he at once replaced Conti with Bouhler.

†Margarete Himmler, born in 1894 and Himmler's senior by six years, is a person whose importance may have been underrated. According to Himmler's childhood friend, Karl Gebhardt, Frau Himmler had been a nurse in a fashionable Berlin clinic, where she had acquired a conviction that all professional physicians were venial. She had therefore stimulated Himmler's faith in mesmerism, homeopathy and Dr. Felix Kersten. Gebhardt did not admit that it was through Frau Himmler that he remained Himmler's physician. Like Sigmund Rascher he was not only a close friend of the Himmler's but deeply involved in Himmler's " human guinea pig " experiments, for which he was hanged in 1947. What part had the former Berlin nurse played in this ? In August, 1952, when, after long periods of internment, the Munich *Spruchkammer* finally disposed of her case, Margarete Himmler showed no reluctance to admit that she had known of her husband's commission to exterminate the Jews. (Evidence of Karl Gebhardt in Case I, printed in *Croix Gammée ou Caducée, Neustadt*, 1950. *Daily Express*, August 23rd, 1952.)

Reichsfuehrer SS.[14] In 1936 Bouhler invited Brack to be head of his liaison office with the Health Department, the office which became known during the 'euthanasia action' as T4—an allusion to No. 4, Tiergartenstrasse, the address of the Fuehrer's Chancellory. In this office Brack had four close associates, Hevelmann, Vorberg, Von Hegener, and Werner Blankenberg, the last named taking his place when he went to Poland in 1942. The medical part of the work was, however, not done by Brack's office but by Herbert Linden of Conti's Health Department, whose fourteen 'chief consultants' conducted circuits of the asylums. It was after these assizes that a 'Charitable Foundation for the Transportation of the Sick' conveyed the chosen patients to the remote and furtive institutes designated for euthanasia.[15]

There were certainly not more than a dozen of these institutes in Germany, but, according to both Karl Brandt and Viktor Brandt, they disposed of more than 50,000 people between December, 1939, and August, 1941.[16] The patients were either gassed or given lethal injections, for the institutes existed for nothing else. 'Here we have no sick but only the dead,' Captain Christian Wirth told a newcomer to the Hadamar staff.[17]

Wirth's first gassing at Brandenburg, which took place in December, 1939, or January, 1940, was witnessed by Brack, who declared that Bouhler and Conti were with him. It was Bouhler who had the inspiration of disguising the gas room as a shower-bath with seats and douches, the method which was used in the super-gas chambers of Auschwitz in 1943-44. Coal gas from a steel retort was used, a method which limited the deaths to twenty or thirty at a time.[18]

Wirth's name does not occur in any of the surviving official correspondence concerning euthanasia, but this was because the last stage in the proceedings was disowned at No. 4, Tiergartenstrasse, and entrusted to a fictitious authority, known as the 'Charitable Foundation for Institutional Care.' It is a particularly striking fact that, during the functioning of the death camps in Poland, Kurt Gerstein noticed that Wirth and his associates still called themselves a 'foundation' (*Stiftung*).

The method of gassing then in use was the canalisation of the exhaust of internal-combustion engines. Wirth boasted to Morgen that he had evolved this by personal experiment, but one may doubt this in view of Brack's statement that he employed a chemist called Kallmeyer as his technical adviser. Kallmeyer is, moreover, named in the letter, so often mentioned in this book, which Dr. Wetzel wrote from Rosenberg's office on October 25th, 1941, to Reichskommissar Lohse in Riga.[19]*

'Herr Viktor Brack, *Oberdienstleiter* in the Fuehrer's Chancellory, is ready to collaborate in the installation of the necessary buildings and gas plants. He thinks it easier to construct the latter, of which we are short, on the spot. He would like to send his chemist, Kallmeyer, to Riga. I request you to communicate with *Leiter* Brack through your Higher Police Leader, I permit myself to observe that Major Eichmann is in agreement. He informs us that the camps are intended for Riga and Minsk where even Jews from the Old Reich may be sent. At the present time Jews who are evacuated from the Old Reich are sent to Lodz and other camps, from which they leave for the East or for labour camps if they are suited. To judge from the actual situation one need have no scruple in using Brack's method to liquidate Jews who are unsuitable for work. In this way incidents will no longer be possible or tolerated such as occurred during the shootings at Vilna—and these shootings were public, according to the report that I have before me. On the other hand, Jews suitable for work will still be sent East to be attached to the Labour Service. Naturally the employable men and women must be separated from each other.'

This is the earliest document yet discovered which refers to permanent gassing camps, and it is the most important link connecting them with 'T4' and the Euthanasia Service. It is worth mentioning that, though Brack has been hanged, Wetzel, who wrote the letter, and Leibbrandt, of Rosenberg's Ministry,

---

*Wirth may, however, have played a lesser part in the evolution of engine-gassing. As a *Kriminalkommissar* he was a subordinate of Artur Nebe, who was commissioned by Himmler during his visit to Minsk in July or August, 1941, to find a humane way of dealing with mass executions (*see Chapter 8, page 208*). This story of von dem Bach-Zalewski's finds some confirmation in the discovery in 1949 in Nebe's former Berlin apartment of an amateur film, showing a gas chamber operated by the exhausts of a car and a lorry.[20]

who pursued the subject, have never been tried at all, while Lohse, who sent a mysterious inquiry on October 4th to which this letter is an answer, is now a free man drawing a Government pension (*see page 512*).

It should be noticed that Wetzel did not propose moving the still somewhat primitive installations from the death institutes. It was not the plant that was moved to Eastern Europe, but Wirth and his operators, the 'nurses and attendants' employed by the 'Foundation for Institutional Care,' since it was the training that mattered most. The ghastly Polish extermination camps were nothing new to these people. One might already be reading about Treblinka and Auschwitz in the protest, sent on May 16th, 1941, by the Frankfort *Landgericht* to Guertner, the Minister for Justice. It records that the Hadamar children shout after the blacked-out buses, 'Here are some more people being gassed'; that the patients are taken to the gas room in paper shirts, the corpses enter the furnace on a conveyer belt and the smoke from the crematorium chimney is visible for miles. At night Wirth's experts, picked by the Gestapo at Columbia House in the Papenstrasse, drink themselves to oblivion in the little Hadamar *Gasthof*, where the regular customers take care to avoid them.[21]*

To this and other protests of the provincial courts the churches added a more public protest—Hitler had underrated that possibility. A still more gruesome picture of Hadamar was circulated to the Ministries for Interior, Justice, and Church Affairs on August 16th by the Bishop of Limburg. This protest, like others made earlier by Cardinal Faulhaber and Theophil Wurm, the Protestant Bishop of Wurttemberg, remained ignored,[24] but they had some cumulative effect. As early as the winter of 1940 Guertner appealed to Hitler for a ruling, but was told by

---

*The staff of the institutes selected for euthanasia were usually replaced with individuals in the uniform of the criminal police or SD, but some genuine nursing staff were recruited for the sake of respectability. Thus *Krankenschwester* Pauline Kneissler testified[22] that she was interviewed by Werner Blankenberg at Gestapo Headquarters, Columbia House, on January 4th, 1940. In March she was posted to Graefeneck Institute, thence graduating to the awful Victorian stucco villa at Hadamar and from there to Kaufbeuren, near Irrsee, in Bavaria, where idiot children were still being exterminated after the American occupation.[23] Kneissler had to collect the patients from the normal institutes.

Lammers that Hitler would not consent to publish the terms of the secret decree.[25] It is probable that on no question was Hitler's personal dictatorship more severely challenged than this one—on which he acted with quite disgusting cowardice.

In the end public opinion won and Hitler had to be content with his 50,000 or 60,000 German victims. Yet public opinion had nothing to say when nearly a million Jews were gassed or done to death in Auschwitz—and Auschwitz was then part of Germany. This phenomenon can still be observed in the belated trials of war criminals. The German press gives publicity to those who are accused of killing Germans—Ilse Koch for instance—but of the thousands who took part in the massacres of Jews not even a dozen have been brought to trial in German courts since the matter has been left in German hands. Over the deaths of Germans the public conscience could assert itself even in 1941, Himmler was stirred and finally Hitler. Decency and good sense prevailed. If they failed to do so regarding another matter, it was because decency and good sense were lacking.

According to Dr. Fritz Mennecke, Hitler's train was held up at Hof near Nuremberg in the summer of 1941 on account of some lunatics who were being loaded into a truck. The crowd were so outraged that they actually jeered their Fuehrer.* Whatever the truth of this story, we have the testimony of Karl Brandt that in August, 1941, he telephoned Bouhler on Hitler's instructions that the euthanasia programme must be stopped.[26]

Himmler, who did not always try to avoid being a commonplace man and who, as Count Ciano observed, 'felt the pulse of the German people,' had never been happy about it. In December, 1940, he had recommended Brack to suppress the Graefeneck Institute,[27] writing that it was better first to educate the public to euthanasia through films. Taking the hint, Viktor Brack persuaded the Tobis company in the summer of 1941 to produce '*Ich klage an*' ('I accuse'), the sentimental story of a professor who is put on trial for hastening the death of his young wife, an incurable invalid.[28]

*Mennecke was one of the 'higher consultants employed on the euthanasia plan and director of the Eichberg Institute. He died in prison in May, 1947, of cavitary tuberculosis, the death-sentence of the Frankfurt *Schwurgericht* having been suspended to enable him to give evidence at the 'Doctors' Trial.'

There is some difference of opinion whether German adult mental patients were still killed after Bouhler had suspended operations. According to Viktor Brack, only idiot children were still sent to the death institutes, but Alfons Klein, a deputy director of Hadamar, declared at his trial in 1946 that 3,000 adult patients had been killed *after* August, 1941.[29]

2. The Polish Death Camps and Their Evolution

We know now that there was no break in the activities of the 'Charitable Foundation for Institutional Care' after August, 1941. The victims were no longer lunatics or incurables, they were Jews. Although Brack remembered being told by Bouhler that the benefits of euthanasia were only for true Germans, there were already Jewish names in the first case-sheets deposited at 'T4' in 1939. According to Karl Brandt, they were sent in 'for possible future measures.'[30] In fact, Jews were sent to the euthanasia institutes—and merely for being Jews—shortly before Hitler's act of repeal in August, 1941, when Waldemar Hoven, the Buchenwald Camp doctor, was told by Commandant Koch that all the Jews in the camp would be sent to the neighbouring institute. The selection was made by Dr. Mennecke[31] and a few days later 300 Jews were shipped to the Bernberg Institute. Hoven, on this occasion, used a special form for the falsified lunacy certificates, known as '14 F 13.'[32]

The main part of the '14 F 13' action took place in November, 1941, under a commission consisting of Dr. Mennecke and Professors Nitsche and Heyde. On November 25th Mennecke wrote to his wife from the Hotel *Zum Elefant* in Weimar that on a second visit to Buchenwald Camp he had examined 1,200 Jews.[33] All that he had to do was to transfer particulars of the arrest of these Jews to the questionnaire forms. The forms, the photographs, and Mennecke's notes all appeared at his trial in November, 1946. These people had gone to Bernberg merely on their records, ranging from those of prostitutes to those of political leaders of the Left.

During the summer of 1941, according to Viktor Brack, Himmler had asked Philip Bouhler to provide psychiatrists and, if necessary, 'specialists from neutral countries' to investigate the emotional life of concentration camp inmates.[34] There arrived consequently at Dachau in November something that resembled the 'travelling circuses,' familiar to the British Army. The 'psychiatrists' sat in the open on a couple of tables, headed by Professor Heyde—who is still at large, having escaped after his death sentence in 1946. In this way, during the Dachau visitation, hundreds of prisoners, Aryans as well as Jews, were examined purely on their political records. In January, 1942, they were gassed at Schloss Hartheim.[35]

By this time the visitations were so numerous that the commandant of Gross-Rosen camp learnt from the Bernberg Institute that too many cases were being sent from concentration camps and that technical difficulties were causing delay. The nearest date which could be offered was March 24th-26th. Bernberg would not accept more than a hundred patients at a time and they must be delivered by bus.[36]

The next step therefore was to dispense with the bogus lunacy certificate and the waiting list for the euthanasia institutes by creating gassing installations in the camps themselves. Thus eventually every German concentration camp acquired a gas chamber of sorts, though their use proved difficult. The Dachau gas chamber, for instance, has been preserved by the American occupation authorities as an object lesson, but its construction was hampered and its use restricted to a few experimental victims, Jews or Russian prisoners of war, who had been committed by the Munich Gestapo.[36a]

It is little more than a coincidence that the trouble with the Bernberg Institute coincided with the first use of a permanent gas chamber in the Birkenwald at Auschwitz. For Auschwitz was never involved in the bureaucratic complications of '14 F 13.' Under the rule of Hoess it exterminated its own sick at least as early as the autumn of 1941 (*see page 117*). As to Jews, there was no need to certify them insane or incurable. In 1940 and 1941 they were put in the punishment company on arrival, where, if they lasted more than ten days, they were driven into the barbed wire, fifty at a time, and shot 'while trying to escape.'

But in other camps the form '14 F 13' still had its use for dealing with individual cases. Morgen came across it in July, 1943, or even later, though on April 27th Himmler had ordered that in future it should be used only for genuine mental cases.[37] Morgen discovered that Heyde was still directing his 'psychiatric' commissions at Buchenwald, but the trial led to Philip Bouhler, 'a high source in direct relation with the Fuehrer' which Morgen was advised to avoid.[38]

A month or two later Morgen again came across Philip Bouhler in Wirth's correspondence at Lublin.[39] Bouhler, it seems, was still keeping an eye on the 'nurses and attendants' in Poland who remained on his pay-roll with a view to resuming the euthanasia programme after the war.

There had been two main transfers from the euthanasia institutes to Poland. The first was described in a letter from Fritz Mennecke to his wife, dated January 12th, 1942:

'Since the day before yesterday a large delegation from our organisation, headed by Herr Brack, is on the battlefields of the East to help in saving our wounded in the ice and snow. They include doctors, clerks, nurses, and male nurses from Hadamar and Sonnenstein, a whole detachment of 20-30 persons. *This is a top secret.* Only those persons who could not be spared were excluded. Professor Nitsche regrets that the staff of our institution at Eichberg had to be taken away so soon.'[40]

The second transfer is mentioned in a letter from Viktor Brack to Himmler, dated June 23rd. Brack wrote it when he was on leave from Poland to attend Heydrich's funeral[41]:

'Some time ago I put at the disposal of Brigadier-General Globocnik a certain number of men for the accomplishment of his special mission. Following a fresh request on his part, I have again sent him personnel.'

So this was how the staffs of Hadamar, Sonnenstein, and Eichberg helped the wounded in the ice and snow. At the German Hadamar trial in Frankfurt in 1947 a burly member of the Death's Head *Verbaende*, called Hubert Gomerski, sat in the massed dock. As a mere crematorium stoker, posted from Columbia House, he was acquitted. But in August, 1950, Gomerski again faced the *Schwurgericht*, where it was proved that he had left Hadamar for Lublin in January, 1942. Eventually he became the shooting expert of Sobibor death camp. He was known as 'the doctor' because of his past experience in handling the sick and his speciality was braining the half-dead with a steel water-can as they were taken off the trains.[42] Another of these 'doctors,' the Treblinka corporal Josef Hirtreiter, who had also graduated under Wirth at Hadamar, was unearthed by the Frankfurt *Schwurgericht* in 1950.[43] He, too, had previously been on trial for 'euthanasia' activities in 1947, when the court had failed to identify him with the 'Hirtreider' named at the Polish Treblinka inquiry in 1945 as a specialist in killing children without wasting ammunition.[43a]

Viktor Brack's explanation of the functions of his Gomerskis and Hirtreiters is to be found in one of his own trial affidavits[44]:

'In 1941 I received an order to discontinue the euthanasia programme. In order to preserve the personnel that had been relieved of these duties and in order to have the opportunity of starting a new euthanasia programme after the war, Bouhler requested me—I think after conference with Himmler—to send this personnel to Lublin and put it at the disposal of SS Brigadier-General Globocnik. Later, however, at the end of 1942 or the beginning of 1943, I found out that they were used in the mass extermination of Jews, which was then already common knowledge in higher party circles.'

Under examination by his counsel at Nuremberg, Brack explained[45] that at first neither he nor Bouhler had any idea of the requirements of Globocnik, 'the director of the entire Jewish extermination programme in the East.' Only at the time of his second request did Globocnik take Bouhler into his confidence. Bouhler then protested that, if his men worked on 'such an inconceivable assignment,' they would not be fit to be employed in mercy-killing. Globocnik kept Bouhler quiet by telling him that his innocent doves would be employed only as inspectors in the labour camps.*

---

*One member of the Hadamar staff, the stoker Klaier, was acquitted of murder in 1950, having served as an overseer in the sorting camp at Sobibor, where he had nothing to do with gassing. A certain amount of euthanasia personnel were no doubt assigned this only relatively innocent rôle, simply because the job could not be given to men who had not been inoculated to daily exterminations.[46]

Yet, months before the transfer of his personnel to Globocnik, Brack had been involved in proposals to create death camps in the East. The installations, which he was prepared to set up for Eichmann at Riga and Minsk according to Wetzel's letter of October 25th, 1941,[47] were in all probability mobile gassing vans, one of which had been attached to Blobel's extermination commando in the Ukraine in the previous month. They were not sent to Riga and Minsk, because they were needed elsewhere. It is not certain whether the first permanent establishment employing these vans was set up near Lodz, where the first deportees from the Reich had been settled, or near Semlin camp, where the inhabitants of the Belgrade Ghetto had been evacuated (*see page 363*). The evidence suggests that the vans were used both at Semlin and Chelmno before the end of 1941.

Wirth was certainly associated with the establishment at Chelmno, for he was already in Poland. According to the statement of Dr. Gorgass, he had been sent by the 'Foundation' that summer to found an institute near Lublin—a plan which was postponed together with Himmler's plans for Lublin concentration camp (*see page 293*).[48]

There must have been at least a family resemblance between Wirth's 'old empty institute' at Brandenburg and the place chosen for the reduction of the Lodz Ghetto, a mouldering chateau called 'The Palace,' of which there exists an unbelievably sinister photograph. It was at Chelmno, a few miles from the Warsaw-Posen-Berlin main line, and it was first used in December, 1941. It was, like its German prototypes, also intended for the disposal of incurables. Thus on May 1st, 1942, the Gauleiter Artur Greiser proposed to Himmler that 25,000 tubercular Polish subjects of his Gau should be admitted to Chelmno for 'special treatment.'[49]

There was, however, one innovation at Chelmno not to be found in the euthanasia institutes. The permanent staff, recruited from the *Foundation* and known as 'Detachment Bothmann,' was quite small. The heavy work—so much heavier than in a mere euthanasia establishment—was done by the patients themselves before their death, for in the cellars of 'The Palace' the stronger Jews might be permitted to live for several weeks.[50] Wirth, as we have seen, claimed to have invented the Jewish

'*Sonderkommando*,' which, possessed of the secrets of the dead and some of their gold, was gassed and cremated by its successors. But the Gestapo officer, Willi Hoettl, says that it was Heydrich himself who revived this legend of the Pharaonic tombs.[51] Heydrich was certainly more obsessed with secrecy than his subordinates. Shortly before his death he created Colonel Blobel's organisation which was entrusted with the effacement of all mass burials, and it was at Chelmno, the first of the 'Pharaonic tombs,' that Blobel began his operations.[52]

When interrogated at Nuremberg, Blobel delicately described this place as a 'disused Jewish cemetery near Lodz,' but it was at Chelmno that Hoess visited Blobel on September 17th to observe his ineffective attempts at eliminating mass graves by dynamite. The method was tried because Himmler had sent instructions to Blobel through the *Dienststelle Eichmann* that even the ashes must disappear. Blobel also used a bone mill, and on his expert advice Hoess ordered a similar installation for Auschwitz from the firm Schriever A.G., Hanover.[52a]

Hoess, on his return, continued to use an enclosed crematorium in the Birkenwald, because bodies burnt slowly and fitfully in the open air and the problem was to hide the appalling stench from the next batch of victims. In the meantime Blobel adopted the method which he was to introduce at Treblinka death camp and at the immense mass graves outside Russian cities, a vast pyre constructed of iron rails and wooden sleepers. Hoess, however, demanded still bigger and better-equipped crematoria, only to discover during the incredible summer programme of 1944 that to get rid of thousands of corpses in a hurry, trenches filled with petrol were best (*see page 429*). The method proved so successful that finally it was used to eliminate the body of Hitler himself.

Blobel's connection with Chelmno, the first of the death camps, must have dated from its very origins, for a gassing van of the kind used at Chelmno had, as he admitted, been issued to his Commando in the Ukraine as early as September, 1941.[53] Blobel remained to the last an intimate of Eichmann and his assistant Wisliceny, who told Dr. Kastner that in autumn, 1941, Eichmann had commissioned Blobel to design the gas chambers. Although this is a third-hand story, it fits with many known facts.

One may, for instance, note how Hoess recorded Blobel's instructions after his visit to Chelmno. Blobel was a drunken Duesseldorf architect for whom even his co-defendants in 1948 could say no good. He sat through the long *Einsatzgruppen* trial, a tall, blond, bearded maniac with bloodshot eyes. He was one of the seven Landsberg 'Red Jacket' men who were hanged on June 8th, 1951, having survived long enough to become heroes and martyrs of the neo-Nazis.[54]

These Chelmno gas vans drove from 'The Palace' to the burial pits in the woods, killing the passengers with their own exhaust fumes on the way. It was simple but it was not efficient. Captain Bothmann told Hoess that the gas pressure was irregular and sometimes failed to kill,[55] a point made also by a Jew who escaped from the *Sonderkommando* in February, 1942. And yet the same vans were used after Bothmann's recall from Dalmatia in 1944.[56] In the meantime one of the vans, known affectionately as the 'Ghetto Autobus,' had got most embarrassingly lost and was located after an acrimonious correspondence in a repair-shop at Warthebruecken.[57]

Rather more information about these vans is available from Russian sources, from the evidence of Otto Ohlendorf, and from the correspondence of the vehicle department of the Reich Main Security Office, for they were used extensively in Russia after the spring of 1942. The report of Lieutenant Dr. Becker from Kiev, dated May 16th, shows that the vans, made by the firm Saurer of Berlin, were still very faulty[58]:

'The men of the special commandos complained to me about headaches which appeared after each unloading. Nevertheless they don't want to change their orders because they are afraid that prisoners, called on to do that work, would take the opportunity to escape.'

'The application of gas is usually not undertaken correctly. In order to come to an end as fast as possible, the driver presses the accelerator to the fullest extent. Thus the persons executed die by suffocation and not by dozing off as planned. My directions have proved that by correct adjustment of the levers death comes faster and the prisoners fall asleep peacefully. Distorted faces and excretions, such as could be seen before, are no longer noticed.'

The inefficiency of the gassing vans produced horrors enough, but it seems they were nothing compared with what happened when the next step was attempted, the application of the engine-exhaust gas to a group of permanent chambers, each holding hundreds of people at a time. The first of these, the Belsec gas installation, which was intended to be ready for the Lublin resettlement on March 16th, 1942 (*see pages 252-253*), broke down constantly. The deportees were left in the 'transfer station' for days on end, where they crouched in the open, naked and without food or water. Sometimes they were left in railway box-cars to suffocate on sidings. This story, brought to London in February, 1943, by a courier of the Polish Exile Government, cannot lightly be dismissed.[59] It can at least be compared with the evidence which a *German* court was prepared to accept in August, 1950, that on one occasion the gas engine at Sobibor had broken down for three days on end, during which an entire transport had to wait under these conditions till the survivors could be gassed.[60]

Between May and June, 1942, Belsec was out of action for six weeks,[61] and in July it was only handling two transports a week.[62] In November—or soon after—it was out of action for good,[63] but the Jewish *Sonderkommando* was occupied in effacing the mass graves till the following June.

Strange to say, all this happened within a few yards of the main line between Lwow and Lublin, where, in April, 1943, a Jewish doctor, who later escaped to Switzerland, noticed the appalling stench of the exhumed bodies as he passed the spot by train.[64] Nevertheless the wildest legends surrounded the place. Dr. Guérin, in a prisoner-of-war camp only twenty miles along the line, heard that the Jews were killed by an incredible electric current passed through water, and this story reached London in November, 1942.[65] It was only after the war that a real survivor appeared to describe the miserable diesel engine which had supplied the carbon monoxide. He was Rudolf Reder, the former director of a soap factory in Lwow, who owed his survival at the age of sixty to his ability to work the camp steam excavator.[66] Reder once saw the victims locked in the gas chamber for hours on end while efforts were made to start the diesel engine. The same scene was described by the German gas expert, Kurt

Gerstein, who visited Belsec on August 20th, 1942, within a few days of Reder's arrival (*see pages 153 and 265*). It took two and three-quarter hours to start the engine and all the time the moaning could be heard in the four gas chambers, in each of which there were 750 people.[67]

At Treblinka death camp, fifty miles from Warsaw, the method was different. The small gas chambers were charged separately from the engines of captured Russian tanks and lorries, but it is clear that these gas chambers, on which construction was begun in June, 1942, were not ready in time for the liquidation of the Warsaw Ghetto, for which they were intended.* Eugen Kogon learnt in Buchenwald from a man, who was deported to Treblinka from the Kielce Ghetto at the end of July, that the people were machine-gunned by the guards as they streamed out of the trains or as they waited crouching in the compound, known as the *Lazarett*.[72] Apparently the gas chambers only began to work after he had spent three or four weeks in Treblinka. It would in any case have been impossible to gas the greater part of the 310,000 Jews who were deported from Warsaw,[73] together with an unknown proportion from other ghettoes, in three gas chambers, each measuring fifteen feet square, in no more than seventy-five working days.[74] There were days when something like 10,000 people left the assembly point in Warsaw, presumably for Treblinka. Therefore a large proportion must have died in the trains. The witnesses, Wiernik and Rajzman, travelled from Warsaw under just bearable conditions,

---

*This is also confirmed in the narratives of Yankiel Wiernik and Stanislas Kon, deported to Treblinka late in August, as well as in that of Sawek Warszawski, who, left for dead in a burial pit, survived to recognise the killer Josef Hirtreiter at the Frankfurt trial of March, 1951.[68] Hoess of Auschwitz conveys the same impression when he says that the tank and lorry engines were often out of action and that ' it was impossible to apply to the internees the treatment which was foreseen in the plan to empty the Warsaw Ghetto.'[69]

On the other hand some note must be taken of the Polish investigation commission's discovery that there was a ' steam' extermination chamber which was finished as far back as the end of April.[70] It is difficult to see how people could be exterminated by steam, but it appears that there was a hutted camp at Treblinka at this time for Jewish families deported from Slovakia (*see pages 388-389*), and that this community was liquidated and that Wiernik saw parts of their huts used in the construction of new gas chambers[71] in 1942-43.

eighty to a box-car. This must have been exceptional, since both men saw trains arriving from places less than a hundred miles away, trains in which 80 or 90 per cent of the passengers had already died.[75]

These stories of naked transports and corpse transports seem to end with the opening of the second season at Treblinka in March, 1943, when there were several transports from Vienna, Luxembourg, and Prague made up of passenger coaches. The Germans even provided medical aid on the journey and, if one may trust Baldur Von Schirach, milk for the children.[76] The open compound, where the sick were killed, was provided with a hospital anteroom and the camp siding was dolled up as a 'Potemkin' railway station with time-tables and advertisements. Since Treblinka now had thirteen gas chambers, the executions may have become rather more humane.[77]

These four Polish camps had been intended for extermination centres and nothing else, but by the beginning of 1943 they employed such large numbers of Jews in the work of loot-sorting, exhumation, and cremation that they became hardly distinguishable from other Jewish labour camps of the SS. In this way they ceased to be 'Pharaonic Tombs' and disclosed their secrets. For as the number of death transports diminished, the rule had to be relaxed by which, with the exception of Wirth's 'column leaders' and a few skilled men like the carpenter Wiernik, the *Sonderkommandos* only lasted a few weeks.

By the second season the 'Einsatz Reinhardt' staff seem to have ceased to worry about secrecy. Thus in Auschwitz Professor Robert Levy met a boy of thirteen from Luxembourg who, after performing for months the most unspeakably horrible of all tasks in the Treblinka burial commando, was allowed to volunteer for a mining camp.[78] During the Warsaw rebellion and afterwards, regular selections were made in Treblinka for labour camps,[79] while at Sobibor this became the general procedure with the transports from Holland during the summer of 1943.[80]

At Sobibor quite an embarrassing situation arose. In July Himmler proposed to convert the women's tailoring workshops in the outer camp to a depot for altering the fuses of captured ammunition.[81] The fact that Pohl and Globocnik had to persuade Himmler to change his mind suggests that, in spite of the

142

allegations that he had witnessed a gassing at Sobibor, Himmler may not have known that this was a death camp,[82] when there were so many others like it.

These places were less familiar to the German hierarchy at home than they were to the Polish population, and it was from the Germans that the need of concealment was greatest. Globocnik's men were not expected to talk. When Corporal Hirtreiter asked for a transfer from Treblinka, he was told by Captain Staenge that 'the circle of those who knew could not be increased,' and the corporal understood the threat in that statement,[83] a threat which, more than the post-war need of discretion, may explain the total disappearance of Wirth and his four camp commanders, the captains Bothmann, Staenge, Neubauer, and Tomalla. It may also explain why only five men from the Wirth commando have been identified and brought to trial. For one should not overlook the remark made by one of these vanished men, Mussfeld, the Auschwitz crematorium chief, to Dr. Nyiszli and the slaves who were his companions: 'Good evening, children, you are all going to be killed very soon but after that it will be our own turn.'[84]

Globocnik, Wirth, and the officers of Einsatz Reinhardt relied on the discretion of their men and they were not deceived. They also relied on their Jewish slaves not breaking out—but there they were mistaken. There were weaknesses in the system from the beginning. The Jewish 'column leaders,' of whom Wirth said to Morgen that he had 'given them a financial interest in the spoliation of the dead,' could not be disposed of like the other slaves. They became indispensable. Lest Morgen's story should seem far-fetched, I would quote the testimony of the Memel judge, Samuel Gringauz, a survivor of the Kovno Ghetto. He declares that the Jewish 'column leader' Liptzy acquired so much jewellery from the executions at 'Fort No. 9' that he was able to 'handle' the Gestapo for two years.[85] At Treblinka and Sobibor the rebellion leaders concentrated on 'handling' the Ukrainian militia, a much simpler proposition since they were undisciplined, without loyalties, drunken, and corrupt, the Achilles heel of the Germans.

After August, 1943, a further circumstance arose to make the death camps very dangerous for the Germans. The gassings ceased. It was no longer possible to replace the working Jews from incoming transports, though the huge programme of exhumation demanded more hands. Exhumation had begun at Treblinka already in March, 1943, the month of the 'Katyn' revelations, when Goebbels discovered the political value of an allegedly Russian mass burial. This, like most of Goebbels's inspirations, was ill-timed, since the Russians were now advancing into an area which was peppered with mass burials. From Kharkov and Smolensk back to the German border Himmler was compelled to order an exhumation and cremation drive under Colonel Paul Blobel and 'Commando 1005.'[86] According to Wiernik, the Germans had to camouflage the smoking pyres at Treblinka from the view of low-flying Russian aeroplanes.

The leaders of the Treblinka rebellion of September 2nd, 1943, were Dr. Leichert, a former captain of the Polish army, and the constructional engineer, Dr. Galewski, whom the Germans trusted so much that they kept him alive more than a year and made him *Judenaelteste* of the camp. The Jews broke into the armoury and obtained weapons, but unfortunately the alarm was mistimed. It was to have gone off just as a trainload of Polish prisoners passed the camp, returning from the gravel quarries of one of Himmler's business enterprises to the camp known as Treblinka I. Thus most of the rebels were massacred and of those who escaped only forty survived the war, of whom fourteen were interrogated by the Warsaw court in 1945. But the Germans had had enough[87] and in November the remains of the camp were blown up; the site, which had been cleared of its mass graves, was levelled and planted with pines.[88]

At Sobibor the mutiny broke out on October 14th, 1943. Some White-Russian Jewish partisans had survived from a gassing in August—and this in the very camp that Himmler was going to turn into a munition works. Their leader, Saszka Pieczerski, was said to have been a *Politruk*, or Political Commissar, with the Red Army. On this occasion about 150 of the 600 Jews and Jewesses in Sobibor, Polish, Russian, and Dutch, got out under Pieczerski's leadership, but few crossed the minefield. Only thirty are known to have survived the war. Pieczerski's second-in-command, Leon Feldhandler, was protected by the Russian partisans, but in April, 1945, he was murdered by a band, affiliated to the Polish Home Army.[89] A few of the Dutch Jews regained their own country (*see page 337*).

In November, 1943, when the last trace of the death camps had been removed and Wirth's men had been banished to the Adriatic, there were still hundreds of thousands of Jews in Poland, either in hiding or in labour camps, but the rebellions induced Himmler to abandon this method of execution at least in the General Government, though from Western Poland victims continued to be sent to Auschwitz and in February, 1944, the Chelmno death camp was reopened. It is nevertheless unlikely that more than a quarter of the Jews of pre-war Poland were brought to the death camps from first to last. At least as many were shot down in or near their native towns and a much larger number died of hardship in the ghettoes and camps (*see Appendix 1*).

3. Zyklon B versus Internal Combustion

In all four of the Polish death camps gassing by engine-exhaust fumes was practised. Only at Majdanek, a concentration camp under the central SS administration, were 'Zyklon B' crystals used and apparently on a small scale. Although the crystals were assumed to be more humane, Wirth resisted any change in his methods which had been evolved in the sinister mental institutes of the Third Reich. He was scornful of Rudolf Hoess, the apostle of hydrogen-cyanide or 'Zyklon B,' describing him to Morgen as 'his untalented disciple'[90] For his part Hoess's recorded contempt for the methods used at Treblinka was due not to humanitarian feelings but to the outraged sense of method of a former bookkeeper. Hoess, moreover, took a possessive pride in 'Zyklon B' gassing, because he had made what was allegedly the first experiment as a result of Eichmann's visit to Auschwitz in 1941, according to Dr. Filip Friedman, on September 15th.[91] Six hundred invalid Russian prisoners of war, together with 250 inmates of the Auschwitz infirmary were locked in the cellar of No. 11, the famous penal block in the main camp. The windows were earthed in and the crystals were merely thrown through the door. But on the following afternoon, when Sergeant Palitsch entered the cellar, many living bodies were discovered and the whole process had to be repeated. The final scene has been described by the Polish officer, Zenon Rozanski, who served in the penal company which provided the burial party.[92]

> 'Those who were propped against the door leant with a curious stiffness and then fell right at our feet, striking their faces hard against the concrete floor. Corpses! Corpses standing bolt upright and filling the entire corridor of the Bunker, till they were packed so tight that it was impossible for more to fall.'

For three days before this incident the penal block had been evacuated by the punishment company on the pretext that it was to be fumigated. Hoess was to declare at Nuremberg more than four years later that it was fumigation which had given him this inspiration. He had performed the gassing with 'Zyklon B' crystals, left over after the decontamination of the camp which had been carried out by the firm of Tesch and Stabenow. But it is highly probable that this was not the first experiment, since there exist letters from Karl Weinbacher, one of the directors of this firm who was condemned to death in March, 1946, tendering for the ventilation and heating equipment for two very small 'extermination chambers,' measuring only ten cubic metres each, for Gross-Rosen concentration camp. The first of these letters is dated July 24th, 1941.[93]

Who was this experimenter whose researches ran parallel with those of Kallmeyer, Blobel, and Wirth? One would like to know more of Lieutenant Ulmer of the SS, who, according to Filip Friedman, submitted a detailed gas chamber project for Auschwitz in 1940. One may also consider the claims of Captain Sigmund Rascher, who, on May 15th, 1941, submitted proposals to Himmler for the first human guinea-pig experiments which eventually he performed at Dachau in February, 1942. This garrulous and murderous quack had become the intimate friend of Himmler, who admired Frau Rascher because she had borne three children after passing the age of forty-eight—a credit to German motherhood.[94] Now, in the spring of 1944, the Raschers were arrested on a charge of having illegally obtained possession of these three alleged children of theirs. Himmler thereupon intervened, pointing out the importance of Captain Rascher's researches; yet, though he stopped the trial he would not release the Raschers. Confined in Dachau, Rascher boasted to Captain Payne-Best that he had invented the gas chambers. Presumably it was for this sort of indiscretion that Himmler refused to release Rascher and had him shot in the neck in the last days of the Third Reich.[95]

Again, the experimenter may have been a civilian, operating on behalf of private enterprise. According to Hoess all purchases of 'Zyklon B' had to be made through Dr. Mugrowski, of the SS Health Institute.[96] Mugrowski employed Kurt Gerstein, who produced the bills for 'Zyklon B' that were later put in evidence at Nuremberg. The gas was always bought from two private firms who had acquired the production rights before the war from the great Frankfort chemical combine, I.G. Farben. These firms were Tesch and Stabenow, of Hamburg, and 'Degesch,' of Dessau. The former were supplying Auschwitz at the beginning of 1944 at the rate of two tons a month,[97] but Hoess's recollections were all of deliveries by Degesch, whose lading bills, produced at Nuremberg,[98] showed that Auschwitz received three-quarters of a ton a month between February 14th and May 31, 1944. Hoess had to collect the crystals from Dessau by lorry after obtaining a special permit from the Inspectorate at Oranienburg*

Hoess recollected receiving ten tons of 'Zyklon B' from Degesch alone, but at the Hamburg trial of March, 1946, the partners Bruno Tesch and Karl Weinbacher, of Tesch and Stabenow, pleaded that two tons a month were not excessive for disinfecting such a huge group of camps as Auschwitz; nevertheless, the British military court decided that such quantities could not have been supplied without a knowledge of their true purpose. An alternative plea that SS orders could not be refused was likewise dismissed and the partners were hanged.[100]

Far different was the fate of Dr. Gerhard Peters, manager of Degesch. In 1948 his evidence had cleared the I. G. Farben

*The surviving correspondence shows that Gluecks, the Inspector-General—a missing man—used to refer to 'Zyklon B' by its own name, but his assistant, Artur Liebehenschel, who had commanded at Auschwitz for a few months, used a camouflage term, 'Material for the transfer of Jews.'[90]

directors of the charge of race murder, since he had been under oath of secrecy not to divulge the knowledge he acquired in the summer of 1943 from Kurt Gerstein.[101] Concerning his relations with Gerstein, Peters was examined again by the Frankfurt *Schwurgericht* in March, 1949, and by the appeal court a year later. On both occasions he swore that Gerstein had not mentioned mass murder, though he had described to Peters the agony endured by the victims through the 'irritant substances' which were introduced among the crystals as a detecting agent. Peters had formed the impression that the gas was intended for condemned criminals and incurables. And yet, as Dr. Kosterlitz, the Frankfurt prosecutor reminded him, Peters had admitted selling Gerstein enough of the stuff to kill half-a-million people. Were all these criminals and lunatics? Despite that ambiguity, the appeal court would not interfere with Peters's sentence of five years' imprisonment, which was, moreover, back dated to 1947.[102] Dr. Peters is now free. Since he is only fifty-two and his technical credentials are excellent, he is still available to a scientific age that may need another back-room boy.

'Zyklon B' gassing was free of the mechanical breakdowns that made carbon-monoxide gassing so monstrous. Hoess could not recall a single instance of anyone being taken out of the gas chamber alive, yet such a case is recorded with the minute care of a pathologist by Dr. Nyiszli. The subject, a girl aged fifteen, was saved by contact with the humidity of the floor, but she was not permitted to live more than a few hours before she was shot in the neck by Mussfeld, the crematorium commander.[103]

This incident more than confirms Hoess's statement that death might take as long as fifteen minutes, according to the weather and the number of victims in the chamber. Rascher told Captain Payne-Best that in spite of Himmler's humane intentions (*see pages 207 and 208*), it had proved necessary to gas too many people at a time to ensure a regular and instantaneous death for everyone.[104] But if Himmler had really wanted to avoid pain, he would surely have been advised to continue with carbon-monoxide, while using a more efficient generator. Hitler, it seems, had decided after the first experiment at Brandenburg to use *only* carbon-monoxide, and the fact that the Birkenau installation was not capable of dealing with large numbers until August, 1942, suggests that the change over to 'Zyklon B' was viewed with misgiving.

Nevertheless, it was certainly Hitler himself who authorised the improved 'Zyklon B' installations at Birkenau which began working in 1943, for the greatest importance should be attached to Pohl's statement that he had heard that the plans came originally 'from Bouhler's agency.'[105] The ultimate working drawings, however, were produced in the constructional department of the WVHA or SS economic administration. This department, known as 'Amt C,' was in the charge of a very uncommon person, Lt.-General Heinz Kammler, who became in January, 1945, constructional officer for the Wehrmacht as well as for the Waffen SS, having designed the huge rocket bases on the French coast and the underground aircraft factories in Germany, a genius in concrete who was probably responsible for the death of more slaves in the last year of the war than all the years of German concentration camp practice put together. Kammler was one of the first people to be trusted with the secrets of the Final Solution. He had been to Auschwitz on February 27th, 1942, and as a consequence an order for two three-door crematorium furnaces was[105b] increased to five. Henceforward there is a wealth of correspondence concerning crematorium construction at Auschwitz, all pointing to Kammler. But Kammler cannot be questioned, for he disappeared during the last battle in Berlin, where he commanded a division.[106] He seems to have been a man born out of his time. He should have built the pyramids.

The two converted barns on the outskirts of Birkenau village functioned adequately between March and August, 1942, for gassings of more than 300 people at a time were then exceptional.* But in August transports were already arriving from France, bringing such a low percentage of active workers that 700 would sometimes be gassed in a day. It was then that plans were produced for a death factory which could dispose of

---

*The essential difference between the Nuremberg affidavits of Rudolf Hoess (D 749) and the much implicated Birkenau medical officer, Ferdinand Entress (NO 2368), suggests that originally one of the two converted barns was used as a dressing room and that, while this remained the case, the gassings were limited to two or three hundred persons. This was sufficient so long as gassing was restricted to the sick, picked out from the *Krankenbau* at the rate of 500 to 800 a week.

thousands at a time. The initial working drawings for the four great crematoria are in fact dated August 3rd, 1942. They bear the inscription 'Bath establishment for special action.'[107] But construction did not proceed quickly. On January 29th, 1943, Major Bischoff, of the Auschwitz construction department, wrote to Kammler as follows:

'*Crematorium No. 2.* The completed furnaces have been started up in the presence of Engineer Pruefer from Messrs. Toepf (of Erfurt). The planks cannot yet be moved from the ceiling of the mortuary-cellar on account of frost, but this is not important, as the gassing cellar (*Vergasungskeller*) can be used for that purpose. The ventilation plant has been held up by restrictions on rail transport, but the installation should be ready by February 20th'[108]

In fact Crematorium No. 2 was not ready till March 13th. On June 13th it was still the only crematorium of the four which was actually working and the carpentry work was incomplete. On November 6th, 1943, an order for young trees to form a green belt between the crematoria and the camp only mentions Nos. 1 and 2.[109] The working of all four crematoria was not put to the test till the following May.

A letter from Messrs. Toepf to Bischoff, dated February 12th, 1943, shows that in each crematorium there were five three-door furnaces with mechanical stokers, ash tips, and corpse lifts, but in the two larger crematoria the gas chambers were on the same level as the furnaces* to which the corpses were run on the rail-wagon, seen and described by Dr. Ada Bimko.[113] The under-

*There is a wide divergence of opinion on the capacity of these furnaces. The Polish commission of inquiry considered that the four new crematoria between them could absorb 12,000 bodies a day, while Dr. Nyiszli puts the figure as high as 20,000, and Hoess on the basis of 2,000 per crematorium in twelve hours at 16,000.[110] Yet in the Hungarian deportations of May-June, 1944, the entire mechanism was not nearly capable of dealing with even 6,000 bodies a day. The old crematoria, bunkers 1 and 2, had to be commissioned again and huge burning-pits had to be dug in the open (*see pages 428-429*). At the Lueneburg trial Dr. Bendel declared that the five furnaces of Crematorium No. 4, where he worked for months, could only consume 1,000 bodies a day, whereas burning in open pits consumed as many in an hour.[111] Apparently the crematoria were superseded altogether after August, 1944,[112] because compared with the burning-pits they were considered uneconomical.

ground gas chambers of the smaller crematoria were approached by a subway, gently graded, down which Dr. Nyiszli saw fathers of families pushing peramulators.

The aspect of the buildings, according to Dr. Nyiszli, who lived in one of them for six months, was not unfriendly, in spite of the chimneys, so ominously big for a mere bath house. The ground over the gassing cellar was converted into a well-kept lawn, in which stood at regular intervals mushroom-like concrete objects,[114] and these, though they might not intrigue the new-comers very much, were the shafts down which, after methodically unscrewing the lids, the sanitary orderly was to scatter the amethyst-blue crystals when Sergeant-Major Moll gave the order, 'Nah, gib ihnen schon zu fressen' ('Now let 'em eat it').[115]

Slowly the gas escaped from the perforations in the sheet-metal columns. Generally the victims would be too tightly packed in to notice this at first, but at other times they would be few enough to sit in comfort, gazing up at the douches, from which no water came, or at the floor, which, strange to say, had no drainage runnels.[116] Then they would feel the gas and crowd together away from the menacing columns and finally stampede towards the huge metal door with its little window, where they piled up in one blue clammy blood-spattered pyramid, clawing and mauling each other even in death.

Twenty-five minutes later the 'exhauster' electric pumps removed the gas-laden air, the great metal door slid open, and the men of the Jewish *Sonderkommando* entered, wearing gas masks and gum boots and carrying hoses, for their first task was to remove the blood and defecations before dragging the clawing dead apart with nooses and hooks, the prelude to the ghastly search for gold and the removal of the teeth and hair which were regarded by the Germans as strategic materials. Then the journey by lift or rail-wagon to the furnaces, the mill that ground the clinker to fine ash, and the lorry that scattered the ashes in the stream of the Sola. This was the usual and orderly procedure, when each crematorium was not called on to cope with more than a few hundred victims, but in the summer of 1944 the death factory was not so orderly. I quote Dr. Bendel, as he gave his evidence at Lueneburg[117]:

'Now a real hell begins. The *Sonderkommando* tries to

work as fast as possible. In frenzied haste they drag the corpses by the wrists. They look like devils. People who had human faces before I can no longer recognise. A barrister from Salonika, an electrical engineer from Budapest—they are no longer human beings, because, even as they work, blows from sticks and rubber truncheons are showered on them. All the time this is going on, people are being shot in front of the ditches, people who could not be got into the gas chambers because they were overcrowded. After an hour and a half the whole work has been done and a new transport has been dealt with in Crematorium No. 4.'

✻　　✻　　✻　　✻

In the course of this chapter there has been frequent mention of the name of Kurt Gerstein. I will, therefore, conclude with a brief account of his mission—perhaps the most astonishing of the whole war—on which he was sent by the SS Health Department to pursuade Globocnik and Wirth to introduce 'Zyklon B' gassing into the Polish death camps.[118]

On April 26th, 1945, an American intelligence team discovered a German civilian living in a hotel at Rottweil in the Black Forest. He was Kurt Gerstein, a thirty-four-year-old mining assessor and former director of the Duesseldorf firm, Lihmon-Fiume. Gerstein handed the Americans a statement of seven pages, typed in French, together with those gas bills that were to appear at Nuremberg, and then vanished from history.[*]

According to his story Gerstein had been a missionary student. In 1936 he had been arrested by the Gestapo for distributing religious tracts and expelled from the National Socialist Party. Under arrest again in 1938, Gerstein heard of the impending euthanasia plan and resolved to join the SS Health Institute in order to expose it. And so this man, whom Pastor Niemoller

---

[*]It was alleged at the Peters trial that Gerstein was arrested by the French and that he hanged himself in his cell in Fresnes prison. I have found no confirmation of this story. During the international Nuremberg trial Gerstein was considered to be alive and the defence had the right to demand that he be produced in court. His unsworn statement could not therefore be produced in evidence. At several subsequent trials it was successfully challenged by the defence, but a small portion of it was, nevertheless, printed in the official selection of documents from the 'Doctors' trial' published in Washington.[119]

described at the Peters trial as 'a confirmed saboteur'[120] and who had been twice in the hands of the Gestapo, was appointed by Mugrowski in January, 1942, to be head of a department handling 'poisonous disinfectant gases.'

On June 8th, 1942, Gerstein was approached by Eichmann's deputy in Prague, Hanns Guenther, and asked to collect 100 kilos of 'blue acid' from the Prague Kalkwerk factory and take it to a secret destination in company with Professor Pfannenstiel, major in the SS (in fact Lt.-Colonel) and 'Ordinarius for health in the University of Marburg an der Lahn.'* Gerstein and Pfannenstiel made their journey two months later and were received by Globocnik in Lublin on August 17. They were ordered to disinfect the mountains of clothing that had accumulated in the death camps and to devise a scheme for replacing the gas engines with 'Zyklon B.'

This was said to be an order from Hitler who had recently visited Lublin, where he had dined with Globocnik. At dinner Dr. Herbert Linden (*see page 128*) had called Hitler's attention to the danger of future discoveries of the mass-burials and thereupon Globocnik had delighted Hitler by declaring that he would like 'to bury bronze tablets, proclaiming his authorship of the deed.' This must be treated as the hearsay story that it is, but the caution does not apply to Gerstein's description of his own visit to Belsec, his account of the gassings which is so identical with Rudolf Reder's and his portrait of Christian Wirth, walking about with a jam tin full of gold tooth fillings. One may also notice Wirth's two Jewish 'column leaders,' a gold assayer of the Berlin 'Kaufhaus des Westens' and a former captain of the Austrian army, 'Knight of the German Iron Cross, First Class,' who played the violin for him.

After behaving like a maniac at the exhibition of the gassing team's incompetence, Wirth begged Gerstein not to recommend any change. As to Gerstein, he got out of making his 'Zyklon B' test by declaring that the stuff had been damaged in transit.

---

*This person is not an invention but another of the missing men. On October 8th, 1942, Sigmund Rascher wrote to Himmler that he had Pfannenstiel's permission to continue his Dachau 'high altitude' experiments in Marburg University. However, a year later Pfannenstiel wrote to Kurt Blome in the Reich Health Department that he could not take in Rascher because of the necessity for keeping his activities secret.[121]

Wirth then took Gerstein in his car to Treblinka, where the excellent entertainment induced Pfannenstiel, the Marburg professor, to make an after-dinner speech on the 'beauty of the work of *our institute.*' Then they drove to Warsaw.

Gerstein had to spend the night in the corridor of the Berlin sleeper, where he chanced to meet Baron von Otter, an attaché of the Swedish Legation, to whom he made a voluble, almost hysterical, confession. Of this incident many details were recalled by the Baron seven years later, and also the fact that Gerstein visited him again in February, 1943.[122] But the Swedish Government did nothing about it till after the war when an *aide-mémoire* on the incident was sent to the British Foreign Office.

Gerstein had bad experiences of neutrality and its ways. He was nearly arrested again when he tried to approach the Vatican through the Bishop of Berlin. In 1944 he claimed once more to have diverted a large quantity of 'Zyklon B,' when Rolf Guenther wanted to liquidate the Theresienstadt ghetto, a project attested by other witnesses (*see pages 472-3*). Even after the war Gerstein's story got a bad hearing, since the unsworn word of a man on the run could not be evidence at law. Yet there are so many means of checking Gerstein's confession that an historian must accept most of it. It casts a beam of daylight on the grizzly world of the Eichmann commando, 'the Institute,' Globocnik, Wirth, and Bouhler—a world of men without pity or responsibility, because respectable Germans in high office chose to condone them and yet to deny their existence.

CHAPTER 7

The Fate of the Reich Jews and the Fight for Exemption

1. The Deportations from the Greater Reich, January, 1942—May, 1943

THE Gross-Wannsee conference of January, 1942, set no time-limit for the evacuation of the Jews of the Greater Reich, but it would certainly have been swifter and more complete had not Heydrich died on June 4th. Even at the end of May, 1943, when the Greater Reich was officially considered to be 'Jew-free,'[1] the number of pure Jews, living at large, probably well exceeded 40,000, while of some 180,000 Jews, who had been deported since the Gross-Wannsee conference, more than 100,000 had gone to the privileged ghetto at Theresienstadt in Bohemia, where 40,000 still survived.*

In the form that was described to the assembled delegates at Gross-Wannsee on January 20th, 1942, Heydrich's Russian plan was only gradually abandoned. Prevented from sending further Jews to the Russian ghettoes early in March through the intervention of the Transport Command of the Wehrmacht, Heydrich sent his deportation trains as far as the Eastern border of the General Government. This change was undoubtedly arranged to coincide with the opening of the first permanent gassing camp at Belsec. The destination of these transports was described rather obliquely in Goebbels's diary entry of March 27th, which is given at greater length on page 251. Here we may note one sentence[3]:

'The ghettoes which will be emptied in the cities of the

---

*The claim that the Greater Reich was 'Jew-free' in May, 1943, becomes still more illusory if Jews in camps and ghettoes on Reich territory are included. Thus one must reckon more than 90,000 Jews in the Reich city and district of Lodz, more than 50,000 in Auschwitz and other labour camps in Upper Silesia, and 18,000 Russian Jews who, according to Dr. Korherr, worked in the Koenigsberg region.[2]

General Government will now be refilled with Jews thrown out of the Reich. This process is to be repeated from time to time.'

It was not repeated after June or July. Utter chaos, created by the combination of internal and external 'resettlements' in the General Government and the continuous opposition of Governor Frank, stopped the plan. The 'Jewish Reserve' towns and the transit camps became hopelessly overcrowded during the weeks that the deportees, mainly unemployable, waited for the Belsec death factory to function (see pages 140 and 153). Local officials complained that the Reich Jews arrived completely destitute, their luggage, food, and linen having been taken off the train at Lublin.[4] A few were selected for agricultural work at the request of the District Headmen, but the overwhelming majority must have been disposed of at Belsec during the summer, though Rudolf Reder found some Czech Jews in the Belsec Sonderkommando as late as August.*[5]

Large numbers of able-bodied males were taken off the train at Lublin and committed to 'KL Lublin,' the camp that became known to the West as Majdanek. It had first been used as a camp for Jews as late as December, 1941, but at the end of 1942 Dr. Korherr was able to report to Himmler that of 26,300 Jews, who had been registered in the camp, only 7,330 survived. A very large proportion of these obscurely slaughtered people came from the Greater Reich, Slovakia, and France. Most revealing is a list of confiscated watches, dated June 6th, 1942.[9a] The 304 owners belonged to the camp registry series 8607-9579 and with very few exceptions they came from Vienna, the Bohemian protectorate, and Slovakia.

On June 15th, 1942, shortly before the last transports left the

---

*Identification of the 'Lublinland' transports is very difficult. The list, compiled by the Berlin Jewish Restitution Centre, shows that six transports, collected from Berlin, Potsdam, and Frankfurt, left in March, April, and June, either for 'the East' or 'Twarnice' (presumably Trawniki transit camp). They were small transports, since the total number sent was only 3,420. Several transports left Vienna for Opole Wlodawa and Isbica.[6] A number of transports were sent to 'Transferstelle Isbica,' from Prague on March 4th and April 27th[7] and from Duesseldorf and Nuremberg in April.[8] A transport left Cassel for Piaski on April 11th.[9] During this period transports also arrived in 'Lublinland' from Slovakia.

Greater Reich for Lublin province, Eichmann told his department chiefs that 40,000 Jews would go to Auschwitz from
France and Rumania. For military reasons, there would be no
deportations of German Jews to 'the eastern zone of operations during the summer.'[10] But this turned out not to be a
final decision of Himmler's. Between August and October about
1,200 Berlin Jews left for the Riga Ghetto and 2,000 for the oil-
boring camps in Esthonia,[11] while a few thousand reached
Auschwitz from Theresienstadt. The puzzling feature of these
orders is the fact that the first mass deportations to Auschwitz
should have come from the Western countries, rather than from
the Greater Reich and that for a short period the deportation
of German Jews was suspended.

The explanation seems to be that Himmler still felt very
timid about exterminating Reich Jews on Reich territory. A
decree had been published soon after the revival of deportations
from the Reich—on December 11th, 1941—which permitted the
summary execution of Jews and Gipsies who had been convicted
by the police of any trivial offence, and this should have been
an adequate cover for massacre, but it applied only to occupied
territory.[12] Consequently Himmler had to bring his difficulties
to the Fuehrer's notice and on April 26th, 1942, Hitler summoned
the Reichstag in order that they might accord him the right to
abrogate statutory law for the duration of the war. This was done
in a unanimous and public resolution[13] of which, however, no
particularly striking use was made for some weeks. Then in July,
1942, an execution took place in Breslau without previous trial,
the victim being Karl Lasch, who was accused of peculation
while acting as governor of Radom province in the General
Government. This individual execution proved to be the trigger
which released the whole murderous powers of the Reichstag
resolution, for Lasch's chief and friend was Hans Frank, and
Frank was not only Governor-General but *Reichskommissar* for
Justice.

After Lasch's execution Frank made a tour of the German
law schools, advocating the return of constitutional rule (*see
pages 38 and 39*). Thus Hitler was forced to act. On August
20th, four days before relieving Frank of his legal offices, he
replaced the somewhat negative acting Minister for Justice,

Franz Schlegelberger, by a vigorous party man, the People's Court judge, Dr. Otto Thierack. The new Minister was 'authorised to deviate from the existing law in order to establish a truly National Socialist administration of justice.'[14]

To extend the Auschwitz plan to the Reich Jews a blanket sentence of outlawry was needed. Thus a minute, signed by Thierack and dated September 14th, 1942, shows that Goebbels had proposed to him that Jews and Gipsies should be 'unconditionally exterminable.' Goebbels considered that 'the idea of extermination through labour was best.'[15] It is very significant that on July 22nd, a month before his promotion, Thierack had invited Goebbels to lecture to members of the People's Court and that Goebbels had then thundered against the continued existence of some access to the courts by Jews and had predicted the deportation of 40,000 Jewish 'enemies of the State,' residing in Berlin.[16] It is equally significant that Thierack went to Goebbels before interviewing Himmler. It gives some credibility to the statements which Himmler made in April, 1945, to Count Bernadotte and Dr. Kersten that his persecution of the Jews had been forced on him by Goebbels's superior influence on Hitler.[17] Unfortunately, Thierack was never cross-examined on the Goebbels minute. He committed suicide in a British internment camp in October, 1946, on learning that he was to be the chief defendant in the third Nuremberg trial, the trial of the German judges.

On September 18th, 1942, Thierack saw Himmler at his headquarters and it was agreed that, under the heading 'Delivery of asocials for the execution of their sentences,' all Jews, Gypsies, Russians, Ukrainians, and non-Germanised Poles could be committed to the concentration camps without preferring a charge. As Thierack informed Martin Bormann on October 13th[18]:

'The administration of justice can only make a small contribution to the extermination of members of these peoples. No useful purpose is served by keeping such persons for years in German prisons, even if, as is done to-day on a large scale, they are utilised as labour for war purposes.'

Thierack considered it better to surrender such persons to the police 'who can take the necessary measures unhampered by the laws of criminal evidence.'

As Minister of Justice, Thierack had only to renounce his interest in the 'asocials.' To surrender them to the police no decree was necessary beyond his private authorisation. Thereafter the Reich Security Main Office notified the Higher SS and police leaders and through them the Gauleiters that the decree of December 4th, 1941, was superseded and that the regular procedure of the Criminal Code no longer applied to Poles, Eastern peoples, Jews, and Gipsies.[19]

These instructions enabled Himmler to do three things. He had for the first time legal cover for the extermination of Reich Jews on Reich soil, he could press-gang free 'Eastern workers' for his concentration camp factories, and he could pursue his lunatic scheme for the German colonisation of the Zamosc region in Poland (see pages 45 and 246).

Prompt action followed the Security Office instructions of December 4th. On the 14th a round-up of foreign workers was ordered 'by a simplified procedure.'[20] The Ministry of Justice was to arrange the transfer of 35,000 persons to the concentration camps before January 31st, 1943. On December 31st about 12,000 people had been collected, but Kaltenbrunner informed Oswald Pohl that the camp inmates—there were more than 400,000— were dying faster than the rate of reinforcement. Himmler wrote to the Inspectorate that the death-rate must be brought down at all costs. Though 136,700 people had been admitted to the camps in six months, 80,000 of them were no longer alive.[21]

Under cover of the reorganisation programme there began the concentration of the Jews from the Reich camps at Auschwitz. On October 5th, 1942, the Inspectorate at Oranienburg ordered that the Jews in Buchenwald, Dachau, Sachsenhausen, Ravensbrueck, Mauthausen, and Gross-Rosen camps should be exchanged with the Poles and Ukrainians in Auschwitz and Lublin camps.[22]

The numbers involved were very small. Of 40,600 Jews, committed to the concentration camps since the seizure of power, most had died or emigrated.[23] Of the few thousands of survivors only 1,600 were expected to be fit for labour at Auschwitz. Moreover, in Buchenwald the transfer to Auschwitz could be avoided by 'influence.' According to Mr. Christopher Burney, a British officer prisoner in Buchenwald, there were more than five hundred of these German Jews, who had been interned since pre-war days, surviving in Buchenwald in 1945, while Eugen Kogon states that two hundred of them had been exempted from the transfer because they had been trained as bricklayers.[24]

On November 26th a decree of Fritz Sauckel, the Reich Plenipotentiary for Labour, extended the exchange operation to all Jews in recognised employment in Reich territory. They were to be replaced by Poles who were due for expulsion from the Zamosc region.[25] At last it seemed that the resistance of the economic ministries to the SS had been overcome and that the Jews in the armament industry, who had been protected since October, 1941, would now be deported. Nevertheless, since skilled factory workers were not to be had merely by expelling Polish peasants from Zamosc, the Jewish armament workers of Berlin and Breslau enjoyed a reprieve of three more months.

In December 1942, there arrived in Berlin from Vienna the sinister figure of Major Alois Anton Brunner, who had been appointed by Eichmann to the emigration office. This man, who was hanged in Vienna in May, 1946, was perhaps the most successful of Eichmann's deportation experts, for among his other battlefields were France, Greece, and Slovakia. Brunner remains, nevertheless, a fairly intangible personality. M. Dunand thought he looked like a Jew and Dr. Georges Wellers found him 'small, ill-formed, delicate in health, with an expressionless face, but small, spiteful eyes, speaking in a monotonous voice which he seldom raised.'[26]

It was Brunner who introduced from Poland the Jewish *Ordnungsdienst*, the arm-band police who arrested their own brethren on the orders of the Jewish Council,[27] a device which Brunner failed signally to exploit when he was in Paris in the following July (*see pages 306 and 327*). In Paris even the Stateless Jews did not share the resignation, born of ten years of oppression, which permeated the Jews who remained in Berlin. This resignation is expressed only too well in the words of Rabbi Leo Baeck, who was then President of the *Reichsvereinigung*.[28]

'Later, when the question arose whether Jewish orderlies

160

should pick up Jews for deportation, I took the position that it would be better for them to do it, because they could at least be more gentle and helpful than the Gestapo and make the ordeal easier. It was scarcely in our power to oppose the order effectively.'

The entries in Goebbels's diary almost cast doubt on this last sentence. Three deportation trains left on January 12th, February 19th and 26th without attracting attention[29], but in the great round-up in the munition factories on the night of February 27th many Jews who were known in Berlin society were involved. The Wehrmacht factories were surrounded by Himmler's Praetorian Guard, the *Leibstandarte Adolf Hitler*, and the Jews were held under arrest in the workshops till the transports were ready.[30] In the meantime their families were confined to their apartments. But on March 2nd Goebbels had to write that the week-end round-up had not quite succeeded. 'Our better circles, especially intellectuals,' had warned the Jews. Four days later Goebbels was equally angry with the Gestapo, who had continued the round-up during a night of tremendous bombing by the RAF.[31] Finally, after a crowd had demonstrated against the evacuation of a home for aged Jews, Goebbels had to suspend the whole action. 'We can save it up for a week or two.'

Hitler, however, would not stand the delay. On March 9th he complained to Goebbels of the presence of Jewish intellectuals in Berlin. 'After a terrific commotion in artistic circles, particularly among actors, a number of Jews married to Aryans had to be released.[32] These partners of 'privileged mixed marriages' were destined to remain long after March 19th, when the last 306 Berlin Jews left for Auschwitz, and long after May 19th, when Berlin became officially 'Jew-free' with the departure for Theresienstadt of 109 members of the *Reichsvereinigung*, including Rabbi Leo Baeck.[33] But it was not only the Jews in mixed marriages who succeeded in staying on. Officially there were 27,281 Jews in Berlin on February 28th, and of these about 6,000 left subsequently for Auschwitz and 3,000 for Theresienstadt. Of the 18,000 or so who remained in Berlin after May 19th less than half were privileged. The others roamed the streets without ration books or identity cards, precariously sheltered at night by Aryan friends. Goebbels on March 11th underestimated their numbers at 4,000, while on April 18th he complained that Jews, who possessed no exemption certificate, were still to be seen in Berlin publicly wearing the Jewish badge.[34]

Chance has preserved the record of the fate of three transports which left Berlin for Auschwitz on March 4th, 5th, and 13th, 1943. First of all, Hoess, the gaoler of Auschwitz, was told by Gluecks's labour office DII at Oranienburg (*see pages 111-112*) that the first transport would consist of armament workers, who must, under all circumstances, be passed fit for employment, for only in this way could the Bunawerk factory be brought up to strength (*see page 109*); that the transport must be unloaded not in the usual place but as near the factory as possible ; that a perceptible increase of the Bunawerk establishment would be expected within a few days.

On March 5th a report was received at Oranienburg from Lieutenant, later Captain, Albrecht Schwarz, the labour-commitment officer for the Auschwitz outer camps, according to which 1,118 people out of this transport of 1,750 were found to be women and children. All the men were spared for labour and 200 of the women. The rest were ' specially handled.' The average age of those who were spared was fifty to sixty. ' If the transports from Berlin arrive in future with so many women and children, besides old Jews, I do not promise myself much immediate results. "Buna" needs above all things young and healthy bodies.'

Schwarz's pessimistic forebodings were justified. The next Berlin transport delivered 1,128 people, of whom only 485 were spared the gas chamber, though this, too, was an ' armament' transport. As to the third transport, 365 were spared out of 964. Thus, out of 3,842 Berlin Jews, 1,682 were available for Buna-werk. It was the best that could be done in the greatest man-power panic since the outbreak of the war. It had taken the disaster of Stalingrad to mitigate the gassings even this much.[35] Eleven days later, on March 16th, representatives of Krupps met Karl Sommer of this same ' DII ' department to discuss the proposed grenade-fuse factory at Auschwitz. Sommer declared that all Berlin Jews had been sent to Auschwitz about a fortnight ago and that, ' according to the statements of the SS,' they are for the most part in Auschwitz camp.[36]

On March 5th a second transport had reached Auschwitz from Breslau, so that 1,450 people were gassed in a day, a high figure at a time when not one of the four new crematoria was available. The fact that the opening of the first crematorium (*pages 149, 150, footnote*) was delayed till March 13th contributed to the slowing down of the deportations, which went on in the Reich cities till the end of May. Auschwitz became so congested with transports from France, Belgium, Greece, Bulgaria, and Poland that in March the Dutch transports had to be diverted to Sobibor death camp[37] and the transports from Prague, Vienna, and Luxembourg to Treblinka. Fantastic figures of the number of Czech and Austrian Jews, who were gassed at Treblinka in the spring of 1943, have been submitted by survivors of the death camp, who have also spoken of a ' Potemkin ' railway station and of sleeping-car trains.[38] But the actual numbers of Jews remaining in Prague and Vienna at the end of 1942 preclude the possibility that more than two or three thousand were sent to Treblinka. The report of the Commission of Inquiry, conducted after the war by Judge Lukazskiewicz of Siedlice, mentions only two Vienna transports which reached Treblinka on March 23rd and April 1st, 1943— presumably one of these was the transport in which the Nuremberg witness Rajzman believed that a sister of Sigismund Freud had perished.[38a]

Apart from the Treblinka deportations, as many as 25,000 Jews from the Greater Reich may have gone to Auschwitz during the six months of the last resettlement action. Another 8,000 Jews were forwarded to Auschwitz from Theresienstadt. Even so, the proportion of Reich Jews sent to the death camps was small when compared with the quotas of Greece and Holland, which were occupied countries.*

' There are now in the Reich area,' Eichmann wrote on

*It is extremely difficult to assess the number of Jews who were actually sent to death camps. According to the figures presented to Himmler by Dr. Korherr there were, at the end of 1942, 74,979 Jews in the Greater Reich, of whom 51,327 lived in Germany, 15,530 in the Bohemian protectorate, and 8,102 in Austria. Dr. Korherr's second report shows that in April the Jews in the Old Reich numbered 31,910, only 16,668 of whom were Jews in mixed marriages and therefore privileged to remain. The inference is that at the end of May, when the Greater Reich was officially ' Jew-free,' there were many more Jews living at large than the 32,000 officially classed as mixed-marriage Jews.[39]

July 8th, 1943, to Eberhard von Thadden, his new contact man in the Foreign Office, 'only those Jews who are partners in Jewish-German mixed marriages and a few Jews of foreign citizenship.'[40] The former probably totalled approximately 33,000 —the number that survived the war[41]—but they were far from representing all the Jews who were still at large, a great number of whom, as Dr. Korherr admitted to Himmler, 'had to be written off as undiscoverable.' All three capitals in the Greater Reich had their underground Jewish populations. In Vienna, which, as Baldur von Schirach had boasted after Heydrich's funeral, was to be Jew-free at the end of 1942,[42] they were known as *U-boats* and were secretly supplied by the Budapest and Bratislava Jewish communities.[43]

Most of the half-Jews and Jews in mixed marriages survived the war, because Hitler would not tie his hands by permitting sterilisation as an alternative to deportation. In the end the deportation of the Jews in mixed marriages was ordered, but only to Theresienstadt, and the movement did not begin till 1945. In the meantime the 'privileged' Jews of the Greater Reich had led the life of hostages of the Gestapo. Heydrich's ruling at Gross-Wannsee and Thierack's agreement with Himmler had deprived them of the last shred of legal protection. Any trumped-up complaint meant deportation.

Much depended on the co-operation of the Gauleiters with the Gestapo. At Frankfurt the year 1943 opened with a régime of terror when the Gauleiter of Hessen, the ex-postmaster Jakob Sprenger, ordered the monthly arrest of at least a hundred Jews in mixed marriages with their offspring.[44] As a result, the wives of judges and high civil servants, the mothers of serving soldiers, an officer of the First World War, and even a wrongly registered Aryan died in the Auschwitz gas chamber. Among the qualifications for deportation were failure to add the designation 'Israel' when signing a postal order, smoking a cigarette in the street, using a tram, receiving a food parcel, and making up a party of *skat*. If a half-Jew complained that these regulations did not apply to him, he would be told by *Kriminalsekretaer* Heinrich Baab or his like: 'That makes no difference to us. We make our own decrees.'[45] Yet Baab, who was tried by the Frankfurt *Schwurgericht* in 1950, was only one among half a dozen Gestapo officials in Frankfurt, and Frankfurt only one among half a dozen German cities where 'privileged' Jews remained. It must not be overlooked that from the beginning of 1943 no Jew or half-Jew could have any doubt of the meaning of deportation. Baab himself would threaten them with 'going up the chimney' and 'making compost.'

Yet even after May, 1943, there existed skeleton organisations of the Jewish communities of Berlin and Vienna. In March, 1943, when Eichmann wanted to deport the surviving members of the Vienna *Reichsvereinigung* to Theresienstadt, the order was contested by Ebner, the regional Security Police commander. Thus a staff of 180 was spared in order to look after the interests of some 6,000 Jews in mixed marriages and their children.*[46] The staff included a relief committee, most of whose members were killed in March, 1945, when an Allied bomb, carefully aimed, destroyed the Gestapo building in which they worked. M. Georges Dunand, who visited Vienna soon afterwards, found a Jewish community hospital, but the arrival of hordes of sick deportees from Hungary had produced Belsen conditions. In this hospital M. Dunand saw the last synagogue in the Greater Reich[47] (*see page 445*).

2. Theresienstadt, the Privileged Ghetto

On January 20th, 1942, Heydrich announced at Gross-Wannsee that Theresienstadt was under consideration as a special ghetto for Jews over 65 years of age and Jews with serious wounds or high decorations from the First World War. This was a change of policy, for hitherto Jews of these categories had gone to Poland and Russia, Hitler having declared that 'the swine got their decorations fraudulently in any case.'[48] Originally, however, Heydrich had intended Theresienstadt to be a transfer camp for the deportable Jews of Bohemia. He had ordered the evacuation of this 18th-century fortress town on the steep banks of the Bohemian Eger on November 24th, 1941, eight weeks after

*Nevertheless, some forty members of the Vienna *Reichsvereinigung* staff were deported to Auschwitz at the beginning of February, 1944, where, according to the quarantine records-keeper, Dr. Otto Wolken of St. Poelten, almost all were gassed. (Filip Friedman, *This was Oswiecim*, London, 1946, page 24.)

becoming *Reichsprotektor*. Transports of complete Jewish families from Prague and Pilsen actually began arriving in the following January before the civilian population of Theresienstadt had been completely evacuated.

The Gross-Wannsee Conference brought almost immediately the first of the privileged Jews from Germany and Austria, not only the aged and the war veterans, but Jews married to Aryans who had lost their exemption, half-Jews who professed the Jewish faith, senior civil servants, and members of the *Reichsvereinigung*.[49] Then there followed a flood who had merely bought their exemptions. The figures, compiled by the *Reichsvereinigung*, are eloquent. During the year 1942 Theresienstadt received 33,200 Jews from the Old Reich, 14,222 from Austria, and 39,722 from the Protectorate. These numbers may have been four times the number deported in the spring and autumn of 1942 to Poland and Russia.[50]

This state of affairs, brought about by the corruption of the Gestapo, could not go on for ever. At the end of 1942 some 49,392 Jews occupied the living-space of Theresienstadt's 7,000 normal inhabitants, but the number sent there was actually 87,093. Some of these had been forwarded on to Auschwitz or Lublin, for instance 648 Jews who arrived from Berlin in October, but it does not seem to have been a large proportion and Dr. Korherr told Himmler that the principle cause of the loss of 37,000 people was 'the incidence of death.'[51] But even if one allows a figure reduced to 30,000 for those who died in the ghetto, it is still a tremendous death rate. Furthermore, at the end of 1942 there was every prospect of the 50,000 Jews within these narrow walls being joined by the greater part of the 75,000 surviving free Jews of the Greater Reich. Something worse even than the catastrophe of Belsen in April, 1945, was imminent.

It is probable that Heydrich, and after his death Mueller and Eichmann, let this go on, knowing that one day Himmler would have to agree to the evacuation of most of the camp. They tolerated a procedure by which Jews could buy a place in Theresienstadt from individuals like *Kriminalsekretaer* Baab and even pay their own fare.[52] It was called 'protective custody,' but once in Theresienstadt the Jews were in the Gestapo's trap and beyond recall, for Theresienstadt was the private preserve of

Hans Guenther, Eichmann's 'Referent' in Prague.* The only Reich Ministry that affected any interest in it was the Foreign Office, which on three occasions conducted diplomatic tourists over the 'model ghetto.'[53] Through these visits Himmler thought that the gas-chamber rumours had been discounted abroad and in April, 1945, he even used Theresienstadt as his passport to respectability, telling Dr. Norbert Masur of the World Jewish Congress the following:

> 'Theresienstadt is not a camp in the ordinary sense of the word but a town inhabited by Jews and governed by them and in which every manner of work is to be done. This type of camp was designed by me and my friend Heydrich and so we intended all camps to be.'[54]

But from the beginning of 1943 entrance to 'the town governed by Jews' was carefully controlled and exit was by way of Auschwitz and the crematorium chimney, a process which reduced the population to 18,000 by October, 1944. Finally, in the last three weeks of the war, there was a third phase in the history of Theresienstadt, unpredicted by its creators. It became a dump for Jewish survivors from Poland and Hungary, pushed westwards and then southwards by the retreat of the Wehrmacht. During this phase Theresienstadt averted a typhus epidemic and several threats of liquidation, and, on May 11th, 1945, it was handed over to the Russians with 32,000 inmates (*see pages 472-4*).[55]

---

*In 1942 the purchase of a place in Theresienstadt was done through the *Reichsvereinigung* of German Jews, which was controlled by the Gestapo. An accord was reached between the Ministry of Finance and *Regierungsrat* Suhr, the legal expert of Eichmann's office, by which a Jew destined for Theresienstadt transferred all his property to the *Reichsvereinigung*, who were supposed in their turn to indemnify the *Judenaelteste* at Theresienstadt. (Case XI, NG 4583, Ministry of Finance memorandum, signed Maedel and dated December 14th, 1942, printed in *Le Monde Juif*, No. 51).

Economically, Theresienstadt came under the control of Oswald Pohl and the WVHA office and ranked as a concentration camp. As such it figures in all this office's circulation lists. Administratively it came under Eichmann, and the commandants of Theresienstadt were selected from Eichmann's staff. The three successive commandants, Karl Rahn, Alfred Seidl, and Heinrich Joeckl, were tried and executed in 1946-47, together with the deputy commandant, Wilhelm Schmidt. All but Seidl, who was tried in Vienna, were sentenced by the Prague Court.

Inside the compact octagon of Theresienstadt's walls there were no SS guards and no murderous German convicts officiating as *Kapos*. This was the privilege for which fortunes were paid. But as a health resort most German concentration camps could give the 'model ghetto' points. In 1942 only 60 per cent of the inmates—and the aged predominated—had a bunk to sleep in.[56] Labour was compulsory and severe, and the reward bare existence. Young farm workers and mica miners did rather better than on nine ounces of bread, two ounces of potatoes and a watery gruel each day, on which diet one witness was hungrier than in Auschwitz,[57] but in the 'Altesheim,' the huge attics of Maria Theresa's barracks, the aged had merely to die, 16,000 of them in 1942 and 13,000 in 1943. Sometimes 130 would die in a day and the crematorium chimney smoked continuously.[58]

The Jewish autonomy in Theresienstadt, of which Himmler boasted, was a dictatorship in the hands of three experienced members of the *Reichsvereinigung,* to whom in 1943 the Germans entrusted the horrible task of preparing 'resettlement lists.' On December 16th, 1942, Heinrich Mueller, chief of the Gestapo, had circulated an order requiring the delivery in Auschwitz by January 31st of 45,000 Jews, 2,000 of them from Holland, 3,000 from Berlin, 30,000 from the Bialystok Ghetto (*see pages 286-287*), and 10,000 from Theresienstadt. Only a quarter were expected to be fit for labour in Auschwitz and of the Theresienstadt contingent a still lower proportion, for the order specified that 'half should be light workers and half incapacitated people.'[59]

The action was timed to begin on January 11th, 1943, after the railways were free of Christmas-leave traffic. In fact the first three trains left Bauschowitz, the station for Theresienstadt, on January 20th, 23rd, and 26th. On February 17th Gerhardt Maurer of Department DII asked Hoess for a report, adding, as was his custom, that by now the Jews should be at work at the Bunawerk factory or in the construction department of Auschwitz camp.*

---

*It is unfortunate that Maurer, who must have received hundreds of such reports, was not tried at Nuremberg. The indictment of the 'Concentration Camps Case' had already been filed in February, 1947, when Maurer was discovered and arrested. He was not called as a witness but extradicted to Poland, together with Artur Liebehenschel and many others connected with the Auschwitz administration, with whom he was condemned to death on December 22nd, 1947 (*see page 111, footnote*).

We possess the reply, sent on behalf of Hoess by the labour commitment officer, Lieutenant Schwarz—the most complete record of death that has survived from the archives of the crematorium. Out of the first transport 420 had been chosen for work from 2,000 people, out of the second 228 from 2,029, out of the third 284 from 993. The remainder were ' separated and disposed of ' and the dates and numbers carefully entered. Schwarz was rather apologetic that 1,442 males had been ' specially handled,' but there had been more feebleness among the males than among the females, since most of them were children.[60]

The second contingent from Theresienstadt did not reach Auschwitz till March and apparently there was short measure, for Himmler's statistician, Dr. Korherr, wrote on April 19th[61] that 8,025, and not 10,000, Theresienstadt Jews had changed their place of residence since the beginning of the year. These Jews had gone to labour in the East and yet they were the least fit for labour. Months went by and no word was heard from them. The misgivings grew, and in August a Jew actually escaped from Auschwitz and made his way back to Theresienstadt. He told the story of the selections for the gas chamber, alone and in secret, to Rabbi Leo Baeck, the venerable ex-President of the *Reichsvereinigung*, who had reached Theresienstadt in May. Rabbi Baeck has related how he decided not even to tell his colleagues on the Theresienstadt Jewish Council.[62]

About this time, August, 1943, Eichmann brought Eberhard von Thadden of Department ' Inland II,' his Foreign Office stooge (in succession to Martin Luther, then languishing in Sachsenhausen), to conduct a German Red Cross delegation over Theresienstadt.[63] Probably the visitors observed some of the uneasiness in the camp. In any case there was a change in Eichmann's methods between September 7th and 14th, when 4,000 Czech Jews left Theresienstadt for Auschwitz. They travelled in family groups, taking their luggage. At Auschwitz they were accorded six months' quarantine in the isolation section of Birkenau camp. They were reasonably well treated and encouraged to send letters. Freddi Hirsch, their *Lagerleiter*, was even allowed to open a school for the children.

For the sequel we are indebted to a Slovak Jewish doctor, who escaped to Hungary in April, 1944. This man, who was in charge of the Birkenau infirmary records, warned Hirsch that his people had been marked down for SB or 'Special Treatment.' It was known all over the camp. Moreover, the Jewish commando at the crematoria was believed to be ready to mutiny if the Czech Jews could procure arms. But on March 7th, 1944, the day the quarantine was to expire, Hirsch killed himself with veronol and 3,791 Jews went to the crematoria with full knowledge of their fate. At the last moment they were told to send off post-dated letters to their friends and relatives.[64]

At the end of December, 1943, Theresienstadt still contained 38,000 Jews, for the new arrivals had exceeded the number of deaths. The overcrowding was therefore relieved by the despatch of another convoy of 3,000 to Auschwitz, where the same story of the six months' quarantine was repeated. These Jews are clearly shown in the Birkenau camp employment list of May 11th, 1944. One thousand four hundred and fifty-two Theresienstadt Jews were still in the Quarantine Section IIb, but 1,575 were described as 'in readiness for transport' (*Vorbereitung zum Transport*) and this in the officialese of Auschwitz had only one meaning, which was 'waiting for the gas chamber' (*see page 119*). In fact there is substantial agreement that all 3,027 Theresienstadt Jews were gassed on or about June 20th.[65]

There was one more transport to the 'family camp' at Auschwitz, but this was part of the strangest incident in Theresienstadt's history. On October 2nd, 1943, Hitler committed the prodigious error of attempting the deportation of the 6,000 Jews of Denmark, a neutral and sovereign State maintaining diplomatic relations abroad (*see pages 345-351*). Thereupon, worried German officials tipped their Danish contact-men and, as a result, only 360 Jews fell into the net and these it was found politic to send not to Auschwitz but to Theresienstadt, where the Danish king could be assured of their safety.

In April, 1944, Mueller, the Gestapo chief, was pursuaded by Colonel Mildner, former commandant of the Security Police in Denmark, to allow the Danes to send a Red Cross delegation to Theresienstadt.[66] But a population of 34,000 was too big for a 'Potemkin village,' so between May 15th and 18th, while the flower-beds were being dug and the house fronts painted, 2,780 Jews left Theresienstadt for Auschwitz. The young and able were chosen in order to show the visitors that Theresienstadt was a home for the aged and privileged and not a transit camp for 'The East.' More than half were Dutch Jews from recent transports (*see page 340*). But the demands of the 'Jaeger plan' (*see page 422*) intervened to save many of these Jews from the fate of their predecessors. Under the 'Jaeger plan' 938 of the Dutch Jews were picked from the Birkenau 'family camp' at the beginning of July and transferred to the Sachsenhausen camp register. They were sent to work at an aeroplane factory at Schwarzheide, near Senftenberg, in Moravia. A rather larger number of Jewesses were distributed to the factories *via* Ravensbrueck and only a few hundreds were gassed to celebrate the end of the 'Family Camp.'

The Odyssey of a small part of this Theresienstadt group can now be traced, thanks to the researches of the Netherlands Red Cross.[67] They left Schwarzheide camp on foot for Leitmaritz on April 16th, 1945. Then they were put on a train which was bombed and abandoned by its SS guards. Finally, they sought protection in the place they had left a year ago—Theresienstadt, now a camp of the Red Cross.

Soon after their departure, a year previously, a streamlined Theresienstadt was got ready for exhibition to the Red Cross. On a preliminary inspection Mildner had found it overcrowded but decent. As it was calculated that the delegation would not go upstairs, it was sufficient to empty and redecorate the ground-floor barrack-rooms.[68]

The visit of June 23rd, 1944, was a success. There were parcels for all the Danish Jews and a message from the Danish King to Rabbi Friediger.[69] Steengracht von Moyland, who had succeeded Weizsaecker at the Foreign Office in April, 1943, was thanked by the Danish Ambassador, who declared that the delegation had been delighted with the hospital and the Jewish theatre.[70] M. Jacques Sabille suggests that the head of the Red Cross delegation, Dr. Juel Heningsen, was quite aware of the 'Potemkin' nature of the display, though his published report was extremely prudent[71]; so prudent that it evoked protests from Jewish organisations throughout the world and from Geneva there came a request to the German Government that the Red Cross should send an *international* delegation to

Theresienstadt. This request was not granted till April 6th, 1945. By this time Theresienstadt was a different sort of place. The Final Solution had been called off and Himmler was working his passage with the Allies (*see page 466*).

For the ludicrous episode of June 23rd Mueller and Eichmann exacted a horrible vengeance. At a time when the German frontiers had been breeched in the East and West, when the Fuehrer Order may even have been revoked by Himmler (*see pages 455-456*) they ordered a huge deportation from Theresienstadt involving, according to the information which Eichmann's office gave M. Paul Dunand of the Red Cross, 10,000 Jews, but probably rather more.[72] The first transport, which left on September 28th, 1944, consisted of 2,300 volunteers, the working *élite* of the camp, who thought they were going to the German factories. And to the factories they went, but the road lay through Birkenau, where they left 900 in the crematoria, including the President of the Theresienstadt Jewish Council, Dr. Zucker. It was an exceptionally generous selection, but it seems that Doctors Tilo and Mengele were prepared to spare anyone who gave the right answers.[73]

After postcards had arrived from some of the deportees, a transport of wives and children was organised by the widow of Dr. Zucker. It reached Auschwitz early in October, where it was gassed apparently without any selection. Dr. Nyiszli found the dressing-room in Crematorium No. 1 strewn with the permits that authorised these poor people to join their husbands and fathers at their place of work—one of Eichmann's flashes of inspiration.[74]*

*The researches of the Netherlands Red Cross have now corrected the version repeated by so many Auschwitz survivors. There were two specially selected transports of able-bodied men which left Theresienstadt at the end of September, 1944. Among the Dutch element nearly 90 per cent were under fifty years of age. The first of the Theresienstadt wives arrived on October 4th in the third transport, of which 60 per cent were women and children. Dr. Nyiszli's transport seems to have arrived on October 6th, but there was another one, closely similar, on October 8th. With the exception of a dozen or two old men, all were women and children ; nevertheless more than 20 per cent were eligible for entry on the camp books and some of the Dutch women from these two transports have been traced to the registries of the ' Outer Commandos,' showing that a selection did in fact take place. The Dutch name-lists show that in the remaining six transports there was the normal proportion of 20-30 per cent eligible for entry. (*Auschwitz Deel* VI, The Hague, March, 1952.)

And so the deception continued. Even when the camp notables, including the President, Dr. Epstein, and Friedlaender, the Austrian general, were arrested, it was thought that their fate would not be shared by the rank and file.[75]

The eleventh and last transport from Theresienstadt—almost certainly the last Auschwitz transport of all—reached Birkenau on October 30th, 1944. The figures, noted by Dr. Wolken, camp secretary of the quarantine section, were absolutely normal; 216 Jews were admitted to the male camp.[76] It is not known how many of the remaining 732 went to the women's camp.

The 'home for the old-aged' in Theresienstadt still contained 15,000 Jews but they were dying fast. Early in 1945 there appeared 5,000 Czech and German Jews who were married to Aryans. They gave the camp a new character and when M. Dunand arrived on April 6th he found that more than a third of the 20,000 inmates were not of the Jewish faith.[77]

3. Sterilisation

Heydrich's proposal for the Jews in mixed marriages had been neither immunity nor privileged deportation, but sterilisation (*see pages 97 and 98*). According to the surviving minutes of the Gross-Wannsee Conference, this announcement excited no protest, but when the department experts or *Referenten* reported back to their various chancelleries and ministries, a wave of obstruction began to grow. Its aim was very limited. The deportation of Jews to unknown places without any safeguards was not opposed for an instant by Messrs. Weizsaecker, Lammers, Stuckart, and Schlegelberger. However, by involving Himmler and his officials in the complexities of German law, these men sought to create a privileged class of Jew out of those who were nearest their own way of life.

It may be noticed that, while Stuckart for instance welcomed the sterilisation plan on behalf of the Ministry of the Interior, because it would 'avoid an endless administrative task,' sterilisation does not appear among the five resolutions in the Gross-Wannsee minutes. The matter was deferred for a further conference in Eichmann's office on March 6th, at which eleven ministries and chancellories were represented by their experts on the Jewish question. It was resolved that till the end of the war both the Jews in mixed marriages and their offspring, the 'Mischlinge,' should remain in a special ghetto. The operation of sterilisation on both classes would require hospital bed-space equivalent to 700,000 days and must be postponed. Concerning this, there was no major conflict between the civilians and the SS, who well knew what could be made of a 'special ghetto' and were probably never serious about sterilisation.[78]

Martin Luther, who again represented the Foreign Office in person, reported that the conference had furthermore resolved that 'the qualification of being a Jew would be determined exclusively by the Higher Gestapo Regional Headquarters, which had jurisdiction over the Jew in question.'[79] This seems to have been not the resolution of the conference, but the point of view put forward on behalf of Heydrich. In fact there had been in this Holy of Holies of the Final Solution—where even the Gestapo could not enter without a pass—a head-on collision between the civilians and the SS. Gottfried Boley, who represented Hans Lammers and the Reich Chancellory, declared at Nuremberg that several of those present had contested the Gestapo's claim, particularly when one of Eichmann's bloodhounds had explained that the Gestapo would keep records of the half-Jews in order to accuse them of secret radio-listening and similar activities.[80]

Heydrich's claims for the Gestapo particularly injured the competence of Rosenberg's 'Ostministerium' and on March 6th the delegates of this conference received a circular from Georg Leibbrandt of Rosenberg's Political Department, pointing out that, while the Security Police in the Eastern Territories might choose experts on the Jewish question, these experts could only act under the authority of the Commissar-General. On April 27th Rosenberg embodied this suggestion in a very long-winded decree,[81] which Lammers was apparently about to embody in a Reich decree at the time of Heydrich's death. It would have ended the rough-and-ready methods by which for the past year any Russians who looked remotely like Jews—or who had been denounced casually as such—were included in the extermination actions. But Himmler, who was in Reval in Esthonia on July 28th, wrote this furious sentence to Gottlob Berger, his liaison-man with Rosenberg's ministry[82]:

'Do not publish the decree defining Jews. Such foolish precision ties our hands. The Eastern Territories will be freed of *all* Jews. I alone am responsible to the Fuehrer and do not want any discussion. You will receive Lammers's note for the record.'*

This sort of language might do for Reval. It would not do for Germany, where, with Heydrich dead, Himmler was trying to dodge the complications of deporting Jews in mixed marriages besides half-Jews. The sterilisation plan was mysteriously shelved after the conference of March 6th, 1942. Schlegelberger, the acting Minister for Justice, circularised the Gross-Wannsee delegates on April 6th[83] suggesting that deportation or sterilisation might be offered as *alternatives*. Schlegelberger, who was sentenced at Nuremberg on December 4th, 1947, to a life imprisonment, which, as an invalid, he has not had to serve, pleaded that he had done this to spare the half-Jews the fate that might[84] await them in Heydrich's 'special ghettoes' if the resolution of March 6th were adopted. Schlegelberger was thereupon visited by Roland Freisler, the 'People's Court' judge, who warned him not to go any further. 'The Fuehrer does not like this sharp measure of the Reich Cabinet at the present time.' Hitler in fact refused to tie his hands when the moment should come to extend race-murder to the half-Jews.

It was Himmler who tried to revive the sterilisation plan after Schlegelberger's failure. His interest in this went back at least to March, 1941, when Viktor Brack had offered the services

---

*At some moment, it is not known precisely when, Himmler must have climbed down, for eventually—though at a time when very few Jews were left in Occupied Russia—the privileged categories were recognised. On March 5th, 1943, Kaltenbrunner himself circularised all the police commanders in Russia to the effect that Jews, wanted for exchange by the protective powers looking after enemy states, should be exempted from resettlement (Case XI, NG 2652a and *see pages 338 and 391-2*). It is possible that a certain number of Russian Jews, either baptised or in mixed marriages, may have qualified for Theresienstadt. According to Eva Mosse-Noack the camp register in April, 1945, contained the names of Jews from Kiev, Smolensk, and the Crimea. (*Frankfurter Hefte*, ed. Eugen Kogon, March, 1952.)

of the Euthanasia Institute to sterilise—or rather to castrate—
3,000 or 4,000 Jews a day in cheap and practical X-ray clinics.[85]
In June of that year Himmler sent Oswald Pohl and Dr. Grawitz,
of the concentration camp administration, to offer human guinea
pigs to a certain Dr. Madaus, who had published a paper on the
sterilising properties of the plant *Calladium Seguinem.*
Dr. Madaus declined, but Dr. Adolf Pokorny of the RKFDV
office (*see pages 36* and *487*) wrote to Himmler suggesting that
three million Russian prisoners of war could be allowed to survive
and work for the Germans, because *Calladium Seguinem* could
be used to prevent their contaminating good German blood.[86*]

Himmler must have been used to this sort of letter, for just
a year later, on June 23rd, 1942, Viktor Brack explained to him
how two to three million Jews could be preserved to work for
the Reich under his original X-ray plan. According to Brack, the
circumstances had now changed so much that the knowledge of
the victims that they had been castrated was of no consequence.[87]
This, as Brack explained at his trial, was an appeal for mercy
through Himmler's economic instincts and, as a direct
consequence, Himmler borrowed Dr. Horst Schumann of the
Graefeneck Euthanasia Institute to make experiments in
Auschwitz. Schumann—one of the men who have disappeared—
was not put off by failure. It was not till April 29th, 1944, that
Brack's successor, Blankenberg, reported to Himmler that the
X-ray method was quite unsuitable for mass sterilisation.[88]

As early as May 29th, 1941, Professor Clauberg,[†] director of
a gynæcological clinic in Silesia, had asked to be allowed to
sterilise women by injection. Himmler put him to work in

---

*At Nuremberg Dr. Pokorny said that he had been pulling Himmler's
leg—no arduous task—and the court, though they did not believe
Dr. Pokorny, acquitted him. But as to *Calladium Seguinem*, it just would
not grow in Germany, not even in a hothouse.

†Clauberg had a large retinue of internee doctors working for him in
Auschwitz. One of the names, mentioned by witnesses at the 'Doctors'
Trial' in 1947, was that of Dr. Wladyslas Dering, who was discovered to
be still in practice, tending Polish troops in Huntingdon Military Hospital.
Eventually the Auschwitz witnesses were brought to England, but, as they
failed to identify Dr. Dering in Brixton prison, his extradition to Poland
was refused and he now directs a hospital in British Somaliland. I think
these facts should be stated in view of some of the extremely erroneous
accounts that have been published.[89]

Ravensbrueck camp in July, 1942, with a view to finding out how long it would take to sterilise a thousand Jewesses. After a year's work Clauberg reported that he could do it in a day.[90] In reality neither Schumann nor Clauberg, who continued to torture wretched girls in Block 10 of the main camp of Auschwitz right through 1943 and most of 1944, achieved a satisfactory method, though in the early days Himmler was optimistic. Thus on October 7th, 1942, the sterilisation working party was convened again in Eichmann's office, where the SS experts on the Jewish question assured them that 'thanks to the new knowledge' 72,700 'First-Degree Mischlings' could be sterilised even in wartime. The conference then resolved that all mixed marriages should be annulled and that the Jewish partners should be deported, while sterilisation should be offered to their children as a 'gracious favour,' the alternative being deportation to a special settlement where the sexes must be separated for ever.[91]

Just as he had done in April, Hitler delayed the passage of a decree on these lines, which might at some future date stand in the way of the total deportation of the Mischlings.* There was no further move till February or March, 1943, when the sterilisation working party met for the third time in Kaltenbrunner's office. No minutes of this conference have been traced, but Gottfried Boley recollected a declaration by Eichmann that the Mischlings must be sterilised or go to concentration camps. According to Boley, no one present doubted that the Mischlings were really to be exterminated.[92] Yet this meeting brought neither deportation nor sterilisation any nearer for the Mischlings. Even the Jews in mixed marriages were not sent to Theresienstadt till February, 1945. Thus 19,000 pure Jews survived the war in Germany, perhaps 33,000 in the Greater Reich and Protectorate. This does not include those who returned from deportation.[93]

Close on a thousand Jews, married to Aryans, did actually

---

*On July 1st, 1942, Hitler observed at table: 'It would be a shame to the German people if it permitted service in the armed forces to the Mischlings and in this way offered them the possibility of equal treatment with those of German blood. The creation of exceptions for Mischlings should therefore be reduced to the very lowest minimum.' Bormann thereupon sent a message to Dr. Picker, requesting him to note this down carefully. (*Henry Picker, Hitler's Tischgespraeche*, Bonn, 1951, p. 313.)

avoid deportation through sterilisation certificates, but this happened only in Holland. On March 20th, 1943, that is within a very few weeks of the last sterilisation conference in Berlin, mentioned by Gottfried Boley, a memorandum was prepared in the Jewish section of the Gestapo at The Hague, according to which the alternative of deportation or sterilisation was to be offered to the 8,000 Dutch Jews in mixed marriage. Himmler was also to be asked for a ruling concerning 21,000 Dutch Mischlings, ' since no measures of this kind have been taken in the Reich.'[94] On May 5th Dr. Zoepf, Eichmann's agent in Holland, learnt from the commandant of the Security Police, Brigadier Harster, that compulsory sterilisation would start in Vught camp. In Westerbork, the transit camp for Auschwitz, this actually happened. Some of the exempted Jews were told that, if they did not accept the operation, they would be sent with next Tuesday's deportation train ' and you know what that means.'[95] Two witnesses, who had been sterilised under these conditions, appeared in 1949 at The Hague trial of Captain Ferdinand Aus Der Fuenten, but as a rule the victims were sterilised by their own physicians. By June 28th, 1943, there existed an album of regulations, approved by Seyss-Inquardt, the *Reichskommissar* for Holland. Those who were certified barren by a Gestapo doctor received a special identity card, were freed from wearing the Jewish badge, and could pursue a restricted range of employments.[96]

On July 9th, 1943, a bombshell fell. The BBC's ' Radio Oranje' service published the regulations in full. Rolf Guenther, Eichmann's deputy, at once summoned Werner of Zoepf's office to Berlin and declared the amazement of the Main Security Office that such an action had begun in Holland without their knowledge. These Dutch Jews would have to be deported, whether sterilised or not. But it leaked out during the conversation that Guenther did not know of Himmler's private arrangements and, in fact, there was an understanding between Himmler and his Austrian friend, General Hanns Rauter, the Higher SS and Police Leader for Holland.

As late as the following January the Main Security Office was still trying to get the sterilised Dutch Jews into the assembly camps. At this time Zoepf's office recorded more than a thousand certificate holders, freed from wearing the star. On March 2nd

Rauter personally informed Himmler that 8,610 Dutch Jews in mixed marriages were at liberty.[97] Rauter agreed that those who had not borne children, should be sent to the East, but the certificate holders were no danger to Germany and should be left free.

At his trial in 1947 Rauter pleaded that in writing this letter to Himmler he had no choice, since Erich Naumann, the new Security Police commander, would not carry on the struggle with the Main Security Office, which had been begun by Harster before his transfer to Rome. The Dutch Jews in mixed marriage were therefore interned. A few were deported and several disappeared in Auschwitz, but the sterilisation-certificate holders were not molested. Apparently Rauter, an old Austrian firebrand of the *Freikorps* days and rather a simple man (*see pages 330 and 336*), never realised that the sterilisations were mostly a fraud. The stamped cards, that freed the owners from wearing the Jewish badge, had for the most part been sold them by Gestapo agents.

This curious history throws some light on Hitler's complete failure to eradicate Jewish blood by extending the Final Solution to the partners of mixed marriage and their children. Even at the end of the war, when all pretence of the existence of civil rights had been abandoned in the Third Reich, it was only possible to deport a few thousand Jews in mixed marriage and those, too, under privileged conditions. Had Germany won the war, the climate would have been still more unfavourable for extending the Final Solution. This, like the euthanasia programme for the insane and incurable, was one of Hitler's defeats.

Part II

The Final Solution in Practice

CHAPTER 8

The Soviet Union I. The Einsatzgruppen

1. The Commanders

IN January, 1946, a queer witness took the stand at the international Nuremberg trial. He was then thirty-eight years old and of such an attractive appearance that two years later, when he was on trial for his own life, women spectators sent bouquets to his cell. But on this, his first appearance, it was not the good looks of Otto Ohlendorf that electrified the court but his avowal, made firmly and without equivocation, that he had ordered the execution of 90,000 people, most of them for the crime of being Jews.

Later, Ohlendorf was to back out of this statement by deposing that the 90,000 executions had been reported to him by subordinates whose reckoning he had no reason to trust. But the numbers were immaterial, since Ohlendorf justified himself on ethical grounds. The future, he predicted, would find his firing squads no worse than the press-button killers of the atom bomb,[1] and had not the same God who gave the Ten Commandments also ordered the Israelites to extirpate their enemies? Thereupon Ohlendorf read the court ten foolscap pages of historic precedents down to 'the extensive descriptions of Schiller and Ricarda Huch' concerning the massacre of gipsies in the Thirty Years War.[2]

Ohlendorf, unlike his six 'Red-Jacket' companions who were hanged with him in Landsberg Gaol on June 8th, 1951, was an intellectual. Trained as a lawyer and an economist, he had joined the Security Service in 1936 from the Institute for Applied Economic Science.[3] Having risen to be head of 'Amt III' of the Main Security Office, he suddenly interrupted a bureaucratic career in June, 1941-June, 1942, to command that extermination unit, functioning behind the Eastern front, which was to land him in the Nuremberg dock. And from this assignment the 34-year-old major-general went quite quietly to the Ministry of Economics, where he became manager of a committee on export trade and delegate to the Central Planning Board.[4] Funk, the Minister for Economics, did not even know that Ohlendorf was a major-general of police or that two years ago he had been a mass executioner, to whom General Ritter von Schobert of the 11th Army would not speak except in the passage.[5] Ohlendorf, in November, 1943, could be compared to a young Oxford don, transferred to the wartime Board of Trade. Even at his trial five years later he still looked that part. But in the last months of the war the horrors of Nikolaiev and Simferopol became even more remote from Ohlendorf's preoccupations. He was now one of the liberal figures in Himmler's entourage, looking with a benevolent eye on the July plotters and chosen by Walter Schellenberg to figure on a Cabinet list which was to make a Himmler Government presentable to the Allies.[6]

The Nuremberg judgment compared Ohlendorf to 'Dr. Jekyll and Mr. Hyde,' but that combination[7] was commonplace in the Third Reich, which inherited from the Weimar Republic an inability to separate the Judiciary from the Executive, the pen from the sword. Ohlendorf had changed to Mr. Hyde, not on the South Russian steppe but in the Prinzalbrechtstrasse in 'Bureau III,' where the twenty young people working under Professor Hoehn' of May, 1936, had become by September, 1939, a far more impressive organisation.[8] 'Bureau III' was no longer a kind of Citizens' Advice Bureau, but an intelligence service peering into the lives of every inhabitant of the Greater Reich. Gallup polls and quizzes, those little parlour games of an age of thinly sugared regimentation, had found their true outlet in a secret police inquisition. The rather old-womanish SD or Security Service had passed through Heydrich's fingers and become the long arm of the Gestapo.

Of the distinctions between the Security Police and the SD and of the numerous ramifications of the Main Security Office, RSHA, the Nuremberg court could never make very much. They were part of the necessary labyrinth of official murder. The court ruled that the SD was a criminal organisation equally with the Gestapo and that any branches of Heydrich's RSHA organisation

Soviet Union, showing maximum Territory occupied by the Germans, 1941-1942.

185

which did not come under either heading were small, few, and insignificant.[9] The SD's so-called information services had full executive powers and its so-called research workers were full-blown secret police agents.

Heydrich was nevertheless more interested in counter-espionage than in his assignment to carry out the Final Solution. He was a career intelligence officer who had held the same post in the navy as the famous Admiral Canaris. It was Heydrich's ambition—though it was only his successor Kaltenbrunner who fulfilled it—to unite the counter-espionage departments of the Wehrmacht and Foreign Office with the counter-espionage section of the Main Security Office. This ambition sprang less from a love of military intelligence work than from the jealous watch, maintained by the SS on the military leadership ever since the days of the Roehm *Putsch*. The *Einsatzgruppen* were formed as much to watch the conduct of the military leaders in Russia as to murder Jews, Gipsies, and political commissars. A young counter-espionage officer could best please Heydrich by volunteering for his *Einsatzgruppen*. Most of the hundred or so officials who attended the three-weeks' training course at Pretzsch on the Elbe near Leipzig, which began at the end of May, 1941, were as a consequence recruited from the ' information ' branches of the RSHA. There was hardly time to turn them into military-looking personages, although twenty-four of them were at once made majors and colonels of the SS. One former *Einsatzgruppe* officer said at his trial that the Pretzsch course had consisted of ' terrain exercises, apparently games of hide-and-seek.'[10]

It was thus a queer intellectual riff-raff which stalked the rear areas of the Russian front in the following months, even if profusely jack-booted and armed with unlimited authority. None of the four group commanders had more than 600 to 900 men serving under him, yet their spheres of activity covered areas as big as the Baltic States, White Russia, the Ukraine, and the Crimea-Caucasus.

Ohlendorf, who was in Russia for exactly a year, commanded group D at the extreme southern end of the front. To the north lay group C, which was commanded in June, 1941, by the former Security Police inspector for Koenigsberg, Otto Rasch. This elderly man, who was declared unfit to plead in September, 1947, on account of Parkinson's Disease, deposed in an affidavit[11] that he learnt of the full meaning of the Fuehrer Order only at the end of August, 1941. This was when Lieut.-General Franz Jaeckeln, the Higher SS and Police Leader, arrived in Zhitomir in the Ukraine. Rasch claimed that he at once started for Berlin in order to protest personally to Heydrich, but in Cracow he changed his mind and tried to telephone. Failing to get through to the Prinzalbrechtstrasse, he had to go back to Kiev, where he arrived in time for the great massacre at the end of September. Shortly afterwards Rasch quarrelled with the Civil Commissar Erich Koch and succeeded in indefinitely prolonging his leave in Germany. Quite late in the war he refused the post of Higher SS and Police Leader for France-North Italy in favour of a peaceful life as Mayor of Wurttemburg and a director of the company, Continental Oil AG, proving in that not-too-frozen Siberia that one could quarrel with Heydrich without being beheaded.[12]

Einsatzgruppe B, which operated mainly in White Russia and the area of the Moscow front, was commanded by Artur Nebe, a personality combining even more contradictions than Ohlendorf's. A police detective under the Weimar Republic, Nebe had been in the Gestapo since 1933. The reorganisation of September, 1939, made him chief of the fifth branch of the RSHA, the criminal police or *Kripo*. When *Einsatzgruppe* B was formed, it was expected to police Moscow, and this explains why so important a person as Nebe accepted a command of only 700 men. In November, 1941, when this prospect receded, Nebe returned to his office in Berlin and his place was taken by Erich Naumann, a minor technical expert from Ohlendorf's department. These five months spent by Nebe in Russia are not mentioned by his friend Hans Berndt von Gisevius, who has made almost a saint of his old chief in his book *To the Bitter End*. Another member of the German 'Resistance,' Fabian von Schlabrendorf, writes solemnly that the massacres of Jews in Nebe's area were carried out by other commanders, for Nebe was all this time in touch with the 'resistance circle' at Central Army Group Headquarters, which was led by Colonel Oster. And yet the operations report, which credited Nebe's group with 45,476 executions during the five months of his command, was prepared by one of his own Criminal Police officials, Dr. Knobloch.[13] Moreover, the claims made on behalf of Nebe were absolutely contradicted at Nuremberg by the Higher SS and Police Leader for the Central Army Group Area, Lieut.-General von dem Bach-Zalewski, according to whom Nebe, as a direct representative of Himmler, was the chief obstacle to his own interventions.

This general was present at an execution near Minsk, where Himmler ordered Nebe to devise a new method for mass killings,[14] and it is at least curious that the only film showing the working of a gas chamber should be found in Nebe's former Berlin flat.[15] Even Gisevius admits Nebe's complicity in this matter. The gas-chamber plans were discussed at daily luncheons at RSHA headquarters between Ohlendorf, Mueller, Schellenberg, and Nebe.[16] The horrible cynicism of these conferences exhausted Nebe so much that he had twice to go on sick leave with a nervous breakdown. In July, 1943, Nebe became a 'human wreck suffering from persecution mania.' If this, according to Gisevius, was Nebe's condition already in July, 1943, it is interesting to see what the former extermination-group commander was doing a year later, three weeks before the plot against Hitler, in which he is alleged to have taken part. On June 28th, 1944, Nebe wrote to the SS Medical Service, offering 'Asocial gipsy half-breeds' from Auschwitz camp for experiments in drinking sea water.[17]* The fateful July 20th passed and Nebe went underground to escape the proscription of the 'Resistance Circle,' but his sporting offer still stood. On the night of August 2nd nearly half the inmates of the 'Gipsy camp' at Auschwitz were gassed, but 915 young men were picked out for Buchenwald and from these the sea-water drinkers were selected (see pages 119 and 448).

Even if Nebe exaggerated his massacre figures to please Himmler, and even if he experimented in mass killing methods

---

*Similar orders by Nebe were seen at this time by Eugen Kogon, in the serum preparation block at Buchenwald.[18] Yet in the last English edition of his book Eugen Kogon retracts his statement that Nebe's connections with the resistance group were due only to opportunism. Without condoning Nebe's acceptance of an *Einsatzgruppe* command, Kogon is now prepared to recognise good intentions in Nebe from the beginning.

only under pressure, he still accepted the rank and the pay, and he did the job. If Nebe's moral scruples amounted to no more than this, he must have been a very craven man, an impression confirmed by another German witness, the SS judge Konrad Morgen, who described how Nebe ran from the room in terror when he disclosed his investigation of the Auschwitz mass murders to Nebe's chief, Ernst Kaltenbrunner[19] (see page 453).

Finally, even Nebe's rôle as a hero of the resistance movement may be an alibi. He was last seen by his friend Gisevius in July, 1944, but he was not arrested till February, 1945. The allegation that Nebe was then summarily hanged rests on the testimony of his friends alone.[20] The mighty mandarins of the RSHA, Schellenberg and Ohlendorf, have exhibited their credentials as resistance fighters and peace negotiators with the Allies. Nebe's friends have done better; they have put his martyr's crown in evidence.

The fourth of the original *Einsatzgruppen* commanders, Franz Stahlecker, who led group A to the Baltic provinces and the Leningrad front, was a less discreet person than Nebe, since he signed at least one of the massacre reports himself. According to Ohlendorf, who recognised his style in the notorious Nuremberg documents 'L 180' and 'PS 2273,' Stahlecker used to exaggerate —and Stahlecker may have had good reason to placate Heydrich this way, for his assignment to an *Einsatzgruppe* was a demotion. He had been head of 'Amt VIa,' the foreign intelligence department of the Main Security Office, a post he may have lost through his intrigues to supplant Martin Luther, Heydrich's contact man in the Foreign Office.[21] The rather shadowy Stahlecker, who was killed in a partisan action in March, 1942, never got back to 'Amt VIa,' where he was replaced by the meteoric Walter Schellenberg.

The soured Ohlendorf, who had seen him at Nuremberg in the rôle of a 'white' witness, declared at his own trial that 'Schellenberg would have taken any opportunity to choose an *Einsatzgruppe*, in which he would have done his utmost to please Himmler.'[22] That Schellenberg opposed the massacres is unlikely. At the end of the war he told the Finance Minister, Schwerin von Krosigk, that the liquidation of the Jews was in itself desirable, but 'since only a third of the Jews were in our hands and the remainder lived outside our reach, the method of dealing with the Jews was worse than a crime. It was a stupidity.'[23]*

If Schellenberg, the suave hero of the kidnapping incident at Venlo, had avoided an extermination-group assignment, it was surely because he perceived a better path of advancement. The readjustment of the RSHA office at the beginning of the Russian campaign gave him control of *two* counter-espionage departments, sections IVa and VIa. A brigadier at the age of thirty, Schellenberg was *de facto* chief of the entire foreign intelligence service when Himmler and the SS finally extricated it from the hands of the Wehrmacht and the Foreign Office. In this way Schellenberg became in February, 1945, Himmler's right-hand man, parrying the force of Kaltenbrunner and urging Himmler to make peace with the Allies. He was the sympathetic character in a white collar who arranged Himmler's interviews with Count Bernadotte[24] at the end of the war (*see page 462*).

It may not prove possible to determine the share of responsibility of this sleekest of Gestapo men for the massacre of Russian Jewry. Schellenberg, who was examined at Nuremberg immediately after Ohlendorf, admitted that he was present in May, 1941, when Heydrich and Quartermaster-General Wagner established the zones of authority of the *Einsatzgruppen*. Later Schellenberg testified that the final draft of the agreement between the RSHA and Wehrmacht was his own handiwork (*see pages 81 and 82*). Even then he had not been able to discover the true nature of the Fuehrer Order concerning Jews and political commissars, which was only communicated orally to the commanders of extermination units.

After this declaration more than three years were to pass before Schellenberg was finally declared not guilty of conspiring in the 'genocide' of the Jewish race.[25] Schellenberg took his stand, as he had done as a witness at the first Nuremberg trial, on the plea that he was never an executive officer but always

---

*It may be objected that this evaluation of Schellenberg's attitude reposes on the word of one man, but it is well confirmed in a memorandum from the Foreign Office, dated May 14, 1943. Schellenberg had heard of the forthcoming British White Book on atrocities in Poland and learnt that it had been proposed to approach the Vatican for materials. He therefore asked von Thadden to prepare a simple and effective explanation for the solution of the Jewish problem in case an Italian group should visit Russia or Poland. (Case XI, NG 4943, printed in *Le Monde Juif*, No. 52, February, 1952.)

concerned with 'information.' Only in one case was the court able to prove that 'information' was a cloak for murder. The evidence concerning the *Einsatzgruppen* had disclosed a horrible game, known as *Aktion Zeppelin,* played by officials of Schellenberg's Amt VI of the RSHA.[26] Certain captured Russian officers were induced to spy on their compatriots in captivity, the object being to detect political commissars who could be summarily executed under the Fuehrer Order. When these Russians were considered to know too much, they were themselves shot by the *Einsatzgruppen* or delivered to the Political Department in Auschwitz main camp to be shot in front of the cork wall adjoining Block 11. For being perfectly cognisant of these murders Schellenberg was sentenced in April, 1949, to six years' imprisonment, but the sentence was backdated and in December, 1950, they liberated the man who had lunched daily with Kaltenbrunner and Mueller. Since Schellenberg was a laborious diarist, there should be a market for his memoirs, edited with what his friend Himmler called 'that tact which is a matter of course and which, I am glad to say, is inherent in us.'[26a]

2. Devolution of Authority

In contrast to the ambitious active men who commanded the *Einsatzgruppen,* the subordinate officers were mostly social misfits. Erwin Schultz, for instance, was, like eight of the twenty-two *Einsatzgruppen* case defendants, a trained lawyer, but he had to forsake the law to be, like his father, an ordinary policeman. Ernst Bieberstein, who joined the Gestapo to spy on the clergy, had left the Lutheran ministry to found a 'Brotherhood of Love.' Vladimir Klingelhoeffer, an opera singer from Cassel, had been reduced to spying on 'cultural activities' before he used his bilingual capacities as a Russian-born *Volksdeutscher* to get into an *Einsatzgruppe*. Lothar Fendler was an army dentist without a job and Voldemar Radetzky a Baltic German, thrown on his beam-ends by the repatriation of 1940. Strauch, the butcher of Minsk, had to become a bank clerk in spite of his lawyer's degree, and Blobel, the expert on exhumation and cremation, had been an architect, ruined by drink. He had joined the Gestapo 'when down to his last shirt.'[27]

This lost legion of unemployed intellectuals had glued themselves to the office desks of the SD since 1933 only to find themselves in the summer of 1941 on the muddy roads of Russia and in the uniform of the *black crows*. There was even one case of *downward* promotion through ideological zeal. Professor Franz Six* abandoned the Economic Faculty of Berlin University, of which he was dean, to become a reporter to the SD on scientific matters and the chief of a commando under Nebe. Six was sent to collect archives from the Kremlin, but, failing to reach his destination, spent 25 days in Smolensk tracing captured political commissars for execution. A plea that he remained 'always a scholar and never a policeman'[28] did not save Professor Six from a twenty-year sentence, which the changed temper of the age commuted in the year 1951 to one of ten years. This, in fact, meant freedom a year later.

The strangest thing about the careers of these men was the ease with which they could quit. Otto Rasch, as we have seen, arranged comfortably to overstay his leave. Heinz Jost, a former director of Amt VI of the RSHA, who took the place of the dead Stahlecker in March, 1942, left his post after three months and became Rosenberg's liaison man with Field-Marshal Kleist. For his dereliction of duty Himmler's only revenge on Heinz Jost (who still retained his police rank of Major-General) was to send him to the front in May, 1944, as a Second Lieutenant.[29] Similarly Brigadier-General Erwin Schultz, who left his commando in September, 1941, when Franz Jaeckeln arrived with the Fuehrer Order, got himself relieved of his command without fatal consequences.[30] Then there was Colonel Jaeger at Riga, who had a collapse when confronted with Jaeckeln's order for the " Bloody Sunday " massacre and was simply transferred by Stahlecker to another commando of the same group.†[31]

*Franz Six, like the commander of his group, Erich Naumann, concealed himself in the disguise of a day-labourer as late as the summer of 1946 (Affidavit No. 4546).

†Rudolf Diels, chief of the Gestapo till April, 1934, deposed at Nuremberg as a prosecution witness that paragraph 47 of the decree concerning military criminal law empowered a commander to refuse a mass execution order. Then, perhaps rather proud of the fact that he had escaped Heydrich's ill-intentions in 1934, he cited his own case. In 1941 he had refused the Gauleiter's orders to arrest Jews in Hanover and had suffered no penal consequences beyond ceasing to be a *Regierungspraesident*. He also men-

An impression is created by Ohlendorf's original Nuremberg evidence that the entire Jewish massacre programme in Russia was carried out by less than 3,000 men—and a few women—serving in the combined *Einsatzgruppen*. This is by no means the case. As the directors of a vast, largely locally recruited, murder organisation, the *Einsatzgruppen* took credit for all that this organisation achieved. But the two Field-Marshals, Brauchitsch and Manstein, emphasised at Nuremberg that the *Einsatzgruppen* were intended to prepare for the political administration of the country.[32] Thus, as soon as a civilian Government was set up in occupied territory, their function changed radically.

Most of the original personnel went to areas near the front, where they had to deal with partisans, but a number of the commando leaders, retaining only skeleton staffs, were attached to the civilian *Reichskommissars* and *Landkommissars*, with the title of Commander of the Security Police (*Bds*) or Local Commandant of the Security Police (*Kds*). In theory they were part of the machinery of civil administration. In practice they took most of their orders through a devolution of command from Himmler and Heydrich, sustaining endless feuds with the civil powers who had been appointed by Rosenberg's Ministry, but whom they were singularly unable to depose.

Most of the massacres of Russian Jews took place after the establishment of these permanent police offices. The *main d'œuvre* consisted mainly of *Selbstschutz* units, non-German militia trained by the *Einsatzgruppen*, but it was found expedient after the first exuberant native pogroms not to recruit too locally. Great numbers of Lithuanian volunteers were sent to Polish, Latvian, and White Russian territory. The Lithuanians were particularly amenable for this sort of work, but different methods had to be used in White Russia in the summer of 1942, when a powerful partisan movement offered an occasional loophole of escape to those of the able-bodied Jews who had survived. The drunken, unreliable Lithuanians were replaced by entire

tioned a certain Graf Faber-Castell, who had refused to shoot 500 Jews in Poland and had not even been dismissed his regiment. (Case IX, No. 5821, Affidavit Diels, printed in *Le Monde Juif*, No. 52, February, 1952). The former chief of the Gestapo, Rudolf Diels, is now an under-secretary in the Bonn Ministry for Interior (September, 1952).

German regiments of *Ordnungspolizei* or regular police, operating sometimes in considerable field formations with, as in the case of the Pinsk Ghetto action of October 29th, 1942, the support of regular troops.[33] The commanders of the Security Police borrowed such troops from the 'Koreucks,' or Rear Area Commands, and several 'Koreuck' reports enumerate Jews who were handed over to the SD, but sometimes a 'Koreuck' would instigate actions on its own, such as the slaughter of the Jews of Glebokie in White Russia in July, 1942. It would seem that by this time the original *Einsatzgruppen*, reduced from four to two and operating far to the east as combat groups,[34] were quite out of the picture.

A problem, by no means cleared up at the Nuremberg trials, is the rôle in this sombre business of the individuals known as 'Higher SS and Police Leaders.' In Germany they were the SS counterpart of the Gauleiters of provinces. As the war spread, more HSPFF were appointed—in Cracow, Warsaw, and Lublin, in Oslo, Paris, and The Hague, in Belgrade and Athens. In Russia there was an SS and Police Leader to each of the three army groups and one for 'special duties.' Their status was determined by a Himmler order, as long before the campaign as May 21st, 1941.[35] This order made them supreme in police matters and under the direct command of Himmler and Heydrich. The *Einsatzgruppen* commanders, who held the rank of 'Commanders of the Security Police and SD' (*Bds*), were definitely subordinate to them.

Thus several *Einsatzgruppen* commanders have described the way in which they were harried by Lieutenant-General Franz Jaeckeln, Higher SS and Police Commander to the Southern Army Group, to carry out massacres of Jews. Jaeckeln gave orders for the massacre of Hungarian Jews at Kamenetz-Podolsk in August, 1941, the massacre of the Dniepropetrowsk Jews in October, and of the Riga Jews in November-December[36]—the bill already exceeds 50,000 deaths.*

With this, the record of a dead Higher SS and Police Leader,

---

*Jaeckeln was one of six German generals, all local commanders, who were tried by a People's Court in Riga on February 3rd, 1946, and hanged in the former ghetto the same afternoon.[37] Such proceedings are not conducive to historical research.

may be contrasted the self-compiled record of a live one, Erich von dem Bach-Zalewski, who was HSPF to the Central Army Group till the end of 1942, when he was made chief of all units engaged in anti-partisan warfare. He was a professional soldier of a Junker military family, who willingly gave evidence at Nuremberg against Himmler and his own fellow police chiefs. As to the *Einsatzgruppen*, though one of them under Nebe operated in his area, von dem Bach-Zalewski claimed he could not give Nebe orders and he had to 'contrive' in order to get hold of any of the notorious *Einsatzgruppen* reports.[38] Personally he always opposed the murder of Jews and Slavs, while in Baranovice and Mogilev he had deliberately set up his headquarters in the Jewish part of the town. If subsequently the Jews of Mogilev were wiped out, it was because he had left.[39*]

The same plea of incompetence to intervene in anti-Jewish measures was repeated by Rauter and Oberg, the HSPFF for Holland and France, and even by Juergen Stroop, who suppressed the Warsaw Ghetto Rebellion. Though Stroop bound his daily massacre figures in an elegant leather album (*see pages 275-276*), he testified at Nuremberg that the killing was done by the Security Police Commander, over whom he had no authority.[40] In this way the patent absurdity of Stroop's case ruined the similar pleas, advanced by his colleagues in other areas.

3. The Complicity of the Wehrmacht

If Himmler's picked police generals could exonerate themselves from the guilt of massacring Jews, how much more so the field-marshals and generals of the Wehrmacht, who maintained that their hands were tied by the agreements which had been made between the High Command and the RSHA in March-June, 1941. German generals and German advocates, pleading

---

*Nevertheless, the circulation lists of the *Einsatzgruppen* reports show that von dem Bach-Zalewski had his headquarters at Mogilev on November 19th, 1941, a full month after the liquidation of the ghetto. Von dem Bach's services as a Nuremberg and Warsaw witness saved him from extradition to Russia. He was sentenced by an Ansbach court in March, 1951, to ten years' 'special labour,' which in practice meant residence in his own home at Laffenau in Franconia. Von dem Bach-Zalewski claimed that it was he who had smuggled cyanide to Goering's cell in 1946.

for the High Command, have repeated endlessly that the men with the SD flashes on their sleeves were not soldiers and not under army orders; that Himmler's protection was complete, that they could not be removed from army areas. On the opposite side, the *Einsatzgruppen* commanders have described cases where they had to take orders from the army, while three high SS officers, witnesses for their organisation, reproached the commanders of army groups and armies for their cowardice in failing to stop the executions.[41]

This criticism has plenty of substance. Some commanders issued orders forbidding units to assist in actions conducted by the SD, but the normal attitude was less positive. On August 5th, 1941, when some hundreds of Jews were murdered by Latvian militia at Rositten, von Kuechler, of the 18th Army, informed the nearest divisional commander that the SD alone were responsible. The divisional commander then instructed his staff to see that throughout his command no criticism or opinion was expressed.[42] But among the Rear Area Commands even this negative attitude was not permissible, since the SD disguised their Jewish massacres as anti-partisan actions in which the Wehrmacht, particularly the *Feldgendarmerie*, was obliged to assist.[43]

One massacre was conducted with such flagrant publicity as to attract the attention of Central Army Group headquarters in Smolensk. It took place in Borissov on October 19th, 1941, shortly after the headquarters had been moved from that town. A commando of Stahlecker's *Einsatzgruppe* A entered Borissov, which was in Nebe's territory, and killed off the whole Jewish population numbering 7,620.[44] A secret report by an intelligence sergeant[45] shows that the occasion was organised as a 'festival of the German police,' in which the SD and the White Russian militia, led by a Volga-German schoolmaster, got drunk together in the town café, the Jews knowing perfectly well the fate that was in store for them. The old Army Group headquarters was the execution ground, German soldiers looked on, and Wehrmacht units were employed to cordon the ghetto.

When the news reached Smolensk,* several staff officers

* Fragments of a diary of a high official of Admiral Canaris's Ausland Abwehr, who travelled in his company, reveal a further discussion of the Borissov massacre at Bock's Headquarters on October 25th. Here it was said

approached General von Bock, urging him with tears in their eyes to take some action to defend the honour of the army. Von Bock protested that he could not proceed against the SS with arms. All he would do was to order Fabian von Schlabrendorf to draw up a memorandum for Hitler on 'these unheard-of crimes.'[46] Nevertheless, von Bock's successor, Guenther von Kluge, had no difficulty in the following May in expelling the SD from his front area, where their behaviour was a menace to security.[47]

Sometimes army commanders issued elaborate manifestos which were intended to reconcile their men to what they might see. Such the order of the day to the 6th Army, published on October 10th, 1941, by Field-Marshal Walter von Reichenau[48]:

> 'The soldier in the Eastern Territories is not merely a fighter according to the rules of the art of war but also the bearer of a ruthless national ideology . . . therefore the soldier must have understanding of the necessity of a severe but just revenge on sub-human Jewry.'

There was not much doubt what this meant. Every soldier of von Reichenau's command knew that there had been a tremendous killing of Jews in Kiev at the end of September as a reprisal for the mining of the city by the Russians (*see pages 233-235*). The wording of von Reichenau's order was copied by von Kuechler of the 18th Army and von Manstein of the 11th[49]; Manstein's order was dated from Simferopol on November 20th—a few days before the first liquidation of the ghetto.[50] This is the more remarkable since Manstein, a severely professional general, was indifferent to National Socialist aims and theories and in great disfavour with Himmler, who devoted much energy to searching his family tree for Slav contamination.*[51]

that the 7,000 Jews were liquidated in the manner of 'sardines tinned in oil,' and that even the SD were only able to carry on 'thanks to an immense consumption of alcohol.' (NOKW 3146, partly printed in *Le Monde Juif*, No. 50, December, 1951.) (For another extract of this diary *see page 234*.)

*Mr. R. T. Paget, K.C., M.P. (*Manstein, His Campaigns and His Trial*, London, 1951, page 166) has made much of the fact that Manstein struck out parts of the Reichenau order and substituted some unexceptionable instructions for the behaviour of his troops. What Mr. Paget omits to say is that Manstein left von Reichenau's sentence, which I have quoted, quite unchanged.

In December, 1949, Manstein was acquitted by the British military court in Hamburg of two indictments concerning the massacres of Jews, but in this connection he was found guilty of neglecting to protect civilian life. The words ' deliberately and recklessly' were struck out.[52] Ohlendorf, who had claimed that most of his 90,000 murders were committed when attached to the 11th Army, was not produced as a witness. Manstein had already answered Ohlendorf at Nuremberg in August, 1946, but Ohlendorf repeated his charges next year at his own trial and in 1948 as a witness in the ' High Command' trial. In fact, neither Ohlendorf nor Manstein were in a position to be considered reliable witnesses. In this welter of recriminations General Eisenhower's alleged statement that ' the German soldier never lost his honour' seems more than ever premature and irresponsible.

The situation was full of contradictions. Thus, Otto Woehler, Manstein's Chief of Staff, protested that there were officers who made a practice of watching executions, and he ordered Ohlendorf to do his business away from the immediate neighbourhood of Manstein's GHQ. Ohlendorf complained that Woehler refused to call him by his rank.[53] Yet it was Woehler who gave Ohlendorf his marching orders and initialled his reports.[54]

At a lower level it was von Salmuth, commander of Manstein's XXXth Corps, who called in Ohlendorf's bloodhounds for the massacre of the Jews of Kodyma, in Transdniestria, supplying for the purpose 300 of his own men and issuing directions for future collaboration in such matters.[55] Von Salmuth duly reported all this to Manstein, yet it was Manstein's contention that he never saw any such reports and that his duties at the front ' left him no time for curiosity on matters on which he could have had no idea.*[56]

*I record—but purely as a footnote—Ohlendorf's many times repeated assertion that, when Manstein removed his GHQ to Simferopol, in the Crimea, he was asked to speed up the liquidation of the Jews ' in order to relieve the housing shortage,'[57] that Manstein was so friendly with Ohlendorf at this time, Christmas, 1941, that he repaired the insults of Ritter von Schobert by inviting Ohlendorf, together with the HSPF, Udo von Alvensleben, to spend the week-end in his castle. Manstein's reply was to deny that he had seen Ohlendorf's face except in Nuremberg prison.[58] The palpable indecency of permitting Ohlendorf to give evidence against the German High Command, after his own death sentence had been passed in April,

There were also cases when the SD complained that the army was doing their work for them. Thus *Einsatzgruppen* report No. 119 mentions a two-day action on September 22nd, 1941, in the ghetto at Uman in the Ukraine. There had been 1,412 victims, instead of 8,000 as anticipated, because the Ukrainian population, together with German soldiers, had already frightened the Jews away by sacking their houses. As a result, the action of Commando No. 5 was 'seriously impaired,' and the report goes on to say that Field-Marshal von Rundstedt, commanding the Southern Army Group, had been informed of the participation of army units in these excesses.[59]

The complaint was acknowledged next day by von Rundstedt, whose headquarters were in this very town of Uman,* in an open order to his troops[60]:

'Action against Communists and Jews is only to be undertaken by the special commandos of the Security Police and SD who carry out such orders on their own responsibility. Participation of members of the armed forces in Ukrainian excesses against the Jewish population is forbidden, also the witnessing and photographing of the measures taken by the special commandos. This order must be made known to the personnel of every unit. All officers and NCOs are responsible for carrying it out.'

Field-Marshal von Rundstedt—now so respectable that he has been impersonated in an American film as a benign but testy old gentleman—owes it to his age and health that he was never brought to trial on the serious charges that were preferred against him. In the light of those charges there is nothing surprising in this order, of which it can be said that not even

1948, was not repeated at Manstein's trial, which was a model of fairness. On January 31st, 1951, von Salmuth's sentence of twenty years' imprisonment was reduced to twelve years, in keeping with Manstein's. Woehler's eight years' sentence had already been considered as served.

*Guenther Blumentritt, Rundstedt's Chief of Staff, is naturally reticent on the subject of these events in Uman. Oddly enough he quotes a long passage by Rundstedt himself explaining how friendly the Ukrainians of that town were with the Wehrmacht. The subject of this reminiscence is a romantic intervention on behalf of a Ukrainian girl who had run off with a German corporal. (*Von Rundstedt, the Soldier and the Man*, London, 1952, *page 115*.)

Pontius Pilate was so anxious to avoid publicity. It was not only that men on leave showed these tasteful snapshots to Lisa and Dorotea—a suggestion that is contained in Otto Woehler's order of July 22nd, 1941[61]—but that men got captured by the Russians with the things in their pockets. Not that anything could stop the Russians knowing. Rosenberg's representative at von Bock's headquarters complained that Jews crossed the lines in sledge wagons and kept the Russians posted.[62] Colonel Haenisch told the Kharkov People's Court that even Hitler knew that documents concerning the gassing vans had fallen into Russian hands.[63]

4. Civilian Responsibility and the Russian Ghettoes

The *Einsatzgruppen* reports consist of daily situation bulletins (*Taetigkeitsberichte*) and monthly résumés (*Ereignismeldungen*). The series finishes at the end of March, 1942. It was followed by a series of weekly reports covering the whole of Eastern Europe, which were more discreet and offered the Nuremberg prosecutors little material. The original series consisted of nearly two hundred reports with a circulation list of sixty to a hundred copies each. They emanated from an obscure office of the Gestapo, directed by Colonel Kurt Lindow, where a certain Dr. Knobloch received the daily code telegrams from Russia and edited them.[64]

It is not easy to see why the murderers left such an abundant testimony behind them, for in spite of their wide circulation list, Knobloch's reports seem to have been designed primarily to appeal to Himmler and Heydrich.* Thus, in addition to much juggling with the daily death bills in order to produce an

*Among the recipients was von Weizsaecker at the Foreign Office. It is possible that the Foreign Office complained of the indiscretion of the reports, for the Nuremberg copy of the 11th monthly résumé covering March, 1942, is accompanied by a note from Heydrich to Ribbentrop with the observation ' submitted for jurisdictional reasons.'[65] Colonel Lindow, who also issued warrants for executing Russian prisoners of war, avoided extradition to the Soviet Union by giving evidence for the Nuremberg prosecution. He was arrested by the Frankfurt *Schwurgericht* in March, 1950, while officiously giving evidence for Heinrich Baab on a charge of murdering prisoners of war (*see pages 164-165*). Lindow is still (late 1952) awaiting trial.[66]

impressive total, there are some rather amateur essays in political intelligence work. These are of some interest to the historian for the light they shed on the evolution of Gestapo methods.

It is, for instance, almost Heydrich's own words that one seems to be reading in the long special report, sent to him in October, 1941, by Franz Stahlecker. They describe the pogrom that occurred in Kovno three days after the invasion[67]:

> ' It was desirable that the Security Police should not put in an immediate appearance, at least in the beginning, since the extraordinarily harsh measures were apt to stir even German circles. It had to be shown that the native population took the first initiative by way of reaction to several decades of suppression by the Jews and against the terror recently exercised by the Communists.'

The purpose was to show that the Germans were creating an *orderly* solution of the Jewish problem. Thus on October 25th, 1941, Wetzel, the Jewish expert in Rosenberg's Ministry for the Eastern Territories, advocated permanent gas chambers because the massacres in Vilna had been public (*see page 131*). The Rumanians gave the *Einsatzgruppen* even better excuses for intervention. Daily Situation Bulletin No. 25 of July 25th, 1941. reads[68] as follows:

> ' There would be nothing to say against numerous executions of Jews if it were not that the technical preparation and the method of execution is defective. The Rumanians leave the executed people where they have fallen without burying them.'

According to Ohlendorf,[69] the Rumanians failed to kill the Jews outright and let the rich ones escape. This was the real objection to local murder organisations. Without discipline or ideological urge the mere expectation of plunder would not make the men kill enough. On January 31st, 1942, Stahlecker contrasted the 5,000 Jews killed in Lithuania by the native militia with the 136,421 killed by his own commandos. ' The enthusiasm of the local inhabitants waned,' he complained to Heydrich.[70]

An improvement in extermination methods became possible with the creation of self-governed ghettoes and the registering of their population through a Jewish council—that is, after the Rosenberg Ministry had set up civil government in the rear of the armies. It was Rosenberg's contention at Nuremberg that his Ministry had no hand in police measures in occupied Russia and indeed the pretensions of the RSHA seem to have been a permanent anxiety to the Ministry. But so far as the Jews were concerned, the differences between the *Ostministerium* and the RSHA were differences of detail and not of intent. Rosenberg had shown that his policy would be in line with Heydrich's within three days of his appointment—on June 20th, 1941, when he issued the 'Brown Folder.'[71] This states that pogroms by the native population must not be stopped unless military security is at stake, that Jews, who have moved into the border provinces during the Russian occupation, must be 'eliminated by Draconian measures' and the rest confined to ghettoes.

The ghettoes were the responsibility of Rosenberg's commissars, at the head of whom was Hinrich Lohse, *Reichskommissar* to the combined Baltic States and White Russia. Lohse reached Kovno at the end of July but later set up his headquarters in Riga. With his ludicrous walrus-like appearance the former Gauleiter of Schleswig-Holstein looked like a small-town party boss and acted the part. Peter Kleist, a Foreign Office representative, has made a full-length portrait of this comic Satrap, allowing him one virtue—humanity towards the Jews.[72] But in Kovno on July 27th, 1941, Lohse delivered an address to his staff which suggests that this virtue may be insisted on too much. Lohse told his men that the ghettoes would receive only as much food as the rest of the population could do without; that, though the regulations of the Rosenberg Ministry were published in a 'Brown Folder,' they were only meant to be applied 'when further measures towards the final solution of the Jewish problem were not practicable' and they would not interfere with his own oral instructions to the Security Police.[73] These instructions were fulfilled so much in the spirit that Lohse's officials were known in Kovno by General von Roques's staff as 'The Headhunters.' Later Lohse made some attempts to intercede for essential Jewish workers, but the survival of the 'Ostland' ghettoes for two whole years owes little to him. The chief cause of this most unexpected development was the demand of the

Armament Office under General Thomas for Jewish labour* and, secondly, the arrival of Jews from the Reich. As long as official pressure was brought to bear on Heydrich and Himmler to spare the survivors of the Reich Jews, the ghettoes gained a reprieve even during the appalling blood bath in White Russia in the summer of 1942.

Ghettoes which were permitted in some sort to survive according to this revised policy were not treated as summarily as other ghettoes. Since it was intended to spare the lives of employable Jews, secrecy was necessary and some element of hope had to be created for the victims. This was not the case in the Ukraine and much of White Russia, where a single action sometimes settled the whole question. For in the Ukraine most of the employable Jews had escaped or had been evacuated by the Russians, and their families and dependants who remained behind were easily disposed of. When the Russians recovered these towns in 1943-44 they found not the barest skeleton of a Jewish community left.

In most Ukrainian towns a *Judenrat* was created solely for the purpose of an extermination action and, after it had registered and assembled the flock, it was exterminated in its turn. Where the *Judenrat* seemed unlikely to lend itself to the deception, it was the first group to be murdered. Thus at Winnitsa in August, 1941, Commando 4b 'adopted a novel method.'[74] The leading Rabbi was told to produce the Jewish intelligentsia within twenty-four hours. The number being insufficient, the Jews were told to go back and bring others. After the third summons 146 leading Jews of Winnitsa were available for execution.

In sharp contrast to Winnitsa, a *Judenrat* organisation survived in Kovno till July 25th, 1944, and three members were alive at the end of the war.[75] Basically, however, the procedure of 'Resettlement' was the same everywhere. Jews who could produce no sort of protection certificate were collected in market places or large buildings, herded into trains, buses, lorries, or

*Colonel-General Georg Thomas, the friend of Ulrich von Hassell and a member of the Wehrmacht 'Resistance Circle,' was arrested in July, 1944, but never brought to trial. After the war his position was secure and he refused to acquire credit with the Allies as a Nuremberg prosecution witness. He has since preserved a silence which does him honour but which an historian must regret.

sledge carts and taken to the woods or moors, where the burial pits had been prepared. If the latter were not ready, they were kept for days in any prisons or barracks that were available, such as the Zentralka and Laticheva prisons in Riga, the Lukishki prison in Vilna, the Turkczynski fortress at Minsk, Fort No. 9 near Kovno, or the 'No. 10 Tractor Plant' outside Kharkov. But in smaller places the procedure was much simpler. There was often not even a registration and the circumcision test, a Semitic appearance or a neighbourly denunciation was enough. Thus numerous Tartars, Gipsies and people of Oriental appearance were often included. Not till April 27th, 1942, did Rosenberg attempt to amplify his original instructions, and even then Himmler rejected the extremely vague list of tests which he proposed and forbade the police to publish it[76] (*see page 175*).

5. Executioners and Methods

In the larger ghettoes there was a careful apportionment of duties. Local militia under the orders of a German Security Police Commandant surrounded the ghetto and guarded the assembly-point inside it. The Jews, whose names were listed by the Jewish Council for resettlement or who possessed no protection certificate, were rounded up in their homes by the Jewish *Ordnungsdienst*. Absentees and unaccountable persons were routed out of their hiding places under floors, stoves, and rafters by German police troops, with bloodhounds. Those who were found were killed on the spot, sometimes by the thousand. Thereafter the 'resettled' Jews were driven to the burial pits, where the actual shooting was invariably done by German police troops, usually operating in squads of twelve. The favourite weapon was the Schmeisser or Sten gun, but often ordinary magazine-rifles were used, with pistols of small calibre for the *coup de grâce*.

The execution-places were remote from the towns and elaborately cordoned, though secrecy was seldom achieved. Thus Bernhard Loesener, *Referent* in the Ministry of the Interior, was shown a letter describing the horrible way in which Reich Jews were killed in the Riga forest (*see pages 97 and 218*). We learn from Eugen Kogon that these details had been quite common talk among the German Luftwaffe staff who were stationed near the killing-place.[77] Major Roesler of the 58th Infantry Regiment complained to General Schirwind, commanding the IXth Army Corps, that the Zhitomir massacres of July, 1941, were witnessed by men in rest billets. These men lounged about in open shirts, gazing into the mass graves where the living struggled with the dead.[78] Von Rundstedt's order confirms the use that was made of the soldier's *Leica* on such occasions. Despite the prohibition, issued by Himmler on November 12th, 1941,[79] many snapshots have survived the war. Those published by Dr. Steiner of Bratislava illustrate all the stages of a mass execution,[80] the huge pit with people undressing, the naked women queueing with babies in their arms to pass the shooting-point, the layers of corpses with the *Sonderkommando* wading among them in order to give the *coup de grâce* with their Schmeisser guns.

These photographs could be the very scene witnessed by the German civilian works engineer, Hermann Graebe, on the disused Dubno Airport in the former Volhynian province of Poland on October 5th, 1942. The words of Graebe's affidavit, which froze the Nuremberg Court with horror and pity when read by Sir Hartley Shawcross on July 27th, 1946, should in no respect be abridged[81]:

'. . . An old woman with snow-white hair was holding this one-year-old child in her arms and singing and tickling it. The child was cooing with delight. The parents were looking on with tears in their eyes. The father was holding the hand of a boy about ten years old and speaking to him softly; the boy was fighting his tears. The father pointed towards the sky, stroked the boy's head, and seemed to explain something to him. At that moment the SS man at the pit shouted something to his comrade. The latter counted off about twenty persons and instructed them to go behind the earth mound. The family I have described was among them. I well remember the girl, slim and with black hair, who, as she passed me, pointed to herself and said: "Twenty-three years old."

' I then walked round the mound and found myself confronted by a tremendous grave. People were closely wedged together and lying on top of each other so that only their heads were visible. Nearly all had blood running over their shoulders from their heads. Some of the people shot were still moving. Some lifted their arms and turned their heads to show that they were alive.[*] The pit was already two-thirds full. I estimated that it held a thousand people. I looked for the man who did the shooting. He was an SS man who sat at the edge of the narrow end of the pit, his feet dangling into it. He had a tommy gun on his knees and was smoking a cigarette. The people—they were completely naked—went down some steps which were cut in the clay wall of the pit and clambered over the heads of those who were lying there to the place to which the SS man directed them. They lay down in front of the dead and wounded. Some caressed the living and spoke to them in a low voice. Then I heard a series of shots. I looked into the pit and saw that their bodies still twitched or that their heads lay motionless on top of the other bodies before them. Blood ran from their necks.

'I was surprised that I was not ordered off, but I saw that there were two or three postmen in uniform near by. Already the next batch was approaching. They went down in the pit, lined themselves up against the previous victims and were shot. When I walked back round the mound, I noticed that another truckload of people had arrived. This time it included sick and feeble people. An old, terribly thin woman was undressed by others, who were already naked, while two people held her up. The woman appeared to be paralysed. The naked people carried her round the mound. I left with my foreman and drove in my car back to Dubno.

'On the morning of the next day, when I visited the site, I saw about thirty naked people lying near the pit—about thirty to fifty metres away from it. Some of them were still alive ; they looked straight in front of them with a fixed stare and seemed to notice neither the chilliness of the morning nor the workers of my firm who stood around. A

---

[*]May not this gesture of the dying have expressed something that the living could not perceive ? ' *Tendebantque manus ripae ulterioris amore ?* ' (Virgil. Aeneid, Book VI, 314.)

girl of about twenty spoke to me and asked me to give her clothes and help her escape. At that moment we heard a fast car approach and I noticed that it was an SS detail. I moved away to my site. Ten minutes later we heard shots from the vicinity of the pit. Those Jews who were still alive had been ordered to throw the corpses into the pit, then they themselves had to lie down in the pit to be shot in the neck.'

Hermann Graebe noticed that no one screamed or begged for mercy or attempted escape. Colonel Paul Blobel, who directed Commando 4a at Kiev and Zhitomir, decided that this was because 'human life with these people in the East was less valuable than it is with us. They did not know their own human value.'[82] A truer explanation lay in the closeness of the family ties of the Eastern Jew. The Germans could always rely on the refusal of individuals to take flight, when it meant abandoning parents or children. The able-bodied and unattached usually tried to escape, as many *Einsatzgruppen* reports record. Sometimes large groups would break away from the edge of the killing-pit into the forests, where for most of them the chances of survival were small. Many were driven to return to the ghetto to face the next pogrom. The strangest case was that of a girl, Bassia Beker, who escaped the death pit at Kostolpol, thirty miles from Dubno, to become an 'Aryan' Pole working in Germany.[83]

The state of mind of the victims, who meekly stripped, shovelled a layer of sand over the twitching bodies of their kinsfolk, and then lay patiently, naked in a temperature below zero, to await a shot in the neck, was nothing but the normal resignation of the condemned. The state of mind of the executioners invites much more speculation. Ohlendorf seemed to think that he had robbed the executions of their horror by making them less interesting[84]:

'Undressing was not permitted, the taking of personal possessions was not permitted, publicity was not permitted. As soon as it was observed that a man experienced pleasure in carrying out these executions, it was ordered that he should partake in no more executions. The men could not report voluntarily. They were ordered.'

Ohlendorf's adjutant was Heinz Schubert, a descendant of the family of the composer, who entered the SD straight from the *Hitlerjugend* and who was only twenty-five when he came to Russia. In 1948 he described with the big-eyed earnestness of a trained retriever the traffic patrols and road diversions with which he had concealed the Simferopol massacres. 'I knew that it was of the greatest importance to Ohlendorf to have the persons who were to be shot killed in the most humane and military manner possible, because otherwise the moral strain would have been too great for the execution squad'—and Schubert repeated the words, '*seelische Belastung*'—the moral strain.[85]*

In the beginning they worried about such things—even Himmler. Von dem Bach-Zalewski told how in August, 1941, Himmler ordered Nebe to carry out in his presence the execution of a hundred inmates of Minsk prison.[86] Von dem Bach-Zalewski watched Himmler closely during the action, saw him stagger at the first volley and almost fall to the ground in a swoon. He observed that, when these raw executioners failed to kill two Jewish women outright, Himmler lost his head and shouted.[87] As a result of his experience, Himmler instructed Nebe to devise more humane means of mass killing. The final result seems to have been an order in the following spring, mentioned by Ohlendorf, to kill women and children only in gas vans.[88]

Von dem Bach-Zalewski claims to have lectured Himmler after this execution near Minsk, telling him that the firing squad were now ruined for life, that they were destined to become either nervous wrecks or ruffians. The latter was the greater probability, for though *seelische Belastung* might afflict some men in the special commandos, it did not afflict them long—and this we may conclude from the strange tale of Alfred Metzner, told in Augsburg Prison, in October, 1947.[89]

Metzner was a Russian *Volksdeutscher*, born in Kiev in 1895, who came to Germany after the First World War to lead the life of a rolling stone, at one time a sailor, at one time a Berlin taxi-driver, at one time married to a half-Jewess. Called up in 1941,

---

*Schubert's death sentence was commuted in February, 1951, to one of ten years' imprisonment. On top of this, he enjoyed full rights of remission and he was one of the twelve prisoners released by the Americans from Landsberg on January 4th, 1952. (*Le Monde Juif*, No. 53.)

he was posted to the Rosenberg Ministry as an interpreter and labour overseer, and at the end of July sent to Slonim in White Russia, where there were more than 20,000 Jews. Almost his first duty was to drive a lorry-load of Jews to the killing pit. He found the executioners drunk and some of them searching the naked living bodies in the most obscene manner for valuables. He saw pregnant women shot in the stomach and many people buried alive. Next day Metzner drove another lorry-load of Jews, who, seeing the blood-bespattered bodies of the previous day's work, tried to escape.

In the extermination campaign of the following year Metzner served in an actual firing squad. He was attached to the *Sonderkommando Amelung*, which was composed of 70 Germans and 130 Latvians. It is not clear why, as a civilian *Stabsleiter*, Metzner should be either ordered or permitted to do this, but he seems to provide the answer in his own allegation that railwaymen, soldiers, and a certain Herr Muck in his own office volunteered 'because something was to be made out of the actions.'

In Metzner's first 'action' 1,200 Jews of the neighbouring community of Shirowitz were to be 'resettled' and a practice shoot was held a few days in advance to test whether the fusillade could be heard in the ghetto. The actual execution lasted three or four hours and Metzner paused only to load his carbine. He could not count his victims on account of the cross-fire of the platoon, but 400 or 500 Jews were buried in a single pit in six layers. 'During this time we drank a lot of Schnappes to keep our spirits up.' In the lower layers the half-killed Jews were suffocated by the weight of bodies and drenched in their blood. 'No one could survive this way.' The graves were afterwards filled in by the neighbouring villagers.

In September-November, 1943, there were still handfuls of Jews surviving in the ghettoes of Slonim, Baranovice, and Nowogorodek. In the face of the overwhelming Russian advance Himmler decreed the liquidation of all such tell-tale traces. The townspeople helped to drive the Jews out of their concealed 'bunkers.' Jews were shot point-blank with Verey-light pistols and Metzner (with Herr Muck) hurled grenades into the cellars. The dead in the streets and the living in the bunkers were included in the last conflagration of the Slonim Ghetto. At

Baranovice dogs rooted out the too-hastily-buried corpses. At Nowogorodek Metzner's special commando did its work without any issue of Schnappes 'out of idealism.'*

The Slonim region was governed in 1941-44 by *Gebietskommissar* Errer, an assistant of the famous Wilhelm Kube at Minsk (*pages 93 and 224*). Errer had a satisfactory hobby. From time to time he would make members of the Slonim Jewish Council bring valuables to his office-desk and then shoot them. Metzner knew about this and at the end of 1943 Errer managed to get him posted to Berlin. Metzner was then released from the Rosenberg Ministry and in June, 1944, appointed interpreter to an East European variety troupe, run by the Ministry of Propaganda. Then came the capitulation. Metzner lived for two and a half years on the black market, a man among many who possessed a past but no identity.

Metzner's story shows how men could be tempted into the extermination commandos by the prospect of plunder. There were also other advantages. The *Sonderkommandos* did not go to the front. They received home leave every three months, at least treble pay, and a brandy ration. Even so, it was not always possible to recruit the commandos from volunteers, and apparently it was not thought desirable to man such small and isolated units from the gaols, as was done in the case of the Dierlewanger special anti-partisan brigade. There remained another source of recruits—the soldier in trouble.

How this was done was explained to Himmler's masseur, Dr. Felix Kersten, by Major-General Georg Keppler, commanding the SS division 'Das Reich'[90]:

'They are late or they fall asleep on sentry duty. They are court-martialled but are told that they can escape punishment by volunteering for special commandos. For fear of punishment and in the belief that their career is

---

*There were, nevertheless, one or two survivors from Nowogorodek and, if the account published by Joseph Tenenbaum is accepted, the *Sonderkommando Amelung*, who did their work 'without Schnappes out of idealism,' could not have had too easy a time. The 223 remaining Jews of the now completely enclosed ghetto tunnelled their way out on September 23rd and had to be rounded up in the neighbouring forest. (Joseph Tenenbaum, *Underground, the Story of a People*, New York, 1952, p. 370.)

ruined anyway, these young men ask to be transferred to the special commandos. Well, these commandos, where they are first put through a special training, are murder commandos. When the young men realise what they are being asked to do and refuse to take part in mass murder, they are told that the orders that have been given them are a form of punishment. Either they can obey and take that punishment or they can disobey and be shot. In any case their career is over and done with. By such methods decent young men are frequently turned into criminals.'

General Keppler should have known what he was talking about. His Panzer-Grenadier Regiment No. 4 was responsible for the massacre at Oradour-sur-Glane, while the 92nd daily report of the *Einsatzgruppen* gratefully acknowledged the help on September 9th, 1941, of a commando of the SS division 'Das Reich' in liquidating 920 Jews of Lachoisk near Minsk.[91]

That man with a cigarette in his mouth, a tommy gun on his knees and his feet dangling into the death pit—might he not have been just one of those mild-eyed corn-haired POWs, rather wistful in their patched tunics, who peopled the English countryside in the post-war years?

CHAPTER 9

The Soviet Union II. The Massacres

1. The Baltic States

On June 22nd, 1941, at the zero hour of the invasion of the East, the German armies faced a string of Russian-occupied territories, stretching from the Baltic to the Black Sea. All had experienced a peasant-bourgeois form of government since the end of the First World War. All had just endured from twelve to twenty-one months of Soviet rule.

For the people of the Baltic States, who had returned to the bosom of Russia after twenty-two years' emancipation, the change was far more violent than it was for the Ukrainians and White Russians living in Eastern Poland, many of whom had welcomed the Soviet system as a relief from Polish landlordism. No such situation existed in the Baltic States, where only the most ill-adjusted part of the population could benefit from the change of rule. Therefore and because of the Western orientation of the Baltic States, the Germans expected the population to be influenced by its experiences towards National Socialist ideals. For some months at least the Germans were not disappointed. The savagery of the Lithuanian and Latvian pogrom-raising bands, coupled with the indifference of almost the entire population towards the more scientific exterminations practised by the Germans, must have provided unusual satisfaction to Hitler and his circle. To those who in pre-war days had accorded an almost Scandinavian respectability to the Baltic Republics, the news of the massacres, such of it as leaked through, was barely credible.

According to the pompous report, sent to Heydrich by the extermination chief Franz Stahlecker, the Latvian and Lithuanian Jews had co-operated with the Russian invader ' after oppressing the country economically throughout several decades.'[1] Yet the simple fact was that the Russians, in their policy of deportations, had entirely identified the Jews with the native middle class. Of the 70,000 people, deported from Latvia and Lithuania during the plebiscite of July 14th-21st, 1940, no less than 25,000 are said to have been Jews.[2]*

The political influence of Jewry was not increased by the Soviet occupation. The new *Seimas* of the Lithuanian Republic, elected during the July, 1940, plebiscite, contained five Jews among its 85 members. Only two Jews were commissars. In Latvia only one Jew, the head of the Health Department, achieved this honour.[4] On the other hand, the Russians maintained the restrictions on the Yiddish press and on specifically Jewish education. Jews who could be identified with the Jewish political parties, the Orthodox, the Zionists, the Social Democrats, and even the Bundists, were deported indiscriminately.[5] So much had the Jews been identified by the Russians with the pre-Soviet life of the country that the Germans had to find their pogrom-raisers among the class whom they had least reason to trust, the extreme nationalists. Thus it was not long before Stahlecker had to explain the disarming of the partisan bands, which put an end to the 'spontaneous cleansing actions' of the first days.[6]

The results had been none the less remarkable. In Kovno, the Lithuanian capital, 1,500 Jews were killed on the night of June 25th and 2,300 on the 26th. Stahlecker was particularly pleased with 'the understanding attitude adopted by the Wehrmacht,' but this was only half the story. An orderly occupation is not promoted by allowing 3,800 people to be killed in the streets of a city normally as stodgy as Stockholm. Field-Marshal von Leeb, commanding Army Group North, ordered von Kuechler of the 18th Army to stop such incidents recurring. Stahlecker had now to take responsibility for the killings himself.[7]

We hear no more of the Lithuanian journalist Klimatis, whose

---

*In spite of the historic rôle of Lithuania in the development of Eastern Jewry, the Baltic States had a lower ratio of Jewish inhabitants than Poland, Bessarabia, or the Ukraine and the ratio was diminishing. The Jewish population of Vilna fell by 10,000 in the first 30 years of the century and 11,795 Jews emigrated from Lithuania between 1928 and 1938. It is certain that the figures of the 1935 census, 153,743 Jews in Lithuania and 94,479 in Latvia, had fallen at the time of the Russian occupation. The emigration was due to economic pressure, the result of the progress of the native middle class in the post-Tsarist atmosphere. The Jews were losing their commercial monopoly and at the outbreak of war the Jewish traders, who had once outnumbered their rivals by six to one, had been reduced to equality of numbers.[3]

four political groups so distinguished themselves on June 25th-26th, but Stahlecker picked 300 of these citizens to serve in his *Einsatzgruppe*. Henceforward the Lithuanians were to do the work, for which they could be trusted, under a different authority, and seven months later Stahlecker was able to write that eight Lithuanians served in his firing-squads to one German.[8] By the summer of 1942 whole regiments of Lithuanian police and *Selbstschutz* had been sent to Poland, White Russia, and Latvia to guard the camps and ghettoes, to run the extermination centres, and to cut down cringing old people and children in the streets during the 'actions.' There was no political significance in it. It is the nasty truth that Lithuanian mercenaries adapted themselves to this sort of work and that some have been honourably received since the war in Western countries in the guise of displaced persons fleeing Soviet oppression.

A few days after the massacre in Kovno, Stahlecker summoned a council of the Jewish community and, declaring that the Germans 'had no reason to intervene in their differences with the Lithuanians,' recommended to them the virtues of moving into a ghetto[9]—for which Stahlecker found the Viriampole district particularly suitable, since only one bridge across the Memel connected it with the town. But there were too many Jews to be fitted into Viriampole, even if flight and deportation had reduced their numbers from 35,000 to 24,000. On July 11th therefore Stahlecker ordered a 'cleansing action.' All Jews not wanted by the labour office were to be committed to prison and executed daily in batches of fifty to a hundred.[10]

The first step towards ghettoes and 'resettlement actions' had already been taken. On July 8th the 180,000 Jews remaining in the Baltic States had been ordered to wear the Jewish badge. But docile though they showed themselves, there were too many Jews to be handled solely by the *Einsatzgruppen*. Stahlecker had only 990 men, more than half of whom had pushed on to the Leningrad front.[11] He was forced therefore to 'pass on the files concerning the measures he had put in force to the civil administration.'[12]

The speech, made at Kovno by the new *Reichskommissar*, Hinrich Lohse, on July 27th (*see page 202*) shows that he knew quite well that the ghettoes were to facilitate some drastic action by the Security Police.[13] In fact the 'cleansing action' had started in his area of government ten days previously. On July 17th a *Sonderkommando* had removed 700 Jewish hostages from Vilna from the Lukishki prison and taken them some six miles along the main railway towards Landworowo. Here at a railway halt known as Ponary, Punar, or Panarai, the Russians had dug huge pits for petrol storage-tanks. These pits were to become the first of the permanent extermination camps.[14]

By the end of August, 1941, ghettoes had been established in Libau and Dwinsk, and the Jewish population was in process of moving not only in Kovno but in Vilna,[15] where two ghettoes were selected in the Strachun and Litzka districts. On September 1st the Germans conducted an action in Vilna quite openly. Hingst, the new town commissar serving under Lohse, posted a notice warning all Jews to stay indoors on account of a 'great provocation,' the shooting of two German soldiers. An area in the centre of the town was then cordoned off and some thousands of Jews taken to the prison and thence to Ponary.[16] The execution of the remaining Jews was then speeded up, and by September 6th the main town of Vilna, which had been one-third Jewish, was completely cleared.

The two separately enclosed Vilna ghettoes were a feature copied later at Riga and at Minsk. Into the smaller or No. 2 ghetto were herded all the Vilna Jews who possessed no *Ausweise* or employment certificates. Originally issued by Lohse's town commissars throughout the Baltic Republics and White Russia, the purpose of these *Ausweise* was to guarantee Jewish skilled and manual labourers against the threat of 'resettlement,' but the Gestapo, by recalling the *Ausweise* and issuing new ones periodically in their place, created a permanent means of torture and blackmail. The certificates were cancelled from day to day. New certificates in varying colours were constantly needed so that no Jew could feel that he had won or purchased security. In this way the No. 2 ghetto became a slaughter pen where the old, the too young, or the merely unlucky waited their turn for the death pits. Thus there were clearance actions in Vilna on seven nights between September 5th and October 28th.[17]

On September 12th, when the actions had made some stir, Field-Marshal Keitel signed an order for the High Command of

215

the Armed Forces forbidding Wehrmacht agencies to issue further employment certificates. As usual the pliant Keitel had yielded to the pressure of Himmler and Heydrich,[18] since at this time the Transport Command and Armament Office of the Armed Forces were serious obstacles to Heydrich's plans. For instance, large numbers of Jews, both from the ghettoes and the rural communities, worked in 'closed columns' on the conversion of the gauge of the Riga-Minsk railway, while at Libau several hundreds of Jews served in the stores and offices of the German Naval Command.[19]

At the end of October, when, as we have noticed (see pages 92 and 131), the orders had already been given for the deportation to the Baltic States of Jews from the Reich, Heydrich made a concerted attack on this opposition of the Wehrmacht agencies, but instead of sending Heydrich to Riga, Himmler sent Lieut.-General Franz Jaeckeln, who had been Higher SS and Police Leader in the Ukraine. Shortly before Jaeckeln's arrival, the Gestapo in Vilna had already cancelled all Ausweise in favour of a new one, coloured yellow, which was issued only to 3,000 heads of families. This was followed between October 21st and 24th by a comb-out of the No. 1 or privileged ghetto, which required new methods. The five to eight thousand Jews who were shot at Ponary included for the first time some who had been delivered personally by the Jewish Ordnungsdienst commander, Jakob Genns (see page 64).

A final action on December 21st-22nd reduced the population of the Vilna Ghetto to 12,000. Thus altogether 25,000 to 30,000 Vilna Jews were killed. The slaughter had been prolonged over several months, being carried out by a permanent execution commando at a permanent killing establishment. Thus it provided the prototype for the Polish death camps and the prolonged 'resettlement actions' of 1942-3. One of the two SD captains in charge of this operation, Martin Weiss, was to make a dramatic reappearance after the war, when, after concealing himself for more than four years as a house-porter in Ochsenfuerth, he was convicted by the Nuremberg Landgericht in February, 1950, of 30,000 murders and sentenced to life imprisonment. Martin Weiss, sharp-faced and very trim, in a bright checked suit, had to be given special protection in court. One of the forty witnesses had a nervous breakdown eight years after the events she attempted to describe. Another witness told how Weiss had personally dragged off her nine-year-old daughter. But the defence witnesses declared that Weiss was a lover of all that was good and beautiful, who read the poems of Adalbert Stifter to his family.[20]

On October 28th the storm broke at Kovno. Half the ghetto population, about 10,000 people, were carried off in a single day to the death pits at Fort No. 9.[21] Ten days later it was the turn of Dunaburg or Dwinsk, a similar number being taken away. Only some labour commandos, numbering less than a thousand, were spared. The victims were taken to the hilly ground at Zolotaya Gorka and disposed of in the usual fashion.[22]

At Riga the pace was slower. The two ghettoes were not created till the middle of October because, as Stahlecker reported to Heydrich, the normal Lithuanian residents of the quarter made difficulties. On October 15th, moreover, Stahlecker wrote that certain authorities of the new civil administration were opposed to mass executions and that he would have to execute the Jews who were not fit for labour in small batches.[23] In the event the fate of the 29,000 Riga Jews was delayed six weeks.*

November 30th, 1941, found the most elaborate measures prepared in Riga. The ghettoes were cordoned, the Jewish working commandos were marched out under guard, while rows of modern blue Riga motor-buses were drawn up outside the ghetto gates. Miles out in the forest, near the railway-halt Rumbuli, the execution-pits had been dug by Russian prisoners of war.[27] Here again the *Einsatzgruppe* résumé for January, 1942, mentions what seems to have been the standard figure for these affairs, a total of 10,600 victims.[28] A daily report, issued while the

---

*It would seem that Colonel Jaeger was told by Stahlecker of the impending mass extermination on November 4th. Jaeger, however, had a nervous breakdown and was relieved by Lieut.-Colonel Eduard Strauch,[24] whom Bach-Zalewski called 'the wickedest man he had ever known.'[25] Strauch, an epileptic with bouts of lucidity, claimed at Nuremberg that he had refused to take Jaeckeln's orders without reference to Heydrich and that he absconded to Koenigsberg on November 27th. His rôle in the Riga massacres was never cleared up. The chief instigator seems to have been Strauch's permanent successor in Riga, Lieut.-Colonel Dr. Lange, with his Latvian aide, Major Arajs, both of whom were handed over to the German courts in the British Zone in May, 1949,[26] but I can find no record of any trial.

massacre was still in progress, declares that Jaeckeln was engaged in a 'shooting action' and that on November 30th 4,000 Jews from the Riga ghetto and an entire transport of Jews from the Reich had been dealt with.[29] This was the notorious 'Bloody Sunday,' but the second Riga action on December 8th was almost on the same scale. One witness, while gathering firewood for the Wehrmacht, saw the preparations in the forest—two lorry loads of German police troops and a long row of machine guns.[30] A third action, also on December 8th, took place not at Rumbuli but at Bikernek, the 'little birch wood,' which was destined to become the permanent execution place for the Riga Ghetto. This action was curtailed. At twelve o'clock, when a column of the condemned was marching out of the ghetto, the police NCO pulled out his watch and remarked: 'You are in luck. It is one minute after time; the action is over.'[31]

At the very least 24,000 people had been murdered in Riga. Stahlecker's estimate is actually 27,800.[32] Of the Riga Jewish community there remained only 4,500 men and 300 women, but within a week of the last action a second transport of Reich Jews, the first of a long series, arrived in Riga to occupy the corpse-strewn rooms of the 'little ghetto.'

Because of the Reich transports and also the presence of Luftwaffe troops near the execution ground, the Riga action created a great deal of gossip. It also made an impression on Heydrich, who invited its organiser, Major Lange of the Security Police, to attend the Gross-Wannsee conference (*see pages 92 and 96*). It is significant that Heydrich explained that the postponement of this conference from December 8th to January 20th was 'due to events in which some of the invited gentlemen were concerned': significant, too, that on December 14th Rosenberg told Hitler that 'in view of developments in the East' he would omit the word *Ausrottung*, extermination, from his forthcoming speech.[33]*

We know something of 'the opposition of certain authorities

---

*' I remarked on the Jewish question that the comments about the New York Jews must perhaps be changed somewhat after the conclusion of matters in the East. I took the standpoint not to speak of the *Ausrottung* of the Jews. The Fuehrer agreed with this and he added that the Jews had thrust the war upon us and that they had caused the destruction. It is no wonder that the consequences should strike them first.' (PS 1517 and XII 63.)

of the civil administration' which delayed the Riga massacres and prevented their completion. Lohse had been reported to Rosenberg's office as early as October for impeding the massacres in Libau. On November 15th he asked for a ruling whether all Ostland' Jews were to be killed without regard to the economic situation.[34] The reply from Rosenberg's office did not reach Riga till December 18th. It was signed by Otto Braeutigam of the Ministry's political department.[*] Braeutigam wrote that by now the Jewish question in the Ostland 'had almost certainly been solved in verbal discussions,' but on principle, economic considerations were not to apply at all. Such matters should in any case be settled with the Higher SS and Police Leaders.[36]

While waiting for this reply Lohse had shown a small degree of independence and this, after the war, saved him from the Allied Military Courts and perhaps the gallows.[†] On November 7th he telegraphed *Stadtkommissar* Hingst, of Vilna, calling attention to the protests of General Braemer, intendant to the military commander, Ostland. On December 1st Braemer circularised the civil commissars, urging them to stop the execution of irreplacable Jewish workers. Lohse himself distributed Braemer's manifesto on the 3rd,[37] including a copy for Jaeckeln.[‡] Braemer was not able to prevent the transports of Jews from the Reich starting at the end of November, but through other agencies Heydrich was induced to preserve the larger ghettoes. Vilna and Kovno each retained native Jewish communities of 15,000 to 20,000, while in Riga and Minsk the gaps created by

[*]This former Consul-General in Batum was traced in 1950, working for an American cultural institution in Munich.[35]

[†]The sentence of ten years' hard labour, passed on Lohse by the Bielefeld Denazification Court in January, 1948, was in fact remitted in the autumn of 1951 on the grounds of ill-health. On October 10th it was disclosed that this man, who had discussed the plans for the first gas chambers in October, 1941, was drawing a pension of 263 marks a month from the Ministry for Interior. The interpellations which took place in the chamber at Bonn are interesting. Lohse's allowance was attacked, not because of his conduct in Russia, but because as Gauleiter for Schleswig-Holstein he had shown himself the enemy of democracy. *Frankfurter Rundschau*, October 11th, 1951.

[‡]Apparently the feud between Braemer and the mass-murderer Jaeckeln did not go very deep, for Bach-Zalewski declares that Braemer attended Jaeckeln's social evenings and always addressed him with the intimate pronoun, 'Du.'[38]

massacre were partly filled with Reich Jews. To rectify the numbers, the Reich Jews, who had no potential war value, went straight to the death pits, such actions continuing at Riga and Kovno till the end of January, 1942, but in Vilna, where there was no action after December 21st,[39] numerous Jews who had been in hiding actually sought security in the ghetto, whose population grew in January to 18,000.[40]

On January 31st, 1942, Stahlecker completed his second long report to Heydrich, accompanied by a map, tastefully marked with coffins at the appropriate points. ' The complete removal of Jewry from the Eastern Territories has been substantially attained with the exception of White Russia as a result of the execution up to the present time of 229,052 Jews '[41] Stahlecker's figure includes 171,661 Jews of Latvia and Lithuania and is possibly an exaggeration since there were at least 50,000 survivors in Latvia and Lithuania* when Stahlecker wrote and it is doubtful whether 190,000 of the 247,000 Jews of the two Republics had been caught in the German net. The survivors were to enjoy relative peace till the summer of 1943.

2. White Russia

Further south Heydrich's men met with less favourable geographical conditions and so registered a lower order of success. On February 27th, 1942, only 33,210 Jews had been shot in the Civil Commissariat of White Russia and eight months after the invasion[42] there were still 139,000 to be dealt with. In this poorest part of occupied Europe distances were big and all-weather roads were lacking. According to Nebe's successor, Erich Naumann, *Einsatzgruppe* B covered an area half the size of

*The survivors at this date may well have been far more numerous, if the territories that had once been Lithuanian are taken into consideration— the Memel and Suwalki regions, incorporated in the Reich in March and September, 1939, and Grodno, incorporated (as part of ' Reichskommissariat Bialystok ') in July, 1941. In Grodno as many as 40,000 Jews may have been collected in the two ghettoes, where they were spared large-scale resettlement till the summer of 1942 (*see page 286, footnote*). The Memel and Suwalki territories also retained their Jewish population. Thus at the end of 1942 Dr. Korherr recorded the presence of 18,435 ' Soviet Russian Jews ' in *Bezirk* Koenigsberg.

Western Europe. His twenty-four commanders could only report to him once a fortnight and he could make no regular inspections till April, 1942, when he acquired an aeroplane.[43]

In the area covered by *Einsatzgruppe* B there had lived about 850,000 Jews, nearly half a million of them in former Polish territory. The *Einsatzgruppen* statistics suggest that less than a third stayed behind after the invasion, but even this figure seems remarkably big for a country offering such opportunities of escape. In the larger former Polish towns, such as Pinsk, Slonim, Kobrin, and Baranovice, the big Jewish communities seem to have stayed utterly inert during the two or three days that preceded the German occupation. This, however, can be understood, when it is realised that no news concerning the treatment of the ghettoes across the German demarcation line was permitted in the White Russian press during the days of the Moscow pact. One of Rosenberg's regional officials reported in July, 1941, that the White Russian Jews had not heard of the German anti-semitic laws and expected to be left in peace if they worked.[44]

Another factor contributed to the inertia of White Russian Jewry and this was the savage hostility of certain elements in the peasant population which had grown up with the phenomenal increase of the Jewish settlements in the late nineteenth century. Since the revolution neither the bourgeois republicanism of the Polish area nor the Marxism of the Russian area had eliminated this hostility, nor was it greatly affected by the wave of pro-Soviet feeling after the German occupation. In the Polish area the Russians had introduced a measure of autonomy during the occupation of 1939-41 and made themselves relatively welcome after twenty years of Polish landlordism. Thus there grew up under German rule a considerable pro-Soviet resistance movement but even here the White Russian Jews were not welcomed.[45]

East of the Beresina river conditions were different because the Jews had weeks or months in which to organise their escape. Those of Witebsk and Bobruisk were virtually deported in order to replace the Volga Germans in the Saratov region.[46] The small number of survivors were dealt with by the *Einsatzgruppen* very expeditiously, and only in Smolensk was it found necessary to create a permanent ghetto, which was dissolved in May, 1943, shortly before the Red Army's return.*[47]

West of the Beresina the absolute lack of any other artisan labour meant a reprieve for many of the hopelessly trapped ghettoes.[48] Tanneries and tailoring workshops in the smaller former Polish towns, sledge-wagon workshops in Minsk and Lida, were protected by the economic agencies of the Wehrmacht. Thus a few Jewish communities, thinned down in the end to groups of a few hundreds each after as many as five ' resettlement actions,' survived as late as September-November, 1943.[49]

Side by side with this survival went the illicit survival of Jews in the partisan-controlled areas. At first it suited the compilers of the Einsatzgruppen reports to identify their helpless victims with armed resistance, but an entry in Goebbels's diary of March 6th, 1942, shows that by this time the Germans were seriously concerned over the presence of Jews among the White Russian partisans.[50] To the non-combatant Jews this anxiety of the Germans only meant that the ' actions ' were carried out with greater savagery, bearing heaviest on the Shtetl, the numerous small Jewish market towns which were useless to the German economy, and on the groups that had fled to the uncertain protection of partisan territory. In the Shtetl there was only a chance of survival where the Germans had established a labour camp ; in

*The extent of the flight of the Jews from the Soviet part of White Russia can be gauged from the Einsatzgruppen reports concerning the liquidation of the ghettoes, established by the Germans in Witebsk, Bobruisk, Mogilev, and Borissov. Witebsk had a Jewish population of 37,013 in 1926 and may have had 45,000 in 1941 according to Solomon M. Schwarz. If one trusts the Einsatzgruppen daily report of December 19th, 1941 (No. 2824), the liquidation of the Witebsk Ghetto was then complete, but only 4,090 Jews had been shot. Bobruisk had 21,558 Jews in 1926 and possibly 28,000 in 1941 according to Schwarz. In December, when Bobruisk was declared Judenrein, some 6,179 Jews had been shot. Mogilev contained from 20,000 to 27,000 Jews and here the total killings, recorded by the Einsatzgruppen, come to 4,844. However, the existence of a labour camp in the old ghetto is recorded on December 19th, 1941, after the ghetto's official liquidation, and it was apparently in this Mogilev labour camp that Himmler wanted to instal a gas chamber early in 1943 (affidavit von dem Bach-Zalewski published in Aufbau, September, 1946). The case of Borissov, being considerably nearer the old Polish frontier, was rather different. About 8,200 deaths are recorded in various Einsatzgruppen reports, including 7,620 in the single massacre of October 18th-19th, 1941. Yet Borissov had normally not more than 20,000 Jews.

the forest there was no chance at all, once the whereabouts of a 'family camp' had been conveyed to the Germans, and this accounts for the great numbers of Jews, listed as killed in what purport to be actions against partisan groups. Thus Major-General Jaeckeln reported that, during 'Operation Marsh Fever in February, 1942, no less than 8,350 Jews were executed in the Miczajewice area, north-east of Minsk. A year later, 2,658 Jews were reported killed in 'bandit-held territory' near Slonim and another 3,300 Jews in the Pripet Marshes during 'Operation Hornung.'[51]

A rather large proportion of the records of Jewish partisan warfare in Eastern Europe concerns the former Polish White Russian provinces, simply because here the able-bodied Jew was less entrapped than in the thicker populated and more strictly policed General Government. But even a pro-Russian chronicler like Moshe Kaganovich emphasises the hostility which Jewish recruits encountered among the partisan groups working with the Red Army. Only a very few thousand fugitives from the ghettoes survived in the 'family camps' till the liberation, and with this exception the Germans were allowed to complete their work throughout White Russia. Not a single inhabited ghetto or labour camp was discovered by the Red Army.[52]

The largest individual Jewish community of White Russia was Minsk, which was just within the pre-war Soviet territory. Here the Jews had numbered 53,686 in 1926[53] and probably 80,000 to 90,000 in 1939. Solomon Schwarz (who accepts the evidence of two Soviet witnesses with rather less than his usual scepticism) considers that 75,000 Jews fell into German hands. I attach more importance to the statement in General Halder's diary that he found only 100,000 out of 233,000 inhabitants remaining in the city after the three days bombardment which preceded its capture on June 28th.[54] This would suggest that less than 40,000 were Jews, but even this was a greater number than the Jewish survivors in Riga, Kovno, or Vilna and one that could not be dealt with very summarily. The two Minsk ghettoes were not ready till the end of July, at which date two of the old-fashioned forts encircling the town were prepared as reception centres for the 'resettlements.'[55]

At the end of September there took place the first round-up.

Alleging 'sabotage and terrorist activities' the *Einsatzgruppe* executed 2,278 Jews[56] who were selected from the ghetto. The accusation was not entirely a blind, for the ghetto was believed to harbour a former member of the Minsk Soviet, one Nat Weinhaus, who was acting in collusion with Stolyarevitch, the leader of the Minsk 'underground.' The German remedy was to institute 'actions' on November 6th and 20th in which, according to the estimate of the Russian commission of investigation, 12,000 and 7,000 Jews were killed. Weinhaus was picked up in the second action.[57] Stahlecker, who took over Minsk from *Einsatzgruppe* B in January, could find only 1,800 White Russian Jews in Minsk who carried *Ausweise*, though the number of survivors was certainly many times greater.[58]

The first Reich Jews from Berlin, Hamburg, Vienna, Prague, and Bruenn reached Minsk after the pogrom of November 6th and the second group after November 20th. They were kept in 'No. 2 ghetto,' completely secluded from the native Jews, a precedent which was followed at Riga. The condition of these 6,500 people, used to a Western standard of living, was quite catastrophic but it was not seriously intended that they should survive the winter. However, in Minsk the Jews had a peculiar and unsuspected friend. *Generalkommissar* Wilhelm Kube had been a founder-member of the National Socialist Party and in January, 1934, he had pronounced the funeral oration at Karinhall over Goering's first wife, but in August, 1936, he had been dismissed the post of Gauleiter for Brandenburg-Grenzmark for blackmailing the wife of Major Walter Buch, the President of the Party Tribunal. Kube spent some time in a concentration camp and only returned to favour in 1941 through the support of Himmler and the friendship of Rosenberg and Lohse.[59]

On his first inspection of the German ghetto in Minsk, Kube, whose lecherous inclinations were the subject of detailed Gestapo reports to Himmler, was extremely moved at seeing girls who looked like Aryans. Moreover, the new *Judenaelteste* told him that there were in the ghetto men with war decorations and who had brothers serving at the front. Thereupon Kube wrote these lines to his friend Lohse in Riga[60]:

'The Jews within the next few weeks will probably die of cold or hunger. They constitute a tremendous danger of epidemics for us, because naturally they are exposed to the twenty-two epidemics which rage over White Ruthenia as much as we *Reichsdeutsche.* Vaccines are not available for them.

'On my own responsibility I am not going to give the SD instruction on "handling" these people, although some formations of the Wehrmacht and the police are already eager to get possession of the Jews from the Reich. The SD have already—without asking—taken away 400 mattresses from them and also confiscated all sorts of things. I am certainly hard and ready to solve the Jewish question, but people who come from our *Kulturkreis* are quite different, I submit, from the bestial native hordes. Are the Lithuanians and Latvians, who are disliked here even by the natives, to be entrusted with the slaughter ? I could not do that. I ask you out of consideration for the Reich and Party to issue unequivocal instructions on the subject which will carry out what is necessary in the most humane manner.'

With warm regards and Heil Hitler,

dein Wilhelm Kube.

One way and another Kube managed to protect these 6,500 Reich Jews till the following July. At first they benefited from the natural causes that preserved the native Jewry of White Russia, the frozen ground that precluded mass-burials for months on end. In February, Stahlecker sent the toughest of his executioners, 'Major Dr. Juris Eduard Strauch,' to keep an eye on Kube in Minsk, but Kube managed to get the Reich Jews excluded from the action of March 2nd.[61] Indeed by keeping his office-employed Jews out of the German ghetto a day or two before the action, he warned the Jews in the Russian ghetto and only 3,412 were killed in place of the anticipated 5,000.[62]

Strauch's complaints against Kube make a fascinating document. In the course of this action, Strauch declares, Kube 'hurt a police officer's feelings' by abusing him in front of Jews. Strauch had even heard that Kube had given sweets to Jewish children. Kube had also attacked General Zenner, commanding the Security Police in White Russia, for failing to surrender Kube's three Jewish barbers. And yet, Strauch declared, Kube always protested that he was the great enemy of the Jews.

Soon after this action Heydrich came to Minsk. To Kube he administered a severe rocket for sending him a list of Jews whom he had registered as illegally removed from Germany. From Strauch he demanded the complete liquidation of the Jews of the Minsk territory, though Strauch has testified that he managed to obtain a deferment till after the harvest.[63] The death of Heydrich on June 4th brought no reprieve. On the contrary 'Action Reinhardt,' dedicated to the hero's *manes*, was extended from Poland to all White Russia. On July 28th and 29th, therefore, the population of the two Minsk ghettoes was reduced from 19,000 to 8,794.[64]

On July 31st a very changed Kube wrote to his friend Lohse[65]* that in consultation with General Zenner and Major Strauch, 'the exceedingly competent commander of the SD,' 55,000 Jews in White Russia had been liquidated in ten weeks. In Minsk there remained 6,000 specially exempted Jews in the Russian ghetto and 2,600 Reich Jews. In the Lida region 16,000 Jews had been murdered and 8,000 in Slonim. On August 7th Lohse commented openly on Kube's report at a conference in the Four Year Plan Office, Goering in the chair. 'I can answer this too. There are only a few Jews alive. Tens of thousands have been disposed of.'[67]

The massacres in the former Polish parts of White Russia and the Ukraine kept pace with the tremendous slaughter in the General Government and did not die down till November, 1942. Himmler forwarded to Hitler a report of the Higher SS and Police Leader, General Pruetzmann, showing that 363,211 Jews had been killed in all Russia in August-October—a quite manifest exaggeration,[68] but there were memorable occasions nevertheless. For instance on October 29th, 1942, the 16,200 surviving Jews of Pinsk were liquidated by two companies of *Ordnungspolizei*, aided by an SS cavalry detachment which guarded the shooting-place, 'a precaution that gloriously justified itself when

---

*The extraordinarily different tone of the second letter to Lohse was explained by Eduard Strauch at Nuremberg during one of the intervals when he was not shamming insanity. Strauch believed that he could only have been complimented by Kube in order to fool Himmler, whom the letter was meant to reach through Rosenberg's office. Kube, according to Strauch, had concocted the letter with General Gottberg of the police, who had been denounced to Himmler as too soft.[66]

fifteen Jews were caught who had got several kilometres away.' The diary of the 15th Police Regiment shows that, apart from a new use of cavalry, other strategic lessons had been learnt:[69]

> *Conclusions.* Axes essential. Roofs to be searched for hidden spaces, also spaces under floors even when there are no cellars. For this, grenades and police dogs are useful. The ground round the houses should be sounded with a hard object for camouflaged holes. The assistance of children in finding hiding places can always be obtained by promising their lives.

By November, 1942, there was scarcely any longer a Jewish problem in White Russia. On the 23rd Kube wrote to Georg Leibbrandt in Rosenberg's office that there were only 30,000 Jews in the Civil Commissariat, a number which it was proposed to halve.[69a] Nevertheless, Minsk, Lida, Slonim, Baranovice, and a further half-dozen White Russian ghettoes survived till September-November, 1943 (*see pages 209-10 and 288*).

3. The Ukraine

Of the three million Jews of pre-war Russia about half lived in the Soviet Ukraine Republic, to which were added the 568,000 East Galician Jews annexed from Poland in September, 1939. These were the true 'Reservoirs of Eastern Jewry,' that had played such an excessive part in National Socialist propaganda. Apparently for this greatest murder consignment of all the two *Einsatzgruppen* C and D were deemed sufficient. But in fact as they advanced into the depths of South Russia the problems of Heydrich's men diminished. In Eastern Galicia 80 per cent of the Jewish population remained,[70] while in Lwow the Jewish population had actually increased, but in the historic towns of the pre-industrial Russian Ukraine, Winnitsa, Zhitomir, Berdichev, Uman, Nikolaiev, and Kherson only a quarter or a fifth of the Jews stayed on and this was equally true of the enormous Jewish agglomerations to the East, the towns along the Dnieper, Kiev, Kharkov, and Dniepropetrowsk. Further East still in the Donetz and Kuban basins and North of the Caucasus only a small percentage of the Jews awaited the Germans.

Not only did the bulk of the three million Jews of pre-war Soviet Russia escape to the interior but also a very large proportion of the 1,800,000 Jews of the annexed territories. Although the number of those who reached the sanctuary of South Siberia and the Volga-Ural region may never be known, it is possible that three quarters of the present Jewish population of Europe are to be found in the Soviet Union, where before the war there was less than a third. This result was not due to any special favour of the Russian Government towards Jewry. It was simply that, as the Germans approached the industrial belt, it became the Russian policy to remove the working population so that the towns should not benefit the enemy. In most captured towns less than half the population stayed. Not to consent to be evacuated was regarded as a hostile act, often visited with dire consequences later.*

Although the liquidation of complete Jewish communities did not begin till after Himmler's visit to the Ukraine in August, 1941, the march across Eastern Galicia was accompanied by pogroms in Lwow, Tarnopol, Zborow, Zloczow, and Drohobicz. In Lwow, where there were more than 100,000 Jews, some 7,000 were killed according to one *Einsatzgruppen* report, but several

---

*Solomon M. Schwarz, in a very elaborately documented work, has emphasised the Soviet failure to evacuate the threatened Jewish populations and he has discovered cases of actual impediment. Intent on proving this thesis, he has proposed a set of figures for Jewish losses and survivals which agree neither with German SD figures nor with Russian post-war estimates. Assuming a figure short of five million Jews for the enlarged Soviet Union of June, 1941, he believes that only 1,850,000 have survived, a loss of more than three millions (*Jews in the Soviet Union*, 1951, page 237).

With this may be compared the estimate of Mr. Joseph Schechtmann, made at the end of 1943 (*Hitler's Ten Years War on the Jews*), that the number trapped by the Germans, including the former Polish and Baltic provinces, was between 650,000 and 850,000[71]—an estimate which receives a surprising confirmation in the secret figures submitted by Dr. Korherr to Himmler at the beginning of that year. Dr. Korherr believed that ' exclusive of those who still remained in camps and ghettoes,' some 633,000 Jews had been ' resettled ' from the occupied Russian territory—and these figures were drawn from the often exaggerated *Einsatzgruppen* and other SD reports (No. 5194). Even if Korherr's figure is accepted at face-value, it can scarcely have risen much beyond 750,000 before the Russian reoccupation, and of this total not more than half a million are to be attributed to pre-war Soviet territory. (For a further discussion of Schwarz's figures *see Appendix 1.*)

survivors have put the figure even higher.[72] The town was taken on June 30th, having undergone a period of anarchy in the eight days since the invasion. The Ukrainian nationalists of Lwow had not been gratified by their inclusion in the Soviet Ukrainian Republic, even though they were favoured at first at the expense of the Poles. Already in May, 1940, the Ukrainian, Polish, and Jewish nationalists of Lwow were being deported indiscriminately to South Siberia and there was a big round-up of Lwow Ukrainians as soon as the Germans crossed the border. According to German reports, three to four thousand were imprisoned.[73] On June 25th, when the Russians were openly preparing their retreat from Lwow, an attempt was made to rescue these men from the Kasimirowka and Lackiego prisons. The Russians killed them all, leaving too quickly to dispose of the bodies.

The first act of the SD was to exhibit large photographs of these 'Jewish killings' in the shops.[74] A Ukrainian militia with blue-and-yellow armbands was quickly recruited and a thousand Jewish hostages were arrested. Then on July 2nd and 3rd, with the connivance of the SD, 'Aktion Petlura' was organised,[75] the symbolic revenge for the murder of the Ukrainian Hetman by a Jew in Paris in 1926. Jews were killed in the prisons, the streets, and in the sports stadium. It was a reprisal action, but seventy-three of the victims were declared to be officials of NKVD, while a further forty were denounced by Ukrainians as NKVD helpers.[76]

Carried out in all the hysteria of liberation, this killing of 7,000 people had a strong resemblance to the Kovno and Jassy pogroms which preceded it by only a few days. Nor was it a novelty in Lwow. The last Lwow pogrom had been in 1918 and the instigators the invading Poles. On that occasion Archbishop Szepticki, the Metropolitan of the Galician Uniate Church, had been a friend of the Jews.[77] The Chief Rabbi, Ezekiel Levin, therefore sought his intercession on July 2nd, 1941, but was picked up on his way to the palace. To make this confusion more confusing, the Russians, too, had been killing Jews, and even the first Einsatzgruppen report[78] admits that some of the corpses left in the prisons by the Russians were Jewish.

Brigadier-General Erwin Schulz, who had been in charge of Commando No. 5 of Einsatzgruppe C, declared at his trial that he aided the escape of most of the Jews who were rounded up in the sports stadium.[79] Since Schulz was not punished for this action, it seems likely that the SD backed out of 'Aktion Petlura' which they had started, when the Ukrainian militia got out of hand. This was a general experience in Eastern Galicia and in Drohobicz it is alleged that there was actually shooting between Germans and Ukrainians. There had been changes of heart regarding the nuisance value of the Ukrainians since September 12th, 1939, when, in the Fuehrer's train at Ilnau, Ribbentrop had outlined a plan for making Galicia (with the approval of the Russians) an independent State. Ribbentrop had also planned to incite 'Melynyk's Independent Ukraine movement' to annihilate the Poles and Jews of Galicia (*see page 34*). Now in July, 1941, Hitler no longer offered any rival project to Stalin's Greater Ukraine. He intended Eastern Galicia to be part of the General Government, an area ear-marked for progressive resettlement by Germans, and this he confirmed on August 1st, when he ordered General von Roques to hand over the civil administration to Governor Frank. The Jews gained a reprieve by this incorporation, for they were spared the immediate horrors of the *Einsatzgruppen* massacres to await the *Einsatz Reinhardt* massacre which began in Lwow in the following March (*see pages 253-4*).

It was nevertheless the plan to incorporate Lwow in the General Government which must have been responsible for the first large-scale Jewish deportation to Auschwitz. The Polish officer internee, Zenon Rozanski, writes that 500 Lwow Jews arrived in Auschwitz main camp soon after the occupation of the city. According to the policy of the *Lagerfuehrer* Fritsch, they were not allowed to last more than a few days. Thirty-seven were done to death on the *Appellplatz* on the day of arrival.[79a]

By the beginning of July, 1941, *Einsatzgruppe* C had already advanced well beyond Galicia. Four commandos were at Korosten, Zhitomir, Berdichev, and Winnitsa, deployed across the width of the Ukraine almost from the Pripet Marshes to the Dniester. In the centre of the line was Commando 4a, which, under the leadership of the drunken Duesseldorf architect Paul Blobel, was to achieve a unique record for Jewish mass-executions. It was no coincidence that from the beginning of the campaign Blobel was attached to the Sixth Army and that this army, which was later to surrender with von Paulus at Stalingrad, was then commanded by the most political of Hitler's generals, Walter von Reichenau, the author of the notorious order on 'sub-human Jewry' (see page 33, footnote).

Blobel first met von Reichenau on June 26th at Sokal, on the banks of the Bug, walking in a large park in a bathing suit[80] and giving meticulous instructions, which included an order to Blobel to reduce the five rifles per victim, customary in military executions, to two in the case of Jews. In spite of the interested nature of Blobel's evidence both details concerning the 'chief Nazi general' are very credible. It was in a bathing suit that, as a dug-out general aged fifty-five, Reichenau had swum the Vistula in September, 1939, at the head of an entire division. This picturesque figure was not destined to take part in the Nuremberg High Command Trial or even to lead the last successful offensive of the Wehrmacht, for which Hitler appointed him in place of Rundstedt in the following December. The 'subhuman Jewry' order got Reichenau a Field Marshal's baton, but on January 17th, 1942, he was dead from a mysterious infection.*

There is nevertheless some confusion in Blobel's evidence whether he received the orders for his first mass killings from Reichenau or from Jaeckeln, the Higher SS and Police Leader. The killing of 2,531 Jews in Zhitomir in the last week of July— the killings reported by Major Roesler to General Schirwind (see pages 204-205)—he attributed to Jaeckeln. Blobel's chief, Otto Rasch, commanding Einsatzgruppe C, tried to keep out of the way, when Jaeckeln ordered the inclusion of women and children, by removing his headquarters from Zhitomir to Novo Ukrainka. This gesture did not affect another execution by Blobel

*The Einsatzgruppen commanders personally recorded their gratitude for Reichenau's order of the day. Thus the daily situation report No. 128 of November 3rd, 1941, reads as follows (No. 3157):
'The commandant of the POW camp Winnitsa stopped the transfer of 362 Jewish prisoners to the Einsatz and even put his second-in-command on trial for assisting. OKH then forbade the Einsatz to enter the transit-camp, but this order was countermanded by OKW. Since the Reichenau order of the day of October 10th better co-operation may be expected. With the Secret Field Police there has never been any friction.'

of 407 Jews on August 7th,[81] an execution which included the Jewish president of the Zhitomir Court.* At this stage, however, the *Einsatzgruppe* received orders that the survivors of the Zhitomir Jewish community (which had formerly numbered about 35,000) should be enclosed in a ghetto. The killings were therefore suspended for the next six weeks, but there were further massacres in the main towns of the Western Ukraine, in Korosten, Berdichev, Uman, and in particular in Winnitsa, where they took place in the public gardens with the assistance of a *Landschutz* regiment of the 36th Division which cordoned the area.[83]

The massacre, conducted by Blobel on September 6th, is interesting for the loftiness of its motive. Some 1,668 Jews were found at Radomysl, half way between Zhitomir and Kiev. They were living fifteen to a room in a ghetto, where it was impossible to feed them and where ' their filth constituted a permanent danger of epidemics.' They were therefore killed out of kindness of heart,[84] a third of them by the co-operative Ukrainians. At Nuremberg Blobel was more modest about his rôle at Radomysl. The work, he said, was done by Jaeckeln's detachments and only four of his own men were there, having been sent to Radomysl to look after some pigs. Furthermore, Jaeckeln stole the pigs so that on the march to Kiev Commando 4a found their sausages gone.[85]

The ghettoes which the Germans had created at Zhitomir, Uman, and Berdichev did not last long. They were liquidated on September 19th and 22nd and on October 5th. At Zhitomir the Garrison Commander agreed with Blobel that the creation of a ghetto had ' not stopped the gossiping and mischief of the Jews.' Accordingly, he supplied Blobel with twelve Wehrmacht lorries and sixty Ukrainian helpers and had the graves dug by 150 Russian prisoners of war. On the previous evening the ghetto was cordoned off and the 3,145 Jews, who remained, waited quietly to be taken to execution. Altogether 7,000 Zhitomir Jews were liquidated in the course of two months.[86]

*The fifth fortnightly *Einsatzgruppen* report made much of the execution of Kieper, the ' Jewish judge of Zhitomir' in the hay market. He was probably merely the president of the Jewish division of the Soviet court, for in a town like Zhitomir, where half the inhabitants spoke Yiddish, such a division was required by the Russian constitution.[82]

On September 19th, the day of the final Zhitomir massacre, the Germans entered Kiev, where the defence had lasted forty-five days and cost the Russians an entire army group in what Hitler described as 'the greatest battle in history'—though some military historians say that Hitler ought never to have fought that battle at all, but concentrated his strength on the Moscow front. In this dearly won prize the Germans were not allowed to make themselves comfortable. On the 24th a big explosion wrecked the Continental Hotel, the headquarters of the Rear Area Command of the Sixth Army. The fires spread rapidly and Blobel, who had arrived on the 21st, had to evacuate his office. Twenty-five thousand people were made homeless and hundreds of German troops were killed, mainly while fighting the fires.[87]*

The decision to treat the Kiev Jews as reprisal victims was apparently taken on September 26th, when the fires were still blazing. According to Blobel, there was a conference between Jaeckeln, Otto Rasch of the *Einsatzgruppe*, and Eberhardt, the town commandant.[89] The *Einsatzgruppe* reports give the full credit for the massacre to Blobel, assigning to Jaeckeln's two police companies merely the rôle of assistants, but at Nuremberg Blobel protested his absence from Kiev and declared, furthermore, that only fifteen of his fifty-three men could be detailed for the executions.[90]†

The notices posted on September 26th required the Kiev Jews to report within three days at the junction of Melnik and Doktorevskaia streets 'for resettlement.'[92] 'At first it was not expected that more than 5,000 or 6,000 people would co-operate

*At Nuremberg the theory that this and other landmines were laid by Jewish agents was disposed of by Colonel-General Jodl, who recollected a captured chart of 50-60 landmines, which had been prepared by the Russian High Command long before the retreat.[88] And yet it is clear that Jodl had permitted the explosions to be blamed on the Jews, for, in giving evidence, he most unguardedly associated von Reichenau's order on 'sub-human Jewry' with 'the events in Kiev'—a point which the Soviet Prosecutor failed signally to bring home.

†There exists, however, one absolutely independent testimony to confirm the version compiled by Dr. Knobloch in Berlin. On October 22nd, 1944, Mr. W. H. Lawrence of the *New York Times* was shown over the Babi Yar ravine by M. Aloshin, the Kiev city architect, who told him that 'a German architect' had boasted to him of the deed. Who can this architect possibly be but Blobel, the 'Red-jacket man' of 1951 ?[91]

in this measure, but, thanks to an extremely clever organisation, there arrived more than 30,000 people who believed right up till the last minute before execution that they would be resettled.'[93] Heydrich always insisted on precision. The daily report No. 106 and the monthly report No. 6 both make the figure 33,771 and all these were killed in the two days, September 29th and 30th, a record not even equalled by the Treblinka and Auschwitz death factories in the summers of 1942 and 1944.

At the limit of the Kiev built-up area, beyond the Lukyanovka Jewish cemetery, the Babi Yar ravine serpentines between sand dunes. According to one witness before the State Commission, the victims received the shot in the neck as they stepped from a plank into the ravine. It seems that they were marched off to the ravine in small groups with their 'resettlement' bundles, but it must have taken some ingenuity to keep 33,771 people crouching in the road for two days on end, particularly as the small-arms salvos must have been almost within earshot.[94] 'The population,' says report No. 106, ' scarcely knew that the Jews were liquidated, but the latest experience suggests that they would not have objected.' The German-controlled Ukrainian newspaper *Krakiviski Visti* reported that ' The Jews set off in groups on foot for an unknown destination,' but is doubtful[95] whether such reports deceived anybody. An *Ausland-Abwehr* officer wrote to Admiral Canaris that, though the *Reichskommissar* Erich Koch had gone to great pains to conceal the massacre from the foreign press correspondents who were shown the devastation in Kiev, they had told him that they knew all about it (*see page 196*). By the end of October everyone in Kiev must have known the truth, for the SD had just distributed among the Kiev poor some of the 139 lorry-loads of Jewish clothing which they had destined for the *Volksdeutsche* of the Ukraine.[96]

In March, 1942, Albert Hartel, a Gestapo expert on church affairs, was driving with Blobel towards a country villa outside Kiev used by Major-General Thomas, the Security Police Commander.* At the Babi Yar ravine Hartel noticed small

---

*Max Thomas, who had been Higher SS and Police Leader in Northern France and Belgium, was of course a different person to Georg Thomas, head of the Wehrmacht Armament Office. He seems to have been killed early in 1944.

explosions which threw up columns of earth. It was the thaw, releasing the gases from thousands of bodies, and Blobel explained: 'Here my Jews are buried.'[97] But Blobel was not quit of the affair. Two months later he was sent for in Berlin by Heydrich, who was about to leave for Prague and his own death. After the passage of more than five years the words of that steel-faced young man were still indelibly stamped on the memory of the Nuremberg defendant[98]:

> 'Well, you have developed a stomach. You are just a cissy, only fit to be employed as a porcelain-manufacturer— but I will push your nose much deeper into it. You will report to *Obergruppenfuehrer* Mueller.'

Henceforward Blobel's unique assignment was to destroy the traces of mass burials in Poland and Russia. We have seen him at Chelmno in September, 1942 (*see pages 136-138*); in the following June he was back in the Babi Yar ravine, where his knowledge and experience showed the exhumation squad where to dig. Blobel admitted at his trial that he removed the contents of a mass-burial pit measuring sixty yards long and more than eight feet deep.[99]*

It is evident that not all the Jews who had remained behind from Kiev's normal Jewish population of 180,000 were massacred at the end of September, for 7,000 Jews were killed in the Kiev area late in October and 8,000 in January, 1942. Even then there was a ghetto in Kiev. In December, 1942, Professor Peter Seraphim, now attached to the Armaments Office (*see pages 56 and 239*), complained to General Thomas that Jews in Kiev were not entitled to any rations.[101] Almost till November 6th, 1943, when the Russians returned, there was a Jewish labour-camp in the suburbs at Syretsk and in the city itself a few hundred Jews were found living 'underground.'[102]

East of the Dnieper *Einsatzgruppe* C now entered the most populous part of Russia. On October 5th Commando No. 5 established itself in the industrial towns of the Dnieper bend,

---

*On September 29th, 1943—a fateful anniversary—the Jewish slaves of Commando 1005, working at Kiev, rebelled and a few escaped to give evidence before the Russian investigation commission in 1944. On November 6th, 1943, there were still some mass graves south and east of the town which Blobel did not have time to destroy.[100]

and on the 13th Jaeckeln, who had moved his headquarters to Krivoi Rog, ordered the liquidation of the Jews of Dniepropetrowsk. More than six weeks had elapsed since the first German troops entered the city, but about 30,000 Jews remained —out of a pre-war community exceeding 100,000.[103] Jaeckeln's police companies and the Special Commando were able to handle 11,000 old people and children in a single action.

It happened that there were Hungarian troops in Dniepropetrowsk on October 13th and among them a Jewish lorry driver from Volove in former Czechoslovak Ruthenia, which had been annexed by Hungary in April, 1939. This man, Majer Neuman, has survived the war—a Jew who saw the massacre of Jews as a member of the Axis forces. He has told of the march of the 'resettled' Jews of Dniepropetrowsk through the streets, eight abreast and carrying their bundles. It took two days, and all the time the machine-gunning could be heard from the anti-tank ditches outside the city.[104] There were further mass executions at the Jewish cemetery of Dniepropetrowsk at intervals till March, 1942.

On the march from Krivoi Rog to Dniepropetrowsk *Einsatzgruppe* C passed through a large Jewish agricultural colony, established in imperial times but now collectivised. These Jews, with the exception of the headmen, were actually spared. It was explained in the official report that the Jews were of low intelligence and therefore not dangerous.[105] Their numbers may even have been increased in 1942 by Jews picked from the Warsaw and Lublin 'resettlements' in order to bring in the harvest, but thereafter they disappeared.*

One of the most famous Eastern Jewish communities, Chernigov, had been occupied on September 12th, but Blobel's commando did not get there till October 23rd. In this case, however, only 260 Jews stayed behind out of 10,000. Rather remarkably there was a second execution five days later of 43 Jews who had returned to Chernigov.[106] Apparently a town

---

*Three of the Jewish collective farm settlements between Krivoi Rog and Kherson were big enough to constitute 'National Districts' of the Soviet Union, Stalindorf, Kalinindorf, and Novo Zlatopolje. According to the evidence, collected by Solomon M. Schwarz, all the surviving populations were liquidated towards the end of May, 1942 (*Jews in the Soviet Union*, Syracuse, 1951, page 197).

was considered safe as soon as the SD had left. According to von dem Bach-Zalewski, Jews would come back even in the teeth of warnings given them by Germans.[107] Thus at Poltava, which was taken on September 19th, there were at first only very small actions. Then, on November 23rd, Blobel's Commando 4a made a swoop and secured 1,538 victims. It must, however, be added that the pre-war Jewish population of Poltava exceeded 35,000.[108]

This technique of the sudden return could be most successful in areas five hundred miles behind the front, where there had been no time for a massed flight after the invasion. At Rowno in the former Polish part of the Ukraine a new SS and Police Leader, General Korsemann, suddenly established his headquarters and on November 6th, 1941, the ' long-planned *Judenaktion* was carried out.' *Einsatzgruppe* C lent a reserve-commando to assist the newly arrived police companies and 15,000 people were killed in two days. However, between 6,000 and 7,000 able-bodied workers received *Ausweise* and were spared till July 13th, 1942, when a surprise action was planned by the SD commander, Major Puetz, and the civilian area commissioner, Georg Marschall, as part of the final liquidation of the Jews of this populous province. Hermann Graebe, the works engineer of the firm Jung A.G. and author of the immortal narrative of the episode at Dubno airport, was present at this action, too. Particularly memorable details in his story are the wiring of the ghetto before the action for flood-lights and the rocket-flares which lit up the open ground beyond the station, as the Jews were entrained for the killing-place at Kostolpol[109] (*see pages 205-6*).

The most easterly of the Ukrainian cities, which contained a really big Jewish community, was Kharkov, which the Germans occupied on October 24th, 1941, but apparently not more than 20,000 Jews remained.* The town commandant was slow in

*The Jewish population of Kharkov before the invasion is a matter of conjecture. There were 81,139 Jews in the last Soviet census to use a separate Jewish register, but this was in 1926 when the population of Kharkov was only 407,000. According to Whitaker's Almanack, it rose to no less than 833,400 in 1939. It is doubtful whether this immense accretion of industrial inhabitants included a proportional number of Jews, for a very interesting breakdown of the 1926 figures shows that 17,000 out of 40,000 Jews of working age were office employees and 15 per cent were out of work.[110]

setting up a ghetto, but finally he gave the Jews from December 14th to December 16th to settle in some workers' huts, attached to the derelict tractor plant No. 10, which was several miles outside the town. This, the removal of the Jews to a relatively remote camp as the prelude to slow extermination, was an improvement on the methods that had just been applied in the Baltic States and it must be assumed that the inspiration was Heydrich's own, since at the same time the survivors of the Belgrade Ghetto were removed to the Semlin and Tasmaidan camps to be slowly absorbed by the gassing vans (*see page 361*). Tractor plant No. 10 was, however, not a prison, for at first the Jews were not closely confined but allowed by day to beg in the streets. They were barefooted and had been robbed of much of their clothing and, since it was forbidden to admit them indoors, many froze to death while hunting for food. From an *Einsatzgruppen* report of February 4th, 1942, it appears that preparations were already being made to shoot them.

There followed the slow and inconceivably ghastly extinction of this once flourishing community. The shootings, conducted in the inevitable gully not far from the tractor plant, went on well into March, two or three hundred victims being taken at a time. Finally in April, 1942, the pestilential huts of the tractor plant, which were crammed full of the bodies of those who had merely died of cold and hunger, were set on fire.[111]*

After February, 1942, the *Einsatzgruppen* reports are not available, so that one may only conjecture the fate of the remnants of Ukrainian Jewry. Another Kharkov trial witness, a Russian driver for the SD, witnessed massacres during the German offensive of June, 1942, at Voronezh and Kursk.[113] From Kamenetz-Podolsk a German *Feldgendarmerie* commander wrote about the same time of this Jewish community which once numbered 24,000: 'We don't sleep here. There are three or four

---

*There must still have been some Jews in Kharkov since the Molotov note of April 26th, 1942, estimates the deaths at Tractor Plant No. 10 at 14,000. There were Jewish witnesses in December, 1943, at the Kharkov trial—after the city had changed hands four times. One of the German witnesses, Lieut.-Colonel Hans Haenisch, civil commissioner for the Melitopol region, declared that 3,000 Jews had been shot in Kharkov in the previous June, because they had welcomed the Russians at the brief reoccupation in the previous April.[112]

actions a week.' This was, however, in the Western Ukraine, where there had been less opportunity of flight. In the great city of Rostov near the mouth of the Don the fate of the survivors during two periods of German occupation is quite unknown,* though one report mentions a massacre of 18,000.[114]

One of the last massacres in the Eastern Ukraine may have taken place on November 22nd, 1942, after the Russians had already broken the Don front. This was the second and final massacre of the Jewish community of Artemovsk on the Donetz.[115] A month later Professor Peter Seraphim of Goettingen University reported to General Thomas of the Armaments Office of the Wehrmacht that there were still Jews in the bigger Ukrainian cities, though officially they received no rations.[116] Professor Seraphim estimated the number of Jews who had been killed in the Civil Commissariat of the Ukraine at 150,000 to 200,000.

There is one more report, dated March 19th, 1943, concerning the infamous Commando 4a (now described as a *Sondergruppe*), which had formerly been associated with Blobel and the Kiev massacre, but which was now involved in the retreat from Stalingrad. Circumstances had changed so much that Major Christiansen directed his men that 'as a rule no more children will be shot,' but collective farm officials and Jews were still to be selected for reprisal measures.[117]

4. The Black Sea Coast, Crimea and Caucasus

The Rumanian share in the 'Final Solution' is considerable and forms the subject of Chapter 15. Here, however, it will be convenient to consider an incredible massacre by the Rumanians, not of their own subjects but of Russian Jews in pre-war Russian territory. This was in the great city of Odessa, whose community of 175,000 Jews ranked with Berlin, Vienna, Lodz and Kiev, and which came into the firing-line on August 5th, 1941, though

*Rostov had 26,356 Jews in 1926. Professor Seraphim's estimate of 40,000 in 1938 may be high. In any case 18,000 seems much too big a proportion for those who had failed to flee after so many months of warning. The only details I can discover of a massacre are in the testimony of a captured German sergeant-major radio-operator who saw a bedridden old woman removed from his billet during a *Grossaktion* which took place in August, 1942, after the German reoccupation. (*Black Book*, 360.)

it was not entered by the Rumanian army till October 16th. Before the city was encircled there was time to evacuate the able-bodied population on instructions from Moscow and it is probable that fully two-thirds of the Jews left by train for Eastern Russia.[118]

On October 22nd a delayed-action land-mine destroyed the former NKVD building, which had become the headquarters of the Rumanian 10th Division and the town commandant's office. Some German officers, including the Port Captain, were among the 220 killed.[119] It is obvious that Marshal Antonescu copied the action taken by the Germans in Kiev some three weeks previously. He ordered that 100 Jews were to be killed for every soldier who had died and 200 for every officer, with the result that 26,000 Odessa Jews were massacred between October 23rd and 25th. A day after the massacre the Germans published reports that partisan resistance was continuing against the Rumanians and that it was directed from the Great Synagogue. This suggests that the Germans may have organised the affair and in fact an *Einsatzgruppen* report, dated October 9th, shows that two of Ohlendorf's commandos were then waiting to enter the city.[120] This was prevented by Rumanian jealousy, but there was certainly SD inspiration in the preparation of execution-pits in the neighbourhood of a disused hutted camp, which could be fired after it had served its purpose—the method later used at Kharkov.[121]* No attempt was made to exterminate the remaining Jews of Odessa, but instead the usual preparations were made for a ghetto and a labour camp. It seems, however, that the Jews were distributed among the Transdniestrian towns with the deportees from Rumania. There was a ban on their returning, but a number were deliberately brought back to Odessa in May, 1942 (*see page 402*), and on April 10th, 1944, the Red Army encountered Jews here for the first time in their great advance which had begun at Stalingrad sixteen months earlier.

The failure of Ohlendorf's two commandos to take part in resolving the Jewish problem in Odessa had been part of a

*The Russian Court at Odessa in May, 1945, put the blame directly on Antonescu, but Trestorianu, the army commander, and Dragalina, the town commandant, denied that they had passed on Antonescu's orders to Generals Gazun and Maziel, who carried out the massacre. The hanging of all four has made the question academic.[122]

considerable political difficulty with Rumania. Having interfered successfully with Rumanian attempts to clutter up the German rear-lines with their deported Jews, Ohlendorf had to renounce his interest in the territory between the Dniester and Bug after a joint staff conference on August 30th had handed it to the Rumanian civil administration. Ohlendorf had to quit his headquarters at Ananiev, when the liquidation of Transdniestrian or Podolian Jewry was by no means complete, and he complained of the lack of co-operation from the Hungarian troops and German colonists 'who considered the Jews quite innocent people' and in some settlements appointed Jewish political leaders.[123]

Under the agreement of August 30th the Rumanians used Transdniestria as a reserve for their own Bessarabia and Bukovina Jews and so it remained till the Russian reconquest, a fragment of the Russian steppe where, though the death-rate from disease was very high, Jews could live and where in fact well over 50,000 survived (*see page 402*). And so it happened that the major part of the activities for which he was tried at Nuremberg were carried out by Ohlendorf and his *Einsatzgruppe* D after he had moved his headquarters to Nikolaiev. His first big-scale actions were in September, when the survivors of the Jewish populations of Nikolaiev and Kherson were resettled. Apparently both of these communities had been reduced by flight from about 30,000 Jews to 5,000.[124] During the course of this action Ohlendorf spared the Jewish agricultural communities, but on October 4th Himmler himself dined in Ohlendorf's mess and forbade any further exemptions[125] (*see page 236, footnote*).

After an action against 2,000 Jews in Melitopol[126] Ohlendorf moved his headquarters early in November to Simferopol in the Crimea, which was the GHQ of Manstein's 11th Army. Here he was presented with his largest problem, for according to the researches of his information department, 65,000 Jews had lived in the Crimea at the beginning of the war and 8,000 Krimshegs or Islamised Jews.[127] An unknown proportion had been trapped, including 10,000 Jews in the Simferopol Ghetto.

It was Ohlendorf's claim that Manstein had asked him to complete the liquidation of the Simferopol Ghetto before Christmas. The main action seems in fact to have ended earlier.

On December 15th, the day that Heinz Schubert made such efficient arrangements for the reception of 700 Simferopol Jews, the total of 9,600 was reached.[128] It was on this account that Ohlendorf gave a Christmas-dinner to Commando 11b and made the men a speech.[129] On December 30th, when the Jewish labour camp at Yankoi was liquidated, Simferopol was declared officially 'Jew-free.'[130] This, however, was premature, since 300 Jews were killed in Simferopol on February 17th and another thousand in the course of March.[131]

The entire Crimea was considered 'Jew-free' on April 16th, 1942, but it was admitted that there were a few hundred Jews in hiding.[132] One of Manstein's witnesses at Hamburg in 1949 spoke of a Jewish market in Simferopol, open and unmolested, as late as the winter of 1942.[133] On July 15th, 1942, a Rear Area Commander reported 1,099 Jews drowned off the coast at Bakchiserai, though it had been reported from the same place that the SD had 'resettled' all the Jews on December 13th, 1941.[134] These mistakes were very common in the depths of Russia.

The Crimean sects of the Krimshegs and Karaims were a nice problem for the SD. Ohlendorf ruled on December 5th, 1941, that they should be spared, but Heydrich decided that the Krimshegs, who were Jewish by race, should be killed, while the Karaims, who were Jewish only by religion, should be spared.[135] To Heydrich it was as important for Tartars as it was for Aryans not to be exposed to the risk of contamination with Jewish blood. Moreover, the Gestapo discovered that 'the fact that the Krimshegs and gipsies shared the fate of the Jews did not particularly excite the population.'[136]

In June, 1942, Ohlendorf returned to Germany and there is very little further trace of *Einsatzgruppe* D in the reports. At Nuremberg the Soviet prosecution produced a resettlement notice which had been posted by Commando 12 at Kislovodsk in the North Caucasus two thousand miles from the Reich. The Jews were to report for 'resettlement' on September 9th, 1942, and it appears that some 2,000 Jews from Kislovodsk and several thousands from Piatygorsk and Essentuki were taken by train the short distance to Mineralny Vody and there shot.[137] Since the Germans were now on the fringe of Asia, they no longer spoke of sending their victims *East*. The Caucasian Jews were told that they would colonise the 'undeveloped parts of the Ukraine.'*

In May, 1942, traces of *Einsatzgruppe* D appear in a report on gassing vans, sent in by a technician employed by the RSHA.[138] Vans had been sent from Simferopol to Taganrog, Stalino, Mariupol, and Gorlovka. Lieut. Becker reported that the vans, besides being defective, were unpopular among the men of the special commandos (*see page 139*). This was confirmed by Ohlendorf at Nuremberg.[139] The vans were issued to the *Einsatzgruppen* in the spring of 1942 chiefly for the purpose of executing women and children. Both Russian and German reports suggest that the principle use was the daily reduction of hospitals, asylums, and orphanages. They were never sufficient for mass executions and, though they were used in the final liquidation of the Minsk and Smolensk Ghettoes, this was only done in 1943 when the numbers involved were small (*see pages 243 and 289*). The gassing vans have a peculiar horror, but their part in the 'Final Solution' in Russia has been over-estimated.

In four short months of 1941 Himmler, Heydrich, Mueller, and the experts of the Gestapo carried out one of the most terrible deeds in the history of man. The murder of about 350,000 Jews in such a space of time was surpassed in Poland and at Auschwitz in the summers of 1942 and 1944, but not the naked savagery of the methods. It was made possible by the conquests of the Wehrmacht, whose chiefs, many of them free men to-day anxiously anticipating employment in a European army, stood by and watched this happen. Their attitude was, as it always will be, that of a strictly professional military caste. They left the unclean thing alone as something outside their professional duties, for which they had no time, and they passively allowed their subordinates to take orders from a handful of beings, whom they regarded as beneath the rank of soldiers.

*The execution-pit at Mineralny Vody was opened under the supervision of the journalist Alexei Tolstoi, who published an account in *Pravda* on August 5th, 1943. According to this, the number of corpses was 6,000; among them were recognised the bodies of well-known Jewish intellectuals from Leningrad, who had been evacuated to the North Caucasus for safety. Abandoned hurriedly by the Germans after Stalingrad, this was the first Jewish mass burial to be discovered by the Russians. (*See* Solomon, M. Schwarz, *Jews in the Soviet Union*, page 339.)

CHAPTER 10

Action Reinhardt, the Extermination of the Jews of Poland, 1942

1. The Action Begins—Chelmno

IT is not clear when the extermination of the Jews of Poland was decided. In Eastern Galicia the massacres were halted in July, 1941, soon after the opening of the Russian campaign, and not resumed till March, 1942. Yet it is unlikely that Hitler had in the meanwhile decided to spare the Polish Jews the fate of their kinsmen in Russia, for the Polish commissions of investigation have concluded that work was begun on the Chelmno and Belsec death-camps as early as October, 1941.

The task which confronted the murderers at the beginning of 1942 was gigantic. The Jewish population of Poland, 2,732,600 in 1931, was not less than 3,200,000 at the outbreak of war. In January, 1942, massed flight to the East, the *Einsatzgruppen* massacres, and an appalling death rate had probably reduced the population to two millions, of whom 1,600,000 still lived in the General Government,* where it had been expected that they would die of hunger.

The postponement of the massacres in the General Government from June, 1941, to March, 1942, sprang primarily from the disagreements between Frank and Himmler. Frank did not approve of Himmler's plan for the German colonisation of Poland, of which Jewish resettlement formed only a part. The

---

*Dr. Korherr estimated at the end of 1942 that voluntary emigration and excess death-rate had diminished the Jewish population of the General Government by 427,920 heads and this was exclusive of the ' resettlement actions.' This figure is consistent with a reduction of 900,000 for the whole of pre-war Poland, of which 250,000 may well have been due to excess death-rate and the remainder to emigration or deportation into the Eastern Soviet Union[1] (*see page 50 and Appendix 1*).

German ethnic 'corridor,' first mentioned on July 21st, 1941 (*see pages 45 and 159*), was probably suggested to Himmler by Globocnik, the Higher SS and Police Leader for Lublin province, who 'wanted to deport all Poles as well as Jews from the General Government, but could do nothing because of the opposition of Frank and his *Landkommissars*.'[2] According to von dem Bach-Zalewski, it was the disastrous repercussions of Globocnik's insistence on going ahead with this plan—at a time when Russian partisans had already appeared in the General Government—that enabled him to obtain Globocnik's recall in September, 1943.[3]

But the career of the man, to whom Himmler entrusted the entire massacre programme in the General Government, should be traced to the beginning. Odilo Globocnik was born in 1904 in Trieste of an Austro-Croat family of small bureaucrats. Too young for the First World War, he became embroiled in the Austrian *Freikorps* movement in Carinthia in the early 'twenties, from which this half-educated builder's foreman gravitated to the Austrian National Socialist Party, the almost inevitable goal of the sons of the dispossessed Imperial Civil Service. In 1933 Globocnik received a prison sentence for his part in the murder of a Jewish jeweller in Vienna,[4] but in July, 1936, he was nevertheless considered a suitable person to lead the deputation of the Austrian National Socialists to Berlin. It was then that Hitler instructed the deputation to respect the pledges against political interference which he had made to Chancellor Dollfuss.[5] Henceforward Globocnik was a principal conspirator in the Anschluss plot. In March, 1938, he wrote the fake telegram from Schuschnigg's office, which requested German protection for the Austrian Government during the forthcoming plebiscite. He also flew to Berlin to bring Hitler a copy of the National Socialists' ultimatum to Schuschnigg.[6]*

Such services demanded a high reward and Globocnik, the

---

*The Austrian conspirators of March, 1938, all of whom received high official appointments, included some of the most noteworthy war criminals of Hitler's Reich. In addition to Globocnik and Kaltenbrunner, the worthy successor of Heydrich, one may mention Josef Buerckel, who conducted the deportations from Alsace and the Saar, Governor Waechter of Cracow Seyss-Inquardt, Reich Commissar for the Netherlands, and Friedrich Rainer, Gauleiter of Carinthia and Dalmatia.

builder's foreman, became the first Gauleiter of Vienna, but in January, 1939, his speculations in illegal foreign exchange lost him his post and all his party honours. But Globocnik was too useful a man to be dropped and, after a very brief expiation in the ranks of the Waffen SS, Himmler pardoned his old friend 'Globus' and, in the month of November, 1939, made him Higher SS and Police Leader for Lublin province.[7]

Globocnik's personal appearance was physically good but the eyes and mouth were both shifty and brutal. As a police-commander he led a life of permanent drunkenness and self-indulgence. He wrote in a German so involved and ungrammatical as to be sometimes unintelligible, and, according to his fellow-conspirator Friedrich Rainer, he was capable of talking in an Austrian dialect of an opaqueness that served as a secret code in his telephone conversations.[8] This capacity for conspiracy was Globocnik's only practical merit. 'Einsatz Reinhardt' could not be conducted by honest men. It demanded active crooks and secret agents, and in Globocnik Himmler got both. Like many uneducated men, who pursue a single idea all their lives, this German race-fanatic—who was probably as much Slav as German—was partly crazy, though this was not always apparent to those who worked with him. The modest official, who reported Globocnik's frustrated aim of deporting both Poles and Jews, found it 'far reaching but excellent in tendency.'

Himmler seems to have first considered the removal of the Jews from Globocnik's 'Lublinland Reserve' in July, 1941. The first step was to be the creation of an enormous Jewish concentration camp at Lublin.* According to a certain Dr. Gorgass,

---

*There seem to have been various changes of plan. Himmler's proposals of July 21st, 1941, were for an entirely new camp, in addition to the expansion of Globocnik's workshop camps at Lipowo, the old airport and in Lublin itself (Case IV, NO 3031). In reality 'KL Lublin' or 'Majdanek' was created by extending a prisoner-of-war camp for Poles and Russians which dated from 1939. The camp was in the Majdan Tatarski suburb, and the surreptitious administrative change was made to defeat the objections of Frank's civil commissar, Governor Zoerner (IMT XII, 144-5 evidence Buehler). At Lipowo camp there were some 2,000 Polish Jewish soldier-prisoners who had been transferred from Germany early in 1941. These men were used at the end of the year to pressgang Jewish labour for the construction work. It would appear that the same team also 'recruited' the first Jewish commandos for the future death camps (see page 124).

Christian Wirth was also summoned to Lublin in order to start a new 'euthanasia institute.'[9] In reality both these plans were deferred, to be revived in October, when the deportations of Jews was ordered from the Reich and the evacuation of the Lublin Ghetto was once again under discussion. On October 17th, a week before the start of the Reich deportations, Frank declared that the ghetto, which had hitherto been open, would be cordoned off, that the highway to the Eastern front would be made to by-pass it, and that 1,100 Jews would be expelled immediately beyond the River Bug.[10] On December 16th Frank made the notorious speech to his Cabinet which contained the words 'liquidate them yourselves'[11] (see page 99):

'We cannot shoot or poison 3,500,000 Jews, but we shall nevertheless be able to take measures which will lead somehow to their annihilation and this will be done in connection with the gigantic measures to be determined in discussions from the Reich. The General Government must become free of Jews, the same as the Reich. Where and how this is to be achieved is a matter for the offices which we must appoint and create here. These activities will be brought to your notice in due course.'

These words imply that Frank expected to direct the extermination of Polish Jewry himself. Furthermore his chief Secretary of State, Josef Buehler, had just been told by Heydrich that no more Jews would be dumped in the General Government. Consequently Heydrich's double treachery in reviving the deportations from the Reich and in appointing Globocnik to run the exterminations in the General Government provoked Frank's opposition. We know that his 'Internal Administration Office' cancelled two trainloads of Hamburg Jews who were to have reached Hrubieczow in Lublin province on October 7th.[12] As a result they did not leave Hamburg till the 26th and and then went no further than Lodz, which was in Reich-incorporated territory and outside Frank's jurisdiction.

Heydrich and Eichmann easily accommodated themselves to the change that had been brought about as much by Frank's truculence as by the opposition of the Wehrmacht Transport

Command. They had only to divert the gassing vans, which were intended for the permanent extermination camps at Minsk and Riga to the neighbourhood of Lodz (*see page 137*). In January a resettlement commissioner of the Gestapo was sent to Lodz, a certain *Kriminalkommissar* Fuchs whose immediate task was to get rid of 30,000 inhabitants of the ghetto. The deportees[13a] from the Reich, of whom a large portion were still unemployed and destitute three months after their arrival, were his first target. But for several months the ' special installation ' was used so discreetly that refugees who reached the Warsaw Ghetto from Lodz did not know of its existence,[13] since the first deportations which began on December 8th, 1941, were only from small communities in the neighbourhood.[14] Then, on January 15th, 1942, some 650 families were taken from the Lodz Ghetto itself to the transit camp at Pabianice and thence by driblets to Chelmno.

The Chelmno death camp could not rival Treblinka by disposing of thousands of people in a day. The Gauleiter for the Wartheland province, Artur Greiser, told Himmler on May 1st that it was expected that 100,000 Lodz Jews could be resettled in six months.[15] In actual fact the decline in the ghetto population between January and September, 1942, the period of the actions, was less than 72,000 and part of this total was due to the ravages of hunger and overwork.* Hans Biebow, the ghetto commissioner, warned the SD at the very beginning of the action that it was quite wrong to suppose that the resettlement would mean better rations in the Lodz Ghetto. The death-rate was still running at 14,000 a year,[19] and in June Biebow had to ask the Labour Office to select Jews for heavy labour only from the rural communities, because in the ghetto the physical standard was too low.[20]

On April 11th, 1943, the Bothmann Commando left Chelmno

---

*Figures, allegedly kept by the Lodz Jewish Council, have been[16] published by Dr. Abraham Melezin. They show that the population of the ghetto was 162,281 in January, 1942, when it fell by 12,000. In February the fall was 10,000 and in March, the record month, 25,000. Then there was a drop of only 14,000 in five months and in August actually an increase of 4,700 due to the incorporation of some rural Jewish communities. In September the fall was 16,500, but it was actually intended to resettle 20,000, including all children under working age.[17] This action was called off on September 12th when the factories were reopened and new *Ausweise* were issued. It was the last resettlement action in Lodz till March, 1944.[18]

for Dalmatia, whence it was recalled by Himmler in February, 1944 (*see page 302*). It seems that the gassing vans had been little used after September 12th, 1942, when the Lodz Ghetto resettlement officially came to an end. The Polish Commission of Inquiry concluded that in this month transports to Chelmno were suspended because the mass-graves were reported to be creating a typhus epidemic and a crematorium had to be installed.[20a] It is significant that on September 17th Hoess came over from Auschwitz to report on Colonel Blobel's exhumation operations at Chelmno and to lend him internees for the work (*see page 138*).

A small portion of the 'resettled' Jews of Lodz were sent to labour camps and to the emptied ghettoes of the Lublin province, but Dr. Kermisz believes that 66 transports left Lodz for Chelmno between January and September and that they brought 55,000 victims.[21] Deportations, conducted on this scale and spread over so wide a period, could be organised with little coercion or panic, the more so since the stories about Chelmno were not generally believed in the ghetto. Even at the very end of the resettlement, in September, 1942, the President of the Lodz Jewish Council, Chaim Rumkowski, accompanied the march of the children to the railway station, confident because his own orphanage had been spared.[22] Those who knew did not care to spread despondency. Thus Lieutenant Rosenblatt, the commander of the Jewish *Ordnungsdienst*, admitted that he selected the old and feeble, knowing perfectly well they would be gassed.[23]

Outside the ghetto the Germans proceeded with less than their usual caution, perhaps because the region had a high proportion of racial Germans, who were even less likely than the Poles to make any protest.* A farmer who lived close to 'the Palace' told Judge Bednarz's commission of inquiry in 1945 that Bothmann's commando had stayed in Chelmno village on

---

*Although the Radagocz railway station was situated inside the ghetto and the deportations invariably took place at night, it was impossible for the 'Aryan side' to ignore them. Pastor Schedler, a Lodz *Volksdeutscher* now living in Wuerzburg, has told in moving language how members of his congregation, who lived on the edge of the ghetto, were kept awake at night by shouts, screams, and sobbing as the Jewish *Ordnungsdienst* dragged the people, designated for resettlement, from the houses (*Friede ueber Israel*, Munich, No. 3, July, 1951).

very friendly terms with the natives, employing local girls in their canteen. In 1944 members of the Jewish 'Waldkommando' were habitually sent into the village under escort to buy vegetables.[23a] Thus a number of civil agencies were acquainted with the Chelmno death camp and its purpose. For instance, in January, 1943, the Party Winter Relief Organisation in Posen complained to the Lodz Ghetto administration that the clothing, sent them from Chelmno camp, did not correspond with the samples shown them there. The clothing was bloodstained and it was still marked with the Jewish star. It was feared that the Polish conscript workers, for whom the clothing was intended, would 'spread the knowledge of the origin of these things' to their homes.[24]

On June 19th, 1942, the sorters of the Chelmno loot in Pabianice camp demanded the same danger money—15 marks a day—as the extermination commando because of the risk of infection. Danger money was also claimed by the Polish cab-drivers, who entered the Lodz Ghetto in the course of the resettlements.[25] Furthermore, the provincial food office in Posen was asked to allot a brandy ration to the loot-sorters, since the Chelmno camp staff were already receiving half a pint per man every day. The sorting, they were told, was 'in the highest degree nausea-rousing.'[26] In the autumn of 1943 the food office complained that, though the brandy distributions at Chelmno camp had ceased months ago, brandy was still being claimed by the ghetto administration. The answer to this was that the unpleasantness of exercising control in the ghetto still called for brandy.[27]

How far did these daily details of office work become public knowledge in Germany? In the early days of his arrest, in May, 1946, Oswald Pohl, the former emperor of the concentration-camp system, was disposed to answer that question. In language far different from his subsequent pleas, he denounced Kaltenbrunner's story that 'only a handful of men knew' as nonsense. 'In the case of textiles and valuables everyone down to the lowest clerk knew what went on in concentration camps.'[28] Equally, the lowest Food Ministry clerks must have asked themselves why certain camp guards needed enough brandy to get drunk every day.

2. The Action Spreads—Belsec

At least 50,000 Austrian, German, Bohemian, and Slovak Jews arrived in the small towns of the Lublin province between March and July, 1942 (*see pages 156 and 389*). To make room for them the locally resident Jews were pushed towards the old Russian frontier, but their real destination was the death camp Belsec, opened on March 16th. On March 27th Goebbels made this entry in his diary[29]:

'Beginning with Lublin, the Jews in the General Government are now being evacuated eastward. The procedure is pretty barbaric and is not to be described here more definitely. Not much will remain of the Jews. About sixty per cent of them will have to be liquidated. Only about forty per cent can be used for forced labour. The former Gauleiter of Vienna (Globocnik), who is to carry out this measure, is doing it with considerable circumspection and in a way that does not attract much attention . . . the ghettoes that will be emptied in the cities of the General Government will now be refilled with Jews thrown out of the Reich. The process is to be repeated from time to time.'

At first Globocnik tried to keep the nature of this movement secret from Governor Frank's Interior Administration Office, with whom he had to work, and some record has survived of the bewilderment of these officials who had had already two years' experience of Globocnik and his 'circus.'[30] The Lublin branch of the office was informed by the SD on January 6th, 1942, that 2,000 Jews from Mielec were to be moved some 150 miles east, to places along the old Russian border, near the River Bug. The German District Headmen at Cholm and Hrubieczow were to see that these Jews did not scatter themselves about the reception area, 'as usually happened.' On the 21st a new order increased the number of deportees to 4,500, presumably the bulk of so small a Jewish community as Mielec.[31]

This was the first removal of a complete Jewish community situated *inside* the Jewish Reserve, and the ominous news spread quickly. Apparently the Jewish Relief Committee for Lublin province knew as early as January 17th. Someone had overheard a telephone conversation in the corridor of the Interior Administration Office.[32] As a consequence the action was postponed to March 8th-16th. On March 7th Captain Turk in the Lublin Office was instructed from Cracow to keep in touch with Captain Hoefle, Globoenik's adjutant. Turk did his best, but for three days he was not even able to find Globocnik's orderly officer and he did not manage to talk to Hoefle till March 16th, the day that the Mielec action was completed.

Turk, who was a rather colourless member of the Reichstag with a blond moustache, has left a memorandum of this interview.[33] He was told by Hoefle that more Jews would be moved into Lublin province, including Jews from the Reich, who would be sorted for labour at Piaski, Isbica, and Trawniki (*see pages 101, 155 and 156, footnote*). In addition to these transfer stations, Hoefle was building a big camp at Belsec, 'the furthest frontier station in the province of Zamosc.' To this camp the Jews from Mielec would be sent forthwith, but later Belsec would be able to take four or five transports a day of a thousand Jews each. 'These Jews are to cross the frontier and will never more return to the General Government.'

Turk was to learn the finality of that sentence, for he was asked by Frank's Health Department three months later for the address of the Mielec Jewish Council who owed some money. On July 28th the Lublin Security Police commander reported 'address unknown' and referred Turk back to Globocnik's office from which a sergeant in 'Abteilung Reinhardt' wrote that the Mielec *Judenrat* had been settled in Russia. 'Definite information cannot be provided about their present residence since the address is not known.'[34]

On March 16th, the day of Turk's interview with Hoefle, the action began in Lublin itself. A ghetto had been set up on March 24th, 1941, but it was not closed and guarded till after October 17th.[35] Thereafter the Lublin Ghetto was not only enclosed but 'noticeably restricted' and divided into three sections. This ominous partition followed the precedent of Riga, Minsk, and Vilna. The action began, according to the former practice of the SD in Russia, in the section which was allotted to Jews who had no employment certificates, the hospitals and orphanages receiving prior treatment.[36] After ten days the action was broken off for nearly a month, during which Krueger issued a police decree from Cracow that all Jews without employment certificates must return to the ghettoes.[37] The last action in Lublin on April 20th-21st was largely a matter of rooting out Jews who had concealed themselves in bunkers and, according to some accounts, as many as 2,500 people were killed in the ghetto itself.[38] In the end only 3,857 exempted workers were left, living in the gipsy huts in the Majdan Tatarski suburb till the following November.[39]

At least 26,000 Jews were resettled in March-April, 1942. The Polish commission of investigation believed that 15,000 of them went to Belsec, the rest to the big labour camps, Majdanek (KZ Lublin) and Trawniki.[40] The reports that Jews were resettled in Russia from Belsec camp may be discounted as part of the camouflage that Heydrich had been creating since the Gross-Wannsee conference. In fact the allusions to the Krivoi Rog Jewish colonies and the Pinsk land reclamation camps may derive from fake field postcards.[41] The proportion which was sent to the death camp nevertheless seems low when compared with the Warsaw resettlement, but it must be borne in mind that Jewish industry in Lublin was a pie into which Globocnik had his fingers. Incidentally, it was precisely the proportion mentioned in Goebbels's diary on March 27th.

Even the closed and guarded Polish ghettoes soon learnt the truth. The President of the Jewish Council of Zamosc was approached from Lublin to find out what happened to the deportation trains. From the Jewish Council at Tomaszow-Lubelska he obtained a clear picture of Belsec camp, which he had confirmed through several Jews who escaped.[42] The Warsaw Ghetto knew of the Lublin manhunts in April 15th, while they were still in progress, and the arrival of Globocnik's murder commando was already expected,[43] but in fact Lwow and Lublin still kept Globocnik's hands full.

Lwow was a much harder proposition than Lublin. In August, 1941, when there had already been massacres, 119,000 Jews were registered with the Lwow Jewish Council.[44] They were not at first ruled by the Gestapo. Katzmann, the Higher SS and Police Leader, told Krueger that the civil administration had caused a typhus epidemic by their failure to create a ghetto during the first winter. Krueger's decree of February 28th, 1942, remedied this, but the removal of 100,000 Jews to the Kleparow quarter could not be completed till April.[45] In March Katzmann had ordered a registration, as a result of which 70,000 people, including 20,000 women, received labour certificates.[46] In spite of the fact that Katzmann controlled the labour exchange, which awarded 'special treatment' to all bearers of forged certificates, the Town Commandant and the representative of the Armaments Office obtained this astonishingly high number of exemptions for the tanneries, saw mills, and tailoring workshops of the Galician capital.

Katzmann's decree ordering the resettlement of Galician Jewry in 'The East' coincided with the transfer to the Kleparow Ghetto. The unexempted Jews were rounded up as they passed the control points. In Katzmann's own camouflage language, 'All work-shy and asocial Jews were caught during the screening and treated in a special way.' By this he meant that some 15,000 people were taken in April, 1942, to Janowska camp and gradually forwarded to Belsec. Their fate was not discovered for several weeks.[47]

There were further round-ups in Lwow in May and June, but they were on a smaller scale, since the Belsec death camp had already become overworked; finally it was out of action for six weeks so that the Lwow deportations were suspended till August.[48] But on May 18th the opening of a new death camp at Sobibor kept a certain number of resettlements going, pending the completion of the Treblinka camp and the opening of the great Warsaw Action.

The largest movement was still from the 'Jewish Reserve' towns in the Lublin province, which were required for Jews deported from the Reich, but there were also resettlements in Silesia and Western Galicia. In May and June the first actions took place in the large ghettoes of Sosnowiece, Dabrowa-Gornicza, Cracow, Tarnow, and Bielitz, actions which provided some of the first victims for the Birkenau gas chamber (see page 110).

Late in June Belsec camp was reopened and there followed a month later the big actions in Przemysl, Rzeszow, and Debica. In Rzeszow (or Reichshof) where there had once been 12,000

Jews, the German District Headman dedicated a wooden eagle, which was thus inscribed:

> 'This eagle, the German sign of superiority and dignity, was put up to mark the liberation of the town of Reichshof of all Jews in the month of July, 1942. It was put up during the service of Major Dr. Heinz Ehaus of the SS, first District Headman and first Station Commander for the NSDAP for the district Reichshof.'[49]

This grandiloquence was typical of German District Headmen, who in reality did not dispose of such matters.[*] For in the following November and December the Gestapo collected the surviving Jews of several neighbouring communities and brought them into the Rzeszow Ghetto to work a slave workshop, where the spoils of the death camps and resettlement actions were repaired—a human hell among many like it, which has been described with the honest simplicity of Defoe by the survivor, Frau Hilde Huppert, and Arnold Zweig, her editor.[51]

3. The Warsaw Resettlement

From data concerning the resettlements, collected by Dr. Josef Kermisz in *Dokumenty i Materialy,* one may conclude that on July 22nd, 1942, when the Warsaw action began, only 250,000 of the 1,600,000 Jews in the General Government had been subjected to the process called 'resettlement.' But the Warsaw resettlement had already been dangerously delayed. The bodily displacement of 380,000 ghetto inhabitants could not wait till the moment when the whole of Polish Jewry were made

[*]The rôle of the District Headmen seems to have been to compete with each other in writing to the *Landkommissars* or provincial governors, requesting the aid of the Security Police to free them of their Jews. Thus, on May 19th, the Headman of the district 'Lublinland' asked the permission of Governor Zoerner of Lublin province to deport 19,735 Jews from six communities, two of which, Lubartow and Piaski, had been increased by the reception of Reich deportees. From Janow-Lubielska the Headman wrote direct to Globocnik's office, asking for the removal of the Jews from eight small communities. The Chelm District Headman was ambitious; he wanted 15,000 Jews removed, including the 6,690 Jews of Hrubieczow.[50] As yet, however, the Belsec and Sobibor death camps could not deal with all these numbers.

desperate by the knowledge that the Germans meant the exterminations to be total. Apparently Globocnik said as much to Viktor Brack early in June, and Brack put it to Himmler in Berlin on the 23rd,[52] after he had attended Heydrich's funeral.

'... on this occasion *Brigadefuehrer* Globocnik advanced the thesis that the anti-Jewish action must be carried out as quickly as possible to prevent unforeseen obstacles forcing us to abandon the action while in full execution. You yourself, Herr Reichsfuehrer, have already expressed the opinion in my presence that considerations of pure propaganda force us to act quickly.'

Brack then suggested the alternative of sterilising the entire Jewish race, but there was no question now of Himmler slowing down the work which Heydrich had begun and which was devoted to his shade. On March 13th, 1942, when Himmler made an extravagant speech on his resettlement schemes, only a short precis of which survives, he was alleged to have said that half the Jews of the General Government must be resettled by the end of the year.[53] But on July 19th he telegraphed Krueger from Lublin that at the end of the year the *whole* Jewish population must be resettled. No Jews must be left in the General Government except in concentration camps and these were to be set up only in the neighbourhood of the main towns, Warsaw, Cracow, Czestochowa, Radom, and Lublin.[54]

The failure to complete the Treblinka gassing installation in April had delayed the start of the Warsaw resettlement and on top of it there occurred transport difficulties. The German summer offensive began on the Kharkov front on June 10th. On the 18th Krueger informed Josef Buehler that the question of reducing the ghettoes would be clarified in August. All non-military traffic on the railways had been suspended for a fortnight, but he had persuaded President Gerteis of the Reichsbahn 'to allow a few trains for the Jews now and then.'[55] But it seems that Himmler had more influence than the High Command on the Ministry of Transport,* from which the Under-Secretary of State, Teodor

*This is an instance of Himmler's power to short-cut the devious paths of German bureaucracy. The usual method of obtaining deportation trains was described precisely at Nuremberg by Eichmann's assistant, Dieter Wisliceny. Eichmann's transport officer, Captain Nowak, had to apply to one of the office chiefs in the Ministry of Transport. This *Amtsleiter* had in turn to apply to the Area Transport Command of the Wehrmacht in the

Ganzenmueller, wrote to Himmler's field adjutant, General Karl Wolff, on July 28th[56]:

'Since July 22nd one train a day with 5,000 Jews goes from Warsaw to Treblinka *via* Malkinia as well as two trains a week with 5,000 Jews each from Przemysl to Belsec. Bedob is in constant touch with the SD in Cracow. The latter agrees that transports from Warsaw *via* Lublin to Sobibor should be interrupted as long as building on this route makes these transports impossible.'

Karl Wolff replied from Winnitsa on August 13th, sending copies to Krueger and Globocnik:

'. . . I was especially pleased to learn from you that already for a fortnight a daily train, taking 5,000 of the Chosen People every time, had gone to Treblinka. . . . I have contacted the departments concerned myself so that the smooth carrying out of all these measures seems to be guaranteed.'

As a witness at the trial of Oswald Pohl on June 5th, 1947, Karl Wolff had 'not the slightest recollection' why he had taken such a close interest in these trains. He was not unduly pressed on the subject. Karl Wolff was a 'good German.' He had gone as Kesselring's peace envoy to Berne in March, 1945, and in May he had signed the capitulation of the army in Italy, as a consequence of which he was allowed to wear his general's insignia in court at Nuremberg. The sight was apparently so impressive that no one thought of asking him what he thought happened to 70,000 people, who were moved in the course of a fortnight to a single improvised camp, from which there was no transport to take them any further. Nor was Karl Wolff asked under what

theatre of war concerned. The latter might impose an effective veto as in the case of the Northern Army Group Transport Command in 1941-2 (*see page 92*). These vetoes, however, seem to have been possible only when the Wehrmacht was advancing and consequently getting some support from Hitler. Thus the Jewish transports from Poland, Hungary, Greece, and Italy in 1944 were allowed to encumber the communications of desperately retreating armies. (See Wisliceny's Affidavit C in 'Nazi Conspiracy and Agression,' Supplement B.)

conditions of hygiene he supposed that 5,000 old people and children could travel in a single goods train.*

On July 22nd, 1942, the Warsaw Ghetto had known of the massacres in Russia a whole year. In February there had been rumours of the Chelmno death camp and in April news of the Belsec death camp.[58] Yet on this fatal day, when the action began, there was not the least co-ordination of the various resistance movements. That had to wait till October, when the first ten weeks' agony of the ghetto was over. This singular failure of the Warsaw Jews sprang from looking to the Jewish Council for leadership and from believing that the huge size of the Warsaw Ghetto made it proof against anything so drastic. But on their side the Germans failed to see that the more they left the ghetto alone, the more this mood of fatalism would play into their hands. Instead they introduced terrorism inside the walls of the ghetto many months before the resettlement.

The indiscriminate shootings by German patrols began as early as September, 1941,[59] but mass executions, fifty victims at a time, dated from April 17th, 1942, the time of the Lublin resettlement. Next there were the round-ups early in July of able-bodied men who were sent to unknown camps on the grounds that they possessed no labour certificates—a hint that in Warsaw, too, the Germans proposed to use their characteristic methods. From now on there was a rush among the intelligentsia and people of means to get enrolled on the books of 'operational' factories.[60] There were other portents between April and July, 1942. On April 14th American subjects had to register at Pawiak prison. On June 10th the relatives of Palestine residents registered, having been told they would be exchanged for German subjects in England. Finally, on July 17th some 700 Jews, classified on account of real or falsified documents as foreigners, were interned in Pawiak

*Karl Wolff was handed over by the Americans to the British for trial in connection with the Ardeatina tunnel massacre, but the evidence implicating him was insufficient to justify a charge. He was, however, sentenced by a German court in the British Zone in 1946 to four years' imprisonment for his reports to Himmler and Field-Marshal Milch on Rascher's 'High Altitude' experiments on human beings carried out for the Luftwaffe. Milch used apparently to address his correspondence to 'Liebes Woelfchen.' 'Little Wolf' has not yet ceased to be a useful man. At the Rademacher trial in February-March, 1952, he testified his belief that even Hitler did not know about the massacre of the Jews.[57]

prison.* All this could only mean that some treatment was in store for the ghetto, which might cause diplomatic difficulties if foreign subjects were involved. There could be no plainer indication that Warsaw was to share the fate of Lublin and Lwow.[61]

On July 20th Dr. Adam Czerniakow, the President of the Jewish Council, was sent for by Auerswald, the ghetto administrator. On the same day a large number of notables of the community were arrested and kept as hostages while the German police companies, mainly old soldiers, who guarded the ghetto, were replaced by Ukrainian and Lithuanian militia.[62] Captain Hoefle now virtually took over the German *Transferstelle* which administered the ghetto. He had full powers from Globocnik, who remained in Lublin in an almost permanent state of drunkenness. In the meantime Auersbach, the economic administrator, faded out and Captain Franz Konrad, 'the king of the ghetto,' took his place. His office, the *Werterfassung*, eventually employed

---

*The registration of the U.S.A. and Palestine groups anticipated the plan, first mentioned in February, 1943, by which 30,000 Jews in occupied territories were to be retained for purpose of exchange on account of their claims to foreign nationality. False papers were no bar to entry into these groups. It was sufficient that the Foreign Powers concerned were prepared to accept the Jews, who were preserved just so long as there was a chance of using them (*see page 338*). The fate of the 'Pawiak Jews' was thus very diverse. Mary Berg left for the French exchange camp at Vittel on January 18th and small groups seem to have left right up till the ghetto rebellion. After the rebellion a further 300 Jews were picked out from the deportation trains and quartered in Warsaw in the Hotel Polski. According to Stroop and his adjutant, Karl Kaleske, they were removed *en masse* by the Security Police commandant, Dr. Hahn, on Kaltenbrunner's orders (IMT XI, 318-9, and PS 3841). It appears that they were taken to Treblinka in July (Yankiel Wiernik, *page 41*).

'Exchange-Jews' still continued to be picked out from the deportees and some were sent in July to the exchange camp at Bergen-Belsen from the Pawiak prison, from the Hotel Polski, and even from Globocnik's camp at Trawniki (*Mary Berg, page 236*). But, on the arrival in October of the first foreign Jews to be employed in the demolition of the Warsaw Ghetto, a clearance was made of the Jews in Pawiak prison. It is alleged that most of them were gassed at Auschwitz on October 25th, when there occurred one of the most dramatic incidents in the history of the camp, the shooting on the selection-siding of an SS *Rapportfuehrer* by one of the Warsaw Jewesses who claimed U.S. nationality, apparently an actress. (Filip Friedman, *This was Oswiecim*, 75, War Refugee Board, Auschwitz report, *page 14*). Dr. Albert Menasche, however, associates this incident with the arrival of the Rome transport on October 22nd. (*Birkenau, Auschwitz II*, New York, 1947, *page 61*.)

no few than 2,000 Jews in sorting and removing assets, besides treacherously trading in employment certificates for which Konrad was not destined to pay till September 8th, 1951, when a Warsaw court sentenced him to death.[63]

The reports of the excellent courier service which reached the Polish Exile Government in London by December, 1942, enabled Hoefle's proclamation of July 22nd to be reconstructed.[64] A collecting station or *Umschlagplatz* was to be established, where the Stavki Street crossed the railway tracks. Here 6,000 Jews had to be delivered daily by the Jewish *Ordnungsdienst*, acting under the orders of the Jewish Council, for resettlement 'in the East.' There was a very large exemption list, which included Jews with valid employment certificates, Jews municipally employed not only by the Jewish Council but also by the welfare associations, besides Jews who could not be moved from hospital.

The extent of the exemptions anæsthetised the will to resist, for the individual strove to acquire and keep his protective scrap of paper as if it had some permanent value. It was believed that the employment certificates had preserved six or seven thousand Jews in Rowno, the nearest of the Russian ghettoes, since the November massacres. No one knew that these, too, had been murdered on July 14th.[65] Thus the first round-up in Warsaw failed to create the right sense of horror. Thousands of shelter-dwellers were sent to join the deportation column, so broken down and so despairing of life that they scarcely needed any compulsion from the Jewish *Ordnungsdienst* (*see pages 64 to 66*). A large portion volunteered for the collecting station for the sake of the big loaf of bread and tin of marmalade, offered as a travel ration by the German Resettlement Office.

Yet the collection of 6,000 Jews a day could not go on without involving the certificate-holders, who should have realised their position after July 24th when 'President' Czerniakow committed suicide. Hoefle had raised his daily quota of lives and on Czerniakow's desk was found a slip of paper between his fingers bearing the figures '7,000.'[66] Czerniakow's body was taken away on a handcart and the Germans forbade any mourners to follow it.[67]

Before the end of July it had been observed from the wagon numbers that the deportation trains returned to the collecting station in twelve to fourteen hours. Soon afterwards a Polish railwayman, the relative of a deportee, brought back a description of Treblinka death camp.[68] Many other Polish railwaymen were aware of the shunting manœuvres that went on beyond Malkinia Junction. By the end of August some of them were offering for sale photographs of the Treblinka ' bath-house.'[69] Furthermore, a Jew escaped from the Treblinka work column during the gassing of the Radom transport on August 16th and made his way later in the month back to the ghetto.

Such evidence could only confirm what in principle had been known from the first. Contrary to the proclamation, hospital inmates and even typhus patients were taken in rickshaws in the very first days to be ' resettled.'[70] On July 28th anyone on the streets could see the march of the Janusz Korczak orphanage, complete with nurses and staff, from its premises in Dzielna Street. At the head walked the white-haired Dr. Korczak himself, carrying two babies, a picturesque and universally beloved figure. No one could suppose that the Germans would saddle themselves with such a burden in the labour camps of Russia.[71]

As soon as the beggars, the destitute and the sick had been disposed of, the Germans attacked the certificate holders. Their certificates were annulled from day to day, their wives and children were rounded up while they were at work, they were paraded before Gestapo commissions in the factories. The SS had now to assist the wilting *Ordnungsdienst* and in the Nalevki and Gesia Streets the tenements had to be broken open by hatchet-gangs of Lithuanian militia.[72] Intervention was no longer easy. Neither the German Armaments Office nor the German factory owners could save their men, unless their certificates bore the new stamp signed ' SS Polizeifuehrer. Aktion Reinhardt.'

The story of Jewish co-operation in the resettlement of July 22nd-October 3rd is not very pleasant. The Jewish Council bureaucrats still believed that they could bargain indefinitely for their own security. There was still no Jewish resistance movement to send them awkward reminders. During the first few weeks Szerynski and Lejkin continued to command the *Ordnungsdienst* and two Jewish officers, Szmerling and Furstenburg, presided over the horrors of the collecting station.[73] Of this an Aryan Polish manager in one of the German-owned factories, who visited the inferno on July 24th and 30th, has left an exceptionally vivid picture.[74] He observed the terror-struck brutality of the *Ordnungsdienst** and the condition of the deportees, who had been waiting up to forty-eight hours for the Treblinka train. They huddled in the Stavki Square or overflowed into the gutted Czyste hospital, an up-to-date institution in a modern capital which had been turned into the cattle-pen of a human abattoir, full of excrement and the odour of despair.

The collecting station could be visited by representatives of the factories. Bearing placards, they would hunt for their men and sometimes extricate a victim from the clutches of the SD, but often this victim would have to part from his family who remained, waiting for the train. Sometimes, when the train was full, the remainder would be dismissed and sent home. Sometimes there would be a second selection at the collecting station, and those who were fortunate would board a train for the great concentration camp at Lublin-Majdanek or the transit camp at Trawniki. On July 31st a transport of a thousand people left for Minsk to serve under the Luftwaffe command—though not for long. According to General Stroop's report to Krueger, 310,332 Warsaw Jews were resettled by October 3rd. At least two-thirds of these went to the death camp Treblinka, possibly as many as three-quarters.[75]†

*The Germans were able to twist even this circumstance to serve propaganda. Thus on May 29th, 1942, Hitler's secretary, Dr. Henry Picker, records the following specimen of table-talk at Field Headquarters:

> ' Hitler mentioned reports that Jewish police in the ghettoes had beaten up their coreligionists in masses in a way that our police would scarcely have dared to do to members of the National Socialist Party, even in the fiercest period of their struggle. This expressed so perfectly the whole crudity of Jewish existence.' (*Hitler's Tischgespraeche.* Bonn, 1951, page 311.)

†Captain Hans Hoefle, Globocnik's resettlement commissar for Warsaw, escaped from an internment camp in Austria early in 1949 when he learnt that he was to be extradited to Poland and tried with Major-General Stroop. Hoefle has never been found. According to *Le Monde Juif,* August, 1949, the indictment charged him with deporting ' more than 200,000 Jews to Treblinka.' Since 310,000 Jews were indisputably deported in the course of ten weeks, this figure suggests that close on 100,000 were sent to Majdanek, Trawniki and elsewhere. Yet such numbers could certainly not have been accommodated in the camps. From the already quoted Ganzenmueller letter it may be inferred that most of the transports to Lublin were merely delayed death trains, pending the clearing of the railway track to Sobibor.

Normally the death train consisted of forty to sixty wagons. It might take as many as 6,000 people with their bundles and provisions or as few as 3,500. On some days there would be two trains, while for several days on end there would be no train at all. Such a lull occurred between August 20th and 25th when Treblinka dealt with numerous transports from other ghettoes.* There was a longer lull late in September.[76]

Nearly half the ghetto population had gone by August 15th. The area could therefore be reduced. A large part of the walled ghetto was situated south of Chlodna Street, the main highway to Posen and the Reich. It was linked with the rest of the ghetto by wooden bridges crossing the street. With the exception of 'the little ghetto,' an island containing the Toebbens and other factories on Prosta Street, the southern half of the ghetto was evacuated and a large number of streets were returned to the municipality, but in some of the empty apartment-houses the loot-sorting commandos of Konrad's Liquidation Office were now established.[77]

On August 16th an employment certificate of a new pattern was issued. It was restricted to 30,000 workers without covering their dependants. It was the prelude to the great round-up of September 5th-12th, when the last 100,000 Jews living in the ghetto were collected in stages at a new collecting station in Milo Street known as the *Kessel*. Work was suspended in the factories where the entire staff had, in theory, to march out. About half the dependants who were not protected by the certificate were apparently allowed to leave the *Kessel*, but many of those who hid in the houses were killed on the spot. Even the Jewish Council employees had to go to the *Kessel*, where they were reduced to

*The real explanation of this lull seems to be that, until enough police troops and militia could be obtained for a mass round-up of the whole ghetto, it became impossible to fill the trains. Dr. Michel Mazor, who is now an archivist of CDJC in Paris, writes that by the middle of August there was no longer a continuous inhabited ghetto but only islands of inhabited tenements round the factories. He himself was picked up in a surprise raid on the Jewish cemetery and put on a Treblinka train, which left at some time during the lull period at the end of August half empty. It was this circumstance which favoured his own miraculous escape from the death train and his walk back to Warsaw, where he was able to live on 'the Aryan side' (*Le Monde Juif*, No. 51, January, 1952. *La cité Engloutie*, Part XII).

3,000. Only 380 were left of the 1,600 *Ordnungsdienst* policemen. The others were kept in a single apartment-house and sent to Treblinka on September 21st.[78]

On September 29th the ghetto was reduced to its final limits, a mere corner in the north-east of the old ghetto measuring about a thousand yards by three hundred. The Jews continued to work in factories outside this area and the little ghetto in Prosta Street remained in its isolation. On October 3rd some 65,000 to 70,000 Jews survived. Less than half had any official right to exist, but nearly all were capable of bearing arms and very few of these were encumbered with concealed parents or children who were potential hostages for their actions.

This conduct of the SD seems careless in view of Himmler's intention, expressed on July 19th, of converting Warsaw and four other ghettoes into concentration camps. Apparently the Warsaw ghetto was already considered to be a concentration camp after the *Kessel* action. On September 12th the Interior Administration and Labour Offices in Cracow handed over their joint control of the ghetto to the SS.[79] The Jews now lived officially in blocks attached to their factories and those who were seen on the streets were shot at. Reunions between the working groups had to be clandestine. Yet there were still a *Judenrat* and an *Ordnungsdienst* and some of the trappings of autonomy. There were whole blocks inhabited by 'wild' Jews who belonged to no factory at all. Beyond the incomplete and hastily run up walls of the new ghetto smuggling and escapes went on as never before, nor had Konrad's Liquidation Office removed all the wealth of the ghetto. Symptoms of the new state of affairs soon appeared. On October 20th most of the Jewish political groups accepted the orders of a committee for resistance. It may have been on this day that the ghetto resistance movement secured its first victim of distinction, the Jewish *Ordnungsdienst* commander, Lejkin.[80]

4. A Change of Plan

The resettlement of 310,000 Warsaw Jews in ten weeks did not absorb all the strength of the SD and its helpers. In the whole of pre-war Poland, including the Russian-annexed provinces, 500,000 Jews may have been killed in these ten weeks. More than 7,000 murders a day seem less incredible when the simplicity of the method is accepted. The special extermination commandos of the Security Police and SD contained perhaps no more than a thousand or two Germans, spread over the whole country. But, before the executions took place, the difficult work had been done by a vast legion of helpers. Old reservist soldiers—the greater part of them Austrians—made up the *Ordnungspolizei, Schutzpolizei* and *Feldgendarmerie* companies, who cordoned the ghettoes, while inside the ghettoes the Security Police relied on Lithuanian, Latvian and Ukrainian militiamen to help them in the filthiest work of all. In many accessory matters ordinary Polish police played their part, while the *Junaks*, or Blue Police, who were recruited from German-speaking Poles, could be relied on for anything. Among civilians even members of the Polish resistance would make a few zlotys by denouncing Jews—and they could be tempted to go further. On November 8th, 1942, after a resettlement action in Cracow, the Prince Archbishop, Cardinal Jan Sapieha, complained to Governor Frank that Polish youths from the conscript labour service had been incited with liquor to take part in the round-ups.[81]

On August 24th, 1942, Governor Frank told his Cabinet in Cracow that there were still 1,200,000 Jews in the General Government. He hoped that 'the possibility of their not dying of hunger would hasten the anti-Jewish measures'—a hope that was justified.[82] Dr. Kermisz's list of the 'actions' of the month of August, 1942, includes twenty-four towns of the General Government, besides thirteen in Reich-incorporated territory and six in former Polish White Russia. Among them is the resettlement of 40,000 Jews, more than half the surviving population of the Lwow Ghetto.[83]

Between August 10th and 22nd one of the trains, provided by Herr Ganzenmueller of the Ministry of Transport, left Lwow nearly every day for Belsec. Even for Frank's General Government the state of these trains was particularly shocking (*see page 140*). On the 20th Kurt Gerstein saw a train arrive at Belsec among whose 6,700 passengers there were 1,450 dead. At Rawa-Ruska the French prisoner of war, Paul Roser,[84] saw corpses lying on the track every morning, a circumstance which is confirmed in a report to Goebbels by his ministerial representative in Lwow[85]:

> 'The resettlement of the Jews (which partly assumes forms not worthy of a cultured people) directly provokes comparison of the methods of the Gestapo with those of the GPU. The railway wagons are said to be in such a bad state that it is impossible to prevent Jews breaking out. The result is that at wayside stations there occur wild shootings and regular man-hunts. It is also reported that corpses of shot Jews lie on the streets for days. Although the Reich Germans as well as the foreign population are convinced of the necessity of liquidating all Jews, it would still be more appropriate to carry these out in a manner that causes less sensation and offence.'

There must have been a good deal of criticism of this kind, but in the face of the passive attitude of most of the Poles it was not thought necessary to conduct the actions with the least circumspection. In September there were again actions in twenty-four communities, including the resettlement of most of the Jews of Czestochowa. In October the biggest action was at Piotrkow, but Tarnow, Stryj, Kolomea, and Cracow[86] all had large-scale affairs, while in the provinces, considered Russian, there took place the great Pinsk and Dubno actions (*see pages 226-7 and 205*).

The winter of 1942 began late and on November 18th it was possible to conduct another three-day action in Lwow. It followed the issue of a new employment certificate, available only to 12,000 workers. These had to wear an armlet with the letter R for *Rustungsamt* (armament office) or W for *Wehrmacht*. Some thousands of hitherto exempted Jews were taken *via* Janowska camp to the new shooting-place, Piasky Gora, the 'Sand Hill.' This replaced Belsec, which was practically out of action. In December the Lwow Ghetto was reduced to a few streets in the Kleparow quarter, in which were packed some 25,000 Jews, both licensed and unlicensed.[87]

Dr. Kermisz's list for November once more includes the names of Lublin, Czestochowa, Piotrkow, Rzeszow, and Przemysl, besides a whole string of Eastern Galician towns which the Germans had already declared officially Jew-free. In some cases a small group of Jews had been allowed to survive, in others an entirely new ghetto had been allowed to form. This situation seems even more self-contradictory in view of the order Himmler gave on October 8th to Krueger, Globocnik, and Quartermaster-General Wagner.[88] In this order Himmler speaks of collecting the protected Jewish workers—whom he calls 'bogus armament workers'—into two concentration camps, Warsaw and Lublin. From now on, he declares, all army contracts for Jewish labour must be placed through the SS. Finally, the Jews will have to be replaced by Poles, so that they may be sent to 'camps in the eastern part of the General Government,' where they will 'some day disappear in accordance with the Fuehrer's wishes.'

The whole order, including the transparent reference to the death camps Treblinka, Sobibor, and Belsec, was circulated next day to a number of rear-area commanders in Poland, as well as to the Ministry of Economics.[89] On October 13th there was a conference at Spala between Krueger and the Wehrmacht where the Jewish workers were formally surrendered to the SS, exception being made for certain specialists such as Jewish dentists. Henceforward, Jews would be hired by the SS to civilian contractors at 4.50 zlotys a day per Jew or 2s. 3d., out of which not more than 1.60 zlotys—or ninepence—was deductable for their keep. The Jews could only be supplied from labour camps, though exception was made in the case of the Warsaw, Cracow, and Lodz Ghettoes. Officially these Jews were 'labour prisoners of the SS and Police.'[90]

But the effect of Himmler's original letter of October 8th and the decrees of October 17th for Lwow and other towns was completely annulled by a decree of Governor Frank's, dated October 28th, and one of Dr. Waechter's for Galicia, dated November 10th. In addition to the three official ghettoes, these decrees permitted Jews to reside in five towns in Warsaw province, eight in Lublin province, four in Radom, and four in Cracow, while in Galicia there were no less than eleven ghettoes and twenty-two licensed residences.[91] Thus, instead of reducing the official ghettoes from five to two, Himmler had agreed to the SS taking over and guarding some fifty-seven widely scattered Jewish communities. Himmler, who was quite often a realistic person, had decided to profit by the experience of the SD, who knew that the best way of finding hidden Jews was to let them return home. Hence the very large number of 'permitted residences.'

And yet the place to which the fugitives returned could often be far worse in its prolongation of living death than any German concentration camp. In a small ghetto, brought under direct SS rule by the decrees of October, 1942, a mere NCO and a labour-overseer of Frank's Interior Administration Office could between them utterly terrorise a thousand or two slaves, huddled day and night in a work-shed and a few slum tenements. Men who had never known responsibility, they were accountable to no one for the lives of Jews from whom the last inch of work had to be squeezed. Thus at Rzeszow Frau Hilde Huppert described what she saw in February, 1943:

'I stood at the window and saw twenty miserable figures wrapped in rags crouching in the lorry. I did not understand what it meant and asked a native of Rzeszow to explain it to me. That, he said, was an incident which repeated itself every six weeks. A few weeks ago these people had left Rzeszow hale and hearty. They were sent to the equipment workshop at Stalowswola,* not far from Rzeszow, from which they returned as living corpses. They had to work eighteen hours a day under violent ill-treatment on a diet on which no one could live. When I asked why they brought such sick people here, he explained that the factory only acquired healthy bodies in exchange for the expended human material. In the afternoon we were subjected to a regular man-hunt, since no one would go there willingly.'

The twenty people from Stalowswola were put to bed in a room in the ghetto, but two days later:

'Toward seven o'clock six Gestapo men arrived and asked to see the sick workers. From their black looks it could be seen that they were up to no good. In the sick-room they

---

*The two slave-workshop camps, Stalowswola and Rozwadow, were situated on the San river thirty-five miles north of Rzeszow and were not evacuated till the Russian advance to the Vistula in July, 1944. They were the subject of a Polish Commission of Inquiry at the end of the war. (*Dokumenty i Materialy*, I, *pages 280-290*.)

ordered the people in bed to get up and run into the square. Whoever could not run would be killed. They chased the poor victims out of bed with blows of the whip and forced the ones who could hardly stand on their feet to run to and fro. The executioners found it so funny that they had to stop their mouths from laughing. Then they began to shoot at the runners. . . .

'As we reached the West Ghetto we stumbled into puddles of blood: our footsteps sounded unearthly in the darkness, we felt the neighbourhood of death. We saw corpses lying in front of our houses. Men carrying lamps were engaged in loading them on hand-carts. Among the bodies were people who were not yet dead and who groaned. Nevertheless, the men had their orders to cart them all away.'[92]

At the end of 1942 Dr. Korherr reported to Himmler that no less than 1,274,166 Jews from the General Government had been 'resettled.' This meant that at least a million had been killed,[93] and yet in Eastern Galicia there were still plenty of Jews, and here the conditions were far more lax than at Rzeszow.* Thus on Christmas Day Dr. Guèrin from 'Stalag 323' at Rawa-Ruska found the narrow winding streets of the ghetto in Stryj thronged with people. The Jewish girls were in their best attire, some of them walking out with German soldiers.[94] Yet 2,000 Jews had been removed from Stryj between November 13th and December 3rd. Barely a quarter remained of the pre-war Jewish population of 11,000 and all of these were to disappear in the actions of February and May, 1943.[95]

I can do no better than give Dr. Guèrin's own explanation, for he is perhaps the only literary witness of what happened in Poland who was neither persecutor nor victim[96]:

'What happened to the Jews between the actions? Those who escaped the massacres resumed their normal life

*Officially there were 297,914 Jews still awaiting resettlement at the end of the year, including 161,514 in the Galician ghettoes. To these should be added 200,000 to 250,000 Jews in labour camps and perhaps 100,000 in hiding or on the run, making from 550,000 to 600,000 in all. The figures apply only to the General Government, where there had been 1,600,000 Jews as late as March.

through a healing power in their race which has known many other massacres. Those who were able to escape gradually emerged from their hiding places. They circulated freely in the town, they resumed their shops and moneylending and again acquired capital. Some Jewish girls appeared in their best clothes, deliberately forgetting to wear the armlet and exciting the jealousy of the Polish girls of their age, for they were often more beautiful, more graceful, and more smartly dressed. It did not occur to the Jews to take to the woods, to disappear for ever from the towns where there was so much danger. It was not lack of courage on their part so much as racial fatalism forcing them to crowd into the ancestral ghettoes in virtue of an ancient gregarious instinct. Death for death, they preferred to enjoy the advantages of urban civilisation to the end and to endure their trials in collectivity, rather than be delivered to themselves in the solitude of the fields and woods, where the Ukrainian police in German pay pursued them with pitiless hatred.'

Three more examples will suffice to illustrate the blind fatalism of the Polish Jew, so accurately observed by Dr. Guèrin. In the case of Sandomierz the ghetto was completely cleared at the end of October, 1942, but in November Jews were moved in from several labour camps and thousands of fugitives joined them in the ghetto in order to acquire a legal status. Nearly all of them were taken to Treblinka on January 10th, 1943, but a few were left to form the nucleus of a third ghetto, which was not liquidated till June.[97]

Bochnia, near Cracow, had enjoyed immunity till August 25th, 1942, because the German *Landkommissar* made huge profits from its Jewish workshops. After the first resettlement, which nearly emptied the ghetto, the workshops were reopened by the SD and again they were filled with Jews, who offered themselves as slaves to be rented by the SD to German entrepreneurs. Bochnia became a permitted residence under the decree of October 28th, but on November 11th a second action halved the ghetto. The survivors were kept in concentration camp conditions till September 1st, 1943, when a third action dispersed

270

them to other camps and killing-places, but there was still a small labour unit in Bochnia in January, 1944.[98]

In the extreme east of Galicia the Jewish community of Zbaraz suffered six actions over a similar period. It was a typical Galician ghetto, neither guarded nor enclosed, but the cruelty and treachery of the Ukrainians was such that hunger and exposure always forced the fugitives to return. Even in this little community the Jewish Council, intent on survival, was forced to the most abominable tyranny and corruption, while the Jewish Ordnungsdienst, who were issued with a liberal allowance of spirits on action days, could be relied on to do the Germans' work right up to the moment of their own decimation. We owe an extremely factual unvarnished description of this Gehenna to Jakob Littner, a Munich stamp-dealer, who survived the last killing in Zbaraz, not by taking to the woods but by living from June, 1943, to March, 1944, when the Russians came, in a hole in the clay underneath the cellar of a Polish farmer's house—one of the most miraculous stories of the war.[99]

This narrative sheds an even more terrible light on the fatalism and helplessness of the Galician Jew. The Warsaw Jew was a more Europeanised product. So, in neglecting to make the Warsaw Ghetto a true concentration camp in October, 1942, Himmler miscalculated. It is true that this might have meant combing out each building separately, but that would have been easier in October than it proved to be in the following April.

The failure to implement Himmler's decree of October 8th is not easily explained. Himmler described the Higher SS and Police Leader for Warsaw as 'from the cavalry, very pleasant, but in no way suited to his functions.[100] He replaced this man, Ferdinand von Sammern-Frankenegg, on the eve of the Warsaw rebellion. Himmler may have been led astray by von Sammern's advice or von Sammern may simply have failed to carry out Himmler's instructions for lack of man-power. All one knows is that Globocnik in a memorial to Himmler, written at the beginning of 1944, remarked cryptically that 'in Warsaw the wrong methods were applied.'[101] The fact is that the situation which provoked the extraordinary historical drama known as the Warsaw Ghetto rebellion is wrapped in mystery.

271

CHAPTER 11

The Liquidation of the Polish and Russian Ghettoes, 1943—1944

1. The Warsaw Ghetto Rebellion

THE months of December, 1942, and January, 1943, saw the activity of 'Einsatz Reinhardt' much reduced. They were the months in which the new combat groups in the ghettoes procured themselves arms. In Warsaw pistols and grenades, bought outside the ghetto, were smuggled past the Polish police and foreign militia who guarded the Jewish cemetery or were introduced through the sewers.[1] But in spite of some liaison with Polish Left-wing groups, the weapons had to be paid for, and it was not till the end of the ghetto rebellion that General Sikorski's appeal from London induced the *Armia Kraiova* or Home Army to contribute. As to the groups that were in contact with Russia, it does not make much difference that Marshal Rola-Zymierski told Mr. Josef Tenenbaum that he wished he could have helped.[2]

The Italian divisions, which were withdrawn from the line in February, 1943, but which still served in Galicia in May, were the best source of supply. At a price they provided arms for resisters and transport for fugitives. In Lwow Italian pistols fetched 2,000 zlotys (£50).[3] But cover was as important as arms. In October, 1942, after the Warsaw resettlement, the German factory owners in the ghetto encouraged the building of underground shelters—ostensibly against air raids—because they had now acquired a vested interest in preventing the liquidation of the ghetto. The SD failed to keep Himmler informed, and it is easy to see why. Even the mass-murderer-in-chief could be bought. Globocnik was hiding his own business deals which he conducted with Toebbens and other German entrepreneurs.

But on January 14th, 1943, Himmler paid a surprise visit to Warsaw. 'I did not know I was going and I did not inform you,' he told Krueger. Himmler had learnt from Colonel Fretter of the Armaments Office that 8,000 of the 40,000 workers in the ghetto were to be resettled on the 18th. Of the remainder he found that 24,000 Jews, camouflaged as armament workers, were employed only as tailors and fur-dressers, and most of them were on the books of 'Walter C. Toebbens A.G.' Fretter was told to convey Himmler's amazement to General Schindler of the Armaments Office. 'Once more I set a final term for the resettlement, February 15th.' The plan was to send Toebbens's 16,000 workers to Lublin camp and to work the remaining factories from prison-barracks in the Warsaw Ghetto. As to Toebbens, who had 'made himself a millionaire on cheap Jewish labour supplied by us,' the Main Security Office would audit his books.[4]

Of the skirmish of January 18th Major-General Stroop wrote later to Krueger: 'The factory managers as well as the Jews resisted the order in every possible way.' One factory manager may even have been· shot by the Gestapo.[5] A still subservient Jewish Council tried to make out the resettlement lists, but of 5,000 'volunteers' demanded for the Trawniki and Poniatowo camps only a few hundreds were obtained. The managers made false returns of their Jews and hid part of them in the prepared bunkers. Only Toebbens tried to persuade his Jewish foremen. He 'had it from Globocnik' that this was positively the last resettlement and that at Poniatowo the Jews would work under Wehrmacht supervision with 'a nursery school, sports stadium, and swimming pool.' Toebbens in fact hoped to maintain his profits by going into partnership with Globocnik at Poniatowo.* But Toebbens was the employer who was least likely to reassure the Jews. For a long time he had been known as the 'resettlement commissioner' and his factory in the little ghetto, directed by his assistants Bauch and Jahn, had the reputation of a 'Bastinado battalion' (Pretzelregiment).[6]

On January 18th, 1943, a miserable column of deportees started to march down Niska Street, but at the junction of Zamenhova Street several of them pulled out firearms and shot at the SS and militia. The Jewish column dispersed, but with fantastic casualties. For three days a house-to-house round-up

---

*A contract, signed on January 31st, was produced at Toebbens's trial in May, 1950.

was conducted. In the north-east corner of the ghetto four of the fifty Jewish combat groups barricaded themselves and after four days von Sammern had to use two field guns to pound up the buildings—without getting the ringleaders. Colonel Fretter's 8,000 Jews were not obtained.[7] The German official figures show that only 6,490 Jews were resettled between October 3rd, 1942, and January 31st, 1943,[8] but von Sammern nevertheless decided to call off the action.

The Jewish leaders for their part were not misled by this relative success. They knew that a far more desperate struggle awaited them. On February 3rd Himmler ordered Oswald Pohl to proceed with the construction of a concentration camp in the ghetto, but only as a provisional measure pending the transfer of both Jews and workshops to Lublin.[9] On February 16th Himmler told Krueger that the rest of the ghetto must be razed to the ground as soon as the camp was ready.[10] The houses where 500,000 'sub-humans' had lived must disappear. The city of Warsaw must be assigned a smaller space for it was a 'constant source of disaffection and revolt.'*

Krueger and von Sammern still hesitated and Globocnik was believed to have said that the concentration of Jewish labour at Lublin could not be achieved till June.[11] On March 13th Krueger tackled the easier proposition of liquidating the Cracow Ghetto. Only 14,000 Jews remained in the Podgorze quarter and the action was completed in two days by Major Willi Haase, seconded by Captains Neumann and Amon Goeth. Most of the Cracow Jews went to the camp at Jerozolimskie Street and thence to the labour camps, Plaszow, Szebnice and Prokocim, but many were killed in the ghetto and one transport went to Auschwitz in time for the opening of the first of the new gas chambers. A Jewish commando still remained in the ghetto to sort the loot. It was a model resettlement action.[12]

On the same day, March 13th, Krueger demanded 2,000 'volunteers' from the Warsaw Ghetto for the transit camp, Trawniki, but only 200 people from the 'wild' apartment houses could be rounded up by the Jewish Council, while 400 'wild'

---

*It is possible to see what was in Himmler's mind. At the end of January 40,000 people had been expelled from the Vieux Port quarter of Marseilles, which was now in course of demolition.

Jews were hidden in the bunkers by the combat groups. The Germans had to get their men by force, for the Jewish Council told them blankly that their power had passed to another authority.[13] Now that the Jewish officials, who had assisted in the great resettlement, had all either been shot by Jews or carried off by Germans, the Council no longer opposed the resistance movement. The Jewish *Ordnungsdienst,* who had seen their colleagues taken to Treblinka, no longer rounded up Jews, indifferent whether they were to wait their turn for Treblinka or be shot as reprisal hostages.

On April 17th Major-General of the Police Juergen Stroop arrived in Warsaw from the Balkans to replace von Sammern. Lichtenbaum, the president, and Wielikowski, the ghetto's delegate to Governor Frank, were at once arrested, apparently in Toebbens's office. On the 19th Stroop's armoured cars entered the ghetto.[14]

The events of the next five weeks may be seen from three totally different angles. The first, which is the symbolic angle, must determine the verdict of history. From this angle the ghetto rebellion was the first national military struggle of the Jews since the rebellion of Bar Kochba in the reign of Hadrian. It was the precursor of the defence of Jerusalem's 'Old City' and the invasion of Sinai. Goebbels himself took notice of the bulletins of the 'Jewish High Command.' Accordingly, the ghetto rebellion has become a Jewish epic in its own right and it must forever remain so.[15]

The second angle is that of Himmler and his resettlement experts. For them there was never any doubt as to the ultimate issue of an action involving at most 60,000 people, and it was in this light that the ghetto rebellion was presented at Nuremberg. In Stroop's leather-bound album the court was shown a photographic record. There was the black pall of smoke hanging over the inconceivably macabre Victorian tenements. There were the terrified flame-lit faces of the deportees and the limp, barely human, bodies of the defenders as they were hauled out of the bunkers. There were the accurate statistics of Jews roasted to death or smoked out of drains for eventual execution. At Nurembeg, therefore, the rebellion was just a massacre.[16]

The third angle, the angle of the German High Command, is

illustrated by Colonel-General Alfred Jodl's comment to Dr. G. M. Gilbert:

> 'The dirty arrogant SS swine! Imagine writing a 75-page boastful report on a little murder expedition, when a major campaign fought by soldiers against a well-armed army takes only a few pages.'[17]*

From this angle the Warsaw affair was an anti-partisan action which was conducted by only 1,100 regular troops who were not even reinforced. Anti-partisan warfare could often be much more burdensome. In the course of the Warsaw Ghetto rebellion the Germans had to proceed against 'the Partisan Republic of Lake Palik' in the region of Minsk, where they claimed the liquidation of 12,000 partisans and civilians; but the operation required 16,622 men and 127 Germans were killed.[18]

At Warsaw no front-line troops were diverted and not for a moment were the communications of the front threatened, since the action was confined within the walls of the ghetto. The Polish population, which was to fight almost as an army a year later, went quietly about its business. As the sour Stroop wrote from his Warsaw prison in 1948[19]:

> 'Since the Polish population showed themselves at the most passive, I considered help from this quarter as of no consequence. There was certainly a liaison with the Polish resistance (underground) movement. I do not believe that this material was of any assistance.'

The rebellion in the ghetto was a psychological surprise for the Germans, but it was not a strategic triumph for the Jews. Under the conditions in which the ghetto lived, military leadership was impossible. On May 9th Stroop believed that he had captured the deputy leader and staff of the resistance committee. Two days later he was told by a prisoner that all the leaders had

---

*Himmler, however, seems to have exaggerated the extent of resistance in the ghetto to avoid the possible reproaches of the High Command. Thus, Jodl stated at Nuremberg: 'I did not quite believe in this heroic fight, but Himmler immediately supplied photographs showing the emplacements which had been built there and said: "Not only the Jews but the Polish nationalists have entrenched themselves there and are offering bitter resistance."' (IMT XV, 308, evidence Alfred Jodl.)

committed suicide.[20] Did such a staff really exist? The now almost legendary figure of Mordechai Tenenbaum-Tamarov reached the ghetto from Vilna as early as July, 1942, and succeeded in creating a combat group from the Zionist *Hechalutz* and the Socialist Bund.[21] He may have been the founder of the movement which in October united the remaining active political groups in the ghetto. A very young man called Mordechai Anielewicz, a member of the *Hechalutz,* is said to have been the elected combat leader. Needless to say, survivors writing in the Moscow Jewish press name a Communist.[22] The Germans at any rate gave all the credit to the *Hechalutz.* Stroop described the grenades hidden in the skirts of the women *Chalutzim* and Krueger praised their endurance. Even Eichmann distinguished them as 'important biological material.'[23]

One may suppose that the Jews fought in independent groups as in the days of Josephus. Stroop was not in a position to call off the attack for 33 days. His 2,090 men included 363 Polish policemen and 166 Polish firemen, who were in no sense combatants. He had 335 Lithuanian militiamen and 228 German security policemen—extermination experts but not trained fighting men. Stroop's soldiers were restricted to a Panzer-Grenadier training reserve battalion of 381 men and an SS cavalry reserve battalion of 440 men, besides 78 sappers and 24 light-AA gunners. The two training battalions had not worn uniform more than three or four weeks. With such a force Stroop was not prepared to take risks. His casualties were sixteen killed and ninety wounded, though this may have been understated to please Himmler.

On April 19th a four-inch howitzer, two light AA guns, a captured French tank, and two armoured cars entered the ghetto. Stroop's report is reticent concerning this first day, but it seems that the display failed to strike terror, so that on the second day he was obliged to allot definite sectors to each unit. Resistance in the apartment houses was general and only 505 Jews were rounded up for Poniatowo camp. The German factory owners were even now unhelpful. Only Toebbens tried to get 4,000 workers to assemble voluntarily. Many stayed in the big 'operational' bunker under the factory and Toebbens's partner Lautz, bearing a white flag, was refused a hearing.[24]

On April 21st Stroop was more successful. The 5,200 inmates of the 'Army Enterprise' were removed peaceably, but Stroop noted the presence of women *Chalutzim* and next day reported thirty-five Polish Communists firing from outside the ghetto. It appeared that armed Jews had been left in the 'Army Enterprise.' They had provided themselves with German uniforms from their own workshops. It was now that resistance became truly desperate. As Stroop wrote in his despatch to Krueger:

'Over and over again we observed that Jews and bandits, despite the danger of being burned alive, preferred to return to the flames, rather than be caught by us.'

On April 23rd Krueger received Himmler's command to comb out the ghetto 'with relentless tenacity.' Stroop therefore decided to destroy the ghetto, block by block, with fire and explosives. The unarmed Jews began to surrender more readily. By the 25th Stroop had taken 25,500 Jews, of whom some thousands, who were regarded as unemployable by reason of age or health, remained corralled in the ghetto. Stroop entered this inconceivably cold-blooded sentence in his war diary:

'I am going to obtain a train for T2 [Treblinka] to-morrow, otherwise liquidation will be carried out forthwith. [Next day he noted that the train left as arranged.]* Not one of the Jews whom we have caught still remains in Warsaw.'

A week had passed and great obstacles remained, in particular

*Unfortunately I have no information concerning the trial of Stroop, who was condemned to death in Warsaw on September 8th, 1951, but at the international Nuremberg trial Stroop had signed an affidavit to the effect that the deportations during the ghetto action were carried out by Lieut.-Colonel Hahn, the *Kds* or Commandant of the Security Police and SD in Warsaw, over whom he had no authority.[25] These two sentences in Stroop's report to Krueger seem to make mincemeat of that plea. Normally, making up deportation trains was the responsibility of the Resettlement Commissioner, Hans Hoefle, whose immediate chief was Globocnik. But it is quite evident that in April, 1943, the 'Abteilung Reinhardt' was no longer in charge in Warsaw and that Himmler had asked Stroop to take over the ghetto as an area of partisan warfare (*see* pages 259-60).

the sewers through which Jews escaped and partisans with arms entered the ghetto. Stroop tried to flood them, but the Jews blew up the control valves. At the very end of the action Stroop thought of smoke candles, which were lowered through the 183 manholes. Thus the last sewer dwellers were driven towards the centre of the ghetto, believing they were being gassed.

On April 28th a huge bunker was taken in which ' 274 of the richest and most influential Jews had lived since October, 1942.' It was here, according to Stroop, that Wehrmacht officers were entertained and business deals concluded with Germans. To reach such bunkers Stroop hesitated to destroy the factories for fear of wrecking the machine-tools, but Krueger's presence in the ghetto on May 2nd may have changed this. On May 4th the Schultz and main Toebbens factories were destroyed. Only 456 Jews came out to surrender. The second Toebbens factory in the ' little ghetto,' where the Jews had manufactured explosive charges, was not cleared till May 11th.

On May 8th Stroop believed that there were less than 4,000 Jews in hiding, but the capture of the alleged headquarters dugout did not end the resistance. On the 13th, realising that combing out might go on indefinitely, Stroop decided to call off the action in three days' time, leaving only the Security Police in the ghetto. ' The Jews whom we catch now go only to T2.'

Stroop's plans must have leaked to the other side. He was informed by Jewish prisoners that they had been instructed not to shoot him. They believed that, when Stroop withdrew, they would be allowed to go on living in the ghetto.

On May 15th Stroop was still able to kill 87 Jews and capture 67, while on the 16th he killed as many as 160, but he stuck to his original intention. The synagogue in Tlomaczec Street and the oratory of the Jewish cemetery were blown up as a symbolical act, though both were outside the ghetto. Underneath that black, smoking wilderness lived many hundreds of Jews. Some had even walled themselves into their bunkers, and between June and September Captain Franz Konrad was still rooting them out. One bunker dweller, a fifteen-year-old girl, was discovered as late as December 13th.[26] But on May 16th, the official end of the action, 7,000 Jews had officially been killed in the ghetto and 7,000 ' taken to T2.' The killed and the resettled Jews numbered

56,060, but 'unascertained numbers,' perhaps thousands, had been buried under the debris or burnt to cinders.

Himmler's reactions may be inferred from Krueger's report to Governor Frank on May 31st[27] that the *Reichsfuehrer* now wanted the Jewish labour camps to be liquidated as well as the ghettoes. General Schindler was trying to intervene with Kalten-brunner, because the Jews who had been retained in industry were 'the best physically speaking, the so-called Maccabæans,' and the Warsaw affair had proved that the females were even stronger than the males.

General Schindler was successful. Although Himmler's decree of June 11th doomed the surviving ghettoes, the work camps were to continue,[28] but the destruction of the Warsaw Ghetto was to proceed at once. The Dzelnia prison would be retained to house the demolition workers, otherwise the ground of the ghetto was to be levelled and made into a park after all sewer and cellar openings had been sealed. By October 9th the chief works engineer of the SS, General Kammler[29] (*see pages 151 and 425*) was able to tell Pohl that a third of the ghetto area had been demolished. The work was partly done by Jews serving in the Dzelnia prison under the notorious Colonel Goecke from Mauthausen.[30]

By February, 1944, there were 2,040 Jews at work and 1,304 free labourers. A branch line of the *Ostbahn* now ran into the ghetto with 19 locomotives, but, as was usual with SS enter-prises, the work was hindered by the appalling living conditions of the slave workers. Pohl's report of April 20th, 1944, shows that of 4,675 hands employed 2,180 were prisoners, but a further 3,000 prisoners were in quarantine for typhus. On June 10th hardly any of the prisoners were at work. However, on July 29th Kammler reported that the demolition was complete but not the levelling. Krueger had ordered the work to stop and the Jewish prisoners to be removed. The Russians were fifteen miles away and two days later the Warsaw rebellion broke out.[31]

The survivors of the five or six thousand Jewish workers—they were mostly Dutch and Greek Jews transferred from Auschwitz and Lublin—were moved to Kutno, after some hundreds of sick had been liquidated on the spot. From Kutno they were taken to Dachau concentration camp. What this meant may be realised from the case of 1,050 Dutch Jews who had been transferred from Auschwitz to 'KZ Warsaw' on October 7th, 1943. Only fifteen lived to be liberated by the Allies in Dachau in April, 1945.[32]*

The ghetto area has been rebuilt, but only the names of the streets belong to the past. In January, 1946, there were 9,000 Jews in Warsaw, some of whom had lived in hiding in the Aryan section and even taken part in the second rebellion. Others had returned from German camps, but to-day the number is certainly smaller.[33] Warsaw has probably fewer Jews than any European capital.

2. The Liquidation of the Remaining Ghettoes in Poland and Russia

To fulfil Himmler's plans after the Warsaw rebellion at least 300,000 Jews had to be moved from ghettoes to camps, and of these 220,000 lived in eight big communities:

Lodz	85,000	Vilna	...	20,000
Bialystok	30,000	Kovno	...	20,000
Sosnowiece - Bendzyn	25,000	Riga	...	15,000
Lwow	20,000	Minsk	...	8,500

The four Russian ghettoes were included in the plan on June 21st, 1943, when Himmler informed Gluecks and Kaltenbrunner that the process must be completed in the 'Ostland' by August 1st. The Wehrmacht workers must go to a camp near Riga, the able-bodied to the quarries, and the rest must be 'evacuated East,' a euphemism that Himmler still used even when the German armies were moving rapidly West.[34]

*The first arrivals in 'KZ Warsaw' were 300 Aryan internees who left Buchenwald Camp on July 23rd, 1943, to construct huts. In addition to the Dutch transport of October 7th there were transports of Greek Jews from Auschwitz on October 8th and 12th, followed possibly by transports from Majdanek. Two trainloads of survivors arrived in Dachau from Kutno on August 6th and September 12th, 1944. They apparently numbered 3,428. Thus more than 2,000 had already died in 'KZ Warsaw.' (Netherlands Red Cross, Auschwitz, Deel VI, March, 1952, pages 123-4.)

The order in which the final actions in the ghettoes were carried out illustrates the difficulties of Himmler's plan:

Lwow	... ...	June 21st-27th, 1943
Sosnowiece	...	August 4th-12th, 1943
Bialystok	... ...	August 21st-September 15th, 1943
Minsk	... ...	September 14th, 1943
Vilna	... ...	September 23rd, 1943
Riga	... ...	November 3rd, 1943
Kovno	... ...	July 25th, 1944
Lodz	... ...	September 5th, 1944

The survival of the Lodz and Kovno ghettoes for more than another year is the strangest feature of this list. By contrast the small open ghettoes, mostly in Eastern Galicia and White Russia, and the rather larger ghettoes of Tarnow and Przemysl were all dealt with by November, 1943,[35] when officially there were no Jews in the General Government outside the labour camps. On August 2nd Frank had told his Cabinet: 'We started here with three and a half million Jews and now only insignificant working parties are left. As for the remainder, we shall say some day that they emigrated.'[36] Nevertheless, in the following January, Frank had to admit that these "insignificant working parties" still numbered 100,000.

The last great resettlement action in the General Government began at Lwow on June 21st, 1943. There were 12,000 certified Jewish workers, confined to their factories, and 8,000 'wild' Jews. Since the Warsaw rebellion the neighbourhood of the Hungarian and Slovak frontiers had encouraged some attempts at organising massed escape. On May 15th Katzmann discovered through the arrest of twenty fugitives that the escapes were directed towards Brody, where a Jewish resistance group was concealed in the woods. Katzmann claimed the capture of thirty-three members of the group in this, his first encounter with any opposition among Galician Jewry. There is some reason to believe that other members of the group escaped to Hungary.[37]

But in the last action in Lwow the Germans met a more dreaded weapon than the few wretched Italian pistols of the ghetto defenders. Katzmann's casualties were 8 killed and 12 wounded, but 120 of his men caught spotted fever and one of them died. He was shown Hebrew leaflets urging the Jews to breed infected lice as well as the actual phials which were said to contain them. This story may have been something more than mere Gestapo propaganda, for in Lwow there was a clinic—the Behring Institute—which had been used by the Red Army as an anti-typhus centre and later run for the Wehrmacht by Drs. Eyer and Haas, of the I. G. Farben organisation. According to Mary Berg, anti-typhus serum used regularly to be smuggled from the Behring Institute into the Warsaw Ghetto.[38] At the same time it is known that the Institute supplied infected lice for the human experiments in German concentration camps.* Possibly the Lwow Ghetto was the one place where the experiments of the SS were turned against themselves.

Katzmann was rather surprised that the number of Jews 'resettled' from June 21st to 27th, 1943, was 20,000, since only 12,000 were registered with the Lwow Jewish Council. Out of this number some 3,000 were not taken to the 'Sand Hill' but entered as having committed suicide in the bunkers. A few thousand more were spared for the labour camp in Janowska Street, where Lwow Jews remained as late as January, 1944. Several Jews who had escaped from this camp were interrogated by a Russian commission after July 27th, 1944, when Lwow was retaken by the Red Army. Among them were members of 'Commando No. 1005,' who had been engaged in cremating the dead of the 'Sand Hill' and who had escaped in the mutiny of November 20th, 1943. They were responsible for the inconceivable descriptions of 'Janow' presented by the Russian prosecution at Nuremberg. It must not, however, be supposed that, as a torture chamber, 'Janow' surpassed Lublin and Auschwitz. It was a 'Julag' or Jewish labour camp of the SS among a score of others. Its abuses were the abuses of the whole of Himmler's system.[40]†

*Haas testified at Nuremberg that he not only brought the serum to the anti-typhus block in Buchenwald but also dispatched phials of infected lice to Waldemar Hoven, the Buchenwald chief medical officer. Hoven admitted at his trial that he had had to destroy fifty defective phials at the end of 1942.[39]

†For instance, the labour camp at Dorohucza near Radom, which served the SS factory 'OSTI No. 2,' producing peat-briquettes and tar-products. At the trial of the SS corporal, Konrad Buchmayer, by the Vienna People's

On June 30th, 1943, Katzmann calculated that in the Lwow Commissariat, that is to say in the whole of Galicia east of the San, he had 'resettled' 434,329 Jews—and by that he meant killed, since he listed separately 21,156 Jews who survived in labour camps and whose number 'was being reduced from time to time.' Oddly enough it was just at this moment that there appeared a forlorn hope for this remnant of the densest Jewish population in Europe. On July 9th the 'partisan army' of the Ukrainian Major-General Sidor Kovpak appeared on the borders of Galicia and occupied the Jewish labour camp at Skalat. Filtering through the German lines west of Kursk, this force had made a fantastic westward march of seven hundred miles to destroy the oil refineries of Boryslaw, in the Carpathians, penetrating to regions which the main advance of the Red Army did not reach for another year.

According to Mr. Joseph Tenenbaum, Kovpak freed several hundred Jews from the Skalat labour camp and henceforward he was joined by Jewish volunteers 'from every town, camp, and hiding-place,'[41] but Mr. Solomon M. Schwarz, quoting other sources, tells a different story. The Jews of Skalat were told that soldiers and healthy men were needed, not concentration-camp inmates who could barely drag their feet—and the thirty young men who nevertheless followed Kovpak were at first driven off and denied weapons. Still more significantly Kovpak made no mention of the liberation of Jews in his own book. It would indeed be something of an historic miracle that a Ukrainian general in the Cossack tradition should be a liberator of the Jews.[42] The fate of the Jews in the East Galician camps after Kovpak's raid is obscure. A year later, when the Red Army returned, there were only 9,000 Jews living in hiding in the entire area, including 827 in Lwow.[43]

After Lwow it was the turn of the twin cities of the Silesian industrial belt, Sosnowiece-Bendzyn. With their 185,000

Court in December, 1950, it was alleged that 1,500 Jews died in this relatively small camp before it was liquidated on November 3rd, 1943 (*Wiener Volksblatt*, December 16th, 1950). Even a small factory-commando of Plaszow camp, employing only 150 Jews and 200 political detainees, had its own *Todesberg*, where a man could be executed for falling asleep at a machine. (Report of the trial of Bernard Fuchs at Hohenneuendorff, *Der Tagesspiegel*, Berlin, May 11th, 1947.)

inhabitants, 45,000 of them Jews, they had returned to the Reich in 1939, resuming their German names, Sosnowitz and Bendsberg. There had been selections in May, August, and October, 1942, but, by reason of the great number of Jews employed in industry, these had been small in scale and the estimate of the physician, Dr. Ada Bimko, that in the final action of August, 1943, 25,000 Jews were sent to Auschwitz in a week is probably not exaggerated. Dr. Bimko believed that 5,000 travelled in her own transport on August 4th and of these only 500 were admitted to the camp.[44] The entire action occupied ten days and presents this matter of interest that reports of the exact forces employed have survived. The whole affair was managed by civil police, *Schutzpolizei* detachments stationed in the neighbourhood. The number of men engaged varied between 250 and 690, and, since no Security Police in military formations appear to have been called in, the resistance described by certain survivors[45] could not have done more than delay the programme by a few days.*

The effects of this action may be seen in a police memorandum to the Ministry for Interior, dated October, 1944. It notes that the population of the two towns had fallen from the 1939 level of 184,739 to 127,350. 'A specially high degree of criminality is no longer to be reckoned with, now that the Jews—who were mostly delinquents—have been resettled.'[48]

The next big ghetto on the resettlement list was Bialystok. This textile city had a population of 110,00 before the war, and its 39,115 Jews were certainly increased by refugees when the Russians took over in September, 1939.[49] A minor massacre took place on July 11th, 1941, after the German occupation, but it was not followed up. Some 8,000 square miles of swamp and forest were annexed to the Reich as the 'Reichskomisariat Bialystok,' a dependency of the *Gau* of East Prussia, governed by Erich Koch. At least 150,000 Jews inhabited this area, which included the big Jewish communities of Bialystok, Grodno, and Lomza besides many smaller ghettoes. They profited from a curious

---

*Dr. Dvorjetski mentions a woman delegate who was smuggled by the *Chalutzim* from Vilna to Bendzyn, where she was killed in a bunker on August 3rd.[46] Jenny Spritzer states that the final transport from Bendzyn to Auschwitz consisted of the employees of the Jewish Council and other specially privileged Jews, some of whom attacked the guards on the Birkenau siding with firearms.[47]

immunity from the fate that overwhelmed their neighbours in White Russia and Lithuania. Even the 20,000 Jews of Grodno, which had been Lithuanian, were spared Stahlecker's massacres. The Jewish communities of Bialystok and Grodno were increased and perhaps even doubled by the creation of subsidiary ghettoes at Jasinovka and Keilbasin for Jews, rounded up from the smaller towns.[49a]

Even the tentacles of 'Einsatz Reinhardt' in the summer of 1942 largely avoided the 'Reichskomisariat,' though a large part of the second Grodno Ghetto was removed to Majdanek. It was only in December, 1942, when a general clearance was ordered for the whole of Reich territory, that Mueller of the Gestapo issued a decree which was to include, besides Jews in Berlin and Theresienstadt, 30,000 Jews in the Bialystok Ghetto. The reduction of the main Grodno Ghetto and the Bialystok 'country Jews' began that month with deportations to Treblinka and Auschwitz. These deportations rapidly embraced the whole of the 'Reichskommissariat,' as well as Makow, Mlava and Cieczanow, which had been added to the *Gau* of East Prussia, but though the Auschwitz crematoria were kept exceptionally busy in December-January, Grodno was not made 'Jew-free' till March 12th, 1943.[49b]

As to the Bialystok main ghetto with its textile factories, so precious to the German economy, Mueller's decree of December 16th, 1942 (*see page 168*), was slow in execution. For the next two months the Auschwitz murder-machine was choked to capacity. Between February 3rd and 12th three trains, conveying 13,000 Bialystok Jews, went to Treblinka. Some Jews were killed in rooting out the bunkers, but there was no resistance with arms, and this despite the fact that long immunity had made Bialystok one of the first ghettoes to organise combat groups.[50]

Globocnik discussed the removal of the Bialystok textile factories to Lublin in his correspondence with Himmler in March and June, 1943,[51] but it was not till August 21st that the ghetto was cordoned and the factories occupied by the SS. As the population was herded into the Jurowiecka Square, 300 Jews tried to breech the barbed wire, but this, the long-prepared action of Tenenbaum-Tamarov, on which the last hopes of Polish Jewry were centred, proved a failure. The defenders took refuge in the bunkers, some of which held out till after September 15th, when the Germans began dynamiting the ghetto. In one of these bunkers Tenenbaum-Tamarov met his death.[52]

A chance survival of way bills in the Koenigsberg office of the German State Railways reveals the fact that five special trains left Bialystok for Treblinka between August 21st and 27th.[53] Two hundred and sixty-six wagons were sent. On such a journey, occupying normally two and a half hours, a box-car would hold from eighty to a hundred Jews. Thus there was room for all the 25,000 survivors.*

With the exception of Lodz, this disposed of the Polish ghettoes. As to the ghettoes in Russia, Rosenberg declared at a conference in his office on July 13th that 50,000 'Ostland' Jews would have to go to the labour camps and 22,000 would be 'resettled.' *Generalkommissar* Wilhelm Kube, whose efforts on behalf of the Reich deportees have been noticed in Chapter Nine, was present in person at this conference, where he put in a plea for Jews at Minsk and Lida, who were building sledge wagons for the Wehrmacht. Gottlob Berger, Himmler's liaison man with Rosenberg, suggested that 4,000 of these Jews could be transferred to an SS camp, but Gauleiter Meyer replied that Himmler wanted the labour camps of the Minsk region cleared as well as the ghettoes.[55] This Himmler confirmed five weeks later. The remaining Jews had to be removed from White Russia to Lublin concentration camp or 'some other place.'[56]

Since April the 6,200 Russian and 2,600 German Jews, surviving from the Minsk massacre of July, 1942, had been slowly whittled down by gas-van executions, directed from the prison. Wilhelm Kube still tried to protect the German Jews, but he was getting into hot water. On July 10th Himmler received Kube's criticisms of the campaign against the 'Partisan Republic of Lake

---

*According to Dr. Jozef Kermisz, the Jews were transported to Treblinka, Majdanek, Blizyn, and Auschwitz camps. It appears from a report to Oswald Pohl on the winding-up of Globocnik's enterprise OSTI, that three Bialystok factories were reassembled at Blizyn as works Nos. 6, 7, and 8. The fate of the bulk of the Bialystok Jews is, however, obscure. It is clear that none was gassed at Treblinka, which was used solely as a distribution centre, for the last transport arrived there only five days before the Treblinka rebellion and both the witnesses Wiernik and Rajzsman agree firmly that there were no gassings in the camp in August.[54]

Palik.'[57] Kube had written of alleged partisans who had been burnt alive in a barn and then eaten by pigs. He spoke of executed men who turned up for hospital treatment after being left for dead. He complained of the Security Police in Minsk and their traffic in the gold teeth of murdered Jews, a business in which they employed a German Jewish dentist.[58] Kube had told Eduard Strauch, the Security Police Commander, that this was 'unworthy of a German and the Germany of Kant and Goethe.'

On July 20th, after his return from Berlin to Minsk, Kube found that Strauch had got to work on the 'German ghetto.' During the action the *Ordnungsdienst* had been enticed away to fight a fire. They had been loaded on lorries and, as Strauch wrote to von dem Bach-Zalewski, 'given special treatment.' The 70 Jews employed at Kube's headquarters had likewise been killed,[59] and Strauch gave the reason. He had discovered that Kube had failed to punish two girl clerks who forged employment certificates. He had even failed to arrest the Jewish electrician who tapped his telephone line for the *Judenrat,* declaring that it was safe to employ German Jews in Minsk because they could not speak Russian.

As a result of these complaints, Kaltenbrunner ordered that office Jews must be returned to manual labour, since the native population was beginning to seek their favour, hoping to be remembered when the Red Army returned.[60] As to Kube, it appears that Rosenberg intended sending Gauleiter Meyer to Minsk to give him a good dressing-down.[61] There was no more intercession from Kube and soon Kaltenbrunner's instructions were out of date, for on September 14th the last of the Minsk Jews were removed. Instead of going to Lublin camp* they were killed on the spot in the *Dushegubky* or gassing vans, and apparently not one of the Reich Jews who had enjoyed Kube's protection survived the war.[62] Finally, on September 22nd, Kube himself was killed by a bomb thrown in his billet by his

---

*On the other hand, the last Jews at Lida left for Lublin camp by rail on September 19th. According to Moshe Kaganovich (quoted in Schwarz, *Jews in the Soviet Union,* p. 323) a number who escaped from the train near Nowo Gorodek had a bad reception from the White Russian partisans. Their long immunity through the intervention of Wilhelm Kube and the Wehrmacht economic agencies had attracted the accusation of collaborating with the Germans.

chambermaid, a partisan. Himmler told von dem Bach-Zalewski that Kube's death was 'a boon to the German people.' Sooner or later 'he would have had to put Kube back in a concentration camp because his Jewish policy bordered on treason.'[63]

The turn of Vilna came next after a respite far longer than that enjoyed by the Minsk Ghetto. Apart from the appalling treachery of the 'Kovno action' on April 15th, there had been no resettlement between December 21st, 1941, and August 5th, 1943.[64] The rule of Jacob Genns had secured the ghetto tranquillity during the worst period of the massacres in Poland (*see pages 65 and 220*). The group FPO (*Fareinikte Partisanen Organizacie*) was able to send emissaries to other ghettoes. Itzig Wittenberg, the commander, ran a radio transmitter and a newspaper, and communicated with Russian parachute groups.[65] In this incarcerated ghetto, from which 30,000 Jews had gone to their death in 1941, there was a flourishing production of cosmetics, mineral water, and Vitamin B tablets, a monopoly in sweeping the chimneys of Vilna from which fortunes were made, a theatre, a football stadium, and—in 1943—an 'Olympic Games' contest. The ghetto children were sent for holidays to the country and Hebrew scholars were employed to translate for the Frankfurt 'Rosenberg Foundation.'*

The massacres of the summer of 1942 swept up to the walls of the Vilna Ghetto without harming it, but in March, 1943, Jews from White Russian rural communities were brought in. Such actions by the SD were generally the prelude to liquidating some of the older inhabitants of the ghettoes. Nevertheless, on April 15th several thousands of Vilna Jews were deceived by the German offer of a transfer to the Kovno Ghetto. But the Kovno train shopped short at the Ponary death pits. Departing from the 'Pharaonic Tomb' policy that had been laid down by Heydrich, the SD commander sent for the Vilna Jewish *Ordnungsdienst* to bury the victims. When these men were returned from their

---

*One may explore the fascinating possibility that the survival of the Vilna and Kovno ghettoes was hidden from Hitler. On July 24th, 1942, he remarked at table, according to Dr. Picker, that it was specially remarkable that 'Lithuania, too, was Jew-free to-day.' Lithuania had acted according to its own experience, having sufficiently got to know the Jews in the short period of the Soviet régime.' (Dr. Henry Picker, *Hitler's Tischgespraeche*, Bonn, 1951, page 118.)

unspeakable task to the bosom of their families,[66] it was realised by everyone in the ghetto that their knowledge and their fears no longer mattered to the Germans. They were doomed.

Some of the younger armed Jews escaped to the woods a few days later. Most of them decided to fight in the ghetto, but the voluntary surrender of Itzig Wittenberg, the partisan leader, in July probably averted the fate of the Warsaw Ghetto from Vilna. The deportations began on August 5th with a slight skirmish at the railway station, but the subsequent transports were orderly, because it was known that the first had gone to a labour camp at Vaivara in Esthonia. The two actions of September 1st-3rd and 23rd-24th disposed of the remaining Jews. There was some resistance in the bunkers, but a general massacre was averted when Jakob Genns in his turn surrendered voluntarily to the Gestapo[67] (*pages 64, 65, and 216*). This was not quite the end of the Vilna Ghetto. Jews, attached to the two fur-lining factories, HKP and Vilna Kajlis, continued to live in isolated prison blocks, besides Jews working for a variety of German authorities. They were evacuated on July 2nd, 1944. On July 13th the Russian found some 600 Jews hiding in the Vilna sewers.[68]

In the two Riga ghettoes the population remained round the figure of 15,000 between February, 1941, and August, 1943, though in 1942 two more transports of elderly people were decoyed to the shooting place at Bikernek.[69] Neither Max Kaufmann, speaking for the Latvian ghetto, nor Jeanette Wolff, speaking for the German ghetto, describe a life comparable to that of Vilna. Resistance never got beyond the plotting stage. The enlargement of the concentration camp at Kaiserswald and rumours concerning Himmler's general evacuation order brought about plans for a ghetto rebellion, which the Germans unearthed in June, 1943. A more serious one was detected in October among the *Ordnungsdienst*, who, after the evacuations had been going on for three months, expected their end. Accused of possessing arms, some forty of them were shot in the main square and 350 in the Zentralka prison.[70]

The last 4,000 Jews left on November 2nd-3rd. The able-bodied survivors, mostly women, went to a labour camp, but 2,000 children and some invalids were loaded with very little food into open railway trucks. The children under twelve years of age were supposed to go to a ' home' in Germany, but the Riga Jews believed that the train was merely shunted to and fro till its passengers died of cold and hunger. A survivor, however, has reported that the train went to Auschwitz and that 600 out of 2,216 passengers died on the ten-day journey.[71]* That Jews from Riga should have been sent all the way to Auschwitz is curious enough, but there were no more death camps in the General Government and the Russians were too near for the Germans to risk any more mass burials in the open. But. as it turned out, the Russians did not occupy Riga till October 13th, 1944, and Kaiserswald was not evacuated till land communication with the Reich had already been severed, when the Jews were removed by sea to Stutthof concentration camp near Elbing.

The fate of the Kovno Ghetto is less fully documented, but it appears that the population of 13,000 which survived after the action of October 28th, 1941, was increased by German and Lithuanian deportations to 20,000. The belief in better conditions in Kovno, which seduced the Vilna Jews in April, 1943, is confirmed in the dry factual description of the survivor Dr. Samuel Gringauz, a former judge of the Memel court. There was little German interference. Thus Dr. Elkes, who became President of the Jewish Council after the 1941 massacres, remained in office till July 25th, 1944, and survived the war.[73]

The relatively prosperous air of the Kovno Jews was noticed in Kaiserswald camp during the deportations of September, 1943. After these deportations the ghetto was left in peace for six months. Then the 140 members of the *Ordnungsdienst* were treacherously taken to Fort No. 9 and shot, and the rule of the SS imposed inside the ghetto.[74] There was still a vestige of autonomy and on July 25th, 1944, Dr. Elkes begged the Ghetto Commissioner, Gewecke, to allow this community of three or four thousand Jews to await the arrival of the Russians, but at the last moment the women were sent to Stutthof camp and the men to Dachau.

By November, 1943, Himmler's order had been largely carried out and about 50,000 Jews of the Baltic States were confined to

---

*According to Dr. Wolken, record-keeper at the quarantine camp, the Riga transport arrived at Auschwitz-Birkenau on November 4th bringing only 596 people,[72] of whom 476 were gassed.

labour camps, either in Esthonia or in the Riga region. The men were mainly employed in the very rigorous lumber, peat-cutting, and shale-oil camps, the women, if they were not sent to Auschwitz, in tailoring workshops. On June 23rd, 1944, the Russians broke through at Witebsk and by the end of July the Baltic States were temporarily severed from the Reich. As early as July 5th it had been decided to evacuate the 4,000 Jews working near the front in the Kivioeli shale-oil deposits,[75] for it was a strict rule of Himmler's that no victims must be left behind to speak. But the German plans could not keep up with the speed of the Russian advance. Thus Reval, the Esthonian capital, fell on September 23rd. The labour camp at Kloga had become encircled four days previously.

Mr. W. H. Lawrence of the *New York Times*, who visited Kloga on October 6th, was told that 1,500 Vilna Jews had been shot, besides 800 Russian prisoners of war and 700 Esthonian partisans. The Vilna lawyer, Dr. Lasarc Olajski, told the Russian commission of investigation that he had escaped when all the able-bodied men had been taken into the woods. The remainder of the camp had been liquidated on the spot before the barracks were fired.[76] There were certainly other incidents of this kind. A week before the evacuation of the 15,000 inmates of Kaiserswald, which took place on August 6th, the unfit in the Jewish section of the camp had been selected for a lethal injection by Dr. Krebsbach, a child specialist of Cologne, who had been the Mauthausen camp medical officer. Krebsbach was sentenced to death by an American court at Dachau on May 27th, 1947.[77]

Of the 50,000 Jews in the Baltic camps in November, 1943, possibly a fifth survived the trek from camp to camp in the last months of the crumbling Third Reich. Between 60,000 and 70,000 of the 245,000 pre-war Baltic Jews escaped the Germans altogether and spent the war behind the Russian lines. It is not known what proportion has returned.

3. The Ghettoes Replaced by Labour Camps

While the evacuation of the Riga, Kovno, Vilna, and Minsk Ghettoes was going on, the fate of more than 70,000 Jews, who had survived the Warsaw and other Polish ghetto resettlements, hung in the balance. They were distributed in the concentration camp Majdanek and a number of labour camps under the control of Globocnik, and it was the complication of Himmler's relation to his old friend 'Globus'—whose dishonesty he could not have doubted for a moment—which decided the abrupt and premature abandonment of this source of labour. The concentration camp Majdanek, which Himmler had planned during his visit to Lublin in July, 1941, was itself the product of his distrust of Globocnik, for it was by introducing the control of Pohl's central office, WVHA, that he had hoped to curb Globocnik's speculations in Jewish labour.[78]

But with the opening of 'Action Reinhardt' Globocnik recovered his control of the Majdanek concentration camp and its subsidiaries. Furthermore, in Majdanek and in the former 'Action Catholique' building in Chopin Street Globocnik kept the loot of the murdered ghettoes. He had merely to write himself receipts from the 'garrison Treasury of Lublin,[79] which Colonel Schellin, the SS economic administrator in Cracow, was not even allowed to see. Major Wippern, Globocnik's treasurer, dispensed with a liberal hand. On October 21st, 1942, Himmler himself applied for a 'Christmas present' for 240,000 Russian *Volksdeutsche* from the Jewish clothing, piled up at Lublin and Auschwitz. It appears that this did not come off. Although 825 wagon-loads of Jewish loot had been accumulated by February, 1943, there was no railway transport to the Ukraine.[80]

But in Berlin Oswald Pohl was trying to get his hands into the gold coins, tooth fillings, and screwed-up wads of foreign currency notes, extricated from each clammy heap of corpses and officially described as 'property originating from thefts or the receipt of stolen or hoarded goods.' According to the instructions of September 26th, 1942, he was to see that the loot was distributed in an orderly fashion, the gold to the Reichsbank, the watches and fountain pens to submarines and SS divisions, and the spectacles to the Reich Medical Office. But there was absolutely no control. The gold, for instance, was brought casually in a suit-case to the Reichsbank cellars by a certain Major Melmer of the SS to become the 'Max Heiliger account,' credited to the Finance Minister, Count Schwerin von Krosigk, the former Rhodes Scholar.[81]

Not till June, 1943, was Pohl stirred into sending his auditor to Lublin, where Globocnik's credit balance for foreign currency alone stood at 100 million marks. By the end of the year it reached 178 millions. The auditing court nevertheless received a bad report from which Globocnik's name was never cleared.[82] Moreover, Globocnik had been appointed by Himmler head of a company called OSTI, which had taken over all Jewish labour in Lublin province, and it was unfortunate for him that his failure as a big-business man coincided with this adverse report. For Globocnik had just complained to Himmler that, in spite of 45,000 Jewish slaves, OSTI was not getting orders. In Poniatowo camp, for instance, where Toebbens had his 18,000 Warsaw Jews, there was only work for 60 per cent. It was all the fault of the army and the German businessmen, he said, because they were jealous of an SS enterprise which was not run for profit, and they preferred to shower their orders on the Lodz Ghetto, hoping thereby to save 80,000 Jews from resettlement.[83]

In addition to 45,000 Jews, employed in the OSTI camps, Globocnik's concentration camp at Majdanek held perhaps as many as 12,000 Jews, mainly the less constitutionally adapted deportees from Greece and Macedonia. This was probably the period, referred to by Oswald Pohl, when Majdanek,[83a] which was intended with all its complicated sub-sections to hold 15,000 internees, actually contained 25,000. On June 21st Globocnik told Himmler[83b] that only half the Jewish section was employed and on light duties at that. Globocnik wanted to 'resettle' ten per cent of the Jews. Himmler apparently replied by ordering a complete clearance. At the end of the month 5,000 unemployable Jews left for the death camp Sobibor in a single train. A quarter died on the journey and the rest waited three days at Sobibor for the gassing to begin (*see page 140*). The remaining 5,500 Jews were to be sent to Auschwitz, but on July 6th Hoess learnt that Globocnik had reserved 1,700 Jews for his OSTI camps in Radom province.

In spite of an adverse medical report, the 2,800 disposable Jews reached Auschwitz on July 8th and 11th. Of 1,500 Jews in the first train, more than half the men and four-fifths of the women were found unfit for work on account of serious debilitation, phlegmones, hernia and hunger-œdema. They were given light duties or sent to the *Revier* and the hospital, whence they graduated to the gas chamber. The second trainload ' produced a better impression ' and only 78 out of 763 Jews and 49 out of 568 Jewesses received ' Special treatment.'[83c]*

The Jewish camp at Majdanek was still not quite evacuated and in September it was again a clearing house for Jews from the Bialystok Ghetto who were intended for Globocnik's factories. But the final tragedy was fast approaching which was to engulf both the factories and the mother camp. For Himmler had not been impressed with Globocnik's explanation of his business failures. On September 7th he ordered Pohl to take over the ten OSTI camps, where General Schindler of the Armaments Office had been closing his eyes to the gross profiteering of Messrs. Schulz and Toebbens and the connivances of Globocnik.[84] Globocnik had to appear before Pohl and Gluecks. He was told that in future OSTI would hire its labour from the Reich Treasury. He was dismissed from the board on September 22nd and Himmler warned him that his transfer meant an adjustment of accounts. The balance-sheet for ' account Reinhardt I ' must be produced before the end of the year.

Technically, Globocnik remained head of ' Action Reinhardt ' till October 19th, but in fact he had been posted at the end of September to his home town, Trieste, where he was duly appointed Higher SS and Police Leader for the Adriatic coastal region. For this von dem Bach-Zalewski claimed the credit. In September he had taken over the military command of the General Government as a ' guerrilla area ' because Russian parachute troops had appeared west of the Bug. As *Chef der Bandenverkaempfungs-Verbaende*, he had seen a specimen of

---

*The circumstances of the Sobibor transport and the final clearance action in November show that the gas chambers, set up in Majdanek after Kurt Gerstein's visit in August, 1942 (*see page 152*), could not have been adequate for the work of a death camp. A Polish clerk in the records department told the inquiry commission, set up by the Russians, that there had been a gassing of 3,500 Jews in June, 1943, but the figures used by this commission—which found that a million and a half people had been murdered in the camp—are thoroughly suspect (*Black Book*, pages 381-390). The impressive Majdanek crematorium, which was photographed in the British press, was only completed in the autumn of 1943 and was used to eliminate the many mass-burials in the camp area. It was not a death factory on Auschwitz lines.

Globocnik's idiotic resettlement of Germans in the Zamosc district and he had persuaded Kaltenbrunner to recall both Globocnik and Krueger.[85]

From Trieste Globocnik bombarded Himmler with self-justification:

> 'The remarkable thing about this account is that the collection of the revenue was not compulsory, since the stocks were merely held on order and only the decency, purity and vigilance of the SS men could guarantee full delivery. Nevertheless, what has been seized, collected, and taken by *Abteilung Reinhardt* has been accounted for and delivered with the greatest promptitude without defrauding.[86]

> 'On October 19th I concluded 'Action Reinhardt,' which I had carried out in the General Government. My establishments in Lublin have achieved an especially dazzling focal point. . . . I have sought to reproduce the image of these moments of danger. It will perhaps be instructive for posterity to look back and see how this danger was averted. I have also tried to give an account of the labour achievement, in which not only the volume of the labour may be perceived, but also how few Germans were needed to set this colossal action in motion.'[87]

Globocnik then went on to ask for some Iron Crosses for his men 'for the outstanding performance of their hard task of which the Warsaw rebellion [for which Himmler had already distributed decorations] was only a small part.' Himmler replied by telling Globocnik that he 'had performed a great and unique service to the German people.'

The ten labour camps of the OSTI concern, which Oswald Pohl had taken over from Globocnik on September 7th, were now approaching the final catastrophe, not only the withdrawal of the Jewish labour but the massacre of a large part of it. On October 4th Pohl was present with no less than twelve Higher SS and Police Leaders and over a hundred other SS officials in a stuffy hotel lounge in Posen, where Himmler made a terrible and ominous speech of which there exists not only an immensely long transcript but also a partial gramophone recording.[88]

'I also want to talk to you quite frankly on a very grave matter. Among ourselves it should be mentioned quite frankly and yet we will never speak of it publicly . . . I mean the evacuation of the Jews, the extermination (*Ausrottung*) of the Jewish race. It is one of the things it is easy to talk about. "The Jewish race is being exterminated," says one party member, it is quite clear, it is in our programme— elimination of the Jews ; and we are doing it, exterminating them. And then they come, eighty million worthy Germans and each one has his decent Jews. Of course, the others are vermin, but this one is an " A1 " Jew. Not one of those who talk this way has witnessed it, not one of them has been through it. Most of you must know what it means when a hundred corpses are lying side by side or five hundred or a thousand. To have stuck it out and at the same time—apart from exceptions caused by human weakness—to have remained decent men, that is what has made us hard. This is a page of glory in our history which has never been written and is never to be written."

Most of Himmler's illustrious audience have suffered a loss of memory concerning this passage. Not so Oswald Pohl.[89]

'After this speech I talked to *Obergruppenfuehrer* Schmidt, von Herff, and other comrades. Their understanding of this speech and their opinions were not uniform at all. We were rather surprised that the Jewish question was now to be solved in such a brutal manner.'

'*We were rather surprised.*' Himmler knew exactly what audience he was addressing when he said, 'most of you know what it means,' and he knew that the only thing that could surprise them was frankness. Pohl clearly saw that a new phase in the Final Solution must be approaching, for he says that he sought an interview with Himmler afterwards to discuss labour allocations and to point out to him that ' It was madness to exterminate these people now,' but Pohl was told to mind his own business.

The sequel occurred a month later, on November 3rd, when five of the ten OSTI camps had to close down. In Pohl's correspondence there are many oblique hints as to what happened that day.[90] Moreover, numerous Germans as well as Jewish survivors of the labour camps have told a story so identical that it must be accepted. A huge selection took place in all the Jewish camps in Lublin province. Eleven thousand men and six thousand women were taken to Lublin (Majdanek) camp. In the most concentrated single massacre of the war they were machine-gunned in death pits, which had been prepared, in the camp enclosure, by Russian prisoners of war. Then they were cremated. Lieutenant Mussfeld, who afterwards commanded one of the Auschwitz gas chambers, told Konrad Morgen that he had executed 20,000 people. 'During the cremation a light dust lay over the whole town of Lublin and permeated the air like smoke.'[91] Prince Christopher Radziwill, one of the original officer-prisoners who had been in Majdanek since 1939, described it this way[92]:

> 'I shall never forget the day the Nazis killed 17,000 Jews at Majdanek while I was in another part of the concentration camp. That evening many of my Polish fellow-prisoners got drunk to celebrate. That is terrible but it is true.'

Konrad Morgen claimed that he had seen the orders to liquidate the Jewish labour companies, which were headed 'by order of the Reichsfuehrer SS.' He believed that Himmler acted on Kaltenbrunner's advice, but it is just as likely that Himmler, disgusted with the low output of the OSTI workshop, ordered the action in a fit of tantrums—without telling anyone. Thus Globocnik wrote from Trieste on January 5th, 1944[93]:

> 'On November 3rd, 1943, the workers were withdrawn from the labour camps and the works shut down. The camp leaders were not informed of this action although the responsibility rested with them. Actually on the very day before the order General Schindler, armaments inspector, Cracow, told the camp leaders that Krueger had assured him that 10,000 Jews would be brought in for armament work.'

And Lt.-Col. Horn, in his winding-up report for OSTI, on March 13th, 1944[94]:

> 'In spite of the best intentions of the German employees it could not be helped that November 3rd, 1943, impressed itself on OSTI, since works Nos. 2, 3, and 5 could not be got going again.'

According to Globocnik, Toebbens at Poniatowo lost through the action a turnover of thirteen million zlotys. For a few more weeks he tried to keep going with paid Polish labour,[95] but on January 13th, 1944, Pohl ordered the WVHA office to take over all camps in the areas of Lublin, Radom, Lwow, and Cracow. This finished the business career of Walter C. Toebbens (see page 68).*

4. The Russians Reinvade Poland

There was no further mass reduction of the number of Jewish slaves in Poland till the Russian invasion of the General Government in July, 1944. In the meantime there were some 70,000 Jews in camps in the Western provinces, mainly in the neighbourhood of Cracow, Kielce, Radom, Tomaszow, Piotrkow, Czestochowa, and Lodz. If one includes the Auschwitz group of camps, the Lodz Ghetto, and the hidden Jews there must have been still a quarter of a million Jews in German-held Polish territory.

In contrast to Heydrich's instructions of September, 1939, some of these agglomerations were very large. The firm Hans Bauer and Karl Schranz (HASAG), of Czestochowa, employed 13,000 Jews, of whom 800 were actually liberated by the Russians on January 16th, 1945.[98] Skarzysko-Kamienna, near Kielce, employed 8,000 Jews, and the camps Blizyn and Starachowice, near Radom, about 5,000 each. The Plaszow concentration camp group near Cracow contained at one time 12,000 Jews. The Plaszow camps had the worst conditions of all under the notorious Captain Amon Goeth, who was imprisoned by the Germans in September, 1944, for embezzlement and executed by the Poles in 1946.[99]† Those camps, where labour was leased by

---

*At the same time the last Jews were removed from the Lwow labour camp in Janowska Street.[96] In February the group of Jewish camps east of Tarnow was evacuated. With the exception of the Carpathicus (Beskiden) Oil Refinery of Drohobicz, which employed Jewish labour till the following April, there were no more Jewish camps east of the Vistula.[97]

†Amon Leopold Goeth, the liquidator of the Cracow and Tarnow Ghettoes, was, like most of the executive of Globocnik's 'Abteilung Reinhardt," an Austrian and a founder-member of the Austrian National Socialist Party. A kinsman and namesake, Amon Goeth, was convicted at Graz in 1948 of plotting to revive the Nazi régime and sentenced to fifteen years' imprisonment, but pardoned in August, 1952. (The Times, August 23rd, 1952.)

private firms from the SS, were rather better, but undernourishment was a matter of principle, and it was here that the typhus epidemic was created which swept the German concentration camps in 1945.

On July 16th, 1944, the Russians attacked towards Lwow, crossing the River Bug on the 19th, taking Lwow on the 27th, and reaching the Vistula on August 3rd. On July 20th Schoengarth, the Security Police Commander for the General Government, ordered that prisons and labour camps should be blown up if they could not be evacuated in time. Numbers were to be kept down by wholesale commitments to the concentration camps in Germany. 'The liberation of prisoners or Jews by the enemy, be it the Polish underground or the Red Army, must be avoided. Under no circumstances must they fall into the enemy's hands alive.'[100]

For the Jews the meaning of this order was generally Auschwitz and the gas-chamber selections. It does not seem that liquidations took place on the spot. In December, 1944, Dr. Reszoe Kastner, the Jewish lawyer who negotiated for Hungarian Jewish lives with the SS, had a significant interview with Eichmann's assistant, Dieter Wisliceny, in the latter's Vienna flat.[101] He was told by Wisliceny how Eichmann had briefed the camp commanders in Poland; in spite of the principle that Jewish lives should be spared, they were to punish drastically any obstruction to the evacuations. Wisliceny believed that the SS had interpreted this instruction correctly by shooting as many Jews as possible on the march.

About 27,000 Jews were evacuated at the end of July, 1944, from nine camps in the Radom and Cracow regions together with nearly 4,000 from the camp in the former Warsaw Ghetto. The Pustkowa camp near Debica was evacuated to Auschwitz on July 28th, only 463 men out of 1,600 escaping the gas chamber, according to Dr. Wolken's list.[102] The Blizyn camp was also evacuated to Auschwitz. The physician David Wajnapel of Radom declared at Nuremberg that hundreds of inmates were machine-gunned on the march.[103] There were further transports to Auschwitz from Plaszow camp and the Cracow sorting commando. It was also during this week that many of the huts at Plaszow were dismantled to be set up in the notorious No. 2

camp at Bergen-Belsen (*see pages 465-466*), but the last 1,600 inmates of Plaszow, mainly women, were not sent to Auschwitz till October, when, according to a survivor, Mila Hornik, 600 were gassed after one of the last of all the selections before the crematoria were blown up.[104]

By the middle of August the Russian advance was halted by resistance both in the Warsaw region and the Carpathians. The front remained static till January 11th, 1945, and in the Warsaw-Lodz-Cracow triangle more than 30,000 Jews stayed in their camps. In this interval occurred the liquidation of the last ghetto in Europe, the great Jewish community of Lodz.

There had been no resettlement from Lodz after the Warsaw rebellion. The ghetto was actually increased in August, 1943, by some hundreds of ragged and starving Jews from the municipal labour camps of the Posen region.* Consequently, at the beginning of 1944, there were no less than 80,062 Jews in the ghetto, of whom the huge proportion of 60,200 were registered workers. On January 22nd Eichmann came to Lodz to meet Hans Biebow, the ghetto commissioner, the local authorities, and the representatives of the SS Economic Administration and to play a characteristic rôle. There were 5,365 children in the ghetto under the age of ten—the age at which they were sent to work. Eichmann ruled that these children should be 'discharged,' except for the children of the *Ordnungsdienst* policemen and other privileged personnel.[107] Three months later, when the Foreign Office was looking for 5,000 Jewish children to barter with the Allies, Eichmann told the estimable Eberhard von Thadden that the only place in occupied territory where there were 5,000 Jewish children was Lodz, but that they would soon be liquidated.[108]

After meeting Eichmann in Lodz, the SS Economic Administration reported to Himmler that to turn the ghetto into a concentration camp would entail too much financial risk—and

*Globocnik had complained to Himmler about Lodz on June 21st, 1943, and on January 5th, 1944, he wrote to him from Trieste that he had not been able to carry out the action in Lodz because of his transfer.[105] In fact the failure was due to Himmler's vacillation, for in June he had promised Gauleiter Artur Greiser to make Lodz a concentration camp. In September he had declared his intention to evacuate the ghetto industries to Lublin and in December he had reverted to the concentration camp plan.[106]

from the dry statistical sentences of their report there falls together a ghastly picture of human misery:

> 'The inner-ghetto population can be halved and the 10,721 carpet workers can be eliminated. The turnover is very small. For the entire population it is 1.50 marks a day, for the factories alone not more than 2.40 a day per head. A third of the man-power is wasted. The plant managers are Jews. There are no Aryans in the factories and not more than three to four enter the ghetto daily. The wages bill in 1943 averaged 1.75 marks a day plus 0.75 expenditure per worker.'[109]

In spite of this report, Greiser was informed by the SS Economic Administration on February 9th that Himmler would go on with the concentration camp plan because 'technical reasons made it impossible to transfer the Lodz Ghetto to Lublin.' At this stage Himmler visited Greiser personally and on the 14th Greiser informed Pohl that Himmler intended outright liquidation. It was to be done gradually and 'Captain Bothmann's special commando is to be recalled from Croatia to complete this action in the Gau, where he has already exercised his activity in the past.' On February 16th Pohl wrote to Greiser, Kaltenbrunner, and (through Rudi Brandt) Himmler. Nothing could restrain his delight that his office was not to be saddled with the Lodz Ghetto and that the solution was to be so simple.[110]

The Bothmann commando returned to Chelmno, where the crematorium had been blown up in April, 1943, but there was little work to do till the Russian July offensive when the ghetto population suddenly dropped by 7,700.[111] At the beginning of August mass evacuation was ordered. On the 4th the workers of factories Nos. 1 and 2 were told that their rations would be waiting for them at the railway station. The stratagem did not quite answer, for three days later the workers of factories 3 and 4 were told to get their rations at the Central Prison. Those from factories 1 and 2 could do the same if they wished. Eventually the 'wild' Jews, unattached to the factories, had to be combed-out street by street as in Warsaw, but most of the employed Jews responded to Biebow's address of August 16th, a copy of which has survived. Biebow pointed out that the German population were already leaving Lodz and that bombing had begun. Then he painted a bright picture of the advantages, enjoyed by the Jews who were employed in the HASAG factories at Czestochowa, and he offered equally fair conditions in camps in Germany—but he added a threat: 'I don't stand here talking like a fool and doing nothing. If you make me use force, there will be dead and wounded.'[112]

On August 21st there were 61,174 Jews in the ghetto, famished, exhausted, and broken in spirit. On the night of September 5th-6th nearly all had left except the sorting commando, which still numbered 870 Jews on January 15th, 1945, when the Russians entered the town.[113]* The deportations to Auschwitz and other camps were spread over many weeks. A typhoid outbreak in Birkenau women's infirmary was caused by a Lodz transport which arrived on June 27th,[114] while Chaim Rumkowski, who was allegedly seen at the crematorium, did not leave Lodz till September 6th.[115] Survivors such as Dr. Nyiszli noticed the famine-stricken condition of the Lodz Jews, even when compared with the Auschwitz inmates.[116] Kristina Zywulska saw great numbers of Lodz Jewesses working in the fields[117] in the camp area, but most of the 'employables' were forwarded to other concentration camps, since a report dated August 1st shows that 60,000 Lodz Jews were still expected.[118]

It is clear that nothing like this number reached Germany, but survivor-estimates of enormous gassings of Lodz Jews must be treated with the usual reserve, Dr. Wolken's list mentions only one 'selection' transport on August 21st.[119]† The death roll in the

---

*In addition to the *Aufraeumungskommando*, which remained till the Russian conquest of Lodz, there was another and more curious survival. With the connivance of Biebow and his deputy Seifert, some 500 Jews, consisting mainly of labour supervisors and their families—there were even thirty children—were kept on in one of the tailoring workshops on pretext of dismantling the huts and removing them to Germany. In this manner the 500 remained in Lodz till October 22nd, 1944, when the women were removed to Ravensbrueck and the men followed the huts to Koenigswusterhausen, a work commando of Sachsenhausen concentration camp. (Bendet Hershkovitch, *The Ghetto in Litzmannstadt. Yivo Annual of Jewish Social Science*, New York, 1950, *page 121.*)

†The list includes only transports which were registered in the quarantine section of Birkenau male camp. At this period it was more usual to send the Jews, who emerged from the selections, directly to the working commandos or to keep them in a special section of the camp, awaiting transfer.

German camps was nevertheless enormous and many thousands of Lodz Jews were engulfed in the final tragedy at Belsen (*see pages 466-467*). Some indication of the fate of the last 70,000 Lodz Jews can be obtained from the Polish census figures, which show that only 17,500 Jews lived in the entire Lodz province in January, 1946.[120]

Hans Biebow, the former ghetto commissioner, was hanged in Lodz on April 27th, 1947.[121] This former insurance agent came, like Toebbens, from Bremen and his career in many respects resembles that of Toebbens. The latter, it is true, exploited the ghetto for personal profit, whereas Biebow (in theory) only served his masters, but both worked their people to death with equal indifference. Biebow was a man who reported all the facts and who apparently would have preferred a properly fed and fully productive labour force, yet knowing all the implications of Heydrich's policy of 'natural diminution through labour,' he stayed on till the end and crowned his work with the almost unbelievable treachery of his address of August 16th, 1944. Biebow's reports are those of a model administrator. The fact that a model administrator consented to fill this part raises the most disturbing and unanswerable question concerning the true implications of the Final Solution.

CHAPTER 12

France

1. The Wooing of Vichy

HITLER, who never expected to conquer France and the Low Countries in six weeks, tackled the problems of occupation as they came without preconceived ideas. There were no demographical plans for the shifting of populations, as in the case of Poland, and for a time France was scarcely considered in connection with the Jewish problem in the light of National Socialist theory. Thus we have seen in Chapter 4 an attempt to treat the Free Zone or Vichy Territory, not as a place to be cleared of Jews, but as a dumping-ground for unwanted Jews from Germany. After Hitler had stopped this action, which was probably a private exploit of Heydrich's, the Security Office completely reversed its policy. It now tried to bring the Vichy Government into line with the regulations as enforced against the Jews in the Reich. Joyfully seconded by 'Ambassador' Abetz and his diplomatic assistants, Schleier and Zeitschel, Heydrich began to instal the machinery of the *Reichsvereinigung* and the *Judendezernat*, that is to say, a single body to represent all Jewish interests, handcuffed to a special police department, through whom alone the Government could be approached. This was the classical model, evolved by Heydrich and Eichmann in Vienna and Prague. In France that result was never achieved and, because of it, less than 65,000 out of a possible 300,000 Jews were deported in the course of the war.

This was only the mechanical reason for the failure. The mechanism itself broke down because of its psychological unsuitability. It took the Gestapo a very long time to learn that the most collaborationist French officials persisted in regarding a French-born Jew and even a naturalised Jew as a Frenchman. It is nevertheless true that in the bargaining game to which they were forced, the Vichy Government was always prepared to sacrifice the stateless or refugee Jews from the Reich Thus, while less than a tenth of the Jews who were deported possessed French nationality, most of the refugee population were exterminated.

The refugees unfortunately lent themselves to this discrimination. Having lived largely on Jewish charity, they were deprived of their source of supply by the flight of wealthy and influential native Jews in the summer of 1940. It was easy for the Gestapo to gather up the shreds of the welfare organisations so as to make another *Reichsvereinigung*, but this writ did not extend beyond the stateless Jews. The French Jews retained some means of livelihood, they were at home, they had Aryan friends and they were *debrouillard*. They could even escape identification by the Gestapo's 'physiognomy brigade.' This differentiation was so great that when the Gestapo created a co-ordinating committee for the Jewish relief organisations—the traditional first step towards a Jewish Council or *Judenrat*—they had to appoint as directors two Jews living in Vienna and the committee was boycotted by French-born Jews.[1]

Late in 1941 the co-ordinating committees of the two zones were amalgamated as UGIF, *Union Generale Israelite Française*. This did not mean that UGIF became a *Judenrat* in the East European sense, though in December, 1941, the Paris branch had to aid in collecting the 1,000 million franc fine and, at the time of the deportations, it distributed relief from Jewish assets confiscated by the Germans. But UGIF never sponsored a Jewish police force to arrest Jews, not even in July, 1943, when Anton Brunner sent his Jewish decoy-gangs from Drancy camp.[2]

If the Germans failed to create an effective ghetto system in France, they failed equally to create a French Inquisition of any consequence. The *Commissariat aux Questions Juives* was never sure of the support of the Vichy Government, and its police obtained less and less co-operation from the regular *gendarmerie*. Yet it was essential to the Germans that the Jews should appear to have been arrested and deported by Frenchmen, and in the first flush of victory the Germans had little reason to doubt that they would obtain this compliance from the conquered. The ' Statut des Juifs ' of October 4th, 1940, by which refugee Jews who had been deprived of their German nationality forfeited all civil rights, was easily exacted and it enabled 40,000 Jews in the two zones to be put in internment camps.[3] Moreover, it forced the Vichy authorities to intern the German Jews who were dumped on them by Heydrich eighteen days later. But in the following February a warning note was sounded by Werner Best. This Gestapo legal expert, who was now Administrative Chief of Staff to the military commander, declared that only the French should be allowed to create a Central Office for the Jews, because of 'the reaction of the French people to everything that comes from Germany.'[4] When it was suggested during this month that Stuelpnagel, the military commander, should be asked to authorise the internment of the remaining refugees, Eichmann's agent, Theodor Dannecker, argued with Abetz that 'legal supplementation from Vichy would be needed.'[5]

On March 6th Abetz informed Ribbentrop that Pétain was far from sharing the enthusiasm for these measures attributed to Admiral Darlan. Having interviewed Xavier Vallat, the former secretary-general of the *Legion de Combattants,* whom the Vichy Government had appointed as its first Commissary for Jewish Affairs, Abetz decided that there would be heavy resistance to any new laws which would lead to the emigration of *French* Jewry.[6] Later Dannecker was to declare that Vallat did not hide his partiality, even for 'acclimatised' foreign Jews, and that the arrest of 3,600 naturalised Polish Jews on May 14th, 1941, had created more stir in Vichy circles than the arrest of 30,000 unwanted Jews from the Reich at the end of 1940.[7]

Captain Theodor Dannecker, the author of this report of July 1st, 1941, was a pettyfogging lawyer of the least possible consequence, so obscure that no one has yet found him. Most of the information he collected for Heydrich was puerile. Yet Stuelpnagel, Rosenberg, and Abetz agreed to send representatives once a week to consult at 72, Avenue Foch, with this nonentity. Such was the awe with which the highest officials then regarded the Gestapo.

Stuelpnagel, the soldier, did, however, put up a little resistance. It was not till December, 1941, that he authorised any deportations of Jews from France and then only in the disguise of a reprisal measure, for France differed from the rear areas in Russia in that the Wehrmacht had not surrendered its rights to the servants of Himmler and Heydrich. Nothing less than a head-on collision between Keitel and Heydrich was necessary before the 'Sipo and SD' could assert its full competence to handle Jewish affairs in France.

This collision began with a thoroughly ludicrous story. On the night of October 2nd, 1941, an amateurish attempt was made to blow up two Paris synagogues. The commander of the Security Police and SD in Occupied France was Colonel (then Major) Helmuth Knochen, a former Gestapo spy, who, having been employed in watching Jewish refugees in Holland, had assisted in the kidnapping of Captains Best and Stephens at Venlo in November, 1939. Knochen sent a report to Stuelpnagel from which it appeared that the explosions were the work of French fascists and that the French police suspected the journalist Eugène Deloncle. Yet Knochen sent his report knowing that a certain Lieutenant Sommer of his commando was under open arrest. Sommer had boasted of the explosions to two French Gestapo informers while drinking in the 'Cabaret Chantilly.' This led to a court of inquiry on October 5th, when Sommer admitted having supplied the explosives to Deloncle and his assistants— all of them Gestapo informers.

Sommer's case was referred to the Main Security Office in Berlin and a report was sent to Stuelpnagel, but it was from another member of the court of inquiry that Stuelpnagel learnt *unofficially* that Sommer had pleaded orders from Knochen. On the 6th, therefore, Stuelpnagel complained to Keitel, as head of the High Command of the Armed Forces, that the SS were increasing his difficulties with the French, which were already bad enough on account of 'the necessary shooting of hostages.' Knochen, against whom Stuelpnagel repeated his charge of forging a report, was sent for by Heydrich and on October 22nd Keitel demanded not only Knochen's recall, but that of Brigadier-General Thomas, the Higher SS and Police Leader for the occupied Western countries. On November 6th Heydrich replied to Keitel through Quartermaster-General Wagner:

'It is important to demonstrate to the world that the French nation has the necessary strength to fight the Jews and Communists. Deloncle seemed to me the best instrument in spite of his ambiguous political record. My Director of Services in Paris did not think it necessary to tell Stuelpnagel because our experience gave little hope of his comprehension. I was fully conscious of the political consequences of these measures, the more so since I have been entrusted for years with the task of preparing the final solution of the Jewish problem.'

Heydrich then went on to inform Wagner that he had transferred Sommer to Berlin, but that Knochen would continue to direct 'Action-Group France.' As to Brigadier-General Thomas, he had already transferred him to Russia. In fact, Thomas had replaced Otto Rasch of *Einsatzgruppe* C at Kiev (*see page 234, footnote*).

Stuelpnagel still demanded Knochen's recall and Wagner reminded Heydrich of an agreement by which 'special commandos' of the Main Security Office had to accept the orders of the military commander in France. Heydrich's reply cannot be traced, but we know that on February 5th Stuelpnagel withdrew his complaint against Knochen, 'because he had expressed his willingness to co-operate.'[8] But if Knochen commanded the Security Police in France right up to the allied reconquest, it was precisely because he did not put himself at the disposition of Stuelpnagel. Furthermore, the new 'Polizeifuehrer West,' Brigadier-General Kurt Oberg, who arrived in Paris from Radom in Poland on May 7th, 1942, was completely independent of Stuelpnagel and took his orders straight from Himmler.

Much later, in July, 1943, Stuelpnagel was strong enough to refuse Knochen military personnel for his Jewish round-ups, but on the occasion of the Deloncle affair he seems to have had his head well washed and this perhaps accounts for the proposal he put to Keitel on December 5th. Stuelpnagel now wanted a hundred hostages executed as a reprisal for three recent attacks on German soldiers. In addition, the Paris Jews were to pay a fine of 1,000 million francs, and a thousand Jews and five hundred Communists were to be deported for forced labour in the East.[9]

Hitler, to whom this was referred, was sly enough to order that the plan should be carried out with the co-operation of Abetz, who had a French wife. Abetz in a tremendous panic at once telephoned the Foreign Office to make sure that the hostages were described not as Frenchmen but as 'Soviet and Secret Service agents of Judeo-Communist and De Gaullist origin'—which happy phrase was conveyed to the Vichy envoy, De Brinon, by Stuelpnagel on December 21st[10] with the news that the deportations were in course of execution. Actually Stuelpnagel was premature. Although 753 Jews had been rounded up in Paris on the 12th and taken with 355 more Jews from Drancy to Compiègne camp, word arrived from Heydrich on the 24th that the Wehrmacht Transport Command had banned extra traffic across the Reich during the Christmas leave period.[11] As a consequence the Paris Jews, who might have gone straight to Heydrich's death pits at Riga or Kovno, were partly set free and partly reserved for Auschwitz.

Dannecker tried to press Eichmann on February 28th for a positive date, but failed to get one. Since the first Auschwitz train did not leave Compiègne till March 28th, Stuelpnagel's administrative staff had three and a half months in which to weed out the prisoners of December 12th. The Gestapo having concentrated on rich foreign Jews and intellectuals, Stuelpnagel proposed to deport only Jews between the ages of eighteen and fifty-five who were medically fit. As a result, only half the 1,098 Jews who were sent to Compiègne boarded the Auschwitz deportation train. Another 550 had therefore to be chosen from Drancy camp. In Compiègne moreover some 97 victims of the round-up died from the hardships of the place in the course of fifteen weeks and fifteen were released early on.[12] On this occasion the Jews travelled to Auschwitz in passenger coaches. Dannecker had expressly asked Eichmann's transport officer, Lieutenant Nowak, for goods vans, but all the vans available were reserved for Russian civilian workers. The Gestapo disliked passenger coaches because they made observation difficult.

With the arrival of the train at Auschwitz on March 30th the first 1,100 deportees from France disappear from view, but a Slovak Jewish doctor, whose very accurate report on Auschwitz was circulated by the War Refugees Board in 1944, states that only 700 survived a fortnight later. The French Jews lived in three of the five completed permanent buildings in the new Birkenau camp and they worked at the DAW factory three miles away.[13] Invalids were already being selected for the gas chamber at this time, five hundred leaving the *Krankenbau* every Tuesday according to Zenon Rozanski and other witnesses.

2. The Great Round-up of July, 1942, and After

Dannecker, who visited Eichmann in Berlin on March 3rd, 1942, claimed the credit of being the first to propose continuous Jewish deportations from France.[14] On March 9th Eichmann informed his faithful Foreign Office stooge, Franz Rademacher (*see page 74*), that the immediate number would be 6,000. Rademacher replied on the 20th that the Foreign Office and the German Embassy in Paris did not object to 6,000 Jews, whether French or stateless, going to the concentration camp, Auschwitz. Rademacher's reply was countersigned by von Weizsaecker, who wrote in the margin words that seem somehow intended to wash his hands: '*Polizeilich naeher charakterisierbare*'—'to be characterised more closely as a police matter.'[15]

As a witness in the Wilhelmstrasse case in 1948, Abetz expressed his surprise that Weizsaecker and Woermann should have co-operated in a matter which normally concerned Martin Luther and his 'party veterans.'[16] Weizsaecker in his own defence quoted a minute of Franz Rademacher's, dated September 13th, 1941, and concerning the Belgrade Jews, 'Eichmann prefers shooting.' This minute (which he had previously sworn he had never seen) showed, said Weizsaecker, that the Jews might be in greater danger in France as hostages than they would be at Auschwitz, 'a name which then meant nothing.'[17]

The name of Auschwitz may indeed have been new to Weizsaecker on March 20th, 1942, but there could be nothing new to him in the proposal to hand Jews over to Heydrich. Weizsaecker had initialled copies of the *Einsatzgruppen* reports (*see footnote on page 200*) and, so far from denying having read them, he boasted that in the autumn of 1941 he had protested to Ribbentrop at these horrors.[18] How then could Weizsaecker have been ignorant of Heydrich's description of the true character of the deportations, which was circulated in the protocol of the Gross-Wannsee conference of January 20th, 1942—a protocol which bore Weizsaecker's annotations ? * (*See footnote on page 96.*)

The Foreign Office mandate to Eichmann with Weizsaecker's approving rider was responsible for the deportation trains which left Drancy for Auschwitz on April 29th and on June 1st, 6th, 22nd, and 28th.[21] In these trains were packed more than 5,000 men and women. The arrival of two of the trains was noted at Auschwitz-Birkenau by the 'Slovak Doctor.'[22] The others probably went to Lublin (Majdanek) concentration camp. The selections were made at Drancy, in the four hideous skyscrapers of the 'cité ouvrière' which affront air passengers arriving at Le Bourget. Jewish camp orderlies, approved by Dannecker's staff, made out the lists and Dannecker himself saw the transports off 'with a nervous twitch and ill-coordinated movements which at a distance resembled those of a drunken man.'[23] At this period there were many exempted classes in Drancy, not only French Jews and those with French wives, but Jews from the countries not yet included in the deportation plan ; furthermore, the old, the unfit, and the children[24] were still protected from the Auschwitz crematorium, though not for long. According to the 'Slovak Doctor's' report, the first direct selection took place when the Drancy train of June 22nd reached Auschwitz station. There two hundred Jews were picked for the gas chamber and eight hundred for the camp.[25]

But already the Germans had taken a step towards a far more radical deportation policy to include French-born Jews, irrespective of political associations or hostage value. In a conference

*The Nuremberg court chose not to believe in this ignorance[19] and to the grief of Baron Ernst von Weizsaecker's champions in England and Germany—seated among the crestfallen defendants in the dock he looked exactly like a bishop—he was sentenced to six years' imprisonment. Eighteen months after his conviction Weizsaecker was released from Landsberg, but nine months later, on August 9th, 1951, he died in hospital at Lindau. In the memoirs which he composed in prison Weizsaecker made only one reference to the persecution of the Jews, and the words which he used might have been uttered by almost any of Hitler's officials[20] :

'To me the Jewish question was part of the general problem "how could we achieve peace quickly without Hitler." Jewry was as little to be helped in the Third Reich as the church or the remains of justice and human liberty. One had to fight the bacillus and not the symptoms of the disease.'

of experts on Jewish affairs from the various ministries, held in his office on March 4th, 1942, Eichmann proposed extending the badge, worn by the Jews of Poland since 1939 and by the Jews of the Greater Reich since September, 1941, to the Jews of all Occupied Europe. Himmler thereupon instructed Major Knochen, who convened a conference on March 14th, where he obtained the concurrence of the Military Government in Belgium and the Civil Commissariat in Holland,[26] but the Vichy Government was not brought into line so easily. The chief obstacle was Xavier Vallat, who had just put the insignificant Dannecker in his place and whom De Brinon described to Abetz as 'the Commissary for the protection of the Jews.'[27]

So great was Vallat's resistance to the Jewish badge that at the end of the month Abetz demanded his replacement. Abetz thought that the new Commissary, D'Arquier de Pellepoix, would get the Jewish badge decreed in the Free Zone within a few weeks, but Dannecker wrote in the margin of Abetz's memorandum ' too big an optimism '[28]—and Dannecker was right. The Jewish badge could never be enforced in Vichy territory even after November 11th, 1942, when it ceased to be a free zone.

On April 17th the new Commissary reported that the Vichy Government would do nothing about a Jewish badge without an order from Stuelpnagel, but Abetz was still chicaning to get the Vichy Government to publish the decree before the Germans did. On May 4th Abetz resigned himself to publishing the German decree for the Occupation Zone first, impressed by ' the part that the Jews had played in the Communist riot at Argenteuil.' Thereupon, as was his habit, Heydrich, having gained a point, demanded another. He summoned Knochen to Prague on May 18th and told him that the French half-Jews must wear the badge, too.[29] But before the incredible difficulties of the new order could be studied by the newly arrived and still bewildered Oberg, Heydrich was stricken down and on June 4th he was dead.

With a long schedule of diplomatic exemptions, which included British and U.S.A. subjects, Major-General Kurt Oberg of the police published the Jewish badge decree for Occupied France on June 1st. The badge had to be worn from the age of six years upwards and a clothing coupon had to be surrendered.[30] The reception of the order was at first lighthearted. Some young

French men and girls wore the badge out of sympathy and in order to give the Security Police trouble. Knochen complained on June 10th of Jews who flaunted their badges in cafés and restaurants frequented by the German army, and of Jewish ex-soldiers who wore the badge below their decorations.

Even more satyrical matter was provided by demands for exemption. Pétain asked De Brinon to intercede for a Marquise and two Countesses, to which modest list he later added the novelist Collette and the widow of Professor Bergson. De Brinon himself had to seek the protection of the Gestapo for his wife, who received her exemption in person from the hands of Major Hagen of 'the commando.'[31] Six Jews were exempted because they worked for D'Arquier's anti-Jewish police and one because he worked for Schellenberg's secret service.

The real implication of the badge was not unappreciated, since Dannecker complained on June 19th that only 83,000 out of 110,000 Jews, officially at liberty in the Occupied Zone, had applied for it. Stuelpnagel's decree of July 8th could not have been quite unforeseen. It entitled the Gestapo to make any public place out of bounds to badge wearers and the list, published on July 15th, was so big that there was little a Jew could do except walk the streets. Even the shops were only available to Jews between three and four in the afternoon. In M. Poliakov's words, 'It was sufficient to buy a box of matches at a tobacconist's at 12.05 to qualify for a journey via Drancy to the crematory ovens of Auschwitz.'[32]

The purpose was, of course, to facilitate a general deportation. On June 11th Dannecker told his colleagues from Brussels and The Hague that the French quota for the next three months was to be 100,000 Jews from both zones, all to be sent to Auschwitz. Eichmann had promised three trains a week after July 13th.[33] Five days later Dannecker learnt that a Jewish deportation programme which required 120 box cars* was out of the question,

*The full programme would have entailed a daily train of twenty box cars and six days had to be allowed for the return of the rolling stock. The limitation to twenty box cars or approximately a thousand passengers to a train was dictated by fuel consumption. The trains from Malines in Belgium, which had 250 miles less to go, were correspondingly bigger at times and so too the trains from Westerbork in Holland. Deportation trains to Auschwitz from Hungary carried habitually 2,500 to 3,000 passengers. On

because Fritz Sauckel had priority for 350,000 French workers to be sent to the Reich. In any case the order had been misunderstood. Eichmann had instructed Rademacher that the French quota was to be 40,000 Jews.[34]

Dannecker was disappointed on other counts. On June 25th he told Leguay, who represented the Vichy Ministry of Police in Paris, that a date must be set for the round-up of 22,000 Jews in Paris and 10,000 in the Free Zone.[35] Leguay hedged. It would take his Government more than three weeks to locate 10,000 'undesirables' and it would need at least 2,500 police. The chief of D'Arquier's private police told Dannecker that Réné Bousquet, the Vichy Minister of Police, would have nothing to do with deportations, but from Heinz Roethke (who was about to be promoted over his head) Dannecker learnt that Bousquet's real attitude would not be known till after Laval's visit to General Oberg in two days time.[36] Laval was then to be persuaded to give D'Arquier full powers over Bousquet and the *gendarmerie*.[37]

After the interview Eichmann complained that Vichy made 'ever-increasing obstacles,' but in fact—perhaps because Abetz sent his Legation Counsellor, Rudolf Rahn, to muffle the mailed first of General Oberg—Laval had been unusually accommodating. Although for the moment he only consented to the deportation of foreign and stateless Jews, he promised later to revise the naturalisations, granted to Jews since 1927 and even since 1919.[38] Laval was also willing to deport children under the age of sixteen from the Free Zone ; children in the Occupied Zone 'did not interest him.' Here one suspects that Laval was deliberately using the Gestapo's language.*

the short runs to the death camps in Poland there were inconceivable trains of up to sixty box cars and more than six thousand passengers.

*Or one may suppose, as M. Georges Wellers does (*Le Monde Juif*, No. 57, July, 1952), that Laval deliberately offered the Germans the 'stateless' children in order to secure exemption for the French Jews and that the protection of French Jewry, for which Laval demanded recognition at his trial. amounted to no more than this. In my view the affair was not so simple. Laval could do nothing to protect the children in the Occupied Zone. Moreover, Laval's proposal to go beyond the Gestapo's wishes by deporting children from the Free Zone occurs only in a second-hand report from Dannecker to Eichmann 'Laval hat vorgeschlagen.' Actually the round-up in the Free Zone was delayed two months and carried out as casually as possible and the children were not arrested. The Gestapo at least had no doubt that Laval had tricked them.

The Gestapo still believed that the French police would round up French subjects. On July 1st Eichmann came to Paris and briefed Knochen and Dannecker to demand the 'indispensable legal basis whereby the French Jews became stateless the moment they crossed the border' (*see pages 333 and 380*). 'A delay in this matter would involve considerable inconveniences in foreign policy, inconveniences which the execution of the *Reichsfuehrer's* order must avoid at all costs.'[39] This sentence in the joint communication sent by Eichmann and Dannecker to Abetz and Stuelpnagel is surely from Eichmann's pen. It reveals the cautious German bureaucrat whom Eichmann's friend, Wisliceny, so precisely described at Nuremberg (*see page 27*).

Extremely ambitious plans were drawn up during Eichmann's visit to 'the commando' for deportation trains starting from Bordeaux, Angers, Rouen, Chalons, and even a train from Marseilles which was to take Jews ferried from Algiers,[40] but the appearance of D'Arquier and Bousquet at 72, Avenue Foch, three days later was less satisfactory. Pétain and Laval had recommended to the *Conseil de Ministres* an immediate deportation of stateless Jews in Vichy territory, but Bousquet, the regular policeman, had passed the responsibility entirely to D'Arquier, the terrified amateur. Dannecker would not be put off by Bousquet's assertion that a new registration of Jews would be needed. The quota of 10,000 Jews for the great round-up, due on July 13th, could be obtained, he said, from the Free Zone internment camps without going to all the trouble of a general registration. Thereupon, but very reluctantly, Bousquet agreed to Dannecker inspecting these camps himself.[41] Dannecker concluded his report to Knochen on a note of triumph: 'I told him that it was not to be supposed that Germany found it easy to welcome so many Jews, but we were determined to resolve this problem for Europe in spite of all the difficulties.'

Dannecker, having been allowed to see for himself, found the reports of the Vichy arrests which had taken place in 1940 grossly overrated. The three main camps of Les Milles, Gurs, and Rivesaltes contained less than 6,000 Jews, including all the survivors of 'Action Buerckel' (*see page 75*). In the course of this uncongenial excursion, which lasted from July 11th to 19th,

Dannecker found the Casino at Monte Carlo full of Jews, while at Perigueux someone with more accuracy than prudence called him a *sale Boche*. Furthermore, during his absence, Heinz Roethke, a barrister of the Berlin court and a new boy at 72, Avenue Foch, was promoted to be head of the Jewish Office.[42*]

Before proceeding to the Free Zone, Dannecker had had another interview with Bousquet and D'Arquier, who brought along seven Vichy police officials, by whom Dannecker was assured that 28,000 stateless Jews still possessed registered addresses in Paris. Convinced that he could count on arresting 22,000 of them, Dannecker chose the Velodrome d'Hiver, a sports stadium in the Boulevard de Grenelle, as a place big enough for a collection centre.[43]

At this interview the Vichy officials agreed that the deportation trains should be guarded as far as the German frontier by French *gendarmerie*, serving with the German regular police. One regrets to have to say that ordinary French policemen performed the main tasks of the round-up, which would not have been possible without them. From the beginning of 1943 it was a different story. The French people were then beginning to feel their strength.

Still there was much non-collaboration, even though Roethke, who was cleverer than Dannecker, postponed the *grand rafle* to July 16th to avoid the repercussions of the national holiday, the *Quatorze Juillet*. Roethke complained to Knochen that only half the numbers had been obtained, that the population had shown sympathy with the arrested children, and that the French police warned the richer Jews in time. The number arrested, including a fair proportion who had to be released, was not 22,000 but 12,886, of whom only 3,000 were grown men, while 4,051 were children.[44] About 6,000 were sent direct to Drancy, while 6,900 were collected at the Velodrome d'Hiver, including all the children.

*Dannecker was recalled to Berlin in October, according to M. Poliakov, on account of the night clubs which he had been running. In the following January he represented Eichmann's office in Bulgaria (*see pages 380-383*). He was posted to Verona in October, 1943, and to Hungary in the summer of 1944. Apparently he remained with the Eichmann commando till the last, but it is not clear whether he reported with them at Alt-Aussee in May, 1945. His fate has not been traced.

It took five days to empty the Velodrome d'Hiver. To pen people like cattle for days on end without food or water, without any of the comforts of existence and sometimes without a shred of clothing, had been the practice of the German police in Poland for the past four months and in Russia for the past year. The ordeal of the Kiev, Lwow, and Lublin Ghettoes was now repeated in the most civilised city in the world. André Bauer, the President of UGIF for the Occupied Territory, reported that it took him twenty-four hours to get Roethke to the stadium, where there were only two doctors, no water except from a single street hydrant, and only ten latrines for 7,000 people. After Roethke's visit some pregnant women and disabled ex-soldiers were released, but there were several births in the stadium, besides numerous attacks of insane frenzy and thirty deaths. On the last day the mothers were separated from their children, never to see them again.[45]

Among all the unspeakable things of the Second World War the story of the 4,051 children in the Velodrome d'Hiver takes a very high place. Knochen and Roethke conferred with the Vichy officials about them on the second day of the round-up. D'Arquier wanted to send them to orphanages, but the Gestapo wanted them to accompany their parents to the deportation camps at Pithiviers and Beaune la Rolande, pending a decision about them from the Security Office in Berlin.[46] On the fourth day of the inferno in the Velodrome d'Hiver Eichmann, a model German bureaucrat and the father of three little girls, the eldest of them five years old, telephoned Roethke that there would be enough trains at the end of August to take the children to 'the General Government.' Consequently, the children were separated from their parents and taken to Drancy.[47]

At the next conference at Avenue Foch on August 13th, Leguay agreed that 300 to 500 children might be mixed with each Auschwitz transport at once and in fact they were mostly deported from Drancy before the 30th. Till then the women internees tried to look after them as best they could in bare and verminous rooms. No attendants went with the children in the sealed box cars, filled at that time with the old, the sick, and the dying, but somehow the children had to be got on to the trains. I quote Dr. Georges Wellers, a survivor of Drancy and Auschwitz[48]:

'It happened sometimes that a whole roomful of a hundred children, as if seized with ungovernable panic and frenzy, no longer listened to the cajoling of the grown-ups who could not get them downstairs. It was then that they called the *gendarmes*, who carried the children in their arms, screaming with terror.'

In Roethke's deportation file there was found an illicit tract, dated November 11th, 1942. It reported that in the box-cars, returning empty from Auschwitz, Belgian railwaymen had found twenty-five bodies of children, aged between two and four.[49] These had never reached the gas chamber.

The vengeance of outraged humanity is seldom spectacular. Eichmann and his chief, Mueller, Dannecker, and Roethke have not even been caught, Oberg and Knochen are still (November 1952) in the Sureté prison, having secured through their lawyers several remissions of trial. There is a strong movement in favour of freeing them.

The Auschwitz trains ran almost to time-table after the great round-up, eight between July 19th and 31st, 1942, and thirteen in August. The Gestapo figures that have survived show that the trains averaged a thousand passengers each, though they might vary as much as from 948 to 1,089.[49a] It is therefore possible— through a fragment of the Birkenau daily *Appell* roster for the male camp—to trace the tragic results of the great round-up. Seven hundred and sixty-nine Jews from the Pithiviers transport were registered in the male camp on July 20th and only 115 on August 16th,* when the groups of children from the Velodrome d'Hiver were already being deported. At this time the transports from Holland were still delivering 80 per cent of their passengers alive, but of the French transports perhaps 70 per cent were missing.

By the end of August 25,000 Jews had been deported from

*Following the transport which arrived on July 20th there were entries of 475, 412, 599, and 370 Jews from France in the Birkenau male camp. Jenny Spritzer, who reached the *Frauenlager* on July 21st, noticed no selection. Two trains which left after the great round-up brought only 240 and 270, but August 2nd and 8th showed an upward trend, 693 and 317 male registrations. Between August 8th and 16th the admixture of the children is shown by four trains bringing no more than 128, 140, 152, and 115 registered male internees. (*Auschwitz, Deel II*, The Hague, May, 1948.)

France,[50] but none from the Free Zone and very few from the provinces. On July 14th Roethke cancelled the train from Bordeaux because the French police, who only arrested stateless Jews, could not collect more than 150. Eichmann was most indignant after all the trouble he had taken with the Ministry of Transport. 'Such a thing had never happened to him. It was reprimandable.' He did not want to pass the matter to *Obergruppenfuehrer* Mueller, because he would be blamed personally, but he wondered whether he should give France up altogether as a base for deportations.[51]

Greater efforts were made to extract Jews from the Free Zone in August, 1942. On the 13th Leguay told Roethke and Knochen that the round-up was on ; but it did not begin till the 26th, when Leguay complained that his unprofessional colleague D'Arquier had given the show away to the Paris press. Nevertheless, 7,100 stateless Jews were arrested. By September 3rd the number deported to Drancy from the Free Zone was still only 9,000, but Roethke wrote that a train would be running to Auschwitz every day by the 15th. He hoped to deport 52,000 more Jews from France before October 30th, when the *Reichsbahn* would have to withdraw the rolling stock.

However, to make up this figure the Vichy Government were expected to revoke the Jewish naturalisations granted since 1933,[52] and their failure to do so was reflected in the actual figures, thirteen trains in September and none in October.[53] There was one consolation for Roethke. On September 23rd he triplicated a telegram to Eichmann, Gluecks, and especially to Rudolf Hoess, the Auschwitz butcher, 'The brother of Léon Blum, the former French President of the Council, was included in to-day's deportation.'[54]

Roethke had now to bargain frenziedly in order to get the naturalisations revoked. In August he had gone so far as to offer immunity to French-born Jews in the Occupied Zone if the post-1933 naturalisations were legally withdrawn. The terms of a decree were drawn up by D'Arquier and—so Roethke was told—submitted to Laval.[55] At intervals in the next twelve months Roethke pressed Knochen for action, reminding him that Laval had approved D'Arquier's draft. Finally, on August 14th, 1943, Roethke managed to obtain an interview with Laval himself.

During those twelve months the Germans had occupied the Free Zone. On the other hand, they had been driven out of North Africa, Sicily, and most of South Russia. Roethke, moreover, was not in Laval's eyes a German of consequence. All this conspired to make Laval less accommodating than he had been when he had made his promise to Rahn and Oberg. He told Roethke that Pétain was disgusted with Bousquet and D'Arquier for drawing up a decree denaturalising women and children. Laval then told Roethke casually that he had lost his copy of the draft. Before a new draft could be submitted to the *Conseil de Ministres*, three months must be allowed to enable Jewish objections to be lodged, even though only thirty Jews might have the right to do so. Until it was done, Laval warned Roethke, the French police could in no wise assist Knochen in his round-ups. And then there were the Italians to be consulted. After this extremely unpleasant interview Roethke had to report to Knochen that he would need more German police.[56]

What inference is one to draw from this document which M. Poliakov has brought to light? There must have been fifty ways in which Laval could be squeezed into revoking the naturalisations, but none of them were used, and suddenly we see the Gestapo singularly powerless, commanding no support from the High Command or the Foreign Office. Hitler must have lost interest in exterminating the Jews in France. This man, who cared nothing for the opinion of the world and who was unamenable to reason, could be undermined completely by slow obstruction.

3. The Italian Intervention

The full tide of obstruction was yet to come. On the night of November 7th, 1942, the Allies landed in French North Africa. On November 11th Admiral Darlan, having joined the Allies at Algiers, invited the Toulon fleet to sail. The Germans at once occupied the Free Zone. But, since this could only be done with the agreement of Germany's ally, the Italian army occupied Nice, Grenoble, and the Alpes Maritimes. In this way the blow to Jewry in the Free Zone was mitigated. The round-ups by the Security Police in the former Vichy towns were so disappointing that only six trains left Drancy for Auschwitz that November. The Gestapo believed—and with some reason—that most of the Jews had fled to the Italian area. For already in Tunis, Greece, and Croatia the Italians had established a reputation for humanity towards the Jews, and even in France they had succeeded in opposing the deportation of Italian Jewish subjects.[57]

On December 4th the Italian Government became party to a German order expelling all Jews from French coastal and frontier areas. The Italian military leaders interpreted this order as applying to French Jews but not to Italian and other foreign Jews, whom they considered to be under their protection. Consequently, on December 29th the Italian Armistice Commission made a formal protest to the French Government concerning an order of the Prefect of Alpes Maritimes which banished all Jews to the German Zone. Laval's response was to send Ribière, the Prefect, to General Vercellin with a proposal that the French Jews be included in his protection and that he should move all the Jews from the Italian Zone into Italy.[58] Vercellin refused and Laval's indiscreet correspondence fell into the hands of Joseph Antignac of D'Arquier's office, who passed it on to Knochen—just when the latter had heard from Mueller that Laval had asked for Gestapo aid in order to remove the Jews from the coast. On the strength of this, Himmler had already sent Major-General Kurt Daluege, the head of the German regular police, to investigate the situation in Marseilles.[59]

Completely foxed, Knochen let Mueller have both versions. Himmler presumably took the line that this was just Laval and there was nothing to be done about it, but the Italian problem was passed to the diplomatists and D'Ajeta of the Italian Foreign Office was soon assuring Count Mackensen that the non-French Jews had now been interned in accordance with the agreement of December 3rd.[60] On February 19th Abetz informed Knochen that the Italians had interned *all* the Jews in their zone, but Roethke, who knew that the Italian Jews had been allowed up to March 31st to repatriate themselves, wrote in the margin ' Incorrect.'[61]

Worse was to come. On February 22nd Knochen again telegraphed Mueller—the matter went too high for Eichmann's competence—that the Italian Fourth Army had stopped the Prefect of Lyons arresting 2,000 to 3,000 Polish Jews in the Grenoble district and prevented their dispatch to Auschwitz 'for labour service.' Knochen was told that Mussolini would discuss the matter personally with Ribbentrop on the 27th.[62]

Mussolini gave Ribbentrop an evasive answer. He agreed, nevertheless, that the military did not possess a correct understanding of the Jewish question. He attributed this in the first place to their 'different intellectual formation.'[63] In short, Mussolini did not interfere with his generals. On March 6th Roethke recapitulated all the unfulfilled Italian assurances to Eichmann, adding that the Fourth Army had liberated two or three hundred more Jews, whom the French police had arrested at Annecy.[64]

On March 18th D'Ajeta ordered the Italian Legation staffs in Vichy and Paris to continue adopting a strong line about the French Prefects, but Marazzani, the liaison officer with the German High Command, informed Hagen of the Gestapo that the Jews in the Italian Zone, who had previously been under house-arrest, were now being interned. This followed an interview between Mussolini and Mackensen, at which Mussolini had again apologised for 'the silly sentimental ideas' of his generals. Ambrosio, the Chief of Staff, would see that they did not interfere again with the French police.[65]

Four days later Mackensen received one of those shocks from which a Nordic nature is not immune. Ambrosio had persuaded Mussolini that the French police were not to be trusted. The registration of the Jews in the Italian Zone would therefore be performed by Italian police, commanded by a certain Lospinoso, formerly chief of police for Bari, although the French police would still be allowed to handle the actual deportations. Mackensen expressed his fear to Bastianini that the Italian generals would continue to hamper the French police, but Bastianini replied that Ambrosio's orders to Vercellin were positive and immutable.[66]

This last manoeuvre so electrified Himmler that he sent the highly recondite grand inquisitor of the Gestapo, Heinrich Mueller, on a visit to Rome. On March 27th Mueller learnt that Lospinoso had left for the Occupation Zone some days ago, but Knochen's inquiries in Mentone were fruitless. On April 6th

Knochen was in such a state of nerves that he telegraphed, not only to Eichmann, but to Schellenberg of the Intelligence Service. He had learnt from the Gestapo in Marseilles that Jews were simply pouring into the Italian Zone. The movement was apparently financed by one Donati, director of the Bank France-Italie. As to Lospinoso, he kept appearing and disappearing and Mueller demanded magisterially that he be brought to Berlin. But Lospinoso was not located till May 26th, when Roethke learnt from the Gestapo in Marseilles that the former chief of police of Bari was living in the Villa Surany at Cimiez—in the uniform of a general. He was in charge of a 'Commissariat for Jewish Affairs' and his adjunct was 'Donati, half-Jew, 37, Promenade des Anglais.'[67]

Lospinoso had indeed begun the expulsion of the Jews of Nice and the coastline. With the aid of Donati's committee he had put them in hotels at Vence and Megève, well within the Italian Zone. When Bousquet protested that the hotels were meant for evacuated children, Lospinoso consented to see a representative from D'Arquier's commissariat—and asked him whether he happened to be a Jew. On July 10th the Marseilles Gestapo reported to Roethke that Lospinoso had moved 22,000 Jews under these humane conditions. A thousand Jews of the poorest class were living 'in the best hotels in Isère and Savoie.' Roethke himself believed that altogether 50,000 Jews were in the Italian Zone.[68]

This game of twisting the Gestapo's tail was bound to end. Already Mussolini had agreed to hand the Occupation Zone over to the Germans, retaining only Nice. On July 22nd Roethke learnt that Donati had left for Rome to intercede for the doomed Jews. Then on July 25th Mussolini was arrested and a new Italian Government was formed under Marshal Badoglio. On August 19th Lopinoso called on the Gestapo in Marseilles to say that, since the change of government, he no longer considered himself bound by the agreement to hand his office over to them.

In spite of this reprieve, the forces working in favour of the Jews showed a lack of decision. The very liberal instructions of the new Italian Foreign Office were not published before September 1st, when it appeared that the Italian Jews were to be repatriated and the stateless Jews brought back to the Nice enclave. In the meantime Donati had been to the Vatican, where he sounded Allied representatives with a view to shipping the stateless Jews to North Africa in Italian liners. Nothing had been concluded on September 8th, when Eisenhower announced the terms of the Italian armistice and the Germans, as a consequence, marched into the Italian Zone.[69]

The Gestapo had planned for this moment. Anton Brunner had gone to Marseilles. He was to direct a massed round-up of Jews without making any distinctions and they were to be shipped to Drancy from Marseilles and Lyons. At Drancy they could be sorted out, since the Italians possessed no effective Jewish registration system.[70]

But though the Germans did not enter Nice till September 11th, the plan to bring the Jews back from Megève into this trap had not progressed very far. Only 2,000 had been moved and the rest were able to scatter among mountain villages. Nevertheless, tragedy seemed about to overwhelm many thousands of Jews who had never left the large towns, but Roethke's threat was largely a vain one. Brunner could achieve no real massed round-up without the complete collaboration of the French police. In Nice Ribière's successor, Chaigneau, destroyed such lists as the Italians left behind them. Brunner was reduced to finding what he could in street man-hunts.[71]

Eichmann, who arrived in Nice soon after the German army, was shocked at the smallness of the bag, but he perceived the explanation. He learnt 'at a party' that 15,000 Jews were hiding in the mountains of the Principality of Monaco. On September 23rd the German Consul in Monaco was instructed by the Foreign Office to arrange for the Security Police to enter the Principality, but the consul could only find a thousand Jews, all of them old residents. Eichmann nevertheless insisted that there were 10,000 to 15,000 Jews. The matter was pursued at intervals. In July, 1944, the consul told von Thadden of the Foreign Office that, following Eichmann's inquiries, most of the thousand Jews had found their way to Switzerland, Spain, or the *Maquis*. There remained forty-five, all of them adequately protected. Only a few had been surrendered to the Security Police and taken to Drancy.[72]

The extent of the German failure may be judged from the

following results. The list found in Roethke's office[73] shows that only three transports left Drancy for Auschwitz in the three months following the fateful September 8th, 1943, when the whole edifice of Italian protection collapsed.

4. The Final Solution Not Achieved

Throughout Roethke's letter file from 72, Avenue Foch runs a refrain. If only Laval would revoke the naturalisation papers granted since 1933—or 1927—we could run the trains every day and fill them. On July 21st, 1943, Roethke believed that the revocation of the post-1927 naturalisations would make 50,000 Jews immediately available. As to French-born Jews, they were only available if they were already under lock and key as hostages, 'Judeo-bolshevists,' or delinquents against the countless new regulations. Thus, out of 52,000 Jews who had then been deported, only 6,000 were French by nationality, while the Free Zone, which had been occupied eight months, had contributed only 13,000 to the quota.[74]

To go back some months before the Italian debacle, transports from Drancy to Auschwitz had been resumed in February, 1943, after the agreed winter pause, but with great difficulty. The round-up of February 11th was composed, according to Dr. Wellers, of children and very old people, the only foreign Jews who could be found at their registered addresses.[75] Next day Knochen reported to Mueller that Bousquet would not let the French police assist in deporting 1,300 French Jews who had been arrested for failing to wear the Jewish badge. Bousquet had offered 1,300 stateless Jews in their place. 'It goes without saying that both categories will be deported.[76]

Colonel Helmuth Knochen, who had served under Professor Franz Six in a bogus-information service of the Gestapo on 'scientific affairs,' was not unduly gifted with a sense of proportion. He told Mueller that the Americans were offering France the Italian colonies and the Rhine and that Laval would certainly hand over more Jews if the Germans bid higher.

On March 6th Roethke wrote to Eichmann that he hoped during April to deport 8,000 to 10,000 Jews a week, but in fact no Jews were deported in April, though five trains had left in

March.[77] In June Roethke had to cancel a round-up. On July 21st he reported that Stuelpnagel refused absolutely to permit the army to assist. Roethke had to rely on the Darnand militia, the D'Arquier anti-Jewish police, and the 'reporter' service of the Gestapo.[78] It was in this month, too, that Major Anton Brunner, the architect of the Vienna, Berlin, and Salonika deportations, tried to produce a sort of Jewish *Ordnungsdienst*. A number of Jews were allowed out of Drancy to collect friends and relatives by various appeals to sentiment or blackmail threats, but *les missionaires* were not a success and they were withdrawn after a few weeks.[79]

In the year that remained till the liberation of Paris another twenty Jewish deportation trains may have left France. It was largely a matter of clearing the camps and also the charitable institutions which UGIF was permitted to run. Dr. Wellers states that in July, 1944, the Paris orphanages and the Rothschild Home for the Aged were cleared.[80] Roethke's file contains the record of an earlier clearance. On April 7th, 1944, Lieutenant Barbie of the Lyons Gestapo reported the dissolution of the Jewish *Colonie des Enfants* at Eyzieux, Ain. 'Captured—forty-one children, aged from three years to ten, and ten attendants. The transport will leave for Drancy to-morrow.'

At Drancy there was a little trouble. 'Dr. von B' said it was Roethke's practice to make special provision for lodging such children. The SS major Brunner said he knew nothing of such instructions and did not approve of them. He would act 'according to the usual methods of deportation.'[81]

Only two transports left for Auschwitz in April, 1944, and one in May, yet on April 14th Knochen made the last despairing attempt at a general round-up, from which even half-Jews were not to be exempt. Brunner was told to remove the Jews from all French camps and prisons to prevent the French authorities from taking them elsewhere[82]—an indication of the changed attitude of the French police. Nevertheless, the invasion of the continent created grave dangers for the Jews in France. For instance, there was a period of a week between the Allied landings in the south of France and the fall of Paris, when the Gestapo, centred on Lyons, ran amuck. Jews were picked up and murdered at random, sometimes in mass executions, but deportation was scarcely possible now that the French railways had been bombed almost to a standstill. Thus the evacuation of Drancy, intended for August 13th, 1944, ten days before the liberation of Paris, had to be cancelled and 700 Jews remained in the camp when the Allies arrived.[83] Dr. Wolken does, however, record the arrival in Auschwitz on September 7th of a hundred Jews from Lyons, which had fallen to the Allies on September 3rd. It is probable that a few railway wagons got round through North Italy.[84]

Dr. Wellers, who had access to the Drancy registration lists, estimates that in the last phase of the deportations between June, 1943, and August, 1944, only 17,000 Jews left France. If this number is added to the earlier figures recorded by the Gestapo, a total is reached which is less than 65,000, and of these 2,800 are known to have returned from Germany.[85*] What proportion does this represent of the Jews who were caught up by the war in France? It is almost impossible to estimate the total number of Jews in France with whom the Gestapo had to deal and of which they themselves were extremely ignorant, but, allowing for escapes, it was still probably not much less than 300,000. With a loss of less than 25 per cent, no Jewish community in Occupied Europe came off so lightly, except in Italy and Denmark, and this was due in large measure to the tactics of Laval, a man who was shot by his compatriots for treason. But it is wrong to ascribe the survival of three-quarters of the Jews in France to the cleverness of any individual. The Final Solution, which was applied so successfully in Central and Eastern Europe, failed in France because of the sense of decency in the common man, who, having suffered the utmost depths of self-humiliation, learnt to conquer fear.

---

*The list dated July 1st, 1944, which was found in Roethke's office shows that up to that date there had been 75 Jewish deportation trains. Normally a thousand Jews travelled in a 20-wagon train, but many of the later transports were much smaller. While the figure I suggest is by no means final, revision is likely to be downwards rather than upwards.

CHAPTER 13

Other Western European Countries

1. Holland

THE case of Holland was almost the reverse of the case of France. Out of a Jewish population of 140,552 on August 2nd, 1941,[1] 110,000 were deported, of whom less than 6,000 returned. To-day the community numbers about 35,000. Barely a fifth of the deportees were stateless refugees without Dutch naturalisation, and of the pre-war native Jews nearly two-thirds perished. The scale of the disaster cannot be explained by any special factors tending to native anti-semitism, for the riots of February, 1941, were well worthy of Holland's tradition of racial and religious tolerance. The reason was the inferior political situation of Holland under German rule as compared to that of France. Even in November, 1942, the Germans did not feel themselves strong enough to take over the civil government of France, whereas Holland was a small country which had been overrun in five days and from the first governed by a German civil commissary. The Dutch Government appointed by the Germans in 1942 was a pure sham.

Nowhere was the Jewish population more completely trapped than in Holland, since very few Jews lived outside the three main cities and more than 60 per cent were concentrated in Amsterdam. Moreover, there was no open front which could be crossed in secret, the nearest neutral sanctuary lying beyond three guarded frontiers. Thus already in 1940 the economic sanctions against the Jews proceeded faster than in France. In October Jewish and half-Jewish firms were sequestered, in November Jews were dismissed from State employment, while early in 1941 their ration books and identity cards received a special stamp. In February a Jewish Council (*Joodse Raad*) was created on the East European model, while early in 1942 the country-dwelling Jews were concentrated in Amsterdam or sent to the peat-cutting camps.[2]

In the earlier stages these cruelties produced something more than sympathy from the Gentile population, namely, physical resistance. On February 9th, 1941, the German police, accompanied by some Dutch collaborationist militia, sacked houses in the historic Amsterdam Jewish quarter, allegedly because they had been shot at from the windows. During a second raid on the quarter on February 11th the Dutch workers from the Kattenburg raincoat factory in the Waterlooplein came to the help of the Jews. A certain Hendrik Koot, a Dutch militiaman, was wounded and later died. Although the Jewish quarter was closely patrolled during the following days, the ostentatious German funeral given to Koot on the 17th provoked further riots, as a consequence of which Himmler ordered the arrest of 400 Jewish hostages.[3]

It may be observed that Artur Seyss-Inquardt, the Civil Commissary, and Hans Rauter, the Higher SS and Police Leader, both of them Austrians, warned Himmler against this. Seyss-Inquardt had been for a brief period Chancellor of Austria in succession to Schuschnigg and as such had arranged the *Anschluss* by telephone. He had been rewarded with the post of *Reichsstatthalter* of Vienna, but had not held it long. His subsequent posts were hardly commensurate with his services, since he was regarded as only a moderate party man. Nevertheless, Seyss-Inquardt's part in the persecution of Dutch Jewry was one of useful though passive condonation.

Rauter was rather a different sort of Austrian. Typical of the class from which Himmler chose his police chiefs, he had been a *Freikorps* leader in the days following the collapse of the Hapsburg monarchy, a turbulent figure who managed to be present in every area where militant German racialism was challenged. The prison interviews with Rauter, published by Dr. De Jong and Professor Postumus, suggest a man with a strong but strictly professional sense of honour, a man not unpleasing to meet, but unusually silly and in love with violence.[4]

Rauter, who had had to hurry back from his sick leave in Bad Gastein, learnt on February 19th that a German police patrol had been sprinkled with vitriol in the old Jewish quarter.[5] He therefore arrested 250 Jews on the 22nd and 140 on the 23rd. They were personable young men, selected in the streets by the *Schutzpolizei* and forced to kneel there for hours on end before being taken to a camp.

On the 25th Rauter plastered Amsterdam with notices that

the Jews had shot first and that the arrests were a reprisal measure,[6] but this did not stop a general strike spreading through the city. In the Rokin, where the strikers forced passengers to leave the trams, the German police fired on the crowd. But, since the war made few military demands on Germany in February, 1941, it was possible to rush to Amsterdam three battalions of regular police and a battalion of the Death's Head *verbaende*, which normally provided concentration-camp guards. The display of force succeeded and, though the sympathetic strike had already spread to Rotterdam, the Amsterdam gas and electricity went on again next day.[7]

For their part in the action, the boldest till the strikes that followed the Allied invasion of the continent, sixty Dutch workmen were deported to German concentration camps, but the full penalty for the loss of German prestige was borne by the 389 Jewish hostages. For a time their relatives received field postcards, but in the summer notices began to arrive from ' Standesamt II, Mauthausen,' declaring that so-and-so had died of pneumonia and that his ashes could be collected from the Gestapo for a fee of 75 gulden. When the notices became numerous they were passed in bulk to the Jewish Council. Then in October, 1941. the Swedish Minister in Berlin complained that Red Cross representatives had been denied access to the hostages and that the deaths of 400 young and healthy men had been announced at regular intervals.[8] The only result was that Martin Luther of Department ' Deutschland ' advised that in future arrested Dutch citizens be kept in Holland, where no protective Power functioned, and that death notices be timed with more realism.[9]

The hostages were literally tortured to death. On May 22nd, 1941, when 59 had died, the remainder were removed from Buchenwald to the ghastly quarrying camp at Mauthausen, near Linz, in Austria. Here they were joined by a further 230 Amsterdam Jews, who had been deported in June. Of the whole 619, only eight were alive at the beginning of 1942,[10] and only one, Max Nebig, at the end of the war, when he described to Eugen Kogon in Buchenwald how the group had undergone a treatment special to Mauthausen. They were driven up and down the 148 steps in the side of the quarry, carrying boulders. On the third day the survivors of the man-made hell formed groups who joined hands and jumped over the rock escarpment. But their act was seen by civilian workers, so that it was necessary to take the last few back to camp, where they were driven on to the high-voltage wire. Nebig saved his life by volunteering for a human guinea-pig operation, after which he was hidden in the TB ward at Buchenwald till the end of the war.[11]

Thanks to the brutish bureaucratic stupidity of the death notices and the traffic in cremation urns, the destruction of the Jews became common knowledge. In August, 1941, when Himmler wanted to send Dutch Communists to Buchenwald, Harster, the Security Police Commander for Holland, persuaded Mueller, chief of the Gestapo in Berlin, to alter the order because 'otherwise political repercussions would make such measures notorious.' Rauter claimed at his trial that he, too, had intervened against sending Dutchmen 'to the stone quarries.'[12] They went instead to what was admittedly no health resort—Sachsenhausen concentration camp.

The mass murder of Dutch Jews was not repeated till July, 1942. Indeed, the pace of the persecution of Dutch Jewry seems to have been slowed down to coincide with the preparations at Auschwitz. Thus the wearing of the Jewish badge, which was decreed for the Greater Reich and Slovakia in September, 1941, was not ordered by Rauter till April 29th, 1942. On the other hand, a branch of the Central Jewish Emigration Office, which later became responsible for the deportations, was established in Amsterdam in September, 1941, under the notorious Captain Aus der Fuenten, precisely when the first mass deportations were ordered from the Old Reich.[13]

On June 23rd, 1942, Eichmann informed Rademacher, his contact man at the Foreign Office, that from the middle of July the Jewish deportation trains from the West would run daily and include 40,000 Dutch Jews in addition to 40,000 French and 10,000 Belgian Jews.[14] It then appeared that for 'psychological reasons' the Foreign Office wanted the 25,000 'stateless' refugees in Holland to be deported first. Nevertheless, naturalised and even native-born Dutch Jews were included among the first arrests, made by Zoepf and Aus der Fuenten, and on this matter, which took the Foreign Office by surprise, there was a conflict of opinion.

The Reich Main Security Office wanted these Jews to be deprived by decree of their Dutch nationality the moment they crossed the frontier 'in order to stop Sweden intervening.' But Dr. Emil Albrecht, the Foreign Office legal expert, pointed out that, if this was done, Sweden would cease to protect German nationals in Curaçao and Dutch Guiana. Then, recalling that the Swedes had pertinaciously tried to visit Mauthausen whenever death certificates had been received in Holland, Albrecht suggested it would be sufficient if the police concealed the whereabouts of the deportees and dispensed with the needless ceremony of sending death certificates to their relatives—prudent advice from an extremely prudent German which the Gestapo accepted. There was no decree denaturalising the deported Dutch Jews and no interference from Sweden either.[15]*

The Jews, who at first presented themselves voluntarily at the Polderweg when summoned by the Jewish Council, were taken by train to Hooghelen, more than a hundred miles from Amsterdam and close to the German frontier. They were then marched to the 'Drancy' of Holland, a lonely camp among the peat bogs known as Westerbork. It had once been a camp for Jewish refugees and it was here that the passengers of the German liner St. Louis were sent in June, 1939, after her fruitless voyage to Havana. By the natural processes of logic, Westerbork had now become the collecting station for the gas chambers of Auschwitz, for which destination some 5,742 left in the second half of July, 1942. Six passenger trains took them across the German Reich, covering the 750 miles in 40 hours.[16] Eichmann had been precise. There was a train from France or Holland every day.

Direct selection for the gas chamber was already practised when the trains reached Auschwitz station, but the proportion was still low. A comparison between a fragment of the Birkenau roll-call roster and the Westerbork lists shows that at the most 18 per cent of the male passengers were missing and in the case of the second train none. Till August 7th more men were taken

---

*So far as I know, the guilt of Dr. Emil Albrecht in making this proposal has never been investigated. Albrecht's Referent on Jewish affairs, Dr. Konrad Roediger, who is now a high judicial official of the Bonn republic, testified at the Rademacher trial that he had had no knowledge of this letter of Albrecht's (Frankfurter Rundschau, February 22nd, 1952).

in than were listed as being of employable age. On August 7th, however, 35 per cent were missing and thereafter fewer men than the theoretically employable number were admitted to camp.[16a] At the end of August the *Joodse Raad* were still picking mainly able-bodied young people for the trains but the proportion must have dropped soon afterwards. From March 2nd, 1943, when the trains were diverted to Sobibor, the gas chamber claimed 97 per cent.

The progress of the deportations was duly reported to Luther's section of the Foreign Office by 'Minister' Otto Bene, the former Consul-General in Milan, who represented the Foreign Office at Seyss-Inquardt's court. On August 13th, however, Bene wrote in a strain that was far from complacent. He had learnt that only 400 of the 2,000 Jews summoned that week by the *Joodse Raad* had turned up at the Polderweg 'because the Jews found us out and got to know what was behind the deportations and labour service in the East.'[17] Presumably the Amsterdam community had discovered that the trains terminated at Auschwitz and that Auschwitz was a concentration camp. Later they got to know more. On October 9th Anne Frank, hidden with her family in an Amsterdam warehouse, wrote in her diary: 'The British radio speaks of their being gassed.' We may notice another diary, that of Dr. Kremer, medical officer in Birkenau camp, who wrote on the 18th[18] (*see page 117*):

'In wet, cold weather attended my eleventh selection on a Sunday morning (Dutchmen). Shocking scene with three women who beseeched us for their naked lives.'

Bene had added in his report to Luther 'It is not known how the trains will be filled.'* Actually four of the trains which left Westerbork that August were only half made up.[19] Consequently, Major Willi Lages, the Security Police Commandant in Amsterdam, had to make different arrangements. A specially chosen detachment of Dutch police was kept at the Tulpkaserne and

---

*Bene's wording suggests that he himself knew something about the deportations which he believed to have been hidden from the Jews, but at the Rademacher trial he testified that he merely passed on the Security Police report and that he had never thought it meant mass-killing (*Frankfurter Rundschau*, February 20th, 1952).

the Jews were brought forcibly to the *Schouwberg*, the former Jewish playhouse. Even so, Rauter complained on September 10th that the co-operation of the Dutch police was almost non-existent.[20] About 15,000 Jews had then been deported, but 25,000 were in hiding, 6,000 were believed to have crossed the Belgian border, and no less than 46,000 were still exempt from deportation, including dependants of the Jews in the peat-cutting camps.[21] Another way of securing exemption was to be employed by the Jewish Council. These employees increased from 8,886 on October 15th to 17,492 at the beginning of December, but at the end of the year they were reduced under Gestapo pressure to 14,500 and to 13,000 at the end of March, 1943.[22]

On September 10th Rauter wrote personally to Himmler that the concentration of the Jews was his 'greatest headache.' He believed that the exempted families of the peat-cutters in the labour camps represented 30,000 people. On September 21st Rauter declared that their arrest and deportation would fill three trains a week. To reach this quota Rauter proposed to pronounce a sentence of outlawry. After October 15th the Dutch Jews could be arrested, not only by the police, but by members of the armed forces and by party members.[23]

These measures, to which Himmler appended the marginal words *sehr gut,* were only partly successful. Winding up the labour camps yielded not 30,000 people but 17,000, and by the end of the year the total number of Jews deported from Holland was 38,606.[24] Nevertheless, the *Reichskommissar*, Seyss-Inquardt, counted on completing the deportations by May 1st, 1943, at the rate of 2,000 to 3,500 a week,[25] but in reality only 12,000 Jews were deported in the first 12 weeks of 1943, and even this result required new expedients.

Rauter had written to Himmler that he would never allow a deportation train to be cancelled: 'What is started is started.'[26] Yet Rauter claimed at his trial[27] that he knew nothing of Captain Aus der Fuenten's descent, on January 20th, 1943, upon the Jewish mental home, *Appeldoornse Bos.* This person arrived at night, accompanied by a hundred Jewish *Ordnungsdienst* men from Westerbork camp and some SS men. Nine hundred lunatics and mentally defective children were taken at once in lorries and loaded on the cattle-truck train which waited in Appeldoorn station, most of them in night-shirts, but many quite naked. The stretcher cases were packed forty to a van. They could not be reached by the attendants, who were locked in a passenger coach, and dead bodies were removed at Hengelo and Deventer before the train had even passed the frontier. Thereafter, the vans, hermetically sealed, lumbered for four days through Germany before they reached Auschwitz, where those who survived, including the attendants, were taken off in lorries and not seen again. The incident at Appeldoorn can be compared with the most fantastic Polish survivors' reports and the most savage details in the *Einsatzgruppen* bulletins, but at Aus der Fuenten's trial in December, 1949, it was confirmed in all its details by the least emotional witnesses in the world, stolid, honest Dutch railwaymen.[28]

Two months later Rauter made a speech to the Security Police officers at his headquarters on the occasion of the return of a comrade from Russia and, unfortunately for him, it was printed in an SS magazine:

> 'I will gladly pledge my soul in heaven for what I have undertaken here against the Jews. He who has discovered the meaning of Jewry as a race and nation cannot do otherwise than we have done.'[29]

In April, 1943, Rauter was inspired by the action of Police Major-General Juergen Stroop in the Warsaw Ghetto. On the 27th he sent for Major Zoepf, Eichmann's representative at The Hague, and informed him that Amsterdam must be 'de-Jewed' quarter by quarter, that the exempts must go to the new camp at Vugt and the half-Jews to the provinces. This was not an easy task, for Zoepf had just prepared a report, entitled 'De-Jewing of the Netherlands,' which showed that half the 71,700 surviving Jews in Holland lived legally and openly in Amsterdam and that at least 27,000 of them had valid exemptions.[29a]

A week later Zoepf received new instructions from Harster, the Security Police commander. The May quota was reduced from 12,000 Jews to 8,000, a figure that was absolutely essential because a 'record number of Jews from the West was needed for the new Bunawerk factory at Auschwitz,' which was now nearing completion. Zoepf could at first find only 5,780 deportable Jews, but after an inroad into the exemption list 8,150 Jews were obtained and deported during May on four transport days.[30] The final action in Amsterdam had to be postponed till June 20th, when the Transvaal quarter was cordoned with the aid of Jewish camp police from Westerbork. According to Bene's report to the Foreign Office, these Jews were delighted to be able to arrest members of the Jewish Council, but in fact the 5,550 Jews obtained in the Transvaal round-up were mainly protected from deportation.[31]

By the end of July, 1943, the Germans had deported 82,000 Jews from Holland. Since the beginning of May the rate had been 2,000 a week, the highest since July, 1942. These Jews had not gone to the Bunawerk factory. They had not even been taken to Auschwitz, where the crematory ovens had been occupied in March-May with the Berlin and Salonika transports and immobilised during the typhoid epidemic of June-July. Every Tuesday since March 2nd a train had left Westerbork and every Friday it had arrived in Poland at the lonely siding of Sobibor, 75 miles beyond Lublin and 1,100 miles from Westerbork. On some Tuesdays the trains were doubled. In this manner a total of 34,313 Jews from Holland reached the secret death camp by the River Bug (see pages 135-6).

Only sixteen women and three men returned after the war to Holland from Sobibor, where the chance of avoiding immediate death in the gas chamber was not one in four, but less than one in forty. From most trains about 40-80 young men were picked for the services of the death camp, but they lasted only a few weeks. On the other hand, the dozen or so girls who would be chosen for the tailoring shops in the outer camp had a chance of being transferred to other labour camps. Hence the high proportion of girls among the nineteen who finally survived out of more than 800.[32]

There was a few weeks' pause after the last Sobibor transport, which left on July 20th. Though more than 25,000 Jews were still to leave Holland, the pace was governed by the growing number of exemptions demanded by various German Government agencies, exemptions which, as usual, entirely refute the myth of the omnipotence of the SS. On March 20th, 1943, Zoepf's bright and efficient secretary, Fraulein Sloettke, had compiled a thirty-one-page guide book on her typewriter entitled 'The Development of the Jewish Stay-behind Groups.' Here one may read that Colonel Veltjens needed twenty-six Jews to buy war materials on the black market, that thirteen 'old party members' had been freed from wearing the Jewish badge, as well as three picture experts, a German Olympic champion of 1896, and the son-in-law of a former Dutch Royal librarian.[33]

Certain categories were quite numerous. Dr. Kalmeyer of the German Commissariat of Justice wanted 370 members of the Amsterdam Portuguese Jewish community, 'who had no affinities with Eastern Jewry,' to be interned separately—and Dr. Kalmeyer succeeded, the more surprisingly since at this very moment the greatest of all the former Spanish Sephardic communities, that of Salonika, was in process of destruction in Auschwitz. Another large list, comprising diamond-cutters and fur-dressers, was wanted by the Armaments Office of the Wehrmacht. The Wilhelmstrasse wanted Jewish subjects of certain countries who could be used in exchange bargains with the Allies, while finally there was a list of Jews who, because they were married to Aryans, might achieve complete freedom through the possession of certificates of sterilisation. On June 15th, 1944, these certificate-holders numbered 1,146[34] (see pages 177-9).

The Austauschjuden or exchange Jews were not at first a large category. Bene's list of February 19th, 1943, comprised 289 English-born Jews, but Fraulein Sloettke discovered that 96 of them had already gone to Auschwitz, because they possessed double nationality. They are perhaps the only group of British subjects who are known to have been sent to Auschwitz, and it must be assumed that most of the 96 found their way to the gas chamber.[35] In March, however, a new list was made out, showing no less than 499 Jews in Holland having some claim to British protection. This list was part of a scheme of European dimensions. A Foreign Office circular of February 20th, signed by Rademacher, had asked for a total of 30,000 exchange Jews who should be representative of all Allied countries, including even the Soviet Union. This plan was for a short time taken perfectly seriously and was probably a product of Himmler's recent tentative dealings with world Jewry through the Slovak Zionist

Relief Committee (*see pages 391-2*). But very shortly afterwards it encountered heavy weather. Kaltenbrunner had gone so far as to instruct his Security Police commanders in Russia to select suitable Jews from the ghettoes when, on April 5th, Windecker, the Foreign Office representative with *Reichskommissar* Lohse at Riga, pointed out a little matter that had escaped the notice of bureaucracy[36]:

> 'Since it is known that many thousands of the local and German Jews have been shot in the course of time in the area of Riga, it is questionable whether any Jews can be considered for the purpose of exchanging them without the executions being used against us abroad.'[37]

Not many days after the receipt of this dispatch the formidable Dr. Martin Luther entered the 'Political Bunker' of Sachsenhausen concentration camp—for life. It was therefore not Martin Luther but a new department-chief, Eberhard von Thadden of 'Inland II,' who sent Windecker a snub, telling him on May 10th that the Foreign Office was quite aware of these 'practical difficulties.' The purpose of the decree was to get 'more information regarding the treatment of the Jewish problem.'[38] And that was how it was regarded in Holland. Rauter suggested on June 24th that an advertisement for 'exchange Jews' might bring to the surface some of the 20,000 Jews in hiding.[39]

Nevertheless, the Gestapo still found other and more desirable uses for the 'exchange Jews' decree, namely, in the sale of privileges. A traffic was discovered in Hondurasian and Paraguayan passports issued in Switzerland. The lucky owners were thereupon told that they were 'exchange Jews' and the meaning was this. There were many Germans interned in the U.S.A. and Latin America, but very few natives of the New World interned by the Germans. Himmler therefore ordered Eichmann to find a special camp for these useful if bogus foreign subjects.[40] A new concentration camp had been under construction at Bergen-Belsen since April and to this camp[41] 367 Jews with Spanish passports were brought from Salonika on August 2nd, while on September 15th a further 305 owners of foreign passports arrived in wagons that had been detached from the Westerbork-Auschwitz death train. There were already 3,000 Jews in

Bergen-Belsen and in the next twelve months a further 3,750 arrived from Holland alone.[42]

From the very beginning, the purposes of Bergen-Belsen were confused and uncertain. Lieutenant Nowak wrote to Zoepf from Eichmann's office on September 9th, 1943, that only Jews from the 'exchange list,' Jews with relatives in Palestine, and 'Honduras and Paraguay' Jews should go there. But many more categories were introduced among the 1,037 Jews who arrived from Westerbork on January 11th, 1944; diamond workers, men decorated with the German Iron Cross and their families, half-Jews belonging to the Dutch Confessional Church—and Trotski's nephew.[43] This confusion of purpose appears in the variety of terms by which Bergen-Belsen was officially described, 'convalescence camp,' 'transit camp,' and 'exchange camp.' It was split into a number of rigidly separated sections, each with its own régime such as the 'Christmas Tree Camp' for alleged American subjects. All these formed part of what was later known as the 'Star Camp or No. 2 Camp,' where in April, 1945, the British army found relatively few horrors (see page 466). But in September, 1944, the 'Star Camp' held already 15,000 people and some draining-off took place. The Jews who were least likely to be negotiable were moved on to Auschwitz. On October 9th, 1944, the Amsterdam diamond-cutters went and 112 of the Jews of double nationality. The Bergen-Belsen Jews, who had been encamped in the middle of Germany in the last year of the war, had learnt all about the Auschwitz selections. This is confirmed by Hoess, the Auschwitz butcher, who testified that the guard at the gas chambers had to be increased when this small group of deportees arrived. Hoess wrote of desperate resistance in the ante-room of death. Some of the SS were disarmed and the resisters, apparently the three hundred who arrived on October 9th, were not gassed but taken out and shot.[44]

It is ironical that Bergen-Belsen, after two years' existence as a 'soft' camp for the privileged, should become in April, 1945, the one place where the British soldier saw naked race murder face to face, the place which to British minds most symbolises the outlook and practices of Himmler and the SS.

In 1944 4,969 Jews were deported in six trains from Holland to the 'model ghetto,' Theresienstadt. These were the privileged

Jews without exchange value, mainly former employees of the Jewish Council. But since 2,424 of them were redeported from Theresienstadt to Auschwitz in September-October, they gained very little from their privileges over the ordinary deportees, who were routed to Auschwitz again after September 14th, 1943. On the eve of a second wave of deportations to Auschwitz on January 27th, 1944, Zoepf reported 'a flood of interventions' and even proposals that the Jews should be allowed to return to Holland after the war,[45] but Dr. Wolken's Birkenau quarantine statistics show that in 1944 the gas chambers absorbed their usual quota.*

On March 2nd, 1944, Rauter wrote to Himmler: 'In ten days' time the last pure Jew will be sent East from Westerbork.'[47] Henceforward the rare deportation trains from Holland went only to Theresienstadt, Bergen-Belsen, and Ravensbrueck. There remained in Holland 8,610 pure Jews who were married to Aryans, a few thousand still working for the Germans and at least 20,000 hiding with Aryan protectors—and this in spite of the fact that head-money was increased from twenty-five to forty gulden for each Jew detected.[48]

Although the threat of deportation was incessant, these numbers remained little changed till the end of the war,† when it soon became apparent that at least 104,000 Jews formerly living in Holland had been murdered. To-day many streets in the Joedenhoek quarter of Amsterdam present the appearance of

---

*About 10,000 Jews left Westerbork for Auschwitz in September-November, 1943, and 4,500 in February-March, 1944. There was a round-up of 3,000 Jews in Amsterdam on September 28th-29th, including 130 employees of the Jewish Council. This has been wrongly called the liquidation of the Amsterdam Ghetto. A trainload of 1,700 Jews from this round-up left for Auschwitz three weeks later.[46]

†The last deportations of Jews from Holland were not till September 5th and 6th, 1944, when Allied patrols had already reached the Dutch border. The 3,500 inmates of Vugt or Herzogensbosch camp were then moved to Ravensbrueck and Sachsenhausen, including a few groups of 'privileged' Jews. Previously on June 3rd the 496 Jews, who had been exempted as skilled employees of the Philips valve factory at Eindhoven, had been sent from Vugt to Auschwitz, where, however, they were spared to continue their work in Germany for the Telefunken Company and nearly 400 of them survived the war—the largest survival-rate of any Auschwitz transport. (Netherlands Red Cross, Research Bureau. 'Etude sur le sort des prisonniers du Kl Herzogenbosch,' The Hague, February, 1952.)

bombing—but they were not bombed. These are the Jewish houses which stood empty during the terrible scarcity months of 1944 and 1945, and which were carried off bit by bit to repair the homes of neighbours.

Major-General Hans Albin Rauter of the SS was tried at The Hague in April-May, 1948, and sentenced to death, although the court accepted his plea that he was unaware of the true character of Auschwitz. Rauter's appeal was dismissed in January, 1949, and he was executed on March 25th.

Major Lages, commandant of the Security Police in Amsterdam, was sentenced to death in June, 1949, and Captain Aus der Fuenten in December. It now seems unlikely that the sentences will be carried out. Major Zoepf and his essential Fraulein Sloettke have escaped detection—like most members of Eichmann's office.

2. Belgium

The story of the deportation of the Jews of Belgium can be told briefly since the incidents fit into the main pattern of deportations from the West. Inasmuch as Belgium was under German military administration, there was an almost total lack of political repercussions.

There were probably 85,000 Jews in Belgium on May 10th, 1939, all but a few of them in the two towns Antwerp and Brussels. Yet on October 28th, 1940, when all Jews were ordered to register with the police, the Germans could obtain no higher figure than 42,000.[49] While part of the difference was due to massed flight across the French border, in the main it must have been due to failure to register. The Germans were in fact never able to lay their hands on the well-assimilated native-born Jewish population and were indeed reluctant to do so. The Military Governor, General von Falkenhausen, was a pronounced opponent of National Socialist extremism and, till his own arrest in July, 1944, more than held his own against Security Police interference. Thus after Knochen's conference in Paris on March 14th, 1942,[50] the military administrator in Belgium, Brigadier-General Eggert Reeder, absolutely refused to impose the Jewish badge and maintained his refusal. But, if Falken-hausen and Reeder pursued a policy intended to placate Belgian opinion, they never had any scruple about sacrificing the foreign and refugee Jewish population. In fact Belgium was the first of the Western occupied countries from which such Jews were deported. On December 5th, 1941, some 83 Polish Jewish families were 'repatriated' to Poland from Antwerp, while a considerably larger number were sent in February-March, 1942, to work in the textile factories of the Lodz Ghetto.[51]

The deportation trains, which began to run from Malines to Auschwitz on August 4th, 1942, were intended for a mass deportation of Jews, both Belgian subjects and foreign. No discrimination was made by Eichmann's office,[52] who later complained to the Foreign Office at the way their instructions were carried out. Consequently, on December 2nd, Luther and Rademacher initialled a strong protest to Werner von Bargen,* the Foreign Office representative with General Falkenhausen in Brussels, because the native-born Belgian Jews were not being included in the deportations.[53] By this time thirteen transports had already left Malines and no Jew any longer reported voluntarily. The deportations had to be carried out through police raids.

According to the very reliable report published by the War Refugees Board in Washington, native-born Belgian Jews were first noticed in camp at Auschwitz after the transport which arrived on August 3rd, 1943,[54] but there was only one attempt at a mass round-up. On September 3rd some hundreds of native Antwerp Jews were taken in furniture vans from their homes to the Caserne Dossin in Malines. Soon afterwards Reeder ordered their release at the instance of Queen Elizabeth and Cardinal Van Roey, and the attempt was not repeated.[55] It was conse-quently impossible to find enough stateless and foreign Jews to

---

*Like Otto Bene at The Hague, von Bargen had to forward the Security Police reports on the Jewish deportations from Belgium to Luther's depart-ment at the Foreign Office. In March, 1952, he gave evidence at the trial of Franz Rademacher as an official in the legal department of the new Bonn Foreign Office. Von Bargen then declared that he had merely forwarded the reports of the *Judenreferent* in Brussels and that, if he had not been very circumspect in his replies to the instructions from Luther's office, he would have been deported himself. (*Frankfurter Rundschau*, March 4th, 1952.)

fill another Auschwitz transport after September 20th, though some 1,800 Jews of various privileged categories were taken in 1944 to Theresienstadt, Bergen-Belsen, and other German camps.

The transports were governed by the same law of diminishing return as in France. Five Auschwitz transports left the Caserne Dossin in August, 1942, five in September, and three in October. In 1943 a single transport left for Auschwitz in the months of January, April, July, and September.* After October, 1942, strong young men from the conscript labour camps were included in the Auschwitz transports and escapes became common. On January 15th, 1943, some thirty or forty cut their way out of a train with smuggled saws.[57] On April 22nd the Belgian railwaymen contrived to leave some doors open when a transport of 1,586 Jews left the Caserne Dossin. Other railwaymen held up the train between Tirlemont and Visé, where the 'Comité de defense des Juifs' had arranged an ambush. The fire of the SS guards was returned and 150 Jews were enabled to escape, though twenty were killed and more than a hundred wounded. The recaptured Jews, including the wounded, were taken back to Malines and put on the transport of July 31st, from which too thirty-nine Jews escaped.[58]

At the trial of Falkenhausen and Reeder, which was not concluded till March 9th, 1951, the Brussels court ruled that both were guilty of ordering the deportation of 25,000 Jews, but that they were not responsible for their subsequent torture and extermination in Germany. Under the Belgian law of remission† the generals' sentences of twelve years' imprisonment each were cut to a third and they were released within three weeks.[59]

---

*The first five Auschwitz transports were passenger-coach trains, carrying 1,000 Jews at a time, but from September, 1942, the Jews travelled in cattle-trucks. The average train held 1,500 people, but sometimes, as on October 31st, 1942, it would take nearly 2,000 people by crowding seventy to a truck. Of the 25,437 Jews who were deported from Belgium, 23,000 travelled in the seventeen Auschwitz transports. Of the 1,276 Jews who returned to Belgium from Germany after the war, only 615 had survived the Auschwitz mill.[56]

†In September, 1952, the commutation of a death sentence on a Belgian servant of the Gestapo created so much public indignation that M. Pholien, the Minister for Justice, resigned. On September 14th, following a mass demonstration, the Government submitted a Bill, annulling the conditional liberation rights of imprisoned war criminals, from which Falkenhausen and Reeder had benefited (see Appendix II).

Falkenhausen and Reeder were in fact imprisoned first and tried afterwards. The scandal of this 'Alice in Wonderland' justice does not, however, alter the fact that these two men uprooted the Jews from their homes and confiscated their property, and that they made no real inquiries concerning the ultimate fate of the innocent people who passed through their hands.

3. Denmark and Norway

At the beginning of 1942 Himmler and Heydrich put pressure on the Foreign Office to get the Nuremberg anti-Jewish laws applied to the occupied Western countries. In Holland, a totally occupied country, this pressure could not be resisted. In France, a half-occupied country, it was half-resisted. We come now to the case of a nation which retained its neutrality under German occupation with a monarchy and constitution both unimpaired. Here the pressure of Himmler and the SS was resisted with 90 per cent success—almost the only happy-ending story in this book.

In January, 1942, it was reported in the American press that the King of Denmark had threatened to abdicate if the German demand for 'Nuremberg' legislation was pressed. As a consequence, Rademacher, the SS's watch-dog over the Diplomatic Corps, advised Cecil von Renthe-Fink, the Reich plenipotentiary in Copenhagen, 'to find occasions to point out that it would be prudent for Denmark to prepare in good time for the Final Solution.'[60] But Denmark was not prudent, and in June, 1942, when the Germans were pressing for a Danish 'Jewish badge' decree, similar to that which had been in force in the Reich since September, 1941, King Christian was reported to have said that he would be the first Danish subject to wear the badge.[61]

Himmler now tried to proceed against the Jews in Denmark in the guise of security measures. On September 24th, 1942, he ordered Heinrich Mueller, the head of the Gestapo, to insert the names of Jews in a list of Danish Communist and resistance leaders whom he proposed to arrest.[62] No doubt Himmler believed he could rely on the co-operation of Renthe-Fink's successor, Karl Werner Best, since he had been legal adviser to the Gestapo; but Best, who had left the Gestapo to get out of the clutches of Heydrich, was now relieved of the worst anxieties of a successful careerist by the death of his old friend. Moreover, as a Reich plenipotentiary in a quasi-neutral country, Best desired a quiet life above all things, so his report to Ribbentrop on January 28th, 1943, was quite daring. Best suggested that, since the proposed measures would certainly create a constitutional crisis in Denmark, the Danes should be asked only to dismiss their Jews from the civil service.[63]

Under Himmler's pressure Ribbentrop returned to the charge and on April 24th Best replied that out of 6,500 Jews in Denmark only 31 were civil servants and only 60 handled German contracts. Of course, there were the 1,351 refugees from the Reich whom the Danish Government had hitherto protected, but Best suggested that the Danes would not be able to do this any longer if the refugees were given back their German nationality. Such a step was, however, impossible under the ' 11th decree supplementing the Reich Law of Citizenship,' which could not be retracted in the case of refugees in Denmark without upsetting the whole legal fabric of the deportations from Germany[64] (see pages 75-87).

Himmler still insisted on the full application of the Final Solution in Denmark, and Ribbentrop, as usual, gave way. On May 22nd he informed Best that, while he could not take instructions from Himmler, the next steps might be discussed with Himmler in the precincts of the Foreign Office, if necessary in Ribbentrop's presence.[65] Nothing, however, was done till August, when a disturbance in Denmark gave Himmler the pretext he required. On August 5th, 1943, Sweden renounced the 1940 agreement by which German troops stationed in Norway were permitted to use her railway system. This action inspired the Danish dock workers at Odense to refuse to repair German ships. There were riots and arrests, and on August 9th the Danish Premier, Scavenius, threatened to resign if the Danish courts were required to try the arrested men. As a consequence, the Germans introduced martial law at Odense. On August 24th—the day that Himmler was made Minister of Interior—the Danish resistance movement blew up the German-occupied Forum Hall in Copenhagen and on the following day all the Danish shipyards were on strike. On the 28th the Scavenius

Government resigned, on the 29th General von Hannecken proclaimed martial law throughout Denmark. The small Danish fleet either scuttled itself or sought internment in Swedish ports.

But even now Best and von Hannecken could not take over the government of Denmark, since they had to rely on a Committee of Ministerial Directors to act for the absent Danish Cabinet. It appeared to Best, nevertheless, that this provided the opportunity for deportations, and on September 8th he asked for police reinforcements and help from the Wehrmacht ' so that the Jewish problem can be handled during the present siege conditions and not later.'[66] But as a Nuremberg witness on July 31st, 1946, Best tried to put the cart before the horse. He claimed that he had only approved of martial law for Denmark after Himmler had fixed the date for the deportations, which, he feared, would cause riots.[67] At the same time he warned certain Danish politicians of Himmler's plans. This explanation accords extremely ill with the report Best made to Ribbentrop on September 23rd, 1943, according to which he had told Ministerial-Director Svennigsen of the Danish Foreign Office that the fact that Jewish notables had been arrested ' had nothing to do with the Jewish question.'[68]

The truth would seem to be that Best, in company with von Hannecken and even the Security Police chiefs in Denmark, was seized at the last moment with a fear of the world publicity which the action ordered by Himmler must entail. On September 18th Rolf Guenther arrived in Copenhagen from Berlin with a special commando of members of Eichmann's office. The station commander of the Security Police in Copenhagen, Colonel Rudolf Mildner, at once perceived what matters would be charged to his responsibility and flew to Berlin to get Kaltenbrunner to withdraw the commando, but without success.[68a] Best, in the meantime, continued to cover himself either way.* Thus

*The Danish Government Commission of Inquiry after the war accepted the statement of Georg Duckwitz, Best's shipping adviser, that on September 29th, two days before the round-up, he had warned the ex-Premier Scavenius and Henriques, the President of the Jewish Community. But the commission observed that Duckwitz had not at the time claimed to be acting with Best's authority. At Nuremberg, however, Karl Hoffmann, who had been station commander of the Gestapo in Copenhagen, deposed that Best had made the arrest of Jews almost impossible by

on the night of the round-up he promised Svennigsen to forward the King's petition that the Jews should be interned in Denmark,[70] but Best had already tried to interest Ribbentrop in a far less honourable proposal, proceeding from Helmer Rostig, a former League of Nations Commissioner in Danzig, now head of the Danish Red Cross. This was that the Jews should be interned in place of the Danish soldiers 'to show that Germany was at war not with the Danes but with the Jews,' and that fifty to a hundred Jews should thereafter be deported for each Danish act of sabotage.[71] Furthermore, on September 28th Best assured Ribbentrop that the deportations would start as soon as the steamer *Wartheland* berthed in Copenhagen, and he complained that through the non-cooperation of von Hannecken the Security Police were unable to proceed with the round-up in Jutland and Fuenen.[72]

Von Hannecken had in fact been engaged in an intrigue to shift the responsibility on to Best's shoulders. He had asked Keitel on the 23rd to suspend the round-up during the period that the Wehrmacht was responsible for maintaining order if indeed it was not possible to cancel altogether such unpopular measures which would mean 'the loss of Danish meat and fats.' Keitel replied that Gottlob Berger, Himmler's chief of personnel, would be in charge of the action. Von Hannecken thereupon refused to lend the Security Police the use of his *Feldgendarmerie* and Secret Field Police—a direct challenge to Keitel and the High Command.[73]

On September 29th Ribbentrop telegraphed Best that he had read his complaint to Hitler in the presence of Keitel, who denied that he had banned the use of Wehrmacht police and swore that he would demand an explanation from Hannecken. But the latter told the Danish Commission in 1945 that, even after the rocket he got from Keitel, he only provided fifty men of a guard battalion to cordon the embarkation on board the *Wartheland*.[74]

At Nuremberg Colonel-General Alfred Jodl, chief of the

forbidding the police to break in the doors of the flats. This was supported at Best's trial in Copenhagen by a telegram from Steengracht, the Foreign Office successor to Weizsaecker, informing Best on October 4th that the RSHA had complained of his action, which had restricted the arrests only to those Jews who chose to answer the knock on their doors.[69]

operations section of the High Command, insisted that these fifty men must have been policemen. He had telephoned von Hannecken to have nothing to do with the deportation order, which was Himmler's affair.[75] This got back to Best *via* Colonel von Engelmann of the *Abwehr*, the German ' MI 5.' Best then telegraphed Ribbentrop on the eve of the action that Keitel's order for co-operation had been revoked[76] and that ' Keitel had misinformed the Fuehrer.'

One is to suppose from all this that, apart from Himmler, who was dead, no German had carried out the Fuehrer's order in Denmark. In reality the misgivings of Germans in office had played less part in saving the Jews than had the geographical position of Denmark and—be it added—the ineradicable humanity of the Danish people. The figures are eloquent: 284 Jews were arrested on the night of October 1st, of whom 50 were released and only 202 embarked in the *Wartheland*.[77] They were mostly people who were too old to hide from the police. Casual arrests in the next few days brought the number to 477, but more than 6,000 full-Jews and 1,376 half-Jews were smuggled into Sweden in fishing-boats between September 26th and October 12th.[78]*

On the morning after the round-up Best suggested that the interned Danish soldiers should be released at once to show that the ' Danish peasant-boys' were not being treated like Jews. Von Hannecken at the same time demanded the abandonment of martial law. It suited Himmler to believe that Denmark was now ' Jew-free' and both requests were soon granted.[79] Best was less successful in trying to get some of the Danish Jews out of the clutches of Eichmann's office. He believed that it might appease Danish public opinion if a Jewess, aged 102, could be brought back from Theresienstadt together with a few other very

---

*About a fifth of the Jews had taken refuge in Jutland, where escape was rendered more difficult by the considerable distance from the Swedish coast. The escapes were arranged by a resistance group, which operated inland at Lyngby, near Aarhus, under the direction of Aage Bertelsen, *Rektor* of the cathedral school in Aarhus. Eventually these escapes were betrayed to a Gestapo agent. Bertelsen went into hiding, but on November 9th his wife was taken as a hostage but released ten days later. Both were able to escape to Sweden. (See Aage Bertelsen, ' *Oktober, 1943* ' (in Danish), Aarhus, 1952.)

old people. On this project von Thadden, the successor to Luther and Rademacher, reported back to his chief, Wagner, on October 25th that the RSHA thoroughly disapproved, 'because it would create an impression of weakness among the Jews if any were brought back to Copenhagen.'[80]

In the meantime the Foreign Office maintained unreal negotiations with the Swedish Government. Unofficially the Danish Jewish refugees were in Sweden, enjoying complete liberty. Officially they were still hiding in Denmark, and the Swedish Government offered to intern them if the Germans would hand them over. On October 4th the Swedish Minister in Berlin begged that Sweden might at least be allowed to take the children, a request that Steengracht formally refused, upbraiding the Minister with the following words[81]:

'In very severe words I criticised to-day's Swedish morning press and told him that I was unable to imagine what further reactions might be possible in Sweden after the newspapers had voiced such incredible language. If the occasion arose, this attitude would force us to answer in a manner not to be misunderstood. It was not appreciated here why Sweden was unequivocably taking the side of Bolshevism, while our blood and the blood of our allies was being expended to keep the Communist danger from Europe and thus also from the Nordic countries.'*

It had been decided early in September that the Danish Jews should go not to Auschwitz but to Theresienstadt. About 360 were sent *via* the German port of Swinemuende and of these twenty died on the voyage and fifty in the camp. The macabre farce of the visit of the Danish Red Cross to Theresienstadt in June, 1944, has been told in Chapter Seven.

---

*On October 1st, three days before this interview with Steengracht, the Swedish Minister had conferred with *Geheimrat* Werner von Grundherr, head of the Scandinavian section of the German Foreign Office. Grundherr told Steengracht that he had given evasive answers on the Swedish internment proposal. The trial of Franz Rademacher in February, 1952, revealed that Grundherr, who had played this part, so characteristic of Ribbentrop's diplomats, was now Ambassador for the Bonn Republic in Athens. He retired under the normal superannuation rules in the following May. (Case XI, NO 4092, and *The Times*, July 15th, 1952.)

Werner Best was sentenced to death by a Copenhagen court in August, 1946, soon after his appearance as a witness at Nuremberg. His appeal was not heard by the High Court till July 20th, 1949, when, in the light of new evidence, his sentence was reduced to five years' imprisonment. He was released on August 29th, 1951.[82]

The case of Norway unfortunately presents none of the diplomatic complications which occurred when the Final Solution was applied to Denmark. Like Holland, Norway was ruled by a German *Reichskommissar* and the Norwegian Cabinet was a subservient affair, made up of picked National Socialist fanatics. The truly remarkable thing is that, after all the usual time-table had been observed, registration, economic exclusion, and finally mass arrest, two-thirds of the small Norwegian Jewish community escaped the net.

Southern Norway was fully occupied by the beginning of May, 1940, but the programme of anti-Jewish measures proceeded slowly. The stamping of Jewish identity cards took place in January, 1942, but was not followed by any mass arrests of the 1,700 Jews, the great bulk of them refugees from the Reich living in Oslo. A reception camp for Jews was established at Berg, near Tonsberg, in the following October, and on November 17th a general registration of Jews was ordered. The round-up in the principal towns took place on the 25th, but only 725 were discovered by the police, assisted by the *Hirden*, Quisling's National Socialist militia. According to Dr. Korherr's report to Himmler, only 691 Jews, all of them stateless, were deported ; 532 Jews sailed from Bergen to a German port on the 26th in the Norddeutscher Lloyd steamer *Donau* and their final destination was Auschwitz. A second deportation of 158 Jews occurred in March, 1943. Of the Norwegian Jews in Auschwitz, only thirteen survived the war.[83]

Of the remaining Jews, fully 900 managed to cross the Swedish border. The others stayed in Norway, either privileged or in hiding. Officially, however, there remained only 64 in October, 1944, all of them married to Aryans and interned in camps.[84] The behaviour of the Swedish Government deserves special praise. After the first sailing of the *Donau*, Dr. Richert, the Minister in Berlin, proposed that his country should receive all the remaining Jews. True to his usual rôle, Weizsaecker refused even to discuss the matter and informed Ribbentrop that he had told Dr. Richert that the project would not stand a chance.[85] There was, nevertheless, a liberal dispensation of naturalisation papers by the Swedish Consulate, of which Terboven, the *Reichskommissar,* complained in March, 1943.[86]

4. Italy

The outstanding rôle of the Italians as the saviours of Jewry in Southern France has been discussed in the previous chapter, and in the sections dealing with Greece and Croatia we shall again see Italian soldiers and officials exercising their subtle wits on behalf of decency and humanity. Unfortunately, these escapades ended in September, 1943, when Italy itself came mostly under the yoke of the Gestapo. Mussolini's officials and perhaps Mussolini, too, still tried to substitute half-measures for deportation to the gas chambers, but after his captivity on the Gran Sasso Mussolini was a deflated balloon and the Verona Government had nothing to bargain with. Furthermore, the Gestapo was aided by the Jewish registration lists, created in the days when Mussolini made discriminatory decrees. It was also unfortunate that many of the native and refugee Jews who made their way south after the Allied landings in Calabria should have waited in Rome. When the Germans occupied the city on September 10th, an event which was in most quarters unexpected, about 8,000 Jews fell into their hands, a sixth of the Jewish population of Italy.

By the end of the month it was known to the German Embassies in Rome and the Vatican City that Himmler intended to send these 8,000 Jews to Auschwitz. On the 30th Bishop Hudal, rector of the German church in Rome, warned General Stahel, the Town Commandant, that the Pope might take a position against the deportations. Stahel decided not to carry out Himmler's orders without the permission of the Foreign Office, but, though the German Embassy itself recommended internment in Italy rather than deportation, Ribbentrop would not intervene[87] and the first round-up took place on October 18th.

The Baron Ernst von Weizsaecker was now Ambassador to

the Holy See. Much was made at Weizsaecker's trial of the warnings which he gave the Vatican and the Jewish community of the impending action, but the only thing which is certain is that he forwarded a copy of Bishop Hudal's protest to Lieut.-Colonel Herbert Kappler, the Security Police Commander—but this was on October 22nd, after the round-up.[88] According to Gerhard Gumpert, Weizsaecker's Legation secretary, Kappler was persuaded that the warning came from the Pope and became too frightened to continue the actions.[89]

If this story is true, it was a triumph of pure bluff, for the round-up of October 18th had taken place without the least intervention by the Vatican. On October 28th Weizsaecker wrote to Ritter at the Foreign Office:

> ' Although pressed on all sides, the Pope did not allow himself to be drawn into any demonstration of reproof at the deportation of the Jews of Rome. The only sign of disapproval was a veiled allusion in *Osservatore Romano* on October 25th-26th, in which only a restricted number of people could recognise a reference to the Jewish question.'[90]

Weizsaecker believed that the Pope had acted wisely. An open protest would have stimulated the SS.[91] M. Poliakov suggests that this negative attitude was typical of Pius XII, who never renounced the 1933 concordat with Hitler and who denounced the National-Socialist system only after the surrender of Germany.[92] In the view of the present author, this failure to notice that Jews were being herded to their death from the very shadow of St. Peter's proceeded not from subtle benevolence, nor from pro-German sympathies, but from plain fear. On September 10th Rudolf Rahn, the Ambassador to the Quirinal, had to fly to Berlin to stop Hitler occupying the Vatican City.[93] For many months Hitler was free to do this and thereby destroy the immense strength of the Pope's diplomatic immunity.

Most of the Jews in Rome were warned in time and went into hiding, particularly in monasteries and convents. Less than a thousand were arrested on October 18th, of whom 615 arrived in Auschwitz on October 22nd. If we may believe Dr. Wollken, 468 were gassed.[94] Thereafter and until June 4th, 1944, when the Allies entered the city, the Jews of Rome led haunted lives, always subject to round-up and arrest. According to M. Max Vitale, 1,127 in all went from Rome to Auschwitz and only 15 returned after the war, to which very small total must be added the 57 Jews who were murdered on March 24th, 1944, in Rome itself in the affair of the Ardeatina Tunnel. This, the subject of several very controversial war trials, may be described briefly.

On March 23rd a bomb was thrown at a company of German Security Police marching through the Via Rosella. On learning that 32 of them had died, Hitler ordered the death of ten Italians for each German. The order was conveyed through Field-Marshal Kesselring, General von Mackensen of the 14th Army, and General Maelzer, Town Commandant of Rome. Finally, it was passed to the executioner, the same Lieut.-Colonel Kappler of the SS who had conducted the great round-up of October, 1943. The 335 victims were shot under Kappler's eyes in the Ardeatina Tunnel. They included people whom the Italian fascist police had selected quite at random. The 57 Jews seem to have been thrown in by Kappler as a matter of course.[95]*

On September 10th, 1943, when the Germans entered Rome, German army units already held most of the towns of Northern Italy. They had been pouring across the passes since July, providing the Jewish population with a warning of their danger. Some moved southwards towards the Allies, while others made for the Swiss frontier—movements which did not escape the notice of the Gestapo. As soon as the armistice was announced, a police commando of the SS left Novara for Lake Maggiore, making numerous arrests of Jews in Licino, Stresa, Baveno, and Pallanza. These Jews disappeared completely, but a number of bodies are said to have been recovered by fishermen from the lake.[96] Incidents of this sort were common but, after a few weeks, casual murder was succeeded by methodical destruction. Early in October Martin Sandberger, a former *Einsatzgruppe* commander in Russia, took over the Gestapo in Mussolini's capital, Verona, while that indispensable figure, Theodor Dannecker, became Jewish Commissary for Italy.

*The prison sentences passed by the British military courts on the three generals continue to-day to attract the severest criticism, but little notice has been taken of the fate of Kappler, by whom the generals maintained they were tricked. He was sentenced to life-imprisonment by a Rome court in 1947. His appeal was not rejected till November, 1952.

The task which confronted these experts was complicated by the extremely dispersed nature of the Jewish population in Italy, but it was also simplified by the availability of a number of empty prisoner-of-war camps, north of the Appenines. The Wehrmacht had succeeded in removing the British prisoners, who were held by the Italians, at a time when Badoglio's dealings with the Allies were still in doubt. Under the Fascist Republic the SD filled these camps with the Italian opposition, the Jugoslav partisans and any Jews they could lay hands on, all being destined for deportation to Germany.[97]

About a fifth of the Jews living in Italy, partly refugees from abroad and partly the remains of the native community who had not gone underground or emigrated, were rounded up during the twenty months of the Fascist Republic. The number of names of Jewish deportees, received by the Search Committee for Deported Jews, is 10,271,[98] of whom some 2,824 were sent to Auschwitz in 1944 from a single collecting centre, the camp at Fossoli di Carpi near Modena. Since this was classed as a mere transit camp, families were not broken up nor the sexes segregated. Although it was handed over to the SD after the Badoglio armistice, the administration stayed in Italian hands and was relatively mild. According to Primo Levi,[98a] it was even possible to get drunk. The Jews were cleared for Auschwitz whenever the camp, which contained other categories of internees, became too full. About 600 Jews, some of them from Tripoli, left on February 22nd, 1944, and of these only 126 men and women passed the selection at Birkenau. On July 1st, however, Dr. Wolken recorded that 180 men from the Fossoli transport were admitted to quarantine and this, according to the Italian Search Committee for Deported Jews, was a mixed transport of only 517 persons. The selection rate was therefore improving.[99]

After one more train in August, 1944, Fossoli di Carpi was given up as a collecting centre. The Allies were approaching the Gothic Line and the province of Modena had become a combat area. The chief transit camp was now Gries, near Bolzano, 180 miles nearer to Vienna and Auschwitz. From Gries a final small transport reached Birkenau on October 28th, shortly before the closing of the gas chambers. Most of the Gries transports, however, went to Mauthausen, where the rate of human destruction was in no way inferior to Auschwitz. Thus M. Max Vitale declares[100] that only 605 Jewish deportees returned to Italy and this includes 140 Jews who were sent back to Gries camp on February 25th, 1945, when the Mauthausen train was blocked by Allied bombing at the Brenner Pass. It also includes 146 survivors of the transport of Jews from the island of Rhodes which reached Auschwitz on September 17th, 1944 (*see pages 378-9*).

The small size of the deportation trains from Italy is note-worthy. None of the Fossoli and Bolzano transports exceeded 600 people. These trains had to pass through the same bottle-neck, in the Brenner Pass, as the great bulk of Kesselring's reinforcements and supplies, and it is indeed extraordinary that Eichmann's office could obtain any rolling-stock at all. The journey to Auschwitz took four or five days, but it was so hazardous that Primo Levi's travel-mates were told to take a fortnight's provisions.

About 5,000 Jews were shipped to Auschwitz and Germany from other Italian towns and camps. A collective transport from Rome, Trieste and Fiume reached Auschwitz in December, 1943, and another very small transport from Trieste on April 4th, 1944. The case of Trieste was peculiar, since as a former Austrian city, it was incorporated in the Reich on September 23rd, 1943, as the capital of a new *Gau*, Trieste-Kuestenland. Friedrich Rainer became *Gauleiter* and his friend of Austrian *Anschluss* days, Odilo Globocnik, whom Himmler had just dismissed from Poland, returned to his home town as Higher SS and Police Leader (*see pages 295-6*).

Before the war there were more than 5,000 Jews in Trieste, but less than half remained behind when the Germans took over. There was a round-up on October 9th and a second on January 19th, when Dr. Morpurgo, secretary of the Community Council, was taken and the old-age home, 'Pia Casa Gentilomo,' liqui-dated. The 70 inmates were kept for seven days in the rice warehouse at Santa Sabba before being shipped to Auschwitz. On the 25th Globocnik dissolved the Community Council and closed the synagogue, and thereafter the Trieste Jews led an underground life, threatened constantly with removal to the Coroneo prison or the rice warehouse. Another small transport left for Auschwitz early in April, while at the end of the month

Jews enjoying Swiss consular protection were deported following the explosion of a bomb in a German officers' mess in the Via Gegha. During the whole period of German occupation some 600 Trieste Jews were deported and only 400 or 500, living in great destitution, were discovered after the entry of the 8th Army on May 7th, 1945. It was a Palestinian sergeant serving in this force who broke open the Great Synagogue on that day.[101]

Rainer and Globocnik had fled. Early in June, 1945, they were denounced to a British patrol in the mountains south of Klagenfurt. Globocnik, with a million and a half murders to his credit, took cyanide. Rainer surrendered and a year later gave evidence at Nuremberg for his former colleague, Seyss-Inquardt, who was condemned to death. He was then extradited to Jugoslavia, where he was sentenced to death by a Ljubjana (Laibach) court on July 20th, 1947.[102]

CHAPTER 14

Jugoslavia, Greece, Bulgaria

1. Jugoslavia : The Belgrade Ghetto

IN no country of Axis-occupied Europe is the fate of Jewry more difficult to trace than in Jugoslavia. In no country are the final figures of losses and survivals more difficult to assess. Pre-war Jugoslavia contained about 70,000 Jews living in widely separated groups which had grown up under the extremely heterogeneous administrations from which in 1918 the new nation had been created. Twenty-two years of political union had failed to make Jugoslav Jewry a single community and the partition of the country in April, 1941, drove the groups still further apart, since under Axis occupation Jugoslavia became a collection of governments of every type, but all of them a prey to anarchy and civil war. Such conditions hampered the efforts of Heydrich and Himmler to impose the Final Solution and enabled many Jews to escape. Although only 10,460 officially registered Jews appeared in the Jugoslav census of 1946, there is good reason to think that many thousands more have survived either in Italy and Albania or by assimilating themselves on the spot with the Gentile population.[1]

After the Blitz campaign of April 6th-17th, 1941, the grouping of Jugoslav Jewry was roughly as follows : About 20,000 Jews came under Hungarian rule in Bachka, the region east of the Great Danube bend. The German military occupation area, Old Serbia, contained 12,000 Jews, including the 8,500 Jews of Belgrade. The newly created independent State of Croatia contained 21,000 Jews, including the 12,315 Jews of Zagreb. Twelve thousand Jews, living in Bosnia-Herzegovina, were disputed between Croatia and Serbia, including the 8,000 Jews of Serajevo, while Bulgaria acquired 7,000 or 8,000 Jews in the former Serb towns of Skoplie, Pirot, and Bitolj. There remained Montenegro, which was run by the Italians as a regency for a future kingdom, and Slovenia, which was partitioned as a permanent annexation between Germany and Italy. These, however, contained few Jews.

The Hungarians in the Bachka were the first to practise deportation. The Government of Laszlo Bardossy had dispatched State Secretary Alajos Kovacz to Rosenberg's great anti-semitic conference at the Frankfurt *Buergersaal* in March, 1941, and there it was learnt that the German Government was ready to assist Jewish deportation on a European scale.[2] Within a month the Hungarians had acquired a new Jewish minority population and by the beginning of August it was decided to hand them over to the Germans. About 16,000 Jews, mainly from Bachka, but also Jews of foreign nationality from the Hungarian Banat province, were merely put across the Danube.[3] The Germans interned them in the ghetto which they had established for the Jews of Belgrade, and which acquired a population in the region of 25,000. Confined, according to German practice, in the miserable huts on the edge of the town which were used by visiting gipsies, this helpless mass of people threatened to die of cold and hunger in the approaching winter. Their plight was therefore the subject of a long dispatch to Ribbentrop from Felix Benzler, the newly created Minister Plenipotentiary to the equally new Serb puppet Government of General Milan Nedic.*

The gravest problem, according to Benzler, was the fact that 8,000 of the Jews in the Belgrade Ghetto were males of fighting age, ' potential saboteurs ' who could not be accommodated in the existing internment camps of Serbia. He believed that in Slovakia Father Tiso's Government had shipped Jews down the Danube in barges to an island in the Rumanian delta. But the report was incorrect and Luther (apparently without consulting Ribbentrop) replied to Benzler's dispatch of September 8th that deportation to Rumania was out of the question and that camps must be found in Serbia for the Jews of Belgrade.[4] To which four days later Benzler retorted that Sabac camp was already in the hands of partisans and that, unless the Jews could be sent

---

*Benzler was one of the former SA leaders, somewhat under a cloud since June, 1934, whom Ribbentrop appointed to diplomatic posts in the Balkans on the recommendation of Martin Luther. In January, 1941, Benzler had been in charge of the resettlement commission for racial Germans in Latvia and Esthonia, and in the following April he was made liaison officer with the High Command in Belgrade.

to Russia or Poland, he would not be able to carry out Ribbentrop's instructions to clear the able-bodied Jews out of the ghetto.

The importance of this reference to Poland and Russia has already been discussed in Chapter Four. In the margin of Benzler's teletype message, Franz Rademacher (*see page 85*) wrote a note that Eichmann had ruled that 'not even German Jews could be sent to the General Government or Russia at present. . . . *Eichmann proposes shooting.*' Rademacher did not write this as a mere Foreign Office postman. To Luther, his chief, he wrote that, if the Jews were dangerous in Serbia, they would be still more so in Russia, while the General Government was already overcrowded with them. 'I cannot imagine that the Jews will go on conspiring once a large number have been shot as hostages.'

But Benzler in his next letter reminded Luther that Ribbentrop had promised him in an interview at Fuschl at the end of August that all the Jews, Freemasons, and 'pro-British Serbs' would be deported from Belgrade, either to the Danube Delta, the General Government, or the German concentration camps. The military governor, General Franz Boehme, now wished to associate himself with Benzler in reminding Ribbentrop of this promise. Luther replied on October 2nd—and it is interesting to perceive Weizsaecker's initials in the margin—that all Boehme had to do was to 'liquidate the Jews himself.' Luther then added the following words:

> 'In other territories other military commanders have taken care of considerably larger numbers of Jews without even mentioning it. I think we cannot ask the Rumanian head of the State, who has enough trouble anyway with getting rid of his own Jews, to take over another 8,000 Jews from foreign countries. The Jews would certainly leave their island within a few days and appear in Rumania. The matter should be discussed with Heydrich, who is due to return from Prague in a few days.'

In the meantime Ribbentrop instructed Luther personally to request Heydrich to make the deportation arrangements, but Heydrich, as might be expected, came down on the side of Luther and Rademacher. According to Ulrich von Hassell's gossip in the Foreign Office, Hans Haeften (*see Chapter 4, page 73*), Heydrich's action was to 'send a specialist to Belgrade to clean out these poor people.'[5]

This *specialist* was not one of Eichmann's bloodhounds from the Kurfuerstenstrasse, but none other than that sleek personage Franz Rademacher, the former legation secretary in Montevideo. Rademacher reached Belgrade on October 18th and after his return on the 25th he informed Luther that the adult male Jews in Belgrade had never numbered more than 4,000. General Boehme had, moreover, shot half of them already as hostages for attacks on German soldiers.[6] Of the survivors, 500 were exempted workers engaged in the construction of the new Semlin Ghetto camp. The remaining 1,500 would be executed before the end of the week, though Benzler and the military administrator, Dr. Harald Turner, still favoured deportation. About 20,000 Jewish elderly people, women and children could be kept in Belgrade during the winter, together with 1,300 gipsies. They could thereafter be removed to the neighbouring Mitrovica island and thence embarked for 'camps in the East.'

On December 8th Benzler came to Berlin, complaining that Mitrovica island was under water and the situation in the Belgrade Ghetto desperate. Rademacher refused to see him and, with the approval of Luther, sent him word that the Belgrade Jews could not be moved even in the spring. To Rademacher Luther admitted that Ribbentrop had indeed asked Heydrich to deport the Belgrade Jews to Eastern Poland, but 'the two directives were not contradictory' and the matter was therefore closed and there was no need to send any more written instructions to Benzler.

Subsequent events abundantly confirmed the existence of 'two directives.' At the Gross-Wannsee conference on January 20th Heydrich agreed that the Jews, who had been expelled to Belgrade by the Hungarians, should be moved to Eastern Poland.[7] The Jugoslav State Commission, which sat after the war, concluded that these deportations actually took place in the spring and one account speaks of a shipment of women and children from Semlin camp as late as July, 1942,[8] but one may search in vain for any record of Serbian Jews either in Auschwitz, Majdanek, or the ghettoes and transit camps of Lublin province, which were filled at this time with Reich and Slovak Jewish deportees (*see page 155*). In fact the Serbian Jews never got to Poland at all. In the laconic words of the International Red Cross's report of its wartime activities[8a]

> ' Three camps were known to be situated in Serbia. The detainees who had been quartered there temporarily were afterwards taken to an unknown destination and nothing further was heard of them.'

It was not till October, 1952, that it was made clear to the world why Heydrich's two directives had not been contradictory. The gigantic camouflage, which they concealed, was revealed ten years after Serbia had been declared ' Jew-free,' but it is still not easy to fill in the details. On December 8th, 1941, Benzler had told Rademacher that, since Mitrovica island was still under water, he had had to remove the remaining Jews from the infected gipsy quarter to Semlin. This was the ' Worlds Fair ' site which had been under conversion as a relief-ghetto since September, but which was quite inadequate for some 8,000 women and children who survived after a distribution to other Serbian camps. As to the male Jews of Serbia, they were fast dwindling away in the competent hands of Colonel Fuchs and his *Einsatzgruppe*. Weizsaecker had prudently informed Benzler on November 22nd that he was to concern himself solely with the deportation question. The ' internal measures against the Jews ' did not come within his brief.

At the beginning of February, within a few days of Heydrich's Gross-Wannsee conference, Colonel Fuchs was replaced as ' *Kds*. Belgrade ' by Lt.-Colonel Emanuel Schaefer. This man was one of Heydrich's most trusted agents. As an officer of the State Police in Oppeln, he had staged the faked Polish attack on a radio station which had been part of the *casus belli* against Poland. Schaefer was rewarded by successive promotion to chief of the Gestapo in Cologne and Security Police commander in Serbia. Like most Gestapo officials, brought belatedly to trial, Schaefer in October, 1952 looked like a bank manager and in keeping with his appearance he pleaded that extermination in Semlin camp had begun before his arrival, that the gassing vans were not under his authority and that he could not forbid their employment. And to support the plea the professional witness von dem Bach-Zalewski—a free man now—described Schaefer as a typical Prussian bureaucrat, glued to his desk.[8b] Yet it was Schaefer himself who had notified the Main Security Office on June 10th, 1942, that two gassing vans were on their way back to Berlin for repairs,[9] a document which, seven years after its production at Nuremberg, brought Schaefer into the dock before the Cologne *Schwurgericht*.

Schaefer found 6,280 Jews in Semlin camp in February, 1942. In May he informed the Security Head Office a little prematurely that Serbia was 'Jew-free.' The Jews in Semlin—they were all women or children—had been taken off quietly from day to day in the gassing vans. After a time the true nature of these vehicles had been discovered in the camp and some of the women were able to bribe the guards to aid their escape[9a] but more than six thousand were gassed from this camp alone. The Foreign Office were consulted till the very last and at Nuremberg Kurt Heinberg, head of the Balkans section 'Political VII,' recollected a mass of dispatches relating to gassing at Belgrade.[10]

At the end of July, 1942, Belgrade was truly 'Jew-free' and in the following October the Belgrade Jewish Bureau of the Gestapo was closed down 'because there were no longer any Jews living in its operational area.'[11] According to the *Berliner Boersenzeitung*, Old Serbia and the Hungarian Banat were the first areas in Europe to merit the description *judenrein*.

One remarkable aspect of the tragedy of the Belgrade Ghetto is the very diverse fate of its authors. Martin Luther died mysteriously in the 'political bunker' in Sachsenhausen camp,[12] where he was last seen by Captain Payne-Best in 1944. General Franz Boehme, who ordered the first massacre of Serb Jews, committed suicide in Nuremberg prison in June, 1947, on the eve of 'the hostages' trial.' Colonel Fuchs, the Security Police commander who carried out the second massacre as planned during Rademacher's visit, and Dr. Harald Turner were both executed in Belgrade on March 7th, 1947.[13]

Felix Benzler testified at Schaefer's trial as a free man who had never been charged with the massacres of Belgrade.[14] Schaefer himself, though now a Brigadier-General in the SS, hid his identity after the war and escaped extradition to Serbia.

He was not discovered till April, 1951, when the Bielefeld denazification court sentenced him to twenty-one months labour camp as a former member of the Gestapo. The real charges were not produced in court for another eighteen months. The case is still *sub judice*.

Rademacher's post-war adventures have already been noticed (*see page 76*). At his incredibly delayed trial at Nuremberg in February-March, 1952, he pleaded that his visit to Belgrade had no influence on the shooting of 1,500 Jews, which had already been ordered by Boehme.* In awarding a punishment which amounted to almost immediate release, the court gave Rademacher the benefit of the doubt, sentencing him to no more than three years and five months imprisonment.[15] Rademacher appealed and while awaiting a second trial jumped his bail—as his codefendant Klingenfuess had done—and fled to the Argentine Republic.

2. Jugoslavia (Croatia)

The Germans declared the independence of Croatia as early as April 10th, 1941, but the Italians got in before them, having been in negotiation with Ante Pavelic, leader of the Croat nationalist *Ustashe* party before 1939. Although the Germans

---

*The shooting of the 1,500 Jews was ordered by General Boehme after a conference with Turner and Fuchs on October 19th. Rademacher had declared to the American interrogation commission that he left Belgrade on the 18th, but that he had altered his expenses account in order to claim payment for a longer stay. But it was shown at Rademacher's trial that he had cashed considerable sums at the German Embassy in Belgrade as late as the 21st. Rademacher then admitted that he had lied to the Americans to save himself from extradition to Jugoslavia as a party to the order of the 19th. Nevertheless, in claiming his expenses, Rademacher had filled in the question 'purpose of journey' with the words 'liquidation of the Jews,' but this, he said, was to draw Weizsaecker's attention to what was going on in Belgrade. Seeing that the court were far from believing that Rademacher's visit had no influence on Boehme, Turner, and Fuchs, the sentence of three years' imprisonment on this count seems ridiculous, but the court were probably influenced by the fact that at least four witnesses, who had like Rademacher acted as messenger-boys for Eichmann's massacre arrangements, were comfortably installed in the Foreign Office of the Bonn Republic. See particularly *Das Freie Wort*, March 8th, 1952.

kept troops in the country, Pavelic, as head of the State, managed to play the Italians against them by accepting a nephew of the King of Italy, Aimone Duke of Spoleto, as King of Croatia, and by encouraging Italian desires for the possession of the Dalmatian coastline.[16]

Pavelic was a ruthless man of great driving force whom in reality neither Germans nor Italians could manage. His personal anti-semitism was little more than a bait for the Germans, since he was himself married to a daughter of the Jew Lorencevic,[17] while 'Marshal' Kwaternik, the organiser of *Ustashe* military terrorism, was in the same position, having married the daughter of the former nationalist leader of the days of the Hapsburg Empire, the Jew Josip Frank. Indeed, according to Kaltenbrunner's intelligence officer, Willi Hoettl, whose business it was to ferret out such things, the whole of the *Ustashe* autocracy was mixed with Jewish blood. Nevertheless, Pavelic decreed the confiscation of all Jewish property in Zagreb on April 14th within four days of forming a Government.[18] It was simply that the trigger-happy *Ustashe* needed plunder and the wealth of the orthodox Serb minority was not enough to satisfy them.

Thus the situation reached its peak of frenzy after the Berlin award of July 12th, 1941. This followed up the Vienna award of April 29th, which had fixed the German and Italian zones of occupation, by trying to draw a frontier between the Serbs and Croats in Bosnia. The *Ustashe* blackguards of Slavko Kwaternik murdered and tortured the Serbs, while the Bosniak Moslems fell upon the Jews. Even the representative of the Wehrmacht at Pavelic's court, the Austrian general and National Socialist leader, Edmund Glaise-Horstenau, was moved to protest.[19] Of the ancient Sephardic Jewish community of Serajevo in Bosnia, which numbered nearly 8,000 before the war, only 1,140 survived in January, 1946. What happened in July and August, 1941, is not clear, but about 2,000 Serajevo Jews escaped to Cattaro and to Albania. A certain number were interned in the south of Italy in a refugee camp at Ferramonte-Tarsia, which was liberated by the Allies in September, 1943, while a few fled to Trieste.[20] The massacres were not completed in 1941, for several hundred Serajevo Jews are believed to have been taken to Auschwitz during the second Croat Jewish deportation in May, 1943.

In October, 1941, when the first deportations from Germany to 'the East' were being organised, Pavelic had largely achieved the enslavement and expropriation of Croat Jewry, except in the areas that had remained under Italian military government. About a third of the 21,000 recognised Croat Jews were interned in labour camps at Jasenovac, Laborgrad, and at Pag island north of Zara,[21] about the same number had sought refuge with the Italians, either in the virtually incorporated towns Ljubljana and Susak, or at Spalato, Ragusa and Mostar in 'Military Zone II,' while some 4,000 Jews were still at large in Zagreb.[22]

Rademacher, in pressing for an extension of the deportations to include Croatia, commented favourably on these evidences of the willingness of the Croat Government to take 'severe measures' against the Jews,[23] but in fact Pavelic was not ready. It was not until August and September, 1942, that he permitted Franz Abromeit, an Austro-Croat member of Eichmann's office, to make a clearance of the three labour camps towards Poland.*

To these deportations, which did not affect the area of Italian military government, there was no Italian objection. The Pavelic Government co-operated with Abromeit and his section of the Eichmann commando through the Minister for the Interior, Andrija Artukovic. This man was discovered in May, 1951, running a bookshop at Surfside, Los Angeles, having entered the U.S.A. illegally under the name of Anic. Such escapes need surprise no one when it is recalled that Ante Pavelic himself and Dido Kwaternik, the son of the 'Marshal,' who had been Minister for Security, are both living in the Argentine Republic.[25]

When it came to demanding the deportation of Jews in the Italian Military Zone II, the Germans encountered diplomatic opposition from the Italians and later, in the game of playing Italians against Germans, from Pavelic too. This is one of those surprising stories which occasionally transform the vast sheaves of documents in the great Wilhelmstrasse trial of 1948-49 into vivid and living history.

*According to the Nuremberg witness, Dieter Wisliceny, Abromeit was not able to collect more than two transports for Auschwitz, totalling 3,000 Jews, but Dr. Korherr, Himmler's statistician and probably more trust-worthy, put the number of deportees from Croatia in the year 1942 as high as 4,927.[24] Presumably the extra two thousand went with the Slovak Jews to Lublin province.

The butterfly fuses of diplomatic sensibility in Croatia had been entrusted by Ribbentrop in April, 1941, to Siegfried Kasche, a ham-fisted party fanatic with bushy eyebrows.[26] Kasche, like his fellow ministers in the Balkans, Killinger, Jagow, Beckerle, and Ludin, had narrowly escaped death in the Roehm Putsch of June, 1934,[27]* and, like them, had been hauled out of obscurity by the too ambitious Martin Luther. The prowess of these ' old party fighters' as policemen-diplomats fills no small part of the following pages.

Kasche's first report of heavy weather with the Italians dates from July 24th, 1942. General Roatta, commanding in Zone II, had declared that the honour of the Italian army would not tolerate the deportation of four of five thousand Jews seeking sanctuary in Dubrovnik (Ragusa) and Mostar. Roatta had even stopped the German Inspector-General of the Todt Organisation from commandeering Jewish apartments.[28] As a result of Kasche's complaint, Prince Otto von Bismarck called on Count Ciano at the Foreign Office on August 17th. The only result was that Kasche was informed coldly three days later by Casertano, his diplomatic colleague in Zagreb, that the matter was beyond the competence of the Italian Army and could only be settled in Rome.[29] However, when Kasche's proposals were forwarded by Casertano, Mussolini wrote the ominous words ' No objection.'[30]

At this crucial stage all progress was sidetracked by Count Ciano, Mussolini's son-in-law and the head of the Foreign Office. Count Ciano ordered General Roatta to conduct an elaborate registration of Jews. All Jews who had connections in the zone, which the Italians hoped to annexe, were to be exempted from the deportation order. This registration took so long that on September 24th Ribbentrop sent Kasche the outlines of a memorial which he was to compose for Hitler to submit personally to Mussolini, Ribbentrop's idea of a diplomatic approach being to propose to Mussolini that two German divisions and an SS battalion should assist the deportations by taking up stations in the Italian military zone.[31] But Hitler did

---

*As a *Gruppenfuehrer* of the SA, Kasche was seen by Hans Gisevius on the fateful June 30th in Goering's palace in the Leipzigerplatz, a prisoner waiting to be shot. For some reason he was reprieved and set free after a few weeks in a concentration camp. (Gisevius, *To the Bitter End*, page 159.)

not see Mussolini. He was visited by Pavelic next day and was apparently convinced of Pavelic's ability to make the arrests in spite of the Italians.

On October 14th Kasche reported that he had learnt from Kosak, the Finance Minister, that the Croat Government would not only make the arrests, but pay the Germans 30 marks for each Jew deported. But six days later Lorkovic, the Croat Foreign Minister, told Kasche a different story. His Government had approached Count Ciano with the proposal that Italy should receive the Jews, while the Croat State received the Jews' property, thereby 'sparing them the fate that awaited them in Poland.'[32] Kasche at once telegraphed Ribbentrop that 'our embassy' had been tricked and that the Vatican had been at work.

The Italian Foreign Office would not accept Pavelic's proposal. Italy, they said, was not Palestine. Prince Otto von Bismarck was therefore told that such Jews as were connected with 'the annexed territories' would be interned on the spot and the remainder handed over to Pavelic, whereupon the Croat Government complained that they would lose the assets of the Jews whom the Italians interned. To increase the befuddlement of the German Foreign Office Kasche learnt on November 10th that, in spite of their outward refusal of Pavelic's offer, the Italian Government had taken some Jews to Italy—to Porto Re in Istria.[33] Two days later Kasche found it necessary to get in touch with Eichmann in person. The Jews, whom the Croats had arrested for the Auschwitz deportations, had been carried off by the Italians to the Dalmatian island of Lopud.[34]

Neither Lopud nor Porto Re would do. Prince Bismarck's proposal to D'ajeta on December 10th was that all the interned Jews should be shipped to Trieste—presumably because Trieste had direct railway communication with Auschwitz and Poland. The Italian reply was that there was no shipping to take the Jews to Trieste. According to the somewhat roundabout sources quoted by M. Jacques Sabille, this was Mussolini's own inspiration.[35] But it is worth noticing what a pathetically small portion of the victims of the Final Solution were involved in all this high diplomacy. The Jews who were arrested in Military Zone II numbered 2,662 and of these 863 had been released as Italian subjects.[36]

For the next few months Kasche had to concentrate on getting Eichmann his quota of Jews not from the Italians, but from Pavelic. A Major Helm of the Gestapo was sent out to be Police Attaché at Zagreb and by March 4th Kasche was able to report to Rademacher that in ten days' time the deportation of 2,000 Croat Jews would be practicable in small groups.[37] The deportations went on till May, in which month 400 Jews were deported from Zagreb.[38*] But, like the Slovaks and the Rumanians, the Croats now discovered that Jews were a negotiable commodity. In this very month the American Joint Distribution Committee succeeded in establishing regular remittances of food and foreign currency to the Zagreb community,[39] while in July Kaltenbrunner's office learnt that 800 Jewish women and children, whom Pavelic was to have deported, were still in Croatian camps.[40]

Pavelic was indeed a very changed man. On April 27th, when he visited Hitler at Klessheim, he had become known as 'the Mayor of Zagreb,' so restricted had his territory become through the activities of Tito's partisans.[41] Henceforward he kept an eye on the reactions of the Western Allies. In January, 1944, he accepted the Red Cross conventions regarding civilian internees and in July the Red Cross were allowed to inspect Jewish labour camps at Jasenovac, Stara-Gradisca, and Gredjani.[42] There were still Jews in Zagreb and other towns, and in April Kasche complained that 'German agencies' had brought in Jews from outside Croatia 'to conduct official and economic transactions' and that in many public positions no substitutes for Jews could be found.[43] Kaltenbrunner ordered an investigation of the position, but it was not till October, 1944, that the rest of the Zagreb Jewish community were sent to the internment camps. Even then they were not deported from Croatia and they received supplies from abroad till the end of the war, but in January, 1946, there were officially only 1,647 Jews living in Zagreb in place of 12,315 before the war.[44]

The fate of the Croat Jews who were protected by the Italians is, one regrets to say, obscure. In May, 1943, after months of

---

*Of all the racial groups in Auschwitz least of all is known of the Croat Jews. They are mentioned in 1943 in the narrative of Dr. Ella Lingens-Reiner and the list, recorded by the secret radio transmission of August 21st, 1944, includes 550 survivors. (*Dokumenty i Materialy*, I, page 120.)

sorting and registration, rather less than 2,000 were removed to the island of Arbe in the Gulf of Cattaro. On August 19th Augusto Rossi, Foreign Secretary under the Badoglio Government, telegraphed the Military Commander in Zone II that these Jews must be protected from the Croatian Government at all costs.[45] Three weeks later Military Zone II ceased to exist. The Germans had occupied Cattaro. The Jews on Arbe island dispersed where they could, and it is probable that many reached the areas protected by Tito's partisans.

3. Greece

In point of numbers the Jewish tragedy in Greece has the closest resemblance to that of Jugoslavia. The declining Jewish population of Greece in 1941 probably did not exceed the 67,200 of the 1931 census. In 1945 the officially registered survivors numbered rather more than 10,000.[46] This figure is, however, more likely to be final than in the case of Jugoslavia, because unhappily the total character of the destruction of the great Salonika community cannot be doubted.

If the Germans believed in March, 1943, that they were saving Greece from Jewish strangulation, they could have spared themselves the trouble, for this was a fast-dying community. Two-thirds of Greek Jewry lived in Salonika, the only Spanish Jewish settlement of Turkish times to prosper and expand since the creation of the Greek kingdom. Yet in the twentieth century the Salonika Jews declined. In 1900, when they numbered 80,000, they constituted nearly half the town's population. On April 9th, 1941, Salonika had probably 260,000 inhabitants, only 46,000 of them Jews.[47] Emigration had been forced by poverty and also by a certain degree of anti-semitism, which became stronger after the expulsion of the Turkish population in 1923-24. But Salonika was not a place where the Germans could count on the native population doing their work for them. This is shown by the fact that they hesitated to apply the Final Solution till a year after the first murderous Jewish deportation trains had left France and Slovakia.

Apart from the usual arrests of Jewish notables 'and the conversion of the Jewish Community Council into something resembling a German-appointed *Judenrat*, there were no specific anti-Jewish decrees till July, 1942. Yet in the winter of 1941 the Salonika Jews were scarcely better off than their brethren in the hungry ghettoes of Poland. The invasion had deprived Greece of her normal produce exchange and in November famine was already in sight. Although in March, 1942, the British Government sent wheat shipments—under safe conduct from the enemy—to Athens, 20,000 of the Salonika Jews starved, and there was an outbreak of spotted typhus.[48] This situation did not prevent the German administration office of the 'Salonika-Agais command' decreeing in the month of July heavy labour conscription for all Jewish males from eighteen to forty-five years old. But the Todt organisation had difficulty in finding three or four thousand men for railway construction among this debilitated mass of people. Consequently, in October exemptions were freely sold and finally Dr. Merten, counsellor to the Military Administration, stopped the conscription on payment of a community fine of 2,500,000 Drachmas.

The Germans began the Final Solution in Salonika, as they had begun it in Poland, by destroying the vestiges of Jewish history, the archives and liturgic scrolls, and finally the gravestones. These were removed for road-metal from the great Salonika cemetery on December 6th,[49] when Major Wulff of Eichmann's office was making a preliminary survey. Shortly afterwards Eichmann paid a brief visit, bringing his adjutant, Rolf Guenther. The deportations were to be carried out by Dieter Wisliceny, who arrived from Vienna with Anton Brunner on February 6th, 1943.[50]

The preliminary steps were now taken in quick succession, the order to wear the Jewish badge on that very day and the creation of a ghetto three weeks later—in fact, three ghettoes, one of them the 'Baron Hirsch' quarter, where Jews were brought from the Macedonian hinterland, being enclosed.[51] This place was a hutted camp near the railway station, which had been constructed in the early 'nineties for Jewish refugees from the Mogilev and Kishinev pogroms, to be inhabited subsequently by 2,000 of the poorest Salonika Greeks. While the changes were taking place at 'Baron Hirsch,' Wisliceny and his associates established themselves in two Jewish villas in the Hodos

Velissariou which they proceeded to get up like a Port Said brothel.[52] According to M. Molho, Wisliceny looked rosy, corpulent and self-indulged, a very different figure to the Wisliceny of the Bratislava trial of 1948 (*see footnote on page 386*). But even now the Jews of Salonika failed to realise what this presence boded, though on March 14th it was learnt that the 2,800 country Jews in 'Baron Hirsch' were to go to Cracow. A train of forty box-cars removed them all on the following day. Henceforward 'Baron Hirsch' was filled, emptied, and refilled, and by the end of the month 13,435 Jews had been shipped off in five trains.[53] By the middle of May, when the Todt labour conscripts were moved, the great bulk of Salonika Jewry had departed, 42,830 persons in sixteen trains.[54]

The 1,000-mile journey to Auschwitz or the 1,200-mile journey to Lublin or Treblinka took from seven to nine days.* Food was supplied to the deportees for ten days, chiefly bread, dried fruit, and olives. One very significant detail was mentioned by Wisliceny at Nuremberg. The food and the trucks, he declared, were provided by the Transport Command of the Wehrmacht.[55]

Since October, 1942, the chairman of the Jewish Council or *Judenaelteste* had been Rabbi Koretz, who, because the Germans had kept him some months in Vienna, had a taint of collaboration. Consequently, on March 17th, when he made a speech in the Monasteriotes Synagogue, extolling the new life in Poland, he was so ill-received as to require police protection. Yet, in spite of the distrust of Koretz, there was practically no resistance to deportation. It was believed that the emigrants would be better off than the labour conscripts, some of whom got married in order to be included in the deportation trains for the 'Cracow Ghetto.'[56] The Germans, moreover, used many subterfuges. Some witnesses who survived Auschwitz have claimed that they were shown grants of land in the Ukraine which were brought by Salonika Jews into the death camp. Furthermore, Mme Vaillant-Couturier has described the fictitious picture-postcards of a place called

---

*According to the report of the Commission of Inquiry held by the Siedlice Court in 1945 a transport from Salonika reached the death camp at Treblinka on March 26th, 1943. This must have been the second transport which left 'Baron Hirsch' on March 17th. (*German Crimes in Poland*, I, page 104.)

Waldsee, by which Salonika Jewesses were made to invite their relatives to join them.[57] Another subterfuge is mentioned by Dr. Albert Menasche. Dr. Merten assured Rabbi Koretz that the deportations were no more than a security measure to remove potential Communists from the military zone. They would not affect the middle classes. Thus 900 intellectuals and people of means were kept in Baron Hirsch camp after the departure of the Todt workers. They were then told a different story. As privileged Jews they would be sent to the 'Free Ghetto,' Theresienstadt. In fact the train, which carried 820 of them away on June 1st, went to Auschwitz.[58]

The Todt workers left in the middle of May. The neutral Red Cross representatives, who had been looking after them, attempted to supply milk to the trains, but were frustrated—and still more so the Red Cross representatives in Germany, who tried, as in the case of the Dutch Jews who had been sent to Mauthausen in 1941, to trace their addresses. This was an embarrassment which added to the growing volume of world knowledge and which Eichmann's office had perhaps not foreseen.[59]

The survivors of the deportations to Auschwitz, Treblinka. and Lublin can be numbered on one's fingers. The journey alone, lasting from seven to ten days and performed with 60 to 65 people packed, regardless of age, health, or sex, in each ill-ventilated box-car from which there was not one minute's escape, must have taken a heavy toll of life. Moreover, most of the Salonika Jews began the journey in low health. Hoess, the Auschwitz gaoler, told Wisliceny that they were *all* of such poor quality that they had to be exterminated,[60] by which apparently he did not mean that they were gassed at once. There were always selections for Birkenau camp, to which, for instance, more than half of the 'intellectuals' transport' of June 1st were admitted. And on arrival Dr. Menasche found Birkenau full of Salonika Jews, who were employed on the construction of a new section of the camp known as DII,[61] but the 4,000 Greek Jews who were sent to join the Dutch Jews in the labour camp on the site of the Warsaw Ghetto at the end of October, were picked from the much healthier transports organised by the Bulgarians in Thrace and Macedonia. Another group of Salonika deportees who were spared the gas chamber consisted of Jewesses who were reserved for the sterilisation experiments of Drs. Clauberg and Horst Schumann in Block 10 of Auschwitz main camp (*see page 176*).

But the Salonika Jews brought the spotted typhus to Auschwitz in the form of the worst epidemic that ever attacked the camp. Birkenau was quarantined during June and no transports arrived for three weeks.[62] Three months later Hoess decided that all the Salonika Jews must be liquidated, and those who survived the typhus epidemic mostly succumbed to the massive selections, both of the sick and the fit, which took place in September and October.[63]*

At Nuremberg Wisliceny attempted to deny his responsibility for this miserable end of Salonika Jewry. He declared that on March 10th, 1942, he had informed Eichmann that spotted typhus raged in the Jewish districts of Salonika and that there was a high rate of tuberculosis, but Eichmann had telegraphed him that the resettlement must proceed at all costs.[65] There was also a certain amount of intervention by Greek personalities. For instance, within a few days of the first deportation, the Salonika Bar presented a petition to Logothetopoulos, the Prime Minister, that the Jews should be interned on a Greek island. This plan was supported in Athens by the Metropolitan Damaskinos, who was later to become Regent for the throne. Damaskinos suggested allotting one of the larger islands occupied by the Italians, together with a communal maintenance fund based on the entire Jewish assets. But Simeonides, the Greek Civil Governor of the German Occupied Zone, wanted these assets for the Greek refugees whom the Bulgarians had expelled from Thrace. Logothetopoulos also inclined in this direction. He declared that Simeonides had not sought his intervention with the Germans and that the 'Salonika Ghetto' was needed for Thracian refugees. Nevertheless, Logothetopoulos protested privately to the German Minister in Greece, Altenberg, that Simeonides had requisitioned Jewish property without consulting the Greek Government.[66]

---

*Most of the June, 1943, transports were routed to Sobibor and Lublin. In July some 2,800 Jews were forwarded on from Lublin to Auschwitz. Apparently the epidemic had now reduced the working strength at Birkenau so much that the second transport was entered in the camp books almost intact (*see page 294*). The documents relating to this peculiar case are published in *Dokumenty i Materialy*.[64]

Rhallis, the successor of Logothetopoulos, came to Salonika in April and Rabbi Koretz again petitioned for the island solution and was therefore removed from office by Merten and interned in ' Baron Hirsch.' Since the arrival of Eichmann's deportation commission Merten was no longer interested in coming to terms with the Jewish Council. According to Wisliceny this was because the Counsellor to the Military Administration had acquired a vested interest in the deportations. Through Simeonides the Military Administration got control of the Jewish houses, and through the Security Police it got the cash which the deportees had to surrender, being credited, according to Wisliceny, with no less than 280,000,000 drachmas, then worth about £1,000,000, at the National Bank of Greece.[67]

Now that the intervention of the so-called Greek Government was worthless, the Salonika Jews could only seek the representatives of Axis or neutral States. South of Larissa Greece was in Italian occupation, and here immunity could be guaranteed at least against deportation. As early as October, 1942, Luther had complained to Ribbentrop that the labour-conscription decrees of Merten and Simeonides had driven the well-to-do Salonika Jews to emigrate to Italian-held territory.[68] On March 6th, 1943, Kaltenbrunner instructed Luther to see that the Salonika Jews who had registered at the Italian Consulate were not recognised as fully fledged Italian subjects, ' seeing that the deportations are to begin in a few weeks.'[69] On this question neither Luther nor his successor, von Thadden, were successful and the Germans were not able to deport Jews with Italian papers from their various occupied territories till after the Badoglio armistice of September 8th, 1943. Owing to Italian intervention, 551 Salonika Jews survived the first wave of deportations and were allowed at the end of June to go by train to Athens.[70] Among them were many women who had been extracted from Baron Hirsch camp at the last moment by M. Castrucci, the Italian Consul. Another group, perhaps larger, succeeded in crossing the German-Italian demarcation-line in secret.*

*At Plati, where the Italian Zone began, refugees from Salonika were allowed to use the Italian military train to Athens. General Carlo Geloso of the Italian 11th Army declared in a memorandum to the Italian War Office that at the beginning of the deportations he had been asked by Colonel-General Alexander von Loehr, Chief of the ' Ost-Agais Command,'

As usual, the flight of a few Jews from torture and slow death was a matter of the gravest concern to the professional bureaucrats of the German Foreign Office. Neutral Governments were instructed by von Thadden at the end of April, 1943, that recent naturalisations in Salonika would not be recognised,[71] but there was one neutral Government that had to be handled with circumspection. The interest of Spain in Eastern Sefardic Jewry dated from the late nineteenth century, when an emotional wave of atonement had made Spain the first nation to welcome the refugees from the Russian pogroms. A decree was published by which Jews in the Ottoman Empire of proved Spanish descent might once again become Spanish citizens. In practice the Jews acquired Spanish consular protection without Spanish nationality till in 1924 the Spanish Government offered to make them Spanish subjects, but there was a great deal of confusion and delay in carrying out the instructions and the number of Jews in former Ottoman areas who obtained Spanish passports was small. As recently as December 29th, 1948, this privilege has been confirmed by General Franco.[72]

According to immemorial habit, the Spanish Government met the problems of 1943 with procrastination. For the protectees the alternative was 'repatriation' to Spain or deportation to 'the East.' After renewing the option twice without getting a decision from General Franco,[73] the German Foreign Office decided to treat 367 Spanish-protected Jews of Salonika as 'exchange Jews' and they became the first inmates of the 'exchange camp,' Bergen-Belsen, leaving Salonika on August 2nd, 1943, together with the privileged Jewish staff of Baron Hirsch camp and the two Jewish Council chairmen, Koretz and Albala[74] (see pages 339-340).

There is no better illustration of the painstaking Foreign Office

to lend his assistance to the removal of the Jews from Occupied Greece, but that he had replied that he could do nothing without the authorisation of his Government. As in the case of Croatia, the matter was taken up with the Italian Foreign Office through the usual diplomatic channels. The Foreign Office then asked for the views of Geloso, who reported against it. Loehr, who was perhaps more implicated in Jewish deportations than any other Wehrmacht commander, was never tried on this count. He was captured by the Jugoslavs, who executed him on February 27th, 1947. for his part in the aerial bombardment of Belgrade without declaration of war. (For the rôle of Geloso, see A. Nehama in *In Memoriam* (op. cit.) and Jacques Sabille in *Le Monde Juif*, No. 49, November, 1951.)

efforts to camouflage and promote the Final Solution than the conversation which took place on December 22nd, 1943, between von Thadden and Señor Diaz, secretary of the Spanish Embassy in Berlin. Diaz declared that his Government was now prepared to repatriate *all* Spanish Jews in occupied territories. Von Thadden said it was too late. The Spanish Government's option had been cancelled in November after five renewals. Only those Jews who had not been sent East could be returned to Spain. This was because the papers identifying the deportees had been destroyed in the last air raid on Berlin and because they were engaged in 'the East' on work so secret that it could not be revealed to enemy intelligence.[75]

Even now the Spanish Government would not take the Salonika Jews who were in Bergen-Belsen camp, but as a compromise they offered them transit through Spain. On February 7th, 1944, these 367 Jews were transported to Palestine by the American Joint Distribution Committee, travelling *via* Barcelona and Casablanca.[76]

On August 7th, 1943, five days after the 'Spanish Jews' had left Salonika for Bergen-Belsen, there took place the last deportation. About 1,800 ragged fugitives, partly from the Macedonian hinterland, were taken from Baron Hirsch camp and put on the Auschwitz train. There remained a few hundred Jews in Salonika living either 'underground' or in the sorting camp at Pavlo Mela,[77] but as many as 2,000 may have found temporary sanctuary in Athens. This sanctuary came to an end on September 10th, when the Germans marched in, but Eichmann's office and its faithful henchmen, the local Security Police command, did not get busy for some time. Registration of the Jews in Athens was ordered on December 18th, when it was believed that there were 8,000 Jews in the city. Only 1,200, however, reported to the *Judenrat*. This disobedience was used by the German Military Governor as a pretext for the confiscation of Jewish property.[78]

It was not possible to fill more than two Auschwitz transports with Jews from Athens, so effectively were they hidden in this great city.* A few hundred were detected after the first registra-

*Wisliceny declared that these two transports left Athens in July, 1944, during the first stages of the German retreat from Greece,[79] but Dr. Wolken's

tion and there were also some hundreds in privileged categories who left Athens for Bergen-Belsen on April 2nd, 1944, taking a whole fortnight on the journey. A year later, when some of the privileged Jews were evacuated from Bergen-Belsen to make way for the horde of living skeletons which was encountered in the camp by the British troops, 155 Athens Jews were put on a ghost train. It wandered about the disrupted railway system of the dying Third Reich, no one knew whither. Finally, the stranded box cars fell into American hands between Magdeburg and Stendhal.[81]

The Athens deportees reached Auschwitz in better shape than the Salonika deportees. The secret camp radio-transmission of August 21st, 1944, enumerated 1,838 Greek Jews surviving in Birkenau.[82] They included 300 of the April deportees who had been picked out for the special commando which served the gas chambers and crematoria. All these men, including some well-known members of the Salonika intelligentsia, worked the death factory during the deportations from Hungary, Lodz, and the Cracow region, and died in the mutinies at the crematoria in September and October (see pages 456-7).

On August 17th, 1944, the last Greek transport reached Birkenau. It contained—and there is a remarkable agreement in the estimates—the entire Jewish population of the island of Rhodes, some 1,200 people.[83] They had fallen into German hands on September 16th, 1943, after an abortive British attempt to induce the Italians to surrender the island. In June, 1944, Lieut.-General Kliemann, the commander of the Rhodes garrison, received the visit of two SS officers, presumably members of Eichmann's office. Immediately afterwards he posted notices ordering all Jews to reside in a particular group of villages, from which they were transferred to a barracks. Then came the order of 'Ost-Agais Command' that they should be off the island by July 17th,[84] but the action was postponed till the beginning of August, when the Jews were embarked in some old caiques. It was believed by the German troops[85] that these caiques were sunk a few miles out to sea, but in fact they reached the Greek

Birkenau quarantine list shows 1,387 Athens Jews who arrived on April 13th and 1,869 Athens and Corfu Jews who arrived on June 30th.[80]

mainland. And then these poor islanders, who lived harmlessly 2,000 miles from the nearest point in the Reich, began their land voyage to the Silesian death factory. It was a time when the Germans were obliged to abandon great quantities of their stores to the Greek partisans. This cluttering-up of their evacuation route with another deportation train was utterly without sense, but like a procession of blind caterpillars, the Wehrmacht submitted to the priority of the ' Fuehrer Order,' even when it faced disgrace and disaster on every front.

4. Bulgaria

The case of Bulgaria is unique among the satellite or puppet governments of Hitler's Europe, for no Bulgarian-born Jews were deported, though in March, 1943, hard-pressed by the Germans, the Bulgarian Government assisted in the deportation of 11,000 Jews from the Greek and Jugoslav territories which were occupied by their forces. As to deportations from pre-war Bulgaria, they were stopped by the weight of popular opinion, and Hitler and Himmler were singularly powerless to do anything about it.

In November, 1941, the Bulgarian Minister in Berlin, Popoff, suggested to Ribbentrop at a party that the Jews of all Europe might be included in the deportations which were then taking place from the Reich, but this was the view of a private individual (*see pages 95 and 99*). No measures were taken against the 28,000 Jews of Bulgaria proper till August, 1942.* Even then it is not clear when and how the German pressure was first applied, but it is probable that in this month of victory in South Russia Prime Minister Filoff was told that his country's claims on Greece, Jugoslavia, and Rumania were in jeopardy. The Bulgarian

*Rademacher claimed at his trial that after Weizsaecker had referred Popoff's proposal to Emil Albrecht of the legal section of the Foreign Office, the latter had commissioned Dr. Konrad Roediger, his expert on Jewish matters, to take up the question with the Balkan Governments. Roediger, who was now a judge of the Federal Constitutional Court, thereupon insisted on giving evidence, in which he declared that he had done everything possible to prevent Popoff's project going further (*Frankfurter Rundschau*, February 8th, 1952 ; *Nuernberger Nachrichten*, February 22nd, 1952).

Government at once announced a programme which included ghettoes, labour camps, and a Jewish badge.

In September Beckerle, the German Minister in Sofia, pressed for deportations, having been instructed through the usual channel of Himmler's authority, the department *Deutschland* of the Foreign Office.[86] Beckerle met with no immediate Bulgarian response and on November 9th the department *Deutschland* learnt from Himmler's intelligence service that the Bulgarian measures had been extremely half-hearted. Only a fifth of the Jews in Sofia wore the regulation badge, manufacture of which had ceased. Gabrowsky, the Minister for Interior, had not merely been friendly to a Jewish deputation, but had stopped the press publishing the appointment of a Commissary for Jewish Affairs. Moreover, Beleff, the Commissary, belonged to the Bulgarian fascist legionaries, the *Ratnizi*, who were opposed to the Filoff Government, while Filoff himself was a lukewarm anti-semite who had ordered many exemptions at the instance of the Metropolitan Stefan and of Balan, the king's secretary.[87]

On the basis of such reports Himmler and Ribbentrop decided to go slow. Apparently the Filoff Government was not interested in Jews in the Occupied Territories. When Theodor Dannecker, the former Jewish *Referent* of the Gestapo in Paris, arrived in Sofia in January, his brief was limited. On February 22nd it was agreed that Dannecker should assist Beleff to arrest 20,000 Jews, half of them from three towns south of Sofia—Radomir, Dubnitza, and Juma—all of which were near the old Serb border and inhabited by Jews of mixed nationality. The other half were to be deported later from Uskub (Skoplice), Bitolj, and Pirot, in former Serb territory. Those Jews who were Bulgarian citizens were to lose their nationality on crossing the frontier.[88]

In fact, only the Jugoslav Jews were deported. The Jews of Uskub were deported in three trains, which left the transit camp that had been established at Kachanig, between March 22nd and 29th,* while the Pirot Jews were taken, together with the

---

*The Court of Inquiry, established at Siedlice in 1945, concluded that a transport from Uskub reached the Treblinka death camp on March 29th, presumably the first of the three transports from Kachanig camp. But Yankiel Wiernik and the Nuremberg witness Samuel Rajzman both assert that there were a number of ' Bulgarian ' transports to Treblinka in March and April. It can at least be said with certainty that not all the transports, organised

Jews rounded up by the Germans in former Greek territory, to the Bulgarian Danube port of Lom Palanka, whence they travelled by barge to Vienna on the first stage of the journey to Poland.[89] A memorandum prepared for Luther on April 3rd shows that 7,240 Jews had left former Jugoslav territory and 4,210 had gone from former Greek territory.

From quiet, remote mountain valleys and country towns that were scarcely more than sprawling villages came this horde of people, little removed from the state of peasants themselves and dwelling at peace with their neighbours, who were among the most tolerant of the races of Eastern Europe. In lambskin caps and brightly coloured shawls they boarded the box-cars, frightened and bewildered, to end their journey, after many days, on a lonely siding in Eastern Poland, where the whips of the pitiless Ukrainian guards goaded them to the fatal bath-house.

Another 6,000 were to have gone from the towns on the Bulgarian side of the border, but they never left, and for this story we have to turn to the correspondence of Adolf Beckerle, another of Luther's policeman-diplomats of April, 1941, but one who understood his background better than most.[90] According to Beckerle, Beleff had tried early in March to round up the Jews of Kustendil, Plovdiv, and Varna. Thereupon a deputation from Kustendil, headed by the Vice-President of the Bulgarian Senate, approached Gabrowsky. But the Minister for Interior had already been warned from 'a very high source.' Consequently, all the Jews who had been arrested in Old Bulgaria were released by March 10th.[91] Certain Bulgarian Deputies had discovered the true meaning of the plan and opposed it. Moreover, in spite of the fact that Beckerle had been assured that the British Palestine offer would be rejected (*see page 408*), the Bulgarian Government had applied in Bucharest for transit visas for Jewish children and had furthermore asked for the Swedish Red Cross ship *Oeresund* to call at Dedeagatch,[92] the Bulgarian Ægean port.

by the Bulgarians, were routed to Treblinka, for the Jews, deported by the Bulgarians from Greek territory, formed the greater part of the labour camp in the former Warsaw Ghetto in the following October (*see page 281*). See *German Crimes in Poland*, I, page 104. *A Year in Treblinka*, page 30, and *Dokumenty i Materialy*, I, page 187.

The meaning of all this was made clearer on April 4th, when Hitler received King Boris. This king, who was to die soon and under suspicious circumstances, was the first in a long series of receding satellite rulers who visited Hitler at Schloss Klessheim in that month, so unpropitious for the mighty Wehrmacht. Even during Hitler's triumphs King Boris had never been afraid of these interviews, lecturing him, according to Dr. Paul Schmidt, in fluent German. On this occasion the king had a subsequent interview with Ribbentrop, telling him his intention to keep the 25,000 Jews of Old Bulgaria in labour camps. Ribbentrop observed that this was 'unacceptable,' but he refrained from discussion.[93]

In April and May the royal plan was held up for lack of camps and barracks. Gabrowsky could only offer Dannecker the expulsion of the Jews from the capital, and even this the king tried to prevent by proposing a total civilian evacuation of Sofia on the grounds of imminent air attack—this was when American bombers, based on North Africa, first raided the Ploesti oil-field in Rumania.[94] The German counter-move on May 20th was to announce over the Berlin radio that the expulsion of the Sofia Jews would start in three days' time.

Rather more than 6,000 Jews were involved, but 2,000 of them had exemptions and 90 per cent. of the remainder reported at the railway station voluntarily, to the accompaniment of demonstrations which showed how little this peasant nation had been corrupted by the East European plague of race-prejudice. As Beckerle wrote in a covering report to the Main Security Office[95]:

> 'The mentality of the Bulgarian people is lacking in the ideological enlightenment which our people enjoy. Having lived all their lives with Armenians, Greeks, and Gipsies, the Bulgarians see no harm in the Jew to justify special measures against him.'

M. Benadev records that the crowd tried to stop the Jews going to the railway station,[96] but according to Otto Hoffmann,[*]

*Not to be confused with Karl Hoffmann, who commanded the Gestapo in Copenhagen at the same time, or Lieut.-General Otto Hoffmann, another SD man, who was head of the Race and Settlement office.

the commander of the Security Police in Sofia, this was because the people of Sofia believed that the expulsion of the Jews would invite bombing by the Allies. Hoffmann also wrote that Beleff had only taken measures of the most temporary kind, since he had put the expelled Jews into school-buildings which would be needed after the holidays, that a crowd had demonstrated before the palace in favour of the Jews, and that the Metropolitan Stefan hid the Chief Rabbi of Sofia in his house.

After the fiasco of May 24th Beckerle's attitude became still more ambivalent. On the one hand, he endorsed Hoffmann's Gestapo report that Prime Minister Filoff's attitude to the Jewish problem was irreproachable and that Beleff had asked Dannecker to prepare deportations *via* the Danube in the following month. On the other hand, he wrote that Filoff meant to keep the Jews in Bulgaria and that Beleff and the *Ratnizi* were playing a double game to discredit Filoff's Government. At the end of June Hoffmann, too, was shaken. He reported that it was no time to exercise pressure on the Bulgarian Government, who regretted their action in turning some 20,000 Jews loose on the countryside, where food shortages and rent inflation had followed. The only consolation was that this source of anti-semitism might become a ' springboard for further developments in accordance with our aims.' But this view was contradicted two months later when Horst Wagner, head of the office ' Inland,' which had taken over Luther's department, *Deutschland,* wrote that the expelled Jews had acquired the sympathy of the peasants and would prove a danger if the Allies dropped parachutists in Bulgaria.[97] Wagner, moreover, informed Kaltenbrunner, head of the Main Security Office, that the situation following the recent death of King Boris —the German Secret Service were suspected of murdering him— was not clear. In fact, the reign of the boy king Simeon meant the Regency of Filoff, and no further measures were taken against the Jews, who, deprived of most of their property, drifted back to the towns.

But the tragedy of the former Jugoslav and Greek Jews, deported by Beleff and Dannecker, was complete. From Treblinka none returned, and from Auschwitz, Lublin, and the Warsaw labour camp only the smallest handful. In the annexed part of

Thrace the towns of Drama, Cavalla, and Xanthia were reported in October, 1945, not to contain a single Jew.[98]*

In the spring of 1943 Himmler, through the usual chain of authority, Kaltenbrunner, Mueller, and Eichmann, had made a concentrated and partly successful onslaught on the Sephardic Jews of Eastern Europe. If its success was not complete, it was because the defeats of the Wehrmacht had robbed Hitler of the compliance of satellite governments. As usual, the carrying out of the Final Solution was full of inconsistencies. While 90,000 Sephardic Jews went to their death from the Balkans, successful efforts were made to rescue a few hundred Sephardim in Amsterdam on the grounds that they had 'no racial connections with Eastern Jewry' (see page 338).

---

*From these three communities came most of the 4,210 Greek Jews who were deported through Bulgaria and the Danube port of Lom Palanka. M. Molho has published a report that the barges were never delivered to the Germans by the Bulgarians, but merely sunk with their passengers in the river.[99] Such reports were always circulated when a deportation by water was involved, as in the case of the Jews of Rhodes. In the absence of any confirmation, one must accept the probability that the survivors of these transports merely merged their identity in the flood of Greek Jews at Auschwitz and Lublin.

CHAPTER 15

Slovakia and Rumania

1. Slovakia

IT is necessary to devote what may seem a disproportionate space to this satellite State of two and a half million peasants, a Ruritania that lasted exactly six years, because this is the story of the first outright failure of the 'Final Solution' and a failure at a time when there was no glimmer of hope for Jewry in Axis-controlled Europe.

The Slovak Republic had been under German protection since its birth on March 14th, 1939. Every move in the 'Final Solution' was copied in Slovakia and the very first Jewish deportation train to Auschwitz was provided voluntarily by the Slovak Government. Yet as early as July, 1942, this Government rebelled. The deportations were not resumed by the Germans themselves till September-October, 1944, and from 28,000 to 35,000 Slovak Jews were enabled to survive the war.* It was but a small proportion of 136,739 Slovak Jews of the 1931 census, but at the outbreak of war this total had already been reduced, first, by the cession of the Kosice province to Hungary in November, 1938, and, secondly, by Jewish emigration since the Munich agreement. It is probable that not more than 89,000 Jews remained in the power of the German-dominated Government of Father Tiso.[1]

The political atmosphere of the new State is not easily described. A deeply Roman Catholic upper class of peasant-proprietors had emancipated themselves from Prague and the socialistic free-thinking Czech ascendancy. This traditionalist society had little in common with the practices of National

---

*A discussion of these tentative figures will be found in Appendix I. The recent statistical study of Mr. Gregory Frumkin (Population Changes in Europe since 1939, N.Y., 1951) suggests a much greater number. Quoting a 'fairly reliable estimate' which is unfortunately not further described, Mr. Frumkin supposes that 67,000 Slovak Jews were killed. Allowing for emigration, this suggests that more than 60,000 survived the war.

Socialism, except anti-semitism, and even this was not an ancient growth. In the days when the Jews provided almost the only town life, it hardly existed, nor was there anywhere in Slovakia a dense proportion of Jews, since within the frontiers of March 23rd, 1939, they were only 3.35 per cent of the population. Thus the Government, which produced the Slovak anti-Jewish code of April 18th, 1939, was divided. On the one hand, there was the traditional anti-semitism of the clerical politicians, Father Tiso, the President, and Dr. Vojtek Tuka, the Premier. On the other hand, there was the imported German article, represented by the Minister for Interior, Sano Mach, who read a paper at Rosenberg's anti-Jewish conference of March-April, 1941, and who subsequently conducted the deportations.[2]

These deportations were facilitated by an inquisition-structure, based closely on German practice—a Central Jewish Office and a Jewish Centre. The latter, known as *Ustredna Zydow*, was a slave organisation similar to the *Reichsvereinigung*. To this structure there was already attached in 1940 a representative of Eichmann's office, Dieter Wisliceny. This extremely interesting person, whose name has already recurred many times in this book, was originally Eichmann's senior in the 'religious cults' section of the SD and in 1937 he had recommended Eichmann for a commission. He was the only member of Eichmann's staff to give evidence at Nuremberg[3]—for the prosecution, since Wisliceny was as ready to betray his comrades after the war as he had been to bargain with his victims during the days of his power. Wisliceny must have at one time made a considerable fortune out of the work he professed to hate and which included the efficient marshalling to their death of a 100,000 Greek and Slovak Jews.*

In August, 1941, the fruits of German indoctrination in Eastern

---

*Wisliceny, a native of Regulovken in East Prussia, was, like most members of Eichmann's ' commando,' trained as a lawyer. His affidavits show an almost model grasp of essentials and some of them considerable experience and skill in placing blame elsewhere. Personal descriptions by Michael Molho, Reszoe Kastner, and Eugene Levai suggest something of a *bon viveur* and man of the world, an impression which is far from borne out in the photographs taken in July, 1948, during his trial at Bratislava, where he was condemned to death. Here we see Wisliceny in decline, a dim German *gelehrte* with timid inquiring eyes and puffy, hanging cheeks.[4]

Europe took shape in massacres of Jews by Hungarian and Rumanian troops. At the same time in Slovakia the historic Jewish quarter of Bratislava was demolished and the inhabitants dispersed to crowded suburbs or labour camps. Next, on September 10th, Sano Mach published a Jewish code of 270 paragraphs, the most devastating feature of which was that it treated as full-Jews the baptised Slovak Jews, numbering from ten to fifteen thousand, who had been exempted from the provisions of the older Jewish code.[5] There was much pricking of ears in the Wilhelmstrasse. The Embassy in Bratislava particularly reminded von Weizsaecker, as a devout Catholic, that a Catholic priest, the head of the Slovak State, had ordered all this. Correspondence of this sort went, as a matter of course, in duplicate to Eichmann's office through Dr. Luther. Thus it was not long before Eichmann approached Franz Rademacher, his Foreign Office contact-man, on the question of including Slovak Jews in the forthcoming deportations to Poland. Rademacher agreed, but thought it should be done as a matter of courtesy through the Bratislava ' Legation.'[6]

The approach was premature. The Slovak President of the Council, Isidor Koso, had just returned from Poland, where, as proof of German humanity in this autumn of 1941, he was shown a Jewish town with its own autonomy and Jewish police. The Slovak Government, however, felt that, if the Jews were to be made to work, it should be for them and not for the Germans ; so in November they began the construction of three great labour camps. These, too, were the fruits of a visit to Poland, where Wisliceny, in the company of Eichmann, had inspected the Jewish workshops at Sosnowiece.[7]

The Slovak labour camps were in fact destined to serve as assembly points for deportation, but it is not clear when and how this change of policy was forced on the Slovak Government. On March 7th, 1942, Sano Mach published a decree confining all Jews to their quarters till the ' Transfer East' of the community was complete.[8] On March 10th a few thousand Jews were put across the Galician border, but this was far from the type of deportation desired by the SS. As Luther recalled to Ribbentrop five months later, they had not sufficed to cover ' labour commitments in the East' and Himmler had had to request the

Wilhelmstrasse to demand 20,000 Slovak Jews.[9] To this Father Tiso agreed in spite of the opposition of the Slovak bishops.

Thus there took place in Bratislava on March 23rd a big round-up of Jews, conducted by the police and the Fascist militia, the Hlinka Guard.* The Jews were taken to Sered camp, whence two days later the first train left for Auschwitz, the future extermination centre being only a 130 miles away, or one night's journey. Ten more trains left for Auschwitz in the next four weeks and four for Lublin (Majdanek), bringing 17,000 able-bodied Jewish workers. In addition, 11 family transports left for the small towns of Lublin province,[10] Lubartow Isbica, Demblin, Opole, and Treblinka, bringing some 10,000 people. According to Dr. Steiner, no less than 7,000 were children, a statement which is partly borne out in the complaint of the German *Kreishauptmann* of Lubartow that, of the 1,600 Jews who arrived on April 17th, not one was fit for labour.[11]

Apart from Sano Mach and certain enthusiasts, the Slovak Government had misgivings from the beginning. The aged Premier, Vojtek Tuka, showed concern over the deportation of baptised Jews and, in about the same degree, over the prospect of the Germans acquiring the Jewish property.[12] Heydrich, who was in Prague, thought it expedient to see Tuka personally, and he came to Bratislava on April 10th. Tuka's memorandum to his Cabinet shows that Heydrich described the proposed extension of the plan to the Western countries, declaring that 'half a million Jews were being moved at that moment.' As to the Slovak Jews, they would be settled permanently in Lublin province as 'protection subjects' of the Reich, while those who had been baptised before the publication of the Jewish codex of September 10th, 1941, would live in a separate settlement.[13]

Heydrich's treachery was effective, for, according to

---

*The Hlinka Guard were the members of the Catholic People's Party of Monsignor Andrej Hlinka, or 'Pater Hlinka.' This venerable figure was primarily a Slovak nationalist, who believed that President Wilson had cheated the Slovaks out of a promise of autonomy. He therefore made common cause with Henlein's Sudeten-Germans in 1938 to secure the break-up of the Prague Republic. It was impossible for a severely Catholic movement to remain staunchly pro-Nazi indefinitely and the rôle of the Hlinka Guard in the deportations disappeared when the Nuncio had rallied the leaders of the church against such action.

Wisliceny's evidence, the Slovak Government now asked that the families of the 17,000 young men and women who had been sent to Auschwitz and Majdanek be permitted to join them.[14] At first Eichmann refused, then, early in May, he saw Tuka and Mach in Bratislava and agreed to raise the number of family dependants in the Lublin region to 35,000, including those who had already left. Under this arrangement 18,000 Jews left between May 15th and June 30th for Lukow, Biala-Podlaska, Miedzyrzec, Cholm, and other towns. This, together with a fresh wave of transports to Auschwitz, brought the number of deportees at the end of June to 52,000.[15]

What was the fate of this mass of people, of whom the Slovak Repatriation Commission could trace only 284 alive at the end of the war ?[16] It seems that the first 17,000 who went to Auschwitz and Majdanek were not selected for the gas chamber. Hoess, the Auschwitz gaoler, told Wisliceny that they were his best workers.[17] But only the very privileged could stand more than three months either in Birkenau or in Majdanek, and in the summer of 1944 the only traces remaining from the Slovak deportations were a few girl clerks in the staff office in either camp and some *Kapos* and infirmary attendants in Birkenau. Of the family transports about 25 per cent had been selected for labour camps in ' Lublinland.' The rest became ' useless mouths ' in overcrowded ghettoes and transit camps, from which they were soon forwarded to the gassing-centres at Belsec and Sobibor. Thus Yankel Wiernik saw the remains of the Slovak Jewish hutted camp, used in the construction of the Treblinka gas chambers, while Rudolf Reder noticed a few Slovak Jews still employed in the Belsec death camp in August, 1942.[18]

But on May 15th, the day the second wave of deportations started, the Slovak Government published a constitutional law which, while it expropriated the deportees, established many exempted categories, among them all Jews who could prove baptism before March 14th, 1939. These would be kept, not in a reserve in Poland, but in Slovak labour camps. In practice the way was open in this intensely Catholic country for any professed convert to demand protection.[19] On June 26th, when the deportations were slowing down, Ludin, the German Minister in Bratislava, telegraphed Weizsaecker that Dr. Tuka was asking for diplomatic pressure to enable the remaining 35,000 Slovak Jews to be deported ' in the face of the unpopularity of these measures among wide circles of the population and the growth of English propaganda.'[20] Luther, on the other hand, maintained that Tuka's request was eye-wash and that the Slovak Government had granted all 35,000 Jews a ' special legitimation.'[21]

According to Wisliceny, what happened next was this[22]: Dr. Tuka kept plaguing him to arrange an official Slovak inspection of the settlements in Poland, but on this subject Wisliceny found Eichmann evasive. Then at the end of July the Papal Nuncio warned Father Tiso that the Jews in Lublin province were being murdered. In August Wisliceny visited Eichmann in Berlin to point out the gravity of these accusations. Finally, Eichmann declared that inspection was out of the question, because the Jews were no longer alive. Eichmann then showed Wisliceny a secret order, signed by Himmler in the previous April, whereby the entire Jewish race were to be exterminated progressively. ' God grant that our enemies never have an opportunity of doing the same to the German people,' cried Wisliceny. ' Don't be sentimental, this is a Fuehrer Order ! ' Eichmann answered.

The deportations came practically to an end at the beginning of September, soon after Wisliceny's return to Bratislava, when the figures exceeded 56,000.[23]* Wisliceny thought that this was on account of the inadequate explanation he had brought back.[24] But is one really to believe that Himmler could apply no pressure to this pocket-government and that he could do nothing until September, 1944, when he had occupied the country ? On February 14th, 1943, Sano Mach actually declared over the Bratislava radio that the rest of the Jews would be deported within two months,[25] but only a few hundreds were sent. In December, 1943, Father Tiso promised Himmler's special envoy,

*The fragment of the daily *Appell* roster of Birkenau male camp suggests that the transports to Auschwitz may have ended after the Nuncio's warning to Father Tiso. Thus 326 Slovak Jews were admitted to the male camp on the 18th July, 117 on the 25th, and 166 on August 1st, but none in the next eighteen days. Following Sano Mach's broadcast, a transport of 854 Slovak Jews left on some date before March 31st, 1943, either for Lublin or for Treblinka and was included in Dr. Korherr's second report to Himmler. (Netherlands Red Cross, ' Auschwitz, Deel II,' The Hague, May, 1948.)

Edmund Veesenmayer, that the deportations would start again in April, but this time nothing happened at all.[26]

One explanation of the riddle was provided at Nuremberg by the witness Dr. Reszoe Kastner of the Budapest Relief Committee, known as Vaadat Ezra wa Hazalah—the *vaadah* and the *Dr. Kastner*, of whom much will be heard in Chapter Sixteen. Dr. Kastner is unique in that, as a Jew, he had many interviews with Eichmann but still lives. It is a pity that his fascinating and withal modest story is only available in typescript, for the rôle which Dr. Kastner was destined to play towards the end of the war was truly extraordinary. During this period he was frequently in contact with Wisliceny, who told him that he had heard Eichmann disclose the gas-chamber plans at an office conference in March, 1942. In July, when Father Tiso and Dr. Tuka had learnt the truth, Wisliceny had indeed gone to Berlin to get the deportations called off—but he did so against payment received.[27] He had been promised 55,000 dollars as a personal *douceur* as far back as March and, while waiting for the final payment, he had shipped off 3,000 Jews as a stimulant[28] to the Bratislava Relief Committee.

At the end of 1942, Kastner declared, Wisliceny made another offer, this time on behalf of his superiors. He would get the deportations stopped everywhere except in Poland on payment of two million dollars. It was on the basis of this offer, the so-called 'Europa Plan,' that a fund was actually put aside by World Jewish Congress within the next three months, though a year was to pass before any part of it could be transferred (*see page 409*). But as long as there was a chance of the 'Vaadah' of Bratislava collecting the money, the Slovak Jews were immune from deportation and in May, 1944, when the Final Solution spread to Hungary, it was Wisliceny who resumed the threads of the negotiation with the 'Vaadah' of Budapest.

There is other evidence that Himmler was made aware of the financial value of the Slovak Jews. On November 24th, 1942, Heinrich Mueller, the head of the Gestapo, conveyed to him a proposal from Gottlob Berger to finance the recruitment of an SS division in Hungary by the sale of emigration permits to Slovak Jews.[29] Berger, on trial in 1948, said vaguely that this project came too late, by which he apparently meant that, since the fall of the Bardossy Government, the Hungarians no longer turned the Slovak Jews back across the border.

Strange to say, Slovakia, with its complicated and elusive Jewish codex, was to become a place of refuge for Jews. This was after March 19th, 1944, when Himmler introduced the Final Solution into Hungary. This situation was again reversed after August 23rd. On that day—rather a momentous one, for it was then that the Germans abandoned Paris and Rumania signed an armistice with the Allies—a rebellion broke out against the German-dominated Slovak Government at Banska-Bystrica, or Neusohl, in a valley of the High Tatra. Part of the Slovak army and several former members of the Government took part, assisted by British-trained parachutists. The rebels relied on the advance of the Russians, who were barely a hundred miles away. But seven months were to pass before the Red Army reached the Tatra and very quickly the German Security Police became masters of Slovakia. The repression of the rebellion was from the beginning an SS affair. Gottlob Berger, Himmler's right-hand man, arrived as Military Commander on August 31st, to be succeeded three weeks later by another SS general, Hermann Hoefle.[30] This man, who was condemned to death by a Bratislava court in March, 1948, furnished a Nuremberg affidavit which contains a statement, not confirmed elsewhere, that Himmler himself arrived in Bratislava shortly after his appointment and that in the presence of Hoefle, Father Tiso, and Ludin, he had insisted on the total deportation of the Jews[31] (*see page 438*).

The deportation was publicly announced as a military operation. The able-bodied Jews, who had been exempted from 'resettlement' in 1942 and who had spent more than two years in labour camps, had all escaped during the rebellion. It appears that the régime in these camps was lax. A portion of these young men, of whom there were 3,000 or 4,000, found their way to resistance groups in the mountains.[32] To be a Jew was therefore a title to arrest. On December 9th Colonel Witiska, who led the five Security Police commandos in Slovakia, reported that of 18,937 persons arrested to date, 9,653 were Jews, and of these 8,975 had been transferred to German concentration camps. The remainder had been 'specially handled.'[33]

Thus, after an interval of two years, new Slovak Jewish arrivals were seen in Auschwitz camp, but most of the 9,000 deportees of September-October, 1944, were sent to Sachsenhausen, Stutthof, Theresienstadt, Bergen-Belsen, and other German camps, so that after the war there was a fair proportion of survivors. A desperate effort had been made to avert this revival of the deportations by reopening the negotiations between the *Vaadah* in Bratislava and Wisliceny, who was then with Eichmann in Budapest. The *Vaadah* proposed to obtain funds through Switzerland from the American Joint Distribution Committee and the intermediary with Himmler was to be Colonel Kurt Becher, a horse-dealer, who had already handled delicate negotiations of the same kind for the SS (*see page 435*). Becher flew from Bratislava to Berlin, but there Himmler told him that the 'military reasons' advanced by Berger and Kaltenbrunner made the completion of the Jewish deportations from Slovakia essential.[34] On September 25th—that is before Himmler's alleged conversation with Father Tiso—Becher returned to Bratislava to find that Witiska had handed over the Jews to the notorious Major Anton Brunner, who had been transferred from France after the fall of Paris. As to the *Vaadah,* who had arranged the traffic to Hungary in the past, they had been shut up in Sered camp and Gisi Fleischmann, the courageous woman who had handled the first negotiations with the SS, had been smuggled on to the Auschwitz train and thence to the gas chamber. Brunner had done all this in a great hurry as soon as he learnt that Wisliceny was on the way.[35]

Following Becher's failure and Brunner's triumph, M. Georges Dunand of the International Red Cross reached Bratislava from Switzerland in an attempt to persuade the German and Slovak authorities to observe the laws of humanity towards rebels and Jews. In his terrible and haunting book, *Ne perdez pas leur trace,* M. Dunand has described his first hopeless interviews with Witiska and Brunner, and how he was powerless to stop the latter treacherously deporting the 'Exchange Jews' (*see pages 338-339*) besides many baptised Jewish children, who were hidden in convents, for, naturally, the hero of the affair of Eyzieux saw to it that the children were sent nowhere but Auschwitz. Even so, M. Dunand's mission did not turn out altogether fruitless.[36]

On November 16th Witiska ordered all surviving Jews to assemble three days hence at the Bratislava *Rathaus* for transfer to Sered camp, but only 50 obeyed this summons.[37] At least 6,000 Bratislava Jews were hidden in bunkers. On January 2nd M. Dunand transmitted to Father Tiso the petition of the indefatigable Professor Burckhardt, President of the Red Cross, to end the deportations. Father Tiso's answer, for which M. Dunand had to wait more than a week, was a downright lie. Father Tiso declared that, though his Government had been compelled to yield to pressure, the Slovak Jews had been spared previous to the rebellion.[38] Nevertheless, the Red Cross, with the aid of the country clergy, succeeded in feeding the hidden Jews of Bratislava, and in February and March Dunand, assisted by Kastner, affected many escapes to Switzerland. Finally, in March, Witiska himself offered to aid this traffic, but in the total collapse of the Third Reich nothing could be organised. On April 4th the Russians were in Bratislava.[39]

For the murder of three-quarters of the Jews of Slovakia some penalties have been paid. Anton Brunner was condemned to death by the *Volksgericht* in Vienna on May 21st, 1946. Wisliceny was not condemned till July, 1948, after standing a three months' trial in Bratislava along with the German Minister, Hans Ludin, the Minister for the Interior, Sano Mach, and the Cabinet Ministers Koso and Vasek. Vojtek Tuka died before the end of the war. Father Tiso was condemned and executed in April, 1947, not without some opposition in a Czechoslovak State that was not yet fully Communist.

2. Rumania Accepts the Final Solution

We come to the story of a nation which began its deportations to Russia before Hitler had even given the signal, but which was constrained within a year to a more merciful course, not through humane feelings, but through jealousy of the Germans. Before the Second World War Rumania may have had a proportion of Jews second among the nations of the world only to Poland. At the lowest accepted estimate there were 725,000 racial Jews in a population, numbering, before the cession of territory to Hungary and Russia in August-September, 1940, about

19,000,000. It may also be said that no country had a worse record in its treatment of the Jewish minority. In 1878, very early in the history of Rumania as a sovereign State, the Jews were promised citizenship in accordance with an article in the Treaty of Berlin, which is said to have been due to Disraeli. Nevertheless, the Rumanian Jews never received more than the status of 'protectees.' In like manner the minorities statute, incorporated in the peace treaty of December, 1919, was never fully honoured in the newly acquired territories of Rumania. Thus, during the six weeks' government of Octavian Goga in January, 1938, some 225,000 Jews of the annexed territories lost their nationality. This partly explains the deportations of 1941-42, which affected relatively few of the Jews of pre-1919 Rumania.[40]

Even before Hitler came to power, Rumania had a 'Brown Shirt' organisation, enjoying the protection of the throne, the Iron Guard of Corneliu Codreanu being firmly established since 1930.[41] A paradox resulted in 1938 when King Carol II tried to dispense with the Iron Guard in his bid for dictatorship. For after his tame surrender of territory to Hungary and Bulgaria at Hitler's bidding in July-August, 1940, it was fear of the Iron Guard, now violently opposed to the alliance with Hitler, that made the King abdicate. Under Ion Antonescu, 'the Marshal,' Rumania, though still a monarchy, became a one-party Iron Guard State. In January, 1941, Antonescu had to call on the German troops, who had arrived in Rumania in the previous October, to quell the Iron Guard *Putsch* of Horia Sima. In a week of fighting 6,000 people were killed; both sides murdered Jews, and in Bucharest the bodies are said to have been exposed in the Jewish butcher-shops.[42] Although Rumania had been blackmailed into joining the Axis on November 23rd, 1940, it was only now that the distraught and dismembered country was ready to drown its miseries in an anti-Russian crusade at the side of Adolf Hitler.

During three years of virtual civil war Government pressure on the Jews had been unrelenting. The denationalising decrees of January 21st, 1938, were constantly amplified. In effect, only the old Sephardic Jewish community of Turkish times and the Jews of German origin were permitted any status. The Polish or Eastern Jews of Bessarabia, Bukovina, and Moldavia were as good as outlawed. Thus the statute of August 9th, 1940, recognised only Jewish families who had possessed Rumanian nationality before December, 1918.[43] For the next eleven months the Jews of Bessarabia and Bukovina passed under Soviet rule and the false assumption that they benefited from the political change made them State enemies as well as foreigners. It is probable, therefore, that before joining in the invasion of June 22nd, 1941, Antonescu had already decided to expel the Jews from the reoccupied territories.

Yet the first Rumanian massacre—the first great massacre of Jews in the entire war—was in territory that the Russians had never held. From the outset the Russians fought stubbornly along the line of the Pruth river, the frontier established in June, 1940. Twelve miles into Rumania, Jassy, the capital of Moldavia, was subjected to air bombing and parachutist attacks. These continued from June 22nd to June 29th, when the immensely rapid advance of the Germans on the left flank enabled the Rumanian troops to get across the Pruth unopposed. In the meantime the disappointment of the Rumanian army at meeting opposition was vented on the Jassy Jews. After the heavy air raid of June 24th, the Iron Guard leaders denounced the Jews for signalling to Russian aeroplanes. Consequently, on the 27th the Jewish community were ordered by the police to give up field glasses, electric torches, and cameras. On the 28th the Iron Guard faked a Jewish machine-gun attack on Rumanian soldiers from the Salchana Synagogue. On that night the Iron Guard broke into the Jewish houses and began the round-up, covered by an air-raid alarm. In the early morning all the Jews were assembled in the Prefecture square. The Rumanian police allowed the women and children to leave, but the men were taken into the Prefecture courtyard for deportation. However, the Rumanian police commander, whom the Germans accused of being ' be-Jewed,'[44] was prepared to sell exemption certificates, but when the exempted Jews tried to leave they were shot as fugitives. Many more were shot in the afternoon, when the column of deportees, including a hundred women who would not leave their husbands, marched to the station.[45]

For what followed there are two accounts, a plain and factual one by Boris Kelpner, the secretary of the Jassy Jewish Community Council, and a flight of fancy, in which, however, the same facts are stated, by Curzio Malaparte, who was then staying with the Italian Consul in Jassy as correspondent of *Corriere della Serra*. It seems that the Iron Guardists packed 5,000 Jews in a single train, 120 to each sealed box-car, and that the train was destined for Bucharest, 300 miles away, but it took a devious route. Six hours later, when it had covered no more than 20 miles, part of it was detached and the Jewish elders of Podul Iloaje, or Pudioara, were invited to receive the passengers. As the train doors opened 1,200 bodies rolled out and a few living beings. Another 800 bodies were removed at Tergu Frumos, 45 miles from Jassy, where the Jewish Council was asked 'if it would like some Jewish Communists.' And so for two days the process continued till the train reached the station of Roman in the foot-hills of the Carpathians, 85 miles from Jassy, where camp-space was found for the thousand who remained alive. Kelpner, who interviewed many survivors, was told that the victims stripped off their clothes in the suffocating heat and that many used them to hang themselves.[46]

Officially, 500 Jews were executed in Jassy for signalling to the enemy and firing on troops, but there is a large measure of agreement that the shootings and the death train accounted for at least 7,000. Stawresco, the Rumanian town commandant, did not stop random shootings till July 1st, while it was weeks before the Jewish community emerged from a cellar existence.*

In Bessarabia and Bukovina there were massacres in most of the towns, though not on this scale. Eighty thousand Jews, more than half the town's population, lived in Kishinev, one of the biggest Jewish communities of Eastern Europe, famous for the great Russian pogrom of 1891. Yet early in July, when Ohlen-dorf's commandos entered Kishinev, they could find only 4,000 Jews, of whom 551 were executed on the pretexts that had already served at Jassy. Later, Jews began to return or come out of

---

*As part of old Rumania, Moldavia was only partially involved in the subsequent deportations to Transdniestria. As a consequence, the Jewish population of Jassy, which must have declined from the normal 35,000 to 28,000 after the massacres, recovered to 32,000 in the summer of 1942. This was the result of the anti-Jewish decrees which had driven many Jews out of the country towns. There was no closed ghetto in Jassy, but the Jews were forced to live in the poorest part of the town.[47]

hiding, and on August 23rd Ohlendorf reported that a ghetto had been created for 9,000 Jewish workers and their families.[48] Exactly three years later this ghetto was liberated by the Red Army, having survived the almost complete evacuation of Bessarabian Jewry.[49]

Among the densely concentrated Jewish population of Bukovina the executions in July-August, 1941, were on a bigger scale, Ohlendorf believed that his men had accounted for 3,106. Czernowitz, where there were 58,000 Jews, was entered on July 6th, and Commando 10b at once began to assist the Rumanians by making lists of leading 'Jewish Communists'[49a] —not that the Rumanians wanted much help. On July 8th and 9th, when the commando shot 100 selected persons, the Rumanians in the suburbs killed 400—a proceeding which shocked Ohlendorf because it was not orderly[50] (see pages 84 and 201), but Jewish survivors mention much bigger figures. Being forced to wear the yellow badge, the Jews were an easy prey for the students of Czernowitz University, from which Professor Alexianu, now Governor of Transdniestria, had directed pogroms under the short-lived Goga Government of 1938.[51]

In the case of the smaller Bukovina towns, particularly Radauz and Czudin, the Jews were killed before the Germans had even arrived by Ukrainian bands from Russian-held Galicia,[52] a circumstance which enabled Antonescu to create two concentration camps for the Bukovina Jews in the name of law and order. From these camps, Edinet and Sekureni, and from a ghetto at Suceava, 12,000 Jews were marched on August 12th to the Dniester bridgehead at Mogilev-Podolsk and this was to be the beginning of the deportation of every Jew living beyond the Pruth. But the newly invaded Russian territory across the Dniester was still under German military government and in the second half of August 27,500 Jews were turned back. They were kept by the Rumanians in improvised camps. In the meantime, on August 30th, it was formally agreed between the German and Rumanian staffs, meeting at Tighina, that the civil administration between the Dniester and the next river, the Bug, should be Rumanian. The whole of Transdniestria, or Podolia, was now available to Antonescu as a Jewish dumping-ground (see page 241).

Bukovina and Bessarabia contained 277,949 Jews in 1930 and

more like 300,000 in August, 1940, but, before these provinces were recovered by Rumania, deportations into the interior of Russia, followed by massed flight, had reduced the Jewish population enormously.* These escapes were certainly more numerous than the subsequent deaths, which were mainly due to exhaustion and hunger on the deportation marches and to the typhus epidemic that accompanied the first efforts at settlement. Yet between the first attempt at deportation in August and the revival in October the Rumanians had had time to plan ahead. The blame must therefore lie fairly and squarely on the mixture of callousness, incompetence, and corruption that constituted Rumanian leadership.

There seems to have been a total lack of discipline, so that at each halt in the journey the victims were pillaged. They had to camp among the bodies of their predecessors who had been murdered for their belongings. Even at the end of the journey many of the so-called reception centres were mere clearings in the forest without any shelter,[54] for the Jews were not intended to stay in Transdniestria. On October 18th, a week from the start of the deportations, Antonescu declared the region annexed to Rumania. In spite of the agreement signed at Tighina, he hoped to push the Jews across the River Bug, where Hitler, who had expressed such admiration for Antonescu's initiative, might be expected to dispose of his Jews for him (*see pages 84 and 360*). Thus a report by Richter, Heydrich's police attaché with the embassy in Bucharest, shows that on October 17th Antonescu was believed to be planning to collect 110,000 Jews in ' two forests across the Bug,' the purpose of the action being ' the liquidation of the Jews.'[55]

For the moment Richter circumvented this move and the Jews remained between the Dniester and the Bug, mainly in the camps of Pechora, Tulchin, Balta, Bershad, and Trostyanets. Gradually they were sorted out. Those accused of collaboration with the Russians, including most of the doctors in the hospitals, went

---

*On the eve of the deportations, at the beginning of September, 1941, a military census was taken of the Jews in Bessarabia (but not Bukovina), including those committed to camps. It showed 126,434 Jews. If these figures are reliable, they indicate that more than 100,000 had left Bessarabia, a point that has certainly not been considered in most of the current estimates of the extermination of Rumanian Jewry[53] (*see page 496*).

for some time to the prison camps.[56] The rest were allowed to settle in towns, mainly in Tulchin, Golta, Yampol, Mogilev-Podolsk, Rimnitsa, and Tiraspol. Here they helped to overcrowd the already close-packed Jewish communities.

Some information is available concerning Czernowitz, from which 30,000 Jews were deported between October 12th and November 2nd. First the entire Jewish community—it was estimated that 50,000 remained—were transferred to a poor quarter of the town at twelve hours' notice.[57] Next day the deportations began. The Jews were not selected, but taken street by street. They were allowed to carry haversacks and to keep their money, but it was exchanged for roubles at a confiscatory rate. But the arbitrary nature of these proceedings began to change on the 23rd, when, in strict accord with Rumanian custom, the Mayor of Czernowitz, Traianu Popovicz, began the sale of exemptions. In this way 16,000 Jews obtained a permit to reside, while another 4,000 stayed in hiding. Thereafter the exempted Jews were allowed to return to their looted homes, where they spent a winter of great privation.

It seems that hardly less than 100,000 Jews left Bukovina and Bessarabia in October and November, but none in December and January. For this Chief Rabbi Saffran of Bucharest has given a remarkable explanation.[58] On December 16th Antonescu dissolved the Rumanian Federation of Jewish Communities and replaced it with a Government-controlled 'Centre' on strict German lines. There was therefore every symptom of the deportations extending to Metropolitan Rumania. The Chief Rabbi decided to make a desperate personal appeal to Nicodemus, the Orthodox Patriarch. The Patriarch was moved to request the Queen Mother Marie and the young King Michael to invite him to the palace to meet the Freiherr Manfred von Killinger, the German Minister. This von Killinger was a former torpedo-boat commander and a *Freikorps* fighter of the early 1920s who had narrowly escaped death in the Roehm *putsch* of 1934 as a high officer of the SA and a close friend of Roehm himself. He was foremost of those recommended to Ribbentrop by Luther in April, 1941, as the likeliest bullies to replace the dignified pussy-cats of the old diplomatic service. And Killinger was worthy of his trust, behaving in Bucharest, according to Ulrich von Hassell, 'like a sergeant-major.'[59] Von Killinger was not a man to be overawed by queen mothers and patriarchs, and the dinner at the palace, to which he was invited according to plan, made no impression on him, but in other quarters royal intervention had some effect. Queen Marie conveyed Rabbi Saffran's pleadings to Mgr. Andrea Cassulo, the Papal Nuncio, who saw the Vice-President of the Council, Mihai Antonescu (not a relative of the Marshal), who in turn ordered Lecca, the Commissar for Jewish Affairs, to send medical supplies to the Transdniestrian towns.

According to Chief Rabbi Saffran's narrative, the attitude of the court was conveyed to Corneliu Kolotescu, the Governor of Bukovina, by the Metropolitan of Czernowitz, Tit Semedrea, who had been appalled by the horrors of the October deportations—although Semedrea had been in his day a follower of the extreme anti-semitic party of Professor Cuza.[60] In fact, there were no more deportations from Czernowitz till July, 1942. Moreover, there was a small alleviation for the Jews in Transdniestria itself. The Governor, Professor Alexianu, permitted the sum of 25 million lei, collected by Rumanian Jews, to be transmitted to Tiraspol through the National Bank, a very urgent need, since less than 30,000 of the deportees were capable of making a living. Private remittances could also be made, but they were paid in German military currency at a tenth their real value. In this way the charity, administered to the deportees, remained till the Russian reconquest a fruitful source of revenue to Rumanian officials.[61]

The effect of these interventions with Marshal Antonescu was to induce him more than ever to remove the Jews outside the zone of Rumanian authority. Consequently, the new deportations in February, 1942, went straight across the River Bug. Alfred Rosenberg, the Minister responsible for the Ukraine, informed Luther on February 11th that Antonescu had sent 10,000 Jews across the river at Vosnezhensk and that 60,000 more were on the way. Luther approached Ribbentrop, through von Weizsaecker, to stop the 'wild' deportations, since Rosenberg had objected to the danger of typhus, which occurred whenever the Rumanians sold the clothing from dead Jews.[62]

On March 13th a conference took place between Eichmann, Wetzel of Rosenberg's office, the author of the famous gas chamber letter (*see pages 131 and 201*), and Rademacher. For the moment it was decided only to warn Antonescu. Nevertheless, the deportations across the Bug continued and on April 14th[63] Eichmann informed Rademacher that he reserved the right to take security measures. By May 12th there were apparently no more deportations. Rademacher now received two reports on Eichmann's 'security measures' from Rosenberg's office. On May 16th he learnt that 28,000 Jews had been brought back to the racial German colonies of Transdniestria, 'where they were liquidated.' The report of May 23rd, signed by Otto Braeutigam, said only that a large portion of the Jews in Transdniestria had died and that others had been transported to Odessa. There is therefore considerable doubt concerning the numbers and the fate of the Jews who were put across the River Bug between February and May, 1942.[64]

More is known concerning the third and last attempt to foist the Bukovina and Bessarabia Jews on to the Germans in the Ukraine. On June 28th, 1942, Kolotescu, the Governor of Bukovina, suddenly decided to deport all the Jews who had been given exemption certificates by Traianu Popovicz, the Mayor of Czernowitz; 4,530 Jews were shipped to Tulchin, which was one of the most crowded of the Podolian ghettoes.[65] They included a number of members of the Czernowitz *Judenrat* in addition to hospital and asylum inmates. The latter were let loose on the countryside for the Germans to round up and shoot according to the practice which had been normal in this Russian occupation zone for the past year. From Tulchin a number were transported across the Bug as part of a mass movement involving 14,000 Jews. As late as the autumn the Germans kept them in camps in the South Ukraine, near the towns of the Uman region which had been so effectively cleared of Jews by the *Einsatzgruppen* in September, 1941. Thereafter all trace is lost of the last group of Jews to be deported from Rumania.*[66]

---

*The most conservative estimate of the number of Jews deported from Bukovina-Bessarabia in 1941-42 is 140,000.[67] In December, 1943, previous to the visit to Transdniestria of M. Charles Kolb of the Swiss Red Cross, Mihai Antonescu declared that 78,000 Jews remained in Transdniestria but M. Kolb could only find 54,300.[68] Some may already have returned to their homes but an examination of the estimates of survivors of Rumanian Jewry suggests that 60,000 had died (*see page 497*).

Antonescu's repeated attempts to put the Jews across the Bug incited Himmler to undertake the deportation of Rumanian Jews from an area that had hitherto been spared. This was the part of Transylvania that had been left to Rumania by the Vienna award of September, 1940, a territory in which Rumanian susceptibilities were peculiarly delicate. It swarmed with racial Germans, and in May von Killinger had threatened to resign when Antonescu forbade these Germans to wear their party uniforms.[69] The fact that the Foreign Office presented its demands for more Jews at this tricky moment may well have turned the scales in Antonescu's mind against the entire policy of deportation.

On June 11th, 1942, Eichmann already announced confidently to his staff that Rumanian Jews would be sent to Auschwitz,[70] while on August 17th Luther wrote to Ribbentrop 'Mihai Antonescu's agreement with the marshal is on record, according to which German agencies are at once to deport Jews from Arad, Temisoara, and Turda.' Two days later Ribbentrop learnt through Luther that Himmler intended to deport the Rumanian Jews, starting on September 10th, to the Lublin region in Poland.[71] 'Those who are fit will be posted for work and the remainder sent for *special treatment.*'

This was another of the murderous documents, which passed under the initialling pencil of von Weizsaecker and for which he claimed to have acted 'in principle only as a postman.'[72] It was also sent to Mihai Antonescu, who apparently passed it on as approved to Richter, the police attaché in Killinger's embassy. On September 20th Luther told Eichmann that Davidescu, the Rumanian Foreign Minister, had given his consent and that Lecca, the Commissary for Jewish Affairs, was on his way to Berlin to discuss the economic details of the deportation plan.

Apparently Himmler's proposals had been put to the Rumanian Government through Luther's *Deutschland* department without any reference to von Killinger, the Minister, who had moreover to put up with the presence of Richter, a Gestapo spy installed in his own office. Thus on August 27th a telegram reached Luther which exploded with Killinger's wrath[73]:

'If such important personages as Ministerial Director Lecca come to Berlin, I ask that they should not be put off in such a way that good relations between Germany and Rumania are affected. I would like also to remark that all letters to the *Obersturmbannfuehrer* Eichmann went *via* the Foreign Office so that the Foreign Office knew of the events. I am not in any way surprised that Herr Eichmann of course did not find it necessary to contact the Foreign Office as I know the methods of the Herren of the SS sufficiently well. Besides I would like to remark that all matters which I report to dept. *Deutschland* get into the hands of the SD within the shortest time.'

Explanations and recriminations went to and fro till on September 12th the offending department, 'Deutschland III,' learnt from the Bucharest Legation, 'Herr Killinger does not want to understand at the present moment.'*

While the SS and the SA bickered, Marshal Antonescu changed his mind, not because Leccas's feelings had been hurt in Berlin but because the latest German interference had been resented from the first. On December 12th von Killinger reported that Antonescu had dropped the deportation plan in favour of Jewish emigration to Palestine.[74]

Once again the narrative of Chief Rabbi Saffran fills the gap. He had heard from a Transylvanian Jewish delegation in the middle of August that the plans for deportation by the Germans were complete and he had tried unsuccessfully to reach Mgr. Balan, the Transylvanian Metropolitan at Sibin. Later Saffran saw Balan in Bucharest in the house of General Vatoianu. Balan showed the correct frigid attitude in front of a rabbi but none the less approached the Antonescus. It is probable that Mihai Antonescu had been misleading Richter, for besides receiving Balan, he also gave audiences to Mgr. Cassulo, who had visited Tiraspol, to the Swiss and Swedish Ministers and to representatives of the International Red Cross.[75] He even ordered

---

*On August 25th, 1942, Luther had received a severe rocket as the result of Killinger's complaint. He was forbidden to take any further initiative in the deportation of Hungarian, Bulgarian, and Croat Jews in the Italian occupied zone and he was told that 'the Herr Reichs Foreign Minister requests that in future, before undertaking negotiations with foreign Governments which fall within the competence of his own office, the circumstances be reported or submitted to him and his ruling awaited.' (NG 2586, folder Ia, sheets 69-70 photostat.)

an inquiry into the German massacre of the Jews who had been deported beyond the Bug to the towns of the Uman region.*

3. Rumania Rejects the Final Solution

There remained in this autumn of 1942 more than 70,000 Jews living between the Rivers Dniester and Bug in a corner of that great Russian Steppe that was now Hitler's *Lebensraum* and from which all trace of Jewish life had been otherwise removed. These Jews lay right across the communication lines of the German Eastern Front, whence final victory or final defeat meant but one thing for them—massacre. Only one tenuous and uncertain line of escape led to the Black Sea port of Constanza, but this was only 150 miles from neutral waters, where no German ship had the right to search.

The first attempt had been a tragedy. On December 16th, 1941, a miserable steamer, the 180-ton *Struma*, broke down off Istanbul when bound from Constanza to Haifa in Palestine. On board were 769 Jewish refugees, including 70 children, none of whom possessed immigration permits. As a consequence, the British authorities would issue no *navicerts* to proceed and the Turkish authorities no permission to land. The helpless *Struma* lay in the Bosphorus for ten weeks, her passengers being maintained by the Istanbul Jewish community. On February 24th, 1942, the Turks towed the *Struma* out to sea, where she sank six miles from shore. Only two people saved their lives by swimming. After this there were some questions in the House of Commons, but the Government insisted that they were wedded

---

*The part, played by Red Cross representatives in preventing the spread of Jewish deportation measures in Axis satellite countries and in averting many massacres and catastrophes during the final collapse of the Reich, has not been appreciated. The fault is in the policy of reticence and anonymity, which the Committee of the International Red Cross has decided to pursue even since the war. The author, who must here acknowledge his debt to several publications of the CIRC, can only express his profound regret at the suppression of the names of the authors of certain narratives. The three fat volumes of the 'report of activities of the CIRC in the Second World War' seem to lapse into all the laconic vagueness of wartime censorship whenever the queston of aid to Jews is discussed. Only M. Georges Dunand and the late Count Bernadotte have broken this ring of silence by publishing personal narratives (November, 1952).

to the Palestine 'White Paper' policy of 1939. Thus on March 17th Mr. Harold Macmillan, Under-Secretary for the Colonies, replied to Mr. Lipson: 'It is not in our power to give guarantees nor to take measures of a nature that may compromise the present policy regarding illegal immigration.'[76]

A year of massacres in Eastern Europe failed to change this policy. On December 17th, 1942, the House of Commons stood in silence after the reading of the United Nations declaration promising retribution for racial murder, but, when Mr. McGovern suggested that the United Nations should offer immediate sanctuary for those in peril, Mr. Eden used a different language. 'Certain security formalities would have to be considered' and there were 'immense geographical difficulties.' How easily then could Herr Stumm, Goebbels's Foreign Press Relations Officer, tell the reporters that the United Nations declaration was an atrocity story to benefit the Christmas sales of the Jewish department stores in London and New York.[77] This apparently evasive attitude of the British Foreign Office was capped in the U.S.A. by the positive obstruction of the State Department under the rule of Mr. Cordell Hull. Of this there was a glaring example in January, 1943, when Dr. Stephen Wise, of the American Jewish Congress, revealed many new details of the massacres in Poland and Rumania in the course of a mass meeting in Maddison Square. As a consequence, Mr. Leland Harrison, the U.S. Minister in Berne, actually received a rap over the knuckles for endangering his diplomatic-mail privileges in a neutral country by sending information to private persons.[78]

It was, therefore, with small prospects of success that the World Jewish Congress approached the State Department in March to allow the transfer to a blocked German account in Switzerland of a sum which was said to be sufficient to purchase the escape of 70,000 French and Rumanian Jews from the SS. Eventually a small part of these funds was used for the ransom of a few Jews from Hungary (see pages 435-8 and 443-4), but the original scheme failed completely. Mr. Henry Morgenthau, Junior, the former Secretary for the Treasury, has rather unfairly attributed a large measure of this delay to the excessive cautiousness of the British Government. But the Nuremberg prosecution were later to unearth a correspondence which showed plainly that the obstacle was Ribbentrop and the German Foreign Office, who undermined the plan out of jealousy of the SS.[79] Marshal Antonescu knew of the World Jewish Congress plan on December 12th, 1942. He had told the 'Zentral' of the Rumanian Jews to find 75,000 applicants for Palestine visas. Killinger learnt from Lecca that the Marshal 'wanted to kill two birds with one stone and get rid of a large number of Jews in a comfortable manner.'[80]

For the next few months the Wilhelmstrasse watched the thin trickle of refugees, who were allowed to find their way to Palestine through the Jewish Agency in Istanbul. On March 11th, 1943, Rademacher learnt that 72 Hungarian and Rumanian Jewish children were expected at Atlit reception camp and that 150 or perhaps even 500 were to follow. 'Do your best to prevent it,' he wrote to Killinger,[81] and the Ambassador no doubt did so.

But at the end of May Killinger had something more serious to report. Antonescu had asserted that Hitler had promised to allow 70,000 Rumanian Jewish children to go to Palestine—the similarity of the figures with those of the World Jewish Congress should be noticed. This concession had been obtained from Hitler on April 12th-13th, when Antonescu went to his field headquarters to discuss Rumania's continuance in the war. Most of the Rumanian field army had been left behind at Stalingrad and Antonescu needed bribing. He had already been in correspondence with the Swiss Red Cross to obtain ships.[82]*

Von Thadden, who, as 'Referent' for Jewish affairs in Department Inland II, had just taken over the functions of Dr. Martin Luther, now rotting in Sachsenhausen, heard at the end of May of a second proposal. The British Government had offered through the Swiss Minister in Berlin to accept 5,000 Jews from Poland, Latvia, and Lithuania, 85 per cent of them children, as Palestine immigrants. Eichmann insisted that they be exchanged

---

*Whether Hitler really promised this to Antonescu will never be known. According to Dr. Paul Schmidt, Antonescu advocated a separate peace with the Western Allies during this visit. Hitler may therefore have made a number of promises of this kind to keep him quiet. Hitler, in spite of his obsession with the power of international Jewish financiers, was never sufficiently averse to Jewish financiers buying their lives to forbid such transactions. It was different when 70,000 children from 'the reservoirs of Eastern Jewry' were likely to survive and reproduce their species.

for 20,000 Germans of military age, and elaborate instructions how these Germans were to be chosen were conveyed to 'Inland II' by Dr. Emil Albrecht, the Foreign Office legal expert. It was, said Albrecht, part of a plan to save 30,000 or 50,000 children 'from the extermination with which they are allegedly threatened.' But while it was true that the Bulgarian Government had agreed to co-operate, it was certain that they would create technical difficulties (see page 381). Albrecht used the word *allegedly* and yet he must have known of Eichmann's instructions to 'Inland II':

> 'This must be done quickly, since the time is fast approaching when on account of our measures the emigra- of 5,000 Jewish children will be technically impossible.'[83]

The British offer was argued and dissected by rival Foreign Office experts continuously till May 2nd, 1944,[84] when the Swiss Minister reiterated that the offer still stood. So von Thadden changed his tune and demanded that the Jews be received, not in Palestine but in England in order to create anti-semitism there, but they must hurry since he had been told by Eichmann that the only place where 5,000 Jewish children could be found was the Lodz Ghetto, 'which would soon be liquidated under Himmler's direction' (see page 301).

In this maze of obstructionism both the charity of the World Jewish Congress, blessed by President Roosevelt, and the greed of the Antonescus foundered equally. In the words of the summing up of the Wilhelmstrasse Case[85]:

> 'Every step which the Foreign Office took, every recommendation that it made, was directed to block efforts made by the leading countries of the world, neutral as well as enemy states, to permit little children to come unto them and to defeat the efforts of the Good Samaritan and turn their efforts into Nazi propaganda.'

—and in parenthesis both Albrecht and von Thadden are free men. They have never been brought to trial either by an Allied or a German court.*

*A charge was laid against von Thadden by the Cologne *Landgericht* in May, 1952, but proceedings had not begun at the time this book went to press.

Later in the year 1943, as the German armies rolled back across the South Russian steppe, the Antonescus began seriously working their passage with the Allies. At the beginning of December, when the Russians had reached the River Bug, Mihai Antonescu saw M. Charles Kolb, delegate of the Swiss Red Cross, and told him that the Germans could no longer carry out their plan ' to transplant the Jews to the Azov region.' The Rumanian Government would therefore repatriate all the Jews in Transdniestria who survived.

Between December 11th and 23rd M. Kolb visited Transdniestria, accompanied by a Rumanian Government mission. So much had the climate changed that on M. Kolb's return 1,800 Jewish orphans were received in Jassy and his report was published in Bucharest. M. Kolb's strongest recommendation was that the fraudulent conversion of the Jewish charitable funds should cease and that the relief for the Jews in Transdniestria should be dispatched in kind.[86]

The report was well timed, for foreign funds were now coming in. On January 22nd President Roosevelt simplified such transactions by the creation of a War Refugees' Board, independent of the State Department. The repatriation from Transdniestria was financed by the World Jewish Congress and the Bucharest Jewish Community, but the speed of the Russian advance was too fast. Between March 15th and April 15th the Red Army overran all Transdniestria and even established a bridgehead in Bessarabia. There was only time to repatriate 14,000 Jews.[87]

M. Kolb reported to Mihai Antonescu that there were 7,000 Jewish orphans in Transdniestria, thereby reviving in that bosom the profitable Palestine project on which the German Foreign Office was so unhelpful. In April, 1944, the Marshal offered to sell to the Red Cross the Rumanian liners *Transylvania* and *Bessarabia* to carry the children to Palestine under the Swiss flag. The belligerents, says the report of the International Red Cross, ' refused the necessary safe conducts,'[88] but it was possible to run a daily small steamer from Constanza to Istanbul, bringing a moderate flow of immigrants to Palestine on the ' White Paper ' quota. One of these convoys, consisting of 204 Jews, left Czernowitz on March 21st, nine days before the arrival of the Russians. As a result a very interesting series of depositions were made to the Jewish Agency[89] concerning life in Czernowitz. This community of 15,000 Jews survived not only at a vital point in the German lines of communication but within twenty miles of Galicia and the appalling blood bath of Polish Jewry. In July, 1942, Czernowitz sheltered 270 Galician Jews who had fled from the liquidation of the ghetto at Snyatin.[90] But it was not till October, 1943, that there was any amelioration in the lot of the Czernowitz Jews, when General Dragalina, successor to Kolotescu, abolished the yellow badge. He also created two communal kitchens to feed 3,000 destitute Jews, but, under the regulations then in existence, it was indeed a wonder that the whole Czernowitz community was not destitute. The Jews could not leave the town, they could not use the streets except between the hours of ten and one, when the prices in the shops were increased. Their bread was sold them at double price, they could use no public transport and the only permissible profession, apart from manual labour, was that of physician. Even so a community fine was imposed shortly before the arrival of the Russians.[91]

As the Russians drew near, the Jews were haunted with the fear that the Germans would murder them on the spot or carry them off to German concentration camps. Von Killinger watched the situation closely and saw to it that no Rumanian Jewish community was allowed to disperse. Yet on March 30th, 1944, the Germans passed through Czernowitz in their retreat without doing either of these things. Doubtless they were short of police and of the units who were accustomed to this work, for the Lithuanian and Ukrainian militia were no longer to be relied on.

In August, 1944, the situation for Rumanian Jewry became far more dangerous. It had been obvious, since Prince Stirbey's mission to Cairo on March 13th, that the Rumanians would crack as soon as the Russians chose to cross the Dniester—and the example of Hungary had just shown what might happen to 400,000 Jews when a satellite government thought of surrender. In fact on the day of Rumania's surrender, August 23rd, Eichmann had already arrived from Budapest to deal with the Jews of the border towns, Arad and Temisoara, the Jews whom he had expected to deport in September, 1942.[92]

Eichmann had no doubt of the futility of his mission. According to his friend Wisliceny, he was to have proceeded to Bucharest and he told Willi Hoettl, Schellenberg's intelligence man in Budapest, that he did not expect to return from his Rumanian mission alive.[93] But Eichmann was not the man to risk his own life in the cause of race fanaticism and within a few days he was back at the Hotel Majestic. It would have been different had vom dem Bach-Zalewski arrived in Bucharest with his special force of tanks, as he was to arrive in Budapest on October 15th, but the General was at this time in Warsaw, fighting the rebels. The Germans in Bucharest on August 23rd were so completely taken by surprise that the Freiherr von Killinger failed to get out in time. He barricaded himself in the Legation till September 2nd when, together with his secretary, Fräulein Petersen, he took his life just as the Rumanian Communists broke in.[94]

Thus the danger of massacre passed from Rumanian Jewry, but in the Transylvanian provinces which had been ceded to Hungary it was too late. Four-fifths of the Jewish population— they had numbered 149,000 at the outbreak of war—had been shipped to Auschwitz by the end of June. As to Bukovina and Bessarabia, all but a few thousands of the Jews had been swallowed in the depths of the Soviet Union or killed during the deportations to Transdniestria. Only in the *Regat*, the Rumania of pre-1919 days, the Jewish population was unimpaired. Bucharest and Budapest were now the only cities west of Moscow to retain as many as 100,000 Jews each.[95] But in Bucharest, as in Czernowitz, the Jews could only own what they could hide. As late as November, 1945, the American Joint Distribution Committee had to support half the population.[96] Even to-day with the strength of Rumanian Jewry reduced by Palestine emigration from 400,000 to 260,000, the harm done during the war has not been repaired.

CHAPTER 16

Hungary

1. Before the German Intervention

WE have seen in the case of Slovakia how a Government, which defied German pressure and abandoned the Final Solution, was forced to return to it, when, on the eve of capitulation to the enemy, the country was occupied by German troops. The case of Hungary is infinitely more dramatic, since even the pro-German Bardossy Government made no pretence of accepting Hitler's plans for the Jews. Nevertheless, it was Hungarian Jewry which more than two years later suffered the most concentrated and methodical deportation and massacre programme of the war, a slaughter-machine that functioned, perfectly oiled, for forty-six days on end.

The Government of Laszlo Bardossy, which, in 1941, embroiled Hungary in war, first with the Western Allies and then with Russia, looked no further than the recovery of the inheritance lost in 1918. These territories, duly wrested from Slovakia, Rumania, and Jugoslavia, contained approximately 300,000 Jews.* In line with the policy of the Antonescu Government in Rumania, the Bardossy Government refused to regard these Jews as Hungarian subjects and, as soon as the Germans announced their intention of deporting Jews to Russia, they began pushing them into German military areas. Among the 102,000 Jews of former Czechoslovak Ruthenia some 17,000 to 22,000 were classed as stateless, having had Polish or Russian nationality in the past. Their deportation was ordered by police decree on August 2nd[2] and soon afterwards marches began under

---

*At the Gross-Wannsee conference Heydrich used the figure of 742,800 for the Jews of Greater Hungary, while a figure of a million was mentioned by Luther to Sztojay in January, 1943.[1] In reality the total was somewhere between 680,000 and 720,000, but this had already been reduced at the time of the Gross-Wannsee conference by some 35,000 deportations from Bachka and Ruthenia.

Hungarian military escort to Kamenetz-Podolsk, which lay beyond the Dniester in the nearest part of Russian territory.

Perhaps unwittingly the Hungarians were paving the way for the first of the five-figure German massacres. When the German High Command protested that this mass of destitute beings was a menace to their lines of communication, the Hungarians refused to take them back. The matter was therefore brought up at a civil government conference held at Winnitsa on August 25th at the headquarters of Quartermaster-General Wagner. Here the police major-general Franz Jaeckeln—later the killer-in-chief in the Baltic States—declared his readiness to complete the liquidation of 11,000 Jews by September 1st,[3] this being apparently the balance remaining after the Hungarians had withdrawn the able-bodied Jews for labour service in Eastern Galicia. Several reports confirm that this massacre took place, as arranged, at a spot on the banks of the Dniester some miles from the town.[4]

One report by a Jewish lorry-driver serving with the Hungarian army declares that Hungarian troops assisted the German police units[5] and, though this is not confirmed, there is no question that Hungarian troops participated in a subsequent massacre. At Ujvidek, or Novy Sad, in Bachka the Jews who had been left behind after the deportation to the Belgrade Ghetto in the preceding August (see page 359) were taken either to the Serb cemetery or the bank of the Danube, where between 700 and 1,500 were shot in an action closely copied from German Security Police practice. It is true that the massacre was stopped by the Regent, Admiral Horthy, and the responsible officers brought to trial, but they were released within a year and not sentenced to death till after the war.[6]

These killings did not represent official policy. Like every other satellite Government, the Bardossy Cabinet saw in the German deportation plan an opportunity to despoil newly acquired Jewish populations, but not to debarrass itself of its own Jewish nationals. Heydrich, who was informed of this situation by Martin Luther,[7] spoke at the Gross-Wannsee conference of forcing an adviser for Jewish affairs on the Hungarian Government, but the recommendation of the conference (see pages 85 and 99) was limited to the deportation to 'the East' of the Jews whom the Hungarians had already turned over to the Germans.[8]

Under the Government of Nicholas Kallay, who succeeded Bardossy in March, 1942, there were no more pogroms or deportations, but Jews were still largely forbidden to exercise their professions and were liable for labour service on the Eastern Front under penal conditions. More latitude was shown the Jews in 'Trianon Hungary,' the territory that had been continuously Hungarian between the two wars. Here Jews from Austria, Slovakia and Poland took refuge after March, 1942, and, though neither welcomed nor assisted by the civil authorities, they were generally not handed over to the Germans. They profited from the jealousy of the Hungarians over their own sovereign rights. This jealousy, which was to play a part even when Hungary became virtually an occupied country, is well illustrated in the following episode.

In the summer of 1942, when some Hungarian Jews, living in France, had been made to wear the Jewish badge, the Hungarian Minister in Berlin, Dome Sztojay (later Premier), protested to Dr. Martin Luther, but was induced not to object if the Italian Jews were made to wear the badge, too. However, on October 5th Sztojay made the additional demand that the Hungarian Government must share the trusteeship for the property of their Jewish subjects in the event of confiscatory measures. He then outlined Kallay's attitude towards actual deportation:

> 'The Prime Minister was interested in the question whether a continuous existence in the East would be made possible for the Jews after their evacuation. There were many rumours in this connection, which he, of course, could not believe. However, these rumours somewhat disturbed Prime Minister Kallay. He did not want to be accused of having exposed the Hungarian Jews after their deportation to misery or worse.'[9]

Luther assured Sztojay that the Hungarian Jews would first be employed on road building and then settled in a Jewish reserve. Sztojay (who had told Luther that he considered himself a true pioneer of anti-semitism) expressed himself 'extremely happy about our suggestions.' Nevertheless, after his visit to

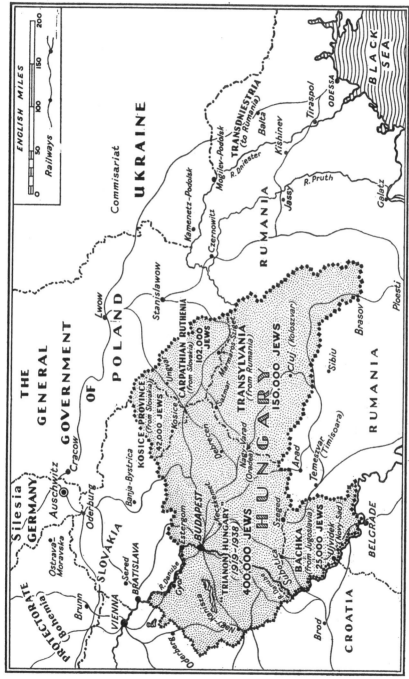

Greater Hungary, showing the acquired Territories with their Jewish Populations.

Kallay, he failed to report back to Luther, and on October 20th Weizsaecker informed Ribbentrop that he had protested at the way Hungary handled the Jewish problem.[10] On December 5th Kallay refused categorically the German demands for parallel measures, among them the Jewish badge and the deportations to Poland.

When it is recalled that for the past six months the Slovak Government had failed to obtain permission to send an inspector to the 'Jewish reserve' in Poland and that assuredly these matters were not hidden from Kallay, it is not surprising that on December 14th Sztojay was ordered to reject Luther's Jewish-reserve proposal.[11] On the contrary, he asked for an extension of the time-limit in which Hungarian Jewish subjects might be repatriated from German-held territory. Finally, on January 16th, 1943, when Kallay had abolished the Office for Jewish Affairs, Luther took Sztojay to task:

> 'We were very much concerned that a country which was friendly to us should be sheltering approximately a million Jews in the middle of Europe. We could not in the long run look on at this danger without taking action.'[12]

But taking action against a rebellious satellite State became an improbable prospect in the following month, the month of Stalingrad. On April 17th Horthy visited Hitler at Klessheim Castle to discuss the terms on which Hungary would remain in the war. Horthy, when reproached with his policy towards the Jews, retorted that, having deprived the Jews of nearly every means of getting a living, he could not 'beat them to death.' At this Ribbentrop declared that they must either be killed off or be sent to concentration camps. Thereupon Hitler delivered a monologue, recorded in the minutes of his interpreter, Dr. Paul Otto Schmidt[13]* :

*At Nuremberg Dr. Paul Otto Schmidt not only confirmed that he had made the minutes personally, but he repeated his own recollections of the meeting, as for instance, the fact that after Horthy had said 'Shall I perhaps beat them to death,' there was rather a lull before Ribbentrop intervened (IMT X, 141, 148). I am at a loss therefore to understand why, in his book, *Hitler's Interpreter*, page 248, Dr. Schmidt should choose to say that, though Hitler asked him particularly to be present ('otherwise Horthy distorts what I say'), Horthy insisted on Schmidt leaving the room, as a consequence of which he records 'I have little information about his conversation with Hitler, as I did not have to interpret.'

'In Poland this state of affairs had been fundamentally cleared up. If the Jews there did not want to work, they were shot. If they could not work, they had to be treated like tuberculosis bacilli, with which a healthy body may become infected. This was not cruel if one remembers that even innocent creatures of nature, such as hares and deer, who are infected, have to be killed so that no harm is caused by them. Why should the beasts who wanted to bring us Bolshevism be spared more ? Nations who did not rid themselves of Jews perished. One of the most famous examples is the downfall of that people who were once so proud, the Persians, who to-day lead a pitiful existence as Armenians.'

These minutes, which are indisputably genuine, contain Hitler's only recorded admission of the massacres in Poland. The remarks are all the more extraordinary in that they were made to the head of a sovereign State of uncertain loyalty. Hitler, according to his practice, overrated the anti-semitism of the Hungarian leaders. Two days later Gottlob Berger wrote to Himmler that 'in Hungarian Government circles there exists a well-founded fear that the accession to the confederation will be tied up with compulsion to liquidate the Jews.'[14] Even Dome Sztojay, after forwarding from Berlin an account of the Klessheim meeting, so far forgot that he was 'a true pioneer of anti-semitism' as to suggest a solution 'which excluded the chance of an eventual intervention by a third party.'[15]

Edmund Veesenmayer—later the Reich plenipotentiary in Hungary—wrote to Himmler still more gloomily that Horthy's only attachment to Germany was his fear of Bolshevism, while Kallay considered all measures against Jews as a crime against Hungarians. He also wrote that the Hungarian Government welcomed Jewish refugees, believing that they would thus be protected from Allied air attacks.[16]

Such reports from Veesenmayer and other SS agents, depicting Hungary as a Jewish paradise, lack objectivity, since the real situation of Jewry in Hungary was extremely wretched. So far from swelling the Jewish population of Hungary to a million, as Ribbentrop and Luther maintained, the refugees scarcely amounted to 16,000 additional heads,[17] and these, like some

200,000 of the existing community, were destitute and in receipt of charity from the Joint Distribution Committee and other bodies.[18] But Veesenmayer was not far out in describing the attitude of the Kallay Government towards the refugees. As that Government became more war-shy, it saw in international Jewish benefactions a bridge for negotiating with the Allies, in particular the contacts of the Budapest Zionist Relief Committee, the *Vaadat Ezra wa Hazalah*—or simply the *Vaadah*—in Switzerland and Istanbul. Later, Himmler himself was to use that bridge.[19]

On August 19th, 1943, when Kallay broadcast a speech on Hungary's need for peace, the country was virtually out of the war. The only pressure which Germany could exert on this awkward neutral power was Hungary's own fear of the Russians. Paradoxically, it was only by retreating that the Germans could once more dictate to Hungary. Thus, on March 16th, 1944, Hitler extorted from Horthy a promise to dismiss the Kallay Government, and this was just three weeks before the first Russian patrols reached the foot of the Jablonica, the historic Tartars' pass into the Hungarian plain.

2. The Deportations

On this, his second visit to Schloss Klessheim, Horthy was practically arrested, being detained 24 hours while he considered the terms of Hitler's ultimatum.* Hitler told him that the Kallay Cabinet had been in touch with the British. The aerodromes surrounding the capital would therefore have to be occupied by German troops. Horthy would have to take orders from a German plenipotentiary and there would be a German Security Police force in Hungary under a Higher SS and Police leader. For the latter, Major-General Winkelmann, Hitler's terms of appointment were precise. He was to 'perform tasks of the SS and police concerning Hungary, and especially political duties in connection with the Jewish problem.'[20]

At Nuremberg the former Reich plenipotentiary for Hungary,

*Dr. Paul Schmidt has described Hitler's devices for detaining Horthy. A fake air raid was staged and the telephone line to Budapest was cut. Orders were given to take Horthy to Budapest as a prisoner if necessary. Dr. Schmidt gives the impression that Horthy lacked firmness and could have bluffed Hitler out (*Hitler's Interpreter,* London, 1951, page 271).

Edmund Veesenmayer,* deposed that, when he reached the Budapest Embassy on March 23rd, Winkelmann and his chief Kaltenbrunner were already in possession.[23] But the plea that Veesenmayer had no authority over Winkelmann has little relevance to the deportations, since they were carried out by Eichmann in person, ensconced in the Majestic Hotel. As to Veesenmayer and Winkelmann, they played the part of complacent stooges while Himmler's orders were carried out. Horthy had been blackmailed, not to keep Hungary in the war, since that, for what it was worth, had been guaranteed by the Russian advance—but to remove 700,000 Jews from a country that was about to become a battlefield. According to Eichmann's assistant, Dieter Wisliceny, the *Einsatzgruppe* of the police, which was intended for Hungary, together with almost the entire staff of Eichmann's office, had assembled—at Mauthausen camp of all places—as early as the beginning of March.[24]

This bodily transportation of the most secret of departments shows the immense importance which the destruction of Hungarian Jewry held in Hitler's mind.

In Hungary, where he arrived at the end of March, Eichmann had, for the first time since his appointment as Grand Inquisitor of the Jews for Europe, to work in the open, since he was to keep close and constant touch with the Hungarian Ministry for Interior. It is for this reason that Eichmann's service-record describes him on September 5th, 1944, by a fictitious title, ' *Bds. Ungarn*,' or Commander of the Security Police, Hungary.[25] Thus there was evolved a new Eichmann, not the cautious, sly German bureaucrat described by Wisliceny, but a cynical

---

*Veesenmayer, a colonel in the general SS, was well suited for the part. He had been employed in the ' Keppler office,' Himmler's liaison with the Ministry of Economics, in each successive storm-centre of German annexationism, and in 1943 Himmler had sent him to coax the Slovak and Hungarian Governments to resume the deportations of Jews. In the meantime Veesenmayer, though an agent of Himmler, had a status in the Foreign Office as ' plenipotentiary for Ireland.'[21] He was a weak creature, whom Kaltenbrunner denounced in the following September as a defeatist, so certain of Germany's ruin as to have attempted a suicide pact with his wife.[22] Though he had given the highest diplomatic sanction to mass murder, these circumstances were eventually credited to Veesenmayer, and on January 31st, 1951, his Nuremberg sentence was reduced from 20 years' imprisonment to 10 years. He has in fact been released.

drunkard and corrupt satrap of the SS, displaying his smart mistress and his horses (*see page 26*).

On March 20th Eichmann's Vienna agent, Major Krumey, summoned the leaders of the Budapest Jewish community. Their apprehension was so great that they brought their families and their luggage, but they were assured that no one would be arrested. Indeed, the Jews who had been arrested overnight at the railway station would be released. Next day, when Krumey and Wisliceny selected a new Jewish Council, headed by Samuel Stern, a highly esteemed member of Horthy's Privy Council, the Gestapo's Jewish experts might well have been believed when they said that 'all would go on as before.'[26]

Disillusionment came not *via* the Gestapo but *via* the Hungarian Government. On March 22nd Sztojay, now promoted Premier, told his Cabinet that Kaltenbrunner had insisted on ghettoes in the chief Hungarian towns and the wearing of the Jewish badge. Horthy had then told Sztojay that he no longer wanted such decrees submitted to him for previous approval.[27] Kaltenbrunner left Hungary on March 26th after securing three more appointments that boded no good for Jewry. Two men who had been active in the 'Arrow Cross' or Hungarian Fascist movement, Laszlo Baky and Vitez Endre, were to run a Jewish Commissariat in the Ministry for Interior, while another 'Arrow Cross' man, Major Ferencsy, was to convey orders to the Hungarian *gendarmerie* from the German Security Service.

On March 31st the Jewish Council had their first interview with Eichmann at the Majestic Hotel. 'Do you know what I am ?' he declared, 'I am a bloodhound.'[28] Other witnesses found him rather slyer, asserting that he had never occasioned executions anywhere, except. when Jews had been linked with resistance movements. Having told the Council that they might sleep in their beds at night, he asked to see the Jewish museum and library, matters which had interested him since 1934 (*see page 25*).

In reality Eichmann was unsure of his position at this moment. On the one hand, Himmler listened to offers made him through Jewish bodies, and, on the other, the Hungarian Minister for Interior, Jaross, tried to gain time; thus on April 7th he issued the first orders for mass arrest by rounding up Jews only in the areas that were least Hungarian. Jaross declared at his trial that he had supposed Horthy to be agreeable to the deportation of ' Communist and Galician Jews.'[29] On this principle the round-ups of April 15th and 16th took place at Ungvar and Munkacs in Ruthenia, and at Nagy-Kanisza near the Croat border, all of them places that were now in combat areas.

The Sztojay Government was slowly gingered up. On April 15th Veesenmayer expected only 5,000 Jews to be produced for deportation every three or four days. Two days later it was to be 50,000 Jews for labour in the Reich in April and 50,000 in May. Sztojay still expected to keep a labour force of 100,000 to 150,000 Jews in Hungary.[30] But there was a way of circumventing this. Baky, Endre, and Ferencsy, taking their orders from the Eichmann commando, confined the Jews in such inadequate quarters that they became an impossible burden to the civil administration—Heydrich's classical method in which Eichmann had been trained. Dr. Reszoe Kastner has described how, as early as April 5th, Wisliceny uttered the warning that ' deportation might be ordered over the mission's head if the Hungarians asked for it in Berlin.'[31]

It is unlikely that Horthy personally gave the order that the mass of interned Carpathian Jewry should be removed to Germany, for, as we have seen, he had washed his hands of the whole affair. According to Wisliceny, Ferencsy came to Eichmann's office as early as April 20th, imploring him to take the Jews off the hands of the Ministry for Interior; Wisliceny declared that Eichmann had the German railway officials waiting in the next office and that Rolf Guenther at once telegraphed General Gluecks, inspector of concentration camps, to get ready at Auschwitz.[32]

Ferencsy's version—at the Budapest trial of January, 1946—was that between April 24th and 28th Endre accompanied Eichmann and Wisliceny on an inspection at Kassa (Kosice), Ungvar, Munkacs, and Marmaros-Sziget. At each of these places from 15,000 to 25,000 Jews huddled miserably in brickfields. Wisliceny proposed moving the Jews to the centre of Hungary, but Endre protested that there was nowhere to put them. He was then persuaded by Eichmann that they had better all go to Germany. Eichmann afterwards told the Budapest Jewish Council that it was the fault of Endre, 'who wanted to eat the Jews with paprika.'[33]

Veesenmayer, in reporting to Ribbentrop the progress of the round-up on April 24th, wrote that from May 15th the Jews would be shipped to Auschwitz at the rate of 3,000 a day.[34] He made no mention of leaving any Jews in Hungary, except that the 50,000 Jews from the Budapest region, who had been promised to the Germans by the Sztojay Government, would have to wait till last. It was apparently these Budapest Jews of whom Horthy was thinking when, on April 28th, he told the Lutheran Bishop Ravasz that Jewish labour companies deported to Germany would remain on the same footing as in Hungary.[35] Yet on the previous day Kaltenbrunner had informed Veesenmayer that Horthy's stipulations concerning the Budapest Jews were impossible. The employment of 50,000 Jews in 'open labour' in the Reich would make the completed evacuation of the Jews from the Reich a mockery. The Budapest Jews must therefore be put in labour camps which were under the control of Himmler.[36]

On May 5th, when the figures of the round-up had reached 200,000, Veesenmayer reported a conference in Vienna between the Security Police and the German State Railway officials, at which the latter had agreed to release enough rolling-stock to bring 12,000 Jews to Germany every day in four trains.[37] This was four times the quota that had been proposed on April 24th, an indication that the selection for labour would now take place in Germany itself.

It must be considered probable that Hitler had ordered Himmler to make these arrangements soon after the successful browbeating of Admiral Horthy at Klessheim on March 16th. It is certain at least that as early as April 9th Hitler told Field-Marshal Milch, Commander-in-Chief of the Luftwaffe, that Himmler was to find 100,000 Hungarian Jews for the construction of underground aircraft factories.[38] There was nothing ungenuine about this project, which sprang from the intense Allied bombing of the German aircraft factories that had begun on February 19th, but, as we shall see, the Jaeger plan was destined to be used, just as the 'Buna' project had been used in 1943, to camouflage the massacre of Jews. To find 100,000 so-called 'Jaeger workers' 400,000 Hungarian Jews had to be sorted at the Birkenau siding.

Reports of Auschwitz survivors suggest that preparations for the reception of the Hungarian Jews were made far back in April, when a report also reached the *Vaadah* in Budapest from Bratislava that the crematoria were being overhauled and that the SS guards at Auschwitz were saying: ' Soon we will be eating fine Hungarian salami.' Indeed, in all their negotiations with the Eichmann commando, the Jewish delegates in Budapest were never in any doubt as to the destination of the deportations.[39]

One transport had already reached Auschwitz on April 28th, 17 days before the main movement. It took close on a thousand Budapest Jews who had been detained since March 19th under various pretexts in Kistarcsa barracks. Apparently this ' political' transport was not selected for the gas chamber.[40] There were, however, no mass round-ups in Budapest till the end of June and, beyond the wearing of the Jewish badge, life for the majority of Budapest Jews was scarcely more vexatious than under the Bardossy and Kallay régimes, though in Ruthenia and the Carpathians conditions grew daily more desperate.

On May 15th, when the main deportations began, Baky reported that 320,000 Jews were concentrated in the camps and ghettoes east of the River Theiss.[41] At Munkacs, where 30,000 Jews were herded into a camp and a few miserable streets, there was already a typhus epidemic. Conditions were scarcely better in the former Rumanian towns, Cluj and Nagy Varad. The first trains, therefore, were packed to capacity and von Thadden reported that 116,000 Jews had left in nine days. Even in four trains a day of 45 box-cars each this meant more than 65 passengers to a box-car.[42] Eichmann explained to Dr. Kastner that, if 90 people were sometimes loaded into one wagon, it was because Ruthenian Jews had plenty of children who took up very little room. Besides, ' the Jews in those regions were not pretentious.'[43]

Thus some 380,000 Jews were deported by June 30th. In Ruthenia, to-day, part of the Soviet Union, in the Kosice province, now returned to Czechoslovakia, and in the Transylvanian provinces, which have been returned to Rumania, only a quarter or a fifth of the Jewish population remains. In ' Trianon Hungary' east of the Theiss the destruction was almost as great. The rounding-up was done entirely by Hungarian *gendarmerie*, who also carried out the obscene searching of women for valuables, about which the Bishop of Szeged complained to Horthy.[44]* The consideration that Sztojay claimed never to have given the order to Jaross and Baky, and that the latter was reprimanded by General Faragho for sacrificing the independence of the *gendarmerie* does not alter the fact that Hungarians did this thing and that most of the Jews who were spared owed their lives to bribery.[45]

Eichmann's assistants, Wisliceny, Krumey, Nowak, and Huensche, went to work with no German police at their disposal. Furthermore, according to Willi Hoettl, who kept close touch with Eichmann in Budapest, the number of the Hungarian *gendarmerie* employed was quite small. The final assembling of the Jews for transportation was in fact largely left to the Jewish Councils.[46] Incredible to relate, the Ruthenian Jewish communities, who had lived quite near the Galician massacres of 1942-43, remained as resigned and fatalistic as the Galician Jews had then been—even in 1944. After entering Slovakia at Presov, the trains took a choice of routes to Auschwitz, all of them following winding single-track lines through lonely wooded Carpathian valleys, where escape had large chances of success. Yet very few escapes were attempted.†

*In spite of the bishop's complaint, the search for valuables was at first perfunctory. Ludin, the German Minister in Slovakia, complained to von Thadden that three deportation trains which had crossed the Slovak border on May 24th had been stopped for several hours in Kysak railway station whilst the German soldiers, who acted as guards, went along the wagons forcing the Jews to give up their hidden wealth. The soldiers then proceeded to get drunk in the station buffet, after which the Jews threw many of the objects that had escaped the search out on to the track as the trains continued their journey. Von Thadden ordered Hezinger, his Foreign Office liaison man with the Eichmann commando, to conduct an investigation and then instructed Ludin on June 6th that the Slovak complaints could not be well-founded, because in Hungary 'the bodily searches were obligatory.' (Case XI NG 5569. Part-printed in *Le Monde Juif*, 51, January, 1952.) (*See also footnote, page 124.*)

†It should perhaps be realised that under the Jewish laws of the Bardossy and Kallay Governments it had become very difficult for the overcrowded Jewish communities of these country towns to exist and that most of the deportees suffered from years of undernourishment. Christopher Burney, in his terrible narrative *The Dungeon Democracy*, notices that, even compared with the Jews of Poland and the Baltic States, the physical resistance of the Hungarian Jews in Buchenwald was very low. 'Morally, too, they seem to have yielded further to the Nazi process of dehumanisation than the others' (*page 67*).

The checking of the trains, as they were turned over to the SS, produced the figure of 381,600 Jews deported by June 30th. This figure should be accepted[47] rather than the widely varying counts of the Hungarian *gendarmerie*, 615,378 reported by Endre on June 21st and 434,351 reported by Ferencsy on July 8th.[48] Except for 9,000 Jews living west of the Theiss, who were sent to Austria, and a few thousands who may have been sent direct to Stutthof and other German concentration camps, the whole mass went to Auschwitz. Changes of frontier have made it difficult to estimate the numbers who returned, while of those who are missing it is impossible to say how many met their death in the gas chamber, but one may notice that von Thadden's memorandum of May 26th records that only a third were expected to be able to work.[49]

It was at a conference on the same day, May 26th, that General Heinz Kammler discussed the arrival of the Hungarian Jews for the Dorsch and Jaeger projects with Albert Speer.[50]

Speer : 'What news of the Hungarian Jews ? '

Kammler : ' They are on the way. At the end of the month the first two transports will be ready for surface work on the bunker sites.'

This announcement appeared so inadequate that Speer proposed taking 90,000 Eastern workers into ' protective custody' by special action. Finally, Fritz Schmelter, a ministerial director in the Armaments Ministry, made this remark:

> ' I can add the following. So far only two transports have come from the SS camp at Auschwitz. For fighter-aircraft construction we have been offered only children, women, and old men, with whom very little can be done. If the next transport does not bring men of an age fit for work, the whole action will have little success.'

Kammler thought it unlikely that they would get 100,000 Jews from Hungary. He probably knew that Oswald Pohl had just reported to Himmler that half the Hungarian Jews who had passed the Auschwitz selections were women and that Pohl found it necessary to employ them on the heavy constructional labour of the Todt Organisation, which was normally performed by men, since no female occupations were available for them.

Himmler thought the women would do—and Pohl was positive he meant it seriously—if they had a ' pure diet of raw vegetables, in particular garlic, which must be imported.'[51] So the women were not used in the Jaeger project, but were sent to Poland and East Prussia, where they dug anti-tank ditches under conditions of incredible neglect and hardship.[52]

Field-Marshal Milch confirmed that the Hungarian Jews and Jewesses could not have been employed in large numbers on the Jaeger project. A report of June 27th shows that 12,000 Hungarian Jewesses had been asked for and that the SS was only now beginning to deliver them in batches of 500.[53] It would seem that these groups of women were actually allotted to the Krupp factories in Western Germany.

Alfred Krupp von Bohlen und Halbach was in an exceptionally privileged position in regard to concentration camp labour. In 1943, when he acquired sole control of the historic firm, Friedrich Krupp A.G., he was already constructing fuse factories in Auschwitz and Wustergiersdorf camps. In July of that year he was actually allowed to collect Jews from Auschwitz for the *Berthawerk* in Essen, a notable exception to the decree of November 26th, 1942, which confined all Jewish labour to Auschwitz and Lublin. The Hungarian Jewesses were allotted to the Elmag plant in Essen, the Suedwerke in Nuremberg, and a number of Krupp factories. In Essen 520 of them lived in a cellar under conditions which, as described at Nuremberg by the firm's physician, Wilhelm Jaeger,[53a] could scarcely have been surpassed in a Polish death camp. Nor could the court elucidate what happened to the 1,500 Hungarian Jewesses who were evacuated from Essen to Bochum in March, 1945.*

---

*Although sentenced to twelve years imprisonment as from April 11th, 1945, Alfred Krupp was released from Landsberg prison together with all his co-defendants on February 4th, 1951. It was explained by Mr. McCloy, the U.S. High Commissioner in Germany, that this had been done with the agreement of his French and British colleagues to bring the sentences into line with those passed on other German industrialists who had used slave labour. For the same reason the confiscation of Krupp's property was annulled, subject to the requirements of the Allied law on the reorganisation of the Ruhr coal and steel industry. It was not till another eighteen months had passed that the Allied ' Deconcentration ' experts published the nature of these requirements. Krupp was no longer to be an amalgamation-king, but his private fortune, estimated to be worth from forty-five to fifty millions sterling was to be returned to him intact.

The male Jews were employed, where possible, on the excavation of six enormous underground hangars, the so-called Dorsch project. Fritz Schmelter, as a witness in the Milch trial, believed that there really[53b] were a hundred thousand of them, in spite of the Field-Marshal's assertion, and that ten thousand soldiers had to be withdrawn from the Russian front to act as guards. So, too, Himmler informed Gabor Vajna, the Hungarian Minister for Interior, when he visited him in the following December. The Hungarian Jews, Himmler declared, had made it possible to increase the Jaeger plan for fighter aircraft by forty per cent.[54]

At Muehldorf, Kauffering, Schwarzheide, and other aircraft factory sites there were indeed Hungarian Jews at work in 1944, but the truth is that the starved and debilitated survivors of the Carpathian ghettoes completely succumbed to the working conditions of these underground hells. One group, according to Christopher Burney, were returned to Buchenwald and then dispatched to Auschwitz for gassing. The majority, however, of the 'selected' Hungarian Jews were merely shuffled from camp to camp to end up in April, 1945, in the holocausts of Belsen and the Buchenwald 'Little Camp.'[*]

We know something of the fate of those who got no further than Birkenau, though the evidence is somewhat conflicting. In February Major Richard Baer succeeded the relatively mild Artur Liebehenschel as commandant at Auschwitz. As early as April Dr. Lingens-Reiner learnt that the Hungarian action was in preparation from the *Lageraelteste*, Heinrich Schuster. Apparently the Birkenau camp commandant, the Austrian Captain Hartjenstein, was unable[54a] to face it. It is at least certain that on May 15th he was exchanged with the commandant of Natzweiler, the 'Beast of Belsen,' Josef Kramer, who had no scruples about attending selections. But the action proved to be of such magnitude that these changes were not enough. Early in June Hoess returned from Oranienburg as 'garrison commander.' Though nominally stationed in Auschwitz for

[*]Wing-Commander Yeo-Thomas, who worked in Rehmsdorf camp, a *Nebenlager* of Buchenwald, between November, 1944, and April, 1945, described it as a 'Jewish extermination camp,' though officially it supplied Jewish workers for the 'Jaeger plan.' (Bruce Marshall, *The White Rabbit*, London, 1952, page 231, etc.)

the next four months, Hoess circulated between Auschwitz and Budapest, keeping contact with Eichmann, and the Hungarian deportation programme had the code name 'Aktion Hoess.'

In April, 1944, there had been a still more significant change. A branch line of the railway was laid between the zones of wire that separated the male and female camps. Thus the debarkation point was advanced to within 200 yards of the crematoria. From the sewing block in the women's camp the whole apparatus of selection could be seen, the girls' orchestra,* the flowering plants, and the commando of elderly women who had to undress the babies[55] (see pages 110 and 151). The strength of the two Jewish special commandos which served the gas chambers was increased from the 224 men, who were entered on the camp books on May 11th, to at least 860.[56] The 'Canada' commando, which sorted the loot, was also increased and most of the former Birkenau village was adapted for additional warehouses.[57] Nevertheless, the mechanism was quite inadequate to deal with the daily arrivals of 12,000 to 14,000 Jews, which occurred between May 15th and 24th.

According to Hoess's statement and the findings of the Polish Judicial Commission, the four new crematoria could deal with 12,000 bodies a day, but this seems to have been a purely theoretical claim.[58] Hoess also declared that it was only on one occasion (apparently not till July) that the gas chambers ever absorbed more than 10,000 victims.[59] At this period the true capacity of all four crematoria, working together, had not yet been tested and it was found wanting (see page 150). It was not possible to gas the usual two-thirds or three-quarters proportion of such gigantic numbers. Thus at first Birkenau camp became choked with deportees from Hungary, who were not entered on

---

*The 'Tango of Death' which, in the narratives of so many Auschwitz survivors, greeted the deportees at the selection point, may have a more prosaic explanation. Dr. Ella Lingens-Reiner writes that the girls' orchestra was created by the Vienna conductress Alma Rosée, who died in the Birkenau Frauenlager in the winter of 1943. At the time of the Hungarian deportations, this orchestra used to play light music on the lawn outside the women's infirmary on two afternoons a week. On several occasions she saw the deportees listening to this music as their train was slowly shunted past. (Prisoners of Fear, London, 1948, page 72.)

the strength but remained waiting transfer to other camps. They filled the new women's section, CII or 'Mexico,' the half-completed men's section, BIII, and parts of the old camp, which became 'two-thirds Hungarian.' Dr. Nyiszli declares that there were habitually 50,000 Hungarian Jewesses in 'Mexico' alone.[60]

Gradually, as the mass of arrivals diminished, the gas chambers claimed their normal quota. Huge additional burning-pits were dug, adjoining the crematorium buildings. 'The White House,' one of the two original gas chambers or 'Little Houses' of 1942 (*see page 104*), was put into commission as a despoiling station for a new shooting-place in the woods.[61] By such supplementary means a death output was maintained exceeding 6,000 a day, but it proved difficult to conceal the cremations in the open air, the flames and smoke from which were seen by the entire camp for weeks. Once the incoming Hungarian transport saw a lorryload of half-burnt bodies.[62] The powers of the camp were worried. On June 16th Hoess, Maurer, and Oswald Pohl discussed the advisability of three new crematorium buildings. In the meantime the camouflage screen of tree trunks which hid the gas chambers was to be doubled.[63] Nevertheless, the handiwork of one camp inmate has survived, who photographed the blazing corpse trenches with the special commando at work.[64]

Hoess's estimate that 400,000 Hungarian Jews were gassed in the summer of 1944, though the lowest of such estimates made in the camp, is too high; but it seems absolutely certain that 250,000 to 300,000 were gassed or shot in this record season of the death factory and all in the space of 46 days. Sometimes news from Auschwitz reached the outer world. On March 19th a courier of the Polish resistance group, PPS, had been arrested in Hungary carrying dispatches from inside the camp, while on April 7th the two Slovak authors of the War Refugee Board report made their sensational escape from Birkenau to Bratislava.[65] Yet news of the annihilation of Hungarian Jewry was slow in leaking through, and it was not till the beginning of July, when they had almost ceased, that the Allied and neutral press reported the massive gassings. Had this happened sooner, 200,000 Jews or more might not have left Hungary.

3. End of the Auschwitz Deportations

The deportation of Hungarian Jewry stopped when it was rather more than half-completed. Partly this was because the Regent Horthy, threatened by the Allies and entreated by the neutral powers and his own clergy, dug in his toes; partly it was because Himmler struggled against Hitler and Kaltenbrunner in an effort to sell the Jews he was ordered to kill.

Hungarian resistance stiffened as the deportations began to threaten Western Hungary and Budapest. It was the old terrible story. The 'Galician Jews,' alien and isolationist, speaking Yiddish and living in ghettoes, were nobody's business. They were mere ballast to throw out to appease the Germans, whereas even Baky, Endre, and Ferencsy hesitated to sacrifice the 'Magyarised' Jews. But Eichmann never intended to rest content with the 50,000 Jews from the Budapest region who had been offered by Horthy and Sztojay. Von Thadden, reporting on May 26th on his visit to Budapest, wrote that the whole Jewish population was to be collected a month hence on a Danube island,[66] though the Jewish Council still believed in the assurances that deportation was only reserved for Eastern Jews. Von Thadden himself did not feel happy about it. On 'D day,' June 6th, he suggested that, if the invasion turned out to be a full-scale affair, it would be better to deal with the Budapest Jews at once while the Allied press had no space for them.[67]*

*It was not only von Thadden who was concerned over the implication of D day upon the Final Solution. Von Thadden had sponsored on behalf of the Foreign Office a grandiose project of Rosenberg's, an international anti-Jewish Congress, meeting in Cracow, where representatives of all Axis and satellite Governments were to swear an oath in the ancient Wawel Castle to remove all Jewry from Europe. On June 12th Martin Bormann wrote to Rosenberg from the Fuehrer's headquarters:

'Yesterday I passed your letter of the 7th to the Fuehrer, who has instructed me to tell you that in these days, when the great destinies of the nation are at stake, the congress may by every evidence pass unnoticed. The Fuehrer therefore wishes me to see that you refrain from calling this congress till further orders.'

Rosenberg nevertheless issued his invitations on June 28th for a congress which was to meet on September 5th. The guests were to include John Amery and the Mufti of Jerusalem. The project was not abandoned till a month later. (IMT, PS 3319 and PS 1752, Max Weinreich, *Hitler's Professors*, pages 223-233.)

The Wilhelmstrasse may have had misgivings, but the Hungarian Ministry for Interior was still taking orders from the Eichmann commando through Veesenmayer and Winkelmann, so on June 15th the Jewish community of Budapest had to move into 2,681 specially assigned houses—a fourteenth part of the space for a fifth of the city's population. The 'Star Houses' were not grouped in a ghetto, since BBC broadcasts had persuaded the town council that this would invite discriminatory bombing.[68] Thus the next move was a series of decrees and street-bans designed to confine the Jews to their new quarters. This was the first step towards the round-ups which began in the first days of July in the suburbs west of the Danube, whence some 17,500 Jews were collected in Budakalacz barracks. But after all these preparations only one solitary train left for Auschwitz on July 8th. The unexpected had happened. Alleging that Baky was plotting to replace the Regent, General Lakatos had succeeded on that day in disarming the Budapest *gendarmerie,* and Messrs. Baky and Endre had not found it advisable to defy Horthy's order which sent them on long leave.[69]

Thus at last the torpid, senile figure of Horthy had been roused into some action, and perhaps the person most responsible for this was the Papal Nuncio, Mgr. Angelo Rotta, who had warned Sztojay on the first day of the deportations that the whole world knew what they really signified. On June 25th Mgr. Rotta delivered Horthy a letter which, though evasively worded, was nevertheless a protest from the Pope. This probably carried more weight than the remonstrances of the Hungarian bishops, who attacked less the principle of the deportations than the cruelties that accompanied them. The pastoral letter of Archbishop Cardinal Prince Seredi, for instance, was a long-winded affair, which failed to name the deportations for what they really were. Its publication was delayed and finally withdrawn on July 8th on an assurance that the Budapest deportation had been countermanded.[70] This and other evidence, collected by Eugene Levai, suggests that the bishops were only ready to exert their power from the pulpit when deportation threatened the Magyarised Jews, among whom there were many converts. Nor should it be forgotten that the uninhibited collaboration of the *gendarmerie* would have been impossible, if the church in

Hungary had consistently denounced anti-semitism in the past.

Since his virtual arrest at Klessheim in March, Horthy had permitted a Ministry, which had been thrust upon him, to pass decrees to which he gave no personal assent in the hope that public opinion might destroy it. As early as the middle of June Horthy had tentatively offered the premiership to General Lakatos, whose pacifist leanings had caused the Germans to demand his dismissal from the command of the First Army.[71] To Lakatos the moment seemed not yet ripe, but on June 21st the members of Sztojay's Cabinet were extremely critical of a report rendered by Endre concerning the deportations. This, combined with the Pope's letter, emboldened Horthy on the 26th to attack General Faragho in council and to demand the recall of Baky and Endre.[72]

The Pope's letter was the beginning of a world-wide bombardment of the Regent's conscience. On the 26th Mr. Cordell Hull delivered a note through the Swiss Legation threatening reprisals against those responsible for the deportations.[73] Sztojay immediately circularised all legations that the deportations differed in no wise from normal foreign labour service in the Reich. Confronted with this situation at next day's Cabinet meeting, Jaross at first threatened to resign and then agreed to exempt converted Jews, a proposal which he conveyed to Mgr. Rotta, but not apparently to Veesenmayer.[74]

The Cordell Hull note was followed by the concrete proposals of the King of Sweden to assist the Hungarian Jews to emigrate (*see page 441*), proposals which were conveyed through M. Raoul Wallenberg, a young man of immense courage, whose mission was to bring him martyrdom. The King's proposals were followed on July 5th by a personal appeal to Horthy from Professor Karl Burckhardt, President of the International Red Cross:

> ' The matters brought to our knowledge seem to us so utterly contrary to the chivalrous traditions of the great Hungarian people that it is difficult for us to credit even a tithe of the information we are receiving. In the name of the ICRC I venture to beg Your Highness to give instructions enabling us to reply to these rumours and accusations.'[75]

Horthy did not answer, but two days later Anthony Eden and Brendan Bracken declared in the House of Commons that '700,000 to 1,000,000 Hungarian Jews' were in process of extermination. The announcement followed on the belated action of the Swiss Government in releasing this accumulation of news from the censorship ban and it is said that Horthy himself read a Swiss newspaper article on the subject which was shown him by his son.[76] Furthermore, on July 14th Mr. Cordell Hull repeated his threat of reprisals in a public broadcast.[77]

It was under this spur that Horthy finally replied to Professor Burckhardt, though not till August 12th and in surprisingly non-committal language[78]:

> ' It is unfortunately not in our power to prevent inhuman acts which no one condemns more severely than my people, whose thoughts and feelings are chivalrous. I have instructed the Hungarian Government to take up the settlement of the Jewish question in Budapest. It is hoped that this settlement will not give rise to serious complications.'

The ambivalence of these sentences is easily explained. Although Horthy had been moved to fight the Fuehrer Order at the beginning of July, he had not dared defy the Germans by removing Sztojay and Jaross from office even after Lakatos's *coup de main* of the 8th. Budapest was still terrorised by the *Einsatzgruppe*. In the barracks at Csepel and Kistarcsa Eichmann could dispose of 150 men, and he used them on the 14th to put 1,450 Jews from Kistarcsa camp on to the Auschwitz train, though, fortunately, Horthy was able to transmit orders through Jaross to stop the train at Hatvan. Nevertheless, two further trains, organised by Eichmann, slipped through on July 19th and 24th and reached Birkenau, where they added 2,000 or 3,000 more victims to the recorded figures.[79] Sztojay was thus put in an intolerable position, for on the 8th he had told the Nuncio, Mgr. Rotta, and the Primate Seredi that the Budapest transports had been cancelled.[80]

Ribbentrop found it necessary to administer his spiritual assistance. He told Veesenmayer to warn Horthy 'not to be frightened by ridiculous Jewish American threats which are well known to us.' Horthy must be told of ' Hitler's utmost surprise ' that he should dream of recalling the Sztojay Government or arresting Endre and Baky. Unless the Sztojay Government was confirmed in office and the deportations resumed forthwith, Ribbentrop 'would recall Veesenmayer and safeguard the interests of the Reich as on March 19th,' and in any case two German armoured brigades would be transferred to Hungary.[81]

Veesenmayer reported back 'Instructions carried out, 5 p.m., July 17th.' Thus Sztojay's Cabinet remained in office and Horthy did not dare appoint Lakatos Premier till August 29th, that is a week after the surrender of Rumania, when Russian divisions were streaming into Transylvania. Nevertheless, after Sztojay's dismissal, Kaltenbrunner thought fit to denounce Veesenmayer, who 'had failed to take any forceful steps to carry out the Fuehrer's instructions for a Hungarian Government unconditionally sympathetic to Germany.'[82]

Veesenmayer might have been excused that failure. In the last six weeks of the Sztojay Government it was not only Hungarian politicians who tried to do a deal with the Allies, but the German SS itself. For all these protests from the outer world had rekindled in Himmler's breast his most characteristic dream that international charity could be harnessed to the waning German war effort. And to realise that dream there was the Eichmann commando, which, ever since its arrival in Hungary, had been bargaining with Jewish lives.

4. The Hungarian Jews for Sale

It began with the entry of the German troops into Hungary on March 19th, when Ferenc Chorin and Baron Moric Kornfeld, partners in the great Manfred Weiss steel combine, were discovered hiding in a monastery. They were taken as hostages to Vienna, where they were able to negotiate the emigration of 45 members of the directing families. In return the SS economic office, WVHA, obtained over the heads of the Hungarian Government a 25-year lease of all the Manfred Weiss-controlled plants. The deal was said to have been an inspiration of Herbert Goering, brother to the *Reichsmarschall*.[83] 'I shall have to account for this *Schweinerei* with Jaross,' Eichmann told Dr. Kastner,[84] and indeed it was harder to acquire Jewish property under the jealous eyes of the Hungarian Government than to get it from abroad—even from enemy countries. The accommodating Herr Dieter Wisliceny, whose transactions with the *Vaadah* in Bratislava have already been noticed (*pages 391, 418, and 423*), was contacted by the Budapest Jewish delegates. On April 5th he received Joel Brand and Dr. Reszoe Kastner, representatives of the Joint Distribution Committee, in the flat of one Winninger, a secret service man employed in Admiral Canaris's *Ausland-Abwehr.* Wisliceny declared that nothing less than the ransom of 100,000 Jews was worth discussing and he proposed a cautionary deposit of two million dollars. A small portion was collected and handed over, but now the members of Eichmann's commando began to shift their ground and to betray the fact that they were not authorised to negotiate.[85] A month was wasted by the *Vaadah* chasing Wisliceny and Krumey, who were at work in the Carpathians ; then, on May 5th, Eichmann sent for Joel Brand, to whom he made an astounding proposition. Brand was to be taken to Istanbul in order to transmit to the Allies an offer to trade the Hungarian Jews for heavy lorries. For a fortnight the whole of Hungarian Jewry would be guarded alive in Germany ' in suspense.'[86]

This crazy mission actually left Vienna on May 19th, when the corpse trenches at Birkenau were already blazing day and night. Brand was accompanied by Colonel Kurt Becher, ' Chief of the Economic Staff of the Field SS, Budapest.' This person, who signed a number of valuable Nuremberg affidavits, played a part not only in persuading Himmler to bargain with the surviving Jews, but also in getting the Fuehrer Order rescinded and in saving the inmates of concentration camps from destruction by the SS at the end of the war. Becher, whom we shall come across frequently, had already had experience in acquiring Jewish property for the SS. A salesman in a Hamburg firm of grain merchants, he became in the summer of 1942—when he was 33 years old—principal horse buyer for the SS personnel department under the jockey-general Fegelein, the brother-in-law of Hitler's mistress, Eva Braun. It was Becher who negotiated the famous Schelderhann stud-farm from the Jewish Baron von Oppenheim, whom he enabled to emigrate.[87] It was Becher who negotiated with the Manfred Weiss combine, and finally it was Becher who, in the guise of buying horses in Hungary for the *Waffen* SS, reported to Himmler the progress of Eichmann's negotiations with Joel Brand. Dr. Kastner considers that Becher obtained private access to Himmler as a protégé of Major-General Schellenberg, whose bizarre belief that the Allies might entertain peace proposals from Himmler was beginning about this time to tickle the *Reichsfuehrer's* fancy.

Although Becher boasted in the Nuremberg witness-box—and perhaps with some reason—that the American magazine *Time* had credited him with saving 200,000 Jewish lives,[88] on this occasion his presence as a colonel on the SS Supreme Staff ruined the chances of Brand's mission. Brand wandered hopelessly about the Near East. He tried to contact the War Refugee Board in Istanbul and the British Embassy in Ankara, and then he made an attempt to reach Palestine to appeal to the Jewish Agency. Thereupon he was arrested by the British Military Intelligence at the Turkish-Syrian border and interned, but he was allowed to see Mr. Moshe Shertok (Sharett) of the Jewish Agency, who transmitted his proposals to London. These were naturally rejected, but in the interests of propaganda they were released to the press on July 18th, when, it appeared, Himmler had asked for 10,000 lorries to be shipped to Salonika 'for use only in Hungary.'[89]

Although after this revelation Veesenmayer still pretended that the negotiations were going on satisfactorily and that the British story had been published only to fool the Russians,[90] Eichmann had written off the Brand plan as early as June 9th, when he told Kastner that, if he had no answer in three days, he would 'let the mills grind at Auschwitz.' Kastner, aware that they had been grinding since May 15th, submitted a new proposal, the purchase of 100,000 Jewish lives for five million Swiss francs. Five days later Eichmann named Himmler's terms: 30,000 physically fit Jews from the still untouched Western Hungarian community could be 'kept on ice' at Strasshof, an Austrian labour camp, at the price of 200 dollars a head, in addition to the cost of their maintenance.[91] Krumey had devised the plan and Becher had transmitted it to Himmler. Actually, only enough money was raised to keep 9,000 of this number 'on ice,' mostly from towns west of

the Theiss, Szeged, Debreczen, Kecskemet, Gyor, and Komorom.*
These 9,000 Jews bought no privileges for their money.
According to Kastner, Eichmann amused himself by substituting
the Auschwitz and Strasshof trains.[92] And there is an ominous
letter written by Kaltenbrunner on June 30th to his friend Karl
Blaschke, *Buergermeister* of Vienna, in which he declares that
only 3,600 of the first 12,000 Jews in Strasshof camp are likely to
be fit for labour. As to the remainder . . .:

> ' The women and children among these Jews, who are
> unable to work and who are all being kept in readiness for
> special action, and will therefore one day be removed again,
> must stay in the camp during the day.'[93]

Significantly, Kaltenbrunner went on to say that details were
to be discussed with Krumey of Eichmann's commando, who was
now in Vienna—the very man who was credited with this plan
to save Jewish lives.

One transport of 1,684 Jews, which was directed nominally
to Strasshof on June 29th, had a less ambiguous fate. It turned
up nine days later in the ' Exchange Camp ' Bergen-Belsen. It
consisted of families from Cluj and other former Rumanian towns
who had been saved from the Auschwitz train at the last moment
as certified emigrants for Palestine. In Budapest they were kept
in a row of guarded houses in the Columbus Street, where, in
addition to signing away their property, they were forced to
procure 1,000 dollars a head in U.S.A. currency. Since the Hungarian Government were as jealous of Himmler's business profits
as his German rivals, Eichmann had to hide all this from
Kaltenbrunner's *Ausland-Abwehr* as well as from Baky and
Endre. He therefore cooked up a story of a dangerous Zionist
conspiracy to account for the confinement in Budapest itself of
Transylvanian Jews, who should have been deported.[94]

The fate of these 1,684 Jews now became of prime importance
to the 250,000 Jews remaining in Hungary. Once the group were
accepted in an Allied or neutral country, a revival of the deportations would become very unlikely. But early in August Becher
brought back the news to the Budapest negotiators that Himmler

*The figures are Wisliceny's (Affidavit C). Kastner gives 18,000 and
Levai 15,000.

was absolutely determined not to leave a single Jew in Europe. It was, however, hinted that, outside of Europe, the Bergen-Belsen Jews might be permitted to go to neutral countries in small groups.[95] In fact, political developments in Hungary were already conspiring to make Himmler reduce his price. There was no longer any possible way of filling up the trains for Auschwitz and, after the dismissal of Jaross, the Hungarian Ministry for Interior refused outright to allow 8,000 Jews to be shipped off from the Budapest labour-conscription companies. It was against this background in the middle of August that the Budapest *Vaadah* learnt from Wisliceny that Himmler favoured sending the remaining Jews to 'a bridge between Hungary and Germany'[96]—a mitigated form of mass-deportation to which the Hungarians in their changed mood might consent.

It appeared that Becher had persuaded Himmler that the Brand negotiations might be resumed through M. Saly Meyer, representing the Joint Distribution Committee in Switzerland. On August 21st, therefore, a token shipment of 318 Jews from Bergen-Belsen was put across the Swiss border at Basel without visas.[97] At the same time Kurt Becher with three SS officers and the hostage, Dr. Kastner, interviewed Saly Meyer at St. Margarethen on the Swiss-Austrian border. Becher offered to suspend the deportations and *stop the gassings,* but the subsequent fate of the Jews must depend on the deliveries of material. But these deliveries were outside M. Meyer's terms of reference and the negotiations could go no further.

There was a second inconclusive meeting on September 1st. Then, on September 28th, M. Meyer offered fifteen million Swiss francs. Kastner proposed that against this payment the Bratislava deportations should be stopped and the projected Hungarian deportations called off, while the remaining Bergen-Belsen Jews should go to Switzerland.[98] But now Becher, who was in Berlin negotiating for the Slovak Jews with Himmler himself (*see page 393*), telegraphed that he was not interested. The fate of the Slovak Jews had been sealed and this, be it remembered, was the moment when Finland, Rumania, and Bulgaria had surrendered. The Allies stood at the very frontiers of Germany, yet Hitler, with the rage of a trapped beast, let the crematorium fires continue burning.

For since the resumption of the Brand plan Eichmann had been busier than ever with deportation measures. A return of clothing for the German concentration camps, dated August 1st, shows that 90,000 Jews were then expected from Hungary.[99] Next day, when Eichmann was sent for by Himmler, the brick works at Bekesmagyar was again got ready as a reception centre for the Budapest Jews. It was believed that the round-up would begin on the 27th,[100] but on the 21st the Corps Diplomatique, headed once more by Mgr. Angelo Rotta, protested strongly to Horthy. The Regent still did not dare send the Germans a categoric 'no,' but Veesenmayer, perhaps on the basis of his own pessimistic reports, perhaps because Himmler wanted to gain time in his struggle with Hitler and Kaltenbrunner, came to terms with Remenyi-Schneider, Jaross's successor at the Ministry for Interior. It was agreed on the 25th that the Ministry should resume entire control of the Jews, provided they were confined to labour camps.[101] Next day the *Einsatzgruppe* left Hungary, though not as it turned out for good. As to Eichmann, he had departed on the 23rd in the depths of depression and was probably in Rumania (*see pages 410-411*), where the situation did not lend itself to German interference in any form, least of all in the shape of deportations of Jews.

On August 29th Horthy at last dismissed Sztojay and appointed General Lakatos as Premier. The Regent at once assured Samuel Stern, President of the Jewish Council, that there would be no deportations from Budapest and no universal commitment to labour camps.[102] On September 22nd General Faragho's armistice-mission left for Moscow. On October 9th M. Molotov's terms were received and the Russians halted on an agreed line, which at Kecskemet passed within 50 miles of Budapest. The threat to the lives of the Hungarian Jews seemed about to vanish as it had vanished in Rumania—but the Germans still had another card to draw from the pack.

5. The Last Deportation and the Fall of Budapest

Dramatic as were the events of October 15th, 1944, the true element of surprise was lacking, since the Germans knew that Horthy would announce a surrender to Russia and Horthy knew that he was in the Germans' power. As far back as September 7th General Lakatos had decided to ask for five German divisions, hoping that the failure to provide them would justify a Hungarian capitulation. But the Germans produced four of the required divisions and they kept them, not in Transylvania, where the front had dissolved, but west of the Theiss and near Budapest.[103] Nevertheless, it was absolutely essential for the Germans to secure Horthy alive and to obtain his sanction—as Regent for a non-existent monarchy—to the nomination of a pro-German Cabinet. For this there was now only one choice of parties, the by no means popular or representative *Nyilaas* or 'Arrow Cross' Fascists.

Three conspiracies were set on foot. Hardly had Horthy announced his surrender to Russia in a Sunday morning broadcast, when Veesenmayer arrived with Rudolf Rahn, the German plenipotentiary to Mussolini. Horthy was informed that his son Nicholas was a Gestapo hostage, having been trapped into meeting an alleged agent of Marshal Tito. This was none other than Himmler's kidnapping expert, Otto Skorzeny,[104] who carried him off with two alleged Russian agents rolled up in carpets. Horthy was also told by the two plenipotentiaries that von dem Bach-Zalewski, the victor over the Warsaw rebels, was on his way to batter in the Hofberg Palace with 42 Tiger tanks,* and that they, Veesenmayer and Rahn, had already persuaded Major Szalasy to form a new National Assembly at Estergom from the Arrow Cross Party. Rahn then relented to the extent of allowing Horthy 24 hours for an answer, and he even offered to persuade the Wehrmacht to withdraw beyond the Reich frontier.[105] Finally,

---

*In a singularly bragging statement to the British Press, Skorzeny, now a resident of Spain, has assumed the credit not only for the kidnapping of Nicholas Horthy, but for the assault on the Hofberg, which, he declared, saved a million German lives. But even if Horthy had succeeded in persuading the Hungarian generals to surrender, the four German divisions could certainly have escaped into Austria, and, in fact, the German counterattack, which drove the Russians temporarily from Pest, was bad strategy and a fruitless waste of lives.

Skorzeny was present at Hitler's headquarters with Ribbentrop, Himmler, Keitel, and Jodl when the *coup de main* in Hungary was decided. The resumption of the deportation of Hungarian Jewry was surely one of the subjects on the agenda, but on this matter 'the toughest man alive' is conveniently discreet. (Interview with Charles Foley, *Daily Express*, April 17th, 1952.)

Horthy agreed to nominate the Szalasy Government if his son was restored to him. Horthy and Lakatos were then driven off in a car for internment in Germany.

On November 2nd, before these events reacted on the battle-front, the Russians gained a temporary footing in the suburbs of Pest, thus freeing a certain number of Jews from danger, but some 200,000 living in Budapest or west of the Danube stayed under the yoke of the Arrow Cross and the Germans. Moreover, Gabor Vajna, the new Minister for Interior, had sworn to carry out the deportations without exemption or foreign protection.[106] Ferencsy was in charge and before the end of the month Huensche of the Eichmann commando returned to Budapest. Even at the end of June the outlook had not seemed blacker, but there was a difference. The Szalasy Government was the feeblest possible. Led by a crazy tub-thumper, it was despised by the Germans and unrecognised abroad. It had no standing in the country and it could not control its own 'Green Shirt' blackguards. Nor were its acts as murderous as it words.

As far back as April 26th the Swiss Legation had sponsored a plan for helping Jews to emigrate to Palestine. After the King of Sweden's intervention with Horthy, this plan was taken over by the Red Cross, who declared in Geneva on July 18th that the Germans had agreed to 40,000 exit permits. This was rather quickly explained away by Veesenmayer, who told Ribbentrop that it was only a question of 7,000 and that Eichmann was going to deport the Budapest Jews so suddenly that the formalities would not be completed in time. In reality, Veesenmayer had discussed the plan seriously with Winkelmann, the Higher SS and Police Leader, but Eichmann, perceiving that this was going to interfere with Himmler's secret negotiations, ruled that the Jews were 'important biological material' who could not be spared.[107]

However, under the short-lived Lakatos Government the Swiss, Swedish, Spanish, and Portuguese Consulates were allowed to register prospective emigrants as under their protection. Since the capitulation of Rumania the road to Palestine was closed, but Mr. Cordell Hull, U.S. Secretary of State, had offered to assist any neutral countries willing to take the emigrants. In the mean-time Horthy granted extra-territoriality to the Red Cross, who took over the houses in which these Jews were concentrated.[108]

At the time of Horthy's arrest there were 15,000 registered Jewish emigrants, whose certificates Gabor Vajna threatened to annul, but was later ordered to confirm. This was because Veesenmayer had informed Szalasy that the German Government would honour the 8,400 exemptions from deportation, conferred by the Sztojay Government. Germany wanted the new Hungarian Government to be protected from attacks in the foreign press.[109] Yet, when the Swiss Red Cross offered to provide the trains, Veesenmayer took refuge behind a Security Police ruling that there could be no railway transit through the Reich.[110] Thereafter Veesenmayer found repeated pretexts for delaying the departure of the Swiss-protected Jews till it was too late to break the Russian encircling ring. The negotiation was doomed by the simple fact that the SS, through whom alone the Jews could be moved, was not offered the Jews' property.

In the end, however, the Swiss Red Cross plan saved many thousands of Jews from the dangers of chaotic deportation because the Szalasy Government never openly repudiated the emigration scheme even after the Germans had made sure that it could not be carried out. Moreover, since it became impossible to distinguish between real and forged consular certificates, the number of protected Jews rose from 15,000 to 33,000, all living in ' Red Cross ' houses.[111]

On November 2nd, when the Russians were in the suburbs, the Jewish labour companies were withdrawn west of the Danube as a security measure. This apparently innocent manœuvre was followed on the 8th by an indiscriminate expulsion of Budapest Jews, who, regardless of age and sex, were marched 120 miles to the now notorious reception camp at Strasshof near Vienna. Thus began the last mass-deportation of free Jewry in Hitler's Europe, a story which reveals the quite open conflict now being waged between Himmler, Schellenberg, and Becher on the one hand, and the team, Kaltenbrunner, Mueller, and Eichmann, on the other.

Three days before this march Becher had had an interview in Zurich with Mr. Roswell Maclelland of the U.S. War Refugees Board, from whom he learnt that Mr. Cordell Hull had allowed five of the twenty million Swiss francs, which had been collected by the Joint Distribution Committee, to be transferred to

Switzerland. Thereupon Becher gave an assurance to M. Saly Meyer that non-workers would not be deported from Budapest, that Jews in concentration camps would have the protection of international law, and that, though all Jews capable of bearing arms would have to leave Budapest, the screening would be done by the Red Cross.[112]

This promise was totally violated. Men up to sixty years of age as well as 15,000 women were conscripted for the Jewish labour companies, while half the civilians deported to Strasshof had emigration certificates. Wisliceny told Kastner that 1,200 people died on this seven-day march, including women aged eighty,[113] and that Eichmann only stopped sending small children after Becher had flown off to Himmler. Becher, it seems, was not able to persuade Himmler to stop the deportation, but Himmler at least agreed to send Lieut-General Max Juettner of the 'Leadership Office' of the SS, together with Hoess of Auschwitz, who was now deputy inspector of concentration camps. They were to watch the march and report back. Years later at Nuremberg Juettner described what he found[114]:

> 'Two-thirds of the way to Budapest we saw columns of Jewish women up to sixty years old, escorted by Honved guards. There were many stragglers lying in the road in the intervals between the columns. Winkelmann told me he was powerless in the matter and would be grateful if I would take it up. I was told that the responsible man was Eichmann. I was aware that I might incur disagreeable consequences in sending for him, but he was not in Budapest, so I saw a captain whose name I do not recall and told him his business. He said he was not under my orders and I threatened to inform Himmler in order that this wrong which cried to heaven should be put right. Three days later I sent Himmler a strong report—apparently without result.'

Unfortunately, Juettner's report reached Himmler together with the news that Mr. Stettinius, successor to Cordell Hull, had cancelled the transfer of five million francs to Switzerland. Consequently, Himmler postponed making a decision on the total abandonment of deportations till he had heard again from M. Saly Meyer.[115] This explains why Eichmann was allowed to return to Budapest on November 23rd, uncurbed and furious over 'the impressions of certain gentlemen who were not in a position to judge whether people, who had been seven or eight days on the road, would be treated as fit for work or otherwise.' Only 38,000 Jewish workers had been provided for the 'South-East Wall,' Eichmann said, in place of the 70,000 promised by Szalasy. Nevertheless, he would stop press-ganging the holders of forged certificates if 20,000 Jews came forward voluntarily. As to Wisliceny, who had returned large numbers of the sick to Budapest, he would bring him before a court-martial.[116]

On November 29th Geschke, the commander of the German Security Police in Budapest, demanded a further 17,000 Jewish workers. They were allowed to travel to the Austrian border by train,[117] but Eichmann now threatened to deport every Jew in Budapest if the twenty million francs were not paid over. Becher had therefore to use a subterfuge. He cabled Eichmann from Switzerland that the first five million francs had been deposited, but that the Allies insisted on the delivery of the rest of the 1,684 Bergen-Belsen Jews. The subterfuge worked. On December 6th a huge train steamed into Bregenz bringing 1,368 Jews, including Kastner's family.[118]

Although Himmler did not get his five million francs till February, the deportations ceased. M. Raoul Wallenberg, the special envoy of the King of Sweden, reported on December 8th that 40,000 people had been deported, only 15,000 of whom were enrolled labourers.[119]* But a further 15,000 had been rescued by the agents of the neutral Powers, the Red Cross, and the Papal Nuncio. These had returned to Budapest, for Eichmann had few German guards at his disposal and had to rely on the easy-going Hungarian militia.

Before December 28th, when the Russians completed the encirclement of Budapest, Kaltenbrunner and Eichmann made one more attempt to sabotage Himmler's plan. At some time before December 15th Kaltenbrunner received Gabor Vajna in person and told him that trains would be available to resume the deportations. For another fortnight Vajna was pestered by

---

*As against Eichmann's 38,000 and Wallenberg's 40,000, Wisliceny estimated at the first Nuremberg trial that there were 30,000, mostly women (IMT III, 286).

Eichmann, 'who was always impertinent and insisted that he had the German might, and especially Kaltenbrunner, behind him.' But Eichmann's threats to seize the children and the aged could now be ignored without incurring those 'disagreeable consequences' that were so recently the terror of SS generals on Himmler's own staff.[120]

Only a small proportion of the 30,000 or 40,000 deportees to Austria returned to Hungary after the war. Wisliceny stated that they were completely emaciated and exhausted after their march and that it was because of his disobedience in sending the worst cases back to Budapest that he was transferred in the following January to another department of the Gestapo.[121] Two-thirds of the Jews who reached Strasshof, mostly women, were distributed at once among the German concentration camps. At Ravensbrueck Mme Vaillant-Couturier saw what happened next[122]:

'There was no longer any room left in the blocks, where the prisoners already slept four in a bed, so there was raised in the middle of the camp a large tent. Straw was spread in the tent and the Hungarian women were brought there. Their condition was deplorable. There were a great many cases of frozen feet, because they had been evacuated from Budapest and had walked a good part of the way in the snow. A great many of them had died *en route*. . . . One day I passed the tent as it was being cleaned and I saw a pile of smoking manure in front of it. I suddenly realised that this manure was human excrement, since the unfortunate women no longer had the strength to drag themselves to the latrines.'

The 10,000 Hungarian Jews, who remained on the Austrian border to dig and quarry for the 'South-East Wall,' which covered Vienna, fared no better. Like the Hungarian Jewesses, digging along the 'Eastern Wall' in Prussia and Poland, they were expendable and worked in conditions of atrocious neglect. In March M. Georges Dunand found the Vienna Jewish Hospital reduced almost to Belsen conditions by the stream of invalids from the camps on the South-East Wall.[123] At the end of that

month Becher tried to persuade Himmler to allow the survivors
to fall into Russian hands, but Himmler was in trouble at this
time because Hitler had received the reports of the freeing of
the Bergen-Belsen Jews in Switzerland. He therefore declared
that the Jews must be marched to Mauthausen camp on foot
(*see page 462*). Baldur von Schirach remembered at Nuremberg
that Himmler had ordered him to treat them well. 'They are my
soundest investment.'[124] About 3,000 Jews, young labourers from
the quarrying camps, were seen by Kastner passing through
Vienna on foot—possibly the only survivors.[125]

It remains to describe briefly the fate of those Jews who were
left in Budapest during the Russian siege of December 28th-
January 17th. After deducting the Jews who 'went underground'
and those who had been deported, there remained over 95,000
recognised Jews in the twin cities. About 63,000 possessing no
protection certificates, were moved after November 29th into an
enclosed ghetto which contained only 162 apartment-houses.[126]
Into this crawling hive of misery Vajna tried a month later to
remove the children's orphanages. The Red Cross, supported by
the Nuncio and the Corps Diplomatique, succeeded in stopping
this and they were equally successful, thanks to the efforts of
Raoul Wallenberg, at the beginning of January, when Vajna
proposed to move in the 33,000 Jews of the 'protected houses.'
At this time the ghetto inhabitants were reduced to a plate of
watery soup a day. But in some respects the 'protected houses'
were worse off, for the Arrow Cross looters regarded their
inhabitants as people of property.[127]

Pest was entered by the Russians on January 16th and 17th,
Buda not till four weeks later. To hunger and bombardment
during the siege were added the terrors of anarchy, which
weighed heaviest on the scapegoat community and which cost
thousands of lives. A few days before the siege began Eichmann
made a brief appearance, when he tried to discover and arrest
the Jewish Council. In this he failed,[128] but there still remained
enough SS during the siege to do his work, and the two most
energetic members of the Jewish Council, Otto Komoly and Janos
Gabor, were executed. Moreover, on the eve of the fall of Pest
a plot was concocted between the German Security Service and
the Arrow Cross leadership to liquidate the ghetto. M. Levai

claims that this was frustrated by General Schmidthuber of the *Feldherrnhalle* Armoured Division.[129]

Capitulation did not end the troubles of the Jewish community, for the foreign legation staffs and Red Cross representatives, who had done so much to help them, were ordered to leave by the conqueror of Hungary, Marshal Malinovsky, and it became impossible to use the funds allotted by the Joint Distribution Committee.[130] It was on this account that Raoul Wallenberg set off on January 17th with two Russian officers to seek Malinovsky in his headquarters at Hergyeshalom. He was not seen again.*

Under a Communist-dominated Government, the persecutors of Hungarian Jewry suffered less for their crimes than for their political affiliations. Four Prime Ministers, Imredy, Bardossy, Sztojay, and Szalasy, were shot or hanged as well as almost the entire Szalasy Cabinet, including Gabor Vajna. Among 122 death-sentences were those of the four greatest Jew-baiters, Jaross, Baky, Endre, and Ferencsy. Most of these men were tried early in 1946 after a very belated extradition from the American Zone in Germany. The surrender of the former Regent Horthy was not demanded,[132] and he lives to-day, at the age of 84, a free man at Estoril in Portugal. Perhaps no one person in the whole of history ever sacrificed so many lives through mere weakness and indecision.

---

*After some months the Swedish Foreign Office was notified that Wallenberg 'was in good health under Russian protection.' Late in 1946 Stalin promised the Swedish Minister in Moscow a full investigation. Yet, in spite of earlier assurances, the Moscow magazine *New Times* declared in February, 1948, that Wallenberg must have been killed either by SS men on the run or by members of the Arrow Cross.[131]

CHAPTER 17

Jewry in the Break-up of the Third Reich

1. The End of Auschwitz

In July, 1944, the Germans failed to deport the Jewish population of Budapest and the Hungarian Jewish massacres at Auschwitz came to an end. Although this was mainly due to the extremely belated revolt of the Regent Horthy and certain members of the Sztojay Government, German objections may also have played their part. The Economic Office of the SS knew that, in spite of the massive selections at Birkenau, the German concentration camps were reaching saturation point. This became inevitable at the beginning of April or earlier, when Hitler took the decision of manning the new underground aircraft factories of the 'Jaegerplan' with Jews from Greater Hungary. It was a momentous decision, for it completely reversed the decree of October 5th, 1942, which removed all Jews from the German concentration camp system and confined them in Auschwitz or Lublin. Not only were the Hungarian Jews forwarded from the selection siding at Birkenau without being registered on the Auschwitz books, but there also began a movement of Jews from the camp itself into Germany, such as an infirmary staff which left for Wustergiersdorf on May 15th to accompany the first selected batch of Jews from Hungary. The 'Philips group' of radio valve workers left for Reichenbach on July 6th, and the survivors of the Theresienstadt family camp (*see page 171*) left for Schwarzheide and Ravensbrueck on July 3rd. Even the gipsies, who for the past three years had been exterminated scarcely less ruthlessly than the Jews, were now found worthy to work for the Reich. On August 1st the last of the *Zigeunerlager* at Birkenau were dispatched to Buchenwald and Ravensbrueck.[1a]

These gipsies had been brought to Birkenau from the Bialystok region during the Jewish resettlement in January, 1943. After a drastic reduction there remained 4,500 of them, including numerous children, who were left in peace for eighteen months.

Not even the active males did any work, and Nebe, the head of the Criminal Police, recommended the use of the 'half-breed asocials' for human guinea-pig experiments (*see page 188*). A few of the gipsies played in the Birkenau Tzigane orchestra. When the final selection was made for Buchenwald and Ravensbrueck, it was found necessary to gas two thousand of the older gipsies and the children. To the very last the gipsies were ignorant of their fate, though thousands of their race had been shot or gassed in Russia and Poland. It seems that, while in Birkenau, they often expressed their approval of the measures meted out to the Jews.[1b]

The immense increase of the German concentration camp population was halted at the beginning of July, 1944, by the suspension of the deportations from Hungary. But the decision, which Hitler had taken in April regarding the Hungarian Jews, was now extended to the Jews of Poland, a country which could no longer be held. For in that month the Russians reached the Vistula and tens of thousands of Jews from Polish and Russian work camps were added to the Hungarian Jews who had been moved to Germany. For instance, at Stutthof, near Elbing, where 70 per cent of the inmates were Hungarian Jews, more Jews arrived from the hastily evacuated Esthonian and Latvian labour camps, as well as the Jewesses from the Kovno Ghetto (*see page 290*). Similarly, the Jews from Kovno and the Warsaw Ghetto labour camp went to Dachau and those from the Radom province partly to Auschwitz and partly to Buchenwald, where there were already 5,500 Hungarian Jews,[1c] once more building up a population in the infamous 'Little Camp.'

An even greater migration was intended. On August 2nd the concentration camp administration at Oranienburg anticipated that the 524,286 inmates of the concentration camps would be more than doubled. A further 90,000 Jews were expected from Hungary, 400,000 rebel Poles from Warsaw, 60,000 Jews from the Lodz Ghetto, 17,000 Polish officers, transferred from POW camps, and 15,000 members of the French Resistance.[2] As a result of Pohl's objections these plans had to be revised. Less than a quarter the number of Lodz and Budapest Jews were moved into Germany and only a seventh the number of the Aryan Poles. Even so, the population of the concentration camps must have risen that winter beyond 600,000 and this was clearly not the limit, since the forthcoming Russian offensive threatened Upper Silesia and the Czestochowa region, where a further 100,000 Jews lived in labour camps. These were mostly Jews who had survived the Birkenau selections. If they were distributed among Western German camps there would be typhus and other epidemics; if Germany civilians worked with them, they would learn the precise meaning of the Final Solution—and the Allies too. For the same reason Himmler could not hope to sell them abroad as he had sold privileged Jews from Hungary, nor could they be allowed to fall into the hands of the Russians, for we have already seen what rigid orders Kaltenbrunner had distributed during the evacuation of the Polish camps (*see page 300*).

Everything led to the conclusion that the remaining Jews in Poland and Silesia would be simply exterminated, and this seems to have been the belief in Auschwitz, where the Jews could have no idea that there were conflicts in the mind of the arch-persecutor and that Himmler hesitated whether to destroy the gas chambers, even when the crematorium chimneys blazed their biggest. For it was on July 24th, at the height of a new extermination season in Auschwitz, that the Russian discoveries at Lublin concentration camp filled the Allied press. The German guards had indeed tried to evacuate the inmates—they no longer included any Jews—but a Polish resistance committee rallied the last 6,000 who seized the camp and delivered it to the Russians along with the German *Kapos* whom they had caught.[3] They also managed to preserve for the inspection of Allied press correspondents six small cells, which were alleged to be gas chambers, the impressive camp crematorium with its five furnaces and with human bones tastefully displayed in the foreground, 535 drums of Zyklon B gas, and several steel retorts of carbon-monoxide gas. In November this was followed up with a mass trial, at which among others the German *Rapportfuehrer*, or camp marshal, and the crematorium director were sentenced to death.[4]

It is remarkable how many high-placed Germans testified that they had been convinced of the truth of the gas chamber stories only after they had heard or read the Allied revelations on Lublin or Majdanek—a place that was never specifically an extermination

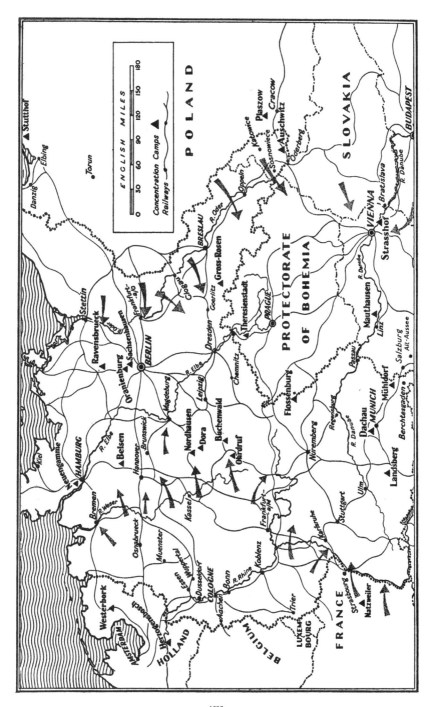

centre. The revelations came, moreover, four days after the plot to murder Hitler, when Himmler was beginning to believe that he might be the person destined to treat with the Allies. For it was from this moment that Himmler began to build up the kind of credit to which he really thought himself entitled at the time of his talks with Count Bernadotte and Dr. Norbert Masur.

In Auschwitz Himmler's shirt of penitence was scarcely noticed, except that in this place of contradictions there were more contradictions than ever. On the one hand the selections and gassings went on till the end of October, merely because in the German bureaucratic grooves there was no other way of disposing of unproductive bodies. On the other hand murder was now occasionally punished and the sick stood some chance of being cured. Furthermore, the number of work commandos increased. By the autumn of 1944 there were at least thirty subsidiary camps, including five collieries and five blast furnaces scattered about Silesia and Sudetenland.[5] These camps, together with the two Bunawerk factories for synthetic petrol and rubber, were known as Auschwitz III, an establishment which grew from 15,000 on April 5th, 1944, to 25,000 on August 21st, and more than 40,000 in October, when the withdrawals began. The entire strength of Auschwitz, Aryan as well as Jewish, rose from 55,600 on August 21st to 90,000 or more,[6*] falling to 64,000 on the eve of evacuation in January, 1945.

The value of the 40,000 Jews in the trained armament commandos, whose health had been better cared for than that of the inmates of the main camps, swayed the balance, for Himmler decided not to massacre them as the Lublin commandos had been massacred on November 3rd, 1943 (see page 298). Moreover, the stimulating personalities, who kept Hitler's mind on the Final Solution, were now less stimulating. Heydrich was dead, Goebbels since July 25th was preoccupied as Reich

---

*In contrast both to this continuous expansion and to the static nature of the old camp, Auschwitz I, the strength of Birkenau, or Auschwitz II, which depended on the arrival of deportation trains, showed the wildest fluctuations: 36,000 men and women on April 5th, 31,000 on ·May 11th, only 19,200 on August 21st, and 30,000 again on October 18th. Between May 11th and August 21st there is a lack of records, but it is probable that during the Hungarian deportations the strength rose to 60,000-70,000 (see page 429).

plenipotentiary for total war, Kaltenbrunner, though as cruel as Himmler, was, like Himmler, wetting his toes in the unpromising waters of negotiated peace. Under such conditions Himmler could indulge his economic instincts more openly and with less fear of delation to Hitler—though not always.

The selections for the gas chamber at Auschwitz ended in October, 1944, but their fate had hung in the balance already in the autumn of 1943, when Georg Konrad Morgen (*see page 124*) was sent there to investigate the gold smuggling that had been traced to the camp. Morgen discovered that the gold came from the selections for the gas chamber. He believed that if he brought a charge against some of the individual murderers in the camp, the official system of mass murder at the crematoria would have to come to light, too. Morgen, therefore, arrested Ernst Graebner, the Political Officer in Auschwitz main camp and the most notorious of the SS executioners. Hereafter Morgen ran into difficulties but he seems to have got further with his alleged plan than might have been expected. Himmler, in sending a criminal investigator like Morgen to Auschwitz, must have known that he would come up against Kaltenbrunner, Nebe and Mueller. One wonders what was the motive. Graebner was not charged till July or August, 1944, and eventually his case was dropped. This maniacal sadist lived to be tried by a 'People's Court' in the Russian sector of Vienna in April, 1946.[7]

Nevertheless, the Reich Security Office was severely shaken by Morgen's visit to Auschwitz. On November 1st, 1943, Graebner was suspended and Hoess's duties were exchanged with those of Artur Liebehenschel, head of the group DI in Pohl's office.[8] Although Liebehenschel only stayed in Auschwitz till February, he instituted many reforms, including a tripartite administration system for the huge group of camps. He stopped the arbitrary executions, punished some of the murderous *Kapos* and *Block-fuehrers* and personally reviewed all disciplinary sentences. With the selections at Birkenau he could not interfere, but it is unlikely that more than three or four transports reached the camp during Liebehenschel's term of office. Throughout occupied Europe the pace of deportation was running down, and but for Hitler's *coup de main* in Hungary in the following month Auschwitz might have ceased to be an extermination centre.[9]

During the Liebehenschel period an incident occurred at Auschwitz whose effects spread far. On January 26th, 1944, a party of 212 Jewish draughtsmen, engravers and printers, survivors of the Dutch and German deportations, left for Sachsenhausen concentration camp, where they were kept in a secret section, directed by Major Bernhard Krueger, the head of 'Amt VI, F4a' of the Main Security Office. This department had been counterfeiting British currency notes since 1940, but it was only when the Sachsenhausen workshop got into stride that the British Government was confronted with the infinite problems of a truly superb issue of five-pound notes.

This strange by-product of the Final Solution survived the war, for in April, 1945, 'Einsatz Bernhard' was transferred to an underground factory at Redl Zipf in Austria. Finally Krueger was told that his 140 surviving counterfeiters must be executed. They were taken to a labour camp at Ebensee, a 'commando' of Mauthausen concentration camp. Krueger disregarded his orders and escaped to Switzerland with a large accumulated private fortune. He has not been found. On the liberation of Ebensee, early in May, the counterfeiters walked out of the camp, well provided with their best handiwork, and about forty were subsequently traced, including Krueger's bookkeeper, the internee Oskar Skala, who provided meticulous information. The Sachenhausen banknotes continue to turn up all over the world, but the real five-pound notes now contain a metal thread.[9a] Recently there have been rumours that survivors of 'Einsatz Bernhard' are at work in Russia.

On July 18th, 1944, the British censorship released the story of the Joel Brand mission (*see page 436*), and it became known to the world that Himmler had tried to sell the bodies of the remaining Jews in Greater Hungary. From this moment the abolition of the gas chamber selections could be expected at any time. In fact it was delayed more than three months.

According to Dr. Kastner it was on August 21st, 1944, that Kurt Becher, in his negotiations with M. Saly Meyer, first offered the abolition of the selections.[10] Something was known about this even in the camp. The internee girl clerks in the staff office believed that the order had gone out on September 2nd, the reason being that the Ministry of Propaganda wanted to conduct an international delegation through the camp to repudiate the Allies' accusations made about Lublin.[11] This is not precisely what happened, but later in September an International Red Cross mission was allowed to interview Baer, Liebehenschel's successor, in his office. ' Of the camp itself (Auschwitz I) we saw only six or eight barracks of red brick.'[12] But the delegation could not help noticing the pale, ashy complexions of the work commandos whom they met on the Silesian roads, or that question from the spokesman of the British POW camp at Monowitz ' whether we knew anything about the very up-to-date shower-baths where the internees were gassed in batches.' It appeared that the spokesman had tried to get information through British soldiers who worked with internees, but that the internees refused to speak.

After the Red Cross visit there was again an improvement in Auschwitz conditions, even in Birkenau where the chances of human survival were once reckoned in weeks. For those not completely broken by a 70-80 hour working week there were even Sunday football matches, concerts, and film shows. The selections were now known as ' going to the pictures,' since it was in the picture theatre that the green cans of Zyklon B were stored.[13] That shadow lingered almost to the last.

On November 26th Becher showed Dr. Kastner a telegram that had just come from Himmler.[14] 'The crematoria at Auschwitz are to be dismantled, the Jews working in the Reich are to get normal Eastern workers' rations. In the absence of Jewish hospitals they may be treated with Aryan patients.' But, according to Becher, Himmler had revoked the Fuehrer Order much earlier. ' Between the middle of September and the middle of October ' Becher had persuaded Himmler to send two copies of an order to Pohl and Kaltenbrunner, making them responsible if subordinate officers failed to stop the liquidation of the Jews.[15] The message, sent to Becher on November 26th, was therefore only a confirmation of an order that had been passed to Mueller and Eichmann and which they had ignored, since in October there were extensive selections at Birkenau of Jews from Theresienstadt, Italy, and the Cracow region. Furthermore, although it is not possible to trace any selections after October 30th (*see page 173*), Dr. Nyiszli declares that the order only reached the crematoria on November 17th.[16]

To one class of internee in Birkenau camp the rumours of the end of the gassings were not good news. The *Sonderkommando*, the exceptionally robust Jews who worked at the crematoria, knew that it meant their death. Experience at Treblinka and Sobibor had taught the Germans that this was the moment when the slaves were likely to rebel. There had been a mutiny as early as December 17th, 1942, in the days of the small gas chambers in the Birkenwald. The *Sonderkommando*, composed of 200 Slovak Jews, had acquired a share of the plunder and it was decided to kill them lest they should bribe their way to freedom. Apparently the Slovaks got wind of the fate in store for them.[17] Thereafter, the commando was exterminated and replaced every few months. In August, 1944, its strength was reduced by 170 men who were sent to Auschwitz I and secretly executed. The remainder, mostly Jews from the Athens and Corfu deportations, were made to live within the enclosure of the crematoria.[18]

But in Auschwitz I there was a secret committee, run by the future Polish Minister-President, Josef Cirankiewicz, which not only warned the *Sonderkommando* of the fate of the 170 men, but smuggled into the crematoria some automatic pistols as well as grenades. The latter were manufactured by the girls in the Krupp 'Union' fuse factory which was in the camp enclosure. On September 21st the committe warned the *Sonderkommando* to stand by for a further selection. Unfortunately, the man who was to have led the revolt, a Jewish officer in the Greek Army, had been killed in an escape attempt so that the plans were ill-co-ordinated and leaked out to an informer. Thus the 150 to 200 men of Crematorium No. IV were taken and gassed.[19]

The secret committee now devised a more ambitious plan for the three remaining crematoria. Arms were to be smuggled by the Polish resistance movement on to a Jewish deportation train. Unfortunately the train left for Birkenau ahead of time and without the arms. Consequently, on October 6th, the men of Crematorium III, realising that they were betrayed, were forced to set fire to their monstrous building to warn the men of No. I who were armed, but the fire was not seen in time. As they tried to cut through the wire the men of No. III were shot down by

Sergeant-Major Moll, the shot-in-the-neck expert of the camp, with his SS guards. A few of them got four miles away before they were rounded up. Nevertheless, Crematorium No. III was completely burnt out in full view of the camp.[20] There was one survivor, M. Charles Bendel, a Paris physician and medical officer to the commando. He tried to commit suicide by taking gardenal but was miraculously brought round by his fellow-internee doctors and hidden in the infirmary. Thus Dr. Bendel lived to tell his fearful story in 1945 at the Lueneburg trial of the Belsen guards and *Kapos*.[21]

The last act of slaughter was late in November when the survivors of the *Sonderkommando* were taken from the remaining crematoria—which were already being demolished—and mysteriously disposed of in the woods. Heydrich's ' legend of the Pharaonic tombs ' was thus respected to the last, but Dr. Nyiszli of Nagy Varad, medical officer and autopsist to Crematorium I, to his surprise found himself still alive. Mussfeld, the mass-murderer of Majdanek, and his guards now spent their time getting drunk and telling Dr. Nyiszli that though he would be killed soon, their own turn would come next. Even now Dr. Nyiszli does not know whether he has the last laugh.[22]

The evacuation of the Auschwitz camps did not wait for the Russian advance. It was spread over three or four months. Birkenau, overcrowded as always, was the first to be dealt with. Part of the women's camp may have been moved to Ravensbrueck as early as September. The sick women were sent in three groups to Bergen-Belsen, which was then officially a convalescence camp, in November-December.[23] The section DII of the male camp was evacuated to Dachau at the end of October, as part of a mass transference of able-bodied Jews to the German armament factories. 2,096 Jews from Auschwitz were registered in Dachau, 1,023 in Buchenwald, 2,045 in Flossenberg, 494 in Mauthausen, 2,522 in Sachsenhausen, and some hundreds in Stutthof.[24]

The women who were sent to Belsen were as yet not numerous. It was only at the end of January, when a big evacuation transport arrived from Birkenau, that Kramer had to open a new *Frauenlager* in what was to be the notorious No. I camp. Kramer himself, the commandant of Birkenau throughout the mass-slaughter season of 1944, arrived in Belsen to take over on December 1st. Josef Kramer, who had been Hoess's adjutant in the first days of Auschwitz in 1940, was not altogether the ape-man that the Allied press made him. He was, nevertheless, a dull, unimaginative brute, who soon made another Birkenau of the so-called privileged camp, Bergen-Belsen.[25]

There were still at least 64,000 people in the Auschwitz group of camps on January 18th, 1945, when in earshot of the Russian guns the general evacuation was ordered. The conditions of transportation had by this time deteriorated abominably. The internees crossed Germany in their prison pyjamas, travelling in open tip-wagons in the depth of winter. Some, who were sent after a halt at Gleiwitz and Wloclawek to Flossenberg and Greiffenberg, travelled the whole way on foot, taking over a month.

Much of this second *Voelkerwanderung* has been identified through examining[25a] the registration numbers in the camps. Thus 13,886 Auschwitz internees have been traced to Buchenwald, 1,379 to Dachau, 3,360 to Dora, 8,365 to Mauthausen, 4,782 to Ravensbrueck, and 2,907 to Sachsenhausen. The most staggering figure is that of Buchenwald and its outer commandos. The greater part were not put to work but merely left in the 'Little Camp,' whose inmates were at no period seriously expected to live and where there were no facilities for existence. The 'Little Camp' became even more crowded than it had been after the round-up of November, 1938 (*see page 14*), with the result that in the last three months of Buchenwald's existence there were 13,066 recorded deaths, more than the combined total for 1942-43.[26] There was, of course, a spotted typhus epidemic, but most of those who died were just *Mussulmen*, the camp slang word for a walking skeleton wrapped up in a bit of blanket. The journey from Auschwitz, at first on foot through the snow under the guns of the SS and then for days on end in open trucks, freezing and without food, was alone sufficient to make a *Mussulman*, and thus it is that Dr. Georges Straka, Reader in Phonetics in Strassbourg University, describes the arrivals from Auschwitz[27] in the winter of 1944:

> 'Sometimes under pressure of blows they would break suddenly into movement like a herd of cattle, jostling each

other. It was impossible to extract from their lips their names, much less their date of birth. Kindness itself had not the power to make them speak. They would only look at you with a long expressionless stare. If they tried to answer, their tongues could not reach their dried up palates to make a sound. One was aware only of a poisonous breath appearing to come from entrails already in a state of decomposition. That was what the transports were like in the winter of 1944-45, that winter when death achieved the prodigious figure of 13,000 detainees in the last three months before our liberation.'

But before the evacuation there were many Auschwitz inmates who had already become *Mussulmen* and who could not be marched through snow-drifts or wedged into tip-trucks. Nor was it practicable to liquidate them on the spot, now that the gas chambers had gone, the installations having been sent, first to Gross-Rosen camp 150 miles to the west, where some optimist thought there would be time to use them, and then to oblivion.* On January 18th, therefore, the sick were left in the infirmaries of the three main camps with a few attendants and some supplies to await the Russians.[28] Why this happened is a mystery, since, after the Majdanek affair Himmler could not have approved of it and Kaltenbrunner, who must have known what was going on through the Auschwitz 'political department,' would have stopped at nothing to prevent it. Someone—the thing was possible even in Hitler's Reich—must have used his own initiative.

The Red Army did not arrive till January 26th. They found 2,819 invalids in the three camps, whom they spared no pains to nurse back to health. In due course a Soviet State Commission arrived and on May 12th the world was presented with its findings.[29]

'However, using rectified coefficients for the part-time

*According to Bruce Marshall's account of the experience of Wing-Commander F. F. E. Yeo-Thomas, who was sent to a branch of Buchenwald, the factory camp Rehmsdorf, at the beginning of January, 1945, Jews were still being selected from the infirmary to be *sent East* for extermination. This could no longer have been at Auschwitz, but it is quite possible that Gross-Rosen camp was still used for this purpose (*The White Rabbit*, London, 1952, *page 223*).

employment of the crematorium ovens and for the periods when they stood empty, the technical expert commission has ascertained that during the time that the Auschwitz camp existed, the German butchers exterminated in this camp not less than four million citizens of the U.S.S.R., Poland, France, Jugoslavia, Czechoslovakia, Rumania, Hungary, Holland, Belgium, and other countries.'

The world has grown mistrustful of 'rectified coefficients' and the figure of four millions has become ridiculous. Unfortunately Russian arithmetic has blurred the stark and inescapable facts that little less than a million human beings perished in Auschwitz, its gas chambers and its camps. There are probably too many incalculable factors to make a closer estimate of the number of Auschwitz victims possible. The number of camp registrations is only partially a guide to the number of Jews sent, because more than 100,000 of the known 363,000 registrations represent Aryan internees from Poland, Russia, and Germany. Moreover, very large groups of Jews in 1944 stayed in the camp without registration, awaiting transfer elsewhere, and they stayed long enough to die of epidemics. Although theoretically not more than 300,000 camp inmates had died by the final evacuation date, January 18th, 1945, the number was certainly higher.

As to the *total* number of Jews brought to the selection place at Auschwitz, it is possible to estimate fairly closely for the Western and Central European countries and the Balkans but not for Poland. There is no real guide to the percentage gassed. It was low before August, 1942, and generally low again after August, 1944, but in the meantime gassings might vary between fifty and nearly a hundred per cent. The following list makes allowances for a number of French and Greek transports which were sent to Majdanek and 34,000 Dutch Jews who went to Sobibor:

Belgium	22,600
Croatia	4,500
France	57,000
Greater Reich (including concentration camps and Bohemia, direct transports only)	25,000 (uncertain)

Greater Reich and Bohemia (via		
Theresienstadt Ghetto)	32,000	
Greece	50,000	
Holland	62,000	
Hungary (wartime frontiers) ...	380,000	
Italy	5,000	
Luxembourg	2,000	
Norway	700	
Poland and Baltic States	180,000	(uncertain)
Slovakia (1939 borders)	20,000	
	840,800	

Of this total, 550,000 to 600,000 may have been gassed on arrival and to this must be added the unknown portion of the 300,000 or more, missing from the camp, who were 'selected.'

2. The Red Cross Intervention

For another two months the Germany that lay between Rhine and Oder remained uninvaded and in it were a dozen concentration camps and more than a hundred satellite camps. They contained about 200,000 Jews[30] and 500,000 Aryan 'politicals,' living in conditions which at best were ceasing to be tolerable and at worst were those of charnel houses of the living dead. Their future lay poised between the wills of a Hitler, who would gladly see them die along with himself and every German as well, of a Himmler who hoped to sell them alive to the Allies as the price of his own immunity, and of a Kaltenbrunner who was deluded enough to think this plot worth frustrating. In attempting to follow the confusions and inconsistencies of the story, the conflict of these three wills must always be borne in mind. It explains the relative failure of the Red Cross missions and the appalling death roll. At least 80,000 inmates of the concentration camps—half this number in Belsen alone—died in the last three months of the war, in a sense perhaps not in vain. Had Himmler been sufficiently master in his own house to keep faith and had he succeeded in his purely selfish negotiations, the troops of the Western Allies would not have seen with their own eyes

461

what had hitherto been regarded as rumour, distorted testimony, or deliberate propaganda.

At the end of January, 1945, while the trains of open wagons dragged their community of the living and the frozen dead from Silesia to Western Germany, Professor Karl Burckhardt, President of the International Red Cross, made contact with the German Foreign Office. He was told that relief would be permitted to reach the camps in lorries if they were provided by the Red Cross and driven by trusted prisoners of war. Then on February 2nd two Swiss Red Cross delegates were allowed into the holy of holies, the inspectorate office of the concentration camps at Oranienburg, where they saw Dr. Lolling, chief of the camp medical services and the deputies for Gluecks the Inspector-General, Hoess and Berndorf. The former, however, with his cold glazed eyes was utterly uncooperative. Only Himmler, he said, could make the arrangements for visits to the camps. As for an interview with the spokesmen of the internees, it was impossible. They could never be brought to Oranienburg in the bombed state of the German railways.[31]

Himmler remained inaccessible and then a catastrophe occurred. On February 6th another 1,100 Hungarian Jews from Bergen-Belsen arrived in Switzerland. It was the signal that Himmler had at last received his five million francs—through the hands of the Swiss President, Jean-Marie Musi. According to Becher, Himmler magnanimously allotted the money to the Swiss Red Cross plan, but the news was published in the Swiss newspapers and it reached Hitler. Becher makes the rather surprising allegation that Walter Schellenberg, whom Himmler had certainly employed in this matter, showed Hitler the reports. Himmler had to endure a scene which was so terrible that he revoked everything. According to Becher, he instructed Pister, the former commandant at Buchenwald, 'to let no camp inmate in the southern half of Germany fall into enemy hands alive.'[32]

Nevertheless a new approach was made to Himmler by the Swedish Red Cross and, because very wisely it was extremely limited in its aims, it had important consequences. Count Folke Bernadotte, nephew of the then King of Sweden and Vice-President of the Swedish Red Cross, obtained an interview with Himmler through Schellenberg on February 17th. Bernadotte asked only for the release of the Danish and Norwegian captives, but in the course of the conversation he learnt that the whole mass of Jewry, interned in the Reich, might be handed over to the Allies. Nevertheless, for the next fortnight there was no sign that even Bernadotte's smaller proposition had been passed to the Inspectorate of the Concentration Camps. Bernadotte instead received a warning through Schellenberg that Kaltenbrunner would prevent any access to the camps and this was confirmed to him by Kaltenbrunner himself on March 5th. 'I do not intend to assist you in the matter you have brought up.'[33]

Having sabotaged the Swedish negotiations, Kaltenbrunner now used Himmler's absence at the front to resume the Swiss negotiations in order to gain credit for himself. He received Professor Burckhardt on the 12th and informed him that a Red Cross representative would be permitted to reside in each camp in order to distribute the relief, while the French and Belgian internees would be exchanged for Germans. As to the Jews, Professor Burckhardt was assured that the children, the aged, and the entire Theresienstadt community would be repatriated.[34]

Although the negotiators probably did not realise it, the chaos in the concentration camps was now too great to make more than a small part of this project possible. On March 1st, Kramer had written to Gluecks from Belsen that there were 42,000 people in the camp, whom spotted typhus was claiming at the rate of 250-300 a day.[35]* And a week later Eichmann used this epidemic as an excuse to forbid the evacuation of the 7,500 surviving 'exchange Jews' from Belsen to Theresienstadt and Landsberg.[36] On the 19th, when the population of Belsen surpassed 60,000, Oswald Pohl arrived with Lolling and Hoess, who deputised for the allegedly sick Gluecks. They brought an order from Himmler to Kramer that 'not another Jew' was to be killed and that the death rate must be reduced at all costs.[37] Hoess, who must have found his new rôle trying at first, told his old adjutant, Kramer, that even he in all his experience had never seen anything like it. 'Tens of thousands of corpses lay everywhere,' he was later

*Brigadier-General Glyn-Hughes ascertained that the typhus epidemic started at Belsen on February 5th among a transport of 'Hungarians.' It is not clear whether these Hungarian Jews came from other German concentration camps or from the 'South-East Wall' (*The Belsen Case, page 33*).

to recall at Nuremberg. Yet it did not prevent Himmler writing two days later to Dr. Hillel Storsch, of World Jewish Congress, that he had 'taken steps' to deal with the typhus epidemic that had broken out at Bergen-Belsen.[38]

On March 23rd Heinrich Mueller, head of the Gestapo, informed Professor Burckhardt that Belsen would be given up and that all the Jews in Germany would be taken to a single place, where relief could reach them from abroad. Yet even now no Red Cross representative had succeeded in entering any of the camps. Mueller explained that this was due to the lack of censors, whose presence would be necessary. The delegation were far from impressed when Mueller offered to allow a representative into Theresienstadt within the next few days 'to put an end to lying enemy propaganda.'[39]

A week later Count Bernadotte succeeded in penetrating into Neuengamme camp in the suburbs of Hamburg, but this was in the nature of a personal favour, since on April 3rd Himmler made his first request to Bernadotte to arrange an interview for him with General Eisenhower.[40] No such favour was accorded the Swiss delegates. On April 3rd they were allowed to interview the camp spokesmen, but it was at Oranienburg in the presence of the whole General Staff of murder, where the poor wretches scarcely dared open their mouths. Hoess, it was observed, was specially reserved about Buchenwald—from which the Americans were then only 40 miles away—and with good reason.[41] Between April 3rd and 10th Buchenwald underwent an immense and chaotic evacuation. Out of 48,000 people, who were now packed into the base-camp, 28,285 were entrained for the south of Germany, particularly for the camps of Ohrdruf, Dachau, Flossenberg, and Leitmaritz. Half the deportees were Jews who lived in the ' Little Camp' and were in no sense protected by the famous ' camp committee,' and of these 4,500 were put on a train for Dachau which arrived many days later with 1,500 dead, having wandered about in search of an unbombed track through Czechoslovakia. The passengers had been issued with only one day's rations.[42]*

---

*The ' illegal committee' at Buchenwald had arms at their disposal, but not enough to fight 3,000 SS guards. They therefore decided on a policy of sacrificing the lives they deemed least worth while. Mr. Christopher Burney admits candidly that the 6,000 Jews, demanded by the SS on April 2nd

At Nuremberg Schellenberg gave the following version of what had happened. Himmler had sent a message to the Swiss President, M. Musi, which was intended for Eisenhower, that Buchenwald would be handed over intact. Nevertheless, the President's son arrived at Buchenwald to find evacuation in full swing. He complained to Schellenberg, who telephoned to Himmler and the evacuation was stopped the same day. Mueller told Schellenberg that Kaltenbrunner had issued the instructions over Himmler's head, and here for once Schellenberg is confirmed by Becher.[43] One should, nevertheless, accept this story with strong reservations. The last evacuation-transport left Buchenwald on the 9th and Himmler's intervention apparently took place on the 10th, when the SS guards themselves were already preparing to leave. Between the 11th and 13th the camp was in the hands of the 'illegal committee' who manned the watchtowers themselves. One is certainly entitled to the suspicion that the SS were incapable of evacuating any more people, and the example of Lublin at once leaps to mind.[44]

The famine-stricken exodus from Buchenwald when the Americans arrived, the cartloads of unburied corpses in the 'Little Camp,' and Frau Koch's human lampshades were far surpassed by what the British troops found at Belsen. There is to-day a danger that this unspeakable tragedy may come to be regarded as no more than an accumulation of accidents. Yet it may well have been the deliberate work of a single man. Belsen, like Theresienstadt, was administered 'politically' by 'IVA 4b'—Eichmann's office, a member of which, Captain Moes, had charge of all matters pertaining to 'exchange-Jews.' On March 1st Kramer wrote a report for Gluecks, the Inspector-General, that Moes would not remove these Jews in order to[44a] make more room in the 'Star Camp,' because the typhus epidemic made movement impossible. And yet at this time the 'Star Camp' was not in the typhus area. Was this the hand of Eichmann? On April 6th Eichmann promised to conduct M. Paul Dunand

were not thought worth fighting over. Similarly, on April 6th, when it was a question of making up 8,000 people for transports to Theresienstadt, the committee weeded out those whom—Jewish or Gentile—they regarded as 'Cretins.' This is not the sort of thing that happens in adventure books for boys, but it was part of the character of the SS State and Mr. Burney is to be praised for his frankness (*The Dungeon Democracy*, pages 74-80).

of the Red Cross over Belsen in order that he might see how the authorities were dealing with the typhus epidemic, but, when M. Dunand came to Berlin, Eichmann had flown.[45] How did it come about that, in spite of Pohl's visit to Belsen on March 19th and his report to Himmler, transports poured into Belsen for another three weeks?[*] Is there not every probability that this was the last leering gesture of the man who was going to 'leap into his grave laughing because he had five million deaths on his conscience'? (see page 27).

Once more it was Kurt Becher, now appointed by Himmler special commissary for the concentration camps, who had to clear up after Eichmann. On April 10th he left Eichmann's office in the Kurfuerstenstrasse for Bergen-Belsen, accompanied by Dr. Kastner disguised in an SS uniform. After seeing Kramer, Becher telephoned Himmler and persuaded him to hand over the camp intact. At first Colonel Harries, commanding the troops in the neighbouring Panzer school, would not capitulate,[46] but on the 12th a truce was arranged, the British commander allowing the camp-guards eight days' parole in order to keep a cordon round the typhus area. No British detachment entered the camp till the 15th, when the front had swept far past Belsen.

Belsen consisted of Camp No. 2, the original 'Star Camp' for the privileged Jews, handsomely laid out and containing some good permanent buildings, and Camp No. 1, which was some distance away. This was a hutted camp, originally used for Russian prisoners of war, but which had been expanded by bringing huts from the Jewish camp of Plaszow in Poland during the evacuations of the winter of 1944.[47] Till the last moment efforts were made to keep the flood of arrivals out of Camp No. 2. Thus, though eventually 15,133 people occupied a camp intended for 7,000, there was no typhus and only the beginning of famine in this section.

It was far otherwise in Camp No. 1, the 'Haeftlingslager.' In this rectangle, measuring one mile by 400 yards, the British troops found 28,000 women, 12,000 men, and 13,000 unburied

---

[*]The Netherlands Red Cross researches show that, while only three transports were directed to Belsen in January, 1945, there were ten in February and eight in March, with two more in the first days of April (Auschwitz, Deel VI, The Hague, 1952).

corpses. Another 13,000 died within a few days of liberation. There is absolutely no means of calculating the number of dead who had been buried since the beginning of February, when typhus arrived, but it is at least certain that 40,000 people, the greater part Polish and Hungarian Jews, died in this plague-compound, of which every rag and stick had to be destroyed by fire.

But the utterly inconceivable thing was this. Two miles away in the stores of the Panzer training school there were[48] nearly 800 tons of food and a bakery capable of producing 60,000 loaves a day. From this store the Wehrmacht had been doling out to Kramer a mere 10,000 loaves a week, when his civilian sources of supply became cut off. Kramer, according to his own testimony, had not attempted to ask for more. That would have meant 'special indents.'[49] Used as he was to seeing human beings die in their thousands in the Birkenau infirmary and gas chambers, he was not used to taking action without signing on the dotted line.

Hoess, who was then acting inspector of concentration camps, had seen the conditions at Belsen on March 19th and a year later he was to offer this explanation[50]:

'Due to the exigencies of war there were practically no building materials at our disposal and, furthermore, rations for the detainees were again and again severely curtailed by the provincial economic administration offices. This then led to a situation where detainees in the camps no longer had sufficient powers of resistance against plagues and epidemics.

'The main reason why detainees towards the end of the war were in such bad condition, why so many thousands of them were found sick and emaciated in the camps, was that every detainee had to be employed in the armament industry to the extreme limit of his physical power. The Reichsfuehrer constantly and on every occasion kept this goal before our eyes . . . the aim wasn't to have as many dead as possible or to destroy as many detainees as possible. The Reichsfuehrer was constantly concerned with the problem of engaging all forces possible in the armament industry.'

One is to gather from this reasoned explanation that six or seven hundred thousand people were herded from camp to camp with the serious intention that they should make armaments. Yet Oswald Pohl's proudest boast was that 230,000 concentration camp inmates—hardly more than a third of the numbers in the last months of the war—were so employed.[50a] So the sickening wastefulness of the concentration camp system went on to the very last.

After the first wave of horror had passed, following the Belsen revelations, there was a disposition in some British circles to seek economic explanations like this one of the mass-murderer Hoess. The lie should be scotched for ever. There was nothing inevitable in the final tragedy at Belsen nor was it anything new in Himmler's SS State. What the British army saw in camp No. 1 could have been seen at any time in the course of more than two years in Block No. 25 in the *Frauenlager* at Birkenau, where the doomed women invalids waited for the gas-chamber lorry for days on end. The soberest of witnesses, such as the Austrian physician Dr. Lingens-Reiner, have described their plight with unanimity; they have told of the living women, who were abandoned without food or clothing, sprawling on top of the already dead and imploring to be gassed. This scene—and how often it must have been repeated at the death camps, Treblinka, Belsec, and Sobibor, during the heavy transport season—was no fruit of personal sadism but the logical outcome of endless speeches and articles, comparing human beings to bacilli and vermin.

Himmler may have been sincere when he told Dr. Hillel Storsch that he had taken steps to 'deal with' the typhus at Belsen, but these steps were left to men like Pohl and Hoess, whom he had taught for years to work their prisoners to death or else get rid of them. What sort of co-operation did Himmler expect? While the typhus raged at Belsen, 1,500 of Himmler's Hungarian SS idled in the neighbouring Panzer school. When the British took over, the epidemic was stamped out in two weeks by the sanitary labours of 360 men.[51]

It seems even more inconceivable that the privileged *Kapos* among the inmates of this Golgotha should still be plying their whips and rubber truncheons when the British arrived, and that at the merest suspicion of picking up a potato the SS guards, in particular the Hungarians, should use their rifles. Brigadier-General Glyn-Hughes, DDMS Second Army, actually saw people wounded and killed and had to give orders to Kramer,[52] but to understand what happened in the last ten days at Belsen one must read the evidence of Mr. Harold Osmond Le Druillenec, a Jersey schoolmaster who had been deported with all his family for sheltering an escaped prisoner of war[53]:

> ' I cannot very well explain my feelings when I first saw one of those pits which already contained many dead and I had to throw my particular corpse on top of those others already there. During the dragging process I noticed on many occasions a strange wound at the back of the thigh of many of these dead. First of all I dismissed it as a gunshot wound at close quarters, but, after seeing a few more, I asked a friend and he told me that many prisoners were cutting chunks out of these bodies to eat. On my very next visit to the mortuary I actually saw a prisoner whip out a knife, cut a portion out of the leg of a dead body, and quickly put it in his mouth, naturally frightened of being seen in the act of doing so. I leave it to your imagination to realise to what state the prisoners were reduced for men to chance eating these bits of flesh taken out of black corpses.'

Later there was a Belsen trial—but not of the real culprits. Forty-four persons were eventually charged, and between September and November, 1945, they were tried by a British military court sitting at Lueneburg. Three, including Kramer, were officers; most of the remainder were SS guards and NCOs of both sexes, the rest were *Kapos*, picked out from among the prisoners. Although eight others in addition to the three officers were sentenced to death, there were no less than nineteen acquittals.

This, the first British war-trial, was criticised from every quarter. The acquittals made anti-British propaganda in the countries that had been liberated by Russia. The verdicts, which had been reached under conditions so different from those under which British justice normally functions, caused grave misgivings in legal circles at home. In their hour of liberation the victims of

Belsen could not have realised that there was no system of human justice, adapted to such immense collective crimes, and that perhaps there never would be.

On December 22nd, 1951, five of the Belsen female guards and *Kapos*, who had received ten-year sentences for their part in beating and tormenting the half-dead and the living skeletons in their care, were suddenly released from Werl prison. The action followed a similar Christmas amnesty granted by the Americans in Landsberg prison. Was the gift of these sinister and unwanted harpies intended in that hour of high policy to placate German opinion, and, if so, what section of German opinion ?

3. Himmler Breaks His Word

Some prescience on the Allies' side might have delayed the publication of the Buchenwald and Belsen discoveries, since it was obvious that the rulers of Germany would be reluctant to allow more hordes of internees to fall into enemy hands. The rescue of the Scandinavians, which Count Bernadotte had been promised, was postponed till after Himmler's meeting on April 19th with Dr. Masur. Even then, though Himmler undertook that no more camps would be evacuated, he failed to keep his promise. According to Hoess's Nuremberg testimony, Himmler was hampered by a Fuehrer Order. Having learnt that the inmates of Buchenwald had broken out and looted the town of Weimar, Hitler decided that no more inmates who were capable of marching should be left behind in the camps.[54] This explanation was apparently not confirmed by Himmler himself, for in Dr. Masur's presence he refrained from blaming either Hitler or Kaltenbrunner:

'It was my intention to hand over the concentration camps undefended, as I had announced. I allowed Bergen-Belsen and Buchenwald to be overrun, but I got no thanks for it. In Belsen they chained up one of the guards and photographed him among the bodies of dead prisoners, and these pictures are now published by the press throughout the world. In Buchenwald the hospital caught fire from a burning American tank and the charred corpses were photographed throughout the world . . . the statements published

470

in hate against us concerning the concentration camps did not induce me to continue my policy of surrendering the camps undefended. Consequently, a few days ago I allowed a camp in Saxony to be evacuated as the American tanks approached. Why should I do otherwise ?'[55]

Dr. Masur had now to explain to Himmler that the Allied press could not be muzzled in return for his concessions. In a democratic country even the Government could not stop the printing of undesirable news. Himmler nevertheless insisted that the power of world Jewry was such that the press could be silenced at any moment. But perhaps to give the full flavour of this interview it should be explained that Himmler had to steal away from a supper party in the Reich Chancellory bunker on the eve of Hitler's birthday in order to drive to a farm belonging to his masseur, Felix Kersten, where he was to interview a Jew, representing the World Jewish Congress.

Far more serious allegations were made at Nuremberg that Kaltenbrunner gave orders—in pursuance of Himmler's instructions dating from early February—that the inmates of the camps in the south, Dachau, Mauthausen, and Theresienstadt, who could no longer be evacuated, should be liquidated *en masse*. The evidence, however, suggests that these were plots by individual civil or SS officials, which were not in the last resort confirmed by the Security Office. Thus the plan to destroy Dachau seems to have been an inspiration of Giesler, the Gauleiter for Munich and Lower Bavaria and incidentally the man nominated in Hitler's will to be Himmler's successor as Minister for Interior. This beauty—another of the putative suicides—wanted to concentrate the inmates of the Jewish camps, Landsberg and Muehldorf, at Dachau and then have the camp bombed from the air.* In fact, Dachau was handed over to the Americans after a partial evacuation on April 24th.

*Nevertheless, Giesler's deputy, Bertus Gerdes, signed a Nuremberg affidavit to the effect that he received many dispatches concerning this plan to bomb Dachau, known as 'Operation Cloud One,' which were signed by Kaltenbrunner. The Higher SS and Police Leader, Karl Freiherr von Eberstein, also knew of 'Operation Cloud One,' but regarded it as an inspiration of Giesler's. In any case, he had no difficulty in obtaining Himmler's instructions to hand Dachau over to the Americans.[56]

In the case of Theresienstadt the conflicts of policy seem particularly mysterious. It was the first concentration camp which Himmler was prepared to use as a passport to respectability and on April 6th Eichmann himself, accompanied by Colonel Weinmann, a former *Einsatzgruppe* chief in Russia, showed M. Paul Dunand of the Swiss Red Cross over the model ghetto. It was a very formal occasion, and in the evening Lieut.-General Karl Frank, Protector for Bohemia and Moravia, gave the delegation a reception in the Hradschin Palace in Prague. Just as we have seen Himmler and Kaltenbrunner on their good behaviour, we may now observe Eichmann taking M. Dunand into a corner of the great *salon* and talking to him with those queer glittering eyes—and telling him that the Jews in Theresienstadt were better off than many Germans. Eichmann then said something which Himmler repeated almost word for word to Dr. Masur a fortnight later. Himmler, he said, had 'wanted the Jews to acquire a sense of racial community through the exercise of almost complete autonomy.' Afterwards they were to be transported to some region where they could live separated from the German population. Eichmann added that he did not approve of all the more humane measures which Himmler intended to introduce towards the Jews, but, *en tant que bon soldat,* he obeyed Himmler's orders blindly.[57]

En tant que bon soldat, it was only that morning that Eichmann had found Rabbi Leo Baeck, former President of the Jewish *Reichsvereinigung,* living openly in Theresienstadt (*see page 161*). 'Herr Baeck, are you still alive? I thought you were dead.' And when Eichmann had verified a mistake in his files, he had said in his cheerful way: 'I understand now. A man who gets himself entered as dead, lives longer.'[58]

Eichmann had promised M. Dunand that not a single Jew should be deported from Theresienstadt, but on April 12th M. Dunand learnt that the SS had destroyed the records, which were kept in the Magdeburg barracks in the ghetto, and this he regarded as a sign that a last-minute mass-execution might be intended.* He therefore went to Berlin to obtain an assurance

---

*According to the affidavits of Wisliceny and Dr. Kastner, Eichmann had proposed the liquidation of Theresienstadt as early as February. Kurt Gerstein's story that he was asked by Hans Guenther how much Zyklon B was needed to gas the entire community in the open moat of the fortress seems to refer to a date in 1944.[59]

from Heinrich Mueller.[60] As a consequence, Becher, the new commissary, came to Theresienstadt on the 16th in the company of Dr. Kastner and Eichmann's assistant, Huensche. They were fortunate in finding a communication still open in a Reich, which was now compressed to the shape of a dumb-bell, and fortunate, too, in finding nothing amiss in 'the model ghetto.' On the previous day Count Bernadotte's agreement had been fulfilled and the 423 surviving Danish Jews had been sent home.[61]

Becher went on to Mauthausen and Dr. Kastner was enabled to escape to Switzerland. Finally, between May 2nd and the arrival of the Russians on May 12th M. Dunand was allowed to fly the Red Cross flag over Theresienstadt,[62] but the ghetto had escaped the dangers of evacuation and even liquidation to incur great risks from overcrowding. Since April 20th no less than 12,863 people, mostly Jews, had been evacuated there from Buchenwald, Dachau, Ohrdruf, Rehmsdorf, and other camps. How many failed to arrive is unknown.* M. Dunand, for instance, rescued three trainloads who had been wandering about the smashed *Reichsbahn* for weeks, but only 1,980 survived out of 3,100 passengers, a fifth of them children.[63]

The newcomers, mainly Hungarian, Polish, and Eastern Jews, had to be isolated from the 21,000 camp inmates on account of typhus. It was unfortunate that only two barrack blocks should be wired off as an isolation camp, since these people became persuaded that the privileged, baptised, and mixed-marriage Jews from Bohemia and the Reich were practising their own racial discrimination—the impression conveyed to Mr. Meyer Levin, who, having, as a war correspondent, seen both, found the

---

*Perhaps the last SS massacre occurred at the very end of April, 1945, in Marienbad railway station, when a train which had contained originally 2,775 inmates of Rehmsdorf camp, a branch of Buchenwald, was bombed. About 1,000 passengers, Aryan political prisoners as well as Jews, escaped into the woods, but were brought back to the station and executed by a shot in the back of the neck. Many more were shot during the march from Marienbad to Theresienstadt, where only 500 or so arrived in the end. IMT XX, 362-3, Doc. D, 924 (evidence of Dutch internees, Peter Langhorst and Baron von Lamsweerd). Wing-Commander F. F. E. Yeo-Thomas's escape from this train is described by Bruce Marshall in *The White Rabbit*, London, 1952.

Theresienstadt isolation block no better than the 'Little Camp' at Buchenwald.[64]

We come now to the case of Mauthausen, where the first Red Cross delegate was admitted on April 23rd. With its numbers increased by Jewish deportees from the 'South-East Wall,' it was still the atrocity camp *par excellence*, run by the horrible baby-faced Ziereis, who had tyrannised over his kingdom since 1939. The delegate was still able to see the work commandos return to camp carrying their dead and the crematorium chimney smoking day and night. In his own words, *Quelque chose de mysterieux et d'horrible planait sur tout.* Nevertheless, the 134 French internees were liberated at his request.[65]

The second delegate—how much one regrets the anonymity of these Red Cross reports—had to spend several days in St. Georgen before he could force his way into the camp and persuade an SS lieutenant to let him share his room. From this lieutenant he learnt of Ziereis's plan to collect the inmates in the underground aeroplane factory at Gusen and blow the place up. In the end Ziereis was dissuaded and went away quietly, leaving the key to his sumptuous house in the delegate's hands. On May 8th, when Patton's troops entered the camp, Ziereis was identified in the camp precincts and shot in the stomach. His dying confession, having been taken down by an inmate in the presence of American officers who could not understand German, is not very reliable. It named Kaltenbrunner as the author of the Gusen plan.[66] Becher, moreover, deposed that Ziereis had told him on April 27th that he had orders to kill at least a thousand inmates a day.[67] Kaltenbrunner retaliated with the evidence of his own white-collar man, Willi Hoettl, that he had ordered Ziereis to deliver Mauthausen to the Americans intact.[68]

One does not get very far with these accusations and counter-accusations. What is more significant is that Theresienstadt, Dachau, and Mauthausen, which were in the section of the Reich that became cut off from Berlin after April 25th, were handed over intact, whereas Ravensbrueck, Oranienburg, and Sachsenhausen, which were in the Berlin area, were largely evacuated. This circumstance is surely very destructive of the

Himmler-Kaltenbrunner legend, as built up by Schellenberg and Becher. Himmler was too afraid of Hitler—even when he was screaming his head off in the Reich Chancellory bunker—and, on the other hand too afraid of the Russians creating another Belsen sensation to keep faith with the Red Cross and World Jewish Congress. Hoess, who during these last days acted as inspector-general of the camps, deposed that, even when he and Mueller protested, Himmler insisted that Sachsenhausen must be evacuated, though there was nowhere to put the inmates except in the woods.[69]

On the 20th a representative of Professor Burckhardt's mission tried to tempt Mueller with the prospect that it might be credited in his favour by the Allies if he delivered under Red Cross supervision Sachsenhausen, Oranienburg, and Ravensbrueck to the Russians according to the Burckhardt-Kaltenbrunner terms. Mueller objected that no Red Cross delegate could reach Oranienburg in time because the Russians were only ten kilometres away.[70] A delegate went, nevertheless, next morning, but, after waiting hours in Hoess's office, which was outside the camp, he learnt that the inmates had been marched off towards Wittstock, 60 miles to the north-west. It was not too late for the Swedish Red Cross lorries to bring up some food to the column and carry off the sick to the Allied lines.

Hoess had transferred himself to Ravensbrueck, 30 miles to the north, and here some devilry was clearly intended. But the delegate, who arrived on the 23rd, learnt that Hoess had met with a motor accident—most opportune, for this day the Russian tanks penetrated Eastern Berlin. Hoess was not seen again till March 12th, 1946, when, as a farm labourer, named Franz Lange, he was arrested in Schleswig. In place of Hoess, the delegate saw the notorious Suhren, commandant of Ravensbrueck, from whom he learnt that 17,000 women were involved. According to Himmler's most recent promise to Count Bernadotte,[71] the 1,500 sick were to stay under the protection of the Red Cross, the Scandinavians were to be taken away in Swedish Red Cross lorries, the remainder would be evacuated by train to Malchow, but the 'Easterners,' that is to say, mainly the Polish and Hungarian Jewesses, would have to cover the 40 miles on foot.[72] At the last moment the Swedish lorries were allowed to take 7,000

Polish Jewesses to Flensburg. It seems that Karl Gebhardt, the director of Hohenlychen hospital, whom Himmler had made head of the German Red Cross, was able to arrange this through the suicide of General Grawitz, chief of the SS medical service.[73]

There now began three utterly pointless marches by starving men and women towards the last pocket of the shrinking Reich, where their gaolers believed themselves safe from the Russians. Suhren's motor-drive with his hostage, Odette Churchill, has become popular history. Less known is his remark to the Red Cross delegate who reproached Kaindl, the Sachsenhausen commander, for the corpses that strewed his line of march, *Bei mir passiert nichts,* ' Nothing of that kind goes on where I am.'

It seems that on the 24th Hoess gave last-minute instructions that women stragglers were not to be shot. The temptation must have been great. One of the guards on the Oranienburg march considered that he was doing the sick a service by shooting them. Another was with difficulty restrained from finishing off nine men lying under a blanket. ' I can't just leave them in a ditch.' When the Red Cross helpers picked up the stragglers, they begged not to be killed from force of habit, for habits died hard in the SS State. Perhaps the finest scene in this German pageant was provided on the 28th, when the wife of an SS officer from Ravensbrueck was seen driving in a carriage pulled by six female skeletons. She was suffering from indigestion from eating too many raisins.[74]*

---

*Evidence given at the Russian-held Sachsenhausen trial in 1948 suggests that Himmler had ordered the inmates of Sachsenhausen, Oranienburg, and Ravensbrueck to be embarked at Luebeck for Norway—as was actually done in the case of the survivors of Neuengamme. On April 20th and 21st, in spite of Hoess's alleged protests, the 650 survivors at Sachsenhausen, who were thought fit to walk, were marched off in the general direction of Luebeck. Between the 26th and 29th they were halted in Below Forest, where the Swedish Red Cross was able to rescue several hundreds of invalids and prevent the murder of the rest by following the convoy, which reached the Allied lines at Schwerin on May 3rd (Netherlands Red Cross, *Etude sur le sort des prisonniers du KL Herzogenbosch,* 1952). About a hundred died on the march, most of them shot by the SS as stragglers. The greater part of Sachsenhausen camp, including all the Jews, had, however, already been evacuated to other places, particularly to Bergen-Belsen.

4. Goetterdaemmerung

On April 30th, when the last victims of the Final Solution still quivered in the Mecklenberg ditches, Hitler was dead and the Russians held most of Berlin. At four o'clock on the previous afternoon Hitler's secretary, Frau Junge, had tapped out on her typewriter the last words of Hitler's political testament—and his final and most terrible admission of failure:

' Above all, I bind the leadership of the nation and its subordinates to the painful observance of the racial laws and to merciless resistance of the world-poisoner of all nations, international Jewry.'[75]

The world-poisoner had survived Hitler and the racial laws had not achieved their end. The war had not meant, as Hitler had prophesied on January 30th, 1939, ' the annihilation of the Jewish race throughout Europe' (see page 21). The death of four to five million Jews had not hidden the reality of his failure even from Hitler himself and, had he lived another three years, he would have learnt that he had made possible the thing he disliked most, a sovereign Jewish State.

It now remains to follow the fortunes of some of the architects of the Final Solution amid the crashing debris of the Thousand-year Reich and, foremost among them, a ludicrous misfit of a man to the very last, the *Reichsfuehrer* and second head of the State, Heinrich Himmler.

On the morning of April 28th the British press published a Reuter's report from San Francisco that Himmler had offered unconditional surrender to the Western Allies through the good offices of Count Bernadotte. The offer had in fact been made on the 24th in the cellar of the Swedish Consulate in Luebeck.[76] The leakage was particularly unfortunate for Himmler, since it revealed his own indiscreet language. He was alleged to have said that Hitler was dying of a cerebral hæmorrhage and that German resistance would not outlast his death forty-eight hours.

Hitler had already resolved to end his own life when this

report was brought to the bunker. He therefore at once erased Himmler from the succession, just as five days earlier he had erased Goering. Before, however, making his will, Hitler ordered the new Commander-in-Chief of the Luftwaffe, Ritter von Greim, to arrest Himmler and execute him.[77] None of this was known to Himmler, who, confident that there could be no other successor to Hitler but himself, had just moved his headquarters to Ploen in Schleswig, where Grand Admiral Doenitz had pledged him his support.

On the 30th Doenitz learnt that the dead Hitler had nominated him Reich President and Supreme Commander of the Forces with a Cabinet list that excluded Himmler. Doenitz thereupon moved his headquarters to Flensburg, whence within two days he opened peace negotiations. As to Himmler, he was still surrounded with a staff of 150 members of the SS administrative offices, including notorious police-generals, who stayed above ground strangely oblivious that they were wanted men. There was Otto Ohlendorf, the organiser of mass-murder in Podolia and the Crimea, Maximilian von Herff, who had assisted at the liquidation of the Warsaw Ghetto, Udo von Woyrsch, who had led the first *Einsatzgruppen* of the police in the invasion of Poland, and Pruetzmann, who had regaled Himmler in 1942 with incredible budgets of Ukrainian and White Russian Jews, slain by the hundred thousand.[78]

Among these grizzly phantoms Himmler maintained all the *simulacra* of power, holding staff conferences and issuing orders and communiqués. Then on May 6th Doenitz formally dismissed him from his functions and the phantoms silently melted away.[79] Finally, on May 23rd, a fortnight after the capitulation of the Reich, the entire Flensburg Government was arrested by the Allies and a shabby 45-year-old SS private with a patch over one eye blundered into a control-post on Lueneburg Heath, within a few hundred yards of the headquarters of the British Second Army.

During a routine search Himmler was easily recognised by his captors, who, however, were unable to stop the *Reichsfuehrer's* teeth biting the cyanide capsule which was concealed in his mouth. It seems that one of Himmler's phantoms had intended a nobler exit for him. On May 9th Ohlendorf, the former extermination chief, had begged Himmler to surrender to the Allies in order to explain and defend the rôle of the SS,[80] but Himmler decided that, whosesoever that honour, it should not be his.

The death mask, made on Lueneburg Heath, which looked like a grinning medieval gargoyle, satisfied all who sought the image of an iron-willed, cold-hearted murderer of millions of Jews and subject people. Later appraisals have not produced so consistent a picture. Was Himmler the cheeseparing economist described by Oswald Pohl, the amiable lunatic and professional invalid described by Felix Kersten, the insignificant stooge described by Willi Hoettl, or the reincarnation of Jenghiz Khan, depicted by Himmler himself in his Posen speech of October 1943. Was Himmler a simpler personage, a man of monumental and undeviating loyalty, who crumbled to pieces when that loyalty was destroyed—the view of Mr. Trevor-Roper? One suspects that Himmler was not quite any of these figures, but that he may have had a little of all of them. To Count Ciano he was 'the only man who really feels the pulse of the German people'[81]—which may explain the popularity of the physically unglamorous *Reichsheini* as well as his absurdity. For Himmler was so intensely German and so intensely middle-class that he combined all the faults and all the virtues of a middle-class German. He typified far more than Hitler the common man, to whom it is still believed that this unhappy century belongs. Himmler could, therefore, neither lie nor let his imagination go without being ridiculous. Capable of believing most of the things that he wanted to believe, he expected them to create no strain on the credulity of others, perhaps the most German of all weaknesses. And here is Himmler explaining to Dr. Masur the reason for the crematoria and the ghettoes:

'Then the war brought us in contact with the proletarianised Jewish masses of the Eastern countries, thereby creating new problems. We could not suffer such an enemy in our rear. The Jewish masses were infected with terrible epidemics; in particular, spotted typhus raged. I myself have lost thousands of my best SS men through these epidemics. Moreover, the Jews helped the partisans.'

To Masur's question 'How could the Jews help the partisans when the Germans had concentrated them all in large ghettoes ? ' Himmler replied:

'They conveyed intelligence to the partisans. Moreover, they shot at our troops in the ghetto.

'In order to put a stop to the epidemics we were forced to burn the bodies of incalculable numbers of people who had been destroyed by disease. We were therefore forced to build crematoria, and on this account they are knotting a noose for us.'[82]

The final adventures of Ernst Kaltenbrunner, who was Himmler's rival during his last year of power, are more obscure. Indeed, was not this scar-faced Austrian, lecherous and excitable, whose job was murder but whose passion was secret diplomacy, a more mysterious person than Himmler ? Kaltenbrunner seems to have left Berlin on April 19th and to have established himself in Innsbrueck in the Tyrol. He claims that he was to have met a representative of Professor Burckhardt and that on the way he meant to liberate the inmates of Theresienstadt—none of which alters the fact that he was sent from Berlin to take over the Security Service in the south, where at this time it was still proposed to make the last stand.[83] According to Willi Hoettl, Kaltenbrunner wanted to see Mr. Allen Dulles in Zurich with a view to ending useless bloodshed.[84] Nevertheless, Kaltenbrunner remained in the Tyrol, removing his headquarters after Hitler's death to Alt-Aussee in a lonely valley of the Salzkammergut. He seems to have had a confused idea of bargaining with the British by revealing the position of Reich treasures that were hidden in a salt mine.[85]

At Alt-Aussee Kaltenbrunner was embarrassed by the presence of Colonel Blobel, the exhumation expert,[86] and of most of the Eichmann commando who had made their way from Prague. All these compromising companions he rejected. Eichmann was last seen by Wisliceny on May 5th, when he was about to ' take to the *maquis* with his men.' According to Wisliceny, Eichmann had discussed this project with Blobel as early as September, describing to him the mountains south of his childhood home in

Linz, which he claimed to know well.[87] Whether the Salzkammergut is capable of indefinitely hiding Eichmann and half a dozen
still-missing assistants one may well doubt. It could not hide
Kaltenbrunner, who, with his adjutant, Schneider, was picked
up a few days later by an American patrol quite close to
Alt-Aussee, their position having been disclosed by Schneider's
wife.

The details and the methods of the Final Solution programme
were little known to the Allies' intelligence teams at the end of
the war. Mueller, Pohl, Eichmann, and Globocnik were not names
to conjure with. The very extended nature of the first hue and cry
enabled the culprits to conceal themselves. Thus, in addition to
Hoess, who hid till March, 1946, Oswald Pohl and his assistant,
Gerhardt Maurer, who kept records of the Auschwitz selections,
were not found till the spring of 1947. These men obtained false
identity papers and by working as day labourers could continue
a long time without attracting attention. This is undoubtedly a
better method than taking to the mountains, though less
romantic. For the latter the Karavanken alps south of Klagenfurt
were the most popular of the delusive sanctuaries. For some
weeks after the capitulation they were roamed by armed
bands of every sort of Axis collaborationist, but these in
the end gave way to British patrols. It was one of these
that early in June discovered Odilo Globocnik, who, however,
achieved the same escape as his master Himmler (*see
page 357*).

The fate of Heinrich Mueller, chief of the Gestapo, presents
the most fascinating possibilities. On April 28th he was in Hitler's
bunker, where he interrogated General Fegelein,[88] the brother-in-
law of Eva Braun whom Hitler executed. According to Willi
Hoettl, Mueller left the bunker in the company of one *Kriminalrat*
Scholz, whom he had employed sending bogus reports on the
short-wave transmitters that had been captured from Russian
spies. It was believed that for some months past Mueller had used
these transmission-sets to establish friendly contacts in Moscow.
There are persistent rumours to-day that he is in Russian employment. The strange thing about this most utterly ruthless of all the
SS personalities is that he did not become a National Socialist till
1939. He had been a regular officer in the Bavarian State Police

who had attracted Heydrich's attention by his study of the Russian police system.[89]

* * * *

After May 8th, 1945, the whole apparatus of National Socialist rule resembled a tangle of burnt rafters, blackened, soaked, and ill-smelling, under which crawled persecutor and victim, no longer very clearly distinguishable. Among the immense horde of foreigners, consisting of prisoners of war, concentration camp inmates, labourers, both conscript and volunteer, and refugees, there was a common impulse to flee this apparently doomed house; but not all could gratify that impulse. There were those who stayed because there was nowhere to go, and among them one group that stayed for months and even years, sometimes in the very camps where they had slaved and where their families had died. These were the survivors of the Final Solution from Poland and the Baltic States, and to a lesser extent from Hungary and Rumania. As late as April, 1946, the Anglo-American Committee on European Jewry and Palestine estimated that there were 87,000 of them in what had been the Greater Reich.[90]

For them the Rheims and Karlshorst armistices had been no golden dawn. They no longer died of hunger and typhus, it is true, nor were they selected for the crematorium if their shoes happened not to fit, but they were without kinsmen, without means, and without a country. They lived among the vanquished, who blamed their race—as they had been taught to do for fourteen years—for every calamity that had befallen them. As Jewish displaced persons, moreover, they were execrated for their preferential rations and for that life of smuggling and subterfuge which they had been forced to acquire when they had tried to survive in the ghettoes.

For the Jewish displaced persons in 1945-48 the lesson to be learnt was the one that had confronted the Warsaw Ghetto survivors early in 1943. The future could no longer be awaited with the ancient resignation of the East. Only through a new use of privation and a new use of loyalty could existence be endured at all. In the trials of a newly created nation and not in the up-to-date installation at Birkenau lay the Final Solution of the Jewish Problem.

Epilogue

THE inquest is over, but it is not the business of the coroner to find the culprits or to judge them. Nevertheless, the reader, who has had the patience to follow even a fraction of this sombre narrative, will have asked himself a dozen questions, and some of these must be discussed even if they cannot be answered.

How much did the man in the street in Germany know and how much did he care? How was it possible that so many hundreds or even thousands of hard-working bureaucrats of all grades went daily to their offices to compose, copy, or pass on the obvious correspondence of race-murder? Why, seeing that every ministry was fighting with every other ministry and that Hitler never knew in the least what was happening any more than Tolstoi's generals at the battle of Borodino, did not one of the righteous men, who said their piece at Nuremberg, make a single active protest? How was it that the mere pathological hate of Hitler and a few companions kept this massive machinery in motion for more than three years?

Others will ask still wider questions regarding the future. Are the Germans the only racial-political group in the world who are capable of setting back the clock to the early ages of man? Is it, on the other hand, the age itself as a whole which is moving that way? Is the discarding of selected victims endemic in the overgrown modern 'democratic' State? Can it happen again and can it happen here? It may be very long before we know the answers to these questions, which recur throughout this inquest on the Final Solution in the form of a sort of repeat design or chintz.

It is difficult to believe that there existed any fully conscious beings in Germany or German-occupied Europe in the last two years of the war who did not know that most of the Jews had disappeared and who had not heard some story that they had been shot or gassed. Nor do I suppose that there was anybody who did not have a friend who knew somebody else who had seen a massacre. More than a hundred million people must have known such things and whispered about them, and yet they could not make the climate unpleasant for the few thousands who carried them out. That, however, need surprise no one. It is as easy for a hundred million persons to be frightened of a secret police force as it is for one.

Conditions of life in a secret police State must not be judged by the standards of a constitutional country, even though England in wartime acquired some of the elements of a police State. The Home Secretary could, it is true, detain persons of suspected political activity without charge or trial and he could suspend newspapers on his own authority. Nevertheless, when a single soldier died from violence in a detention barracks nothing could stop the Sunday papers blazoning it as a sensation. Clearly the wartime powers of the Cabinet were far removed from those of the Reich Main Security Office. What would have happened if the press had got wind of the death of hundreds of thousands of persons detained in the Isle of Man ?

The Nuremberg pleas of 'ignoramus,' made by the war criminals and the implicated witnesses, had the effect of befogging a very obvious fact. In the police State, be it the German or the Russian model, there is never any doubt of the existence of special camps. On the contrary, they become a part of everyone's life—but no one is curious. And this lack of curiosity embraces some of the most powerful persons in the State, who remain unknown because no one wants to know about them. Outwardly the police have become full of glamour. Funny helmets and the braided tunics of village bandsmen have been succeeded by varnished knee boots, white collars, natty military caps, too many motor bicycles, and too many major-generals. But it is all anonymous and remote. The foreign press knew nothing of Heydrich during seven years of his police dictatorship. They only discovered him when he became Protector of Bohemia. During the human sacrifices that attended his pompous funeral in June, 1942, even the German public had probably little idea what manner of man had been snatched from them. And after the war the Allied War Crimes Tribunal believed that the contemptible Streicher was an important and symbolic figure, who should be tried before the world when they had not even looked for Mueller and Eichmann.

It is the atmosphere of anonymity which is most terrible. It numbs the faculty of reason and fair play and substitutes fear. Probably no nation has ever been so frightened as was the German nation during the war. And the higher the Germans rose, the more frightened they became till we reach the case of Heinrich Himmler, who was made head of the police State almost by chance and whom Hitler retained just because he was a frightened man who could be informed on and intimidated. The characteristic plea of the Nuremberg defendants, in spite of its falsity, indicates the state of mind that had prevailed. One by one they testified that they could not have resigned or got themselves transferred to other posts. If they had tried, they would have been sent to a concentration camp or shot. Finally, we reach the climax of absurdity in the Nuremberg yarn of Steengracht von Moyland. He told how Walter Hewel, Ribbentrop's personal liaison officer with Hitler, had disagreed with Goebbels. 'If Goebbels had told Hitler of my attitude,' Hewel informed Steengracht, 'Hitler would have merely pressed a button and called Rattenhuber, the chief of his Security Service, and had me taken away and shot.'

But before the July 1944 plot to murder Hitler, not even the obscurest of wartime officials was ever taken away and shot— either by Rattenhuber or any other Caliph's executioner—and the only State Secretary who ever found his way to a concentration camp was Martin Luther, who was packed off, not by the SS, but in spite of the protection of the SS, having plotted treason against his chief, Ribbentrop, on their behalf. And, as to Hewel and Rattenhuber, they were together at Hitler's stuffy little court till the last and were caught by the Russians in the same Berlin cellar.

Were these the men to stand up for the rights of humanity? They were, it is probable, mostly no more cruel and callous than the German or, indeed, the human race as a whole; but they were a great deal more frightened and a great deal more lacking in artifice. Cruelty and unreason were implicit in the system that had brought them employment and advancement, and to both they had to do lip-service. After they had occupied their desks for some years, they had to invent a mumbo-jumbo language about biological material, inferior strains of blood, 'asocial' and

' unlabourworthy' types, and so forth—to hide from themselves what they were doing.

Like the aerial bomber, the bureaucrat does not see his kill. It is possible that Eichmann never saw a single one of the millions of Jewish corpses of which he boasted, and Himmler, after the experience at Minsk, which von dem Bach-Zalewski described (*see page 208*), probably never wanted to watch another execution. Ordinary Germans were able to see more. Towards the end of the war in particular it must have been hard to avoid seeing something of the plight of the concentration-camp victims pouring into the last pocket of the Reich. The lowest depths of human misery were on public view. Yet Professor Marc Klein has described how the German crowds in the railway stations in February, 1945, watched with absolute indifference the passage of the train from Gross-Rosen to Buchenwald, an immense procession of open trucks, in each one of which a hundred living skeletons crouched in their ragged prison pyjamas under the guns and rubber truncheons of the SS guards and *Kapos*. So, too, the Norwegian witness, Hans Capellen, declared that the Dachau internees, who worked on bomb-disposal in Munich, were cursed and blamed by the crowd for the bombing (IMT. V, 238).

It is wrong to suppose that there was anything particularly unnatural in such incidents. The nearer the misery of fellow human beings, the less is it likely to be appreciated. Men who are beaten, starved, overworked, and frozen are not pretty. Guilty or innocent, they slouch and scowl alike, and they will kill each other for a potato. The honest citizen, who saw them, probably thought how wise Hitler had been to lock up such criminals and savages. The ordinary German should be judged, not for the way that he supported this system, for the more he was bombed and the more he was defeated, the more he had to support it, but for listening in the first place to the silly promises of the authors of the system.

The German of 1933 was a sort of caricature of European civilisation which had grown more frivolous, greedier, and less critical, as material progress undermined some of the older disciplines. The German of 1933 had accepted the bribes and the conditions, but what he got was the ' guns-for-butter' State and, when this led to war, he still expected the account to be paid up. He still believed that the capitalist powers lived on cheap food, obtained by exploiting native populations in backward continents while poor Germany was encircled and blockaded. In this way the dangerous men who half-think really hoped that they could stop the wartime decline in their living standards by plundering and enslaving the conquered and by murdering a part of them—till in the end it was the dead of Auschwitz who provided the wigs, spectacles, and dentures that are now expected of the welfare State.

This record of the ordinary German gives no grounds for supposing that such things cannot happen again, or that there is anything in the present policy of the Western Powers towards Germany that is not conducive to another legend of the 'Diktat,' another crusade of vengeance and racial hate. And yet, in an age that has seen every ideology and every economic creed turned into ludicrous nonsense, we still believe in the powers of sweet reason, as if the French Revolution had never happened.

The mood of Nuremberg has passed. Men whose conduct was far worse than that of most of those who were found guilty and hanged are alive and free; others are released from their prisons from time to time in some confused notion of appeasement. The penitence that was once fashionable among German leaders is less and less in evidence and, when Germany is again united and armed, it will be still less so. The Remer trial has revealed a new breed of heroes and patriots, those who served Hitler's Reich with zeal but can show that they joined the plot to kill Hitler at 11.59 p.m.

And the potential victims? There are still nearly a million Jews in the range of former German wars and several millions more in the deep recesses of the Soviet Union, in the Near East, and North Africa, but the next victims of racial supremacy are not necessarily the Jews. Of the racial problems with which Hitler's Reich believed itself confronted, the Jewish problem was apparently the only one that demanded a Final Solution, but there were always advocates for a final solution for the Slavs. Himmler's Office for the Strengthening of German Folkdom was full of them. They are mostly alive to-day, though as yet modestly employed, but their field of vision is large. For it is not just a

Danzig corridor and a Sudetenland that will irritate the skin of the new nationalism, but a quarter of the territory of the Old Reich, inhabited by seven million Poles.

This, alas, is a book of much evidence and few summations; a book of facts, from which as yet little conclusion can be drawn. But these facts, so far as they can be pieced together, provide analogies that may be of value at the present day. For, while we live in a world where police States abound, these police States do not leave their office correspondence lying about. But here was a police State on the vastest scale, which left documents by the hundred ton and key witnesses by the thousand.

Job on his dunghill wished 'that mine adversary had written a book' and his prayer has been answered, for indeed there is nothing that this adversary did not commit to paper. I have spent close on four years among these documents and I have found their company neither gloomy nor depressing. For on many pages darts and gleams that thing which prevents all government becoming a living hell—human fallibility. Eichmann fails to fill his death trains, the satellite-government Ministers refuse to answer letters, someone gets the figures wrong, and someone else gives the show away too soon. And so the immense disaster was partly whittled down. How much worse it would have been if the French had not been inconsistent, if the Italians had not been easygoing, the Hungarians jealous, the Rumanians corrupt, and the Germans themselves wedded to protocol. It is possible that murderous racialism is something ineradicable in the nature of ants and men, but the Robot State which will give it full effect cannot exist and never will.

Beckley, November, 1952.

Appendix I

Statistical Summary of the Final Solution

Since the reading of the Nuremberg indictment in November, 1945, naming the figure of 5,700,000 Jewish victims of Germany, the round number of six millions has become a generally accepted assumption in most circles that are interested in the matter. But in the course of writing this book I have been forced to the conclusion that, while it cannot be determined even within a half-million degree of accuracy, the true figure may be considerably smaller. In submitting the following estimates I realise that I may be accused of belittling the sufferings of persecuted communities, but I believe that the nature of this book is a guarantee of my good faith in that respect. The figure used at Nuremberg was supplied by the World Jewish Congress at a moment when little reputable data were available. Constant repetition of that figure has already given anti-semitic circles on the Continent and in Germany in particular the opportunity to discredit the whole ghastly story and its lessons. I believe that it does not make the guilt of the living German any less, if the figure of six million turns out to be an over-estimate and that the accurate assessment, *if it can ever be obtained*, will not weaken the Jewish case for sanctions against recurrences of these symptoms. Whether six millions died, or five millions, or less, it was still the most systematic extermination of a race in human history. Moreover, once the principle of the murders is proved, there is no particular magic in additional millions. As a German, Walter Dirks, has written: ' It is shameful that there should be Germans who see a mitigating circumstance in reducing the sum from six millions to two millions !'[1]

In April, 1946, the ' Anglo-American Committee of Inquiry regarding the problems of European Jewry and Palestine,' published an analysis of the Nuremberg indictment figure of 5,700,000—or to be exact 5,721,800 missing European Jews.[2] I use these more detailed statistics purely as a point of departure. Some of them appear to me sound, even over-cautious, others are demonstrably ill-founded. But first I must emphasise that the prosecution at Nuremberg was by no means certain that all these Jews had died. The indictment, read by Mr. Sydney Alderman on November 20th, 1945, goes as follows:

' Of the 9,600,000 Jews who lived in the parts of Europe under Nazi domination, it is conservatively estimated that 5,700,000 have disappeared, most of them deliberately put to death by the Nazi conspirators.'[3]

But next day in opening the case for the prosecution Mr. Justice Jackson said:

' 5,700,000 Jews are missing from the countries in which they formerly lived and over 4,500,000 cannot be accounted for by the normal death-rate nor by immigration ; nor are they included among the displaced persons.'[4]

The higher of my two estimates is slightly bigger than Mr. Jackson's minimum figure but it is still a long way short of the six millions that have

489

received such wide acceptance. This difference of a million and a half is largely to be traced to the highly conjectural estimates of the losses in territory, at present controlled by the Soviet Union, and in Rumania, where figures have been adduced that have no relationship with the facts as known.

I have drawn much of my evidence from the figures compiled for Heydrich and Himmler by the *Sicherheitsdienst* or SD, generally referred to as the Gestapo. These balance-sheets became the gruesome exhibits of the later Nuremberg trials, and it must be observed that, if they contain inaccuracies, they are generally due to over-statement. Their value is relative but it is at least higher than that of estimates which are based solely on alleged pre-war and post-war population returns, the latter being reached by deducting from the former the figure it is desired to prove.

Already before the war there were widely differing estimates of the Jewish populations of Russia, Poland, Hungary, Rumania, and the Balkans, although in most of these countries there was a separate civil registry for Jews. Even in Western Europe, where the use of statistics was less open to reproach, the estimates of Jewish populations are neither more consistent nor more reliable. Since the war few European governments have conducted any census of which detailed figures are available. In the case of Russia particularly, to which the largest group of Jews escaped, there is no present basis for assessing the number of survivors. In April, 1946, the Anglo-American Palestine Committee accepted a figure of 2,665,000 Jews. In January, 1947, the American Jewish Joint Distribution Committee proposed 2,255,000. In 1951, Mr. Solomon Schwarz decided on 1,850,000 for the vastly increased Soviet Union of the post-war era. The Institute of Jewish Affairs in 1950 had calculated as low as 1,600,000.[5] Thus, there is a whole million difference between the highest and lowest of these estimates, none of which are realistic. For it is quite possible that the number of non-Russian Jews who were moved to the depths of the Soviet Union exceeded the number of Russian Jews who were trapped by the Germans, and in this case the number of Jewish survivors should exceed the approximate three million Jews who lived in the Soviet Union of 1939.

There is one source of inestimable value in dealing with debatable figures and this is the 'Korherr report' (Nuremberg documents, NO 5192-4) which was submitted to Himmler in March, 1943. This report tallies with so many counter-checks that its honesty may be assumed where counter-checks are lacking, as for instance in the critical case of Poland. Dr. Korherr was an actuary, employed by Himmler to compile a balance-sheet from the resettlement lists as kept in Eichmann's office, which he referred to discreetly as the RSHA. He describes himself as 'Inspector for Statistics to the *Reichsfuehrer* SS' and his first report, 16 stencilled sheets headed 'The Final Solution of the European Jewish Question,' was sent to Himmler's secretary, Rudi Brandt, on March 23rd, 1943, though the figures are not made up beyond the end of the year 1942. An attempt was made to sum up the total of the various figures in the document and with the omission of Russia and Serbia a figure was reached of 1,873,549 Jews, dead, deported, or emigrated, including 'Special Treatment.' Then Dr Korherr concluded: 'Since the seizure of power the number of Jews in Europe, which was over ten millions in 1933, has been halved ; the decline of over four millions is due to German influence.'

On April 10th Himmler wrote through Rudi Brandt to Dr. Korherr that the words 'including special treatment' on page 9 should be erased and the words 'including transport to the Russian East from the Eastern provinces' be inserted. At the same time Himmler wrote to Kaltenbrunner:

> 'I regard the report as general purpose material for later use and extremely good as camouflage. At present it must neither be published nor communicated to anyone. I shall continue to be informed through the short monthly reports of the RSHA how many go and how many remain behind.'

In the meantime Kaltenbrunner had asked Korherr to prepare an abridged version of the report, six and a half pages in length, for presentation to Hitler. This Korherr sent to Brandt on April 19th, including with meticulous accuracy the returns for transports from France, Holland, Belgium, Norway, Slovakia, Greece, and Bulgaria during the first three months of the year.

> 'Before the war the Old Reich and the Ostmark (Austria) got rid of more than half of their civilised and sterile Jewish population, above all through emigration, whereas in the East the separation of the fruitful Jewish masses, dangerous for the future, was undertaken for the first time during the war and especially since the evacuation measures of 1942.'

Since May 17th, 1939, Dr. Korherr declared, two and a half million Jews had disappeared from the Reich and from Poland. 'The duration of the Jews in the Old Reich is nearing its end.'

Germany (Pre-1938 Frontiers)

Shortly after Hitler's rise to power, in June, 1933, a census was taken of the pure Jews of Germany and it showed 499,682. By the outbreak of war emigration had reduced this number according to the *Reichsvereinigung* to 215,000—a rather problematic figure which must be our starting point.[6] A second *Reichsvereinigung* census, dated October 1st, 1941, shows 163,696 registered Jews, a loss exceeding 50,000, of which only 8,000 heads can be attributed to deportation. One has to decide what portion of the remaining 43,000 escaped by voluntary emigration. Dr. Korherr, in observing that there had been 7,659 natural deaths of Jews in the Old Reich even during the great deportation year, 1942,[7] concluded that the death-rate among German Jewry was 8.5 per thousand, that is six or seven times the death-rate for Europe as a whole. On this basis the volume of such deaths since September, 1939, might be 30,000 and the number of voluntary emigrants only 13,000 (*see page 29 and footnote*). These 30,000 deaths must, I think, be directly attributed to the Final Solution and for the moment the basis for the calculation of the losses is therefore 215,000 minus 13,000 = 202,000.

But on April 1st, 1943, Dr. Korherr estimated that close on 120,000 Jews had been deported from the Old Reich and that 31,910 remained besides a great number 'who must be written off as undiscoverable.' These figures suggest that there had been far less than 215,000 Jews in Germany at the beginning of the war, for the discrepancy is as high as 20,000. Dr. Korherr reported that 16,668 Jews were in mixed marriage. A proportion of these were sent to Theresienstadt, from which they mostly returned at the end of the war. The Anglo-American Committee's estimate allows for 20,000 German Jewish survivors, including the Jews who stayed 'underground.' If a total of 22,000 is accepted and allowance made for the discrepancy in Dr. Korherr's figures we get a death roll of from 160,000 to 180,000.

Mention must, however, be made of an estimate by a most painstaking statistician which is strikingly lower. Dr. Bruno Blau maintains that only 123,000 Jews from the Old Reich can be considered as killed. Starting with the *Reichsvereinigung* figure of 164,000 in October, 1941. He allows 19,000 for survivors who remained at liberty, 8,200 for survivors from Theresienstadt and othe camps, and 13,800 for natural deaths. In my own view a very large part of the latter should be attributed to the Final Solution and a still larger allowance should be made for 'hardship' deaths before October, 1941.[7a]

Austria

In March, 1938, at the time of the Anschluss, the Jewish population of Austria was 185,246. In December, 1939, a report from the Gauleiter's office contained an estimate of 70,000 Jews,[8] living almost entirely in Vienna. This figure is certainly too high, since 4,000 had already been deported to Nisko in Poland (*see pages 44-5*). The Anglo-American Committee prefers to start on a basis of 60,000. At the end of 1942 Dr. Korherr estimated that 47,555 Jews had been deported from Austria and that 8,102 Jews remained. If one adds 7,000 'natural' deaths—half Dr. Korherr's estimate of 14,509 since March, 1938—and 4,000 wartime voluntary emigrants, the figure for September 1st, 1939, becomes 66,600. Of these there survived on October 24th, 1947, some 8,552 Austrian-born Jews in Vienna and a few hundreds in Linz and other towns. Allowing for the voluntary emigrants the loss should be 58,000, but perhaps some portion of Dr. Korherr's 'natural deaths' should be laid to the account of the Final Solution.[9]

In the recent work on population of Gregory Frumkin[9a] it is stated that at one time it was estimated that only 40-50,000 Austrian Jews had been killed. Mr. Frumkin does not say why he prefers an unnamed estimate of 80,000, which is more than the entire Jewish population at the outbreak of war.

Czechoslovakia

The census of 1930 showed 356,830 Jews in the republic, distributed as follows: 117,551 in Bohemia-Moravia, 136,737 in Slovakia, and 102,542 in Ruthenia. The first two groups were subject to an annual decline and the last to a prolific increase. There was a big emigration mainly from Bohemia-Moravia after the Munich agreement and the Anglo-American Committee assessed the population as 315,000 at the outbreak of war, including 90,000 in the Protectorate (Dr. Korherr's figure is 92,000).

Taking the Protectorate or Bohemia-Moravia figures first, Dr. Korherr believed that 69,779 Jews had been resettled by the end of 1942, though this was a relative expression, since more than 50,000 of them had at first gone no further than Theresienstadt, which was inside the Protectorate itself. There were 15,530 Jews still living at large, while nearly 7,000 had disappeared through natural death-rate and voluntary wartime emigration. In contrast to the 1943 survival figure of 15,530, there were no less than 32,000 Jews reputed to be living in the former Protectorate in 1946,[10] but these included not only 15,000 Jews who had survived through mixed marriage or other privileged positions, but also 8,000 Jews who survived

Theresienstadt, 6,000-8,000 Ruthenian Jews, and some thousands of repatriated soldiers and emigrants. To obtain a fair estimate of the number of Jews killed under German rule is, therefore, not easy. I suggest that 15,000 + 8,000 be deducted from 90,000 with a further allowance of 4,000 for wartime emigration. This gives a loss of 63,000 Jews, nearly half of them through Auschwitz, a figure not very much lower than Dr. Korherr's estimate of resettled Jews, made at a time when 'resettlement' was virtually at an end. Mr. Frumkin, however, prefers a figure of 71,000.

The 135,000 Jews of Slovakia had relatively smaller losses through voluntary emigration, since the 40,000 Jews who were ceded to Hungary in November, 1938, believed themselves safe. On the other hand the 95,000 in the new Slovak State reduced themselves to less than 90,000 by voluntary emigration before the beginning of the deportations (*see pages 335-6*). Against this there were 56,691 Jews deported in 1942, according to Korherr's list, though Wisliceny's estimate is only 52,000. In 1944 there were a further 9,000 deportations and a fair number of executions. Data for the 40,000 Jews in the Kosice province, which had been ceded to Hungary, are lacking, but M. Levai[11] believes that there remained 65,500 Jews after the war in the Hungarian 'lost provinces,' a survival rate of 20 per cent. On this basis the Anglo-American Committee's estimate of 30,000 Jews, surviving in all Slovakia, seems far too low.

In a paper read in Paris in December, 1947, Dr. Frederic Steiner, of Bratislava, estimated that, while only 284 returned of the 52,000 deported in 1942, the greater part of the deportees of 1944 from independent Slovakia survived, in addition to a portion of the Jews of Kosice province where, however, he estimated that the Hungarians in 1944 only deported 30,000 out of 46,000.[12] On this basis the survivors for all Slovakia might be as numerous as 50,000. I suggest that this be considered the high figure and 40,000 the low figure, giving a death roll of 85,000 to 95,000. Mr. Frumkin's estimate of 67,000 postulates an even greater number of survivors, something in the neighbourhood of 60,000.[13a]

In the case of Ruthenia the 102,000 Jews were reduced in 1941 by the deportation of 17,000 to 20,000 Jews to Podolia and East Galicia, of whom there are possibly no survivors (*see page 412*). The remainder were involved in the Auschwitz deportations of 1944. According to the Anglo-American Committee, between 6,000 and 8,000 survivors who chose Czechoslovak citizenship after the Russian occupation migrated to Bohemia, but on the basis of M. Levai's figures for Greater Hungary, showing a 20 per cent survival, there should be about 17,000 Ruthenian Jews alive after the war, most of them presumably remaining in Ruthenia, making a total death roll of 85,000.

To sum up these rather complicated conclusions, the death roll for all Czechoslovakia within the pre-Munich frontiers should be between 233,000 and 243,000.

France

The figures used by the Anglo-American Committee in April, 1946, show a loss of 140,000 Jews, based on the survival of 180,000 Jews out of 320,000. On the other hand, the American Jewish Joint Distribution Committee estimated in January, 1947, that 195,000 had survived out of 300,000, while in 1950 the Institute of Jewish Affairs put the population at 225,000.[13] These terminal figures are mere conjecture. While the figure of 320,000 may have been applicable to France in September, 1939, it makes no allowance for emigration at the time of the fall of France and subsequently. Furthermore, the SD were never able to trace the whereabouts of even 300,000 Jews.

Writing in March, 1952,[14] Dr. Georges Wellers asserts that half the deportees from France were Jews and that they numbered 110,000. The puzzling feature of this estimate is that it has no relation whatever with Dr. Wellers's own researches, based on the Drancy lists and published in 1946. According to these, 68,000 Jews were deported between the great *Velodrome d'Hiver* round-up of July 19th, 1942, and the liberation, that is to say less than 75,000 in all, allowing for the very sparse deportations which took place previous to the round-up of July 19th.[15]

The Gestapo lists suggest an even lower figure. An exact estimate of March 27th, 1943, shows 49,902 and a rough estimate of July 21st, 1943 shows 52,000. A third list from Roethke's file shows that a further 16 trains left France before July 1st, 1944, but many of these are known to have been half-transports of less than 500 people each. These 16 trains, with perhaps one or two more which slipped through during the German retreat from France, certainly conveyed less than the 17,000 Jews, mentioned in Dr. Wellers's estimate for the last twelve months of the German occupation.[16] It is also believed that 2,800 Jews returned to France after the war from Germany. I suggest therefore that the real figure, including some hundreds of murders by the Gestapo, should be found between 60,000 and 65,000.

Belgium

The figures used by the Anglo-American Committee are not convincing. 90,000 are allowed for the Jewish population in 1939 and 33,000 for the survivors, including 8,000 refugees. This means a loss of 57,000. But the Belgian Government's lists show only 25,437, who were deported to Auschwitz from Malines, of whom 1,276 returned (*pages 342, 344, and footnote*), to whom may be added a few thousand Polish Jews ' repatriated ' from Antwerp to the Lodz Ghetto early in 1942. In 1941 the Germans were only able to discover 42,000 Jews by registration. It is therefore suggested that most of the missing 48,000 had fled to France, where they were later picked up for deportation as stateless Jews. If that was the case, they cannot be counted among the Belgian losses since they have already figured in the French deportation list. In all probability, however, the majority of the missing 48,000 merely avoided registering—a circumstance which makes it equally impossible to trace their whereabouts since the war.

Allowing for both the Lodz and Auschwitz deportations, the death roll would seem to be between 25,000 and 28,000, but the only figure which is certain is 24,161 for the deportations from Malines.

Luxembourg

According to the Anglo-American Committee, 500 survived the war out of 3,500, and this is only too credible. Luxembourg was incorporated in the Reich and 512 Jews were deported to Lodz in the general Reich deportation of October-November, 1941. Another Luxembourg transport reached Treblinka in March, 1943 (*see pages 142-3*). There were probably transports to Auschwitz as well.

Scandinavia

Dr. Korherr estimated the two deportations from Norway at 690, a little less than the Norwegian Government's figure (*see pages 351-2*). From the Danish deportation 70 died in or on their way to Theresienstadt. The latter figure is too' small to effect the general balance and is omitted.

Holland

In the case of Holland the most careful revision of the death lists has been made by the Netherlands Red Cross with the result that the first estimate of 115,000 missing[17] has been somewhat modified. The estimates in May, 1949,[18] showed nearly 6,000 repatriated and 104,000 still missing, figures which conform closely with the Westerbork camp lists and SD reports. It is doubtful whether much further revision is possible and the figure of 104,000 deaths can be used as the nearest approach to a positive enumeration in the whole of this survey.

Italy

The figures used by the Anglo-American Palestine Committee show a loss of 20,000 of the native Jewish population of Italy in April, 1946. The figures issued by the Vice-President of the Union of Italian Jewish Communities in the following September and quoted by M. Max Adolf Vitale, the President of the Jewish Deportees Search Committee, at the Paris historians' conference at the end of the year, show a slightly bigger loss, namely 22,000. It is, however, evident that at least 60 per cent of this loss was due to emigration, for the sum-total of missing names, both of native and refugee Jews, is according to these two sources[19] 10,271, less 605 who returned after the war. This, however, is by no means a final figure. The statement of September 10th, 1946, shows that there was ' certain notice of death ' only in 1,126 cases and that 2,304 had sent communications since their deportation. That the majority of these had died of privation was still only a supposition at this time.

The composition of the figure of 10,271 is a little peculiar. Approximately 4,500 left Fossoli di Carpi and Bolsano-Gries in known Auschwitz transports, while a further 600 were traced to Mauthausen, but as many as 5,000 are listed as having been sent to Germany or Poland (presumably Auschwitz and Mauthausen) from centres other than Rome, Fossoli, and Bolsano, of which presumably there are no train records. Furthermore, only 272 of the 605 Jews who returned were Italian-born and no less than 146 were survivors from the 1,200 Jews of the island of Rhodes who were deported to Auschwitz in September, 1944. These Jews were Italian subjects, but it is not clear whether the Rhodes deportation is included in the total number of the missing. Taking all these things into consideration, I suggest that the number of victims among the deportees from Italy be placed tentatively between 8,500 and 9,500.

Jugoslavia

The Jugoslav census of 1931 showed 68,405 persons classed as Jews. The Anglo-American Committee seem to assume that this population grew by 7,000 in the next ten years, whereas one should not overlook the possibility that it remained static or even diminished through emigration. Of this population, only 10,446 were classed as Jews in the census of 1946.[20] Here again two factors must be considered, first the numbers who fled to Italy, particularly from Bosnia, and secondly the numbers who, having lived as Gentiles for years, did not choose to reveal themselves as Jews after the war. I suggest, therefore, that the apparent loss of 58,000 Jews be regarded only as a top figure and rather in excess of the most recent estimates. Thus the Office of Jewish Information, New York, accepts 55,000 and Mr. Gregory Frumkin only 50,000.[20a]

Greece

The Anglo-American Committee's figures show a survival of 10,000 Jews out of 75,000. The former figure, based on 5,000 in Athens, 2,000 in Salonika, and the rest mainly in Thrace and the islands, is probably correct. The pre-war estimate is rather doubtful, since the Jewish population of Greece had been declining ever since the turn of the century and the losses through emigration since 1931 are no more likely to have been made up than in previous decades. At the Paris Conference of Historical Commissions in 1947 M. Assher Moissis estimated that 60,000 Greek Jews had been deported, a figure only slightly in excess of the known records of Jewish transports. It would seem, therefore, that a deduction of 10,000 survivors from the 1931 census figure of 67,200 should provide a fair estimate of loss.[21]

Rumania

The discrepancies in current estimates are enormous. The Anglo-American Committee allowed 850,000 Jews for the 1939 population and 335,000 plus 40,000 to 45,000 in Russian-annexed Bessarabia, for the post-war population, a loss therefore of 470,000. M. Matatias Karp, however, estimates an all-round loss of 400,000, but there is evidence that even this figure is far too high.[22]

If we take first the 1939 figure, it must be observed that there was no census that year and that there had been none since 1930, and of this census there are three published estimates, all claiming to be accurate to a single digit, 725,318,[23] 756,930,[24] and 778,094.[25] There is still a fourth and allegedly official figure. Under the law of January 21st, 1938, all Jews in Rumania were required to submit proof of citizenship. It was calculated that 617,396 registered, that 44,848 abstained, and that there were 30,000 who were not qualified to register. This makes a total of 692,000,[25a] a figure of which it may be said that it is just as likely to be accurate as the others.

If we turn to the figures for 1945, the loss in population must be reduced by the numbers, who were deported by the Russians from Bukovina and Bessarabia in 1940-41, and by the numbers who fled to Russia when the Rumanians reoccupied the provinces. According to the military census, conducted in Bessarabia in August-September, 1941, these numbers may have reached 120,000 (*see page 399, footnote 13*).

There are obviously too many discrepancies to arrive at any results by comparing pre-war and post-war estimates. One can proceed more safely by examining the wartime occurrences as far as they can be assessed. There were two distinct movements of extermination. First the series of deportations across the Dniester and Bug between August, 1941, and July, 1942, and secondly the deportations from Northern Transylvania conducted by the Hungarians in May-June, 1944. In the first group of deportations the Jews in Bessarabia were apparently reduced from 126,434 to 17,081,[26] while about 35,000 were deported from Czernowitz. M. Levai's estimate of 140,000 Jews deported may, I think, be accepted.[27] A census of March, 1943, showed 72,412 Jews surviving beyond the Dniester. Although M. Charles Kolb of the Swiss Red Cross could only account for 54,300 in the following December, the difference may be explained by a continuous drifting back (*see pages 402 and 409*). It seems, therefore, probable that 70,000 of the 140,000 deportees perished, and to these it may be necessary to add 12,000 for the murders committed under the direction of the *Einsatzgruppen* in the summer of 1941.

In Northern Transylvania, handed over to Hungary in August, 1940, there were 148,649 Jews according to the Hungarian census and 151,125 according to the Rumanian.[28] M. Levai, in his detailed study of the subject of the Hungarian deportations of 1944, declares that only 6,000 Jews were permitted to remain, but that 20,000 returned from Germany after the war.[29] Some thousands must certainly be allowed for escapes to 'Metropolitan' Rumania. One may accept, at any rate as a top figure, 120,000 deaths in Northern Transylvania. The total losses to Rumanian Jewry, exclusive of the somewhat dubious situation of those who escaped to Russia and Siberia, may therefore be between 200,000 and 220,000.

Hungary

The data are less open to dispute than in the case of other East European countries and the committee's estimate of 220,000 surviving in April, 1946, out of 400,000 Jews in the 'pre-Munich boundaries' may even be too high. It includes 15,000 Jews due for repatriation from Russia and 5,000 refugees in Germany, Austria, and Italy. M. E. Namenyi, however, estimated the survivors in December, 1945, at 190,000, allowing 144,000 for Budapest— which is a reduction somewhat exceeding 40,000 in the city's pre-war Jewish population.[30] M. Namenyi believes that no less than 60,000 of the surviving Jews in Hungary returned from deportation in Germany, a proportion that seems too high. I suggest that the loss of 180,000 Hungarian Jews, the Anglo-American Committee's estimate, be regarded as a low figure and 200,000 as a high figure.

Poland

It has been generally assumed that more than 3,000,000 perished— an assumption that fails to take into account the several factors discussed in Chapter 3. Since there are no means of finding out the number of Jews who have chosen to remain in the Soviet Union, apart from the 157,400 who were repatriated to Poland in 1946, it will probably never be possible to assess the losses of Polish Jewry within a quarter of a million.

The starting-point of the Anglo-American Committee's assessment is a figure of 3,351,000 Jews in Poland in 1939. This is not a census figure but an allegedly official estimate. The last Polish census on December 9th, 1931, showed 2,732,600 'racial' Jews, an increase of 622,000 in the past ten years.[31] Assuming the same prodigious rate of increase, a figure of 3,250,000 Jews would not be impossible in September, 1939, but it is doubtful whether such a figure allows enough for emigration. Against this putative figure we have at the end of June, 1946, when the option to return from Russia expired, a figure of 240,489 registered Jewish survivors in Poland,[32] to which must be added the committee's estimate of Polish Jewish refugees in other European countries in April, 1946, apparently 110,000 scattered as far afield as Sweden, Southern Italy, and Rumania.

On top of this official survival of 350,000 Jews there is the conjectural number who remained in the Soviet Union, either in their old homes to which they had returned in annexed Eastern Poland, or in Siberia and the Volga-Ural region and in Biro-Bidjan. Whether or not all are living to-day, this must have been a gigantic figure, since those who reached inner Russia, either by flight or by deportation, must have several times outnumbered the 157,420 who elected to return to the new Poland in 1945-46. Thus, according to the estimate of the Polish Government,[33] the voluntary emigrants from the General Government and incorporated provinces in 1939-41 numbered approximately 300,000, a figure which is consistent with Dr. Korherr's statistical returns (see page 50). To these must be added the refugees and deportees from the Russian-annexed provinces, including the mass-flight that followed the invasion of June, 1941. In the case of Eastern Galicia there was insufficient time for the flight of so densely massed a Jewish population. In the winter of 1941 Brigadier-General Katzmann of the police was able to discover as many as 450,000 of the original 573,000.[34] But this was not true of Polish White Russia with its huge escape areas. It was estimated before the war that Polish White Russia contained 486,000 Jews and Soviet White Russia 375,000, but of this combined population of 861,000 the Germans could only trace 172,000 in the 'Civil Commissariat of White Ruthenia' in 1941. Even the tremendous slaughter-claims of the Germans for the former Polish White Russian towns in the extermination campaigns of 1941, 1942, and 1943 seem scarcely to reach 130,000.

This certainly does not mean that four-fifths of the White Russian Jews escaped or that the massacres in the Polish section were limited to 130,000, for there was undoubtedly a large population which by repeated flight to small villages and forest camps avoided registration. To the Gestapo figures of an approximate 130,000 Jews, killed in Polish White Russia, there must be added the greater part of this fugitive population, whose fate it was to die of hunger and hardship or at the hands of antisemitic partisans, whose bag could not be included in the Gestapo's totals. The proportion who survived the war by fighting in partisan bands or by crossing the Russian lines must have been quite small. Perhaps to be on the safe side a full 100,000 should be added to the 'registered deaths.'

It may, therefore, be reckoned that 250,000 Jews escaped from Polish White Russia and 120,000 from Eastern Galicia. In addition to these figures, there was a considerable reduction in the Jewish population of former Polish Vilna and its province, before the Germans arrived in 1941 (see page 213). It certainly exceeded 30,000. Thus the flight from Poland into Russia may have been in the neighbourhood of 700,000 when all these sources are considered.

It must not, however, be concluded that there were 700,000 Jews from pre-war Poland living in the Soviet Union at the time of the repatriations of 1946. Some portion of this number must have been mopped up by the Germans in the course of the advance through Russia. A very much bigger deduction must also be made for those who succumbed in the course of transplantation. In Southern Siberia the death-rate was very high for Poles, Lithuanians, Rumanians, and Jews alike, but it is disputable whether such losses, if they can ever be known, should be laid at the door of the Final Solution. Apart from this unknown quantity, I conclude that the number of Jews who perished in the old Poland was between 2,350,000 and 2,600,000.

The Soviet Union

(Including the Baltic States, but excluding the annexed territories formerly belonging to Poland, Rumania, and Czechoslovakia.)

The astonishing variety of estimates of the number of Jews surviving in post-war Soviet Russia has already been mentioned. Equally diverse are the estimates of the slaughter, proffered by the prosecution during the *Einsatzgruppen* trial. The *Einsatzgruppen* reports themselves are too unco-ordinated and end too soon to produce any satisfactory result, but there was at least one German attempt at a general balance-sheet. Dr. Korherr wrote in his first report to Himmler on March 23rd, 1943, that 633,300 Jews had been 'resettled' in Russia and the former Baltic States. Since the figure excluded Jews who had been transferred to ghettoes and labour-camps, it was clearly implied that they had been killed.

This figure had been supplied to Korherr by the RSHA and it was presumably based on *Einsatzgruppen* and other police reports and therefore subject to exaggerations. Nevertheless, it must do as a basis in default of any other, but first it is necessary to deduct the Jews who were killed in areas formerly belonging to Poland, in White Russia, and Vilna Province, and these may have numbered 150,000 by the end of 1942. Then there must be added the Jews massacred in 1943-44, after the composition of the report, in pre-war Russian territory and the Baltic States during the retreat from Stalingrad to the Polish border. Even at this period a considerable proportion of the Jewish population survived, but it was largely an unregistered population living underground. The portion, on whom the Germans could lay their hands with certainty, survived mainly in the Riga, Minsk, and Kovno Ghettoes and in the labour-camps, particularly in Esthonia, the Riga area, and the Reich-incorporated part of Lithuania. From all these sources a figure of 100,000 might be produced and very little of it survived the war. Calculated in this way, the total number of victims might reach 580,000, but the same observation must apply as in the case of Polish White Russia, namely, that there was a big unrecorded death-rate among the fugitive Jewish population which the Gestapo had no means of assessing. This unrecorded death-rate might well bring the total for pre-war Soviet Russia, plus the Baltic States, to 700,000 or even 750,000, figures which, I suggest, should replace the 1,050,000 of the Anglo-American Committee's report.

Writing late in 1943, before the discovery of the *Einsatzgruppen* reports and the bandying of figures of a million and even two millions by the Nuremberg prosecution, Mr. Joseph Schechtmann estimated that from 650,000 to 850,000 Jews had been trapped by the Germans. This figure, based on such Russian reports as came to hand, seems an astonishingly fair one within its very wide limits,[35] but to-day it is the fashion to regard such figures as a form of dupery by the Soviet press in order to pretend that the authorities had· rescued the majority of the Jews from their peril. It is the thesis of Mr. Solomon Schwarz that the wartime policy of the Russian Government was a poorly camouflaged anti-semitism and that the escape of the Jews was hindered in every way. Mr. Schwarz believes that of the whole Jewish population of the Greater Soviet Union of June, 1941, that is nearly 5,000,000, only 1,850,000 survived the war, that no less than 4,000,000 Jews were trapped in Russia and the annexed provinces, and that only 1,000,000 of them escaped.[36]

To reach this conclusion Mr. Schwarz chooses to ignore the German police reports altogether and to assess the numbers who were trapped on a purely arbitrary system of his own. Rejecting the German massacre returns for Kiev, Dniepropetrovsk, Kharkov, and other large Jewish urban populations, which suggest an escape-rate of three-quarters and more, he proposes that only a fifth of the Jewish population escaped from White Russia, a third from the Ukraine, where there had been more than a million and a half Jews, and a half from the Russian Republic. Equally, Mr. Schwarz rejects the post-war estimates of Jewish populations published by the Moscow Yiddish newspaper *Ainikeit*, because they are disconcertingly opposed to his thesis. Since Mr. Schwarz is not above quoting *Ainikeit* as a reputable source when it suits his case, it may be useful to repeat some of this newspaper's figures here, bearing in mind that they come from a Jewish source and that they cast a light, however dim, on the present-day situation of what must be the overwhelming bulk of the surviving Jews of Europe[37]:

Kiev (August, 1946) ...	...	...	...	100,000
Odessa (April, 1946) ...	...	...	...	80,000
Dniepropetrovsk (June, 1946)		...	...	50,000
Winnitsa (September, 1946) ...		...	...	14,000
Zhitomir (March, 1946)	...	...	...	6,000

These figures were recorded at a time when the homeward trek from the deep interior had only begun.

Conclusion

If an analysis of the nature of this destruction is attempted, it will be found that more than a third of the missing Jews of Europe died, not from direct physical violence, but from overwork, disease, hunger, and neglect, but this proportion varies from country to country. In the case of Germany, Austria, and Bohemia, it may be as high as 80 per cent., whereas in Russia it was probably low, because of the summary nature of the exterminations. In the case of the deportees from the Western countries and Greece and most of the deportees from Hungary, this percentage of non-violent death was determined by the Auschwitz selections and probably averaged 25 per cent. In Rumania the peculiar fate of the deportees to Transdniestria brings the percentage of ' slow deaths ' up to nearly 50 per cent. In Poland, where hunger and disease had reaped a big harvest before the exterminations began, this proportion may exceed a third.

Apart from the gassings in Auschwitz and the Polish death-camps, more than a million Jews must have died by the firing squad or during the round-ups in the ghettoes. Auschwitz, in spite of its immense symbolic significance, probably contributed less than a fifth of the victims (*see pages 460-1*).

SUMMARY OF EXTERMINATION ESTIMATES

	Low	High	Anglo-American Committee's Figures, April, 1946
Germany (1938 frontiers)	160,000	180,000	195,000
Austria	58,000	60,000	53,000
Czechoslovakia (1938)	233,000	243,000	255,000
Denmark	(less than 100)		1,500
			(chiefly refugees in Sweden)
France	60,000	65,000	140,000
Belgium	25,000	28,000	57,000
Luxembourg	3,000	3,000	3,000
Norway	700	700	1,000
Holland	104,000	104,000	120,000
Italy	8,500	9,500	20,000
Jugoslavia	55,000	58,000	64,000
Greece	57,000	60,000	64,000
Bulgaria (pre-1941 frontier)	—	—	5,000
Rumania (pre-1940 frontier)	200,000*	220,000*	530,000
Hungary (1938 frontiers)	180,000	200,000	200,000
Poland (1939 frontiers)	2,350,000*	2,600,000*	3,271,000
USSR (pre-1939 frontiers), plus Baltic States	700,000*	750,000*	1,050,000
			6,029,500
			Less dispersed refugees 308,000
Sum Total	4,194,200*	4,581,200*	=5,721,800

*Owing to the lack of reliable information at the time of writing, these figures must be regarded as conjectural.

Appendix II

The Fate of Some of the Participants in 'The Final Solution' (October, 1952)

THE list which follows should promote some disturbing reflections. First, the number of people who have been able, in spite of the notoriety of their former activities, to stay underground for more than seven years is truly prodigious. Of the 202 persons named in the list, 35 have not even been traced, while a further 20, whose whereabouts are known, had not been brought to trial in October, 1952. Among the untraced are the names of Heinrich Mueller and Adolf Eichmann, the two greatest mass-murderers after Himmler.

Luck has played an inordinate part in the fate of these persons. Those who were extradited under the very simple procedure, which prevailed up till November, 1947, to the countries which are now regarded as behind the Iron Curtain, received very short shrift. While the Polish Government favoured elaborate, highly publicised trials, the Russians would sometimes try a batch of generals in the morning and hang them in the afternoon, as they did at Riga on February 3rd, 1946. At the other end of the scale is the fate of those who were handed over to the jurisdiction of the German courts after the winding up of the United Nations War Crimes Commission in 1948. The names of Horst Wagner, Eberhard von Thadden, Georg Leibbrandt, Otto Braeutigam, and Ernst Wetzel occur with some frequency in this tale of murder, but not one of them has been re-arrested. A less fortunate colleague, Franz Rademacher (see page 364), was belatedly tried in February-March, 1952, when his counsel had the happy inspiration of subpœna-ing some of his coadjutors, who, like Rademacher, had signed dispatches relating to mass-deportation of Jews to 'The East.' Most of these gentlemen were by now established in the Koblenzstrasse, the successor to the Wilhelmstrasse as the Foreign Office of the infant Bonn Federal Republic. As a result, Rademacher was judged to have been in most cases a mere postman—the name by which the late Baron von Weizsaecker had described his own rôle. In two cases Rademacher was judged to have used some personal pressure, and on this account he received a sentence of three years and five months' imprisonment—a sentence which he avoided by breaking bail and flying to Argentina.

The mildness of German justice towards war criminals is not restricted to those tried in German courts, for all the defendants before the British and American tribunals who escaped the death penalty were sent to serve their sentences in their own country, profiting fully by the German penal procedure, according to which a third or even a half of a sentence may be remitted for good conduct in prison. Remission has been earned by submissive conduct in prison irrespective of the nature of the crime. Let us take the case of the Ravensbrueck women guards, convicted by the British Hamburg court in February, 1947. Margarete Mewes, who received a sentence of ten years, was let out of Werl at Christmas, 1951, while Alfrede Moenneke and Ilse Vettermann, sentenced to 10 and 12 years respectively, left Werl on June 14th, 1952. Mewes had the effrontery to boast that she had been given a pretty little room in the Governor's house and allowed to go out shopping—a story that had officially to be denied. Similarly, five of the Belsen women, who were sentenced to ten years' imprisonment at Lueneburg on November 15th, 1945, were released from Werl a bare six years later. One has only to read the Lueneburg evidence as published to see how these women had interpreted the functions of a prison under the SS State.

The laws of remission apply equally to the time spent before trial in internment or prisoner-of-war camps. In some cases pre-trial detention has been deemed equivalent to a six years' sentence—less remission—and the defendant has been discharged after serving his term with all the privileges of an officer-prisoner under the Hague conventions. The German penal code also provides for leave of absence from prison, and this has been accorded to the long-term inmates of Werl and Landsberg, including the Field-Marshals Manstein and Kesselring, and the SS General Kurt Meyer, all of whom are on parole at the moment of writing.

In the case of sentences passed by the German *Spruchkammern* or Denazification Tribunals, there is an element of the ludicrous. The term ' Arbeitslager' or labour-camp can be used to cover compulsory labour, which the culprit may or may not be called on to serve while residing in pursuance of the court order in his native town, a device applied in the case of elderly SS police-generals and others who worked their passage with the Allies as Nuremberg trial witnesses.

Even a death sentence may lack the finality which it implies. At the international Nuremberg trial of 1945-46 the 11 of the 21 defendants who did not escape death sentence were hanged a fortnight later. But the seven men who were condemned to death at the 'Doctors' trial, on August 27th, 1947, were not hanged till the following June, having achieved this delay through the tactics of their defence counsel. During those ten months there was a marked change in the climate of public opinion towards what were thought to be vindictive sentences, influenced by the notorious case of the American Dachau Tribunal. This tribunal, which was abolished in December, 1947, had tried 1,500 Germans and condemned 420 of them to death. In the autumn of that year it became the subject of a commission of investigation under Justice Gordon Simpson of the Texas Supreme Court. The commission recommended that 29 men, who were still under sentence of death, should be reprieved, and it declared that statements had been obtained both from defendants and witnesses by highly questionable means.

On November 3rd, 1947, at the height of this scandal, the trial of the Concentration Camp Central Administration was concluded at Nuremberg. Only four out of 15 defendants were condemned to death. In fact only one of them, Oswald Pohl, was executed, and then not till June 8th, 1951, when the enormity of his crimes excluded him from the final Allied pardon. Another nine Nuremberg trials followed this case, but in only one of them, the *Einsatzgruppen* case, which was concluded in April, 1948, were there death sentences. Since the charge was open and undisguised mass-murder, 14 of the 21 defendants were condemned to die. In actual fact only four were executed. One of the 14 men, who wore the red jacket of the doomed, is already at liberty, but the *Einsatzgruppen* commanders, Ohlendorf, Braune, Naumann, and Blobel were hanged in Landsberg prison on June 8th, 1951. With them perished Oswald Pohl, Schallmair, the Commandant of

Muehldorf camp, and Hans Schmidt, the Buchenwald adjutant. It was the last death sentence to be carried out at the orders of the Western Allies.

During the three to three and a half years that these men waited in suspense there was time to turn squalid butchers into patriots and martyrs. In July, 1952, when the Bonn Federal Government sought a legal decision outlawing Remer's Socialist Reich Party (SRP), the prosecution declared that the party venerated these men as 'the Seven Great Germans' and placed them in the same niche as the dead of the two world wars. There have also been death sentences which, though never commuted, have simply not been carried out. Thus, Lieut.-General Kurt Oberg, the Higher SS and Police Leader, and Colonel Helmuth Knochen, the Security Police Commander for Northern France and Belgium, were both condemned to death by British courts in 1946, but sent to Paris to face further charges. And there they are still, waiting in the Cherche-Midi prison, their offences at least eight years old and their names a dim memory. In like manner Lieut.-Colonel Eduard Strauch, the mass-murderer of the Minsk Ghetto, was shipped after his Nuremberg death sentence to Brussels to answer for excesses committed during the Ardennes counter-offensive of 1944. He is apparently in a lunatic asylum.

Time has been the friend of the war criminal, for the public sense of fair play is offended by charges which it takes years to produce. In December, 1950 the British Government circulated a note, declaring that it would no longer regard extradition from the British Zone in Germany as obligatory even when a *prima facie* case had been made out for it. This was because the original undertaking had been made on the understanding that the Governments of the United Nations would complete their trials within a brief period. This act of clemency had a somewhat back-handed result. The Russians at once delivered five German generals to the Czechoslovaks, who hanged them all on August 25th, 1951.

The last extradition from the British Zone took place on October 29th, 1950, and it was the German outcry which followed this case—it concerned the liquidator of the Cracow Ghetto, Major Willi von Haas—that seems to have provoked the British note. On November 14th there was an interpellation in the *Bundestag* of the new republic in the name of all parties except the Communists. It called for the end of all extradition proceedings by the Allies. When the interpellator declared that the Government of Wurttemburg-Baden had refused to carry out arrests in such cases, there were prolonged cheers and still more when the interpellator proceeded to say: 'Anyone who is delivered up to Poland begins his march to the gallows.'

It was easy to believe such a generalisation, and yet on November 15th, 1947, the Polish Ministry of Justice had stated that of 296 German war criminals who had been brought to trial 48 had been acquitted or dismissed from the case ; 1,602 Germans had by then been surrendered to the Polish Government. It seems that the Ministry of Justice has been very slow in dealing with this list and even on the scene where Frank and Globocnik conducted their terror the political climate is changing. Willi von Haas has not been tried, neither has Erich Koch, the former Gauleiter of East Prussia and Bialystok, who was shipped to Poland in February, 1950. Even Juergen Stroop, the liquidator of the Warsaw Ghetto, was not hanged till September, 1951.

APPENDIX II

In France it is notorious that the butchers of the Gestapo have been pursued with less zeal than have their real or alleged French collaborators. Late in 1951 it was revealed at the trial of some obscure informer that no steps had been taken to try Major Barbie, of the Lyons Gestapo, the hero of the episode of the children's home at Eyzieux (*see page 327*). The number of German war criminals sentenced to death by French tribunals certainly does not reach three figures, but on April 11th, 1952, the French Minister for Justice declared that 10,519 Frenchmen had been executed since the liberation, only 846 of them having been tried by legally appointed tribunals. There were then 2,400 French collaborationists still serving prison sentences seven and a half years after the liberation. But at the prison for German war criminals at Wittlich, in the French Zone, there were only 185 left and 18 of these were released to celebrate the following ' Quatorze Juillet.'

At the end of 1951 the number of German war criminals detained in the three Allied prisons, Landsberg, Werl, and Wittlich, was 855. This was when the German demand for their release was at its most vociferous. On December 16th the bulletin of the Federal Government Information Office did not hesitate to demand a retrial of all the inmates of Werl, using the words 'war criminals' in inverted commas. It may be supposed that Dr. Adenauer and his colleagues cannot be expected to act otherwise, but the disquieting side of the situation is this: If there are major criminals hiding outside Germany to-day, the only Government that can demand their extradition is the Federal Government of Bonn. In most parts of the world Eichmann, the man who boasted of his 5,000,000 dead, and Heinrich Mueller, the man who had more reason to make that boast, could proclaim their identity without fear of the consequences.

(Names directly implicated printed in CAPITALS)

ABETZ, Otto. Ambassador to France, 1940-44. Sentenced to 20 years' hard labour by Paris military tribunal, July 22nd, 1949. Appealed to The Hague International Court, March, 1952. At present in civil hospital.

Albrecht, Emil. Chief of Legal Section, Foreign Office. Has not been charged.

ANTIGNAC, Captain Joseph. Chief of the Vichy ' Police aux questions juives.' Condemned to death Paris, July 9th, 1949. Commuted to life imprisonment.

ANTONESCU, Marshal Ion, Prime Minister of Rumania, and ANTONESCU, Mihai, President of Council. Arrested in Bucharest, September 18th, 1944. Executed by sentence of Bucharest People's Court, June 1st, 1946.

ARAJS, Major Viktor. Head of the Latvian 'Perkonkrust' party in Riga. Helped to organise the mass killings of 1941. Reported in July, 1949, detained in British Zone, Germany, but later escaped, and is at large.

BAAB, Heinrich. *Kriminalsekretär*, Frankfurt Gestapo. Life imprisonment, Frankfurt *Schwurgericht*, March, 1950.

Bach-Zalewski, Lieut.-General Erich von dem. Higher SS and Police Leader, central Russian front. Sentenced March 31st, 1951, to ten years' ' special labour ' by Munich *Hauptspruchkammer* and his property confiscated. Said to be living in nominal house-arrest at Laffenau (November, 1952).

BAKY, Laszlo. Commissary for Jewish Questions in Hungarian Ministry for Interior. Shot by sentence of Budapest People's Court, January, 1946.

Bargen, Werner von. Foreign Office representative with military government in Belgium ; promoted deportations of Jews, 1942-43. Employed in Bonn Foreign Office since the war, but retired in June, 1952, after the Rademacher case.

Bene, Otto. Consul-General, Foreign Office representative with Civil Commissar of the Netherlands. Kept detailed reports of deportations of Dutch Jews, 1942-43. Employed in Bonn Foreign Office, March, 1952.

Benzler, Felix. Minister to puppet Serb Government, Belgrade, 1941. Demanded total deportation of Belgrade Ghetto. Has not been charged.

BERGER, SS General Gottlob. Head of the *Hauptamt* (administration office) of the SS and Himmler's personal liaison officer with the Rosenberg Ministry. Condemned by American tribunal, Nuremberg, April, 1949, to 25 years' imprisonment. Sentence commuted to 10 years on January 31st, 1951. Freed a year later.

BEST, Karl Werner. Reich plenipotentiary, Denmark, and in charge of the Jewish deportations of October, 1943. Sentenced to death, Copenhagen, 1946. Sentence commuted to 12 years' imprisonment July 20th, 1949. Released August 29th, 1951.

BIEBOW, Hans. Ghetto Administrator, Lodz, 1940-44. Hanged by sentence of Lodz court, April 24th, 1947.

BLANKENBERG, Werner. Section Chief in the Fuehrer's Chancellory. Succeeded Brack as head of euthanasia activities. Supplied staff for the Polish death camps, 1942-43. Absolutely untraced.

BLOBEL, Colonel Paul. Commanded special commando 4a in Russia. Organised Kiev massacre. Director-in-chief of exhumation activities, 1942-44. Condemned to death, Nuremberg, April, 1948. Not executed at Landsberg till June 8th, 1951.

BOEHME, General Franz. Responsible for shooting Jewish hostages in Serbia, October, 1941. Committed suicide in Nuremberg prison before facing trial, June, 1947.

BOEPPLE, Dr. Ernst. Joint Secretary to Ministry for Interior, Cracow. Collaborated with Globocnik in the resettlement of the Polish ghettoes. Condemned to death, Cracow, February, 1950.

BORMANN, Martin. Chief of the Party Chancellory and Hitler's personal secretary. Believed killed by a Russian shell on leaving Hitler's bunker, April 30th, 1945.

BOTHMANN, SS Captain. Commanded Chelmno death camp in 1942-43 and 1944. Not traced.

BOUHLER, Philip. Chief of the Fuehrer's Chancellory and head of the euthanasia programme. Believed to have killed himself at Karinhall during the battle of Berlin, May, 1945.

Bousquet, René. Vichy Minister for Police. Implicated in the great round-up of Paris Jews, July, 1942. Sentenced June, 1949, five years' 'national indignity.'

BRACK, Viktor. As department chief in the Fuehrer's Chancellory, went to Poland to install the gas chambers. Condemned to death at the 'Doctors' Trial' and executed at Landsberg on June 2nd, 1948.

BRAND, SS Captain. Resettlement Commissar, Warsaw, 1942-43. Said to have been arrested in Austria, summer, 1947.

BRANDT, SS Lieut.-General Rudolf. Himmler's personal adjutant. Condemned to death in the 'Doctors' Trial' for procuring medical experiments, but was also a party to many of Himmler's orders in connection with the 'Final Solution.' Executed at Landsberg, June 2nd, 1948.

Brauchitsch, Field-Marshal Walter von. Was to have been tried by a British military court with Rundstedt in 1949, but was released on grounds of age and health. It was never established whether he was told of Hitler's order to exterminate the Jews at the conferences preceding the invasion of Russia.

BRAEUTIGAM, Otto. Liaison Officer with the High Command in the Political Department of the Rosenberg Ministry. A charge of complicity in the extermination of Russian Jews preferred by Nuremberg *Landgericht* in January, 1950. Not yet tried.

BRUNNER, Anton Alois. Eichmann's most successful Jewish deportation expert (Major SS). Functioned in Vienna, Berlin, Salonika, Paris, and Bratislava. Hanged by sentence of Vienna People's Court (Russian Sector), May, 1946.

Buch, Major Walter. President of the Party Tribunal. Recommended pardon for the murderers of November 9th, 1938. Committed suicide in an Allied internment camp while awaiting trial, 1949.

BUEHLER, Josef. State Secretary to Governor Frank in Cracow. Pressed for extermination of Polish Jewry at Gross-Wannsee Conference. Sentenced to death, Warsaw, July 20th, 1948.

BUERCKEL, Josef. Gauleiter for Vienna and then Saarland-Lorraine. Responsible for Jewish deportations from both in 1939-40. Died November, 1944.

Conti, Leonardo. Head of Department of Health in Ministry for Interior. His part in setting up gassing camps not established. Suicide at end of war.

Cukurs, Herbert. Deputy to Arajs (*q.v.*) during Riga massacres. Reported in 1949 to be running a pleasure-boat business in Rio de Janeiro.

DALUEGE, SS Lieut.-General Kurt. Head of the *Ordnungspolizei*. Signed the orders to deport Reich Jews in October, 1941. Hanged in Prague, October 20th, 1946.

DANNECKER, SS Captain Theodor. In charge deportation of Jews from France, 1942, Bulgaria, 1943, and Italy, 1944. Total disappearance.

D'ARQUIER, de Pellepoix. Vallat's successor as the Vichy Government's Commissaire aux questions Juives. Condemned to death, 1947.

Dering, Dr. Wladyslas. Named by the Soviet State Commission as an assistant to Dr. Schumann in his experiments in Auschwitz. Arrested at Huntingdon in 1947, but charges dropped for lack of evidence. Now directs a hospital in British Somaliland.

EICHMANN, SS Lieut.-Colonel Karl Adolf. Head of the Jewish Office of the Gestapo, 1940-45. Last seen at Alt-Aussee, May 3rd, 1945.

ENDRE, Vitez. Commissary for Jewish Affairs in Hungarian Ministry for Interior. Shot by sentence of Budapest People's Court, January, 1946.

ENTRESS, Captain Ferdinand. Polish *Volksdeutscher* doctor implicated in the extermination of the sick at Auschwitz. Condemned to death at Cracow, November 22nd, 1947.

Falkenhausen, General Alexander von. Convicted by Brussels court on March 7th, 1951. Sentenced to 12 years' imprisonment, but released within a few weeks.

FERENCSY, Major Laszlo. Liaison Officer between Eichmann and the Hungarian militia, 1944. Sentenced to death by Budapest People's Court, January, 1946.

FISCHER, Dr. Ludwig. *Landkommissar* for Warsaw. Executed in Warsaw, March 8th, 1947, for his part in the liquidation of the Warsaw Ghetto.

Foerster, Dr. Albrecht. Gauleiter for Danzig-West Prussia. Condemned to death at Danzig on April 29th, 1948. Charges included deportation of Jews.

FRANK, Hans. Governor-General of Poland, 1939-45. Executed in Nuremberg prison, October 16th, 1946.

Frank, Karl. Protector of Bohemia-Moravia, 1943-45. Executed in Prague, May 22nd, 1946.

Freisler, Roland. President of the Berlin People's Court. Killed during a session by Allied air attack, October, 1944.

FRIEDL, SS Major Gustav. Security Police Commandant, Bialystok. Directed liquidation of Bialystok Ghetto, September, 1943, for which he was tried and hanged in Bialystok, January, 1950.

FUCHS, SS Lieut.-Colonel. Security Police Commander, Belgrade, 1941-42. Condemned to death in Belgrade, November 22nd, 1946.

FUENTEN, SS Captain Ferdinand Aus Der. Directed Eichmann's branch office in Amsterdam and arranged the deportations of 1942-44. Sentenced to life imprisonment, The Hague, December 27th, 1949.

Funk, Walter. Reich Minister for Economic Affairs. Sentenced at Nuremberg to life imprisonment, October 1st, 1946.

Ganzenmueller, Teodor. Under-Secretary in the Reich Ministry for Transport. Arranged deportation trains from Warsaw to the Treblinka death camp in 1942. Has not apparently been charged.

GERSTEIN, SS Lieut. Kurt. In charge of disinfectant gases department of SS Health Institute. Confessed to supplying Zyklon B gas for the death camps. Has disappeared without trace.

GIESLER, Paul. Gauleiter for Lower Bavaria and Munich from 1943. Planned extermination of Jews in Dachau at end of the war. Said to have committed suicide.

GLOBOCNIK, SS Lieut.-General Odilo. Higher SS and Police Leader, Lublin and Trieste. Directed Einsatz Reinhardt massacres, 1942-43. Contradictory accounts: (a) killed by partisans in Istria, May 1944; (b) took poison in Karavanken Alps, June, 1945, to avoid arrest by a British patrol.

GLUECKS, SS Lieut.-General Heinrich. Head of Amt D of the SS Economic Office and Inspector-General of Concentration Camps. Went underground during the Red Cross negotiations of April, 1945, and has not been seen since.

GOEBBELS, Dr. Josef. Minister for Propaganda and, since July, 1944, Plenipotentiary for total war. As Gauleiter for Berlin, directed the chief deportation actions and was Hitler's chief secret abettor in the Final Solution. Committed suicide in Hitler's bunker with his family, May 1st, 1945.

GOERING, Hermann. *Reichsmarschall* of Germany, Prime Minister of Prussia, Plenipotentiary for the Four-Year Plan, and Reich Minister for Air. Committed suicide in his cell at Nuremberg, October 16th, 1946

GOETH, SS Captain Amon. Directed liquidation of Cracow and Tarnow Ghettoes, 1943, commanded Plaszow Jewish camp, 1943-44. Sentenced to death, Cracow, September 5th, 1946.

GRAEBNER, SS Lieut. Ernst. *Kriminalsekretär*. Head of Gestapo's political section in Auschwitz main camp to November, 1943. Sentenced to death by Vienna People's Court, May, 1946.

GREISER, Artur. Gauleiter for Wartheland Province and Lodz. Implicated in exterminations at Chelmno death camp (which he advocated for tubercular Poles as well as Jews). Sentenced to death at Posen on July 20th, 1946, in spite of a personal intercession by the Pope.

Grundherr, Geheimrat Werner von. 'Minister' to Oslo and Foreign Office, *Referent* on Scandinavian affairs. Employed to keep the Swedish Government off the scent during the deportations of Jews from Norway and Denmark. Ambassador of German Federal Republic to Athens, 1951-52.

GUENTHER, SS Major Rolf, and GUENTHER, SS Captain Hans (Eichmann's second in command and agent in Prague), sons of the party anthropologist, Professor Hans F. K. Guenther ('Rassen-Guenther'). Both are apparently still on the run.

HAAS, SS Major Willi von. Directed liquidation of the Cracow Ghetto, March 13th, 1943, as Globocnik's Resettlement Commissioner. Extradited to Poland from British Zone, Germany, November, 1950. Not yet tried.

HAHN, SS Lieut.-Colonel. Commanding Security Police, Warsaw. Directed final deportations during the ghetto rebellion. Has not been traced.

Hannecken, Lieut.-General Hermann von. Military Commander, Denmark. Released from prison in Copenhagen, August, 1951.

HARSTER, SS Brig.-General. Commanded Security Police, Holland, till 1943, then ditto Rome. Twelve years' imprisonment, The Hague Court, June, 1947.

HARTJENSTEIN, SS Captain Fritz. Commandant, Birkenau and Natzweiler. Although condemned to death by the British Wuppertal Court on June 5th, 1946, he is still awaiting a second trial in France. (June, 1952.)

Heinberg, Kurt. Chief of Political Section for Balkans, Foreign Office. Admitted implication in the chain of orders relating to the extermination of Serbian Jews. Removed from Bonn Foreign Office, May, 1952.

Herff, SS Lieut.-General Maximilian von. Higher SS and Police Leader, Russian Central Front. Executed at Minsk, February 6th, 1948.

HEYDRICH, Reinhardt. Head of the Security Police and SD, and Protector, Bohemia-Moravia. Died from a partisan's bomb, June 5th, 1942.

HIMMLER, Heinrich. *Reichsfuehrer* SS, Chief of German Police, Minister for Interior, and General Plenipotentiary, Reich Administration. Committed suicide at British control post, Lueneburg Heath, May 23rd, 1945.

HITLER, Adolf. Leader of the German Nation and Reich Chancellor. Committed suicide in Reich Chancellory bunker, April 30th, 1945.

HOEFLE, SS Captain Hans. Adjutant to Globocnik and Resettlement Commissioner for Warsaw Ghetto. Escaped from an internment camp in Austria while waiting extradition to Poland in 1947.

HOEFLE, SS Lieut.-General Hermann. Higher SS and Police Leader, Slovakia, after the August, 1944, rebellion. Condemned to death at Bratislava, July, 1948.

HOESS, SS Lieut.-Colonel Rudolf Franz. Commandant of Auschwitz and later Deputy to Gluecks as Inspector of Concentration Camps. Condemned to death Warsaw, March 29th, 1947. Executed in Auschwitz camp a few days later.

Hildebrandt, SS Lieut.-General Richard, and Hoffmann, SS Lieut.-General Otto. Successive chiefs of Race and Settlement Office (Rusha). Sentenced to 25 years' imprisonment for responsibility for deportation measures, March 10th, 1948. On January 21st, 1951, Hoffmann's sentence was commuted to 15 years.

HORTHY, Admiral Miklos von Nagybania. Regent of Hungary. Extradition refused by Americans in 1946. Now living (October, 1952), aged 84, at Estoril, in Portugal.

Hoven, SS Captain Waldemar. Buchenwald Camp Medical Officer. Sentenced to death Nuremberg, August 20th, 1947. Executed June, 1948.

HUENSCHE, SS Captain. Member of Eichmann's office, active in Hungary, 1944. Last seen at Alt-Aussee, May 3rd, 1945.

JAECKELN, SS Lieut.-General Franz. Higher SS and Police Leader, Northern Army Group. Tried by the Russians at Riga, February 3rd, 1946, and hanged in the ghetto on the same afternoon.

JAROSS, Andor. Hungarian Minister for Interior. Hanged by sentence of Budapest People's Court, January, 1946.

Juettner, SS Lieut.-General Max. Chief of the Leadership Office of the SS and one of Himmler's personal adjutants. Denazified and at liberty.

KALTENBRUNNER, SS General Ernst. Head of Security Police and SD in succession to Heydrich. Hanged in Nuremberg prison, October 16th, 1946.

KAMMLER, SS Lieut.-General Heinz. Head of Amt C, the Construction Department of the SS, and later of the Wehrmacht, too. Said to have been killed while commanding a division in the Battle of Berlin, April, 1945. Not confirmed.

KAPPLER, SS Lieut.-Colonel Hubert. As Commander of Security Police, organised Rome deportations to Auschwitz. Sentenced to life imprisonment by a Rome court in 1947, sentence confirmed, November, 1952.

Kasche, Siegfried. Minister to the Croat State at Zagreb. Condemned to death at Zagreb, June, 1947.

KATZMANN, SS Major-General Fritz. Higher SS and Police Leader, Lwow Commissariat, and organiser of the massacre of more than 400,000 Jews in East Galicia. On the run. Rumoured as late as summer, 1952, to be in Egypt.

KILLINGER, Manfred von. Minister to Bucharest, 1941-44. Committed suicide in the Bucharest Legation, September 3rd, 1944.

KLAUBERG, Professor. Sterilisation experiments in Auschwitz main camp, 1942-44. Not traced.

KNOCHEN, SS Colonel Helmuth. Security Police Commander, Northern France-Belgium. Condemned to death in British Zone, Germany, but extradited to France for a second trial, October 10th, 1946. Still (November, 1952) waiting trial in Cherche-Midi prison, Paris.

KOCH, Erich. Gauleiter for East Prussia, *Generalkommissar*, Bialystok and Ukraine. Complicity in Kiev massacre of September, 1941. Extradited to Poland from British Zone, Germany, 1950, but still waiting trial in Mokatow prison, Warsaw. (October, 1952.)

KORSEMANN, SS Lieut.-General. Higher SS and Police Leader,

Rowno, November, 1941, and Crimea-Caucasus, 1942-43. Said to have been executed in Russia.

KONRAD, SS Captain Franz. Sentenced to death for his part in the liquidation of the Warsaw Ghetto and hanged in Warsaw, September 8th, 1951.

KRAMER, SS Captain Josef. Commandant of Birkenau and of Bergen-Belsen camps. Condemned to death by British Lueneburg Court, November 17th, 1945.

Krebsbach, SS Captain. Camp Medical Officer, Kaiserswald. Made final selection on liquidation of camp in July, 1944. Sentenced to death at Dachau (Mauthausen case), May 27th, 1947.

KREMER, SS Captain Professor Hans Hermann. Conducted selections at Birkenau crematorium, September-October, 1942. Sentenced to death Cracow, November 22nd, 1947.

KRUMEY, SS Major. Eichmann's representative in Vienna and Hungary. Said to have been captured in Italy.

KUBE, Gauleiter Wilhelm. *Generalkommissar*, White Russia, July, 1941-September, 1943. Murdered by his White-Russian chambermaid, September 22nd, 1943.

KUTSCHERA, SS Major Fritz. Security Police Commander, Serbia, 1941 ; Mogilev, 1942-43 ; and Warsaw, 1943-44. Killed by Polish Underground at the end of January, 1944.

Lammers, Hans. Chief of the Reich Chancellory. Sentenced at Nuremberg, April, 1949, to 20 years' imprisonment, largely on account of his part in anti-Jewish decrees. Sentence commuted January 31st, 1951, to ten years' imprisonment. Freed from Landsberg prison, December 16th, 1951.

LANGE, SS Major. Commander, Security Police, Latvia, 1941-42. Organised Riga massacres and attended Gross-Wannsee Conference. Reported in July, 1949, that he would be handed over to German courts in British Zone for trial, but has since escaped.

LAVAL, Pierre Philippe. Prime Minister of France, April, 1942-September, 1944. Executed in Fresnes prison, October 15th, 1945.

Leibbrant, Georg. Director, Political Department, in the Rosenberg Ministry. Released from Allied detention, May, 1949, but charged by the Nuremberg *Landgericht*, January, 1950, with participation in the Final Solution. Has not been brought to trial.

LIEBEHENSCHEL, Artur. Department Head in the Concentration Camp Inspectorate and Commandant at Auschwitz, November, 1943, to May, 1944. Sentenced to death, Cracow, November 22nd, 1947.

Lindau, SS Colonel Kurt. Gestapo official responsible for *Einsatzgruppen* reports and for execution warrants for captured Political Commissars. Arrested during the Baab trial, March, 1950, at instance of Frankfurt *Schwurgericht*. Not yet brought to trial.

Linden, Dr. Herbert. *Ministerialrat* for Health in the Ministry for Interior. Committed suicide at the end of the war. His part in setting up death camps in Poland has not been established.

Loehr, General of the Luftwaffe Alexander von. Chief of Ost-Agais Command and accessory to the deportation of Jews from Greece. Sentenced to death, Belgrade, February 27th, 1947.

Loesener, Bernhard. *Judenreferent* in Ministry of Interior till end of 1941. Released from Allied detention, 1949, and subsequently denazified.

LOHSE, Hinrich. *Reichskommissar* for the Occupied Eastern Territory. Sentenced at Bielefeld to 10 years' imprisonment, January, 1948. Released on account of ill-health, 1951, and awarded a pension by the Federal Republic.

Ludin, Hans Elard. Minister to Slovak State, Bratislava. Sentenced to death, Bratislava, December, 1946.

LUTHER, Dr. Martin. Directed Foreign Office Department 'Deutschland,' May, 1940-April, 1943, when he was imprisoned in the Sachsenhausen 'political bunker'; seen there by Major Payne-Best in 1944, but the circumstances of his death are unknown.

MACH, Sano. Slovak Minister for Interior. Sentenced to death, Bratislava, July, 1948.

MANSTEIN, Field-Marshal Erich von. Sentenced by British Hamburg court, December 19th, 1949, to 18 years' imprisonment. Commuted to 12 years. On medical parole since August, 1952.

MENGELE, SS Lieut. Dr. In charge of selections for the crematorium at Auschwitz, 1943-44. Not traced.

MEYER, Gauleiter Alfred. Secretary of State in Ministry for Occupied Eastern Territory and Rosenberg's Deputy. Not traced.

Milch, Field-Marshal Erhard. Chief of Staff of the Luftwaffe. Sentenced at Nuremberg, 1947, to life imprisonment for procuring human guinea-pigs and slave labour, largely Jewish, for the underground aircraft factories. Sentence commuted in January, 1951, to 15 years' imprisonment.

Mildner, SS Colonel Dr. Rudolf. Head of Gestapo, Upper Silesia and Denmark. Prosecution witness at Nuremberg. Released in 1949 and apparently not subsequently tried.

MUELLER, SS Lieut.-General Heinrich. Chief of Amt IV of RSHA (the Gestapo). Disappeared from the Fuehrer's bunker on April 29th, 1945. Many subsequent rumours.

MUERER, SS Lieut.-Colonel Dr. Ghetto-Commissioner, Vilna. Reported to have been arrested in Austria in the summer of 1947. May have been extradited to Russia.

MUGROWSKI, SS Brig.-General Dr. Joachim. Head of the SS Health Institute. Sentenced to death at Nuremberg, August 27th, 1947, but not hanged till June 2nd, 1948. His very important rôle in the gassings of Auschwitz was not fully investigated.

MUSSFELD, SS Lieut. Carried out the Majdanek massacre of November 3rd, 1943, and directed Crematorium II at Auschwitz in 1944. Not traced.

NAUMANN, SS Brig.-General Erich. Commanded *Einsatzgruppe* B in Russia, November, 1941-43, then Commander, Security Police, Holland. Condemned to death Nuremberg, April 8th, 1948. One of the seven 'Red-Jacket' men executed in Landsberg prison, June 8th, 1951.

NEBE, SS Major-General Artur. Head of the *Kriminalpolizei*. Commanded *Einsatzgruppe* B in Russia to November, 1941. Said to have been executed in February, 1945, for complicity in the July Plot, but this has not been established.

NOWAK, SS Captain. Eichmann's Transport Officer and liaison with the Reich Ministry of Transport. Not traced.

OBERG, SS Lieut.-General Kurt. Higher SS and Police Leader, Northern France and Belgium. Sentenced to death by a British court in

Germany, but extradited to France on October 10th, 1946. Still awaiting trial (November, 1952) in the Cherche-Midi prison, Paris.

OHLENDORF, SS Major-General Otto. Commander, *Einsatz-gruppe* D. Condemned to death Nuremberg, April, 1948, and hanged in Landsberg prison, June 8th, 1951.

PAVELIC, Ante. 'Poglavnik' or Leader of the Croat State, 1941-45. Said to be living in the Argentine Republic.

Pétain, Philippe. Marshal of France and Head of the French State, 1940-44. Died in nominal freedom on the Ile d'Yeu, October, 1951, at the age of 95.

PETERS, Gerhard. Manager of the firm DEGESCH. Supplied Zyklon B gas to the SS Health Office. Sentenced by Frankfurt *Spruch-kammer* to five years' imprisonment, March 23rd, 1949. Now at liberty.

POHL, SS Lieut.-General Oswald. Head of the SS Economic Administration (WVHA). Condemned to death at Nuremberg, November 3rd, 1947, but not executed till June 8th, 1951.

Pokorny, SS Lieut.-Colonel Dr. Adolf. Member of the Office for Strengthening German Folkdom ; author of mass-sterilisation proposal. Acquitted at Nuremberg, August 27th, 1947.

PRUETZMANN, SS Lieut.-General Hans. Higher SS Police Leader to Southern Army Group, Kiev, October, 1941-September, 1943. Committed suicide, Lueneburg, May, 1945.

PUETZ, SS Major. Security Police Commander, Rowno, 1942-43, and director of the second Rowno massacre. Not traced.

RADEMACHER, Franz. *Amtsleiter* of Department Deutschland III, Foreign Office, under Martin Luther, May, 1940-April, 1943. Sentenced for complicity in Belgrade Ghetto executions and deportation of Belgian Jews, Nuremberg *Schwurgericht,* March 17th, 1952, three years' and five months' imprisonment. Broke bail while waiting appeal in September, 1952, and escaped to the Argentine Republic.

RASCH, SS Brig.-General Otto. Commandant, *Einsatzgruppe* C in Russian campaign (Kiev massacre). Declared unfit to plead in the *Einsatzgruppen* case, February 5th, 1948.

RASCHER, SS Major Dr. Sigmund. In charge of medical experiments for the Luftwaffe. Boasted to Major Payne-Best of having invented the gas chambers. Executed by Himmler's orders in Reichenau camp, February, 1945.

RAUTER, SS Lieut.-General Hans Albin. Higher SS and Police Leader, Holland. Condemned to death by the special High Court at The Hague, April 3rd, 1948, and executed in the following November.

REICHENAU, Field-Marshal Walter von. Commanded Sixth Army and Southern Army Group. Implicated in the Kiev and other Ukrainian Jewish massacres. Died of a mysterious infection, January 17th, 1942.

Reeder, Brig.-General Eggert. Head of the Wehrmacht's civil administration in Belgium, 1940-44. Sentenced by Brussels court, March 9th, 1951, to 12 years' imprisonment largely on Jewish deportation charges, but released three weeks later after nearly six years in detention.

RIBBENTROP, Joachim. Reich Minister for Foreign Affairs. Arrested in a Hamburg boarding-house June 14th, 1945, and hanged in Nuremberg prison, October 16th, 1946.

ROETHKE, SS Captain Heinz. Head of the Paris branch of Eichmann's Office of Jewish Affairs from July, 1942. Has not been traced.

ROSENBERG, Alfred. Reich Minister for the Occupied Eastern Territories, 1941-45. Hanged in Nuremberg prison, October 16th, 1946.

Ruebe, SS Sgt.-Major Adolf. *Kriminalsekretär* to the Minsk Gestapo. Sentenced by Karlsruhe *Schwurgericht* to life imprisonment, December 16th, 1949.

RUNDSTEDT, Field-Marshal Gerd von. Was to have been tried by a British court for his illegal order of June 21st, 1942, to hand captured British Commando troops over to the Gestapo. In the summer of 1949 the proposal was abandoned on account of Rundstedt's health. He died in 1953. His complicity in the extermination of Jews in Southern Army Group Area in July-December, 1941, was not investigated.

SALMUTH, Colonel-General Hans von. Sentenced to 20 years' imprisonment at Nuremberg on October 28th, 1948, for his part in the massacre of Jews at Kodyma (Transdniestra). Commuted to 12 years' imprisonment January 31st, 1951. Due for release early in 1953.

SANDBERGER, SS Colonel Martin. Commander, Security Police, Esthonia and North Italy. Massacred Jews at Pskov while commanding an *Einsatzkommando*. Condemned to death April 8th, 1948. Sentence commuted to life imprisonment January 31st, 1951.

Sauckel, Fritz. Reich Plenipotentiary for Labour, 1942-45. Implicated in misuse of Jewish concentration camp inmates. Hanged in Nuremberg prison, October 16th, 1946.

SCHAEFER, SS Brig.-General Emanuel. Security Police Commander, Belgrade and Trieste. Hid his identity till April, 1951, when a denazification court sentenced him to 21 months' labour camp as a member of the Gestapo. Charged with the gassing of 6,000 Jews from Semlin camp, but case postponed for further investigation. Cologne *Schwurgericht*, October, 1952.

SCHELLENBERG, SS Major-General Walter. Acquitted of 'genocide' charges connected with the *Einsatzgruppen* Jewish massacres, but found guilty of complicity in murder of Russian prisoners of war. Sentenced to six years' imprisonment at Nuremberg, April, 1949, but released December, 1950.

Schirach, Baldur von. Gauleiter for Vienna. Implicated in deportation of Jews in October, 1941-March, 1942, and early 1943. Sentenced at Nuremberg to 20 years' imprisonment, October 1st, 1946.

Schlegelberger, Dr. Franz. Acting Minister of Justice, April, 1941-September, 1942. Involved in mass-sterilisation proposals. Life sentence, Nuremberg, December 4th, 1947. Released on parole as an incurable invalid, February 4th, 1951.

SCHOENGARTH, SS Brig.-General Karl. Security Police Commander, Cracow province, 1941-44, then in Holland till end of the war. Sentenced to death by British military court at Enschede, February 11th, 1946.

SCHULZ, SS Brig.-General Erwin. Led Commando 5 of *Einsatzgruppe* C, June-September, 1941. Sentenced at Nuremberg to 20 years' imprisonment, April, 1948. Commuted to 15 years January 31st, 1951.

SCHUMANN, SS Captain Heinz. Ohlendorf's Adjutant. Organised mass executions at Simferopol. Sentenced to death, Nuremberg, April, 1948. Sentence commuted to 10 years, January, 1951. Released January, 1952.

SCHUMANN, SS Major Professor Horst. Conducted sterilisation experiments on Jewish women at Ravensbrueck and Auschwitz, 1942-44. Has not been traced.

SCHWARZ, Captain Albert. Labour Commitment Officer, Auschwitz. Kept record of gas-chamber selections. Sentenced to death at Cracow, November 22nd, 1947.

Schwerin von Krosigk, Count Lutz. Minister of Finance. Sentenced at Nuremberg in April, 1949, to ten years' imprisonment. Released February 4th, 1951.

SEIDL, SS Captain Siegfried. Member of Eichmann's Commando. Commandant of Theresienstadt and Bergen-Belsen camp. Sentenced to death by People's Court in Russian Sector, Vienna, October 4th, 1946.

SEYSS-INQUARDT, Artur. Reichskommissar for the Occupied Netherlands, 1940-45. Hanged in Nuremberg prison, October 16th, 1946.

SEIBERT, SS Colonel Walter. Ohlendorf's second-in-command. Sentenced to death Nuremberg, April, 1948. Sentence commuted to 15 years' imprisonment, January, 1951.

SIX, SS Colonel Professor Franz. Employed for a short time in the Einsatzgruppen, detecting political commissars among the Russian prisoners of war. Promoted the International anti-Jewish Congress, which was intended for 1944. Sentenced April, 1948, to 20 years' imprisonment. Commuted January, 1951, to ten years. Released September 30th, 1952.

SOMMER, SS Captain Karl. Deputy Head of D II, the Labour Allocation Office for the concentration camps. Kept records of the Auschwitz selections. Condemned to death Nuremberg, November 3rd, 1947. Sentence commuted to life imprisonment January 31st, 1951.

SPORRENBERG, SS Brig.-General Jakob. As Security Police Commander at Lublin from August, 1943, to July, 1944, carried out the Majdanek massacre. Sentenced to death Warsaw, September 22nd, 1950.

SPRENGER, Jakob. Gauleiter for Hessen-Nassau. Conducted a private reign of terror in 1943-44 directed against the Jews who had been exempted from deportation. Committed suicide at the end of the war.

STAENGE, SS Captain. Commandant, Treblinka death camp. Served in Dalmatia from November, 1943. No trace.

STAHLECKER, SS Brig.-General Franz. Commanded Einsatzgruppe A in Baltic provinces and White Russia. Killed by Esthonian Partisans at Krasnowardeisk, March, 1942.

Steengracht von Moyland, Adolf. Successor to Weizsaecker as Secre tary of State in the Foreign Office, April, 1943. Implicated in deportations from Denmark and Norway. Sentenced at Nuremberg in April, 1949, to seven years' imprisonment. Released February, 1950.

STRAUCH, SS Lieut.-Colonel Eduard. Commanded Security Police, White Russia, 1942-43. Condemned to death at Nuremberg, April, 1948, but extradited to Belgium for a second trial as Police Commander during the Ardennes counter-offensive. Sentence commuted to life imprisonment, July 19th, 1952. Said to be in a lunatic asylum.

Streckenbach, SS Brig.-General. Commander, Security Police, Poland, 1939-40, and subsequently Director of Amt I, the Staff Department of the Reich Main Security Office. Played an unprobed part in the organisation of the Einsatzgruppen. Apparently not traced.

STREICHER, Julius. Editor of Der Stuermer and Gauleiter of Franconia. Hanged in Nuremberg prison, October 16th, 1946.

STROOP, SS Major-General Juergen. Liquidated the Warsaw Ghetto, April-May, 1943, then Higher SS and Police Leader, Greece. Sentenced to death by American Dachau Tribunal, March 22nd, 1947, for shooting hostages in Greece. Extradited to Poland, 1948. Retried and executed in Warsaw, September 8th, 1951.

STUCKART, Franz. Secretary of State in Ministry for Interior. Drafted the Nuremberg Laws and their later amendments. Sentenced to the term of detention which he had served to April, 1949, and immediately released.

Stuelpnagel, Otto von. Military Commander, France, 1940-44. Originally a party to the Jewish deportation orders, but later put up some resistance. Hanged in August, 1944, having failed to commit suicide at Verdun after the July Plot.

SZALAZY, Major Andor. 'Arrowcross' Prime Minister of Hungary, October, 1944-February, 1945. Condemned to death, Budapest, 1946.

SZTOJAY, Dome. Prime Minister of Hungary, March-August, 1944. Condemned to death, Budapest, January, 1946.

TESCH, Bruno. Partner of the firm Tesch und Stabenow. Sentenced to death by British Hamburg court, March, 1946, for supplying 'Zyklon B' gas for Auschwitz.

THADDEN, Eberhard von. From May, 1943, expert on Jewish affairs in Department 'Inland II' of the Foreign Office. Released by the Allies from detention in 1949, but charged by the Nuremberg *Schwurgericht* in December, 1950, when he hid in the British Zone. Arrested and charged again by Cologne court, June, 1952.

THIERACK, Otto. Minister for Justice, 1942-45. Committed suicide in a detention camp on learning that he would be charged at Nuremberg, October, 1946.

THILO, SS Captain Dr. Directed selections for the Auschwitz gas chambers with Mengele, 1942-44. Not traced.

THOMAS, SS Lieut.-General Max. Higher SS and Police Leader, France-Belgium, July, 1940-September, 1941, then ditto Ukraine. Said to have been killed in 1944.

TISO, Monseigneur Josef. President of the Slovak State, 1938-1945. Hanged in Bratislava, August, 1946.

TOEBBENS, Walter. German labour contractor in the Warsaw Ghetto and Lublin province. Escaped from a train when being extradited to Poland, November 22nd, 1946. Tried in absence by Bremen *Schwurgericht*, May, 1949. Sentenced to ten years' labour camp, but is still at large.

TUKA, Dr. Vojtek. Prime Minister of Slovakia. Died 1944.

TURNER, SS Colonel Harald. Military Administrator, Serbia. Implicated in Belgrade Ghetto massacre. Sentenced to death in Belgrade, March 9th, 1947.

Vajna, Gabor. Hungarian Minister for Interior, October, 1944-February, 1945. Hanged Budapest, January, 1946.

Vallat, Xavier. Commissary for Jewish Questions to the Vichy Government, March, 1941-March, 1942. Not implicated in deportations, but sentenced to ten years' imprisonment, December, 1947. Released December, 1949.

VEESENMAYER, Edmund. Reich Plenipotentiary to Hungary, March-November, 1944. Sentenced to 20 years' imprisonment Nuremberg, April, 1949. Commuted to ten years' imprisonment, January, 1951, and released one year later.

Waechter, Baron Gustav von. *Landkommissar* of Cracow province,

Galicia. Said to have died as a monk in a convent in Rome, September 10th, 1949.

WAGNER, Colonel-General. Quartermaster-General of the Armed Forces. Unprobed complicity with Himmler's police in Russia. Committed suicide after the plot of July 30th, 1944.

WAGNER, Horst. *Amtsleiter* of Foreign Office Department ' Inland,' 1943-45. Successor to Martin Luther. Has not been charged.

WAGNER, Robert. Gauleiter of Alsace-Baden. Condemned to death by a French military court at Strasbourg, 1946. Charges included the deportations of October, 1940.

WEINMANN, SS Colonel. Security Police Commander, Bohemia, 1943-45. Formerly an extermination-commando chief in Russia. Not traced.

WEISS, SS Captain Martin. *Kriminalsekretär* to Vilna Gestapo. Sentenced to life imprisonment by Wuerzburg *Schwurgericht*, February, 1950.

Weizsaecker, Baron Ernst von. Chief Secretary of State, Foreign Office, to April, 1943. Sentenced at Nuremberg, April, 1949, to seven years' imprisonment. Sentence commuted to five years, but cancelled on October 15th, 1950, when Weizsaecker had served less than three years. He died at Lindau on August 6th, 1951.

WETZEL, Dr. Ernst. Head of the ' Race-Political Office ' of the party. Transferred in 1941 to the Rosenberg Ministry. Author of the famous gas-chamber letter to Lohse. Has not been traced.

WIRTH, SS Major Christian. *Kriminalkommissar*. Head of the Death-Camps Organisation in Poland, 1942-43, then under Globocnik in Dalmatia. The story that he was killed by partisans in Istria in May, 1944, needs investigation.

WISLICENY, SS Captain Dieter. Eichmann's Deputy in Slovakia, Greece, and Hungary. Sentenced to death Bratislava, July, 1948.

WITISKA, SS Lieut.-Colonel. Commander, Security Police, in Slovakia from August, 1944, when he deported 9,000 Jews. Not traced.

Woehler, Major-General Otto. Manstein's Chief of Staff in the Crimea, 1941. Implicated in Ohlendorf's massacres of Jews. Sentenced to eight years' imprisonment, October 8th, 1948. Released autumn, 1950.

Woermann, Ernst. Under-Secretary to Weizsaecker and Steengracht in Foreign Office. Seven years' imprisonment. Released February, 1950.

WOLFF, SS General Karl. Himmler's Deputy and liaison officer with Hitler. Not charged in connection with the Final Solution, but sentenced to four years' labour camp by a German court in 1946 for his part in low-pressure experiments in Dachau. Freed August, 1949.

ZOEPF, SS Captain. Head of Eichmann's office at The Hague. Not traced.

ZOERNER. *Landkommissar*, Lublin province, 1939-44. Said to have been executed in Poland.

CHRONOLOGY OF THE FINAL SOLUTION

THE FINAL SOLUTION	CORRESPONDING POLITICAL AND MILITARY EVENTS
1938	**1938**
October 28th. First deportation order concerns Polish Jews in the Reich.	September 29th. *The Munich Agreement.*
November 9th. Death of vom Rath. "The night of broken glass."	
November 12th. Goering's conference on retributive measures against the Jews.	
1939	**1939**
January 24th. Goering appoints Heydrich to the Jewish Emigration Office.	March 15th. Annexation of Bohemia-Moravia.
April 18th. Puppet State of Slovakia adopts anti-Jewish laws.	
July 4th. German Jewry placed under the authority of a *Reichsvereinigung.*	
July 26th. Eichmann in charge of Prague branch of the emigration office.	August 21st. The Moscow non-aggression pact.
September 1st-21st. SS and Wehrmacht instigate numerous pogroms in Poland.	September 1st. Poland invaded.
	September 3rd. *Britain and France at war with Germany.*
	September 17th. Russians occupy Eastern Poland.
September 21st. Heydrich's plans for ghettoes in Poland.	September 27th. Surrender of Warsaw.
October 6th. Hitler announces his resettlement policy for Poland, including Jewish seclusion.	October 8th. Evacuation of *Volksdeutsche* begins in Latvia.
October 12th. First deportation of Jews from Vienna and Bohemia to Nisko in Poland.	
October 25th. Expulsion of Jews from Jaroslav across the San to Soviet Territory.	
October 28th. The Jewish badge imposed at Wloclawek.	

EASTERN EUROPE	WESTERN EUROPE	CORRESPONDING EVENTS IN THE WAR
November 8th. Hans Frank made Governor-General. November 15th. Germans forced to readmit Jews expelled across Russian lines. November 23rd. Jewish badge compulsory throughout General Government.		November 8th. Attempt to assassinate Hitler in Munich. November 30th. Russia attacks Finland.
1940 January 30th. Heydrich's conference on resettlement of Jews and *Volksdeutsche.* February 12th. Goering opposes resumption of Jewish deportations to Eastern Poland, except from Lodz. March 23rd. Goering decrees suspension of deportations. March 29th. German Foreign Office denies rumours of impending deportation of Berlin Jews. April 14th. Frank declares that Cracow will be made Jew-free. April 30th. First enclosed and guarded ghetto established at Lodz.	**1940** May 10th. Luther appointed to Foreign Office Department Deutschland. June 20th. Hitler's mention of Madagascar to Mussolini.	**1940** January 22nd. V a t i c a n broadcast attacks German conduct in Poland. March 12th. Russia makes peace with Finland. April 9th. German invasion of Denmark and Norway. May 10th. *Germans invade Western countries.* May 15th. Holland capitulates. May 28th. Dunkirk evacuation. June 10th. Italy enters the war. June 21st. *France signs armistice.* June 28th. Rumania cedes Bessarabia and Bukovina to Russia.

CHRONOLOGY OF THE FINAL SOLUTION

EASTERN EUROPE	WESTERN EUROPE	CORRESPONDING EVENTS IN THE WAR
1940	**1940**	**1940**
July 12th. Frank declares that he has persuaded Hitler to stop deporting Jews to the General Government.	July 2nd. Luther's department circular on deportation to Madagascar.	July 19th. Hitler's Reichstag speech, proposing peace with Britain.
August 9th. Rumania outlaws Bukovina and Bessarabia Jews who have come under Russian rule.	August 15th. Eichmann supplies detailed Madagascar scheme. August 19th. Abetz proposes deporting Stateless Jews to Vichy territory.	September 15th. Ion Antonescu becomes dictator in Rumania.
October 16th. Ghetto decreed in Warsaw.	October 4th. Vichy "Statut des Juifs" deprives refugee Jews of their civil rights.	October 7th. German troops in Rumania. October 28th. Italy attacks Greece.
November 15th. Warsaw Ghetto sealed off.		
1941	**1941**	**1941**
January 11th. Frank obtains postponement of Himmler's Jewish deportation plans. January 22nd-23rd. Iron Guard revolt in Rumania. First Jewish massacre of the war.	January 31st. First attempt at creating a "Judenrat" in France.	

February 17th. Rumanía enters the war.	February 22nd-23rd. Deportation of 400 Jewish hostages from Amsterdam.	February-April. 72,000 Jews deported to Warsaw Ghetto.
March 1st. Bulgaria at war.		
March 2nd. Hitler outlines plans for occupation of Russia.	March 4th. Construction of *Buna-werk* factory authorised at Auschwitz.	March 30th. Hitler's "F u e h r e r Order" conference. Possibility that Jewish extermination was mentioned.
End March. British troops in Greece.	March 30th. Vichy Government appoints "Commisaire aux Questions Juives."	
April 6th. Germans invade Jugoslavia and Greece.		
April 10th. Croatia proclaims independence.		
April 24th. Bulgaria occupies Thrace.		
May 15th. Pétain broadcast pledges co-operation with Germany.	May 14th. Germans intern 3,600 naturalised Paris Jews.	End of May. The *Einsatzgruppen* formed at Pretzsch, in Saxony.
June 22nd. *Russia invaded.*		June 25th. Rumanian pogrom at Jassy.
		June 28th. German-inspired pogrom at Kovno, in Lithuania.
		July 2nd. "Action Petlura" pogrom in Lwow.
		July 8th. Jewish badge decreed in Baltic States.
July 21st. Rumania recovers all Bessarabia.	July 31st. Goering commissions Heydrich to proceed with total evacuation of European Jewry.	July 21st. Himmler plans Majdanek concentration camp.
August 14th. Germans occupy Smolensk.		August 2nd. Decree expelling Stateless Jews from Hungarian Ruthenia.

CHRONOLOGY OF THE FINAL SOLUTION

EASTERN EUROPE	WESTERN EUROPE	CORRESPONDING EVENTS IN THE WAR
1941	**1941**	**1941**
August 15th. Hungarians deport Jews from Bachka to Serbia.	Middle August. Slovak Government disperses Bratislava Ghetto.	
August 18th. Rumanians attempt to deport Jews across the Dniester.	End August. Hitler promises Goebbels that Berlin Jews will be deported East.	
September 1st. Massacre of Jews, expelled by Hungarians, at Kamenetz-Podolsk.	September 15th. Slovakia a d o p t s Nuremberg Laws. Jewish badge decreed throughout Greater Reich.	September 19th. Germans occupy Kiev.
September 19th. L i q u i d a t i o n of Zhitomir Ghetto in Ukraine.		September 27th. Heydrich, Protector of Bohemia.
September 23rd. Experimental gassing at Auschwitz.		
September 28th-29th. Massacre of 34,000 Jews from Kiev.	October 2nd. Paris synagogues blown up by secret action of the Gestapo.	
	October 4th. Heydrich's conference on forthcoming Reich deportations.	
October 12th.-13th. M a s s a c r e at Dnietropetrowsk.	October 20th. First deportations from Reich decreed (to Lodz).	October 12th. Part evacuation of Moscow.
October 19th. Foreign Office collaborates in Belgrade Ghetto massacre.		
October 28th. Wetzel letter, proposing gassing camps at Riga and Minsk. End October. Vast massacres of Riga, Vilna, Kovno, and Dvinsk.	November 4th. L o d z deportations completed.	
November 6th. 15,000 massacred at Rowno.		

End November. First massacre at Rostov.

December 8th. Riga massacres concluded. (27,000).

December 22nd. Vilna massacres completed (32,000).
December 30th. Simferopol (Crimea) massacres completed (10,000).
End December. First permanent gassing camp opened at Chelmno, near Posen.

1942

January 15th. "Resettlement action" begins in Lodz.

January 31st. Stahlecker reports 229,052 Jews killed in Baltic States-White Russia.

February - March. Extermination of 14,000 Kharkov Jews at No. 9 Tractor Plant.
March 16th.—Belsec Death Camp opens. "Einsatz Reinhardt" massacres begin at Mielec, in Poland.

First half November. First Reich Jews arrive in Riga, Minsk, and Kovno.
November 27th. Ribbentrop takes up proposal to extend deportations to all European Jewry.
December 5th. Stuelpnagel proposes deportation of 1,000 Paris Jews who are arrested on the 12th.

1942

January 20th. Heydrich admits extermination plan at Gross-Wannsee conference.

End January. First deportations to Theresienstadt.
February 3rd. Oswald Pohl in charge of concentration camps.

End November. Threat to Moscow over.

December 7th. Japan attacks Allies and U.S.A.
December 11th. Germany declares war on U.S.A.
December 19th. Von Brauchitsch dismissed from Russian command.

1942

January 6th. First Molotov note on German crimes in Russia.
January 15th. Allies pledged to punish war criminals.
January 17th. Death of Field-Marshal Reichenau.
January 26th. First U.S. troops cross Atlantic.

February 15th. Fall of Singapore.
March 15th. Hitler promises Russia will be annihilatingly defeated in the summer.

CHRONOLOGY OF THE FINAL SOLUTION

EASTERN EUROPE	WESTERN EUROPE	CORRESPONDING EVENTS IN THE WAR
1942	**1942**	**1942**
March 17th-April 21st. Most of Lublin Ghetto resettled.	March 20th. Weizsaecker signs Foreign Office approval of deportation of 6,000 Paris Jews to Auschwitz.	April 26th. Reichstag approves Hitler's abrogation of German law.
April-July. "Resettlement" extends to the whole of Poland.	March 23rd. First Slovak Jews at Birkenau camp, Auschwitz.	May 13th. Russians fail to retake Kharkov.
	March 28th. First train Paris-Auschwitz.	May 31st. First of the big air raids on Germany (Cologne).
May 15th-June 30th. "Family transports" from Slovakia to Lublin province.	April 2nd. Sauckel's total labour scheme upsets Auschwitz programme.	June 5th. Death of Heydrich.
		June 10th. Von Bock opens Don-front offensive.
June 18th. Transport demands of offensive in Russia threaten "Einsatz Reinhardt" resettlement programme.	June 1st. Jewish badge decreed in France and Holland.	June 22nd. Laval bargains for return of French prisoners of war.
July. Massacres extended to Minsk, Lida, Slonim, and Rowno.	June 15th. Eichmann declares military reasons prevent Reich deportations.	July 1st. Germans reach Alamein (Egypt) and the Don river (Russia).
	June 23rd. First gas-chamber selection from train at Auschwitz (Paris).	
July 22nd. Warsaw resettlement begins. (310,000 resettled by October 3rd.)	July 16th. The great Paris round-up. First deportation train from Holland.	
August 10th-22nd. 40,000 Jews resettled from Lwow.	August 4th. First deportation train Belgium-Auschwitz.	Middle August. Germans in North Caucasus.
August-September. Deportations from Zagreb (Croatia) to Auschwitz.	August 26th-28th. Round-up of 7,000 Stateless Jews in Vichy Free Zone.	August 19th. The Dieppe raid.

September 9th. "Furthest East" Jewish massacre at Kislovodsk, Caucasus.
September 16th. Lodz resettlement ends.

October 3rd. Warsaw resettlement ends.

October 28th. End of first phase of "Action Reinhardt." More than fifty Polish ghettoes recognised by decree.
October 29th. 16,000 Jews killed at Pinsk.

November 18th. Lwow Ghetto becomes in theory a labour camp.

1943
January 18th. First resistance in Warsaw Ghetto.

February 5th-12th. First Bialystok Resettlement.

October 4th. All Jews in concentration camps to go to Auschwitz.
October 14th. Jews in Holland virtually outlawed.
October 18th. Jews and "Easterners" in Reich renounced by Ministry of Justice to Gestapo.

November 25th. Deportation, Bergen (Norway) to Auschwitz.
November 26th. Jewish armament workers in Reich to be replaced with Poles.

December - January. Strong Italian moves to protect Jews in their sector of France.

1943
January 20th-26th. Deportations Theresienstadt-Auschwitz.

February 27th. Round-up of Jewish armament workers in Berlin for Auschwitz.

September 16th. Germans enter Stalingrad.
September 30th. Hitler repeats prophecy of destruction of world Jewry.
October 7th. U.N. War Crimes Commission to be set up.

November 7th. *Allies land in North Africa.*
November 11th. Germans occupy Vichy territory. Italians occupy Nice.
November 22nd. Russian counter-offensive begins.

December 17th. United Nations declaration, pledging punishment for extermination of Jewry.

1943
January 14th. "Unconditional surrender" agreed at Casablanca.
January 28th. Sauckel's general mobilisation decree.

February 2nd. *German 6th Army surrenders at Stalingrad.*
February 15th. Russians take Kharkov.

CHRONOLOGY OF THE FINAL SOLUTION

EASTERN EUROPE	WESTERN EUROPE	CORRESPONDING EVENTS IN THE WAR
1943 March-May. S e c o n d resettlement from Croatia. March 13th. Cracow Ghetto liquidated. March 15th. Deportations begin from Salonika and Thrace. March 22nd-29th. Bulgarians assist in deportations from Thrace and Macedonia. April 19th - May 16th. Liquidation, Warsaw Ghetto.	**1943** March. Deportation trains from Holland routed to Sobibor death camp, those from Vienna, Luxembourg, Prague, and Macedonia to Treblinka. March 13th. First of new crematoria opens at Auschwitz. April 27th. Total resettlement of Amsterdam Jews abandoned as impracticable.	**1943** March 16th. Russians lose Kharkov. April 16th. Hitler admits the exterminations to Admiral Horthy, Regent of Hungary. End April. Fall of Martin Luther. Goebbels publishes Katyn disclosures.
May 24th. Bulgarian Government disperses Sofia Jews in defiance of German orders. June 11th. Himmler decrees liquidation of all Polish ghettoes. Decree extended to Russia on 21st. June 21st-27th. Liquidation of Lwow Ghetto.	May 19th. Berlin declared "Judenrein."	May 9th. *G e r m a n s surrender in Tunisia.* July 5th - 15th. Failure of German offensive in Russia. July 9th. Allies invade Sicily. July 25th. Mussolini arrested. End July. Russian guerrilla force under Kovpak penetrates Carpathians 500 miles behind German front.
August 4th-12th. Deportations from Sosnowiece-Bendzyn to Auschwitz.	August 14th.* Laval refuses to co-operate in Jewish deportations from France.	August 5th. Sweden refuses Germany transit. Riots in Danish shipyards.

August. Exhumation of mass burials at Kiev and in the death camps as Russians advance.	August 24th. Himmler becomes Minister for Interior.	August 17th. Kallay's Hungarian peace speech.
August 19th - 27th. Liquidation of Bialystok Ghetto.		
September 11th-14th. Liquidation of Minsk and Lida ghettoes.	September 11th. Germans begin round-up of Jews in Nice.	September 8th. Allies publish Italian armistice terms. By 10th Germans control Rome and Northern Italy.
September 23rd. Liquidation of Vilna Ghetto.	September 11th-18th. "Family transports," Theresienstadt to Auschwitz.	
September-November. Complete liquidation of White Russian ghettoes follows fall of Smolensk.		September 25th. Russians retake Smolensk.
October 14th. Himmler's Posen speech admits extermination programme.	October 1st. German deportation of Jews from Denmark largely circumvented.	October 13th. Italy at war with Germany.
	October 18th. First deportation, Rome-Auschwitz.	October 20th. U.N. War Crimes Commission set up at Moscow conference.
November 3rd. Liquidation of Riga Ghetto; massacre of remaining Jews in Lublin concentration camp.	November 1st. Hoess removed from Auschwitz. Long lull in extermination activities, except for some trains from Holland.	November 6th. Russians retake Kiev.
December 11th-23rd. Swiss Red Cross mission visits Jews deported by Rumania to Southern Ukraine.		December 15th-19th. First trial of German war criminals at Kharkov.
1944	1944	1944
February 14th. Himmler decides to reduce Lodz Ghetto.	March 16th. Horthy accepts German police control of Hungary and deportation of Jews.	January 6th. Red Army enters former Polish White Russia. Jewish partisans in action.
		January 26th. Russians publish investigation of Katyn mass burial.
		March 15th. Red Army crosses the Bug.

CHRONOLOGY OF THE FINAL SOLUTION

EASTERN EUROPE	WESTERN EUROPE	CORRESPONDING EVENTS IN THE WAR
1944	**1944**	**1944**
March-April. Jews of Transdniestria, Bessarabia, and Bukovina fall into Russian hands.		March 28th. Red Army enters Galicia.
	April 3rd. Conference of experts on Jewish question at Krummhuebel.	April 10th. Bukovina, Bessarabia, and Odessa retaken.
April 14th. First transport Athens-Auschwitz.		
	May 15th - June 27th. 380,000 Jews deported from Greater Hungary, mostly to Auschwitz, where at least 250,000 are gassed.	June 4th. Allies enter Rome. June 6th. *Allies invade Western Europe.* June 23rd. Russian offensive opens. Minsk falls July 3rd, Vilna July 8th, Lwow July 27th. Warsaw reached July 31st.
	July 6th. Horthy temporarily arrests the deportations under Allied pressure.	July 20th. *The plot to kill Hitler.*
July 24th. Russians overrun Lublin concentration camp. Jewish camp in Warsaw Ghetto evacuated. July 25th. Kovno Ghetto evacuated. August 6th. Kaiserswald camp (Riga) evacuated beginning August. 27,000 Jews in camps east of Vistula removed to Germany. August 23rd. Eichmann attempts to organise deportation of Jews from Rumania as Rumanians surrender.	August 23rd. Drancy camp (Paris) liberated.	August 23rd. Rumania surrenders; *Paris liberated.*
September 5th. Lodz Ghetto evacuated.	September. Jews in Dutch camps sent to Germany. Deportations Theresienstadt-Auschwitz. Last transport France-Auschwitz. Red Cross visit Auschwitz camp H.Q.	September 5th. Sweden denies sanctuary to war criminals. September 11th. British enter Holland.

September 13th. Russians reach Slovak border.
September 14th. *U.S. troops reach German frontier.*
October 15th. Horthy arrested by the Germans after announcing surrender of Hungary.

November 3rd. Russians overrun two-thirds of Hungary and reach outskirts of Budapest.
November 5th. British troops in Salonika.
November 7th. Russians reach Lake Balaton.

December 16th. Rundstedt launches the last German offensive in the Ardennes.
December 28th. Budapest besieged.

1945
January 11th. Russians take Warsaw; 18th, take Cracow; 22nd, reach Oder, in Silesia.

February 4th. *Yalta Conference.*
February 14th. Russians complete occupation of Budapest.

March 5th. U.S. troops take Cologne; 7th, cross the Rhine at Remagen.

End October. Last selection for gas chamber at Auschwitz.

November 3th-December 8th. About 35,000 Budapest Jews deported to Vienna region and German concentration camps.

November 26th. Himmler orders Auschwitz crematoria to be destroyed.
December 6th. Hungarian Jews from Belsen reach Bregenz, in Switzerland.

1945
January 17th. More than 80,000 Budapest Jews fall into Russian hands.
January 26th. Russians liberate 2,819 invalid survivors in Auschwitz camps.

February 2nd. Red Cross delegates discuss plans with SS to relieve the concentration camps.

March 12th. Kaltenbrunner receives Professor Burckhardt.

September 23rd. Massacre at Kluga camp, Esthonia, as Russians take Reval. Revival of deportations from Slovakia following Banja Bystrica rebellion.

End October. Survivors of Cracow concentration camp (Plaszow) sent to Auschwitz.

November. Trial at Lublin of Majdanek camp staff.

1945
January 16th. Russians liberate 800 Jews at Czestochowa and 870 in Lodz.

CHRONOLOGY OF THE FINAL SOLUTION

EASTERN EUROPE	WESTERN EUROPE	CORRESPONDING EVENTS IN THE WAR
1945	**1945**	**1945**
March. Poland, Slovakia, and Hungary cleared of Germans.		March 23rd. British cross Rhine at Wesel.
	April 6th-10th. 15,000 Jews evacuated from Buchenwald "Little Camp."	April 11th. U.S. troops reach Elbe.
		April 13th. *Russians occupy Vienna.*
	April 15th. British Army finds 40,000 alive and 13,000 dead at Belsen (mainly Jews); estimated that 30,000 died.	April 20th. U.S. troops in Nuremberg.
	April 23rd. Mauthausen camp opened to Red Cross.	April 23rd. Russians in outskirts of Berlin.
	April 23rd-May 4th. Part of inmates of Sachsenhausen, Oranienburg, and Ravensbrueck camps evacuated to Schleswig on foot. Last massacres by SS guards.	April 24th. Himmler's peace offer transmitted through Count Bernadotte.
		April 30th. *Hitler kills himself in the Reich Chancellory bunker.*
	May 2nd. Red Cross takes over Theresienstadt.	May 2nd. Berlin surrenders to the Russians.
	May 3rd. Eichmann "Commando" last seen at Alt Aussee in Salzkammergut.	May 7th. *General Jodl signs unconditional surrender at Eisenhower's headquarters.*
	May 10th. Theresienstadt liberated.	
		May 23rd. Himmler takes poison in the course of arrest.
		June 14th. Ribbentrop captured in Hamburg.

Bibliography

THE materials used in the preparation of this book come under the following headings:

1. Documents and statements in evidence at the Nuremberg trials.
2. Documents collected by Jewish and other commissions for use in these and other criminal prosecutions.
3. Historical and statistical reports.
4. Non-Jewish memoirs which throw light on the extermination of the Jews.
5. Survivor narratives.

A certain degree of reserve is necessary in handling all this material and particularly this applies to the last section. For instance, the evidence concerning the Polish death camps was mainly taken after the war by Polish State commissions or by the Central Jewish Historical Commission of Poland. The hardy survivors who were examined were seldom educated men. Moreover, the Eastern European Jew is a natural rhetorician, speaking in flowery similes. When a witness said that the victims from the remote West reached the death camp in *Wagons-Lits*, he probably meant that passenger coaches were used instead of box-cars. Sometimes the imagery transcends credibility as when a gang of food-smugglers in a ghetto are described as exceptionally tall men with pockets running the whole length of their bodies. Thus readers, who are by no means afflicted with race-prejudice, but who find the details of murder on the national scale too appalling to assimilate, are inclined to cry *Credat Judaeus Apella* and dismiss all these narratives as fable. The witnesses, they will say, are Orientals, who use numerals as oratorical adjectives and whose very names are creations of fantasy, Sunschein and Zylberdukaten, Rotbalsam and Salamander.

And yet the wildest horrors recounted by these humble people are confirmed time and again in German reports and orders. Gradually it becomes possible to reduce their narratives to scale. Moreover, from several accounts of the same incident there emerges an unbreakable highest common factor, while in addition to this cumulative significance impressions recorded from the receiving end give a new twist to the often oblique language of German bureaucracy and they are necessary to complete the story.

1. The Nuremberg Trials

References to the proceedings of the International Military Tribunal at Nuremberg—the original Nuremberg Trial of 1945-46—are given under the initials IMT. The volume and page numbers refer throughout to the English edition of the proceedings, published by His Majesty's Stationery Office as *The Trial of German Major War Criminals* in 23 volumes (1946-52). The documents, which were put in evidence at this trial, were listed under many initials. Those which are quoted in this book bear mostly the initials PS, but some appear under the initials L, EC, R, M, RF, and USSR. As a rule the parts which were put in evidence—except for the RF and USSR documents—will be found in the American edition of the trial which was printed in Nuremberg, *The Trial of German Major War*

Criminals, in 42 volumes. English translations of most of this material are printed in *Nazi Conspiracy and Aggression* (Washington, State Department, 11 volumes, 1946-48). It is unfortunate that neither the Nuremberg nor the Washington series contains the RF and USSR documents, but a considerable portion of the former, the documents collected for the French Government's prosecution team, have been printed in the publications of the 'Centre de Documentation Juive Contemporaine.'

Many of the numbers in the text of this book refer to the twelve later Nuremberg trials which were conducted by American tribunals. Excerpts of evidence and selections from the documents used in these trials have been printed in *Trials of War Criminals before the Nuremberg Military Tribunals,* Washington, Government Printing Office, 1951-52. Less than a tenth of the material has been published in these 15 immensely bulky but not very satisfactory volumes. In the majority of cases the documents quoted in *The Final Solution* can only be studied in full in the photostats of the originals, which are deposited in various libraries. Where, however, a printed version is available of the relevant portion either in *Trials of War Criminals* or in other publications, it is mentioned in the text-reference in *The Final Solution.*

In the absence of any printed version, excerpts from the oral evidence are given the page numbers of the stencilled transcript as circulated in court. The documents are given their court numbers, all of which begin with the initials NO, NG, NI, or NOKW. The trials themselves are referred to by their serial numbers, and these are as follows, together with the relevant volumes in the 'Trials of War Criminals' series:

Case	I Karl Brandt *et alii*	The 'Medical' Case. (I-II.)
Case	II Erhard Milch.	The 'Milch' Case. (II.)
Case	III Alstoetter *et alii*	The 'Justice' Case. (III.)
Case	IV Oswald Pohl *et alii*	The 'Concentration Camps' Case. (V-VI.)
Case	V Friedrich Flick *et alii*	The 'Business Men' Case. (VI.)
Case	VI Carl Krauch *et alii*	The 'I.G. Farben' Case. (VII-VIII.)
Case	VII Wilhelm List *et alii*	The 'Hostages' Case. (XI.)
Case	VIII Ulrich Greifelt *et alii*	The 'RUSHA' Case. (IV-V.)
Case	IX Otto Ohlendorf *et alii*	The 'Einsatzgruppen' Case. (IV.)
Case	X Alfred Krupp *et alii*	The 'Krupp' Case. (IX.)
Case	XI Ernst Weizsaecker *et alii*	The 'Wilhelmstrasse' Case. (XII-XIV.)
Case	XII Wilhelm von Leeb *et alii*	The 'High Command' Case. (X-XI.)

Convenient summaries of some of these 12 trials will be found in a very much shorter series, *Law Reports of Trials of War Criminals Selected and Prepared by the United Nations War Crimes Commission,* London, HM Stationery Office, 1947-49, 14 volumes. Case II is discussed in Vol VII, Case III in Vol VI, Case VI in Vol X, Case VII in Vol VIII, Case VIII in Vol XIII, Case X in Vol X, and Case XII in Vol XII.

Selections from the NO, NG, NI, and NOKW documents used in these twelve trials have also been printed in the following works:

Bayle, François. *Croix Gammée ou Caducée.* Neustadt im Pfalz,

Commissariat aux affaires allemandes, 1950. (More than 1,500 pages of extracts from *The Medical Case* containing much material that will not be found in Vols I and II of *Trials of War Criminals*.)

Alexander Mitscherlich and Friedrich Mielke. *Wissenschaft ohne Menschlichkeit*, Heidelberg, 1949. Translated into English by Heinz Norden as *Doctors of Infamy*, New York, 1949. Covers the *Medical Case*.

Le Monde Juif (formerly Bulletin du Centre de Documentation Juive Contemporaine, 1946-52). Numerous sequences of later Nuremberg documents edited by Leon Poliakov, Jacques Sabille, Jules Billig, Michel Mazor, etc., have been printed in more than 60 numbers of this monthly review, which, apart from *Trials of War Criminals*, constitutes the largest printed source.

Henri Monneray. *La persecution des Juifs en France et dans les autres pays de l'Ouest, presentée a Nuremberg*, Paris Centre de Documentation Juive Contemporaine, 1947. (Mainly RF documents from the international trial.)

La persecution des Juifs dans les pays de l'Est, ditto, 1949 (particularly cases III, IV, and IX).

Henri Rousset. *Le pitre ne rit pas*, Paris, CDJC, 1950 (documents mainly illuminating the character of Himmler).

Leon Poliakov. *La Breviaire de la Haine*, Paris, 1951.

A great many RF documents, collected for the International Tribunal of 1945-46, were never put in evidence and therefore not given serial numbers. Some of them form the basis of the following two studies, published by the Centre de Documentation Juive Contemporaine:

L. Poliakov. *L'Etoile Jaune*, Paris, 1949. *La Condition des Juifs en France sous l'occupation Italienne*, Paris, 1950.

2. Other Trials Held under the United Nations War Crimes Commission

So far no attempt has been made to publish an official series concerning the British trials held at Wuppertal, Hamburg, and Lueneburg, or the American trials held at Dachau under the terms of the United Nations War Crimes Charter. A private enterprise, William Hodges and Co.'s 'War Crimes Trials' series, embraces the Lueneburg *Belsen Trial*, which is of great importance to this work. The companion publications of this series on the Wuppertal *Natzweiler Trial* and the Dachau *Hadamar Trial* are of only incidental importance. The following summaries of trials by Allied nations under the charter will be found in the *Law Reports of Trials of War Criminals* series:

Tesch and Stabenow (the Zyklon B case), Hamburg, June, 1946.

	Vol I
The Belsen case, Lueneburg, September-November, 1945.	Vol II
Franz Ferdinand Hoess, Cracow, March, 1947.	Vol VII
Amon Goeth (Cracow, August-September, 1946).	Vol VII
Artur Greiser, Posznan, June-July, 1946.	Vol XIII
Josef Buehler, Warsaw, June-July, 1948.	Vol XIV
Hans Albin Rauter, The Hague, April, 1948.	Vol XIV
The Dachau concentration camp trial, December, 1945.	Vol XI

The last of the British trials was that of Field-Marshal von Manstein at Hamburg in August-December, 1949. A little information is available in R. T. Paget, KC, MP, *Manstein, His Campaigns and Trial*, London, 1951, and Paul Leverkuhn, *Verteidigung Manstein*. Since that highly controversial case most of the belated trials of war criminals have been conducted by Polish or German tribunals. The latter at least have received a reasonable amount of reporting in the local press, while the author has been assisted by copies of prosecution briefs for the Rademacher and Schaefer cases and a court summary of the Toebbens case ; but printed proceedings of these and other trials, throwing light on the Final Solution, are not available, and perhaps never will be. An exception is the trial of Heinrich Baab of the Frankfurt Gestapo in March, 1950, which was admirably reported by Miss Kaye Boyle in *The New Yorker* on September 9th, 1950 (" The People with Names ") and reprinted in her book *The Smoking Mountain,* London, 1952.

For the very important Dutch State trials of Major-General Hans Rauter and Captain Aus der Fuenten the author has had to use original court materials, but a first-class summary of the Rauter case with some facsimile documents is printed in the Rijksinstituut's bulletin, *Nederland in Oorlogstijd*, for March, 1951. The splendid publication *Het Proces Rauter* (Nijhof, The Hague, 1952) came out too late to be of assistance.

Some of the documentary evidence used in the Polish trials was supplied by the Central Jewish Historical Commission of Poland and has been published by them in the original German text in the excellent three-volume series *Dokumenty i Materialy*, Lodz, 1946 (editors, Nachmann Blumental, Michal Borwicz, Filip Friedman, Jozef Kermisz, and Jozef Wulf). These volumes also contain many depositions in Polish by Jewish survivors. There is a further volume of German documents, edited by Nachmann Blumental, *Slowa Niewinne*, Cracow, 1947. A great deal of the evidence, taken on commission, concerning Auschwitz and the death camps has been published in English by the Central Commission of Investigation of War Crimes in the following works:

German Crimes in Poland, two volumes, Warsaw, 1946-47.

Polish Charges against German War Criminals, Warsaw, 1948.

3. Historical and Statistical Reports

Some of the following material takes the form (perhaps prematurely) of written history. The best of it consists of data collected in connection with the problems of relief, restitution, and resettlement. But even the earlier works, overtinged though they are with wartime propaganda, contain valuable corroborative evidence.

American Federation for Polish Jews. *The Black Book of Polish Jewry*, New York, September, 1943. Various editors. (In spite of its early date, this work is of value chiefly for its foreign press excerpts.)

Anglo-American Committee of Inquiry. *Report on the Problems of European Jewry and Palestine*, Lausanne, April, 1946. (Contains a detailed breakdown of the much-debated figure, produced by the World Jewish Congress, of 5,700,000 Jewish victims.)

Belgian Ministry of Justice, War Crimes Commission. *La Persecution antisemitique en Belgique, 1940-45*, Liege, 1947.

BIBLIOGRAPHY

The Jewish Black Book Committee. *The Black Book*. The Nazi Crime against the Jewish People, New York, 1946. (Contains translated excerpts of numerous Russian State Commission reports which are not otherwise available.)

Bloom, Solomon F. *Dictator of the Lodz Ghetto* in ' *Commentary,*' New York, February, 1949.

Committee of the International Red Cross. *Documents sur l'activité de la Croix Rouge en faveur des civils detenus dans les camps de concentration en Allemagne*, Serie II, Geneva, 1946. For observations, *see page 405 fn.*

Conference des Commissions Historiques et des Centres de Documentation Juifs. *Les Juifs en Europe 1939-45*, Paris (CDJC), 1947.

Dvorjetski, Marc, *Ghetto a l'Est*, Paris, 1950 (translated from a work in Yiddish, *Struggle and Death of Jerusalem in Lithuania*, New York, 1948). (Well-documented history of the Vilna Ghetto, 1941-44.)

Dunand, Georges. *Ne Perdez pas leur trace*, Neuchatel, 1950. (History of the Swiss Red Cross mission to Slovakia, 1944-45.)

Du Prel, Max Freiherr. *Das Deutsche Generalgouvernement Polen*, first edition, May, 1940 ; second edition, March, 1942. (A guide book for German troops, containing some data on the situation of the Jews collected by officials of Governor Frank's Ministry for Interior.)

Friedman, Dr. Filip. *This was Oswiecim*, translated from Yiddish by Joseph Leftwich. (A history of Auschwitz, containing several important testimonies, edited by the former chief of the Central Jewish Historical Commission of Poland.)

Frumkin, Dr. Gregory. *Population Changes in Europe since 1939*, New York, 1951.

Herzberg, Abel J. *Kroniek der Jodenvervolging*, The Hague, 1951. (History of the fate of Dutch Jewry. Contains a valuable account of Bergen-Belsen camp.)

Institute of Jewish Affairs. *Hitler's Ten-Year War on the Jews*, New York, 1943. (Important articles by Josef Schechtmann, Boris Shub, and others on the condition of Jewry at the time of the German conquests.) *Jews in Nazi Europe* (statistical data supplied to the Inter-American Jewish Conference), Baltimore, November, 1941. (Stencil.)

International Tracing Service. *Catalogue of Camps and Prisons*, Arolsen, British Zone, Germany, 1949, and Supplement, 1951. (Particularly important information on Polish labour camps.)

Kastner, Dr. Reszoe. *Der Bericht des juedischen Rettungskomitees aus Budapest*, 1942-43. (Vaadat Ezra wa Hazaala.) For observations, *see page 391.* Stencil, Geneva, 1946.

Kulischer, Eugene M. *The Displacement of Population in Europe*, Montreal, International Labour Office, 1943. (Considerable data concerning Himmler's racial resettlements.)

Levai, Eugene (ed by Lawrence P. Davies). *The Black Book of the Martyrdom of Hungarian Jewry*, Zurich, 1948.

Melezin, Abraham. *Demographic Processes among the Jewish Population of Poland, 1939-45*, Lodz, 1948 (in English and Polish).

Molho, Rabbi Michel (ed.). *In memoriam, Hommage aux victimes juives des Nazis en Grèce*, Salonika, 1948.

Netherlands Red Cross (General Direction). Auschwitz Deel I, *Het Dodenboek van Auschwitz*, The Hague, 1947. Auschwitz Deel II,

De Deportatietransporten van Juli, 1942, The Hague, 1948, Auschwitz Deel VI, *De afvoertransporten vit Auschwitz en Omgeving naar het Noorden en het Westen en de grote evacuatietransporten,* The Hague, 1952. '*Sobibor,*' February, 1947. *Etude sur le sort des prisonniers, evacués de Kl. Herzogensbosch,* February, 1952.

Poliakov, Leon. *La Breviaire de la Haine,* Paris, 1951. (The first attempt at a comprehensive survey of the 'Final Solution.')

Schwarz, Solomon M. *The Jews in the Soviet Union,* Syracuse, 1951. (For observations on this controversial work, see Appendix I.)

Steiner, Frederic. *The Tragedy of Slovak Jewry,* Bratislava, February, 1949. Documentation Centre, CUJCR. (Mainly photographic material.)

Starr, Joshua, and Shapiro, Leon. *Recent Population Data.* Articles on the statistics of Jewish survival in Germany, Poland, the Balkans, etc., published in *Jewish Social Studies,* New York, January, April, June, 1946.

Tenenbaum, Josef. *In Search of a Lost People,* New York, 1949. *Underground, the Story of a People,* New York, 1952 (Poland and Russia).

Trevor-Roper, H. E. *The Last Days of Hitler,* London, 1947.

Weinreich, Max. *Hitler's Professors,* New York, YIVO, 1946. (Contains long extracts from the 70 documents on Jewish matters discovered by Szako Friedman, a member of the YIVO staff, in the ruined Rosenberg Ministry and partly put in evidence at Nuremberg.)

Wielek, H. *De Oorlog die Hitler won,* Amsterdam, 1947.

Wischnitzer, Mark. *To Dwell in Safety,* Philadelphia, 1948. (A study of massed deportations during and after the war.)

Zjakowski, Zosa (Szako Friedman). *The Organisation of UGIF in Nazi-occupied France,* Jewish Social Studies, New York, July, 1947.

4. Memoirs of Germans and Others which Shed Light on the Final Solution

Bernadotte, Count Folke. *The Curtain Falls,* New York, 1945.

Blaettler, Franz. *Warschau 1942. Tatsachenbericht eines Motorfahrers, etc.,* Zurich, 1945.

Gilbert, Dr. G. M. *Nuremberg Diary,* New York, 1947. (Studies of some of the Nuremberg defendants and witnesses, including Hoess of Auschwitz, by a court psychiatrist.)

Gisevius, Hans Bernd. *To the Bitter End,* London, 1948.

Goebbels, Josef. *The Goebbels Diaries,* translated by Louis Lochner, London, 1948.

Guèrin, Dr. J. *Rawa Ruska, Camp de represailles (Stalag 325),* Marseilles, 1945.

Hagen, Walter (Willi Hoettl). *Die Geheime Front,* Linz-Wien, 1950. (Memoirs of an intimate of Kaltenbrunner and a member of the Foreign Political Secret Service. Gossipy but, when necessary, discreet.)

Hassell, Ulrich von. *The von Hassell Diaries,* London, 1948. (Many allusions to the extermination of Jewry.)

Kersten, Felix. *Klerk en Beul,* Amsterdam, 1947. Translated as *The Memoirs of Felix Kersten,* New York, 1947. (Recollections of Himmler by his Baltic-German masseur.)

Kienast, E. *Der Grossdeutsche Reichstag, November, 1943.* (Some hundreds of short biographies and passport-size photographs, including several characters who avoided publicity, such as Philip Bouhler and Globocnik.)

Kleist, Peter. *Zwischen Hitler und Stalin*, Bonn, 1950. (Some information on the Reichskommissars in Russia by a Foreign Office man seconded to the Rosenberg Ministry.)

Malaparte, Curzio. *Kaputt*. Translated by Professor Foligno, New York, 1946.

Masur, Norbert. *En Jude talar med Himmler*. (The fascinating conversation of a representative of the World Jewish Congress with Himmler in April, 1945.) Stockholm, 1946.

Morgenthau, Henry, Jnr. *The Morgenthau Diaries, VI, Colliers Magazine*, November, 1947. (History of a plan to rescue 70,000 Jews.)

Payne-Best, Captain S. *The Venlo Incident*, London, 1950. (Personal recollections of Himmler, Heydrich, Mueller, Schellenberg, Martin Luther, and Sigmund Rascher.)

Picker, Dr. Henry. *Hitlers Tischgespraeche*, Bonn, 1951. (Shorthand records of several allusions by Hitler to the Final Solution.) Another copy of Dr. Picker's reports was found in Martin Bormann's safe. It was translated into French by M. Charles Genoud and published in Paris in 1952 as *Libres Propos d'Hitler*. At present M. Genoud appears to be sueing Dr. Picker on behalf of Hitler's sister, Frau Paula Wolff, for breach of copyright.

Schlabrendorf, Fabian von. *Offiziere gegen Hitler*, Zurich, 1946. (The Borissov massacre.)

Weizsaecker, Baron Ernst von. *Erinnerungen*, Munich, 1950.

Zalewski, Erich von dem Bach. *Leben eines SS Generals*. (A series of affidavits taken on commission, but not put in evidence at Nuremberg, published in *Aufbau-Reconstruction*, New York, 1946, Vol. 12, Nos. 34-36.)

5. Survivor Narratives

A number of books by Jewish concentration-camp survivors have been excluded from this list, not as any reflection on their merits, but because they add nothing to the sources that have been quoted in the text. Several of the authors quoted, *e.g.*, Christopher Burney, Zenon Rozanski, Eugen Kogon, are not Jews, but they were in an exceptional position to observe the Final Solution in practice. Not all the works quoted are equally reliable, but certain works, which are written with exceptional objectivity, are marked with an asterisk.

A. Soviet Russia

Except for some depositions collected by Commissions of Investigation, the material that has been translated into Western languages concerns mainly the former Baltic States and the annexed Polish territories.

The Black Book, New York, 1945. (See particularly accounts of Minsk.)

*Dvorjetski, Marc. *Ghetto a l'Est*, Paris, 1950. (Vilna.)

*Gringauz, Samuel. *The Ghetto as an Experiment of Jewish Social Organisation*. *Jewish Social Studies*, New York, January, 1949. (The Kovno Ghetto by a former judge of the Memel Court.)

Kaufmann, Max. *Churb'n Lettland's; die Vernichtung der Juden*

Lettlands, Munich, 1947. (The Riga Ghetto, Kaiserswald and Stutthof camps.)

People's Verdict, The. (Extracts from the Krasnodar [July, 1943] and Kharkow [December, 1943] State trials.) London (Hutchinson), 1944.

Schwarz, Solomon M. *The Jews of the Soviet Union*, Syracuse, 1952.

Tenenbaum, Josef. *In Search of a Lost People*, New York, 1949.

Underground, The Story of a People, 1952.

*Wolff, Jeanette. *Sadismus oder Wahnsinn. Erlebnisse in den deutschen Konzentrationslagern im Osten*, Grenz, Thuringen, 1946. (Riga Ghetto.)

B. Poland

It seems useless to list the large number of works published in Yiddish, particularly in Buenos Aires and New York, which the author cannot claim to have read. Among the relatively restricted list which follows, apart from certain individual narratives, the collections of survivor-narratives made by Rabbi Silberschein of Geneva and Rabbi Guttmann of Jerusalem, and the collections in *Dokumenty i Materialy* have the most value.

Berg, Mary. *Warsaw Diary.* Translated by Norbert Gutterman, New York, 1945. (Although aged only 15 when she left Warsaw, this witness was more objective than most, but saw things from a relatively sheltered angle.)

Beth Ammi, Mariam. *Le droit à la patrie, Temoignages traduits du Yiddisch*, Paris, 1946.

The Black Book, American Jewish Black Book Committee, New York, 1945. (Numerous reports Warsaw, Lwow, Bialystok, Bochnia, etc.)

The Black Book of Polish Jewry, New York, September, 1943. (Much information from couriers of the exiled Polish Government as well as from refugee-survivors.)

Bloom, Solomon F. *Dictator of the Lodz Ghetto*, in 'Commentary,' New York, February, 1949.

Blumenthal, Nachmann. *Slowa Niewinne*, Cracow, 1947. (German documents and survivor-narratives in Polish.)

*Dokumenty i Materialy, published by Central Jewish Historical Commission of Poland, Lodz, 1946. (German documents.) Vol I, Obozy (camps); Vol II, Akcje i Wysiedlenia (resettlement actions); Vol III, Getto Lodzkie. (Vols. I and II include survivor-narratives in Polish.)

German Crimes in Poland. Edited in English by Central Commission for War Crimes, Warsaw, two volumes, 1946-47. (Survivor-narratives concerning the death camps.)

Guttmann, Rabbi T. *Dokumentenwerk*, Jerusalem, 1945. Vol I, 62 letter on the Nisko settlement; *Vol 2, massacres in Bochnia-Jasienica, narrative of Israel Weitz.

Hersey, John. *The Wall*, New York, 1951. (Although written as a novel, this is in fact a very able synthesis of a whole number of survivor-reports from the Warsaw Ghetto.)

*Hershkovitch, Bendet. *The Ghetto in Litzmannstadt (Lodz)*, Yivo Annual of Jewish Social Science, New York, Vol V, 1950.

*Littner, Jakob. *Aufzeichnungen aus einem Erdloch*, Munich, 1948. (A Munich stamp-dealer's experience in the Galician ghetto of Zbaraz.)

BIBLIOGRAPHY

*Masor, Michel. *La cité engloutie,* published in *Le Monde Juif,* Paris, 1950-52, numbers 33 to 51. (An astonishingly reticent survey of the economic problems of the Warsaw Ghetto by a former official of the ' Inter-aid ' who escaped from a death-train in 1942.)

Muszkat, Dr. Marian. *Polish Charges against German War Criminals,* Warsaw, 1948. (Evidence before State commissions, principally on death-camps.)

Netherlands Red Cross Information Bureau. *Sobibor,* The Hague, 1946. (Dutch survivors of the death-camp.)

Rabbi A. Silberschein (General Editor). *Die Judenausrottung in Polen,* stencilled reports, Geneva, 1944-46:

1st series, reports from Hrubieczow, Sanok, Radom, Drohobicz.
2nd series*, ' Das martyrium des Warschauer ghetto.'
3rd series, Die Vernichtungslager (*see* Auschwitz).
4th series, Warsaw and the rebellion.
5th series, reports from Lwow, Snyatyn, Sandomierz, *Kosow.

Tenenbaum, Josef. *In Search of a Lost People,* New York, 1949. *Underground, the Story of a People,* 1952. (A quantity of selections from narratives in Yiddish. Not very critical.)

Wiernik, Yankiel. *A Year in Treblinka,* New York, 1945. (Translated.)

*Zweig, Arnold. *Fahrt zum Acheron,* Potsdam, 1951. (The experiences of Frau Hilde Huppert of Teschen in the Rjeszow Ghetto and elsewhere.)

C. Rumania

The Black Book, New York, 1945. (Some commission evidence from the State trials.)

Carp, Matatias. Report (which includes the narrative of Chief Rabbi Saffran) in *Les Juifs en Europe,* Paris, CDJC, 1947.

Guttmann, Rabbi T. *Dokumentenwerk ueber die juedische Geschichte in der Zeit des Nazismus,* Vol. I, Jerusalem, 1945. (Important narratives from Jassy and Czernowitz.)

D. Auschwitz

This is not a complete bibliography of books on Auschwitz, but only of those books which are referred to in the text of *The Final Solution.*

Baum, Bruno. *Widerstand im Auschwitz,* Potsdam, 1951.

Dokumenty i Materialy, Lodz, 1946, Vol. I, Obozy (camps). (Numerous Auschwitz documents and reports.)

Friedman, Filip. *This was Oswiecim,* London, United Jewish Appeal, 1946. (This contains the list preserved by Dr. Otto Wolken, *Lagerschreiber* in the Birkenau quarantine section, of selections and gassings between October, 1943, and October, 1944.)

German Crimes in Poland, Warsaw, 1947, Vol I.

Jules Hofstein, Marc Klein, Robert Levy. See *Temoignages Strasbourgeois.*

Levi, Primo. *Sé questo e un uomo,* Turin, 1947. (Deported from North Italy to Auschwitz III (Monowitz) February, 1944.)

*Lingens-Reiner, Dr. Ella. *Prisoners of Fear,* introduction by Arturo Barea, London, 1948.

*Nyiszli, Dr. Miklos. *Le SS Obersturmfuehrer Docteur Mengele*, printed in *Les Temps Modernes*, Paris, April-May, 1951. (Not a study of Mengele, but the unique story of five months' survival in one of the Auschwitz crematoria. The author was deported in May, 1944, from Nagy-Varad [Oradea Mare], now Rumania.)

Menasche, Dr. Albert. *Birkenau, Auschwitz II*, New York, 1947.

Philips, Raymond (edited). *The Belsen Trial*, London, 1949.

*Rozanski, Zenon, *Muetzen Ab, Eine Reportage aus der Strafkompanie des KZ Auschwitz*, Hanover, 1948. (One of the rare accounts of Auschwitz life which go as far back as 1941.)

*Spritzer, Jenny. *Ich war No 10291. Tatsachenbericht einer Schreiberin der politischen Abteilung aus dem Konzentrationslager Auschwitz*, Zurich.

*Temoignages Strasbourgeois. *De l'université aux camps de concentration*, Paris, 1947. (Collection of narratives of deported professors and readers of Strasbourg University, including the Auschwitz experiences of the Jewish professors Mark Klein, Robert Levy, Jules Hofstein, and Robert Waitz.)

Vaillant-Couturier, Mme. Evidence in IMT, V, 182-196. (Birkenau 'Frauenlager' in 1943-44.)

Waitz, Robert. *See* Temoignages Strasbourgeois.

*War Refugee Board. *German Extermination Camps, Auschwitz and Birkenau* (stencil), Washington, Office of the President, November, 1944. (Four narratives of Polish and Slovak internees who escaped. The most important document is that of the anonymous Slovak Jewish doctor who escaped to Hungary in April, 1944. There is a French printed version in *Camps de Concentration* (Service d'information des Crimes de Guerre, Paris, 1945). The complete version exists only in stencil in Silberschein, *Judenausrottung in Polen*, Geneva, 1944, Part III. The author, who had been registrar of one of the Birkenau infirmaries, was exceptionally accurate and conveyed his report to the Swiss Red Cross as early as June, 1944, thereby making history (*see page 429*)).

Wellers, Dr. Georges. *De Drancy a Auschwitz*, Paris, CDJC, 1946. (Extensive information on deportations from France.)

Zywulska, Kristina. *I Came Back*, New York, 1948.

E. Theresienstadt (Terezin)

Baeck, Rabbi Leo, in *We Survived*, ed. Eric H. Boehm, Yale, 1949.

*Jacobson, Jacob. *Terezin, the Daily Life, 1943-45*, Jewish Central Information Office, London, March, 1946. Report No. 6 (stencil).

*Mannheimer, Max. *From Theresienstadt to Auschwitz*, ditto No. 3, July, 1945.

F. German Concentration Camps at the End of the War

Burney, Christopher. *The Dungeon Democracy*, London, 1946.

*Committee of the International Red Cross. *Documents sur l'activité de la Croix Rouge en faveur des civils detenus, etc.*, Serie II, Geneva, 1946.

Herz, Abel. *Kroniek der Jodenvervolging*, The Hague, 1951. (Bergen-Belsen.)

BIBLIOGRAPHY

Kogon, Eugen. *Der SS Staat. Das System der deutschen Konzentrationslager*, Berlin, 1947. English translation, *The Theory and Practice of Hell*, London, 1951.

Marshall, Bruce. *The White Rabbit. The Story of Wing-Commander F. F. E. Yeo-Thomas*, London, 1952.

Philips, Raymond. *The Belsen Trial*, London, 1949.

Rousset, David. *L'Univers Concentrationnaire*, Paris, 1946.

Temoignages Strasbourgeois. De l'Université aux Camps de Concentration, Paris, 1947.

Text References

CHAPTER 1

1 Walter Hagen (Willi Hoettl). *Die Geheime Front,* Wien-Linz, 1950.
2 For Goebbels's direct access to Hitler in Jewish affairs, *see The Goebbels Diaries,* London, 1948, *page 220.* For an example of Bormann's rôle, Dr. Henry Picker, *Hitler's Tischgespraeche,* Bonn, 1951, footnote to *page 313.*
3 Reichsgesetzblatt, 1, 1146-47.
4 Reichsgesetzblatt, 1, 372.
5 Case XI, transcript (judgment) 28254.
6 Quoted in *The Black Book,* New York, 1946, *page 122.*
7 Reichsgesetzblatt, 1, 109.
8 Case XI, NO 2174. (Affidavit Albrecht.)
9 Jakob Littner. *Aufzeichnungen aus einem Erdloch,* Munich, 1948.
10 *Jews of Nazi Europe,* Baltimore, 1941 (stencil), Ger 4. *The Black Book,* New York, 1946, *page 127.* Eugene Kulischer. *The Displacement of Population in Europe,* Montreal, 1943, *page 97.*
11 Mark Wischnitzer. *To Dwell in Safety,* New York, 1948, *page 196.*
12 *The Black Book, page 128.*
13 IMT, PS 3358.
14 IMT, IX, 90. (Evidence, Goering.) PS 3063. (Report by Walter Buch.)
15 IMT, XIII, 122. (Evidence, Funk.)
16 Ibid., IX., 91-93. (Evidence Goering.)
17 Hans Berndt Gisevius. *To the Bitter End,* London, 1948, *page 332.*
18 *The Von Hassell Diaries,* London, 1948, *page 21.*
19 Walter Hagen (Willi Hoettl). *Die Geheime Front,* Wien-Linz, 1950, *page 20.*
20 IMT, PS 3051.
21 IMT, PS 274.
22 IMT, XX, 146. (Evidence, Werner Best.)
23 IMT, IX, 252. (Evidence, Goering.)
24 IMT, PS 3058, and Eugen Kogon. *The Theory and Practice of Hell,* London, 1950, *page 163.*
25 IMT, PS 3063.
26 IMT, PS 1816. (Incomplete minutes of conference in the Air Ministry, Berlin.)
27 IMT, IX, 261. (Evidence, Goering.)
28 Case XI, NG 3565.
29 Reichsgesetzblatt, I, 1579-81 ; I, 1676 ; I, 864.
30 IMT, VIII, 235-238. (Evidence, Bodenschatz.)
31 Case XI, NG 1537.
32 Case XI, NG 1522-23.
33 Hjalmar Schacht. *Abrechnung mit Hitler,* translated as *Account Settled,* 1949, *page 129.*
34 Case XI, NG 1532-33.

35 Case XI, NO 4586. (Aff. Wohltat.)
36 IMT, XXII, 395. (Final speech, Schacht.)
37 IMT, PS 710.
38 *Black Book of Polish Jewry*, New York, 1943, *page 91*.
39 Norman H. Baynes. *The Speeches of Adolf Hitler, 1942*, Vol. 2, *page 742*.
40 On January 30th, 1942 (German hero's day); September 30th, 1942; February 24th, 1943; March 21st, 1943; and November 9th, 1943.
41 *Jews in Nazi Europe*, New York, 1941. Cz 2 (stencil). *Hitler's Ten Year War on the Jews*, New York (Institute Jewish Affairs), 1943, *page 55*.
42 *Hitler's Ten Year War, page 53. The Black Book, page 133. Jews of Nazi Europe*, Cz-5.
43 Information, Dr. Kafka to Jewish Information Centre, MS, London, 1945.
44 *Hitler's Ten Year War on the Jews, page 53*.
45 *The Black Book, page 132*.
46 *Jews of Nazi Europe*, Baltimore, 1941.
47 Alfred J. Fischer. *Zionist Review*, October, 1946.
48 Jewish Telegraphic Agency, Vienna, October 17th, 1948.
49 This and subsequent details are obtained from Eichmann's personal file, captured in the SS main office and numbered at Nuremberg NO 2259. A complete photostat copy can be consulted at the Centre du Documentation Juive Contemporaine, Paris, together with Eichmann's photographs (unfortunately only passport size).
50 Reszoe Kastner. *Bericht des Juedischen Rettungskomitees aus Budapest* (stencil), Geneva, 1945. Eugene Levai. *Black Book of Hungarian Jewry*, Zurich, 1948.
51 Leon Poliakov. *Adolf Eichmann ou le rêve de Caligula* in *Le Monde Juif*, June, 1949, and *Breviaire de la Haine*, Paris, 1951.
52 Case IV, NO 2259.
53 *Hitler's Ten Year War, 1943, page 27*.
54 Case IV, NO 2259.
55 IMT, III, 288 (examination, Wisliceny) and Affidavit C. (Wisliceny.)
56 Poliakov in *Le Monde Juif*, June, 1949, and IMT 280. (Examination Wisliceny.)
57 Reichsgesetzblatt, 1, 1097.
58 *Hitler's Ten Year War, 1943, page 27*.
59 Case XI, NG 4934. (*See also page 82* in this book.)
60 Mark Wischnitzer. *To Dwell in Safety*, 1948.
61 Bruno Blau. *Jewish Social Studies*, New York, April, 1950. (Even in the five months beginning May, 1941, when the Russian escape route was closed, the Jewish population of the Old Reich fell by 6,276. *Page 171*.)
62 Case XI, NO 5194.
63 Case XI, NO 3973.
64 *The Goebbels Diaries*, translated by Louis Lochner, London, 1948, *pages 41, 112-14*. Case XI, NG 971. (Report by Dierwege.)
65 Ibid., *page 159*.
66 Louis Frey. *Surrender on Demand*, quoted in *Le Monde Juif* November, 1948.

CHAPTER 2

1 R. T. Paget, K.C., M.P. *Manstein, His Campaigns and Trial*, London, 1951, *pages 20, 128, 133.*
2 *German Crimes in Poland*, Polish Government Publication, Warsaw, 1946, I, *pages 137-45.*
3 IMT, XX, 355, and document D 421.
4 *The Von Hassell Diaries*, London, 1948, *pages 76* and *95.*
5 IMT, XX, 282. (Evidence, Robert Brill.)
6 Manstein Trial, *Times, Daily Telegraph*, November 4th, 1949.
7 Evidence, Brig.-General Erwin Lahousen, IMT, I, 274.
8 *Offiziere gegen Hitler*, Zurich, 1946, *page 34.*
9 R. T. Paget. Op. cit., *pages 18, 90.*
10 IMT, I, 265-66. (Lahousen.)
11 PS 3363. (A decision on its authenticity in Case IX, Transcript 95.)
12 The speech is quoted in *Black Book of Polish Jewry*, New York, 1943, *page 15.*
13 Fuehrer-Order, IMT, PS 686.
14 *Memoirs of Dr. Felix Kersten*, translated Ernst Morwitz, New York, 1947, *pages 42, 83-95, 176, 181.* Also IMT, PS 1919, *The Posen Speech*, October 9th, 1943.
15 IMT, PS 660, Case VIII, NO 1880. (Law reports of trials of war criminals, XIII, 7, London, H.M. Stationery Office, 1948.)
16 Case VIII, NG 3225. (Extracts from both reports printed in Billig, *L'allemagne et le Genocide*, 1950, *pages 19* and *37.*)
17 *Nazi-Soviet Relations*, Washington, State Department, 1947, *pages 106-107.*
18 Eugene Kulischer. *Displacement of Populations in Europe*, Montreal, I.R.O., 1943, *page 47.*
19 IMT, II, 421. (Reichsgesetzblatt, 1, 2042.)
20 Kulischer. Op. cit., *page 72.*
21 Himmler to all Gauleiters and to group leaders of RKFDV, Case VIII, NO 4059.
22 IMT, II, 425, and PS 661.
23 Evidence of Hans Frank, IMT, XII, 109.
24 G. M. Gilbert. *Nuremberg Diary*, New York, 1947, *page 156.*
25 IMT, XII, 106.
26 IMT, XII, 117.
27 *The Goebbels Diaries*, London, 1948, *page 216.*
28 Evidence, Hans Frank, IMT, XII, 108.
29 *Archiv fur Wanderungswesen und Auslandskunde, 1942.* (Quoted in Kulischer, op. cit., 1943, *page 22.*)
30 Quoted in judgment of Case VIII, transcript 96.
31 Archives of Lodz Ghetto Administration in *Dokumenty i Materialy*, Lodz, 1946, 1, *pages 228-30.*
32 Case IV, NO 1257. (Printed in *Persecutions juives dans les pays de l'Est*, Paris, 1949, *pages 163-66.*)
33 Case VIII, Judgment. (Transcript 82.)
34 Minutes of conference, presided by Goering at Karinhall, IMT, EC 305.
35 Captured report of *Einsatzkommando* Bromberg, published in *German Crimes in Poland*, 1, *page 143.*

36 *Black Book of Polish Jewry*, 1943, *page 73.*
37 *German Crimes in Poland*, 1, *page 130.* Du Prel, *Das General-Gouverne-ment*, 1st edition, *page 101.* Abraham Melezin, *Demographic Processes Among the Jewish Populations*, Warsaw, 1947. (Statistics of the *Judenrat.*)
38 Case VIII, NO 5322. (Minutes of conference at RUSHA head office presided by Heydrich, January 30th, 1940.)
39 Eugene Kulischer. Op. cit., *page 47.*
40 Information, Dr. Emil Kafka to London Jewish Information Centre, 1945. (Typescript.)
41 Letter printed by Rabbi T. Guttman in *Dokumentenwerk ueber die Juedische Geschichte in der Zeit des Nazismus*, Jerusalem, 1943, *pages 62-66.*
42 Du Prel. *Das General-Gouvernement*, 2nd edition, May, 1942.
43 *Gerichtsurteil*, circulated by Hamburg *Schwurgericht* I, July 15th, 1950. *Veit Harlan Prozess.*
44 *Les Juifs en Europe*, Paris, 1947, *page 192.* (Paper by Wilhelm Krell citing Vienna *Kultusgemeinde* figures. *The Black Book, page 133.*)
45 *Law Reports of Trials of War Criminals*, XIII, *page 20* (the RUSHA case), and NO 3011.
46 *Hitler's Ten Year War on the Jews.* (Quoting *Weltwoche*, Zurich.)
47 Law reports, XIII, 20. Case VIII, NO 5322. *Trials of War Criminals*, IV, *page 855.* (Conference conducted by Heydrich, January 30th, 1940.)
48 IMT, EC 305. (Karinhall conference, February 12th, 1940, quoted in Josef Tenenbaum, *In Search of a Lost People, page 264.*)
49 Case VIII, NO 3031. Du Prel, *Das General-Gouvernement*, 2nd edition, *page 325.* (For Globocnik's part, *see* Case VIII, NO 5875, *Trials of War Criminals*, IV, *page 865.*)
50 Case XI, NG 1530, and Case VIII, NG 5322. *Trials of War Criminals*, IV, *page 855.*
51 *The von Hassell Diaries*, London, 1948, *page 115.*
52 Case XI, NO 2480. (Transcript 28469.)
53 Minutes of conference, April 1st, 1940, printed in *Dokumenty i Materialy*, III, *page 167.*
54 Case XI, NG 3175.
55 *Dokumenty i Materialy*, III, *page 167.*
56 Ditto, *page 168.*
57 Frank Diary, July 12th, 1940. (PS 2233.)
58 Evidence of Baldur von Schirach, IMT, XIV, 364.
59 IMT, USSR 172, Minutes of October 2nd, 1940, and IMT, XV, 11.
60 IMT, PS 1950 and PS 2233. (Frank Diary.)
61 IMT, EC 344 (Quoted in Poliakov, *Breviaire de la Haine, page 461*), and IMT, PS 2233. (Frank Diary.)
62 Abraham Melezin. *Demographic Processes*, etc., op. cit.
63 *Gazeta Zydowska*, quoted in *Jews in Nazi Europe*, 1941, pol 15. (Stencil.)
64 Frank Diary, PS 2233.
65 *Dokumenty i Materialy*, II, *page 6.*
66 Du Prel. *Das General-Gouvernement*, 2nd edition, *page 323.*
67 Manstein Trial. *Times*, August 30th, 1949.
68 Silberschein. *Das Judenausrottung in Polen* (stencil, Geneva, November, 1943), 1st series, *page 6.*

69 *Nazi-Soviet Relations*, Washington, 1947, *page 128.*
70 Frank Diary, PS 2233.
71 Silberschein. Ibid.
72 *Von Hassell Diaries*, London, 1948, *page 99.*
73 *Jews in Nazi Europe*, pol 10 (stencil). *German Crimes in Poland*, 1, *page 127.*
74 NO 5194. (Korherr to Himmler, March 23rd, 1943.)
75 Wiener Library Bulletin, September, 1947.

CHAPTER 3

1 *Hitler's Ten Year War on the Jews*, 1943, *page 132.*
2 Information, Jewish Information Centre, London. Similar Reich decree, Case XI, NG 1143.
3 *The von Hassell Diaries*, London, 1948, *pages 178, 250, 272.*
4 L. Poliakov. *L'etoile jaune*, Paris, 1949. *Dokumenty i Materialy*, III, *page 23.*
5 Order of May 10th, 1940, in *Dokumenty i Materialy*, III, *page 83.*
6 Dvorjetski. *Ghetto a l'Est*, Paris, 1950, *page 128.*
7 *Black Book of Polish Jewry*, pages 206-10.
8 *Diary of Mary Berg*, New York, 1945, *page 29.*
9 IMT, PS 2233, Frank Diary. (Quoted in *German Crimes in Poland*, II.)
10 Papers of Dr. Israel Rothbalsam. (Quoted in L. Poliakov, *Breviaire de la Haine*, 1951, *page 112.*)
11 Du Prel. *Das General-Gouvernement*, 2nd edition, 1942, *page 323.*
12 *Dokumenty i Materialy*, III, *page 65.*
13 Speech quoted in Max Weinrich, *Hitler's Professors*, New York, 1947, *pages 107-10.*
14 PS 2233, Frank Diary. (Report of conference in Palais Bruhl, quoted in *German Crimes in Poland*, II.)
15 *Dokumenty i Materialy*, III, *pages 74, 83.*
16 Ibid., III, *pages 95, 176.*
17 Nachman Blumental. *Slova Niewinne*, Warsaw, 1947 (quoting Lodz *Ghettoverwaltung* archives), *page 99.*
18 *Dokumenty i Materialy*, III, *page 219.*
19 Ibid., III, *page 178.*
20 Eugene Kulischer. *Displacement of Populations in Europe*, IRO, Montreal, 1943, *page 52.*
21 *Black Book of Polish Jewry*, 1943, *page 38.*
22 A. Silberschein. *Die Judenausrottung in Polen*, Geneva, 1944, IV, *page 8* (stencil).
23 Ibid., IV, *page 5.* (Report of a refugee in Switzerland.) *Diary of Mary Berg*, New York, 1945, *page 82.*
24 Silberschein, *page 15.* Quoting *Gazeta Zydowska*, Cracow.
25 Ibid., *page 11.*
26 Abraham Melezin. *Demographic Processes Among the Jewish Population* (English and Polish), Warsaw, 1948.
27 IMT, PS 1061. (Report of Brig.-General Juengen Stroop to Higher SS *Polizeifuehrer*, Cracow. 'The Warsaw Ghetto exists no more.')
28 Report by joint organisations TOZ-OSE, published in *Black Book of Polish Jewry*.

29 'La Cité engloutie,' 1942. *Le Monde Juif*, No. 33, July, 1950.
30 Du Prel, 2nd edition, *page 349*.
31 Michel Mazor. 'La Cité engloutie' in *Le Monde Juif*, No. 37, November, 1950.
32 Curzio Malaparte. *Kaputt* (translated Professor Foligno), New York, 1946, Ch. V.
33 Quoted in *Le Monde Juif*, No. 27, January, 1950.
34 *Black Book of Polish Jewry, page 50*.
35 From *Gazeta Zydowska*. Quoted in *Jews of Nazi Europe*, Baltimore, November, 1941 (stencil), pol 21. *Dokumenty i Materialy*, III, *pages 177-79, 184, 190-92*.
36 *Mary Berg, page 152*.
37 Frank Diary, IMT, PS 2233. Quoted in *German Crimes in Poland*, II.
38 Ditto.
39 *Mary Berg*, New York, 1945, *page 116*.
40 Silberschein. *Ausrottung*, IV, *page 16*.
41 Ditto, *pages 7, 49*.
42 Franz Blaettler. *Warschau 1942. Tatsachenbericht eines Motorfahrers*, Zurich, 1945.
43 Silberschein. *Ausrottung, etc., page 49. Diary of Mary Berg*, New York, 1945.
44 Silberschein. Op. cit., IV, *page 8*.
45 *Black Book of Polish Jewry, page 87*.
46 Silberschein. *Judenausrottung*, I, *pages 59* and *84*.
47 *Black Book of Polish Jewry, page 103*.
48 Solomon Bloom. *Dictator of the Lodz Ghetto*, in *Commentary*, New York, February, 1949, *pages 110-122*.
49 *Black Book of Polish Jewry, page 67*.
50 Bloom. Op. cit., *page 116*. Josef Tenenbaum. *In Search of a Lost People*, New York, 1949, *page 106*.
51 Quoted in full, *Dokumenty i Materialy*, III, *page 264*.
52 Michel Mazor. 'La Cité Engloutie' in *Le Monde Juif*, No. 49, November, 1951.
53 Marc Dvorjetski. *Ghetto a l'Est*, Paris, 1950.
54 Samuel Gringauz in *Jewish Social Studies*, New York, January, 1949. Case IX, NO 2262. (Complaint by Lieut.-Colonel Strauch of the Security Police to Major-General von dem Bach-Zalewski on the conduct of *Reichskommissar* Kube.)
55 *Mary Berg*, op. cit., *page 40*. (The quotation from *Voelkischer Beobachter* in *The Black Book*, New York, 1946.)
56 Dvorjetski. Op. cit., *page 109*.
57 Case I. (Evidence for Wolfram Sievers, printed in *Trials of War Criminals*, Vol II, *page 40*.)
58 Dvorjetski, *page 156*.
59 Wiener Library Bulletin, January, 1950.
60 Dvorjetski, *page 125*.
61 *Dokumenty i Materialy*, II, *pages 4-7*.
62 Dvorjetski, *page 130*.
63 *Dokumenty i Materialy*, II, *pages 178, 190*.
64 *Dokumenty i Materialy*, II, *page 199*.
65 Du Prel. *Das General-Gouvernement*, 1st edition, *page 65*.

66 *Black Book of Polish Jewry, pages 206-10.*
67 Ibid., *page 321. The Black Book,* 1946, *page 194. Jews of Nazi Europe,* 1941 (pol 25).
68 Ibid. (pol 23).
69 Case IV, NO 1811.
70 *Jews of Nazi Europe* (pol 25).
71 Case IV, NO 3031.
72 'Begruendung,' by *Vorsitzer* of the Bremen *Schwurgericht,* May, 1950. (Typescript presented to CDJC, Paris.)

CHAPTER 4

1 Case XI, NG 2586. (Minutes of the Gross-Wannsee Conference.)
2 Case XI, NG 1838. (Affidavit, Otto Abetz.)
3 Case XI, NG 4893.
4 Peter Kleist. *Zwischen Hitler und Stalin,* Bonn, 1950, *page 12.*
5 Case XI, Transcript 8571-72. (Evidence, Weiszaecker.) Ernst von Weizsaecker, *Erinnerungen,* Munich, 1950, *page 338.*
6 *Die Neue Zeitung,* February 6th, 1952.
7 Charge against Rademacher. *Landgericht,* Nuremberg-Fuerth, January 19th, 1950.
8 Case XI, NG 4895.
9 Case XI, NG 1838.
10 Case XI, NG 4933.
11 Case XI, NG 4934.
12 Eugene Hevesi in *Contemporary Jewish Review,* August, 1941. Mark Wischnitzer, *To Dwell in Safety,* Philadelphia, 1948, *page 206.*
13 Documents on German Foreign Policy, 1918-45, Series D, Vol IV, London, 1951, No. 372.
14 Case XI, NG 2586b.
15 Case XI, NG 2586-J.
16 Affidavit by Wisliceny at the Bratislava trial, partly printed by L. Poliakov in *Breviaire de la Haine,* 1951, *page 53,* and in *Le Monde Juif,* June, 1949.
17 Case XI, NG 2586j.
18 Max Weinreich. *Hitler's Professors,* New York, 1946, *pages 98-9.*
19 Dr. Paul Schmidt. *Hitler's Interpreter,* London, 1951, *page 178.*
20 Case XI, NG 2586-J. (Report, Luther to Ribbentrop, August 19th, 1942.)
21 Case XI, NG 1838. (Affidavit, Otto Abetz.)
22 IMT, XIV, 354, 364. (Evidence, Schirach.)
23 Felix Kersten. *Klerk en Beul, Himmler von nabeij,* Amsterdam, 1947, *pages 197-98.*
24 Case I, NO 426. (Affidavit, Viktor Brack, *Trials of War Criminals,* Washington, 1950, Vol I, *page 842.*)
25 Case XI, NG 2586-J. (Printed by David Rousset in *Le pitre ne rit pas,* Paris, 1949.)
26 IMT, XI, 14. (Evidence, Keitel.)
27 IMT, V, 84, and RF 1207.

28 Max Weinreich. *Hitler's Professors,* New York, 1946, *pages 98-9* and *106-15.*
29 IMT, XII, 15. (Evidence, Keitel.)
30 IMT, VI, 179.
31 IMT, XXI, 32, 40. (Evidence, Brauchitsch.) Case XII, NOKW 3140. (Halder Diary.) Extract in *Law Reports of Trials of War Criminals,* XII, *page 23,* London, H.M. Stationery Office, 1949.
32 Case IX, Transcript 525. (Evidence, Ohlendorf.)
33 Case XII, NOKW 3140. (Halder Diary.)
34 IMT, III, 246 and 269. (Evidence, Ohlendorf.)
35 IMT, XXI, 31. (Evidence, Brauchitsch.) XXI, 68. (Evidence, Schellenberg.)
36 IMT, III, 248.
37 Case IX, NO 4145. (Affidavit, Blome.) Transcript 4374. (Evidence, Erwin Schulz.)
38 Case IX, Transcript 312-13.
39 Case XI, NG 4934.
40 IMT, PS 710. (Photostat copy annexed to an invitation to the Gross-Wannsee Conference of January 20th, 1942.)
41 IMT, XI, 250-1. (Evidence, Goering, March 20th, 1946.)
42 Fragment of Goebbels's diary discovered since the published portions and deposited with State Department, Washington. (Typescript in Rijksinstituut fur Oorlogsdokumentatie, Amsterdam.)
43 *Dokumenty i Materialy,* Lodz, 1946, III, *page 197.*
44 Case VIII, NG 1020.
45 *The Goebbels Diaries,* unpublished fragment, *see* 42.
46 Case VIII, NG 839.
47 IMT, L, 61.
48 Case XI, Transcript 28530.
49 Case XI, NG 2499.
50 Case XI, NG 4905, and Transcript 28531.
51 Case XI, NG 4905.
52 IMT, PS 3914.
53 *Dokumenty i Materialy,* III, *page 201.* (*Schutzpolizei* report, Lodz, November 13th, 1941.)
54 Ibid.
55 NG 2421. (Photographs from files, Gestapo, Hessen-Mainfranken.)
56 W. Krell in *Les Juifs en Europe, 1939-45,* Paris, CDJC, 1947. ' Juedisches Nachrichtenblatt,' quoted in *Jews of Nazi Europe* (stencil), Baltimore, 1941 (section Ger 3-4).
56a Communication H. Tuch, Berlin-Dahlem, see footnote.
56b Ella Lingens-Reiner, *Prisoners of Fear,* London, 1948, *page 119.*
57 Ibid., Ger 15-16.
58 *The von Hassell Diaries, page 202.*
59 Case XI, NG 4447.
60 *Dokumenty i Materialy,* III, *page 201.*
61 IMT, XII, 181. (Evidence, Josef Buehler.)
62 ' Dictator of the Lodz Ghetto,' Sol Bloom in *Commentary,* New York, February, 1949.
63 *Hitler's Ten Year War on the Jews,* 1943, *page 30.*
64 NO 5194. Report by Dr. Korherr to Reichsfuehrer, SS.

65 Rabbi Leo Baeck in *We Survived*. (Ed., Eric Boehm, Yale, 1949.)
66 IMT, PS 3921.
67 Case I, NO 365 *Trials of War Criminals*, Washington, 1950, Vol. 1, *page 870*.
68 IMT, PS 3663. (Photostat published in Max Weinreich, *Hitler's Professors*, New York, YIVO, 1946, *pages 145-50*.)
69 IMT, PS 3047. (Lahousen diary.)
70 PS 2273. (Stahlecker to Heydrich.) IMT, 193-95. (Max Kaufmann, *Churbn Lettland*, Munich, 1947, *page 125*.)
71 Jeannette Wolff. *Sadismus oder Wahnsinn*, Grenz im Thuringen, 1947, *page 125*.
72 Case IX, NO 3257, and Max Kaufmann, op. cit. Case IX, NO 5548. (Affidavit, Karl Winter, partly printed in *Le Monde Juif*, No. 50, December, 1951.)
73 Case IV, NO 4072. (Captured Gestapo file.) Kaufmann, op. cit. Communication from H. Tuch, Jewish Restitution Office, Berlin-Dahlem, reproducing Gestapo reports to Higher Finance President, Berlin-Brandenburg.
74 IMT, VII, 114. Soviet prosecution document.
75 *The Black Book*, 1945, *page 324*. (Evidence before Soviet State Commission, Kovno.)
76 IMT, PS 3428, and PS 3665. Documents found in Rosenberg Ministry, Berlin.
77 Communication, H. Tuch. See 60.

CHAPTER 5

1 Case XI, NG 2586-J. (Luther memorandum to Ribbentrop.)
2 Case XI, NG 4766c.
3 Case XI, NG 2586-F.
4 Case XI, NG 2586-J. (For entire account of conference which follows.)
5 Case XI, NG 2586-G.
6 Case XI, Transcript 28526, NG 1949a.
7 Frank Diary, PS 2233, and IMT, II, 393.
8 Case XI, NG 2586-J.
9 Case XI, NG 2586-G.
10 Walter Hagen (Willi Hoettl). *Die Geheime Front*, Linz-Wien, 1950, *page 24*.
11 Wiener Library Bulletin, Vol. 5, No. 1, January, 1951. (Quoting original RSHA file in YIVO Library, New York.)
12 Case VI (I.G. Farben), NI 500.
13 Case IV, Transcript 1798. (Evidence, Pohl.)
14 Case IV, Transcript 8080.
15 Case IV, Transcript 1280.
16 Case IV, Transcript 8080.
17 Case IV, NO 385.
18 IMT, XI, 362. (Evidence, Hoess.)
19 IMT, D 749. (Affidavit, Hoess.)
20 Case VI, NI 11984. (Affidavit, Perry Broad.)
21 IMT, PS 034.

TEXT REFERENCES

22 Affidavit Kramer in *The Belsen Trial*, ed. Raymond Philips, London, 1949, *page 732*.
23 Zenon Rozanski. *Muetzen ab* (Caps off). Eine Reportage aus der Strafkompanie des KZ-Auschwitz, Hanover, 1948.
23a Kristina Zywulska. *I Came Back*, N.Y., 1949, *page 197*.
24 G. M. Gilbert, Ph.D. *Nuremberg Diary*, New York, 1948, *page 269*. L. Poliakov. *Breviaire de la Haine*, Paris, 1951, *page 226*.
25 IMT, Affidavit SS 67 (Morgen).
26 Case IV, NO 2124.
27 *The Belsen Trial* (op. cit.), *page 183*.
28 Case IV, NG 2587. *Black Book of Polish Jewry, page 87* (1943).
29 *Urteil im I.G. Farben Prozess*, Offenbach, 1949, *page 124*.
30 IMT, D 749. (Affidavit, Hoess.)
31 WRB report on Auschwitz-Birkenau, Washington, President's Office, November, 1944 (stencil).
32 *Urteil im I.G. Farben Prozess*, Offenbach, *page 125*.
33 WRB, op. cit.
33a Ella Lingens-Reiner. *Prisoners of Fear*, London, 1948, *pages 69-70*.
34 IMT, XI, 362. (Evidence, Hoess.)
35 IMT, XI, 238 and 256, and doc. PS 2376, also cross-affidavit KR 1.
36 Case IV, NO 2125. (Affidavit, Schwarz.)
37 Case IV, Transcript 1273. (Evidence, Pohl.)
37a Netherlands Red Cross. *Auschwitz, Deel II*, The Hague, May, 1948.
37b Filip Friedman. *This was Oswiecim*, London, 1946, *pages 24-5*.
38 Letter, dated April 24th, 1946. (Copy in Rijksinstituut fur Oorlogs-dokumentatie, Amsterdam.)
39 Ibid., Filip Friedman. *This was Oswiecim*, London, 1948.
40 Trial of Franz Rademacher, *Das Freie Wort*, February 23rd, 1952.
41 Friedman. Op. cit.
41a Lingens-Reiner, op. cit., *page 74*.
42 IMT, V, 194.
43 *German Crimes in Poland*, Warsaw, 1946, I, *pages 61-2*.
44 WRB report, Auschwitz-Birkenau (op. cit.), *Urteil im I.G. Farben Prozess, page 126*. Netherlands Red Cross, *Auschwitz, Deel II*.
45 Zenon Rozanski. *Muetzen ab* (op. cit.) and WRB report.
46 Netherlands Red Cross. *Het Dodenboek van Auschwitz* (Auschwitz deel 1), The Hague, June, 1947.
46a Rozanski, op. cit., *page 79*.
46b War Refugees Board report, *pages 10, 16*, and *18*. Lingens-Reiner, op. cit., *page 67*.
47 Case IV, Transcript 1917-20, and NO 3408. (Diary lent by Judge Sehn of the Cracow tribunal.)
48 Dr. Albert Menasche. *Birkenau (Auschwitz II)*, New York, 1947, *page 84*.
49 Dr. Miklos Nyiszli in *Las temps modernes*, May, 1951, *page 1858*. Dr. Ada Bimko in *The Belsen Trial*, London, 1949, *page 67*.
50 *The Belsen Trial, page 73*.
51 *Dokumenty i Materialy*, I, *page 74*.
52 *Dokumenty i Materialy*, Lodz, 1946, I, *pages 100-105*.
53 Dr. Miklos Nyiszli in *Les temps modernes*, April, 1951.
53a Jeannette Wolff. *Sadismus oder Wahnsinn*, Grenz im Thuringen, 1947.

53b Primo Levi. *Sé questo e un uomo,* Turin, 1947. Yankiel Wiernik. A *Year in Treblinka,* New York, 1945.
54 IMT, PS 2172 (Annexe II). IMT, XX, 347-51. (Evidence, Morgen.)
55 Bruno Baum. *Widerstand im Auschwitz,* Potsdam, 1949.
56 WRB report, Washington, November, 1944 (stencil), *page 25.*
57 Marc Dvorjetski. *Ghetto a l'Est,* Paris, 1950, *page 288.*
58 *Het Dodenboek van Auschwitz,* The Hague, June, 1947. (Netherlands Red Cross.)

CHAPTER 6

1 *Mein Kampf.* Translation published by Hurst and Blackett, 1939, *page 553.*
2 IMT, XX, 380.
3 IMT, Affidavit, Konrad Morgen (SS 65).
4 IMT, XX, 397.
5 IMT, XX, 382.
6 Trial of Josef Hirtreiter, *Frankfurter Rundschau,* November 11th, 1950.
7 IMT, Affidavit, Konrad Morgen (SS 67).
8 Case I, Transcript 2413. (Evidence, Karl Brandt.)
9 Case IX, NO 3143 and NO 3160.
10 PS 630. (Found in files of Ministry of Justice.) Case I, Transcript 2413.
11 Kienast. *Der Grossdeutsche Reichstag,* November, 1943, *pages 168* and *449.*
12 Dr. Henry Picker. *Hitler's Tischgespraeche,* Bonn, 1951, *page 418.*
13 Case I, Transcript 7658. IMT, XI, 130.
14 Case I, NO 426. (Affidavit, Viktor Brack.) *Trials of War Criminals,* I *page 842.*
15 Case I, Transcript 1879. (Evidence, Viktor Brack.)
16 Case I, Transcript 2481, NO 426. (Affidavit, Viktor Brack.) *Trials of War Criminals,* I, *page 810.*
17 Trial of Josef Hirtreiter, *Frankfurter Rundschau,* November 11th, 1950
18 Case I, Transcript 7413-7772. (Evidence Viktor Brack.) *Trials of War Criminals,* I, *pages 876-89.*
19 Case I, Transcript 7743, and NO 365. (*Trials of War Criminals,* I, *pages 803, 870,* and *888.*)
20 Letter to the author and photographs from Mr. Joseph Zigman, Information Services Division, Office of the US High Commissioner, Germany.
21 Case I, NO 844. Mitscherlich and Mielke. *Wissenschaft ohne Menschlichkeit,* Heidelberg, 1949, *page 190.* Translation, *Doctors of Infamy,* New York, 1949, *page 105.* François Bayle, *Croix Gammée ou Caducée,* 1950, *page 763.*
22 Case I, NO 470. (Affidavit, Kneissler.) Mitscherlich, 186.
23 *The Times,* July 3rd, 1945.
24 Case I, NO 846. (Mitscherlich, 192.) IMT, IV, 334, and PS 615.
25 Case I, NO 239. (Mitscherlich, 193.)
26 Case I, NO 2635. (Transcript of Mennecke's examination before the Frankfurt *Landgericht.*) Case I, Transcript 2481. Examination, Karl Brandt (Mitscherlich, 118).
27 Case I, NO 018. (*Croix Gammée ou Caducée,* 1950, *page 758.*)
28 Ibid., *page 843.*

29 *The Hadamar Trial*, London, 1948, *page 20.*
30 Case I, Transcript 7758. (*Trials of War Criminals*, 1950, I, *page 810.*)
31 Case I, NO 2634. (Excerpt from Frankfurt *Landgericht* judgment.)
32 Affidavit, Waldemar Hoven, Case I, NO 429. (*Trials of War Criminals*, 1950, I, *page 847.*)
33 Case I, NO 907 and NO 3060. (Mitscherlich, 209.)
34 Case I, Transcript 7635. (Mitscherlich, 207.)
35 Affidavit, Muthig, Case I, NO 2799. (Mitscherlich, 210.)
36 Case I, Transcript 1913. (Mitscherlich, 209, *Doctors of Infamy, page 120.*)
36a *Konzentrationslager Dachau.* Geschildert von Dachauer Haeftlingen, Vienna, 1946, *page 39.*
37 PS 1933, IMT, III, 158 ; NO 1607, Case I. (Mitscherlich, 212.)
38 Case I. Affidavit Morgen (Document, Karl Brandt, 20), Mitscherlich, 213.
39 IMT, XX, 385.
40 Case I, NO 907. (Mitscherlich, 208.)
41 Case I, NO 205. (*Trials of War Criminals*, I, *page 721.*)
42 Sobibor case. *Frankfurter Rundschau*, August 22nd, 1950.
43 *Frankfurter Rundschau*, November 11th, 1950.
43a *German Crimes in Poland*, I, *page 105.*
44 Case I, NO 426. (Affidavit, Viktor Brack, *Trials of War Criminals*, I, *page 842.*)
45 Case I, Transcript 7613. Mitscherlich, 214, *Trials of War Criminals*, I, *page 733.*
46 Sobibor case. *Frankfurter Rundschau*, August 26th, 1950.
47 Case I, NO 365. *Trials of War Criminals*, I, *pages 870, 888.*
48 Case I, NO 470, NO 3010. Affidavits, Dr. Gorgass. (*Trials of War Criminals*, I, *page 803.*)
49 Case I, NO 2467. *Trials of War Criminals*, I, *pages 769, 776.*
50 *German Crimes in Poland*, Warsaw, 1946, Vol. I, *pages 109-118.* Marian Muszkat. *Polish Charges Against German War Criminals*, Warsaw, 1948, *pages 206-212.*
51 Walter Hagen. *Die Geheime Front, page 38*, Linz, 1950.
52 Case IX, NO 3197. (Affidavit, Paul Blobel.)
52a Case IV, NO 4467. Hoess's memorandum on his journey. Case IV, 4498b. An affidavit by Hoess, produced at his trial in Cracow in 1947 in which many details of the memorandum are explained.
53 Case IX, NO 3824. (Affidavit, Blobel.) Printed in *Trials of War Criminals*, IV, *page 212.*
54 Reszoe Kastner, Affidavit, IMT, PS 2605.
55 Case IV, NO 4467 and NO 4498a. (Transcript of Cracow court.) Muszkat. *Polish Charges, page 208.* (Evidence of Michal Podchlebnik.)
56 Case IV, NO 519 and NO 534.
57 IMT, PS 501.
58 *Dokumenty i Materialy*, Lodz, 1946, III, *page 279.*
59 *Black Book of Polish Jewry*, 1943, *pages 135-38.*
60 Sobibor case. (*Frankfurter Rundschau*, August 24th, 1950.)
61 IMT, V, 240. (Evidence, Paul Roser.)
62 Case IV. Interrogation, Karl Wolff, *Trials of War Criminals*, V, *page 279*, 1951.

63 Josef Tenenbaum. *In Search of a Lost People*, New York, 1949, *page 123*. Evidence, Leon Weliczer.
64 Silberschein. *Die Judenausrottung im Polen*, Geneva, 1944, V, *page 22* (stencil).
65 *Rawa Ruska*, Marseilles, 1945.
66 Muszkat. *Polish Charges, page 229. Dokumenty i Materialy*, I, *page 221*. *Belsec* (in Polish), Cracow, 1945, by Rudolf Reder.
67 IMT, PS 1553. *Trials of War Criminals*, I, *page 865*. This is incomplete ; full version in document books of Cases I and IV.
68 *Frankfurter Rundschau*, March 2nd, 1951.
69 D 749. Affidavit, Rudolf Hoess (IMT).
70 PS 3311 (report of Warsaw Judicial Commission) and IMT, II, 40.
71 A Year in Treblinka (op. cit.). Muszkat, *Polish Charges, etc.*, *page 192*.
72 Kogon. *Theory and Practice of Hell*, 1950, *page 170*.
73 IMT, PS 1061. Figures quoted by Major-General Juergen Stroop.
74 A Year in Treblinka.
75 Ibid. and *Dokumenty i Materialy*, I, *page 183*.
76 IMT, XV, 62.
77 IMT, VIII, 16. (Evidence, Rajzman.)
78 *Temoignages Strasbourgeois*, Paris, 1947, *page 497*.
79 Poliakov. *Breviaire de la Haine, page 225*. (Evidence, Rothbalsam.)
80 Netherlands Red Cross. *Sobibor*, February, 1947.
81 Case IV, NO 482.
82 *Frankfurter Rundschau*, August 22nd, 1950. (Sobibor case.)
83 *Frankfurter Rundschau*, November 11th, 1950. (Hirtreiter case.)
84 Miklos Nyiszli in *Les temps modernes*, April, 1951, *page 1885*.
85 Samuel Gringauz in *Jewish Social Studies*, New York, July, 1947.
86 *A Year in Treblinka, page 28*. IMT, VII, 129-32. (Affidavit, Gerhard Adamitz.)
87 *A Year in Treblinka. Dokumenty i Materialy*, pages 182-90. IMT, VIII, 16. (Evidence, Samuel Rajzman.)
88 *German Crimes in Poland*, Warsaw, 1946, I, *page 96*.
89 Josef Tenenbaum. *In Search of a Lost People, page 286*. Sobibor (Dutch Red Cross Report, 1947). *German Crimes in Poland*, I, *page 181*. *The Black Book, page 374*. (Interrogations by Ilya Ehrenberg.)
90 IMT, XX, 389.
91 IMT, D, 749. Affidavit, Rudolf Hoess. Filip Friedman, *This was Oswiecim*, 1946, *page 18*.
92 Zenon Rozanski. *Muetzen Ab* (Caps off). *Eine Reportage aus der Strafkompanie des KL Auschwitz*, Hanover, 1948, *page 53*.
93 Case IV, NO 4344. (Printed in *Trials of War Criminals*, V, pages 362-64 (Washington).
94 IMT, XXI, 2, and Case I. (Evidence, Karl Wolff. Printed in *Croix Gammée ou Caducée*, pages 358-59.) IMT, XX, 258. (Evidence, von Eberstein.) IMT, III, 160, and PS 1602.
95 Captain Payne-Best. *The Venlo Incident*, 1950, *pages 186, 227*.
96 Case IV, NI 034. (Affidavit, Rudolf Hoess.)
97 *Law Reports of Trials of War Criminals*, London, 1946, I, *page 28*.
98 IMT, PS 1553, and V, 271-72 and 295.
99 Case IV, NO 2360 and 2362, Transcript 1906.

100 *Law Reports of Trials of War Criminals,* London, 1946, I, *page 28.*
101 *Law Reports of Trials of War Criminals,* London, X, *page 24.* Case VI, NI 1211. (Affidavit, Dr. Peters, Frankfurt, August, 1947.)
102 *Frankfurter Rundschau,* April 29th, 1950. *Berliner Neue Zeitung,* March 22nd and 29th, 1949.
103 Dr. Miklos Nyiszli in *Les temps modernes,* April, 1951, *page 1865.*
104 Captain Payne-Best. *The Venlo Incident,* London, 1950, *page 227.* Unpublished statement by Hoess to Dr. G. M. Gilbert in Rijksinstituut fur Oorlogsdokumentatie, Amsterdam.
105 Case IV, Transcript 1590. (Evidence, Oswald Pohl.)
105b Case IV, NO 4472. Bischoff to Wirtz, March 30th, 1942. Photostat at CDJC Paris.
106 Case IV. Transcript 1281.
107 *German Crimes in Poland,* Warsaw, 1946, I, *page 32.*
108 Case IV, NO 4473. Printed in *Trials of War Criminals,* V, *page 619.*
109 Case IV, NO 4466. Printed in *Trials of War Criminals,* V, *page 624.*
110 *German Crimes in Poland,* I, *page 88.* Miklos Nyiszli in *Les temps modernes,* April, 1951, *page 1665.* IMT, D 749. Affidavit, Hoess.
111 *The Belsen Trial,* edited Raymond Philips, London, 1949, *page 132.*
112 *German Crimes in Poland,* I, *page 89.*
113 *The Belsen Trial,* London, 1949, *page 68.*
114 *Les temps modernes,* April, 1951, *page 1665.*
115 Ibid. and Filip Friedman. *This was Oswiecim,* London, 1948, *page 54.*
116 Dr. Ada Bimko in *The Belsen Trial, page 68.*
117 Ibid., *page 138.*
118 IMT, PS 1553. (Also in Cases I and IV); partly printed in *Trials of War Criminals,* Washington, 1950, I, *page 865.*
119 *Frankfurter Rundschau,* April 29th, 1950.
120 *Frankfurter Rundschau,* ibid.
121 Case I. See François Bayle, *Croix Gammée ou Caducée,* 1950, Rascher to Himmler, October 8th, 1942, *page 361* ; Sievers to Karl Brandt, September, 1943, *page 90* ; Pfannenstiel to Kurt Blome, November 18th, 1943, *page 129* ; NO 290 in *Trials of War Criminals,* I, *page 213,* Washington, 1950.
122 Communication from Baron von Otter to Centre de Documentation Juive Contemporaine, November 10th, 1949.

CHAPTER 7

1 Bruno Blau. ' Jewish Population in Nazi Germany,' *Jewish Social Studies,* New York, 1949, *page 172.*
2 NO 5193. Dr. Korherr's statistical reports to Himmler.
3 *The Goebbels Diaries,* translated by Louis Lochner, London, 1947, *page 102.*
4 *Dokumenty i Materialy,* Lodz, 1946, II, *pages 49* and *194.*
5 Ditto, II, *page 224.*
6 Wilhelm Krell in *The Black Book,* 1945, *page 132,* and *Les Juifs en Europe,* Paris, 1947, *page 192.* (Conference of Jewish historical commissions.)

7 *Dokumenty i Materialy*, II, pages 33, 50.

8 Ditto, II, *page 194.*

9 NO 4072, Gestapo files, Nuremberg. *International Tracing Service* list of camps and prisons, Arolsen, 1949.

9a A correspondence concerning the Jews rounded up for Majdanek in December, 1941, is printed in *Dokumenty i Materialy*, I, *pages 129-137.* The list of watches is printed on *pages 154-57.*

10 Case XI, NG 183. IMT, RF 1217.

11 Communication from H. Tuch, Jewish Restitution Centre, Berlin-Dahlem.

12 Case III (German judges) in *Law Reports of Trials of War Criminals*, London, 1947, Vol VI, *pages 11-13.*

13 PS 1965 and IMT, III, 35.

14 *The von Hassell Diaries*, London, 1947, *page 235.* Evidence of Hans Frank, IMT, XII, 117. Case III (*Law Reports of Trials of War Criminals*, VI, *page 7).*

15 IMT, 687, PS, and IMT, IV, 389.

16 Case XI, NG 417.

17 Felix Kersten. *Memoirs,* translated by Ernst Morwitz, New York, 1947, *page 234.* (Conversation of April 19th, 1945.) Folke Bernadotte, *The Curtain Falls, page 43.*

18 Case III, NG 558. (Thierack to Bormann.)

19 IMT, I, 179, and III, 43-4.

20 PS 1063D, IMT, XV, 118. Case IV, NO 1523, in *Trials of War Criminals*, Washington, 1951, Vol V, *page 373.*

21 IMT, PS 2171, Annexe 2, and Eugen Kogon, *The Theory and Practice of Hell, pages 221-22.*

22 *Dokumenty i Materialy*, I, *page 53.*

23 Case IV, NO 5194. (Korherr to Himmler, March 23rd, 1943.)

24 Christopher Burney. *The Dungeon Democracy*, London, 1945, *page 63.* Eugen Kogon, op. cit., *page 167.*

25 IMT, L, 61, and II, 296, XV, 120. (Evidence, Fritz Sauckel.)

26 Georges Dunand. *Ne perdez pas leur trace! Page 100.* Georges Wellers, *De Drancy a Auschwitz, page 110.*

27 Information by former members *Reichsvereinigung* to Wiener Library, London, 1945 (typescript).

28 Rabbi Leo Baeck in *We Survived*, Yale, 1949, *page 289.*

29 Communication from H. Tuch, Jewish Restitution Centre, Berlin-Dahlem, showing Gestapo deportation lists.

30 Information, Wiener Library, *see 24.*

31 *The Goebbels Diaries*, London, 1949, *pages 196, 209.*

32 Ibid., *page 225.*

33 Information, Dr. Jacob Jacobson to Wiener Library, 1945 (typescript).

34 *The Goebbels Diaries, page 260.*

35 *Dokumenty i Materialy*, I, *pages 108-109, 117.* (Cracow court archives.)

36 Case X (the Krupp directors' trial), NIK 6565, printed in *Trials of War Criminals*, Washington, 1951, IX, *page 719.*

37 Informatiebureau van het Nederlandsche Roode Kruis. 'Sobibor,' pamphlet published at The Hague, February, 1947.

38 Evidence of Samuel Rajzman. IMT, VIII, 16, and in *Dokumenty i Materialy*, I, *page 187.* Yankiel Wiernik, *A Year in Treblinka*, New York, 1945.

38a Polish Central War Crimes Commission. *German Crimes in Poland*, Warsaw, 1946, Vol. I, *page 104.* IMT, VIII, *page 18.*

39 NO 5193. Korherr report.

40 Case XI, NG 2652-E.

41 Bruno Blau in *Jewish Social Studies*, New York, 1949, *page 172.*

42 IMT, PS 3886.

43 Reszoe Kastner. *Bericht des Juedischen Rettungskomitees aus Budapest*, Geneva, 1946 (stencil), *page 9.*

44 *Frankfurter Rundschau*, March 7th, 1950.

45 Ditto, March 10th, 1950.

46 Reszo Kastner. Op cit., *page 154.*

47 Georges Dunand. *Ne perdez pas leur trace!*, Neuchatel, 1950, *page 201.*

48 Case XI, NG 2586, *Diary of Ulrich von Hassell* (November 1st, 1941), *page 202.*

49 Jacob Jacobson. Report to Wiener Library on Theresienstadt, 1945.

50 NO 5194. Dr. Korherr's reports to Himmler.

51 Ibid.

52 Report on the Baab case by Kaye Boyle in the *New Yorker*, September 9th, 1950, *page 50* ('The People with Names').

53 Affidavits, Eberhard von Thadden, in Case XI, NG 2007, April 11th, 1947 ; NG 2512, June 18th, 1947.

54 Norbert Masur. *En Jude Talar med Himmler*, Stockholm, 1945. (From a transcript in German kindly provided by the author.)

55 *See* Jacobson report and Czechoslovak Government's English pamphlet, 'Theresienstadt,' 1946.

56 Jacobson report.

57 Max Mannheimer, employee of Amsterdam 'Joodseraad,' report to Wiener Library, 1945 (typed).

58 Jacobson report.

59 IMT, PS 1472.

60 Documents from Auschwitz archives used in trial of Hoess, etc., *Dokumenty i Materialy*, I, *page 116.*

61 NO 5193. Korherr to Himmler.

62 Interview with Rabbi Leo Baeck by Eric Boehm in *We Survived*, Yale, 1949.

63 Case IV, NO 2007 and NO 2512.

64 The report was distributed in stencil by the War Refugee Board in November, 1944, and put in evidence at Nuremberg as Document No. L 22. The most complete of several versions was circulated by Dr. Silberschein in Geneva as '*Judenaussrottung im Polen, IV.*' The episode of Hirsch and the Theresienstadt family transport will be found on *page 19* of the latter version.

65 *Dokumenty i Materialy*, I, *page 105.*

66 Mildner affidavit. IMT, PS 2377.

67 WRB report. *See* Silberschein, *Judenausrottung*, IV, *page 37.* Professor Marc Klein, *Temoignages Strasbourgeois*, 1947, *page 432.*

68 Rabbi Leo Baeck in *We Survived*, 1949.
69 Jacobson report, *page 15*.
70 Evidence, Steengracht von Moyland, IMT, X, 102.
71 Jacques Sabille in *Le Monde Juif*, November, 1949.
72 Documents CICR, etc. (op. cit.), Geneva, 1946, *page 100*.
73 *See* personal experience, described in Max Mannheimer's report on Theresienstadt to Wiener Library.
74 Miklos Nyiszli in *Les temps modernes*, April, 1951, *page 1881*.
75 Jacobson report.
76 Dr. Norbert Wolken. *Lagerschreiber*, quoted in Filip Friedman, *This Was Oswiecim*, 1946, *page 23*.
77 Report on relief activities CICR, Geneva, 1947, Vol. II, *page 648*.
78 Case XI, NG 2586-I, and NO 2419. (Affidavit, Gottfried Boley.)
79 Case XI, NG 2586-J.
80 NO 2419.
81 NG 4848. (Order concerning the definition of the term ' Jew ' in the occupied Eastern territory, pursuant to article 8 of the Fuehrer-Order dated July 17th, 1941.)
82 Case XI, NO 626.
83 Case XI, NG 2586-J.
84 IMT, XX, 238 and 242. Evidence, Schlegelberger.
85 Case I, NO 205. (*Trials of War Criminals*, Vol I, *pages 721, 733*. Transcript 7582. Mitscherlich and Mielke, *Wissenschaft ohne Menschlichkeit*, *page 237*.)
86 Case I, NO 035 (original letter). IMT Doc. SS 035 (affidavit, Dr. Pokorny), and IMT, XXI, 11.
87 Case I. François Bayle, *Croix Gammée ou Caducée*, 1950, *page 672*.
88 Case I. (Document NO 819, printed in François Bayle, op. cit., *pages 687-93*. Eugen Kogon, *Theory and Practice of Hell*, London, 1950, *page 159*. Mitscherlich and Mielke, op. cit., *page 235*. *Doctors of Infamy*, *pages 139-40*.)
89 François Bayle (op. cit.), *page 705*. (Witness, Dr. Dora Kleinova.) *Daily Telegraph*, February 23rd, 1951. (An absolutely erroneous account in Josef Tenenbaum, *In Search of a Lost People*, New York, 1949, *page 292*, and repeated by the same author in *Underground, the Story of a People*, New York, 1952.)
90 Case I, NO 819.
91 Case XI, NG 2586-M.
92 Case XI, PS 2645. Printed as an IMT document.
93 Bruno Blau. ' Jewish Population in Germany ' in *Jewish Social Studies*, New York, 1949, *page 172*.
94 Unpublished file of documents kept by Fraulein Sloettke of the Jewish Section of the Gestapo at The Hague labelled 'Abbau der rueckstellende Gruppen.' At present at Rijksinstituut fur Oorlogsdokumentatie, Amsterdam (by courtesy of Dr. Louis de Jong).
95 Judgment in case of Captain Ferdinand Aus der Fuenten, The Hague, December 27th, 1949, typescript 55 (Rijksinstituut).
96 Sloettke file. Report of conference, Seyss-Inquardt and Rauter.
97 Trial of Hans Albin Rauter, April 1st, 1948, court transcript 24. See also *Nederland in Oorlogstijd*, March, 1949.

CHAPTER 8

1 Case IX. Evidence, Ohlendorf, *Trials of War Criminals*, IV, *pages 272-73.*
2 Ibid, page 659. (*War Criminals*, IV, *page 386.*)
3 IMT, III, 244.
4 IMT, XIII, 132.
5 Case IX, Transcript 555-58.
6 H. R. Trevor-Roper. *The Last Days of Hitler*, London, 1947, *page 182.*
7 Case IX. Evidence, Ohlendorf, *Trials of War Criminals*, IV, *page 242. Ditto, IV, page 510.*)
8 Case IX, Transcript 491.
9 IMT, XXII, 473, 477.
10 Case IX, Transcript 4374.
11 Case IX, NO 2830 and Transcript 312-13.
12 Case IX, Transcript 313.
13 Fabian von Schlabrendorf. *Offiziere gegen Hitler*, Zurich, 1946, *page 40.* Affidavit, Kurt Lindow, Case IX, NO 4327.
14 Affidavit, von dem Bach-Zalewski (not in evidence). (Extract in *Aufbau-Reconstruction*, New York, Vol 12, 1946, No. 34.)
15 Photographs kindly supplied to author by Mr. Joseph Zigman, Office US High Commissioner, Germany, Office of Public Affairs.
16 IMT, XII, 268-69. (Evidence, Gisevius.)
17 Case I, NO 179. (*Trials of War Criminals*, I, *page 421.*)
18 Eugen Kogon. *The Theory and Practice of Hell*, 1950 (' Der SS Staat,' 1946), translated Heinz Norden, *page 144.*
19 IMT, XX, 395. (Evidence, Konrad Morgen.)
20 Hans Berndt von Gisevius. *To the Bitter End*, 1946, *page 579.*
21 IMT, L, 185. (RSHA list, January, 1939. *Ulrich von Hassell Diaries*, London, 1947, *page 176.*)
22 Case IX, Transcript 639. (Evidence, Ohlendorf.)
23 H. R. Trevor-Roper. *The Last Days of Hitler*, footnote, *page 29*, quoting captured diary of Schwerin von Krosigk.
24 Count Folke Bernadotte. *The Curtain Falls*, New York, 1945, *pages 105, 117.*
25 Case XI, Transcript (Judgment) 28562.
26 Case IX, Transcript 891.
26a IMT, PS 1919. (The Posen speech.)
27 Case IX, Transcript 6828, 6858, 8864-67, NO 3197. (Affidavit, Blobel.)
28 Case IX, NO 4546 (affidavit, Franz Six), Transcript 6807, 6623.
29 Caes XI and IX, NO 5884. (Gottlob Berger to Rudi Brandt. Personal letter on Jost's case, May 4th, 1944, Transcript 6791.)
30 Case IX, NO 3644.
31 Case IX, Transcript 5244. (Evidence, Eduard Strauch.)
32 IMT, XXI, 39 and 56.
33 IMT, VII, 335, USSR 119a.
34 IMT, III, 263. (Evidence, Ohlendorf.)
35 NOKW 2079. (*Trials of War Criminals*, X, *page 1243.*)
36 Case IX, NO 3257, IMT, PS 197.
37 Max Kaufmann. *Churbn Lettland, Die Vernichtung der Juden Lettlands*, Munich, 1947, *page 67.*

38 IMT, IV, 28. (Evidence, von dem Bach-Zalewski.)
39 Unnumbered affidavit von dem Bach-Zalewski in *Aufbau-Reconstruction*, New York, Vol 12, 1946, No. 36.
40 PS 3841 (affidavit, Stroop), IMT, XI, 319.
41 Affidavit, Police Major-General Ernst Rode, IMT, IV, 23.
42 Case XII, NOKW 2150. (Journal, 10th Infantry Division.)
43 IMT, Affidavit 17 ; IMT, IV, 22.
44 IMT, L, 180. (Stahlecker to Heydrich.)
45 IMT, PS 3047. (Soenicken to Lahousen.)
46 Fabian von Schlabrendorf. *Offiziere gegen Hitler, page 51.*
47 Affidavit No. 16 (Panzer-General Hans Roettiger), IMT, IV, 21.
48 D 411, IMT, IV, 14.
49 *Law Reports of Trials of War Criminals*, London, XII, *page 53*. High Command Case NOKW 3411, printed in *Trials of War Criminals*, Washington, Vol. X, *page 1214.*
50 IMT, XXI, 71, PS 4064. (Order of the day, 11th Army.)
51 *Aufbau*, Vol. 12, 1946, No. 36. (Affidavit, von dem Bach-Zalewski.)
52 Paul Leverkuehn. *Verteidigung Manstein*, Hamburg, 1950, *page 11*.
53 *Times*, December 15th, 1949 (Manstein trial). NOKW 2523, *Trials of War Criminals*, X, *page 1236.*
54 IMT, III, 270. (Evidence, Ohlendorf.)
55 *Law Reports of Trials of War Criminals*, XII, *page 55*. NOKW 650, 568, 579, and 2963, *Trials of War Criminals*, Washington, Vol X, *pages 1215-20.*
56 IMT, XXI, 57. (Evidence, Manstein.)
57 IMT, III, 249. (Evidence, Ohlendorf.)
58 Case IX, Transcript 681. (Evidence, Ohlendorf, *Trials of War Criminals*, IV, *page 294*.)
59 NO 3403. (Daily situation report No. 119, October 20th, 1941, printed in *Trials of War Criminals*, IV, *page 424*.)
60 Case XII, NOKW 541.
61 Case XII, NOKW 2523. (*Le Monde Juif*, February, 1952.)
62 IMT, PS 1682.
63 *The People's Verdict*, London, 1945, *page 54*.
64 IMT, III, 204, and PS 3542. (Affidavit, Kurt Lindow.)
65 Case IX, NO 4327. (Printed in *Trials of War Criminals*, IV, *page 99*.)
66 Kay Boyle. 'The People with Names,' *New Yorker*, September 9th, 1950.
67 L 180. (Report on *Einsatzgruppe* A to October 15th, 1941.)
68 Case IX, NO 2651.
69 Case IX, Transcript 724. (Evidence, Ohlendorf.)
70 PS 2273. (Report on *Einsatzgruppe* A to January 31st, 1942, captured by Russians in Riga [also USSR 357a, IMT, VII, *pages 333-35*].)
71 IMT, PS 702.
72 Peter Kleist. *Zwischen Hitler und Stalin*, Bonn, 1950, *page 166*.
73 IMT, PS 1138.
74 Case IX, NO 2947 (August 9th, 1941), and NO 2652 (August 1st-15th, 1941).
75 Samuel Gringauz in *Jewish Social Studies*, New York, January, 1949.
76 Case XI, NO 4848.
77 Eugen Kogon. *The Theory and Practice of Hell*, London, 1950, *page 174*.

78 IMT, VII, 90, Document USSR 2.
79 IMT, Document USSR 297, IMT, VII, 91.
80 *The Tragedy of Slovak Jewry*, Bratislava, February, 1949, *pages 112-13.*
81 PS 2992, IMT, XIX, 457.
82 Case IX, Transcript 6745.
83 Mariam Bath Ammi. *Le droit à la Patrie*, Paris, 1946, *pages 106-10.*
84 Case IX, Transcript 524. (Evidence, Ohlendorf, *Trials of War Criminals*, IV, *page 249.*)
85 Case IX, Transcript 6881, NO 3055. (Affidavit, Schubert.)
86 Case IX, NO 2653.
87 *Aufbau*, New York, 1946, Vol. 12, No. 34.
88 IMT, III, 251, 259. (Evidence, Ohlendorf.)
89 Case IX, NO 5530, and NO 5538. (Metzner affidavits.)
90 *Memoirs of Dr. Felix Kersten*, New York, 1947, *page 153.*
91 Case IX, NG 3143.

CHAPTER 9

1 IMT, Document L, 180, dated January 31st, 1942. (Report on *Einsatzgruppe* A activities to October 15th, 1941. No. 23 of 40 distributed copies, signed on one of the enclosures ' A. Stahlecker.')
2 Eugene Kulischer. *The Displacement of Population in Europe*, published by IRO, Montreal, 1943, *page 63.*
3 Joseph Schechtmann in *Hitler's Ten Year War on the Jews*, New York Institute of Jewish Affairs, 1943, *pages 173-77.*
4 Max Kaufmann. *Churbn Lettland, Die Vernichtung der Juden Lettlands*, Munich, 1947, *page 50.*
5 Schechtmann, op. cit., *page 169.*
6 IMT, L, 180.
7 *Law Reports of Trials of War Criminals*, Vol XII, London, 1948, *page 31.* (The High Command case. Résumé of evidence against von Kuechler.)
8 IMT, Document PS 2273. (Second report by Stahlecker, October 16th, 1941, to January 31st, 1942, captured by the Russians at Riga and identical with Document USSR 357a.) *See* IMT, III, 193. Has no date or heading and begins on *page 56.*
9 Case IX, NO 2934. (*Einsatzgruppen* Daily Report No. 19, July 11th, 1941.)
10 IMT, document L, 180.
11 Ditto. Contains a detailed breakdown, including thirteen women auxiliaries.
12 Case IX, NO 2655. (Fortnightly Report No. 5, September 30th, 1941.)
13 Peter Kleist. *Zwischen Hitler und Stalin*, Bonn, 1950, *page 159.*
14 Marc Dvorjetski. *Ghetto a l'Est*, Paris, 1949, *page 25.* Evidence of Abraham Susskever, IMT, VIII, 26.
15 Dvorjetski, op. cit., *page 46.*
16 Dvorjetski, op. cit., *page 38.*
17 Dvorjetski, op. cit., *page 62-79.*
18 Case XII, NOKW 1686. (*Trials of War Criminals*, Washington, 1951, X, *page 832.*)

19 Joseph Schechtmann in *Hitler's Ten Year War on the Jews*, New York, 1943, *page 191*. Affidavit, Lieut.-Commander Dittmann in IMT, XIV, 225 (witness for Admiral Raeder).
20 *Nuernberger Nachrichten*, February 4th, 1950.
21 IMT, Document D 968, and XXI, 178.
22 PS 2273 and Kaufmann, 280.
23 IMT, Document L, 180.
24 Case IX, Transcript 5244. (Evidence, defendant Strauch.)
25 Affidavit, von dem Bach-Zalewski (not in evidence), published in *Aufbau*, New York, Vol. XII, No. 36, September, 1946.
26 Information supplied by Committee of Baltic Survivors in Britain, July 9th, 1949. Eugen Kogon, *The Theory and Practice of Hell*, London, 1950, *page 174*.
27 Kaufmann, 97.
28 Case IX, NO 3405. (Monthly *Einsatzgruppen* Report No 9.)
29 Case IX, NO 3259.
30 Kaufmann, 108.
31 Ditto, 115.
32 IMT, PS 2273. (Stahlecker to Heydrich.)
33 PS 1517 and IMT, XI, 63. (Evidence, Rosenberg.)
34 PS 3663, IMT, XII, 65.
35 Charges against Leibbrandt and Braeutigam. (Communication from Paul Dohmann, Staatsanwalt. Landgericht, Nuernberg-Furth, to CDJC, Paris, January 18th, 1950.)
36 PS 3666, IMT, XII, 66.
37 IMT, PS 3664.
38 *Aufbau*, Vol. 12, *page 35*, September, 1946. (Unpublished affidavit.)
39 Dvorjetski, 93.
40 Ditto, 108.
41 PS 2273.
42 IMT, PS 3876.
43 Case IX, Transcript 860.
44 Solomon M. Schwarz. *Jews in the Soviet Union*. Syracuse, 1951, *page 310*.
45 Hugh Seton-Watson. *Eastern Europe, 1918-41*, Cambridge, 1945, *page 329*, Schwarz, op. cit., *pages 322-26*.
46 Joseph Schechtmann in *Hitler's Ten Year War on the Jews*, New York, 1943, *page 190*.
47 IMT, VII, 44. (Soviet Prosecutor's case.)
48 PS 2273.
49 *Le Monde Juif*, April, 1949.
50 *The Goebbels Diaries*, translated by Louis Lochner, London, 1948, *page 74*.
51 IMT, PS 113, and PS 3743.
52 Joseph Tenenbaum. *Underground, the Story of a People*, New York, 1951, and Schwarz, op. cit., *pages 322-25*.
53 *American-Jewish Year Book*, 1938.
54 Case XII, Document NOKW 3140. (Diary of General Franz Halder [entry for November 12th, 1941], printed in *Trials of War Criminals*, Washington, 1951, X, *page 1196*.)

55 Case IX, NO 2651. (Fortnightly *Einsatzgruppen* Report No. 1, July 31st, 1941.)

56 Case IX, NO 2655. (Fortnightly *Einsatzgruppen* Report No. 5, September 30th, 1941.)

57 Evidence before the USSR Extraordinary Commission at Minsk, 1944, witness J. S. Machiz. (A unique account, excerpts of which will be found in *The Black Book*, New York, 1946, *pages 453-64.*)

58 PS 2273.

59 NO 2262. (Kube's inspection of the ghetto is described retrospectively in a very long report sent by Strauch to von dem Bach-Zalewski on July 25th, 1943. It forms part of the large Kube file, found in the ruins of the Rosenberg Ministry, Berlin. Various accounts of Kube's dismissal have been published. That this is the correct one is shown by the stencilled copy of a circular signed by Hess as Hitler's adjutant. The copy is in the possession of the CDJC, Paris.)

60 PS 3665 (from the captured Kube file). (Facsimile in Weinreich, *Hitler's Professors*, published by YIVO, New York, 1946.)

61 NO 2262. (Strauch to von dem Bach-Zalewski.)

62 Case IX, NO 3241. (Daily *Einsatzgruppen* Report No. 128.)

63 Case IX, Transcript 5264. (Examination of Eduard Strauch.)

64 PS 3428. (Quoted in IMT, XII, 67, and Case IX, Transcript 142.)

65 PS 3428. (Kube to Lohse, July 31st, 1942 [from the captured Kube file], *Black Book, pages 453-64.* The latter, a survivor's account, agrees remarkably.)

66 Case IX, Transcript 5267. (Strauch cross-examined.)

67 Minutes of this conference were presented at Nuremberg as Document USSR 170. Extract in IMT, VII, 170.

68 Case IX, NO 511. (Report on Anti-Partisan Warfare No. 5, dated December 20th, 1942.)

69 Document USSR 119a, quoted in IMT, VII, 335. (Other extracts in the *Black Book, pages 349-52,* and David Rousset, *Le pitre ne rit pas,* Paris, 1947.) PS 3428 from the captured Kube file.

70 '*Endloesung der Judenfrage in Galizien,*' bound copy of report by Gruppenfuehrer Dr. Franz Katzmann to Krueger, Higher SS and Police Leader in the General Government, June 30th, 1943.

71 *Hitler's Ten Year War on the Jews,* New York, 1943.

72 Case IX, NO 2651. (Fortnightly *Einsatzgruppen* Report No. 1, July 31st, 1941.) Joseph Tenenbaum, *In Search of a Lost People,* New York, 1948, *page 115.* Dr. A. Silberschein, *L'extermination des Juifs en Pologne,* vme serie, Geneva, 1945 (stencil), *page 8.*

73 NO 2651.

74 Silberschein, op. cit.

75 Tenenbaum, op. cit., *page 115.*

76 NO 2651.

77 Tenenbaum, *page 115.*

78 NO 2651.

79 Case IX, Transcript 930-39. (Evidence of Erwin Schulz.)

79a Zenon Rozanski. *Muetzen Ab, page 219.*

80 Case IX, Transcript 1507.

81 Case IX, NO 3253. (Affidavit, Otto Rasch.)

82 NO 2653. (Fortnightly *Einsatzgruppen* Report No. 8, August 31st, 1941.)

83 Affidavit of Erwin Bingel, NO 5301, Cases XII and IX.
84 NO 2665. (Fortnightly *Einsatzgruppen* Report No. 5, September 30th, 1941.) NO 3149. (Daily *Einsatzgruppen* Report No. 88, September 9th, 1941.)
85 Case IX, Transcript 1547-51. (Examination of Paul Blobel.)
86 Case IX, NO 3140. (Daily *Einsatzgruppen* Report No. 106, October 7th, 1941, printed in *Trials of War Criminals*, Washington, 1951, IV, *page 147*.)
87 IMT, R 102. (Fortnightly *Einsatzgruppen* Report No. 6, October 31st, 1941.)
88 IMT, XV, 25, 306, 360. (Examination of Colonel-General Alfred Jodl.)
89 Case IX, Transcript 1571. (Examination, Paul Blobel.)
90 Case IX, R 102, and NO 3140.
91 Quoted in *The Black Book*, New York, 1945, *page 360*.
92 *Black Book, page 363*. IMT, VII, 94. (Evidence of Michael Tanklevski.)
93 NO 3159. (*Einsatzgruppen* Daily Report No. 128, November 3rd, 1941.)
94 *Black Book, page 363*.
95 Joseph Schechtmann in *Hitler's Ten Year War on the Jews*, New York, 1943, *page 195*.
96 R 102. (*Einsatzgruppen* Report No. 6 for September, 1941, quoted in IMT, XXI, 70.) Case XII, NOKW 3147. Printed in *le Monde Juif*, No. 56, June, 1952.
97 Case IX, NO 5384. (Affidavit, Albert Hartel. Cross-examination in Transcript 2898-2900.)
98 Case IX. (Examination of Paul Blobel, Transcript 1618.)
99 Case IX, NO 3197. (Affidavit, Paul Blobel.)
100 *New York Times*, October 22nd, 1944, quoted in *The Black Book, page 360*. IMT, VII, 105, and Case IX, Transcript 6741. (Judgment.)
101 PS 3259. (Report forwarded to General Thomas.)
102 Ilya Ehrenberg, quoted in *The Black Book, page 362*.
103 NO 2832. (Daily Report No. 135, November 19th, 1941, *Trials of War Criminals*, Washington, 1951, IV, *page 180, The Black Book, page 355*.)
104 Narrative of Majer Neuman of Volove. (Précis kindly supplied to the author by Miss Helga Melchior, Stockholm.)
105 NO 3153. (Daily Report No. 108, October 10th, 1941.)
106 NO 2832. (Daily Report No. 135, November 19th, 1941, printed in *Trials of War Criminals*, IV, *page 180*.)
107 *Aufbau*, New York, Vol XII, No. 36, September, 1946.
108 NO 3405. (Daily Report No. 156, January 6th, 1942. For population figures *see American Jewish Year Book, 1931*, and Joseph Schechtmann in *Hitler's Ten Year War on the Jews, page 185*.)
109 NO 2827. (Daily Report No. 143, December 8th, 1941, printed in *Trials of War Criminals*, IV, *page 185*. The second Rovno massacre is described in the Graebe Affidavit, PS 2992. Survivor-estimates, closely agreeing with the *Einsatzgruppen* report, in *German Crimes in Poland*, Vol. I, *page 151*, and in *The Black Book, page 113*.)
110 *See* reference ' Kharkov ' in Juedisches Lexikon.
111 Report of Kharkov trial in *The People's Verdict*, London, 1945, *page 122*, and in *The Black Book, page 368*.
112 *The People's Verdict, page 54*.

113 *The People's Verdict, page 100.*
114 Schwarz, op. cit., *page 231.*
115 IMT, VII, 108. (Soviet prosecution.)
116 PS 3256, IMT, II, 413-14.
117 PS 3012. (Report from ' Sondergruppe 4a.')
118 Joseph Schechtmann in *Hitler's Ten Year War on the Jews, page 202.*
119 Case IX, NO 3403. (Daily Report No. 125, October 26th, 1941.)
120 Case XII, NOKW 629, printed in *Trials of War Criminals,* Washington, 1951, Vol. X, *page 1237.*
121 *Hitler's Ten Year War, page 202.*
122 A little information on the Odessa trials from the Moscow Jewish newspaper *Ainikeit* in *The Black Book, page 303.*
123 IMT and Case IX, R 102. (Monthly *Einsatzgruppen* Report No. 6, October, 1941.)
124 Case IX, NO 3148. (*Einsatzgruppen* Report No. 95, September 15th, 1941.)
125 Case IX, Transcript 526. (Evidence, Ohlendorf.)
126 Case XI (High Command), NOKW 1677 and 1678.
127 IMT, PS 3843.
128 Case IX, NO 2834. (Report No. 150, January 2nd, 1942.)
129 Case IX, Judgment, Transcript 6775.
130 Case XI (High Command), NOKW 2281. (Report, Garrison Commander, Yankoi.)
131 Case IX, NO 3339 (Report No. 170, February 18th, 1942), NO 2662 (March 11th, 1942).
132 Case IX, NO 6824. (Fortnightly report of SD activities in the East.)
133 Paul Leverkuehn. *Verteidigung Manstein,* Hamburg, 1950.
134 Case XI (High Command), NOKW 1698, NOKW 1690.
135 Case IX, Transcript 517-18. (Evidence, Ohlendorf.)
136 IMT and Case IX, PS 3843.
137 IMT, VII, 336. (Soviet prosecution.)
138 IMT, PS 501. (Becker to Rauff, Kiev, May 16th, 1942.)
139 IMT, III, 251. (Evidence, Ohlendorf.)

CHAPTER 10

1 Case IV, NO 5194. (Korherr to Rudi Brandt, March 23rd, 1943, ' The solution of the European Jewish question,' initialled Himmler [not available in print].)
2 Case VIII, NO 5875. (Mueller to Hoffmann, *Trials of War Criminals,* IV, *page 864.*)
3 IMT, XII, 185.
4 Eugen Kogon. *The Theory and Practice of Hell,* London, 1950, *page 172.*
5 IMT, XVII, 211.
6 IMT, XVI, 181.
7 IMT, XVI, 169. (Evidence, Seyss-Inquardt.)
8 IMT, XVI, 191. (Evidence, Friedrich Rainer.)
9 Case IV, NO 470. (*Trials of War Criminals,* I, *page 803.*)

10 IMT, PS 2233. (Frank Diary, quoted in *German Crimes in Poland,* 1946, Vol 2.)
11 Ditto and IMT, XII, 393.
12 Nachmann Blumenthal. *Slowa Niewinne,* Warsaw, 1947. IMT, XII, 144. (Evidence, Josef Buehler.)
13 *Diary of Mary Berg,* New York, 1945, *page 135.* Rumkowski, the Lodz *Judenaelteste,* was seen in the Warsaw Ghetto on February 27th, 1942.
13a Mariam Bath Ammi. *Le Droit à la patrie, page 147.*
14 *German Crimes in Poland,* I, *page 109.* Marian Muszkat, *Polish Charges Against German War Criminals,* Warsaw, 1948, *page 204.*
15 Case I, No. 246. (Printed in *Trials of War Criminals,* I, *page 776.*)
16 Abraham Melezin. *Demographic Processes Among the Jewish Population,* Lodz, 1947.
17 Josef Tenenbaum, *In Search of a Lost People, page 106.* Sol Bloom, 'Dictator of the Lodz Ghetto,' *Commentary,* New York, February, 1949, *pages 111-22.*
18 *Dokumenty i Materialy,* Lodz, 1946, III, *page 203.*
19 *Dokumenty i Materialy,* Lodz, 1946, III, *pages 243-45.* (Biebow to Fuchs.)
20 Nachmann Blumenthal, *Slowa Niewinne,* Warsaw, 1947, *page 150. Dokumenty i Materialy,* III, *pages 245-47.* (Biebow to Ventski.)
20a Marian Muszkat. *Polish Charges against German War Criminals,* Warsaw, 1948, *page 206.*
21 Dr. Josef Kermisz in *Dokumenty i Materialy,* I, XVII (introduction).
22 Tenenbaum. *In Search of a Lost People, page 106.* Sol Bloom in *Commentary,* February, 1949, *pages 111-22.*
23 Case I, Transcript, printed in *Trials of War Criminals,* II, *page 40.* (Evidence for Wolfram Sievers.)
23a Muszkat, op. cit., *page 207.*
24 *Dokumenty i Materialy,* III, *pages 228-30.*
25 *Dokumenty i Materialy,* II, *pages 74-81.*
26 Ditto, III, *pages 228-31.*
27 Ditto, III, *page 238.*
28 Case IV, Transcript (not printed), 1928.
29 *The Goebbels Diaries,* London, 1948, *page 102.*
30 Report to Dr. Fohl, Cracow, October 21st, 1940, in *Dokumenty i Materialy,* I, *page 220.*
31 *Dokumenty i Materialy,* II, *pages 4-14.*
32 Ditto, II, *page 12.*
33 Ditto, *pages 32-33.* Photograph of Richard Turk in Kienast *Der Grossdeutsche Reichstag,* November, 1943.
34 *Dokumenty i Materialy,* II, *page 39.*
35 Max Freiherr du Prel. *Das Deutsche Generalgouvernement Polen,* 2nd edition, May, 1942, *page 315.*
36 Marian Muszkat. *Polish Charges against German War Criminals, page 184.* Mariam Bath Ammi, *Le droit à la patrie,* Paris, 1946, *page 12.*
37 Nachmann Blumenthal. *Slowa Niewinne, page 86.*
38 *German Crimes in Poland,* I, *page 153.*
39 Evidence Israel Eisenberg, IMT, XX, 311.

40 Note of M. Mikolajczik in *The Black Book*, page 92 ; *German Crimes in Poland*, II, page 94.
41 Ditto, *The Black Book*, page 136.
42 Muszkat. *Polish Charges, etc.*, page 227.
43 Mary Berg. *Warsaw Diary*, pages 140-41.
44 Josef Tenenbaum. *In Search of a Lost People*, page 118.
45 IMT, II, 388-92 and Document L 18. ('Final Solution of the Jewish Question in Galicia,' Dr. Fritz Katzmann to Krueger, June 30th, 1943.)
46 Ditto.
47 *The Black Book*, page 197. Silberschein. *Judenausrottung im Polen*, Geneva, 1944, fifth series.
48 *German Crimes in Poland*, II, page 95.
49 *Dokumenty i Materialy*, introduction to Vol. II, *pages xvi, xxvii*, and *116* The wooden eagle is in the Miejski Museum, Rzeszow.
50 *Dokumenty i Materialy*, II, pages 53-55.
51 Arnold Zweig. *Fahrt zum Acheron*, Potsdam, 1951. (Narrative of Hilde Huppert.)
52 Case I, NO 205. (Brack to Himmler. Printed in *Trials of War Criminals*, I, *page 721*.)
53 IMT, PS 910. (The speech is mentioned in Count Eduard Raczynski's note to the Allied Powers, printed in *The Black Book of Polish Jewry*, 1943, *page 120*.)
54 Case VIII, NO 4474, printed by L. Poliakov in *Breviaire de la Haine*.
55 IMT, PS 2233. (Diary of Hans Frank, quoted in *German Crimes in Poland*, II.)
56 Case IV. (Interrogation of Karl Wolff, printed in *Trials of War Criminals*, V, *page 277*, 1951.)
57 François Bayle. *Croix Gammée contre Caducée*, Neustadt, 1950, *page 21*. IMT, III, 160. (Milch to Wolff), *Das Freie Wort*, Baden, February 3rd, 1952.
58 Michel Mazor. 'La cité Engloutie' in *Le Monde Juif*, August-September, 1951.
59 Mary Berg. *Warsaw Diary*, New York, 1945, *page 95*.
60 Ditto, *page 159*. Silberschein. *Judenausrottung im Polen*, Geneva, 1944, fourth series, *page 10*.
61 Ditto, Mary Berg, *pages 139, 163*.
62 The Raczynski note in *The Black Book of Polish Jewry*, New York, 1943, *page 120*.
63 '*Tagesspiegel*,' July 20th, 1951 ; '*Die Welt*,' July 26th, 1951.
64 Reports by Ambassador Count Eduard Raczynski and Messrs. Siegelbaum and Schwartzbart of the Polish National Council, reprinted in *The Black Book of Polish Jewry*, 1943, *pages 119-32*.
65 Michel Mazor. 'La cité Engloutie' in *Le Monde Juif*, August-September, 1951. Affidavit of Hermann Graebe, IMT, PS 2992.
66 Josef Tenenbaum. *In Search of a Lost People*, page 33.
67 Silberschein. *Judenausrottung im Polen*, fourth series, *page 18*.
68 Michel Mazor. 'La cité Engloutie' in *Le Monde Juif*, August-September, 1951.
69 Silberschein. *Judenausrottung im Polen*, IV, *page 28*.
70 Ditto, *page 15*.
71 Ditto, *page 21*. Mary Berg. *Warsaw Diary*, page 174.

72 Report by Ignazy Schwartzbart in *The Black Book, page 129.*
73 Silberschein, op. cit., IV, *page 8.*
74 Published by 'Wiadomosci Polskie,' London, December 7th, 1943. Translated in Silberschein. *Judenausrottung im Polen,* IV, *page 24.*
75 Stroop's figures in IMT, PS 1061.
76 *The Black Book,* New York, 1945, *page 129.*
77 Ditto, *pages 130-33.*
78 Silberschein, IV, *page 33;* Mary Berg, *pages 183, 188;* Tenenbaum, *In Search of a Lost People, page 33.*
79 Nachmann Blumenthal in *Dokumenty i Materialy,* I, Introduction, *page 8.*
80 Tenenbaum. *In Search of a Lost People, page 39,* and *Underground, the Story of a People,* New York, 1952, *page 90* (varying versions). *Diary of Mary Berg, page 196.*
81 IMT, PS 2233. (Frank diary, quoted by Leon Poliakov in *Le Monde Juif,* December, 1950.)
82 Ditto, quoted in *German Crimes in Poland,* II.
83 Dr. Josef Kermisz. Introduction, *Dokumenty i Materialy,* II.
84 IMT, V, 240. (Evidence, Paul Roser.)
85 Quoted in Max Weinreich, *Hitler's Professors,* New Yerk, YIVO, 1946, *page 168.*
86 Kermisz, op. cit., xxxiv-xxxvi.
87 Tenenbaum. *In Search of a Lost People, page 118. The Black Book, page 434,* evidence of Israel Herz. Silberschein, *Judenausrottung,* V, *page 17.*
88 Case IV, NO 1611, printed in *Trials of War Criminals,* V, *page 616.*
89 Case XII, NOKW 134.
90 The decree in the case of Lwow is given in Katzmann's report, lMT, L, 18.
91 Both decrees in *The Black Book of Polish Jewry, pages 138-40.*
92 Arnold Zweig. *Fahrt zum Acheron,* Berlin, 1951, *pages 59-61.*
93 Case XI, NO 5194. (Korherr to Rudi Brandt, March 23rd, 1943.)
94 Dr. J. Guérin. *Rawa Ruska, camp de represailles,* Marseille, editions *Oris,* September, 1945, *page 178.*
95 Dr. Josef Kermisz. Introduction to *Dokumenty i Materialy,* II.
96 Guerin, op. cit., *pages 155-56.*
97 Silberschein, op. cit., V, *pages 40-44.*
98 *The Black Book of Polish Jewry, pages 89-91. Dokumenty i Materialy,* I, *page 47* (narrative of Mila Hornik). Rabbi T. Guttmann, *Dokumentenwerk,* 2, Jerusalem, 1945, *pages 47-65* (narrative of Dov Weitz).
99 Jakob Littner. *Aufzeichnungen aus einem Erdloch,* Munich, 1948.
100 Case IV, NO 1257. (Himmler to Pohl and Krueger, January 15th, 1943.)
101 IMT, PS 4024, and XX, 268-274.

CHAPTER 11

1 Silberschein. *Judenausrottung im Polen,* IV, *page 48.*
2 Tenenbaum. *In Search of a Lost People, pages 88-89.*
3 IMT, L, 18. (Katzmann report.)
4 Case IV, NO 1811. (Himmler to Krueger and Pohl.)
5 IMT, PS 1061. Silberschein, op. cit., IV, *page 57.*

6 'Begruendung,' signed by Schneider, assessor of the Bremen *Spruchkammer,* concerning charges against Toebbens, June 1st, 1949; in Centre de Documentation Juive Contemporaine, Paris.

7 Tenenbaum, op. cit., *page 40. The Black Book of Polish Jewry, page 148.* Silberschein, IV, *page 67.*

8 Mazor. 'La cité engloutie' gives the German official total of deportations at the end of January, 1943.

9 Case IV, NO 2514.

10 Case IV, NO 2494.

11 Case IV, NO 1265.

12 *Law Reports of Trials of War Criminals,* London, 1948, VII, Trial of Amon Goeth.

13 Tenenbaum, op. cit., *page 41.* Mary Berg, *page 229.* Silberschein, IV, *page 58. The Black Book of Polish Jewry, page 158.*

14 Henceforward the account of the Warsaw Ghetto rebellion is Stroop's (IMT, PS 1061) unless otherwise indicated. The most complete text will be found in *La Bataille du Ghetto de Varsovie,* edited by David Knout, Paris, CDJC, 1946.

15 *The Goebbels Diaries,* London, 1948, *pages 268, 273.*

16 The photographs were shown in court on December 14th, 1945 (IMT, II, 404-9). Some will be found in David Knout, op. cit., and in *German Crimes in Poland,* Vol II.

17 G. M. Gilbert. *Nuremberg Diary, page 69,* 1947.

18 Case IV, NO 2608. IMT, PS 1475, XXI, 182.

19 Photostat in *Blater fur Gezichte,* August-October, 1948, published by the Jewish Historical Institute in Poland.

20 Stroop's own account, PS 1061.

21 Marc Dvorjetski. *Ghetto a l'Est,* Paris, 1950, *page 157.* Tenenbaum, op. cit., *page 100.*

22 *See* particularly an account from the Moscow Yiddish newspaper *Ainikeit* in *The Black Book, pages 436-444.*

23 Krueger to Frank in the Frank diary, quoted by Soviet prosecution, IMT, XI, 337. Veesenmayer to von Thadden, July 25th, 1944, in Case XI, NG 1806.

24 Tenenbaum, op. cit., *page 51.*

25 IMT, PS 3841.

26 Tenenbaum, *page 73.*

27 Frank diary, quoted by Soviet prosecution in IMT, XI, 337.

28 Case IV, NO 519. (Pohl to Himmler, February 9th, 1944.)

29 Case IV, NO 2496. (Himmler to Gluecks and Kaltenbrunner, June 11th, 1943.)

30 Case IV, NO 2516.

31 Case IV, NO 2515.

32 R. Stern in *Die oorlog die Hitler won, page 381,* Amsterdam, 1947.

33 *Jewish Social Studies,* New York, April, 1948.

34 Case IV, NO 2403, printed in Henri Monneret, *La persecution des Juifs dans les pays de l'Est,* 1948, *page 118.*

35 Josef Kermisz. Introduction to *Dokumenty i Materialy,* II.

36 PS 2233, extract printed in *German Crimes in Poland,* II.

37 IMT, L, 18 (Katzmann report), *The Black Book,* 1945, *page 445.*

38 Mary Berg. *Warsaw Diary,* New York, 1945, *page 85.*

39 Transcripts from Case I, evidence of Haas and Hoven, printed in Francois Bayle, *Croix Gammée ou Caducée*, Neustadt, 1951, *pages 132-3, 182, 258.*

40 *The Black Book*, 1945, *pages 307-10.* Tenenbaum, *In Search of a Lost People*, 1948, *page 123.* IMT (Soviet prosecution), VII, 119-129.

41 Tenenbaum. *Underground, the Story of a People, page 421.*

42 Solomon M. Schwarz. *Jews in the Soviet Union, page 333.*

43 Tenenbaum. *In Search of a Lost People, page 120. Underground, page 434.*

44 R. Philips. *The Belsen Trial*, London, 1948, *page 66.*

45 Collection of *Schutzpolizei* reports in *Dokumenty i Materialy*, II, *pages 61-72.* Tenenbaum, *Underground*, op. cit., *pages 378-381.*

46 Marc Dvorjetski. *Ghetto a l'Est*, Paris, 1950, *page 218.*

47 Jenny Spritzer. *Ich war Nr 10291, Zurich*, n.d., *page 78.*

48 Case III, NG 2660.

49 *German Crimes in Poland*, I, *page 150.*

49a *The Black Book*, New York, 1946, *pages 346-48.* (Evidence before U.S.S.R. Commission of Inquiry, Grodno.)

49b IMT, V, 267, and document R 91. *German Crimes in Poland*, Vol. I, *page 157.* War Refugee Board's report on Auschwitz, November, 1944 (stencil), *page 13.*

50 Dr. Josef Kermisz in Introduction, *Dokumenty i Materialy*, II. Tenenbaum, *In Search of a Lost People, page 95.*

51 Case IV, NO 2187. (Globocnik to Rudi Brandt.)

52 Tenenbaum, op. cit., *page 100.*

53 *German Crimes in Poland*, I, *page 102.*

54 Case IV, NO 2187. (Report by Lieut.-Colonel Horn, March 13th, 1944.) *Dokumenty i Materialy*, II, Introduction, *page lxiii.*

55 Case XI, NO 3304. Case against Gottlob Berger.

56 Case XI, NO 1809. Case against Gottlob Berger.

57 Case IX, NO 3028.

58 Case IX, NO 4317, and IMT, II, 412.

59 Case IV, NO 2262. (Strauch to von dem Bach-Zalewski.)

60 Case IV, NO 1247. (Kaltenbrunner to Himmler.)

61 Case XI, NO 4315.

62 *The Black Book*, 1945, *page 464.*

63 *Aufbau-reconstruction*, New York, Vol 12, No. 36, September, 1946.

64 Dvorjetski. *Ghetto a l'Est*, Paris, 1950, *pages 245-251.*

65 Ibid., *pages 254-6.* (Evidence of Abraham Susskever, Nuremberg witness, in *The Black Book, pages 445-7.*)

66 Dvorjetski, ibid., *page 235.*

67 Ditto, *page 292.*

68 Ditto, *pages 298-300.*

69 Max Kaufmann. *Churbn Lettland*, Munich, 1948, *page 140.* Jeanette Wolff, *Sadismus oder Wahnsinn?*, Grenz im Thuringen, 1947, *page 11.*

70 Kaufmann, op. cit., *pages 196-210.* Jeanette Wolff, op. cit., *page 31.*

71 Ditto, *pages 28-32.* Hermann Voosen, typed statement to Jewish Information Centre, London, 1945.

72 Filip Friedman. *This was Oswiecim*, London, 1948.

73 S. Gringauz in *Jewish Social Studies*, New York, January, 1949.

74 Jeanette Wolff, *page 29.*

75 Case IV, NO 3040. (Minutes of conference in Rosenberg's office, July 5th, 1944.)
76 *New York Times*, quoted in *The Black Book*, 1945, IMT, Document U.S.S.R. 39, VII, 112.
77 Kaufmann. *Churbn Lettland's, page 357*. Voosen, statement to Jewish Information Centre, London. *History of the UN War Crimes Commission*, London, 1948, Appendix IV.
78 Case IV, NO 3031. (Memorandum by Himmler, June 21st, 1941.)
79 Case IV (evidence, Lieut.-Colonel Josef Vogt), printed in *Trials of War Criminals*, V, *page 789*, Washington, 1950.
80 Case IV, NO 606 and NO 1257.
81 Case IV, NO 724. IMT, XX, 266, and PS 4045.
82 Case IV, NO 062.
83 Case IV, NO 1270.
83a Case IV, Transcript 1340. (Evidence, Pohl.)
83b Case IV, NO 485.
83c *Dokumenty i Materialy*, I, *pages 138-41*.
84 Case IV, Transcript 1320. (Evidence, Oswald Pohl.)
85 IMT, Frank defence exhibit, Affidavit No. 8 and XII, 18.
86 Case IV, NO 059. (Globocnik to Himmler, Trieste, December 9th, 1943.)
87 IMT, PS 4024. (Globocnik to Himmler, Trieste, November 4th, 1943.)
88 IMT, PS 1919.
89 Case IV, Transcript 1268. (The scene is described by Pohl in Case IV, Transcript 1795.)
90 Case IV, NO 2187.
91 The figure quoted is that of the War Refugees Board report from Auschwitz, based on the statement of Majdanek office-girls who were sent to Auschwitz, and is rather lower than most survivors' estimates. Morgen's story is printed in *Nazi Conspiracy and Aggression*, Supplement B, *page 1309*, an account of an interrogation of Kaltenbrunner.
92 Sam Welles in *Time*, July 14th, 1947.
93 Case IV, NO 064. (Globocnik to Himmler, Trieste, January 5th, 1944.)
94 Case IV, NO 555, printed in *Trials of War Criminals*, 1951, V, *page 535*.
95 Case IV, NO 063, printed in *Trials of War Criminals*, 1951, V, *page 714*.
96 Case IV, NO 1036. *Trials of War Criminals*, 1950, V, *pages 545-48*.
97 *Catalogue of Camps and Prisons*, British Control Commission, Arolsen, 1949.
98 *Dokumenty i Materialy*, I, *page 36*.
99 *Law Reports of Trials of War Criminals*, London, 1948, VIII. *Dokumenty i Materialy*, I, *pages 45-50*.
100 IMT, L, 53. (Copy to Security Police Commander, Tomaszow, July 24th, 1944.)
101 Kastner. *Bericht*, typescript, Geneva, 1946, *page 148*.
102 Filip Friedman. *This was Oswiecim*, London, 1948.
103 IMT, XX, 312.
104 *Dokumenty i Materialy*, I, *pages 45-51*.
105 IMT, XX, 268-274, and PS 4024.
106 All these documents are in Case IV, NO 519, partly printed in *Persecutions dans les pays de l'Est*, Paris, CDJC, 1949.
107 Ibid.

108 Case XI, Transcript (Judgment 28361)
109 Case IV, NO 519. (*See 106.*)
110 Ibid.
111 Abraham Melezin. *Demographic Processes among the Jewish Population, etc.*, Lodz, 1946 (Lodz Jewish Council statistics).
112 *Dokumenty i Materialy*, Lodz, 1946, III, *page 267.*
113 Melezin, op. cit., and *German Crimes in Poland*, I, *page 157.*
114 Evidence, Dr. Ada Bimko, in *The Belsen Trial*, ed. Raymond Philips, London, 1950.
115 Dr. Albert Menasche. *Birkenau (Auschwitz II)*, New York, 1947.
116 Miklos Nyiszli in *Les temps Modernes*, April, 1951.
117 Kristina Zywulska. *I Came Back*, New York, 1950.
118 IMT, PS 1166, Annexe 11. (Major Burger of WVHA, return of clothing.)
119 Filip Friedman. *This was Oswiecim*, London, 1948.
120 Starr and Shapiro in *Jewish Social Studies*, New York, April, 1946. Of these, 14,152 lived in the town of Lodz. Tenenbaum, *Underground*, New York, 1952, *page 182.*
121 *History of the United Nations War Crimes Commission*, London, 1948, Appendix IV.

CHAPTER 12

1 'The Organisation of UGIF in Nazi-controlled France.' Zosa Szakowski in *Jewish Social Studies*, New York, July, 1947.
2 Ditto. Georges Wellers, *De Drancy à Auschwitz*, Paris, CDJC, 1946, *page 106.*
3 Case XI, NG 4895. Conference reported for Abetz by Ernst Achenbach.
4 IMT, PS 3614, Document II. Conference reported for Werner Best by Mahnke. Printed in *Persecutions des Juifs en France, etc.*, Paris, CDJC, 1948.
5 Case XI, NG 4895.
6 Case XI, NG 2442 and 2432. (Abetz to Ribbentrop.)
7 RF 1207. Report by Dannecker to Knochen, July 1st, 1941, 'The Jewish Question in France and its Treatment.' Partly printed in IMT, VI, 84-8, and *Persecutions des Juifs en France.*
8 The whole of the foregoing account is from a series of documents of the French Nuremberg prosecution which were not put in evidence. Printed in *Persecutions des Juifs en France, etc.*, 1948, as Documents Nos. 65-78.
9 Case XI, NG 3571. Stuelpnagel to Wagner.
10 RF 1211. Printed in *Persecutions, France, etc.*
11 Knochen to Heydrich, December 18th, 1941. Printed in *Le Monde Juif*, CDJC, Paris, No. 14, December, 1948.
12 Georges Wellers in *Le Monde Juif*, No. 15, January, 1949.
13 Report on Auschwitz (stencil) circulated by the War Refugee Board, Washington, November, 1944, 'German extermination camps, Auschwitz and Birkenau.' A fuller version in Rabbi L. Silberschein, *Judenausrottung im Polen* (stencil), Zurich, 1944, third series. (Henceforward referred to as 'WRB Report, Auschwitz.')

14 RF 1216, Dannecker to Knochen, March 3rd, 1942, printed in *Persecutions des Juifs en France, etc.,* 1948, CDJC.
15 Case XI, NG 4594-C. A photographic facsimile with Weizsaecker's minute is printed in *Le Monde Juif,* September, 1947.
16 Case XI, NG 1838. Affidavit, Otto Abetz.
17 For Rademacher's minute, Case XI, NG 3358, and *Chapter 4, page 17,* in this book. For Weizsaecker's evidence, Case XI, Transcript 8584.
18 Case XI, Transcript 8577, and Weizsaecker, *Erinnerungen,* 1950, *page 338.*
19 Case XI, Transcript of Judgment 28293 and 28330.
20 Weizsaecker, *Erinnerungen,* Munich, 1950, *page 338.*
21 Handwritten list from Roethke's office file. Original in CDJC, Paris (XXVI-C, 254).
22 WRB report, Auschwitz.
23 Georges Wellers. *De Drancy à Auschwitz,* Paris CDJC, 1946, *page 34.*
24 Op. cit. and RF 1216, Document 13 (Best to Stuelpnagel), printed in *Persecutions des Juifs en France, etc.,* 1948.
25 WRB report, Auschwitz.
26 Leon Poliakov. *L'étoile jaune,* Paris, CDJC, 1949, *pages 22-4.*
27 RF 1207, Dannecker report, July 1st, 1942, in *Persecutions, France.*
28 Poliakov. *L'étoile jaune,* Paris, 1949, *page 30.*
29 Knochen to Lischka, *L'étoile jaune, page 35.*
30 *L'étoile jaune, page 40.*
31 Ibid., *page 64.*
32 Ibid., *page 52.*
33 RF 1217, printed in *Persecutions, France, etc.,* 1948.
34 Case XI, NG 183.
35 RF 1221, Dannecker to Knochen, printed in *Le Monde Juif,* July, 1949.
36 RF 1219, Roethke to Dannecker, June 26th, 1942, printed in *Le Monde Juif,* July 1949.
37 RF 1220, printed in IMT, VI, 90.
38 RF 1223, printed in *Persecutions, France, etc.*
39 RF 1225, printed in *Persecutions, France, etc.*
40 RF 1223, printed in *Persecutions, France, etc.*
41 RF 1222, printed in *Le Monde Juif,* No. 21, July, 1949.
42 RF 1225, printed in *Persecutions, France, etc.*
43 RF 1234, printed in *Persecutions, France, etc.*
44 RF 1225, Document 17, *Persecutions, France, etc.*
45 Georges Wellers in *Le Monde Juif,* No. 22, August-September, 1949.
46 RF 1225, 19.
47 RF 1233, printed in *Persecutions, France, etc.*
48 Georges Wellers. *De Drancy à Auschwitz,* Paris, CDJC, 1946, *page 58.*
49 Georges Wellers in *Le Monde Juif,* No. 22, August-September, 1949.
49a Document in CDJC, Paris. (See 21.)
50 RF 1234 (21), printed in *Persecutions, France, etc.*
51 RF 1226, printed in IMT, VI, 91 (English).
52 RF 1234, printed in IMT, VI, 92 (portion in English), and *Persecutions, France, etc.* RF 1227, printed in *Persecutions, France, etc.*
53 Handwritten list, CDJC, XXVI-C, 254 (original document).
54 RF 1227, facsimile in *Persecutions, France, etc.*

55 Poliakov. *Breviaire de la Haine*, 1951, *page 203*.
56 Unnumbered document, translated in Poliakov, *Breviaire de la Haine, pages 204-6*, footnote.
57 Case XI, NG 2586-J. Memorandum by Martin Luther to Ribbentrop, August 19th, 1942.
58 Case XI, NG 2268. Leon Poliakov, *La condition des Juifs en France sous l'occupation italienne*, Paris, CDJC, 1946, *pages 23, 62*.
59 Ibid., *page 54*.
60 Ibid., *page 63*, and Case XI, NG 4890 (Abetz to Roethke).
61 Poliakov. *Condition des Juifs, etc., page 73*.
62 Ibid., *page 77*.
63 IMT, D 734, minutes of conference Ribbentrop-Mussolini.
64 RF 1230, Roethke to Eichmann, March 6th, 1943 (*Persecutions, France*).
65 Poliakov. *Conditions des Juifs, page 78*. Case XI, NG 2242.
66 Case XI, NG 2242. Report by Mackensen for Ribbentrop.
67 Poliakov. *Conditions des Juifs, page 98*, Document 28 (Lt. Moritz, Marseilles, to Roethke), May 26th, 1943.
68 Poliakov, op. cit., *pages 108-115*.
69 Ibid., Documents 37-42.
70 Ibid., Document 42.
71 Ibid., Introduction, *pages 38-40*.
72 Case XI, NG 4978.
73 Document CDJC XXVI-C, *page 254*.
74 Document CDJC, I, *page 54*, part printed in Poliakov (op. cit.), Document 34, *page 115*.
75 Wellers. *De Drancy à Auschwitz, page 49*.
76 Case XI, NG 4956. Printed in David Rousset, *Le pitre ne rit pas*, Paris, 1949, *page 127*.
77 RF 1230 in *Persecutions, France, etc.*, and Document CDJC XXVI, *page 254*.
78 Document CDJC I, 54, printed in Poliakov, op. cit., *page 115*.
79 Wellers. *De Drancy à Auschwitz, page 100*.
80 Ibid., *page 106*.
81 RF 1235, printed (English) in IMT, VI, 93.
82 Case IV, NO 1411. Knochen to Brunner.
83 Wellers. *De Drancy à Auschwitz, page 121*.
84 Filip Friedman. *This was Oswiecim*, London, 1948, *page 23*. List preserved by Dr. Otto Wolken of St. Polten, *Lagerschreiber* in camp B IIa.
85 CDJC Document XXVI-C, *page 254*, and Wellers, *De Drancy à Auschwitz, page 108*.

CHAPTER 13

1 *Auschwitz, Deel I*, Information Bureau of the Netherlands Red Cross, The Hague, June, 1947.
2 IMT, Document PS 1726. Report of the Repatriation Commission of the Netherlands Government.
3 *Le Monde Juif*, No. 29, March, 1950, quoting *Nederland in Oorlogstijd*. Wielek, *De Oorlog die Hitler won*, Amsterdam, 1947, *pages 30-35*.

4 *Nederland in Oorlogstijd*, March, 1950.
5 Rauter to Christiansen, printed in *Nederland in Oorlogstijd*, March, 1950.
6 Case XI, NG 2285. Printed in *Le Monde Juif*, *page 29*, March, 1950.
7 Case XI, NG 2805. Mohr to Woermann, ibid.
8 Case XI, NG 2710. Memorandum by Albrecht, ibid.
9 Case XI, NG 3709. Luther to Albrecht, November 4th, 1941.
10 Weekly report, Commander Sipo und SD Nederland, December 28th, 1941. Printed in *Nederland in Oorlogstijd*, March, 1950.
11 Eugen Kogon. *The Theory and Practice of Hell (Der SS Staat)*, London, 1950, *pages 167-9*.
12 Trial of Hans Rauter, The Hague, April 1st, 1948. Court transcript (typed), *pages 25, 36*.
13 Transcript, Trial of Ferdinand Aus der Fuenten, The Hague, March 13th, 1949, at Rijksinstituut voor Oorlogsdocumentatie, Amsterdam,
14 Case XI, NG 183.
15 Case XI, NG 2333. Albrecht to Rademacher.
16 *Auschwitz, Deel II, De Deportatietransporten July 15th-August 24th, 1942*, Information Bureau of the Netherlands Red Cross, The Hague, May, 1948.
16a Ibid.
17 Case XI, NG 2631. Report from *Gesandter* Bene, August 13th, 1942.
18 NO 3408 and Case IV, Transcript 1917-20. The diary was provided for the Nuremberg prosecution by Judge Sehn of the Cracow court.
19 Auschwitz, deel II, The Hague, 1948, op. cit.
20 Rauter to Himmler, September 10th, 1942. Photostat at Rijksinstituut voor Oorlogsdocumentatie.
21 Case IV, NO 1339. Rauter to Himmler, September 24th, 1942. Facsimile in *Nederland in Oorlogstijd*, March, 1950 (part only).
22 Original Gestapo file, *Abbau der ruckstellende Gruppen*, *page 37*, at Rijksinstituut voor Oorlogsdocumentatie (Sloettke file).
23 Case IV, NO 1339. Rauter to Himmler, see supra.
24 Sloettke file, *pages 37-45*.
25 Case XI, NG 2631. Bene to Woermann.
26 See supra, photostat, Rijksinstituut.
27 Excerpt of interrogation in *Nederland in Oorlogstijd*, March, 1950.
28 Judgment of The Hague Court, December 27th, 1949, transcript *pages 17-25*.
29 Trial of Hans Rauter, The Hague, April 1st, 1948, transcript *pages 31-2*.
29a Zoepf to Harster, April 27th 1944. Photostat in Rauter case, Rijksinstituut, ' Sloettke file,' *page 111*, ' Entjudung der Niederlande. '
30 Sloettke file, *pages 112* and *114*.
31 Case XI, NG 2631. Bene to Woermann, June 25th, 1943.
32 *Sobibor*. Pamphlet published by the Information Bureau of the Netherlands Red Cross, February, 1947. Wielek, *De Oorlog die Hitler won*.
33 Sloettke file, *pages 8-39*.
34 Zoepf to Schoengarth, June 15th, 1944, Sloettke file, *pages 178-86*.
35 Sloettke file, *page 45*.
36 Case XI, NG 2586-O.
37 Case XI, NG 2652-A.
38 Case XI, NG 2652-G.

39 Sloettke file, *page 127*. Minutes kept by Fraulein Sloettke of Rauter's conversation with Zoepf, June 24th, 1943.
40 Affidavit, Eberhard von Thadden, printed in *Le Monde Juif*, No. 17, March, 1949.
41 The name of Bergen-Belsen appears on the circulation list of an order from Gluecks, dated April 27th, 1943. IMT, PS 1933.
42 *Auschwitz, Deel II*, Information Bureau of Netherlands Red Cross, May, 1949. Sloettke file, *page 144*. Michael Molho, *In Memoriam, pages 96-7*. Abel Herzberg, *Kroniek der Jodenvervolging, page 228*, The Hague, 1951.
43 Herzberg. *Kroniek der Jodenvervolging, pages 220-28*.
44 IMT, D 749. Affidavit, Rudolf Hoess. Netherlands Red Cross, *Auschwitz, Deel VI*, 1952.
45 Sloettke file, *page 169*.
46 Judgment, Aus der Fuenten trial, The Hague, December 27th, 1949, transcript, *pages 17-25*. Filip Friedman, *This was Oswiecim*, London, 1946, quoting Dr. Wolken.
47 Trial of Hans Rauter, Transcript 24 and Document E 14 (Rijksinstituut).
48 Sloettke file, *page 169*.
49 *Persecutions des Juifs en France, etc.*, CDJC, Paris, 1948, *page 204*. NG 2380 (Case XI). Fortnightly Report No. 10, Military Governor, Belgium-Northern France, November 19th, 1940.
50 Leon Poliakov. *L'étoile jaune*, Paris, CDJC, 1949, *page 24*.
51 *Black Book of Polish Jewry*, 1943, *page 319*. *The Black Book*, New York, 1945, *page 144* (figures not reliable).
52 Case XI, NG 183.
53 Case XI, NG 5219.
54 WRB report, *Auschwitz*, Washington, Executive Office of the President, November, 1944, *page 18*.
55 *Les crimes de guerre, commis sous l'occupation de la Belgique* Persecution anti-semitique, Liège, May, 1947, *page 28*.
56 Ditto, *page 36*. IMT, GB 75 (Belgian Government's report). *Persecutions des Juifs en France, etc.*, CDJC, Paris, 1948, *page 223*.
57 ' La resistance juif en Belgique, *Le Monde Juif*, No. 19, April, 1949.
58 Ibid. and *Persecution anti-semitique, etc.*, Liège, 1947, *page 34*.
59 *The Times*, March 10th, 1951.
60 Case XI, NG 3931.
61 Leon Poliakov. *L'étoile jaune, page 70*.
62 Case XI, NG 4275.
63 Case XI, NG 5121. Printed in *Le Monde Juif*, No. 24, October, 1949.
64 Case XI, NG 5121, ibid.
65 Case XI, NG 4807. Sonnenleitner to Wagner.
66 Case XI, NG 3923.
67 IMT, XX, 147. Evidence, Werner Best.
68 Case XI, NG 5208. Printed by Jacques Sabille in *Le Monde Juif*, No. 24, October, 1949.
68a IMT. Affidavit, Kaltenbrunner, I and XI, 239.
69 IMT, XXI, 167. (Evidence, Hoffmann.) Jacques Sabille in *Le Monde Juif*, No. 25, November, 1949. Document from the trial of Werner Best by courtesy of the Danish Embassy in London.
70 Case XI, NG 5208, anl Jacques Sabille, *Le Monde Juif*, No. 24.

71 and 72 Documents from Werner Best trial by courtesy of the Danish Embassy.
73 Case XI, 3923, and Case XII, NOKW, 356.
74 Case XI, NG 5206 (affidavit, von Hannecken), and Jacques Sabille in *Le Monde Juif*, No. 25.
75 Evidence, Alfred Jodl, in IMT, XV, 308 and 411.
76 Document, courtesy of Danish Embassy (Werner Best trial).
77 Case XI, NG 3907 and 3920. IMT, D 547.
78 Nella Rost (Stockholm) in *Les Juifs en Europe, 1939-45*, CDJC, 1947.
79 Case XI, NG 3921, and Case XII, NOKW 355.
80 Document from Werner Best trial, courtesy of Danish Embassy, London.
81 Case XI, NG 4093. Printed by Jacques Sabille in *Le Monde Juif*, No. 26, December, 1949.
82 *The Times*, August 30th, 1951.
83 Deportation estimates in Korherr's report to Himmler, NO 5194, and in *Les Juifs en Europe, 1939-45* (paper by Nella Rost).
84 Case XI, NG 5217. Printed in *Le Monde Juif*, No. 27, January, 1950.
85 Case XI, NG 2641. Printed in *Le Monde Juif*, No. 27, January, 1950.
86 Case XI, NG 5217. Printed in *Le Monde Juif*, No. 27, January, 1950.
87 Case XI, NG 5027 and 5088. *Le Monde Juif*, No. 20, June, 1949.
88 Case XI, NG 5027.
89 Case XI, Document Weizsaecker, No. 241.
90 Case XI, NG 5207. Weizsaecker to 'Inland II,' printed in *Le Monde Juif*, No. 20, June, 1949.
91 Case XI, Document Weizsaecker, No. 241.
92 *Le Monde Juif*, No. 20, June 1949, and No. 34, December, 1950.
93 Evidence of Rudolf Rahn before Munich *Schwurgericht*. *The Times*, February 17th, 1950.
94 Filip Friedman. *This was Oswiecim*, London, 1948.
95 *Law Reports of Trials of War Criminals* (Kesselring, Mackensen, Maelzer), London, VIII, 1949.
96 Verbal information, Dr. Gaddo Glass, Comitato della communita, Trieste.
97 *Catalogue of Camps and Prisons*, International Tracing Service, Arolsen. British Zone, Germany, July, 1949.
98 Statement by Vice-President, Union of Italian Jewish Communities, to Wiener Library, September 10th, 1946.
98a Primo Levi. *Sé questo e un uomo*, Turin, 1947.
99 Filip Friedman, op. cit. Arolsen list, op. cit.
100 Max Adolfe Vitale in *Les Juifs en Europe, 1939-45*, Paris, CDJC, 1947.
101 'Relazione del comitato della comunita al Consiglio,' June 23rd, 1946, Trieste (courtesy, Dr. Glass).
102 *History of the Allied War Crimes Commission*, London, 1948, Appendix V.

CHAPTER 14

1 Starr and Shapiro in *Jewish Social Studies*, New York, April, 1946.
2 Max Weinreich. *Hitler's Professors*, New York (YIVO), 1946, *page 116*.
3 *The Black Book*, New York, 1945, *page 158*. Eugene Levai, *Black Book of Hungarian Jewry*, Vienna, 1949, *page 39*.

4 Case XI, NG 3354. This file of documents is the source for the next two pages.

5 *The Von Hassell Diaries*, London, 1948, *page 204.*

6 *Law Reports of Trials of War Criminals*, VIII, *page 39*, Case VII, 'The hostages trial,' London, 1948.

7 Case XI, NG 2586-G.

8 *The Black Book, page 158.* IMT, Document U.S.S.R., O 36.

8a *Report of Activities of CIRC in Second World War*, Geneva, 1948, Vol. II, *page 251.*

8b *Koelnische Rundschau*, October 7th-10th, 1952.

9 IMT, Document PS 510. Schaefer to Widderhausen at office ' IID, 3a ' of the RSHA.

9a *Koelnische Rundschau*, October 10th, 1952.

10 Case XI, NG 2570. Affidavit, Kurt Heinberg.

11 Boris Shub in *Hitler's Ten Year War on the Jews*, New York, Institute of Jewish Affairs, 1943.

12 Major S. Payne-Best. *The Venlo Incident*, London, 1950, *page 126.*

13 *History of the Allied War Crimes Commission*, London, 1948, Appendix V.

14 Communication, Nuremberg-Fuerth *Landgericht* to Centre de Documentation juive contemporaine, Paris, January, 1950.

15 *Nuernberger Nachrichten*, February 8th, 1952. *The Times*, March 18th, 1952.

16 *The Ciano Diaries*, ed. Malcolm Muggeridge, London, 1947, *page 336.*

17 Walter Hagen (Willi Hoettl). *Die geheime Front*, Wien-Linz, 1950.

18 *Hitler's Ten Year War on the Jews*, New York, 1943, *page 105.*

19 *The Von Hassell Diaries*, London, 1948, *page 186.* IMT, XVI, 176, evidence, Glaise-Horstenau.

20 International Tracing Service, Arolsen, 1951. *Supplementary List of Camps and Prisons.*

21 *Hitler's Ten Year War, etc., page 106.*

22 *The Black Book, page 158.*

23 Case XI, NG 182. Rademacher to Weizsaecker.

24 IMT, III, 276-89. Case IX, NO 5094 (Korherr report). Affidavit C (Wisliceny), Appendix 2, printed in *Nazi Conspiracy and Aggression*, Washington, 1948, Supplement B.

25 *Aufbau-Reconstruction*, New York, May 18th, 1951. Hagen, *Die geheime Front*, op. cit.

26 Photograph and biography, *Der Grossdeutsche Reichstag*, November, 1943.

27 Hans Gisevius. *To the Bitter End*, London, 1948, *page 159.*

28 Case XI, NG 3560. Printed in *Persecutions dans les pays de l'Est*, Paris, CDJC, 1949, *page 241.*

29 Case XI, NG 2368.

30 Case XI, NG 2346. Printed in *Le Monde Juif*, August-September, 1951.

31 Case XI, NG 3165.

32 Case XI, NG 2367. Printed in *Le Monde Juif*, October, 1951.

33 Case XI, NG 3457.

34 Case XI, NG 2345.

35 Jacques Sabille in *Le Monde Juif*, October, 1951.

36 Ibid.

37 Case XI, NG 2348.
38 *Hitler's Ten Year War on the Jews, page 105.*
39 *Report of Activities of CIRC in Second World War,* Vol. I, *page 647.*
40 Case XI, NG 2413.
41 Dr. Paul Schmidt. *Hitler's Interpreter,* London, 1951, *page 248.*
42 *Report of Activities, CIRC,* Vol. III, 1950, *page 76.*
43 Case XI, NG 2349. Major Helm to attaché-group, RSHA.
44 Starr and Shapiro in *Jewish Social Studies,* New York, April, 1946.
45 Jacques Sabille in *Le Monde Juif,* October, 1951.
46 Report of Anglo-American Committee, European Jewry and Palestine, April, 1946.
47 Rabbi Michael Molho. *In Memoriam, Hommage aux victimes juives des Nazis en Grèce,* Salonika, 1948, *page 1.*
48 *Ibid., page 40. Ibid., page 48,* and report, CIRC, 1950, III, *page 524.*
49 Joshua Starr in *Jewish Social Studies,* January, 1950.
50 IMT, III, 282. (Examination, Dieter Wisliceny.)
51 Molho. *In Memoriam, page 61.* Wisliceny, IMT, Affidavit C and document, CDJC, Paris, LXXXVII, *page 65.*
52 Molho, *page 80.*
53 Case IV, NO 5193. Second statistical report on Jewish resettlement, submitted by Dr. Korherr to Himmler, April 19th, 1943.
54 Molho, *page 94,* quoting official *Judenrat* statistics.
55 IMT, III, 284.
56 Molho, *page 87.*
57 *German Crimes in Poland,* Warsaw, 1946, I, *page 41.* IMT, V, 192 (evidence of Mme Vaillant-Couturier).
58 Molho, *page 94.* Dr. Albert Menasche, *Birkenau,* New York, 1947, *pages 13-15.*
59 Report, CIRC, I, *page 645,* and III, *page 524.*
60 IMT. Wisliceny, Affidavit C.
61 Dr. Albert Menasche, op. cit.
62 War Refugee Board report on Auschwitz (stencil), Washington, 1944.
63 A file of documents showing that the sick were quarantined or given light duties, *Dokumenty i Materialy,* I, *pages 113-14* and *139-41.*
64 *See* particularly Menasche, *Birkenau, page 60,* and Mme Vaillant-Couturier, IMT, V, 192.
65 Wisliceny in IMT, III, 281.
66 The foregoing paragraph is based on the account of M. Levy Tazartes in *In Memoriam,* Salonika, 1948.
67 IMT, III, 284.
68 Case XI, NG 4960.
69 Case XI, NG 4957.
70 Molho. *In Memoriam, page 94.*
71 Case XI, NG 4958.
72 Wiener Library bulletin, September-November, 1949.
73 Case XI, NG 2586-O and 2652-f.
74 Molho, op. cit., *page 96.*
75 Case XI, NG 5262.
76 Molho, *page 95.*
77 Molho, *page 100.*

78 Case XII, NOKW 1754.
79 Wisliceny, Affidavit C (IMT).
80 Filip Friedman. *This was Oswiecim*, London, 1948.
81 Molho, *page 97*. Abel Herzberg, *Kroniek der Jodenvervolging*, Amsterdam, 1951, *pages 220-38*.
82 *Dokumenty i Materialy*, I, *page 120*.
83 Otto Wolken in Filip Friedman, *This was Oswiecim*, and Case XII, NOKW 1715 (Affidavit, Erwin Lenz).
84 Case XII, NOKW 1801-2.
85 Case XII, NOKW 1715.
86 Case XI, NG 2582. Printed in *Persecutions dans les Pays de l'Est*, Paris, 1948, CDJC, *page 249*.
87 Case XI, NG 5351. Printed in *Le Monde Juif*, April, 1950.
88 Case XI, NG 2582-B. Printed as above.
89 Chaim Benadev in *Les Juifs en Europe, 1939-45*, Paris, CDJC, 1947, *page 124*.
90 Case XI, NG 4180.
91 Case XI, NG 4144. *Le Monde Juif*, April, 1950.
92 Ibid.
93 Case XI, NG 062. *Le Monde Juif*, April, 1950.
94 Case XI, NG 2537. Hoffmann to attaché-group RSHA, printed as above.
95 Case XI, NG 2357.
96 Ibid; and Benadev in *Les Juifs en Europe*.
97 Case XI, NG 2753 and 3302. Printed in *Le Monde Juif*, April, 1950.
98 Starr and Shapiro in *Jewish Social Studies*, New York, April, 1946.
99 Michael Molho. *In Memoriam*, Salonika, 1948, *pages 101-2*.

CHAPTER 15

1 Figures mainly from *Hitler's Ten Year War on the Jews*, New York, 1943. Dr. Frederick Steiner in *Les Juifs en Europe, 1939-45, page 217*, Paris, CDJC, 1947. *The Black Book*, New York, 1946, *page 137*.
2 Max Weinreich. *Hitler's Professors*, published YIVO, New York, 1948, *page 118*.
3 *Les Juifs en Europe, page 217*. *Hitler's Ten Year War, page 62*.
4 Photograph in Dr. Frederick Steiner, *The Tragedy of Slovak Jewry*, CUJCR, Bratislava, 1949, *page 50*.
5 *Hitler's Ten Year War, page 62*.
6 Case XI, NG 4409. Endroes to Weizsaecker, and NG 2586-J, Luther memorandum.
7 IMT. Wisliceny, Affidavit C.
8 *The Black Book*, New York, 1946, *page 138*.
9 Case XI, NG 2586-J. Memorandum, Luther to Ribbentrop.
10 Facsimile of German road-bills in Steiner, *Tragedy of Slovak Jewry*.
11 *Dokumenty i Materialy*, Lodz, 1946, II, *pages 47-50*, and Frederick Steiner in *Les Juifs en Europe, 1939-45, page 219*.
12 Case XI, NG 4404. Ludin to Luther, April 18th, 1942.
13 Steiner. *Tragedy of Slovak Jewry*, Bratislava, 1949, *page 6*.
14 Evidence of Dieter Wisliceny in IMT, III, 277.

15 Boris Shub in *Hitler's Ten Year War on the Jews*, New York, 1943, *page 66.*
16 Steiner in *Les Juifs en Europe, 1939-45, page 219.*
17 Evidence, Wisliceny in IMT, III, 281.
18 Yankiel Wiernik. *A Year in Treblinka*, New York, 1945. Rudolf Reder in *Dokumenty i Materialy*, II.
19 Boris Shub in *Hitler's Ten Year War*, 1943, *page 64.*
20 Case XI, NG 4404. Ludin to Weizsaecker.
21 Case XI, NG 2586-J. Luther to Ribbentrop, August 17th, 1942.
22 IMT, III, 278.
23 Case IV, NO 5193. Korherr to Himmler.
24 Ibid., III, 281.
25 *The Black Book*, New York, 1946, *page 140.*
26 Case XI, NG 2867, 4749, and 1823-24. (Case against Veesenmayer.)
27 Reszoe Kastner, affidavit in IMT, PS 2605.
28 Ditto, Introduction to *Bericht des Juedischen Rettungskomitees aus Budapest* (stencil), Geneva, 1946.
29 Case XI, NG 2550. Mueller to Brandt.
30 Case XI, NG 5921.
31 Case XI, NG 2866. Affidavit, Hermann Hoefl.
32 *Report of Activities of CIRC in Second World War*, Geneva, 1948, Vol. I, *page 645.*
33 Photostat copy in Steiner, *Tragedy of Slovak Jewry*, Bratislava, 1949.
34 Reszoe Kastner. *Bericht, etc.*, op. cit., *page 97*, and affidavit, Case XI, NO 4824.
35 Kastner. *Bericht*, and Georges Dunand, *Ne perdez pas leur trace!* Neuchatel, 1950, *page 79.*
36 Dunand, ibid., *pages 110, 148.*
37 Dunand, op. cit., *page 110*, and CIRC report, Vol. I, *pages 645-7.*
38 CIRC report, Vol. I, *pages 645-7.*
39 Dunand, op. cit., *page 212.*
40 *Jews of Nazi Europe*, report of World Jewish Congress, Baltimore, November, 1941 (stencil) (section ru 3).
41 Hugh Seton-Watson. *Eastern Europe*, 1944, *page 207.*
42 *Hitler's Ten Year War, page 88.*
43 Ibid.
44 *Cartea Negra*, by Matatias Karp, Bucharest, Vol. II, 1947, reviewed by Joshua Starr in *Jewish Social Studies*, New York, January, 1950.
45 Boris Kelpner in *Dokumentenwerk ueber die Juedische Geschichte in der Zeit des Nazismus*, edited by Rabbi T. Guttmann, Jerusalem, January, 1945, Vol. II.
46 Kelpner, op. cit., and Curzio Malaparte, *Kaputt*, translated by Professor Foligno, New York, 1946.
47 Starr and Shapiro in *Jewish Social Studies*, New York, April, 1946.
48 Case IX, NO 2952 and NO 4858.
49 Starr and Shapiro in *Jewish Social Studies*, April, 1946.
49a Case IX, NO 2653. *Einsatzgruppen* daily report, August 31st, 1941.
50 Case IX, Transcript 4408. Evidence, Ohlendorf.
51 *Hitler's Ten Year War on the Jews*, 1943, *page 85.*
52 Deposition of Manfred Reifer in Guttmann, *Dokumentenwerk, etc.*, op. cit., Jerusalem, 1945, I, *page 19.*

53 Starr and Shapiro in *Jewish Social Studies,* April, 1946.
54 See particularly deposition of Meyer Sternberg of Czernowitz before Jewish Anti-Fascist Commission, USSR, in *The Black Book,* New York, 1946, *page 306.*
55 Case XI and IMT, PS 3319.
56 Deposition of Hermann Scherff of Czernowitz, *Dokumentenwerk, etc.,* II, *page 22.*
57 Ditto, II, *page 32.*
58 Matatias Karp in *Les Juifs en Europe, 1939-45, pages 199-207,* quoting report by Chief Rabbi Saffran.
59 *The Von Hassell Diaries,* London, 1948, *page 200.*
60 *Les Juifs en Europe,* op. cit., *pages 199-207.*
61 *Dokumentenwerk, etc.,* II, *page 24.*
62 Case XI, NG 3990 and NG 4817.
63 IMT, PS 3319.
64 IMT, PS 3319, and Case XI, NG 4817.
65-66 *Dokumentenwerk,* II, *page 29.*
67 Eugene Levai. *Black Book of Hungarian Jewry,* Zurich, 1949, *page 67.*
68 *Report of Activities of CIRC in Second World War,* Geneva, 1948, Vol. I, *page 654.*
69 *The Von Hassell Diaries, page 166.*
70 IMT, RF 1217. Printed in *Persecutions des Juifs dans les pays de l'Ouest,* Paris, CDJC, 1947.
71 Case XI, NG 3558 and 3559.
72 Case XI, Transcript 9194. Evidence, Weizsaecker.
73 Case XI, NG 2195.
74 Case XI, NG 3986.
75 Matatias Karp in *Les Juifs en Europe, 1939-45.*
76 L. Poliakov in *Le Monde Juif,* No. 17, March, 1949.
77 *The Times,* December 18th, 1942. BBC Home Service, 9 p.m. News, December 18th, 1942.
78 *The Morgenthau Diaries,* by Henry Morgenthau, Junior, in *Collier's Magazine,* November, 1947.
79 Ibid.
80 Case XI, NG 3986. Richter to Killinger.
81 Case XI, NG 178 and NG 2184.
82 Case XI, Transcript (Judgment) 28354-60, and NG 3987.
83 Case XI, Transcript 28355.
84 Case XI, NG 1794 and Transcript 28361.
85 Case XI, Transcript 28362.
86 *Report of Activities, CIRC,* Vol. I, *page 653,* and *Dokumentenwerk,* II, *page 30.*
87 *Report of Activities, CIRC,* Vol. III, 1950, *page 522.*
88 Ditto, I, *page 654.*
89 *Dokumentenwerk,* Jerusalem, 1945, II, *page 28.*
90 Silberschein. *Judenausrottung im Polen,* Zurich, 1945 (stencil), fifth series, *page 30.*
91 *Dokumentenwerk,* II, *page 28.*
92 Case XI, Affidavit, Reszoe Kastner, NO 2817.
93 IMT, PS 2738. Affidavit, Willi Hoettl.

94 Walter Hagen (Willi Hoettl). *Die Geheime Front*, Wien-Linz, 1950, *page 307*.
95 Starr and Shapiro in *Jewish Social Studies*, New York, April, 1946.
96 Report of Anglo-American Committee of Inquiry, *European Jewry and Palestine*, Lausanne, April 20th, 1946, *page 54*.

CHAPTER 16

1 Case XI, NG 2586.
2 IMT, PS 2605. Kastner affidavit.
3 IMT, PS 197.
4 *Hitler's Ten Year War on the Jews, page 68. The Black Book, page 154.*
5 Report by Majer Neuman of Volove (Ruthenia), by courtesy Miss Helga Melchior, Stockholm.
6 Affidavit, Reszoe Kastner, IMT, PS 2605. Ditto, *Bericht des Juedischen Rettungskomitees, Budapest, 1942-45* (stencil), Geneva, 1946 (introduction). Eugene Levai, *The Black Book of the Martyrdom of Hungarian Jewry*, Zurich, 1948 (ed. P. Davies), *page 6*.
7 Case XI, NG 4667.
8 Case XI, NG 2586.
9 Case XI, NG 1856, NG 1800. Printed in *Persecutions dans les pays de l'Est*, Paris, CDJC, 1948.
10 Case XI, NG 1800.
11 Eugene Levai. *Black Book, etc., page 29*.
12 Case XI, NG 1798.
13 IMT, IX, 314, and X, 97, Document D, 736.
14 Case XI, NG 1815, and Transcript (Judgment) 28385.
15 Levai, op. cit., *pages 33-5*. (Sztojay's report verbatim.)
16 Case XI, NG 2192. Veesenmayer to Himmler, May 19th, 1943.
17 Kastner. *Bericht des Rettungskomitees, etc.* (op. cit.), *page 9*. Refers to *Rettungskomitee* report of November 22nd, 1943.
18 Levai, *page 36*.
19 A very important account of these contacts in Kastner, *Bericht, etc., pages 11-16*.
20 Case XI, NG 2947.
21 Case XI, Veesenmayer defence document Vb, *page 211*.
22 Ditto, Vb, *page 207*.
23 Ditto, Vb, *page 213*.
24 IMT, III, *page 285*. Evidence, Wisliceny.
25 Case IV, NO 2259. (Eichmann's SS personal file.)
26 Levai, *pages 80-83*.
27 Levai, *page 89*.
28 Levai, *pages 108, 86-7*.
29 Levai, *page 112*.
30 Case XI, NG 2191 and 1815.
31 Kastner. *Bericht, page 24*.
32 IMT, Wisliceny, Affidavit C. (*Nazi Conspiracy and Aggression*, Washington, 1947, Supplement, Vol. B.)
33 Levai, *page 134*.
34 Case XI, NG 2233.

35 Levai, *page 117.*
36 Case XI, NG 2196.
37 Case XI, NG 2262.
38 IMT, Document R, 134.
39 Kastner. *Bericht, page 30.* IMT, PS 2605 (affidavit, Kastner).
40 Levai, *page 254.* WRB report, Auschwitz and Birkenau, 1944, *page 33.*
41 Levai, *page 138.*
42 Case XI, NG 2190.
43 Kastner. *Bericht, page 39.*
44 Levai, *pages 148-9.*
45 Levai, *page 146.*
46 Walter Hagen (Willi Hoettl). *Die Geheime Front,* Wien-Linz, 1951, *page 39.*
47 Case XI, NG 2263.
48 Levai, *page 235.* Kastner, *Bericht, page 65.*
49 Case XI, NG 2190.
50 Case II, NOKW 336. Printed in *Trials of War Criminals,* 1951, II, *page 555.*
51 Case IV, NO 592, Transcript 1815. Printed in *Persecutions dans les pays de l'Est, page 233.*
52 See especially Jeannette Wolff, *Sadismus oder Wahnsinn,* Grenz im Thuringen, 1947.
53 Case II, NOKW 359. *Trials of War Criminals,* II, *page 557.*
53a IMT, III, *pages 322-3. Law Reports of Trials of War Criminals,* London, 1949, Vol. X, *pages 100-102.*
53b Case II (Milch). Evidence, Fritz Schmelter, printed in *Trials of War Criminals,* II, *page 582.*
54 Case XI, NO 1874. (Affidavit, Gabor Vajna.)
54a Ella Lingens-Reiner. *Prisoners of Fear,* London, 1948, *page 71.*
55 IMT, V, 190. (Evidence, Mme Vaillant-Couturier.) Filip Friedman, *This was Oswiecim,* London, 1948, *page 53.*
56 *Dokumenty i Materialy,* II, *pages 103-5.* Miklos Nyiszli in *Les temps modernes,* April, 1951, *page 1661.*
57 Kristina Zywulska. *I Came Back,* New York, 1950, *page 110.*
58 IMT, PS 3868. (Affidavit, Rudolf Hoess.) *German Crimes in Poland* 1946, I, *page 88.*
59 IMT, D, 749. (Affidavit, Rudolf Hoess.)
60 *Les temps modernes,* April, 1951.
61 Ditto, and Zywulska, op. cit., *page 163.*
62 Zywulska, *page 190.*
63 Case IV, NO 2359, Transcript 1932-5.
64 *German Crimes in Poland,* I, *page 88.*
65 Case XI, NG 2061. Levai, *page 227.*
66 Case XI, NG 2190.
67 *Le Monde Juif,* February, 1950.
68 Levai, *pages 163, 182.*
69 Levai, *page 250.*
70 Levai, *pages 195, 232.*
71 Case XI, NG 1848. (Affidavit, Lakatos.)
72 Levai, *pages 235, 243.*
73 Levai, *page 228.*

74 Levai, *pages 201, 244.*
75 *Documents sur l'activité du CICR,* 1946, *page 60. Report of the ICRC on its Activities in the Second World War,* Geneva, 1948, I, *page 648.*
76 Levai, *page 229.*
77 *The Times,* July 8th and 15th, 1944.
78 Documents CICR, op. cit.
79 Levai, *pages 255-7*
80 Levai, *page 219.*
81 Case XI, NG 2739. (Ribbentrop, from special train Westfalen, to Veesenmayer.)
82 Case XI. Veesenmayer defence document Vb, *page 213.*
83 Levai, *page 290.* Evidence, Kaltenbrunner. IMT, XI, 306.
84 Kastner. *Bericht, page 41.*
85 Kastner. *Bericht, pages 24-8.*
86 Levai, *pages 264-5.* Kastner, *Bericht, pages 33-7.*
87 Case IV. Defence document, Frank, *page 16.* Printed in *Trials of War Criminals,* Washington, 1951, V, *page 682.*
88 Ibid., *page 684.*
89 *The Times,* July 18th, 1944.
90 Case XI, NG 2379.
91 Kastner. *Bericht, pages 48, 55.*
92 Ibid., *page 53.*
93 IMT, PS 3803, XI, 313.
94 Kastner. *Bericht, pages 52, 59-61.*
95 Ibid., *pages 76-9.*
96 Kastner. *Bericht, pages 85* and *98.*
97 NG 2994. Wagner to Veesenmayer.
98 Kastner. *Bericht, page 98.*
99 IMT, PS 1166.
100 Levai, *page 314.*
101 Levai, *page 321.*
102 Levai, *page 326.* Kastner, *Bericht, page 92.*
103 Levai, *page 328.* Case XI, NG 1848 (affidavit, Lakatos).
104 Levai, *page 336.* Paul Schmidt, *Hitler's Interpreter,* London, 1951, *page 272.*
105 Case XI. Veesenmayer defence document Vb, 128. (Affidavit, Rahn.)
106 Levai, *page 352.*
107 Levai, *page 278.* Case XI, NG 1806.
108 *Report of Activities, ICRC,* Vol. I, *pages 649-50.*
109 Case XI, NG 3157.
110 Kastner. *Bericht, page 125.*
111 Kastner, *pages 117-8.* Levai, *page 381.*
112 Kastner. *Bericht, page 115.*
113 Levai, *page 369.* Kastner, *page 149.*
114 Case XI, NG 5218. Affidavit, Juettner.
115 Kastner. *Bericht, page 127.*
116 Kastner. *Bericht, page 129.*
117 Kastner. *Bericht, page 148.*
118 Kastner. *Bericht, page 132.*
119 Levai, *page 381.*
120 Case XI, NG 1874. (Affidavit, Gabor Vajna.)

121 IMT, III, 286. Evidence, Wisliceny.
122 IMT, V, 195. (Evidence, Mme Vaillant-Couturier.)
123 Georges Dunand. *Ne perdez pas leur trace! page 201.*
124 Kastner. *Bericht, page 170.* IMT, XIV, 374 (evidence, Baldur von Schirach).
125 Kastner. *Bericht, page 171.*
126 Levai, *page 373.*
127 Levai, *page 387. Report of Activities, ICRC,* Vol. I, *page 652.*
128 Levai, *page 392.*
129 Levai, *page 403.*
130 *Report of Activities, ICRC,* Vol. I, *page 653.*
131 *Le Monde Juif,* January, 1950.
132 Levai, *page 475.*

CHAPTER 17

1a Detailed analysis of these movements in *Auschwitz, Deel VI, die Afvoertransporten, etc.,* Netherlands Red Cross, The Hague, March, 1952 (stencil).
1b Jenny Spritzer. *Ich war Nr 10291, page 77.* Kristina Zywulska, *I Came Back, page 193.*
1c PS 2171. Report of the Psychological Warfare Division, Buchenwald. Eugen Kogon, *The Theory and Practice of Hell* (Der SS Staat), London, 1950, *page 168.*
2 IMT, PS 1166. Report of Major Burger in Amt D of the WVHA.
3 Kogon, op. cit., *page 247.*
4 IMT, VII, 128, Document U.S.S.R. 29. This is a report of the Russo-Polish Majdanek Commission. Other details in *The Black Book,* New York, 1945, *pages 381-90.*
5 See 'Supplementary List of Camps and Prisons,' International Tracing Service, Arolsen, British Zone of Germany, 1951.
6 April 5th, 1944, figures, from NO 021 (Pohl to Himmler) in *Trials of War Criminals,* Washington, 1951, Vol. V, *pages 384-5.* May 11th, figures in *Dokumenty i Materialy,* I, *pages 100-105,* Lodz, 1946. August 21st, figures in ibid., *page 120.* October 18th, figures ibid., *page 117.*
7 Evidence of Georg Konrad Morgen in IMT, XX, 390 and 393-6.
8 *German Crimes in Poland,* I, *page 79.* IMT, XI, 363, evidence, Hoess.
9 Jenny Spritzer. *Ich war Nr 10291,* Zurich, n.d., *page 96. Dokumenty i Materialy* (Obosy), I, *page 77.*
9a *Auschwitz, Deel VI, page 14.* Case XI, NG 5508, Major George McNally, *The Great Nazi Counterfeit Plot.* See *Readers Digest,* June, 1952.
10 Reszoe Kastner. *Bericht des Juedischen Rettungskomitees, etc.,* Geneva, 1946 (typescript), *page 91.*
11 Filip Friedman. *This was Oswiecim,* 1948, *page 77.* Jenny Spritzer, op. cit., *page 77.*
12 *Documents sur l'activité du CIRC en faveur des detenus civils, etc.,* Geneva, June, 1946, *page 91.*

TEXT REFERENCES

13 Kristina Zywulska. *I Came Back*, New York, 1949. *page 232.* Case IV in *Trials of War Criminals*, V (evidence, Bielsky), *pages 650-54.*
14 Kastner. *Bericht, etc.,* op. cit., *page 131.*
15 IMT, XI, 306, and Document PS 3762. (Becher affidavit.)
16 Miklos Nyiszli in *Les temps modernes,* Paris, May, 1951, *page 1885.*
17 *War Refugees Board Report on Auschwitz and Birkenau,* 1944 (stencil), *page 13.*
18 Albert Menasche. *Birkenau,* New York, 1947, *page 91.* Bruno Baum, *Widerstand im Auschwitz,* Potsdam, 1949, *page 20.*
19 Ibid. and Filip Friedman. *This was Oswiecim, page 76.* Georges Wellers in *Le Monde Juif,* April, 1949.
20 Wellers, ibid. *The Belsen Trial,* ed. Raymond Philips, London, 1949, *pages 133, 180.*
21 Robert Levy in *Temoignages Strasbourgeois,* Paris, 1947, *page 464.*
22 Miklos Nyiszli in *Les temps modernes,* Paris, May, 1951, *page 1885.*
23 Kristina Zywulska, op. cit., *page 209.*
24 Menasche, op. cit., *page 102, Auschwitz, Deel VI.*
25 *The Belsen Trial, pages 160-65, 732.*
25a *Auschwitz, Deel VI,* passim.
26 Eugen Kogon. *The Theory and Practice of Hell,* London, 1950, *pages 168, 223, 142.*
27 *Temoignages Strasbourgeois, page 89.*
28 *Temoignages, etc., page 499. German Crimes in Poland,* I, *page 70.*
29 IMT, VII, 127.
30 Dr. Kastner (*Bericht, page 161*) quotes Dieter Wisliceny as estimating 250,000 at the beginning of February, 1945.
31 *Documents sur l'activité du CIRC, etc., pages 22-3, 94.*
32 Case XI, NG 2675. Affidavit, Kurt Becher.
33 Count Bernadotte. *The Curtain Falls,* New York, 1945, *pages 43-7, 65-6.*
34 *Documents CIRC, pages 22-3.*
35 *The Belsen Trial,* London, 1949, *page 166.*
36 Kastner. *Bericht, page 161.*
37 IMT, D, 749. Affidavit, Hoess.
38 Himmler to Storsch. Photostat in *The Memoirs of Dr. Felix Kerstem,* translated Dr. Ernst Morwitz, New York, 1947, *page 228* (originally in Dutch, *Klerk en Beul*).
39 *Documents CIRC, page 97.*
40 Bernadotte. *The Curtain Falls, pages 81, 87.*
41 *Documents CIRC, page 98.*
42 Eugen Kogon, op. cit., *page 255.* IMT, PS 2171.
43 Case XI, NG 2675. (Affidavit, Becher.)
44 Kogon, op. cit., *page 256.*
44a *The Belsen Trial, page 166.*
45 *Documents CIRC, page 99.*
46 Kastner. *Bericht, etc., page 176.*
47 H. Wielek. *De Oorlog die Hitler won,* Amsterdam, 1947, *page 410.*
48 *The Belsen Trial, page 53.*
49 Ibid., *page 178.*
50 IMT, XI, 351-2.
50a Case IV, Transcript 1347. (Evidence, Pohl.)
51 *The Belsen Trial, page 40.*

52 *The Belsen Trial, page 34.*
53 Ibid., *page 61.*
54 IMT, D, 749. (Affidavit, Hoess.)
55 Norbert Masur. *En Jood talar med Himmler,* Stockholm, 1946 (German transcript kindly supplied by author).
56 Gerdes affidavit, IMT, III, 240. Kaltenbrunner's reply, XI, 276-7. Eberstein affidavit, IMT, XXI, 261-2.
57 *Documents CIRC, page 99.*
58 *We Survived,* Yale, 1949, *page 296.*
59 *Documents, CIRC, page 100.* IMT, Wisliceny affidavit C. Kastner, *Bericht, page 161.* IMT, PS 1553, Affidavit, Gerstein.
60 *Documents CIRC, page 100.*
61 Kastner. *Bericht, page 179.*
62 *Documents CIRC, page 130.*
63 *Documents CIRC, pages 132-3.*
64 Meyer Levin. *In Search,* London, 1951, *page 271.*
65 *Documents CIRC, page 134.*
66 IMT, XI, 304, PS 3870.
67 IMT, XI, 306, PS 3762.
68 IMT, XI, 242.
69 IMT, XI, 354. Evidence, Hoess.
70 *Documents CIRC, page 102.*
71 Ibid.
72 *Documents CIRC, page 112.*
73 Evidence, Gebhardt, Case I. Printed in François Bayle, *Croix Gammée ou Caducée,* 1950, *page 224.*
74 *Documents CIRC, pages 116-27.*
75 Trevor-Roper. *Last Days of Hitler, page 197.*
76 Bernadotte. *The Curtain Falls, pages 113-8.*
77 Trevor-Roper, op. cit., *page 187.*
78 Case IX, NO 1128. Pruetzmann to Himmler. IMT, PS 3046, Lahousen Diary.
79 Trevor-Roper, *page 246.*
80 Case IX, Transcript 504. (Evidence, Ohlendorf.)
81 *Ciano's Diary, 1939-43,* London, 1947, *page 472.*
82 *En Jood talar med Himmler,* Stockholm, 1946 (German transcript kindly supplied by Dr. Norbert Masur).
83 IMT, XI, 252-7. (Evidence, Kaltenbrunner.)
84 IMT, XI, 259. (Affidavit, Hoettl.)
85 Beverley Baxter, from Alt-Aussee in *Sunday Express,* September 9th, 1951.
86 Case IX, NO 3197. (Affidavit Paul Blobel.)
87 Affidavit by Wisliceny at Bratislava trial, 1948, quoted by L. Poliakov in *Le rêve de Caligula. Le Monde Juif,* June, 1949.
88 Trevor-Roper. *Last Days of Hitler, page 185.*
89 Walter Hagen (Willi Hoettl). *Die Geheime Front,* Wien-Linz, 1950, *page 73.*
90 *Report of the Anglo-American Committee of Inquiry regarding the Problems of European Jewry and Palestine,* Lausanne, April 20th, 1946, *pages 58-9.*

REFERENCES

APPENDIX I

1 *Frankfurter Hefte*, March, 1952.
2 Report, etc., His Majesty's Stationery Office, Miscellaneous No. 8 (1946).
3 IMT, I, 6.
4 IMT, I, 62.
5 The details of the Institute of Jewish Affairs' estimate are given in *Frankfurter Hefte*, March, 1952 ; those of the Joint Distribution Committee in *The Jewish Chronicle*, March 17th, 1947.
6 Bruno Blau in *Jewish Social Studies*, New York, April, 1950.
7 NO 5194. Not printed ; photostat in Centre de Documentation juive contemporaine, Paris.
7a *Wiener Library Bulletin*, VI, 3-4, August, 1952, page 25.
8 IMT, PS 1949.
9 Wilhelm Krell in *Les Juifs en Europe, 1939-45*, Paris, CDJC, 1948, *page 190.*
9a Gregory Frumkin. *Population Changes in Europe since 1939*, N.Y., 1951, *page 38.*
10 Bruno Blau in *Jewish Social Studies*, New York, April, 1950.
11 Eugene Levai. *The Black Book of the Martyrdom of Hungarian Jewry*, Zurich, 1948, *page 434.*
12 *Les Juifs en Europe, 1939-45*, Paris, CDJC, 1948, *page 220.*
13 *The Jewish Chronicle*, March 17th, 1947 ; *Frankfurter Haefte*, March, 1952.
13a *Frumkin, op. cit.*, page 50.
14 *Le Monde Juif*, Paris, CDJC, March, 1952.
15 Georges Wellers. *De Drancy a Auschwitz*, Paris, 1946, *pages 45* and *108.*
16 Original documents at CDJC, Paris, No. I, 54, and XXVI, 73.
17 Report of Netherlands Government put in evidence at Nuremberg, IMT, PS 1726.
18 *Bulletin von het Central Bureau voor Statistiek*, May, 1949.
19 *Les Juifs en Europe, 1939-45*, Paris, 1948, *page 45.*
20 Starr and Shapiro in *Jewish Social Studies*, New York, April, 1946.
20a Frumkin, op. cit., *page 155.*
21 *Les Juifs en Europe*, Paris, 1948, *pages 48* and *52.*
22 Ibid., *page 207.*
23 *Statesman's Year Book*, 1944.
24 Institute of Jewish Affairs. *Hitler's Ten Year War on the Jews*, New York, 1943, *page 78.*
25 *Statistisches Handbuch der Europaeischen Nationalitaeten, page 228* (1939).
25a Institute of Jewish Affairs. *Hitler's Ten Year War on the Jews*, New York, 1943, *page 83.*
26 Joshua Starr and Leon Shapiro in *Jewish Social Studies*, New York, April, 1946.
27 Levai, op. cit., *page 59.*
28 Starr and Shapiro. *Jewish Social Studies*, April, 1946.
29 Levai, op. cit., *page 59.*
30 E. Nameneyi in *Le Monde Juif*, July, 1950.
31 Hugh Seton-Watson. *Eastern Europe between the Wars*, Cambridge, 1945, *page 430.*

589

32 Wiener Library Bulletin, September, 1947, quoting the Central Committee for Jews in Poland.
33 *German Crimes in Poland*, Warsaw, 1946, I, *page 126*.
34 IMT, L, 18. Katzmann's report, *Final Solution of the Jewish Question in Galicia*, June 30th, 1943.
35 Institute of Jewish Affairs. *Hitler's Ten Year War on the Jews*, New York, 1943, *page 187*.
36 Solomon M. Schwarz. *The Jews in the Soviet Union*, Syracuse, 1951, *page 220*.
37 Ibid., *pages 229-230*.

INDEX

Reference may also be made to the alphabetical list of 211 names in Appendix II : " The Fate of Some of the Participants in ' The Final Solution ' "

Index

A

Aarhus (Denmark), Rescue of Jews, 349 fn.

Abel, Dr., Anthropologist, 36

Abetz, Otto, 30, 72, 75, 305, 307, 309, 313, 315, 505

Abromeit, Franz, *Capt.* SS, 366

Action Bernhard,' 26 fn., 454

Action Cloud One,' 471 fn.

Action Hoess,' 428

Action Petlura' (Lwow), 229

'Action Reinhardt': 244-71. Origin of name, 101. Mention by Konrad Morgen, 125. Auxiliaries employed, 142. Extended to Polish White Russia, 225. Action opens at Mielec 252. Exemption cards, stamped Einsatz Reinhardt, 261. Financial winding up, 295-96. Globocnik's report to Himmler on ditto, 296

'Action Zeppelin,' 190-91

Ainikeit, Moscow Yiddish paper quoted, 500

Albala, *Judenaelteste,* Salonika, 376

Albrecht, Dr. Emil, 95, 333, 380 fn., 408, 505

Alderman, Sydney, 489

Alexianu, Prof., 398, 401

Aloshin (of Kiev), 234

Alt-Aussee, 27, 480-81

Altenberg, German Minister in Greece, 374

Alvensleben, Udo von, *Maj.-Gen.* SS, 98

Ambrosio, *Gen.* Vittorio, 323.

Amelung, *Lt.* SS, 209

American Jewish Congress, 406

Amery, John, 430 fn.

Amsterdam: pro-Jewish riots, 329-31. Jews sent to Westerbork, 333-34. Plan for total roundup, 336. 'Transvaal' action, 337. Portuguese community exempted, 338. Fate of

diamond workers, 340. Amsterdam post-war, 341-42

Ananiev (Transdniestria), 24

Anglo-American Committee on European Jewry and Palestine, 482, 489-90, Appendix I *passim*

Anielewicz, Mordechai, 277

Ankaisina (Madagascar), 77

Annecy, 323

Antignac, Joseph, 323, 505

Antonescu, *Marshal* Ion: Premier of Rumania, 395, Hitler's comments on his anti-Jewish measures, 84. Responsibility for Odessa Massacre, 240. Action in Bukovina, 398. Plans to clear Jews out of Transdniestria, 399, 401. Attitude to British Palestine plan, 404, 407, 409, 505

Antonescu, Mihai, Rumanian Vice-President of Council, 401, 403, 409, 505

Antwerp, 91, 343

Appeldoornse Bos, 335-36

'*Appell*' in Birkenau camp, its significance, 112, 120, 319, 333-34, 390 fn.

Arad (Rumania), 403, 410

Arajs, *Major,* Riga, 217 fn., 505

Arbe island, 370

Ardeatina Tunnel massacre, 258 fn., 354

Armament Workers, Jewish: exempted status in Germany, 28, 86, confirmed at Wannsee conference, 98, last reprieve, 144. In Poland, 267

Armia Kraiova, 144, 272

'Arrow Cross' party, 420, 440-41, 446

Artemovsk (Ukraine) massacre, 239

Artukovic, Andrija, 366

Athens, 377-78, 456

Auerbach, Philip, 120

Auersbach, German administrator, Warsaw Ghetto, 59, 69, 259

Aus der Fuenten, Ferdinand, see Fuenten.

F

599

G

H

I

N

O

P